Praise for Daniel Jonah Goldhagen's

# THE DEVIL THAT NEVER DIES

"No other writer has held mass murderers, deniers of truth, and propagators of hate to a higher standard of moral accountability than Daniel Jonah Goldhagen....His latest, *The Devil That Never Dies,* doubtlessly will shatter the way people think about anti-Semitism—both in its past incarnations and in its present-day existence....When the world's man-made atrocities, moral failures, and blatant hypocrisies occur, he has proven himself time and again to be a righteous chronicler on behalf of the persecuted and the dead."

— Thane Rosenbaum, *Huffington Post*

"A frightening exposition on how anti-Semitism has become a global phenomenon....*The Devil That Never Dies* is bursting with information and insight." — Neal Gendler, *American Jewish World*

"Former Harvard professor Goldhagen comes out swinging in this frontal assault on anti-Semitism and its practitioners and does not pause for breath until the final page....A frightening photograph of a mutable demon so many fail to recognize and continue to embrace."

—*Kirkus Reviews*

"An important new book....A chilling explication of the explosion of anti-Semitism in the last two decades, fueled by the Internet and other modern means of global communications, as well as a sophisticated analysis of the interrelated international institutions and political trends that underpin it. It is essential reading."

— Rick Richman, *Commentary*

"Explosive....Goldhagen's main points are hard to contradict."

— David Mikics, *Tablet Magazine*

"Effective and disturbing.... Rhetorically and sometimes physically violent anti-Semitism over the past dozen years or so is shocking in part because it does not seem to shock."

— Jeffrey Goldberg, *New York Times*

"Daniel Goldhagen's new book hits hard. This tour de force makes a chillingly compelling case that global anti-Semitism is on the rise.... Goldhagen's material can overwhelm and be tough going for the faint of heart. Yet his passionate compulsion to make his case beyond a shadow of a doubt is understandable, and he does so with brilliance.... In *The Devil That Never Dies,* he does everything within his formidable intellectual power to confront anti-Semitism and make us aware that this devil is real."

— Sharon Rosen Leib, *San Diego Jewish Journal*

"Important and timely.... The dangers Goldhagen outlines in this brilliant work should sound a clarion call for governmental and societal intervention."

— Benjamin Weinthal, *Jerusalem Post*

"An in-depth look at anti-Semitism around the world."

— *Vox Tablet*

"Goldhagen is writing as a prophet, offering the world an apocalyptic call to self-examination and repentance. We should all be grateful for the call and hope that he is not preaching only to the converted."

— David Nirenberg, *Washington Post*

# THE
# DEVIL
# THAT
# NEVER
# DIES

# THE
# DEVIL
# THAT
# NEVER
# DIES

## THE RISE AND THREAT OF GLOBAL ANTISEMITISM

### DANIEL JONAH GOLDHAGEN

BACK BAY BOOKS
Little, Brown and Company
*New York   Boston   London*

Back Bay Books / Little, Brown and Company
Hachette Book Group
1290 Avenue of the Americas, New York, NY 10104
littlebrown.com

Originally published in hardcover by Little, Brown and Company, September 2013
First Back Bay trade paperback edition, April 2016

Back Bay Books is an imprint of Little, Brown and Company, a division of Hachette Book
Group, Inc. The Back Bay Books name and logo are trademarks of Hachette Book Group, Inc.

The publisher is not responsible for websites (or their content) that are not owned by the
publisher.

The Hachette Speakers Bureau provides a wide range of authors for speaking events. To find
out more, go to hachettespeakersbureau.com or call (866) 376-6591.

ISBN 978-0-316-09787-1 (hc) / 978-0-316-27745-7 (int'l) / 978-0-316-09786-4 (pb)
LCCN 2013941806

10 9 8 7 6 5 4 3 2 1

RRD-C

Printed in the United States of America

*For my parents, Erich and Norma Goldhagen*

# Contents

# Preface to the Paperback Edition

THE LAST TWO years have, sadly, confirmed the findings, analysis, and conclusions of this book. In the time since the hardcover was published, we have witnessed the growing and ever more undeniable antisemitic demonization of Israel; been confronted by the violent verbal and physical attacks on Jews, particularly in Europe; seen the results of new surveys fleshing out the case I made here that the new antisemitism is indeed global in reach and outpouring; and watched the diplomatic success and growing impunity of Iran prophesying and threatening the annihilation of Israel. Even people, media, and politicians who had long denied the obviously ominous threat of antisemitism have begun to speak candidly about it and call for something to be done to counteract it.

During the summer of 2014, the Gaza war became the occasion for global antisemitism to erupt in a torrent of expression, with waves of verbal and physical violence. Israel was of course a principal target. But what become obvious was that antisemites across Europe and beyond were directing their naked and murderous antisemitism not merely at Jewish Israelis but at *Jews,* and at all Jews, often openly urging their annihilation. "They are not screaming 'Death to the Israelis' on the streets of Paris," Roger Cukierman, the president of the umbrella organization for French Jewish institutions, explained. "They are screaming 'Death to Jews.'"

This was nothing new. Yet during that summer the antisemitic vitriol and violence was widespread, brazen, so unabashedly calling for the death of the Jews that it could no longer be denied by the apologists and deniers who had pretended that antisemitism barely existed in the United Kingdom, France, Germany, and elsewhere, and that those of us who dared to speak about this enduring diabolical scourge were hysterical or acting in bad faith. During this summer of truth, European media and political elites alike became alarmed at the rampant calls for mass murder and the related violence, and began to decry the antisemitism coursing through their countries in alarming terms. Chancellor of Germany Angela Merkel denounced the antisemitism assaults as "an attack on freedom and tolerance and our democratic state." French prime minister Manuel Valls declared: "To attack a Jew because he is a Jew is to attack France. To attack a synagogue and a kosher grocery store is quite simply antisemitism and racism." Even *The Guardian,* which has been staunchly "anti-Israel" for years and been seen by some as antisemitic, at least for the moment changed its tune. It published a major article entitled "Antisemitism on rise across Europe 'in worst times since the Nazis,'" from which these quotes were taken.

And not just in Europe. This book addresses squarely the vast scope of antisemitism, including the enormous number of antisemites around the world, which by and large, for reasons that the book explains, almost everyone wants to pretend is not so. Speaking the plain truth makes a broad and diverse range of people either politically or personally uncomfortable, including, in large measures, Jews who are members of the elites of their own countries and who don't want to be excluded from the club for making waves. Since this book's publication, the Anti-Defamation League (ADL) conducted in 2014 an extensive survey of antisemitism in one hundred countries, the *ADL Global 100.* Its findings are noteworthy in several ways. They show that the data-driven contention in this book that there are perhaps 1.5 billion antisemites in the world is, if anything, an underestimate. The ADL found that, according to its enormously conservative criteria for classifying someone as an antisemite, 26 percent of the people in the countries surveyed, roughly 1.1 billion adults, are antisemitic. Projecting that percentage all over the world and including teenagers suggests that on the order of 1.5 billion people are antisemitic—and even this figure understates the actual number of antisemites owing to the restrictive methodology by which the ADL counted them.

For the *ADL Global 100* to consider a person antisemitic, that person had to espouse at least *six* antisemitic views. This book maintains that one incontrovertible and serious antisemitic belief is an undeniable indication of antisemitism, yet for the survey, it was not sufficient. Not even five such views were deemed enough. Holding demonizing views of Jews, which the book explores in depth, such as "Jews are responsible for most of the world's wars," "Jews have too much control over global affairs," or "Jews have too much power in international financial markets," are clear expressions and indications of antisemitism—they *are* antisemitism—but for the survey they didn't count unless a person happened to affirm six or more disparate views of this kind. For a person to be considered a racist in this country, all one has to say is "blacks are lazy" or any one of many other familiar prejudicial statements about blacks or Hispanics, even when they are less demonizing than the antisemitic ones in the survey. Why then is the standard used for antisemitism in this survey and in general so out of whack that it leads to an enormous undercounting of the number of antisemites around the world?

The most significant finding from the ADL survey is that only 28 percent of the respondents are not antisemitic, as indicated by their rejection of all of the blatant antisemitic remarks with which they were presented. This means that three out of four people surveyed in the one hundred countries hold at least one view that reveals them to be antisemites. One out of every two people holds at least three such unmistakably powerful antisemitic views.

These enormous numbers constitute the survey's findings, even though the survey did not include questions regarding religious beliefs that deprecate Jews. No question touched on classical Christian or Islamic antisemitic canards. Had the survey asked whether respondents agreed that "all Jews are guilty for the death of Jesus" or that "Jews are the children of apes and pigs," it would have surely found, even by its conservative methodology, that even more people are antisemitic. The religious dimension of antisemitism is crucially important for understanding anti-Jewish animus. When powerfully demonizing and dehumanizing views of Jews are at the center of their adherents' religious sensibility and general worldview, it makes them even more susceptible to accepting other antisemitic canards. When applying more reasonable criteria, such as whether a person holds any serious antisemitic beliefs, only about one-third of the people even of the ADL's least antisemitic countries are free of this most pernicious prejudice. In the 2015 *ADL Global 100* follow-up survey, the United Kingdom goes from appearing low on antisemitism at 12 percent holding six or more powerfully antisemitic views to, according to a more realistic and conventionally applied standard of prejudice (which I discuss in the body of this book), 64 percent of the people being antisemitic.

The power of antisemitism in the world today creates a force field that distorts reality, with Jews deemed to nefariously control the United States, international finance, and other levers of power. Jews loom so large in the antisemitically inflamed public discourse that one out of five people around the world believe that there are more than seven hundred million Jews in the world, when the actual number is a meager fourteen million. The distortion of reality that antisemitism both reflects and produces is particularly striking in the disjuncture between what is actually going on in the Middle East and in the Islamic world on the one hand and on the other how the causes of disorder and violence are represented in the minds of people. Much of the Middle East is consumed by larger and smaller wars, larger and smaller eliminationist and exterminationist campaigns, larger and smaller mass murders. Syria, Islamic State, Sudan, Iraq, Turkey renewing its decades-long assault on Kurds, Hezbollah in Lebanon, Iran, Yemen, Libya, Egypt, Hamas in Gaza—all are sites or sources of eliminationist assaults, mass murders, colossal repression, dictatorships, sectarian wars, butchery, or medieval and modern cruelty. Israel sits squarely, democratically, a relative bastion of freedom, and at peace with itself and, unless provoked, at peace with its neighbors. Yet, as surveys have repeatedly showed, Israel has been over the last several years considered by many the greatest threat to world peace, and Jews—not Israelis—"are responsible for most of the world's wars."

How such wild and fantastical views that constitute the heart of antisemitism could grip, and could have come to grip, a good portion of the global community is one of the many perplexing subjects regarding antisemitism that have baffled observers, and that this book finally explains.

New York, September 2015

# Preface

THE DEVIL, WITH us for two thousand years, is back. This devil has already insinuated himself into hundreds of millions. He has warped religions. He has inflamed minds and hearts the world over. Unleashed riots and pogroms. Led to the expulsion of millions. He has so perverted people's sensibilities that he has convinced them to brutalize and torture masses of people in the name of goodness and God. He has gone further, inducing people to commit mass murder again and again, including one of humanity's most cataclysmic assaults, the attempted murder of an entire people, felling six million of them in one historical instant.

The devil, after a period of relative quiescence, has reappeared, flexes his muscles again, and stalks the world, with ever more confidence, power, and followers. The devil is not a *he* but an *it*. The devil is antisemitism.

In thinking about how to characterize antisemitism and to open this book, I considered many options before settling on conceptualizing it as a devil. Some may think it a metaphor, and perhaps an overdrawn one, yet I mean it not only metaphorically but also conceptually. Sadly, it is not overdrawn. According to how religion depicts the devil, and how those who believe in his existence have understood him, antisemitism is a devil. Compared with the *known* doings of the unseen devil of religions, antisemitism has been far more destructive, a far greater plague on humanity. And it threatens similar destruction again.

Whether you believe in a supernatural devil or just understand such a force conceptually and metaphorically, if you are interested in learning about the world's real devil, this book is for you. Its story is anything but uplifting, but it is important—for Jews and non-Jews alike, for the religious and the secular, for Christians and Muslims, for humanists and students of politics, for all those concerned with goodness and evil, and for those who want to understand critical aspects of today's globalized world, and want it to be a less dangerous, less devilish place.

# PART I

## ANTISEMITISM

# 1

# The Devil

ANTISEMITIC EXPRESSION HAS exploded in volume and intensity in the last two decades, particularly in the last ten years. The upsurge has been so meteoric and the canards advanced so prejudicial that if anyone in 1990 or even 1995 had predicted the current state of affairs, he would have been seen as a fanciful doomsayer. This resurgence of antisemitism and its expression has taken place not merely in select countries but around the world, and especially unexpectedly in Western countries. It has taken place in the halls of parliament and in the streets. Among elites and common people. In public media, places of worship, and in the privacy of homes. Where Jews live and where they do not. It has done so with classical tropes and with new ones, in long familiar forums and in recently invented ones.

Antisemitism has moved people, societies, indeed civilizations for two thousand years, and has done so despite the otherwise vast changes in the world and in these civilizations and societies — economic, scientific, technological, political, social, and cultural. It has been a powerful force, an animating idea, the glue of many societies and cultures for much longer than practically any major belief system or ideology or political form, or many of our major cultural forms. It long predates and, until very recently historically, has been more widespread than genuine democracy as an animating ideology and political system. It long predates the Western idea of liberty becoming widespread, which was not until the modern period. Among intergroup prejudices, antisemitism's longevity is unparalleled. Even the anti-black racism of the West has not existed as long, coming into being in something resembling its classic form much later, when imperial Europeans started to explore and carve up the rest of the world in the fifteenth century. If we consider matters aside from prejudice, antisemitism's singular nature and peculiar power comes into still sharper relief. It long predates the advent of capitalism, and the technological and industrial revolutions that created the foundation for modern economies and prosperity, which have thoroughly altered the world directly and indirectly in every respect. Yet regarding Jews, these changes led not to a diminution of antisemitism but were often used only to deepen and intensify it. Antisemitism long predates the world-altering changes in conceptions of the world that included and were brought about by the Copernican revolution in the earth's and therefore human beings' places in the universe, by the revolution in understanding the early modern period that the very contours of the world were round, and by Europeans' "discovery" of other continents and their conquest of and incorporation of the rest of the world into a world system with its diversity of peoples and cultures. Antisemitism long predates an acceptance of the general equality of human beings, and the moral standing and capacity of women as social, cultural, economic, and political facts. It long predates the current conception of childhood as a time when human beings ought to have their human capacities cultivated and their moral autonomy and rights respected. Antisemitism long predates the emergence of science, a set of rigorous practices to develop objective and correct bodies of knowledge that permeate education, thinking, social relations, and social practices—which, significantly, has barely affected the hold of the nonsense that composes and that flows from antisemitic thinking. Indeed, science has often been perverted to justify such thinking and practice. This includes the foundational revolution in the conception of human beings owing to Darwin, which was used only to intensify antisemitism by merging it with a new body of derivative social Darwinian thought that rendered Jews a biologically based race of evildoers. Antisemitism long predates entire disciplines of thought, including political science, sociology, psychology, anthropology, economics, and cognitive neuroscience, yet despite the emergence of these sober ways of studying the individual and social world, they have made little dent in antisemitism's spread and power.

And it long predates many cultural and art forms, from classical music to the novel to film, each of which—as akin to older art forms, such as drama, philosophy, and history—has been the vehicle for antisemitic expression, often by some of the most distinguished practitioners of each: William Shakespeare, Johann Sebastian Bach, Charles Dickens, Richard Wagner, T. S. Eliot, and on and on. Antisemitism long predates, has been more widespread and more powerful until recent times, and in many instances continues to be more powerful, than many of the defining and most essential features of our world today.

The calumnies against Jews have been the most damaging kind. Jews have killed God's son. All Jews, and their descendants for all time (in other words, all Jews forever) are guilty. They are the enemies of God. Jews are in league with the devil. Jews desecrate God's body, the host. Jews parented the Antichrist. Jews seek to destroy his Church. Jews themselves are demons or devils. Jews sought to slay God's prophet Muhammad. Jews are the enemies of Allah. Jews kill Christian children and use their blood for their rituals. Jews kill Muslim children. Jews wreak financial havoc in the countries in which they live. Jews have started all wars. Jews corrupt the moral fabric of societies and lead non-Jews astray in every conceivable way. Jews poison wells. Jews seduce and defile non-Jewish women. Jews are sexually licentious. Jews are behind prostitution. Jews are all criminals. Jews are fundamentally dishonest. Jews form an insidious international conspiracy. Jews are fifth columnists, betraying their homelands during times of war and peace. Jews control the media. Jews corrupt art and culture. Jews are like vermin, rats, strangling octopi, pests of all kinds. Everything Jews say is a lie. Jews seek to dominate nations. Jews seek to destroy nations. Jews seek to enslave humanity. Jews are behind the predations of capitalism. Jews are behind communism. Jews run the Soviet Union. Jews do not contribute anything positive to society. Jews do not do productive or honest labor. Jews are a race apart. Jews are genetically programmed to be malevolent. Jews are highly intelligent and cunning, making them a very dangerous enemy. Jews invented AIDS. Jews are responsible for 9/11. Jews control the United States. Jews caused the Iraq War. Jews are responsible for the financial meltdown of 2008. Jews are a vanguard of the West to enslave Muslims and destroy Islam.

Over the course of antisemitism's mind-boggling time span—while conceptions of the world, and humanity in its many aspects, and political, social, economic, and cultural practices and disciplines have come and gone and, when existing, have undergone such fundamental internal changes as to become unrecognizably new — antisemitism has maintained its core demonology, at least in several of its powerful strains. Christians since the dawn of Christianity have deemed Jews, for example, to be Christ-killers. This has also been the official and widely taught view of the Christian churches, including the once hegemonic Catholic Church, until very recently historically. (Today, many but hardly all Christians not only don't harbor this view, but forcefully reject it.) Even when there were world historical conflicts among different branches of Christianity, the nature of the Jews and their putative evil was one tenet that they shared, and that united them. In the Arab and Islamic world, where antisemitism, here a stepchild of Christianity, came into existence with the establishment of Islam in the seventh century, the central anti-Jewish charges and construction of Jews have also remained constant. The Arab and Islamic antisemitic discourse has at its core the notion that Jews are the prophet Muhammad's enemies and impediments to Islam's triumph, and, having allegedly raised their hands in violence against the prophet and his emissaries, that they need to be conquered with the sword, and once so, at best be tolerated in a diminished state, until they one way or another — Muslims have often emphasized the sword as the appropriate means — are eliminated. It is not surprising that this antisemitic discourse has, whatever its variations and at times softening, retained this stable and core conception of Jews because it is grounded in the Qur'an and the Hadith, neither of which have, akin to Christianity and the Christian bible, undergone a widespread, fundamental reformation or modernization in understanding or in the practice they inform, and therefore receive a less literal reading and orientation toward the world.

Antisemitism has been highly elaborated and widely encoded in texts — more than any other ethnic prejudice by far. It has not been a mere reflex of prejudice of *we don't like them,* or *they are bad or threatening or inferior* for this or that reason, which ultimately is what most prejudices are. Vast antisemitic literatures exist in many languages, on every continent, and in different civilization traditions. They run the gamut from the most rudimentary rabble-rousing to the most seemingly learned and sophisticated treatises and tomes. The degree to which antisemitism has been spread, adumbrated, specified, elaborated, turned into slogans, been the bases for seemingly learned disquisitions, served as the pseudo-foundation for science and for the arts, been the basis of social and cultural forms and political movements is breathtaking. The antisemitic litany has existed and been elaborated in virtually all forms of information: written, oral, symbolic, imagistic; in all information vehicles: newspapers, pamphlets, magazines, graffiti, jokes, posters, books, the Internet; and in all art and cultural forms: poetry, novels, plays, operas, liturgical music, painting, film, television series. Tens of thousands of antisemitic books have been published, many of which have been huge bestsellers in countries around the world. Now, with the Internet, the proliferation of antisemitic writing, posting, chatting, social networking, tweeting is effectively boundless, and the ready access people around the world have to it is near instantaneous.

Antisemitism's reach is unparalleled, both historically and today. Hundreds of millions of people have, in the past and today, subscribed to the foundational antisemitic paradigm—which, as we shall see, holds Jews to be in their essence different from non-Jews and noxious—taken part in or imbibed the elements and elaborations of various anti-semitic discourses, and believed antisemitism's calumnies. Antisemitism is practically an article of faith, in the literal and figurative sense of the term, in much of the Arab and Islamic worlds, as it still is, if in subdued form among many Christians, among whom it was for centuries a central article and formal doctrine of faith, taught and believed-in hand-in-glove with the notion of Jesus' divinity. As we will see from the survey data, hundreds of millions have been and are moved by antisemitism's associated passions, including hatred. And hundreds of millions have been and are willing to support anti-Jewish programs, including violence, including—indisputably in the past and all but indisputably today—large-scale lethal violence. The range of people believing in and fomenting antisemitism is also unusually broad. From the uneducated peasant and day laborer to university professors and leaders of countries, from people on the political left to those on the political right, from the secular to devout believers in God, from people organized behind antisemitic programs to those having only imbibed available social and cultural notions, from the poor to the wealthy—all these factors, which usually greatly and differentially influence people's prejudices and other belief systems, have had little influence on antisemitism's general spread and power. The people who are in general the least prejudiced, the educated and the elites, have often been at least as prejudiced as the so-called common man and woman of their societies.

The norms against antisemitic expression in public, which were in place in the Western world for roughly half a century after the Holocaust, have been largely breached, in many places overturned, and in many others inverted so that in ever more places and contexts affirming one's prejudices and hatreds of Jews is now a norm. The post-Holocaust inhibitions against antisemitism's public expression are unlikely to be restored anytime soon. The enormous increase in antisemitism and in its expression in the public sphere is accelerating. And publicly and widely expressed antisemitism, and its validation by elites and opinion leaders, has a self-reinforcing dynamic, of persuading more and more people of antisemitism's truths, who then further contribute to its expression or to the demand for its expression.

For all its longevity and permutations, antisemitism is nonetheless straightforward and simple to comprehend. Antisemitism is prejudice against or hatred of Jews. It is easy to recognize and understand when reading classic antisemitic literature, seeing cartoons about the vile qualities and deeds that political Islamists attribute to Jews, hearing insults likening Jews to pigs and dogs, encountering charges that they are responsible for all wars or for AIDS, or that they want to destroy humanity, a particular religion, or goodness. Yet antisemitism is also complex. It has many features that are not so readily grasped. And people disagree over whether some features are antisemitic and their bearers antisemites. Is it antisemitism (and is the person who employs it an antisemite) to use classical antisemitic tropes, such as Jews are more loyal to Israel than to their own countries, or Jews have too much power over a country's economy, even if the person does not openly express "hatred" of Jews? Is it antisemitic to be anti-Israel, to focus on Israel's real and alleged shortcomings and transgressions, while ignoring, even apologizing for or covering up, much worse transgressions by nearby states?

That these and antisemitism's many other aspects are not obvious indicates how deeply misunderstood antisemitism is, and how necessary it is for us to explore what constitutes (1) antisemitism, (2) antisemitism's historical and recent development, (3) its general character today, (4) its various dimensions, and (5) its current multiple forms.

Doing so reveals alarming truths:

Antisemitism is back, but not simply in its old form, more precisely put, not simply in any of its old forms, whether age-old Christian, Islamic, or Nazi. It has a changed content and character, rendering it continuous with past forms of antisemitism *and* substantially new, making it immensely more dangerous than at any time since the Nazi period, and likely laying its own new foundation for a continuing and ever-evolving future. In great measure, its character is eliminationist. Its different dimensions produce a variety of antisemitisms. It is worldwide and dangerous, threatening politically and physically Jewish communities around the globe, including Israel's very existence, and intellectually and morally the corruption of the minds of non-Jews. I dubbed this era several years ago "globalized antisemitism," or, more in keeping with the already changing times, "global antisemitism," a name that aptly characterizes antisemitism's current character: we live in a globalized or global world and, like so many other things, antisemitism has been globalized. Antisemitism is global geographically and, produced in regions, places, and nodes around the world, available for people who want (and often do not want) to hear, see, or read it. It is not two dimensional, static, staying in whatever form it currently takes, in one place or region, but is three dimensional with constant movement and exchanges around the globe. Its content is influenced profoundly by, and indeed influences in return, the global order.

Antisemitism's European heartland has seen three principal eras of antisemitism. The first was the long Christian era, from its dawn to the nineteenth century. Christianity's politics, psychological needs, and theology defined antisemitism's contours, including identifying Jews with the devil, casting Jews as the dark and perfidious people of a dangerously dark and false religion. With Islam's advent in the seventh century, a derivative and parallel form of religious antisemitism emerged. Burgeoning Islam took over and transposed the Christian animus toward Jews in accord with its narrative and political needs. The second European era of modern racist antisemitism began in the nineteenth century. Secularizing European civilizations, inspired by nationalism politically and by social Darwinian quasibiological notions socially and culturally, defined Jews as a racially constituted, irredeemable and powerful alien people—in its most extreme variant, essentially as secular devils in human form. The most disastrous of this era's many antisemitic variants was, of course, in Germany, yet these "modern," now better conceived of as Nazi, notions about Jews also were incorporated, starting in the 1930s and then gaining steam, into a "modernizing" Islamic antisemitism, the stepchild of which is what we see today. The third era of global antisemitism, dating from the 1990s, has spread antisemitism beyond the European heartland, and beyond the Islamic cone, and defines Jews as a demonic global threat.

Within each era, antisemitism has had variations and different, even competing strands. Nonetheless, in each era antisemitism has had an overall thrust. Antisemitism's first two eras are important, not only because each one's central features are still with us. Yet the new global antisemitic era demands the bulk of our attention. It is the era we are living in, and is by far the least well understood.

Antisemitism has become so commonplace that it is now taken for granted. Frightening manifestations of the phenomenon are treated as an expected norm, which means that when we ask people—often true of Jews as well as non-Jews—to confront its growth, presence, and power, many do not see what the big deal is. Imagine if, in Arab countries or at home, the things antisemites say with vitriol about Jews were said about any other group, such as blacks. Imagine if political leaders regularly declared in national speeches and interviews, and their country's television networks and newspapers routinely broadcasted, that blacks foment wars and are intending to commit a genocide, or that all blacks may be targeted for violence or must be killed. Would we, in the United States, or in European countries, would African leaders and peoples, want to have anything to do with them? Yet this has been happening to Jews routinely in many countries. People around the world, including political leaders and elites, shrug it off, assuming they pay it attention at all. Antisemitism has made such inroads into the public spheres of country after country, and around the international community, that it has become an integral and accepted feature of our time. Antisemitism's many lesser manifestations, such as antisemites' frequent desecration of Jewish cemeteries in Europe, hardly seem worth noticing.

Antisemitism has perplexed people for centuries. Why is there so much hatred against Jews? Ordinarily, we would expect such a numerically small, historically mainly impotent people to have been ignored or, at most, been the object of some local prejudices. But instead Jews have been the targets of an enduring, widespread, and volcanic animosity, the world's all-time leading prejudice.

Why are people around the world—this is especially relevant to Europeans—so susceptible to antisemitism? How even after antisemitism's unquestionable absurdities led to the Holocaust can Europeans and others accept variants of the same absurdities as truths? The Holocaust might have inoculated Europeans, and non-Europeans, against antisemitism, and certainly should have put them on their utmost guard against any hint of eliminationist politics and exterminationist intentions. Yet to a sufficient degree neither has occurred: the world is once again plagued by such politics and such plans.

This devil changes form, but it never dies.

# 2

# The Jews

WE DO NOT need to know much about Jews in order to study anti-semitism. Prejudice is an attribute of the prejudiced people and not of their victims. This is especially true for antisemitism and Jews. Anti-semites' accounts of Jews are regularly such a figment of fantastical imaginings that many antisemitic images and accounts of Jews, including several civilizations' principal antisemitic discourses, might as well be describing a people that never existed. And, as a matter of fact, most antisemites historically have never met Jews; the object of their canards and hatreds has been wholly invented.

Nevertheless, examining the character of Jews will introduce them to those who are not familiar with Jews and their history, and will provide a valuable backdrop for those who might be prone to wondering whether the charges of antisemites are true.

Beginning with the obvious, Jews are human beings. As with any large religious, ethnic, or national group, they are of different ages and sexes, from different families, different towns, different cities, regions, even different countries, making their livings in different ways occupying different professions, existing within different communities, cultures, and political and economic systems, having different politics, different levels of religiosity and attachments to being Jews. Jews, especially in modern times, have been enormously socially diverse. There are also individual-level differences: psychological dispositions, mental health or illness, values, intel-ligence, educational attainment, degree of physical vigor, aspirations, and more. Add historical time, level of economic, technological, and organizational development, Jews' vast geographic, national, and linguistic spread, and the differences among Jews and the variety of Jews become staggering—arguably greater than most other peoples. This makes antisemitic prejudice that much more absurd because it has so improbably imputed to Jews a relative constancy of character and disposition over enormous stretches of geography and time.

Jews trace their origins through the Jewish Bible to Abraham, who, according to sacred tradition, sometime in the second millennium before Jesus founded their monotheistic religion. Centered in ancient Israel, Abraham's descendants began a long, tortuous, and often tortured (by others) history. Nevertheless, Jews managed to create a religion that has endured, with its many developments and schisms, interpretations and reinterpretations, for more than three thousand years. Their religion gave rise directly to Christianity and, less directly, to Islam—two other far more influential, powerful religions. These newer religions and their adherents contested the Jews' custodianship of the tradition from which the new religions originated.

Jews never became as populous as either of these two religious offshoots' followers. Unlike Christians' and Muslims' zealous, missionary, and even martial proselytizing, Judaism is not a proselytizing religion and has considerable impediments deterring potential converts. This inward-looking orientation has been significant for Jews' relations with the worlds of non-Jews, and for antisemitism's especial strangeness, because Jews have not competed for non-Jews' bodies and souls.

Jews were determined to remain Jews despite the aggressive attempts by other peoples and religions to eliminate them, to convert them, namely to get them to formally renounce Judaism and adopt Christianity or Islam or, in the case of the Soviet Union, to shed their Jewish identity. Jews' complementary capacities to hunker down when under social, political, and cultural siege, and when expelled from their homes to adapt by moving to new regions or countries, are other distinctive features—from the Babylonian expulsion starting in 597 BCE to the draconian Roman occupation and, most astoundingly, to the centuries of extensive persecution, ghettoization, expulsions, and periodic mass murders that Jews suffered in Christian Europe starting intensively with the First Crusade of 1096 and culminating with the Holocaust.

That remnants of this pulverized European Jewry, and the many Jews Arab countries expelled in 1948, could, together with the Jews already in Palestine, survive and prosper under a state of siege, and ongoing existential threat, for more than sixty years, is but the latest installment of this profound determination to adapt and survive.

This enormous resolve produced a historically singular pattern: a numerically small people, always a minority, maintaining their identity not just as immigrants or into the second or third generation, but across generations and centuries, and not only in one or another region or country where numerical density or special circumstances might have favored it, but in country after country, indeed around the world, often even in hostile and unpropitious circumstances. It also meant that with such longevity in different countries and regions, with different majoritarian cultures and religions surrounding them, Jews naturally became that much more diverse in their own customs and practices, in their linguistic expression, in the food they ate, and more, so much so that Jewish communities and people from different regions and countries often became more different from one another than they were from the majoritarian communities in which they lived. They typically spoke the language of the majority society or developed Jewish vernaculars that were an admixture of Hebrew and the local language, with the local language usually overwhelmingly predominating. Yiddish, with the largest population of speakers and concentrated in Central and Eastern Europe, is by far the best known. Its vocabulary was about 85 percent German in origin, 10 percent Hebrew, and 5 percent Slavic, with a grammatical structure that came from German yet was written with the Hebraic alphabet. Mirroring Yiddish, with various degrees of fidelity, were approximately thirty other such Jewish dialects of majoritarian languages, including Dzhidi (Judeo-Persian); Ladino (Judeo-Spanish), which is very close to Castilian Spanish; Yevanic (Judeo-Greek); and various Judeo-Arabic dialects.

If, in the fourteenth century, or in the nineteenth century, a Moroccan Jew were somehow to have gone to Poland and found himself among Polish Jews, he would have felt the environment to be much more foreign than familiar. He would have likely not been able to communicate with them. Their communal organization, relations with Polish society, mode of dress, customs, concerns would have been far more different to him than those of his fellow non-Jewish Moroccans back home. To be sure, they would have likely shared a powerful, in many ways overriding common identity of religion and some common practices, such as observing the Sabbath or having a Passover Seder or observing the practices of Jewish dietary laws, known as kashrut. In this respect, the Moroccan Jew and the Polish Jews would have recognized one another as belonging to a common people, and the Moroccan Jew would have likely been welcome among his Polish counterparts as a Jew. Yet such affinities are a far cry from the kind of thick identities and familiarities that people of a common community, that people who consider themselves to share an identity as a people, typically share.

Jews' wherewithal and determination to maintain their identity for centuries came from the Jewish religion. Judaism, encoded and passed on through the generations, in a sacred set of texts forming the Jewish bible and in a body of commentary on Jewish law, ethics, customs, and practices codified in the Talmud, provided not only a map for the world and daily living, but also historical grounding, a sense of place, namely a vivid collective memory of an ancient homeland and, critically, a sense of peoplehood that went beyond merely sharing a belief in or adherence to a common religious orientation or God. In this sense, Judaism has been different from other religions. From the beginning, the notion existed that Jews formed a *people,* an identifiable ethnic group, like a large family—after all, they were the twelve tribes—and not merely a freely come together collection of believers. More than just a religious group, and still more than merely an ethnic group, the bible refers to Jews as *Am Yisrael,* the People of Israel, or better translated as the Nation of Israel, an ethnic group with an overriding corporate sense of community that also possesses a territorial home. Even when in a diaspora with no foreseeable prospect of reestablishing their country, Jews thought of themselves as a nation, with a fixed idea of a national home's existence—the land of ancient Israel and Jerusalem as its capital. Only in the post-Enlightenment period, and then ever more so in the twentieth century, when the prospect of citizenship and genuine acceptance in other countries seemed possible, did this notion of nationhood begin to break down—though Jews' sense of peoplehood and their commonality as an ethnic group, even while deeply identified (as Germans, French, English, Argentineans, or Americans) and loyal citizens of their own countries, has endured.

Jews' tenacity in maintaining their identity through the ages and in town, region, and country, was not merely for their right to worship and live according to the religious dictates as they desired, but also to maintain their people. Either religion or ethnicity alone would not have been sufficient, as the many assimilated and gone, forgotten peoples living in diasporas unwittingly attest. It was mutually reinforcing religion and ethnicity — Judaism and Jewishness — that provided Jewish communities around the world the solid foundation to resist the natural tendencies to assimilate.

The centrality of this identity of being a people, shown during more than two hundred years since the Enlightenment, became indisputable finally in Palestine and then Israel. In Europe, the United States, Israel, and elsewhere, Jews' attachment to Judaism, specifically their belief in the Jewish deity and their following of Judaism's religious practices, was much and ever increasingly attenuated compared to what had previously existed for centuries. Yet their identity as Jews persisted.

For two millennia, Jews lacked even the most rudimentary capacity to defend themselves physically, had no effective political representation, and were subjected to considerable discrimination, occupational restrictions, social disabilities, and general hostility. They therefore trod gingerly. They gauged whether their practices, including economic and social practices, might offend non-Jews. Often ghettoized, often expelled from their homes, always in danger of one or another of these fates, if not of being physically assaulted or killed, Jews made few if any political demands. Instead they sought to bend like reeds and approached the political authorities as supplicants asking or pleading for understanding, permissions, protections.

Social discrimination prevented them from owning land in much of Europe and from joining guilds and having jobs in many professions, so Jews concentrated themselves in those occupations open to them. Jews were far more literate and educated than non-Jews, owing to the culture of learning derived from the Jewish biblical injunction to teach the children of Israel to read. Their greater education allowed them to excel in those economic and social spheres permitted to them, including scholarship and those professions requiring or bringing an advantage to those with the ability to read and write, among them commerce of many kinds and, as they opened up to them in modern times, law, medicine, journalism, and university life. Most famously, some Jews became prominent bankers in much of Europe, precisely because the Catholic Church, considering usury (earning interest) to be a sin, forbade Christians from engaging in this necessary economic function. Rabbi Eliezer ben Nathan of Mainz in Germany explained in the twelfth century that because Jews "own[ed] no fields or vineyards whereby they could live, lending money to non-Jews [was] necessary and therefore permitted."[1] Despite these educational advantages and occupational successes, the popular view of Jews' wealth is a myth: most Jews remained poor into the modern period, including the vast majority of Jews in the Eastern European and Russian demographic heartland of Jewry. This was also true of Jews in Arab and Islamic countries.

Today, Jews remain extraordinarily diverse and are Jewish ever less because of religiosity or ethnicity. More than ever, they adopt the idiom of their own countries. The Jews of France and even the Jews of Germany (as alienated and uncomfortable as they remain) are far more like French and Germans than they are like one another, or for that matter like Jewish Americans, let alone the Jews of Israel. Each community of Jews differs substantially from one another in its characteristics and in its political relationships to its own countries. Yet, within certain regions, there are political commonalities.

Owing to the history of persecution and the existence of considerable antisemitism (however much of it may be latent), European Jews are generally timid communities. Regarding their Jewishness, they are inward-looking. With the partial exception of German and French Jews, they are poorly organized politically and reluctant to take public demonstrative political stands either for themselves (they are not corporately active either as liberals or conservatives) or to press foreign-policy concerns regarding Israel, and thus have little collective influence over their countries' politics. In Western Europe, they are generally well off economically, well-behaved members and exemplary citizens of their communities, but without substantial political engagement or influence. Around Europe Jews know that they are on the defensive, with their institutions, especially synagogues and community centers, guarded like fortresses or bunkers. In much of Central and Eastern Europe, Jews are surrounded by even more overt antisemitism.

Jewish Americans live in a society that has always been considerably more pluralistic and less antisemitic than those of Europe. Here, Jews are self-confident, economically well off, with leading positions across the elite professions, including politics. They are not ashamed or fearful of being known as Jews. Jewish Americans individually and collectively are active politically overwhelmingly not as Jews, but like others, as Americans. The distinction is evident in the way Jews are referred to elsewhere: French Jews, British Jews, German Jews, or Polish Jews (where the immediate nationality comes first) versus the United States, where *Jewish Americans* is how Jews are typically conceived of and described—their Jewishness an adjective of the primary identity of American, making them linguistically and conceptually no different from African Americans, Italian Americans, or Asian Americans.

Jewish Americans vigorously pursue their general political aspirations, whatever they are—as voters, as opinion leaders in academia and the media, as financial contributors to political parties and candidates, and as active politicians. Regarding domestic politics, they are overwhelmingly liberal, progressive, Democrats—in voting, monetary contributions, political affiliation, and political officeholding—having marched and carried the banner of greater social justice from the civil rights era until today. When necessary, they pursue their organized interests, including and particularly in foreign policy, on behalf of their understanding of American values and interests, which includes support of Israel. Their attachment to their Jewishness varies enormously. For most that attachment is less grounded in religion as most Jewish Americans are either secular or not particularly religious, many having but weak attachments to Jewish identity. Rather, their Jewishness resides in some combination of a vaguely articulated notion of being culturally Jewish; membership in the Jewish people while identifying themselves foremost as Americans; a sense of shared history, including the persecution of Jews, often family members, during the Holocaust; and concern for Israel.

Jews in other non-English-speaking countries are small in number. Canada with close to four hundred thousand Jews and Australia with more than one hundred thousand, and to a lesser degree South Africa with seventy thousand, have vibrant communities existing in countries that are somewhere between the United States and Europe in the degree of hospitableness toward Jews, of their public spheres being contested by and poisoned with antisemitism, and of danger of antisemitic physical violence. They are thus — measured by the difficult position Jews find themselves in almost everywhere in the world — reasonably well off, capable of representing their interests politically, but by no means with the open and self-confident presence that American Jews have as a community or as individuals. In the rest of Asia, Africa, Oceana, and Latin America, only four countries have Jewish populations exceeding twenty thousand, all in Latin America, forming but tiny percentages of the Argentinean (.4 percent), Brazilian (.05 percent), Mexican (.04 percent), and Chilean (1.2 percent) people. In these countries, Jews have little effective communal representation and face to varying degrees considerable antisemitism and the threat of violence, with Latin America, including these countries, becoming during the last few decades ever more depopulated of Jews as they have progressively emigrated owing to hostility and the danger they face. Finally, in the Arab and Islamic world, Jews have effectively ceased to exist since the various countries tolerate but minuscule numbers of aging Jews, where before Israel's establishment there had been close to a million in the region, with the communities in many of the countries having had uninterrupted histories going back thousands of years. It is inconceivable that these countries, coursing with impassioned and virulent antisemitism, could be home to sizable Jewish communities before a substantial and right now hard-to-imagine one-hundred-eighty-degree turn in the character of the public sphere and in the extent of personal prejudice, which is unlikely to occur anytime in the foreseeable future.

Jews in Israel form the majority in an avowedly Jewish country. Not surprisingly, there Jews socially resemble the majoritarian peoples of other countries much more than do the Jewish minorities of Europe, of the United States, or of any other country. They occupy all spheres of society, economic classes, and professions. They span all political affiliations and aspirations. Their Jewishness, including in its many diversities, embodies society, culture, and politics. They are varied ethnically and in their historical understandings. Jews in Israel serve in the military and defend themselves with a vigor and tenacity that set them apart from Jews over the centuries and contemporary Jews elsewhere. A large and more influential minority have one or another European heritage with family histories overwhelmingly grounded in the Holocaust. The majority originate from the Middle East and its different history of persecution by the countries and peoples surrounding and hostile to Israel, which expelled them or their forebears at the time of Israel's founding. In Israel, being a Jew is just being a Jew. It is unproblematic to say: *I am a Jew,* just as it is for most Italians, French, or Swedes to say *I am an Italian,* a *Frenchman,* or a *Swede.*

What gives Jews, far flung around much of the world, common characteristics in the sense of common attributes or dispositions? Nothing. More pointedly, what common dispositions do they have for acting in ways that substantially affect their neighbors in town after town, region after region, country after country? None. If asked to reflect on the humanity of a collection of Europeans or Christians, even from the same country, let alone from a variety of countries, people would see the absurdity of saying that all such Europeans or Christians are the same, or all share the same distinctive attributes, or, more, all share the one master, defining attribute that motives them to harm others. Yet that is precisely what has been the norm for tens of millions, indeed hundreds of millions of people through the ages, and even today, to say with regard to Jews.

The diversity of Jews over time and today — similar to Europeans or Christians — and their many, depending on time and place, communal and individual differences of concerns and practices, render finding the common denominator, especially with regard to how Jews relate or would relate to non-Jews, an exercise in absurdity. True, Jews have certain social characteristics or tendencies, but they are prosaic, nothing special compared to other people. Jewish Americans are more liberal and less martial than non-Jews, but in Israel Jews are more conservative and more martial than many other people. And the liberality of Jewish Americans in the context of American politics would place them squarely in the middle of the European political spectrum, which far more supports welfare-state policies, governmental regulation of society, and social justice. Historically, Jews have been powerless, the pawns and victims of powerful churches, rulers, prejudiced majorities, and mobs, and while they are not so impotent today, especially in the United States and in their national home of Israel, the notions of Jews' commonality and earth-shattering power, and malevolence, continue to be a figment of the antisemitic imagination.

Antisemitism, grounded in reductionist views of Jews, has been and continues to be nonsense. But sadly for Jews and for non-Jews, such nonsense has had world historically destructive consequences — and could again.

# 3

# The Singular Prejudice

ANTISEMITISM IS ONE thing and it is many things.

Antisemitism is a prejudice against Jews. This means conceiving of Jews—men and women, children and seniors—as having noxious qualities or as undesirable only because they are Jews. Animus in forms ranging from mild distaste to intense hatred typically accompanies such a conception. Antisemites apply their conceptions and animus to Jews as a group and to individual Jews even before they know anything about the individuals. They do so regardless of countervailing evidence.

Antisemitism is many varieties of prejudice against Jews, with diverse dimensions and components, including its varied sources, its many manifestations, and the many different actions it leads its bearers to contemplate and undertake. Antisemitism is thought. It is emotion. It is speech. It is action. It is inaction. Antisemitism exists and can be identified if *any of these* in an anti-Jewish form are present, and a person is antisemitic if he has or engages in *any of them*.

A person thinking antisemitic thoughts, prejudicial thoughts against Jews, is an antisemite regardless of his emotions, his words, his actions, or inactions. A person with an aversion or hostility toward Jews, which he feels as instinctive, even without having more coherent prejudicial thoughts or uttering words or taking actions against Jews, is an antisemite. A person, say for political gain but without inner conviction or hostility, speaking the language of antisemitism is an antisemite. A person who engages in antisemitic action against Jews, regardless of his views of them, is an antisemite. When it comes to prejudice, as with many other things, when you do bad things (your inner thoughts and emotions notwithstanding), you are what you do. And if a person fails to see that obviously prejudicial words or action against Jews is prejudicial and therefore antisemitic, this emerges from prejudicial perceptual bias, and it too constitutes antisemitism.

Antisemitism, like *democracy, modernity,* or *conservatism,* has multiple manifestations, is a complex phenomenon, and defies pithy all-encompassing definitions. We have some sense of what each means, but defining each encounters difficulties, as the many existing competing definitions and analyses of each one demonstrate. Further complicating this are the varieties of democracy, modernity, conservatism, or antisemitism that actually exist, which render seeming truths and essential dimensions of one democracy, one country's version of modernity, or one brand of conservatism false or even at odds with a second or a third, let alone a tenth. If we reduce each phenomenon merely to its common features — such as *democracies* are political systems that use elections to determine who governs — then many essential and actual aspects of that phenomenon are lost, not only stripping it of its complexity and richness but likely misconstruing its real character and functioning. In mapping the many aspects or dimensions of the variety of democracies, modernities, or brands of conservatism, the plethora of each one's components and their combinations can become bewildering. Mapping both how each one came about, often through very different routes, and how they actually function, adds several more layers of considerable complexity. All this is true for many other individual concepts we use to map the complexities of worldly phenomena — from *ideology* to *freedom* to the general category of *prejudice.* Not surprisingly, this is also true for a phenomenon as enduring and varied as antisemitism, a sense of which we can get by looking at a few prominent and assorted antisemites:

Horst Mahler is a notorious German lawyer, Neo-Nazi, and open antisemite who conspicuously became a member of the Neo-Nazi NPD political party in Germany in 2000, defended the party against the government's legal attempt in 2001 to ban it, and then left the party. Having been a leftist revolutionary and one of the founders of the infamous Red Army Faction terrorist group in 1970, before migrating to the radical right, he has nonetheless remained constant to his lodestar antisemitism, merging Marxist anticapitalist antisemitism with his classical Nazi anti-semitic notions. Mahler asserts at once that the "the systematic extermination of Jews in Auschwitz is a lie," and that "billions of people would be ready to forgive Hitler if he had committed only the murder of the Jews"; that Hitler was a savior of Germany and not just of Germany; and that "Jewish financial capital" controls a "secret government" the members of which constitute the "directors of the global economic and financial system."[1] He has been convicted several times before German courts for Holocaust denial and other antisemitic statements, which are illegal in Germany. In Mahler, we see an unreconstructed Nazi antisemitic view of Jews' influence in the world, who sees Germans cowed and shackled by the Jews, whose mass murder, in the name of the German people, he justifies.

Norman Finkelstein is not quite so brazen about the past but has been even more poisonous about the present. Finkelstein has been a leading and damaging source of antisemitism, especially in Germany, though also in the Western world more broadly, as one of the best known (non-Arab or Muslim) anti-Israel ideologues and a college campus speaking darling. He has been overwhelmingly politically oriented in his antisemitism of one part denying truths about the Holocaust and one part characterizing Israel in Nazi-like tones. He falsifies and fabricates history, finds favor with Holocaust deniers (even if he does not explicitly deny that the Holocaust occurred), says that Holocaust survivors lie and invent what happened to them, and attacks scholars of the Holocaust (including me) as wholesale inventors of their accounts. He has written an infamous, mendacious book assaulting the truth about the Holocaust and has baldly stated that "Holocaust studies" is "mainly a propaganda enterprise."[2] Finkelstein's antipathy, which has an obsessive quality, toward having the truth told about the Holocaust (his parents he parades, like court Jews, as survivors) politically serves his main obsession, which has been to blacken the name of Israel. He long treated Israel as the heir of Nazism, as essentially a Nazi-like country, and those, especially Jews, who defend Israel as Nazis or Nazi-like. Finkelstein has spoken in blatant antisemitic idiom about Israel, including, "I think Israel, as a number of commentators pointed out, is becoming an insane state. And we have to be honest about that. While the rest of the world wants peace,

Europe wants peace, the US wants peace, but this state wants war, war and war." And, "[Israel] is a vandal state. There is a Russian writer who once described vandal states as Genghis Khan with a telegraph. Israel is Genghis Khan with a computer. I feel no emotion of affinity with that state. I have some good friends and their families there, and of course I would not want any of them to be hurt. That said, sometimes I feel that Israel has come out of the boils of the hell, a satanic state." And what has Israel been doing? According to Finkelstein, who, in calling Israel a "satanic state," conjured up here the age-old antisemitic likening of Jews to the devil: "Israel is committing a holocaust in Gaza."[3]

Hassan Nasrallah, the leader of Hezbollah, is a stand-in for the views of other Arab and Islamic leaders, political Islamists in general, and Arabs and Muslims throughout the Middle East and in much of Asia. He has been one of the most popular leaders not only in his own country but, until siding with Assad during the Syrian civil war, throughout the Arab and Islamic world. He was certainly its most popular and visible leader during the Lebanon War in 2006 and in its aftermath, when the Arab and Islamic world believed him to have defeated Israel militarily, owing to the casualties Hezbollah caused and the difficulty the Israelis had in dislodging Hezbollah from southern Lebanon. He too, like antisemites around the world who deny or minimize the extent and the horror of the Holocaust, casts doubt on the Holocaust, saying: "The Jews invented the legend of the Nazi atrocities. It is clear that the numbers they talk about are greatly exaggerated." But this is a secondary concern of his, as his many antisemitic pronouncements about Jews and Israel abundantly emphasize. His twofold intention is to persuade others of Jews'—and not just Israel's—depravity and to eliminate the Jews and their political home from the Middle East. On Hezbollah television, Nasrallah declared Jews to be "Allah's most cowardly and avaricious creatures. If you look all over the world, you will find no one more miserly or greedy than they are." Why are they this way? Drawing on the Qur'an's depiction of Jews, Nasrallah calls Israel the "the state of the grandsons of apes and pigs—the Zionist Jews" and condemns them as "the murderers of the prophets." And how evil are they? Jews demonically control the world's superpower and threaten the entire world. In February 2012, he declaimed publicly:

I say that the American administration and the American mentality lack nothing from Satanism. But that kind of behavior and that kind of mistreatment of holy books [referring to the Qur'an burning incident in Afghanistan in February 2012] and prophets, and the prophets' sanctities, and others' sanctities; this behavior is Israeli and let us say it is Jewish, between quotation marks, — now they will say that this is anti-Semitism — [but] the Holy Qur'an told us about this people: how they attacked their prophets, and how they killed their prophets, and how they affronted their prophets, and how they affronted Jesus Christ, peace be upon him, and how they affronted Mary, peace be upon her, and how they affronted Allah's great messenger Mohammad, May God exalt and bring peace upon him and his family. This [behavior] pattern about affronting holy books, and prophets, and messengers, and sanctities; this is their mentality, and maybe they want to push things more and more toward a religious war worldwide.[4]

Hezbollah's very first Facebook posting was in English so the entire world would not mistake Nasrallah and Hezbollah as anything but inveterate, eliminationist antisemites: "O Allah, Please Clean This World From Jewish Contamination."[5] The notion of Jews controlling the United States was a standard Nazi one and has been a staple of antisemites ever since. The view today that if not for Jews' insidious control of the United States, the United States itself would be a better country, the Middle East would be far better off, and the world would be a better place comes also from those whose antisemitism is principally focused on the United States itself. In their widely discussed book *The Israel Lobby,* John Mearsheimer and Stephen Walt peddle such antisemitism dressed up in the garb of academic seriousness and respectability, with their invention of the bogeyman known as the Israel Lobby into which they subsume and thereby delegitimize people who vocally or in various ways materially support Israel. Indeed, their book is the best cloaked major antisemitic tract in English of the last several decades. A small sampling of the antisemitic tropes it draws upon or echoes: Jews working collectively in concrete organizations for nefarious ends. Jewish conspiracy. Jews as fifth columnists. Jews pulling levers behind the scenes. Jews harming the broader societies in which they live. Jews starting or

*In 1942, President Franklin Roosevelt is depicted as serving the Jews.*

causing wars, in this case the attacks of 9/11, the Iraq War, and the war on terror. It is as if Mearsheimer and Walt scoured the antisemitic manual, updated any number of its most effective techniques, and dressed them up in language and tone and academic trappings—*we teach at Chicago and Harvard*—for respectability. Their hollow denials that they are antisemites and their empty self-presentation as brave truth-tellers have since been definitively exposed as false by Mearsheimer's unabashed endorsement (and Walt's support of Mearsheimer in this matter) of the blatantly antisemitic book of Gilad Atzmon, one of Britain's most prominent jazz musicians and most notorious antisemites. Atzmon, born in Israel, draws a link between the most famous antisemitic characters of literature and Jews of today: "Fagin is the ultimate plunderer, a child exploiter and usurer. Shylock is the blood-thirsty merchant. With Fagin and Shylock in [a person's] mind, the Israeli treatment of the Palestinians seems to be just a further event in an endless hellish continuum." Given the long historical malignant character he attributes to Jews, Atzmon, not surprisingly, blames the Jews for Hitler's persecution of them and, in an almost unsurpassable flight of hate-filled raving, accuses the Jews of using the Holocaust as "a license to kill, to flatten, no nuke, to wipe, to rape, to loot and to ethnically cleanse. It made vengeance and revenge into a Western value."[6] In short, according to Mearsheimer and Walt, Jews, and the non-Jews they have co-opted or allied themselves with (Mearsheimer and Walt are careful to formally insist some non-Jews are also part of the Israel Lobby), insidiously control American foreign-policy making, betray American interests, duped the United States into launching an unnecessary war against Iraq, thereby impoverish the United States, produce enmity for it across many countries, wreak destruction halfway around the world, and cause the death of a large number of innocent Americans. Indeed, in an earlier article — before they sanitized their presentation for the book — Mearsheimer and Walt wrote even more openly in the vein of antisemites past and present. They warned in ominous tones about the power of "Israel and its American supporters": "If their efforts to shape US policy succeed, Israel's enemies will be weakened or overthrown, Israel will get a free hand with the Palestinians, and the US will do most of the fighting, dying, rebuilding and paying."

Jews — conniving, powerful, working behind the scenes in conspiratorial concert — ultimately serve their putative Israeli master, betraying

Al-Watan, *Qatar, March 23, 2003. President George W. Bush is a gun-slinging sheriff in the Iraqi oil fields. His badge is a David Star.*

their homeland and their neighbors. But there is actually no such thing as the Israel Lobby (which Mearsheimer and Walt, to cover their backs, concede, buried in their book). There are many supporters of Israel — indeed, by far and away most Americans are, with five times more siding with Israel in March 2013 than with the Palestinians (64 percent to 12 percent) — and Jewish Americans, who comprise less than 2 percent of the American people, generally and strongly support Israel. This should not be surprising as Israel has been for decades the lone genuine democracy in the Middle East and a staunch American ally, including during the Cold War. As has long been known and discussed, Israel's supporters, given their preponderance in a democracy and their passion for the beleaguered, existentially threatened democracy with which many sympathize and identify, have no doubt been influential in Washington. But most of them do not formally or informally belong to a lobby, which in American politics is an organization or group of organizations that seek to directly influence governmental officials and which has the clear connotation of something not in the public interest, or worse. Yet Mearsheimer and Walt deploy this bogeyman concept of the Israel Lobby as their principal conspiracy trope that is an update on the notorious antisemitic tract *The Protocols of the Elders of Zion* (discussed at length in chapter 9). They paint a picture of American foreign-policy making that is fantastical, bearing hardly any relationship to what actually goes on or went on, with Martin Peretz, the former owner of the *New Republic,* getting more references in a book that concentrates overwhelmingly on the causes of the Iraq War than does the powerful Secretary of Defense and architect of the war, Donald Rumsfeld, who is mentioned on only five pages! Karl Rove, the behind-the-scenes architect of George Bush's presidency and overwhelmingly considered to have been Bush's major political strategist, always with an eye on doing what was best for Bush and Republicans, especially with safeguarding their domestic agenda and electoral fortunes, gets one reference — as many as I do! Vice President Dick Cheney was, by political analysts across the political spectrum, widely considered the most powerful person (aside from or even including Bush) in the administration. Add the journalist Jeffrey Goldberg to Peretz and me, and Mearsheimer and Walt's *Israel Lobby* has roughly as many index references to us as to Cheney.

Indeed, Cheney, Rumsfeld, Colin Powell, Karl Rove, and even Bush himself were all deeply enmeshed in the American and Republican power establishment, all mindful and most intimately connected to America's financial and economic corporate powers and leaders, especially the mighty defense establishment and critical oil industry, with its fortunes intimately tied to the Middle East. The notion that the hard-bitten practitioners of power, and all the powerful economic and political interests they represented and wanted to safeguard, were all duped by a bunch of Jews into launching a massive war they otherwise would not have wanted—and which they therefore would have known would damage their own political fortunes massively—is on its face ludicrous and can be made, as Mearsheimer and Walt demonstrate in their book, its fake sober tones notwithstanding, only by suspending reality and substituting for it a parallel antisemitic unreality.

As with antisemites historically, who, whatever their other differences, can find common ground in their distemper with and aggression toward Jews, the renowned, wide-eyed Norwegian "Father of Peace Studies," Johan Galtung, and the American foreign-policy self-styled hard-headed analysts of power Mearsheimer and Walt see eye to eye: the mendacious and nefarious Jews are to blame. Galtung, the founder of the entire discipline of *peace studies,* has publicly done his work since establishing the Peace Research Institute in Oslo in 1959, while keeping his antisemitism to himself—until in 2011 he judged that it was time, and perhaps the world was receptive enough, for him to come out into the open, speak his mind, and warn everyone about the threat of Jews. Galtung is unequivocal: "The Jews control U.S. media," and use it to warp the American people and politics to support Israel. According to Galtung, Jews have been so pernicious in the past that they produced the justifiable antisemitism of those who wanted to be rid of them, which eventually led the Nazis to want to eliminate the world of their evil. He has sponsored public discussions of the The Protocols of the Elders of Zion, which he recommends that people read, and has likened the investment bankers of Goldman Sachs to these Jewish elders. He has even hinted that Israel's intelligence agency, Mossad, may have been behind the Norwegian mass murderer Anders Breivik, who in 2011

slaughtered seventy-seven Norwegians by bombing government buildings and gunning down members of a youth camp. The giveaway:
Breivik was a Freemason, an organization that, according to Galtung,
"has Jewish origins."

Helen Thomas, for years the dean of Washington's White House
press corps, honored with a plaque on her chair in the first row of the
White House press briefing room, and with the right to ask the first
question at presidential news conferences, never said a word of her true
feelings about Jews publicly for all the decades she served the UPI news
agency and then the media conglomerate Hearst. In 2010, perhaps
because her guard had been lowered owing to her advancing age of
eighty-nine or perhaps because she no longer wanted to muzzle her true
views and feelings, she responded to a question about Israel on camera,
referring to the Jews: "Tell them to get the hell out of Palestine." "Go
home," she added. Asked where home would be for all the millions of
Jews born in Israel and citizens of the country, Thomas wildly declared,
"Poland, Germany and America, and everywhere else."[7] Thomas, too
late, apologized and said that these remarks did not represent her views.
But that was when she was trying to keep her job. Several months after
losing it, finally deciding to speak openly about her beliefs, she
showed that her off-the-cuff remark was no slip of the tongue but a
window into her antisemitic soul. Addressing in December an anti-
Arab-bias workshop in Detroit, she declared what was to her obvious
and necessary to say, revealing the core of her true conviction, which
was not merely focused on Israel but antisemitic to the core: "Congress, the White House, and Hollywood, Wall Street, are owned by
the Zionists. No question in my opinion. They put their money where
their mouth is.... We're being pushed into a wrong direction in
every way."

Israel, the Holocaust, old antisemitic tropes, dressed up or not dressed
up and just trotted out to explain deeds, events, situations, and conflicts
large and small that the antisemites deplore or detest, are the common
currency of today's antisemites. Ultimately they are grounded in age-old
animus and belief and felt viscerally, no matter their seeming coolness
and rational presentation. Mel Gibson's private and public outbursts
exemplify this, especially as his 2004 *The Passion of the Christ,* a blatantly

antisemitic film even according to the Catholic Church's own guidelines for depicting the last days and death of Jesus (discussed in chapter 10), was presented by him (and others) in the highfalutin tones of religiously faithful narration. The ancient antisemitic canards, creating a general frame of understanding for Jews, have also led Gibson to express more contemporary demonological notions. When a police officer in Los Angeles stopped him in 2006 for drunk driving, Gibson, obviously moved by bigotry (verging on paranoia) against Jews to think that he was being persecuted by them, demanded to know whether the officer was a Jew and in a rant exploded at him, "Fucking Jews...the Jews are responsible for all the wars in the world." Gibson's even more recent private utterances, as reported by one of his confidants, which repeatedly included calling Jews "Hebes," "oven dodgers," "Jewboys," and other gutter-level epithets laced with wild antisemitic assertions, only confirm his public outbursts, which only confirm that the manifest antisemitism of his very public film was driven by his private hatreds.[8]

Fashion designer John Galliano, unfiltered, less canny than the programmatic antisemite Gibson, erupted at least twice in crude, drunken rages in bars and cafés. One time in 2011, in a tirade caught on video, he directed it, puzzlingly, at a group of Italian women, whom he must have imagined were Jewish: "I love Hitler...People like you would be dead. Your mothers, your forefathers would all be fucking gassed and dead." Another time the same year, a gallery curator, Geraldine Bloch, reported that Galliano grabbed her hair and shouted, "Dirty Jew face, you should be dead," and told her to "shut your mouth, dirty bitch, I can't stand your dirty whore voice," after which he turned to her boyfriend, and (demonstrating hatred that extended beyond Jews) shouted, "[Expletive] Asian [expletive], I'll kill you!" He shouted at Bloch that she was ugly: "I can't bear looking at you...you're nothing but a whore." Bloch reported that this was all part of Galliano's antisemitic outburst: thirty antisemitic remarks in forty-five minutes.[9]

What does it all mean? Finkelstein, the leftist, a Jew, denies he is an antisemite, as he has preached to the converted and converts more by spreading venom against those who want the truth to be known about the Holocaust and who do not want Israel mortally weakened or destroyed. Mahler, a neo-Nazi, rages against a world that does not recognize his truths, unabashedly celebrating his Jew-hatred. Nasrallah, the political Islamic leader on the world stage, takes his and his follow-ers' antisemitism for granted as the foundation for his exterminationist program. Mearsheimer and Walt, self-styled political realists, dress up their decidedly surreal antisemitism in high-flown and self-important defense of American virtue and values against the depredations of Jews. Gibson, a dyed-in-the-wool, old-style Catholic antisemite, spins out his New Testament hatred publicly in cinematic calumny and incitement, and in private and uncontrollable outbursts. Galtung, one of the world's most renowned peace activists, reveals, after years hiding underneath his cloak of universal moralism and love, a burning and psychotic-like hatred for one people. And like so many others, Thomas, the dean of Washington journalism on the one hand, and Galliano, the fashion designer on the other, harbored their political and personal antisemi-tism until it too burst out when advancing years and the elixir of alcohol lowered their guards.

The pronouncements of these antisemites suggest several central fea-tures of antisemitism.

People ascribe to Jews a panoply of powers and malevolence and a record of destruction that is simply out of this world. Then, because Jews do not say that they plot or do these horrid things, indeed in their every pronouncement about all matters that relate to these and other antisemitic calumnies Jews say the opposite, antisemites make a second fundamental accusation, which only some of them articulate, but which underlies most of what they say about Jews: Jews lie and lie and lie — as individuals, as small groups, as a people — and they do so naturally, conspiratorially, and programmatically as a matter of consciously coor-dinated policy of the reified entity of world Jewry.

A third startling thing comes out of these examples. Antisemites can point to no concrete evidence that these vast powers and malevolence, and the coordination required to pull them off without manifest evi-dence of their machinations becoming public, are actually the properties of Jews. So antisemites repeatedly, chronically fabricate things, falsify things, describe an eerie world of their figmental or fantastical imagina-tions and making, pretend to analyze it, condemn it, and propose ways of eliminating the source of the problem. That they often are consciously lying is not surprising: from their perspective, they do so in the service of higher values, including the need to make people, communities, the world aware of the more fundamental truth of the Jewish threat, in which they wholeheartedly believe. As the doctrine of national security often leads governments around the world to think themselves justified in playing loose with particular truths in order to protect the greater interest and security of the nation, so too do antisemites deem the need to alert and convert people about the Jews a higher calling than strict fidelity to the facts.

It is, fourth, noteworthy that these antisemitic pronouncements, wildly at odds with reality, and often hateful, are being made by people of high intelligence and extraordinarily high achievement. These are not the uneducated, unwashed venting common, crude prejudices. Mahler has steeped himself in the famously difficult philosopher Hegel and has won a case before the European Court of Human Rights. Mearsheimer and Walt are political science professors at leading American universities. Galtung is an intellectual and movement luminary in Europe and beyond. Finkelstein is a man of obvious intelligence, capable of stringing together well-crafted if crackpot arguments. Nasrallah is a highly adept political leader, who has managed, as the head of a millennialist movement and army of Hezbollah, to negotiate and manipulate the incredibly complex and minefield-ridden political scene in Lebanon, with its powerful sectarian divisions (Sunni, Shiite, Christian, Druze), in conflict with the Israelis, and while pleasing and serving Syrian and Iranian masters. Helen Thomas was one of the most renowned members of the White House press corps for decades. Mel Gibson is, if not of the highest intelligence, at least cunning and among the most successful actors and producers in Hollywood. And John Galliano, as the head designer of Christian Dior, was at the fashion world's pinnacle. What makes this particularly shocking is that, presumably Nasrallah aside, all of them have had considerable, often enormous personal exposure to Jews, being in industries and in institutions where many Jews work, and undoubtedly having many Jewish colleagues, even close ones, some of whom they would call friends, and those friends, out of self-interest or misplaced loyalty, would even rise to the antisemites' defense.

The fifth noteworthy thing is the diversity of antisemitic orientations, tones, charges, and explicit or implied prescriptions antisemites adopt. The orientations vary from straight neo-Nazi in the case of Mahler; to reductionist anti-Zionist on Finkelstein's part; to Nasrallah's political

Islamist mixing of Islamic, classical Christian, and Nazi antisemitic elements; to Mearsheimer and Walt's fifth-columnist fusillade; to Mel Gibson's classical Christian antisemitism; to Helen Thomas' and Galliano's inchoate antisemitism. Their tones also vary considerably, from the abstract philosophical of Mahler, to the faux sober academic and more restrained of Mearsheimer and Walt, to the baiting of Finkelstein, to the elaborately theatrical or spontaneous inebriated (depending on the moment) of Gibson, to the unhinged of Galtung, to the missionary and politically mobilizing of Nasrallah, to the inhibitionless outbursts of Thomas and Galliano. And the charges in sum run a good part of the antisemitic gamut, although they vary considerably, holding the Jews responsible for an enormous range of ills and harm, from the world historical to the personal, wreaking havoc abroad and domestically, in the past and the present and, if unchecked, of course, the future. It is the latter notion, namely that the Jews are supposedly still at it, that leads any number of them to make or imply prescriptions, from Mearsheimer and Walt's desire for people to mobilize against Jews' (craftily called the Israel Lobby's) power and machinations domestically; to Thomas' blast that Jews just get the hell out of Israel and go back to where they came from (shades of sending blacks back to Africa); to Gibson's wish to turn back the clock and continue Christian religious incitement against Jews; to Finkelstein's many antisemitic, anti-Israel urgings (some of which he has of late repudiated); to Nasrallah's hope that Jews across the world be annihilated; to Mahler's similar declaration, invoking a philosophical and moral absolutism, that "in the destruction of the Jews reason prevails."[10]

And the sixth thing is that despite this diversity, antisemites share common features that unite them: distortions about Jews, turning Jews into corporate groups and organized massive conspiracies, an obsessiveness about Jews, an overt or underlying animus, and verbal, seemingly irrepressible, hyperbole in their denunciations of Jews. Antisemites' pronouncements about Jews and Israel are wild, divorced from reality.

Antisemitism exists as tangibly as does any book, newspaper, television program, Internet site, or national constitution, such as the U.S. Constitution. It is akin to how the American Constitution is sometimes described, as a living, breathing document, a *living constitution,* because the Constitution exercises powerful influence on the United States and its people today, and also because it is subject to changing, indeed evolving, understandings and therefore ever-changing influence. Antisemitism (though not a single written document), too, is a living thing, a prejudice, that influences people and their fates, societies and their fates, and countries, even civilizations and their fates—Christian civilization for close to two millennia, and Islamic civilization. It has also been central to ideologies and politics in movements and countries too plentiful to enumerate. Across Europe in the nineteenth and twentieth century, antisemitism became a powerful political ideology and mobilizing force for nationalism and within the domestic politics of many countries, from Russia, Ukraine, and Poland to Germany and France. Major political and cultural thinkers from the left to right—including Karl Marx, Immanuel Kant, Voltaire, Georg Wilhelm Friedrich von Hegel, and Richard Wagner—and countless politicians and political pamphleteers and agitators were preoccupied with the place and dangers of Jews in their countries and the world at large. Antisemitism was central enough to the political lives of European countries that it would be hard to understand the general character of cultural, social, and political existences of Germany, France, Poland, Russia, and so on without frequent reference to and emphasis upon it.

What makes antisemitism's centrality in political ideologies so important and so natural is that political ideologies are, whatever else, not mere descriptions of the world but calls to action. Like all political ideologies, antisemitism has been a program for righting the world. This differentiates it from many other common prejudices, which are mere accounts of dislikes, some of which can produce horrific oppression and discrimination, such as slavery or segregation, but which nevertheless do not deem a specific group to be devilish in deed and in need of being defeated. The putative problem of Jews has typically been integrated into the broadest possible understanding of the most essential and troubling questions of the belief systems, ideologies, and social and political organization of antisemites' worlds. This political-action orientation has for centuries animated antisemitism and antisemites, long before the existence of Israel—to which it is today principally applied. So, for Christianity and Christians, what ought to happen to the Jews, alleged killers of Jesus, was a central question for ages. Analogously, though less intensively, Islam and Muslims posed a similar question for Jews as the putative enemies of Muhammad and the keepers of a tradition that (like the Christians) they were claiming as now theirs. For European peoples and countries in the nineteenth and twentieth century, the problem of the supposedly alien and malevolent, irredeemable "race" of the Jews was an acute political problem, in need of a remedy. This was so in country after country, and unlike virtually any other belief system, antisemitism was transnational and capable of uniting peoples of otherwise antagonistic orientations. For antisemites today around the world, what to do with, to, and against Israel, indeed for many how to destroy it, and along the way, the influence of Jews in the United States, has been raised to one of our time's central problems.

Because antisemites through the ages have seen the problem of the Jews to be so acute, because they could in one way or another sign on to Heinrich von Treitschke's most notorious formulation in 1879, later wholeheartedly adopted by the Nazis, "the Jews are our misfortune," their antisemitic, religious, and secular ideologies have produced notions about how to deal with the threat Jews allegedly pose. And these notions and proposals have led to policies and programs that have moved people, communities, countries, and civilizations to engage in systematic discrimination. To establish ghettos. To force Jews to convert. To explode in anti-Jewish riots and pogroms. To expel and otherwise exclude Jews. To mark Jews publicly. To hunt down Jews and torture them. To slaughter Jews en masse. Antisemitism has been and continues to be *inherently* — and this is not similarly true of many, indeed most, prejudices — an extraordinarily dangerous prejudice, political ideology, and basis for political mobilization, policy, extreme violence, and elimination.

This continual eliminationist impulse — across time, geography, levels of development, religions, and political orientation — is not accidental, but built into antisemites' underlying beliefs and animus. It started with the Christians' call for Jews to disappear and accept Jesus as the Jewish biblically prophesied messiah. Its lethal practice began with Christians in Roman Alexandria mass murdering the city's Jews in 414. Eliminationism continued through the Middle Ages, with Christians ghettoizing Jews in virtually every European country, often for centuries and under the authority of the papal bulls, including in such economic and political capitals as Frankfurt, Krakow, Madrid, Prague,

Rome, Venice, and Vienna. Such ghettoization or restrictions on where Jews were permitted to live ended in many places only with the Enlightenment, though in Russia, for example, Jews continued to be confined to dwelling in a region known as the Pale of Settlement. Through the Middle Ages, Christians expelled Jews across Europe, with virtually every country, or some of their principal regions or cities, ridding themselves of Jews at one time or another, from England in the west, which expelled Jews in 1290 and did not let them back in for more than three hundred years; to Germany in the center, where during the fourteenth to sixteenth centuries Germans of one region and city after another — the country was divided into scores of sovereign city and regional states — drove out Jews so that the country was virtually Jew-free; to Spain in the south in the most infamous expulsion in 1492; to Hungary and Lithuania in the east in the fourteen and fifteenth centuries. The Middle Ages saw Christians frequently massacring and mass murdering Jews on a large scale, from the Christian warriors of the First Crusade slaughtering ten thousand Jews in France and Germany in 1096; to the vast and multiple assaults on Jews during the black plague from 1348 to 1350, when Germans slaughtered the Jews of three hundred fifty communities in what can be seen as a precursor of the Holocaust; to the mass murders of the Catholic Church–run Spanish Inquisition, most notoriously by burning Jews at the stake, which also had the quality of being a precursor of the Holocaust; to the Chmielnicki massacres of 1649 to 1656, when Ukrainians slaughtered more than one hundred thousand Jews in cities and towns across Poland, another apparent precursor of the Holocaust.

The eliminationist drive inherent in antisemitic thought and sentiment seemed to culminate in the modern period, with the racist antisemites calling for Jews' annihilation, and the Germans attempting, with the support of many other Europeans, to make good on this call. Yet it has continued today in the desire of many Arab and Islamic peoples to destroy Israel and its people, with ever more calls to do the same to Jews elsewhere.

Antisemites prejudge Jews both consciously and non-consciously, which leads them to discriminate against Jews in their thinking and often in their conduct. Antisemitism leads them to reduce the complexity of a Jewish person or of Jews to what can be called their *Jewness*. It renders their many individual or social roles — as men or women, professionals of one kind or another, Americans or some other nationality, conservatives or liberals, athletes or musicians — as irrelevant, leaving only or predominantly their Jewness. Real or imputed objectionable qualities and deeds of people who are Jewish are instantly attributable to their Jewness.

The term *Jewness* captures what antisemites conceive of as the essence and core noxiousness of Jews. It describes Jews' primary quality, as antisemites perceive them, a quality that both resides within the Jew and is the source of his or her noxiousness or malevolence of aspiration and deed. It is this essential quality that ultimately needs to be dealt with, often by elimination, if the imputed dangers Jews pose or harms they are causing are to be resolved. The term *Jewishness* inadequately captures this quality because it either describes Jews' self-identity or their cultural characteristics or attachments, both of which antisemites are less if at all concerned with. For antisemites, the essence of individual Jews, and the essence of Jews the world over, is their *Jewness*. How different antisemites conceive of this essence has varied substantially over time and place. For much of European history, and in much of the Arab and Islamic world for the last many decades, a German antisemite's confessional statement pertains to the malignancy of notions about the essence of Jews: "If one were to assemble in one entity all the attributes of all that is reprehensible and contemptible that entity would exactly be the Jew."[11] Today, in the West in particular, a more tempered view of the essence of Jews, of Jewness, coexists with and is certainly more widespread than this one. But whatever the variation in the content antisemites attribute to Jewness, that antisemites have this common orientation toward and fixation on Jewness, that is, the essence of Jews, cannot be reasonably disputed.

Antisemitism frames how a person approaches Jews, what he expects of them, and how he interprets their actions. Antisemites blame Jews for things they do not do, or see the Jews' Jewness as the cause of things to which their Jewishness is unrelated instead of correctly focusing on any of the people's many attributes that may be relevant to their conduct. Such erroneous thinking then, in an instantaneous feedback loop, further confirms the antisemite's assumptions and reinforces the power of his prejudice and animus. Framing leads to blaming, which further strengthens the frame to blame.

This framing effect exacerbates antisemites' penchant to disproportionately condemn Jews, which they do in three ways: By being on the lookout for Jews' alleged misdeeds, which often includes a bias for exaggerating their actions. By criticizing Jews but not non-Jews who do similar things. And attacking Jews far more intensely than similarly acting non-Jews. This can all be seen in how people condemn Israel and Jews for real or imagined transgressions compared to the transgressions of neighboring countries and peoples.

Many academics sign petitions to boycott Israel and even to boycott Israeli academics (though, in a classically bigoted manner, this de facto applies only to the Jewish and not Palestinian citizens of Israel). In the United Kingdom, such petitions have become hot-button issues, with the British University and College Union, which is the representative organization of university professors, having overwhelmingly passed in 2007 a resolution to boycott Israeli institutions and scholars. In 2013, the Teachers Union of Ireland, representing educators at all levels, voted a boycott, specifically to "cease all cultural and academic collaboration with Israel, including the exchange of scientists, students and academic personalities, as well as all cooperation in research programmes."[12] The British and Irish academics' pious pretentions to being merely impartial and impassioned defenders of human rights generally is on the face of it not believable, given their selective singling out of Israel and its scholars juxtaposed against their repeated and systematic failure to criticize, let alone take up as a cause, the violent oppression of other groups in countries around the world, particularly in the Arab and Islamic worlds.

Such anti-Israel petitions and calls to action have been less controversial and gone more smoothly in the United States than in Britain, probably because they have not succeeded, however briefly, to institutionalize a boycott through professional organizations. Nevertheless, nine hundred leftist academics, seeking to couch their antisemitism in the universal terms of human rights, delivered a petition in January 2009 to newly elected president Barack Obama demonizing Israel with wildly inflammatory tropes including "collective punishment," "apartheid regime," "racist regime," "besieged Bantustans," "crimes against humanity," and "ethnocidal atrocities." Most revealing was what happened when American economics professor Fred Gottheil circulated a second petition to the 675 American signatories of the first anti-Israel petition for whom he could find e-mails. Gottheil's Statement of Concern asked the signatories to support the cause of highly oppressed, indeed often persecuted, people in Middle Eastern countries other than Israel. The groups are women, gays, and lesbians. Gays and lesbians were not just discriminated against informally in these Middle Eastern countries but prohibited, persecuted, and subject in some of the countries to execution. Women, according to the United Nations gender-inequality index, suffer massive discrimination in many of these countries, being subject to imprisonment and even sometimes execution for acts allowed to men, acts that anyone concerned with human, political, or civil rights would deem a person's right to exercise.

So how did these academics respond? Gottheil explains:

> Only thirty of the 675 "self-described social-justice seeking academics" responded, 27 of them agreeing to endorse the Statement. But these 27 signatories represent less than five percent of the 675 contacted. In other words, 95 percent of those who had signed the Lloyd petition censuring Israel for human rights violation did not sign a statement concerning discrimination against women and gays and lesbians in the Middle East.
>
> Surprised? If so, prepare for yet a bigger surprise. As many as 25 percent of the Lloyd petition-signing academics were faculty associated with gender and women studies departments. Yet of these, only 5 endorsed the Statement calling for attention to the discrimination against women in the Muslim countries of the Middle East. Put more bluntly, 164 of the 169 faculty who had chosen to focus their life's work on matters affecting women, and who felt comfortable enough to affix their names to Lloyd's petition censuring Israel, chose not to sign a Statement of Concern about documented human rights violations against gays, lesbians, and women in the Middle East.[13]

Scholars are trained in the art of dispassionate analysis, often in the application of principles and the working out of moral positions, which they resoundingly claim to be doing when condemning Israel and Jewish Israelis, and when discriminating against them. So what does this say about the power of prejudice, and about the likelihood that people less schooled in dispassionate analysis and applying principles to social action will be able to curtail antisemitism's power on their perception, judgments, and conduct? What does it say about the way in which the language of general humanitarian principles and of universal human rights is used as cover for people's true motivation—antisemitism—for attacking Israel and its Jews?

This is typical of the selective concern characterizing the impassioned critics of the Jews' country. Indeed, virtually every real or alleged misdeed of Israel or Jewish Israelis toward Palestinians becomes headline news for the critics and elicits fierce, uncompromising condemnation, while the countries in Israel's region (often in conflict with Israel) and the Palestinians themselves, when they do similar, or much and many more worse, things, had for decades been greeted with silence, apology, or justification, often even applause. The examples are effectively endless. This selectivity—one of prejudice's classic hallmarks—is easy to show in two respects.

If the proverbial Martian had landed on earth and, knowing nothing of people's identities and supposed nature or perfidy, surveyed the world's horrors and the reaction of people in other countries to them, including media and academics, he would be uncomprehending. Not having been inculcated with antisemitic notions, he would not be able to make sense of the degree of criticism and vituperation directed at Israel. He would certainly have used the most fundamental measure of horror, the number of people killed by their governments, and since the Six Day War, the time marking the beginning of Israel's supposedly expansionist policies, he would have noted genocides in Cambodia in the 1970s, in Guatemala in the 1980s, in Rwanda and Bosnia in the 1990s, China's ongoing imperial eliminationist occupation of Tibet, and the genocide in the Democratic Republic of the Congo in the 2000s. He would have noted especially the eliminationist and genocidal assaults and mass murdering in the countries in conflict with Israel: Iran's mass murder of an estimated half a million of its own children as human mine sweepers and in human wave attacks. Saddam Hussein's mass murder of perhaps half a million people, including the systematic targeting of Kurds and the Marsh people Shia, even using chemical and biological weapons against them.

Hafaz el Assad's slaughter of upwards of forty thousand people in Hama, Syria, when they asked for nothing more than their freedom from his tyranny. Assad slaughtered in a few days far more people than Israel has killed in all its operations against those who attack it, yet barely a word of protest was heard from around the world. The Russians' mass murder of between fifty thousand and one hundred thousand people, and whole-sale destruction, in Chechnya from 1994 to 1996. The Palestinians' own systematic occupation and making war on various countries, including Jordan in 1970 and Lebanon in 1975, not to mention the openly geno-cidal orientation of their leaders and governing organizations, and of so many of their people toward Israel and Jews. And finally, Sudan, which for more than two decades has carried out eliminationist and extermina-tionist assaults first on the people of South Sudan and then in Darfur, with a mass murder toll of perhaps 2.5 million people and the destruc-tion of the lives of many millions more as the political Islamic Sudanese regime terrorized, assaulted, and expelled them from their homes and regions, and typically burned and razed their homes and villages. None of these historic horrors, dwarfing anything the Israelis have done, has received even one one hundredth the condemnation directed at Israel and the Jews of Israel. They have elicited almost no comment, let alone condemnation, let alone calls to action, from the cadres of states, political elites, academics, media elites, and organizations that routinely condemn Israel for the death of every Palestinian. No widespread calls for toppling these regimes, let alone for dissolving the countries. No boycotts. No comparisons to Nazism. Mainly silence, except for the enthusiastic sup-port such countries as Sudan receive from the same anti-Israel regimes, institutions, and people.

And these are merely some of the eliminationist and genocidal assaults that could be mentioned. Beyond them, there are the vast num-ber of lesser horrors that these countries or their dictatorships and peo-ples have perpetrated, as well as other eliminationist and exterminationist regimes and programs of North Korea and other communist countries, a slew of sub-Saharan African countries, a bevy of Latin American dic-tatorships, and the brutal dictatorships of the Arab and Islamic world. How many people's lives have been extinguished or utterly ruined by ruthless dictators and totalitarian regimes around the world without the impassioned, even obsessive anti-Israel forces raising hell?

With the various protests and rebellions against state authority beginning in 2010 known as the Arab Spring, it became fashionable for people in the West, until then overwhelmingly silent or apologetic for the same Arab and Islamic dictatorships that have oppressed and brutalized their people with barely any exception for decades, to discover and suddenly become outraged at how murderous and horrible these regimes are. So long as the regimes oppressed their people without the people stirring too much—and even when they did, as in Hama to which the Syrian regime responded with mass murder—much of the media, academics, and governments contentedly conducted business as usual, pretending that these murderous regimes were their peoples' legitimate rulers. But then, mention the words *Facebook* and *social media,* and have small-to-middling protests (as a percentage of a country's population) brandishing the word *freedom,* and the West's opinion makers and governments suddenly find these same regimes illegitimate and insist they must go.

So the question remains: Why did the people in the West, especially the avowed champions of democracy, self-determination, and human rights, who were attacking Israel and its Jews so vociferously for the previous decade or two or four, also not recognize that these same regimes—in Egypt, Libya, Tunisia, Syria, not to mention Iraq under Saddam, not to mention the Hitlerian al-Bashir regime in Sudan, and Hamas itself—at the time perpetrating similar or worse horrors than they later did during the Arab Spring, were illegitimate? Why were they criticizing Israel a hundred to one compared to these murderous regimes, when their denunciation of these regimes during the Arab Spring shows unequivocally the condemnation these rulers and their henchmen had all along deserved? Aside from the international community's indifference to dictators in general and the ways they brutalize their own people, it was in no small measure because these countries were opponents of Israel. Casting a truthful light on them would have also undermined a specific, actually manifestly nonsensical, antisemitic accusation against Israel that was intoned so frequently that it became for many conventional wisdom: Israel was greatly responsible for these countries' deplorable politics and underdevelopment. Indeed, to have condemned them would have broken the united front against Israel, cast an unwanted light upon these regimes' predations, and revealed how comparatively good Israel is.

A person does not have to hate Jews in his heart to be an antisemite, or for his antisemitic statements or acts to be deemed antisemitic. To be an antisemite, he merely has to subscribe to *or* spread antisemitism. Many white racists believe or say (today in private) prejudicial or racist things about, or act in prejudicial or discriminatory ways toward, African Americans. If someone says African Americans are not as intelligent as whites or discriminates against them in hiring or promotion, we say, regardless of his emotions, that he is a racist. No one says that if such a person does not *hate* African Americans, then he is not a racist. The standard is no different for antisemites. And when we rightly conceive of speech as a form of action, and one that powerfully affects the world — after all, most writers and speakers are trying to influence other people's understandings and willingness to support or to undertake certain acts or policies — then it becomes much harder to say that even though a person is acting in a way that prejudicially targets and harms Jews, he has nothing against Jews, and therefore does not deserve the customary term that describes such prejudice affixed to him, which is antisemitism.

Hatred or a deep-seated animus in one's heart for Jews, while often, actually typically, present among those who believe or spread prejudicial things about Jews, is not the issue, even if it is a major component of many people's antisemitism. There is no hatred against an ethnic, religious, linguistic, or cultural group without prejudice, but there is prejudice without hatred. Prejudicial perception, thinking, speaking, and acting are the defining aspect of antisemitism. Thus, there are objective indicators of antisemitism. These include:

> *False charges against Jews,* which may be expressed or merely believed. Antisemites are predisposed to believing all manner of criticism or accusations against individual Jews, groups of Jews, or Jews as a people, and then to convey them to others. This dimension of antisemitism is about the content of what a person thinks about Jews when beholding or dealing with them as individuals or as groups. It is perhaps the best understood and most frequently cited aspect of prejudice.

*Essentializing* Jews, which means that a person sees the *Jewness,* however he does, as the essential, defining, often close to all-defining feature of the person who is Jewish. That the Jew is an American, a German, an Israeli, or some other nationality, a man or woman, young or old, a conservative or a liberal, a professional of one kind, and so on, matters far less and often not at all because in the eyes of the person who beholds him he is foremost and often exclusively just a Jew. This is a quality of how a person conceives of what a Jew is and Jews are. It is a form of dehumanization because it radically fails to recognize the plurality of human qualities and attributes of a person who is a Jew, reducing his entire being to this one aspect of his identity, which is, to boot, often of tertiary or no importance to the Jew himself, who may be a Jew only in name.

*Selectivity of focus* on and criticism of Jews, which itself has three aspects: Putting Jews, and not others, under a microscope. Being unable to overlook or keep in proper perspective real or putative small and even large foibles, missteps, or transgressions of Jews that one does for non-Jews. And subjecting Jews to criticism or leveling accusations at them for such deeds that one does not similarly do for non-Jews who do the same things. This kind of selectivity is the hallmark of certain kinds of antisemites who try to remain respectable and deny their antisemitism by striving to say things about Jews that are not so outlandishly false, while ignoring similar and more objectionable or worse things that non-Jews do. But all antisemites, no matter how much or how little they care about their seeming respectability, fail to apply their stated or implied principles of conduct, of evaluating conduct, and of criticism equally to Jews and non-Jews. This aspect of antisemitism is about how the antisemite thinks of Jews in relation to non-Jews.

*Labeling non-Jews as Jews* is a common move, conscious and not, that antisemites make. There are two cognitive logics prompting this, depending on whether the antisemite knows that what he is saying is false. One is that because he deems a person evil or malevolent or harmful, and believes that the Jews are evil or the source of evil, he concludes that that person must be a Jew. The second is for a person to label someone a Jew in order to powerfully delegitimize that person or to produce enmity for him. If an antisemite wants to feel justified in harming a person, physically or otherwise, there is no better way than to create blanket authorization for feeling this way. When Lara Logan, a CBS television correspondent, was attacked and assaulted sexually while covering the protests in Cairo's Tahrir Square in 2011, her attackers screamed "Jew! Jew!" Egyptian soldiers, her ostensible protectors, had previously hassled her and her crew, seemingly reflexively accusing them of "being Israeli spies."[14] Logan is not Jewish. This kind of antisemitic delegitimization and disinhibition has been practiced by antisemites through the ages, including and particularly by leaders. Christian, racist, Arab, and Islamic antisemites have used *Jew* and *Jewish* as free-floating labels for evil, which today many also do with *Israel* or *Israeli,* as many others do with the sometimes euphemistic, sometimes noneuphemistic stand-in for them, *Zionism and Zionist.* This can be seen all over Europe, where soccer fans, inflamed by passions and perhaps disinhibited by alcohol, routinely shout and chant that opposing teams and fans are "Jews," accompanied by antisemitic slurs and epithets, including such items as "Hamas, Hamas, Jews to the gas," and regular hissing meant to simulate the sound of the gas chambers.[15]

*Resistance to corrections,* which is a person's reluctance, unwillingness, even incapacity to reform his antisemitic orientation in each of its aspects: his conception of what a Jew is or Jews are, the content of his views about Jews and what he says about them, and his understanding of how Jews stand in relation to non-Jews. Thus, if a person who may believe false things about Jews (even non-antisemites may occasionally believe things that are not true about Jews) is shown that they are false, and he does not mend his views, this demonstrates that he is an antisemite. Similarly, an antisemite does not give up his reductionism and dehumanization of Jews even when it is brought to his attention. And he does not desist in his selective attention and criticism of Jews, even when he is asked to apply the underlying principles governing his practice to non-Jews equally and without prejudice.

Humans have a strong proclivity to harboring prejudice. It is the nature of human thought, undoubtedly because it was evolutionarily adaptive for people to do two things: to generalize readily from a few examples, which means to overgeneralize, because that is the best way to make sense of the world's otherwise bewildering complexity; and to be particularly attuned to danger or potential danger, including that of other people. Together these two adaptive cognitive tendencies lead people to be overly ready to see disturbing or dangerous qualities in unknown people who seem different, and then to generalize these qualities to the groups to which such people are deemed to belong. This is what prejudice is. We must all struggle, then, against letting what is useful and adaptive, which is to generalize and to be on our guard, from becoming something misleading and injurious—which is prejudice. When we realize that all generalization contains a misleading or false element precisely because all the things, people, or acts are not the same or exactly the same, yet generalizations hold them to be the same, we should be particularly on guard about the nature of our generalizations about other groups of people. Some false generalizations become both so negative and so hardened in people's minds that they rise to the level of prejudice, and then some become so entrenched and so divorced from reality and reality testing and correction that they become pathological. Antisemitism is the foremost prejudice of this kind, and it fundamentally differs from all other prejudices owing to its unparalleled constellation of features, many of which are singular or at least highly unusual among prejudices.

The third hardwired factor that exacerbates this general evolutionary problem of people being prone to prejudice is that people are not particularly good analysts, not just regarding group life but in general. Few are trained in the assessment of data, or information, and the structure of inference, which is how one draws appropriate conclusions, including generalizations, from data. The fourth factor is a well-known tendency humans have to resist change to many kinds of ideas, particularly generalizations, known as *confirmation-bias*. Humans appear hardwired to privilege new data that confirm what they already believe and to pay less attention to, or discount, data that disconfirm, challenge, or should lead to a revision of what they already believe, including or especially generalizations about the world. This makes a generalization, a negative stereotype, a prejudice, or an animus toward, about, or against another group difficult to dislodge once locked in place.

These four hardwired cognitive features of humans make the problem of prejudice inherent and serious. I mention them, and the constellation they produce, for two specific reasons. First, being cognizant of these hardwired cognitive features helps us point to general processes, factors, and outcomes that explain the general tendency toward prejudice, including antisemitism, and also to identify the distinctiveness of antisemitism's many singular features among prejudices that the general factors cannot explain. Second, in deciding whether to consider someone prejudiced or not, we need to think about what differentiates real prejudice from the ordinary and unavoidable cognitive errors that humans make. And as antisemites routinely seek to inoculate themselves from being called what they are—antisemites—by saying that those decrying antisemitism do so when there is none, we must be clear about when people's statements or beliefs constitute antisemitism.

Because of these cognitive limitations, we should show some indulgence for people who make understandable errors about Jews and who even hold on to such views in the face of countervailing evidence. In general, we should be liberal in allowing for individual errors in casual beliefs about Israel or Jews before applying to people the moniker of antisemitism. Such errors differ from systematic bias and animus against Jews and from people believing in any aspects of the foundational antisemitic paradigm—which we explore in depth in the next chapter—which holds Jews to be in their essence different from non-Jews and noxious. Regarding people who make understandable casual errors, we should give them ample opportunity to recognize their mistakes and to change their views, as people of goodwill would do. Well-meaning people can have an uninformed, casual prejudicial view or two (as distinct from those central to the foundational antisemitic paradigm and discourses) without being antisemites.

Yet when people make such errors systematically, with passion, with little reference to reality, and then hold on to their errors tenaciously, they have crossed well over the line from the understandable errors of human intellectual fallibility into the realms of prejudice and animus, into the realm of antisemitism. Exactly where and when we draw the line between understandable cognitive errors about Jews and antisemitism can be difficult to determine and can be debated as a principle and in how it applies to specific utterances, acts, or people. Take the common notion that Israel, by doing whatever it is doing, is the cause, or at least a principal cause, of political Islamic terrorism against the United States. This notion, as nonsensical as it is—after all, political Islamists as a matter of course conceptualize and call the United States "the Great Satan"—might be believed by a person who casually follows politics. It might also be genuinely believed by some who pay more attention but who simply analyze poorly the issue of terrorism's cause—for reasons that have nothing to do with their views of Jews. And it might be held by a variety of people who are well informed about the facts, about the fundamental antipathy of political Islamists for the West, for Infidels, for the United States as the embodiment of all that they hate and as the cause of their countries' and people's abject state of development, yet who persist in blaming the Jews in Israel, do so with a passion, and stick to this view no matter how many times the facts are thrust before them. In each case, the same belief is held by different people, but with a different status and meaning for each of them. If a person is not paying attention, or is simply a bad analyst, and thinks something seemingly plausible that casts Jews in a negative light, that person is not an antisemite. But if a person pays a great deal of attention, persists in a prejudicial absurdity, and if that absurdity is linked, let alone interwoven into a web of other related beliefs about Jews which that person holds, then he is an antisemite.

Other people who subscribe to the foundational antisemitic paradigm, or its central damaging beliefs and tropes, can at once be well-meaning toward Jews *and* be antisemites. As we have seen, being an antisemite does not even require that the person conceive of himself as an antisemite. It does not require that a person have hate in his heart, since many undeniable antisemites are cool, even cynical bearers of prejudicial views against Jews. It does not require that someone be a non-Jew, as the identity of a person is irrelevant to evaluating the character and meaning of his beliefs and animus. Some people of Jewish origin have thrown their minds, hearts, and prospects in with antisemites. Some have done so for gain—currying favor and advantage from the non-Jewish world. Others have done so because their general politics or ideology and social affiliations powerfully propel them in antisemitic directions. Others, out of touch with reality, have done so driven by their own psychopathology, believing that their family and community members are as malignant as the antisemitic paradigm purports them to be. But no matter people's subjective states, identities, or professed allegiances, people's status as bigots or as nonbigots is defined by their beliefs, passions, and deeds.

Antisemitism and antisemites are characterized by a cognitive bias and confirmation bias that casts Jews negatively as noxious, malevolent, or dangerous. Consider a well-known general characteristic of Jewish Americans, that they are extremely philanthropic. This is barely if ever mentioned among antisemites, except to say that Jews use their money to buy influence and in particular, à la Mearsheimer and Walt among others, to corrupt the political system and harm the United States by getting it to support Israel's policies and alleged predations. While Jews' philanthropy, particularly in a country that so prizes private giving, and many other otherwise admirable characteristics of Jews as individuals (when they are in evidence) or of Jews generally or as an organized community gets ignored by antisemites, seemingly every small or large real or imagined transgression of individual Jews or of Jews more widely is highlighted, exaggerated, and incorporated into the antisemitic discourse about Jews. Even when Jews do something seemingly admirable, such as actively participating in politics — which is generally seen as a virtue in a democracy — it is often cast as something that just conceals a more fundamental negative and even nefarious or deeply damaging act. This, drawing on the foundational antisemitic paradigm, is kindred to the long-existing antisemitic trope and frame of thinking that even when Jews seem to tell the truth, it is fundamentally a lie because the seeming truth serves a darker purpose.

The *general* tendency for people to make cognitive errors about groups of the sort discussed here cannot begin to account for the existence of so many errors *specifically* about, and animus *specifically* toward, Jews that do not exist for the innumerable other ethnic, religious, regional, communal, social, and political groups that have populated the world historically and today. The *human nature* explanation fails because this *general* propensity cannot explain the many *distinctive,* indeed singular, features of antisemitism. These include antisemitism's extent, its longevity, its varieties, its intense passions, its tenacity, its licentiousness, its divorce from reality, its very powerful existence in regions and countries without Jews, and its propensity to violence, including unparalleled mass murder. Perhaps most of all, a *general* propensity to make cognitive errors cannot explain antisemitism's *particular* content, which has across much time and in many places treated Jews as real devils, as being in league with or serving the devil, or explicitly or de facto as secular devils in human form. This is an exceedingly unusual and complex prejudice, not a reflex of group life, with accreted centuries of imagined conspiracy and malfeasance, and thus there is no way to understand this as mere consequence of the failings of humans as social analysts.

These human cognitive and psychological tendencies, which make people poor (meaning overactive) generalizers, hypersensitive to perceiving danger, bad social scientists, and prone to confirming and therefore holding onto views, especially central or cherished views, have synergistically amplified the powerful, fear-inducing prejudice of antisemitism — including its central place in many worldviews and civilizations that has helped people understand the nature of their worlds and the misfortunes and sufferings it brings them — and imbued antisemitism with an unmatched appeal and tenacity.

This is so because antisemitism, the continuity of its foundational paradigm and core elements notwithstanding, has proven itself enormously adaptable, managing to be tailored to the political, social, and cultural circumstances of time and place. This is one of the reasons that it has endured through all the social, economic, cultural, and political changes of the ages when so many other bodies of thought, social practices, and institutions have not. Antisemitism has had this self-transformative quality for two reasons. It has been so deeply entrenched in the cultures, including or especially the religious cultures, of countries and peoples, that its adherents have held on to its foundational paradigm and basic animus while updating its particular elaborations as circumstances changed. And the animus has been based on such a profoundly demonic conception of Jews, as we shall soon more fully see, that it has been possible for its adherents to believe just about anything about Jews, and therefore to make any malignant quality or accusation, old or recently invented, stick. A prejudice such as the typical and often profound racism found in the United States against African Americans, namely that they are inferior in intellectual capacity, does not make plausible many of the gamut of charges that have been central to anti-semitism, which focuses on the supposed high intelligence of Jews, who, with their clever machinations, are said to pull the strings, financial and otherwise, behind the scenes to exploit, impoverish, and in other ways injure non-Jews. Thus, the antisemitism of different centuries, in different countries, among people of different religions, has developed into many variations on the theme of the Jews' acute and multifarious noxiousness and danger (after all, evil geniuses do harm in sundry and inventive ways), rendering antisemitism at once a recognizable, unitary widespread phenomenon (it maintains its core elements), and a series of variations — so much so that it makes sense to speak sometimes of anti-semitisms in the plural, or of different streams of antisemitism.

Antisemitism's grip on so many minds and hearts, and its endurance and adaptability over millennia in a dazzling array of social, political, and cultural circumstances, reveals tenacity to be one of its constituent features. Why has it been so tenacious as to make it singular also in this respect among prejudices? Part of its tenacity has resulted from its near ubiquity in many countries and communities, and across entire civilizations. This past consensus about the constitution and character of Jews and Jewness, about their alien quality, their malevolence and danger, has been tacitly, naturally transmitted, as are many other cultural notions from generation to generation. For centuries, children were reared in social milieus in which they imbibed this seemingly natural, unquestioned view of Jews. Just as children growing up in a uniformly Christian world naturally believe in the divinity of Jesus, just as whites growing up in the antebellum South came naturally to believe in the inferiority of blacks, just as children growing up in a Muslim country and community naturally believe that Allah is God, so too regarding the alien nature and pernicious essence of Jews. Yet this natural process was augmented by purposeful agents of hatred. Explicit and robust public discourses disseminated and reinforced antisemitism. The most authoritative religious and political institutions also actively and powerfully propagated the prejudice. Christianity and its encoded antisemitism, churches, particularly the Catholic Church, and Christian clergy were crucial for spreading it. Islamic institutions and people have done the same, though with similar intensity only starting in the twentieth century, and especially in the past two decades. Social and political movements and political rulers and leaders of all types have also powerfully spread and legitimized antisemitism. They have pushed antisemitism because they believe that the Jews pose danger and also because they know that it is a winning appeal, given their communities' and societies' and countries' vast antisemitic reservoirs. Whether political leaders have sought to mobilize people behind a nationalist movement or communism, a right-wing, fascist, or Nazi agenda, a religious politics, or a revolutionary politics, or to deflect attention from any number of undesirable domestic or foreign issues, antisemitism has been smart politics. It has been so powerful that leaders and political movements not resorting to it have risked losing out to others who would mobilize antisemitism to their cause.

In fact, antisemitism has always been fundamentally a political phenomenon, a part of elites' and publics' stances about how to govern their communities. Complementing its strategic uses, antisemitism has also appealed to people for specific social and personal reasons beyond it seeming to be true because of the conventional means of social transmission (parents to children, preachers to parishioners, ordinary people in the fields, in beer halls, at watercoolers sharing stories and rumors that explain their troubles)—and the solidarity such shared beliefs can produce. As a common enemy strengthens the bonds of a community, by redirecting its members' attention from their internal differences or other problems that may exist, antisemitism variously integrates people, gives them a sense of common purpose, which many prize, and also can divert attention from issues best deemphasized, left alone, or explained away. This has been exploited through the ages, from Christian religious leaders, to kings and nobles during the Middle Ages and early modern times, to modern communal and political leaders in Europe in the nineteenth and first half of the twentieth centuries, to Arab and Islamic political and religious leaders in the latter part of the twentieth century and into the twenty-first. In providing cohesion and deflecting communal discontent, and in holding out promise for making things better—which is what an antisemitic program does—antisemitism performs important social and political functions, and has an enormous appeal. It was no mere quip when leading nineteenth-century German socialists referred to antisemitism as the "socialism of fools." By this they meant that instead of looking to a genuine political program of communal solidarity that, in their view, offered real promise of solving social ills and bringing shared prosperity to a country's people, antisemitism so widespread and powerful in Germany (and elsewhere) — and in this sense they were certainly correct — offered a fictive and false substitute for the real thing, a form of self-defeating solidarity. They might have added that fools abounded in this world, but given the vast antisemitism around them, they might have thought saying so was superfluous. Today, fools of many stripes and in large numbers still latch on to antisemitism for many of the same, or analogous, reasons.

Antisemitism could also be seen as not the socialism of fools, but the religion of fools. It is easy to see antisemitism in this light, as it has been so often tied to religions, and even secular religions. A critical function or offering of religion is an explanation of the inexplicable, which includes the seeming and real injustice and suffering that exists in the world. How can the world be so unjust? How can the gods or God have created or allowed for such injustice and suffering? Why are the good not repaid on earth for their goodness? Antisemitism helps answer general, fundamental questions that allay doubts and fears — it is the Jews who are at fault! Antisemitism also appeals especially powerfully to those people who, by dint of social and economic position or individual personality, are prone to grasping on to such compensatory beliefs, because antisemitism provides prepackaged, easily adopted, and easily used and overused notions that serve such needs extraordinarily well. Everyone thus gets the benefit of explanation and comfort, and some people in particular get the satisfaction that can come from venting an intensity of belief and emotion.

Antisemitism's tenacity has proven that much greater and distinctive because many efforts have been made, and the real-world developments have occurred, that should have considerably tempered antisemitism even more than it has been in those areas where it has declined. To take just two examples: Major Christian churches and denominations, most famously the Catholic Church, have since the Holocaust forcefully repudiated antisemitism. Yet tens of millions still cling to the calumny that Jews for all time are responsible for Jesus' death, and tens of millions more believe a far more elaborated antisemitic litany that has grown out of this calumny. The Catholic Church has even declared doctrinally that antisemitism is a sin, and while antisemitism has declined among

Catholics and Christians in general in the last half century, it still is widespread and powerful. Second is the evidence of antisemitism's horrors, which should have been so bracing to nonmurderous antisemites as to lead them all, as it did for Christian churches and many Christians, to renounce the prejudice that had produced the Holocaust. Yet such horrors did not have this general, let alone near-universal or enduring, effect. Antisemitism's hold on people and cultures was and is so tenacious that even in the face of such a calamity, antisemitic discourse is more powerful than ever and its litany of charges against Jews persists.

In its longevity, its adaptability, its protean nature, its tenacity, its many variations, its vast reach numerically — across cultures, countries, continents, and cross sections of populations — antisemitism has no parallel. Yet all of these features combined compose not even a figurative half of what makes antisemitism distinctive and singular. Antisemitism's content, the anti-Jewish litany and its character, historically and today, is the other half. Its demonology has no parallel in prejudice's annals past or present.

There are three categories of prejudicial beliefs. The first can be called *common prejudices*. A group's offending attributes can be intellectual (the people are less intelligent), moral (they are dishonest), cultural (they don't share proper values), psychological (they are too emotional), dispositional or aspirational (they want to change us), or behavioral (they take our jobs, cause crime, et cetera). Such beliefs range widely in character and intensity. Many are garden-variety intergroup prejudices that hold the different groups to have certain distasteful or problematic qualities. In the melting pot of American intergroup relations of my youth, such prejudices were common, given regular expression in ethnic jokes. Italians were cowardly. Irish were drunkards. Jews were cheap. Poles were stupid. Such views, the kind that many European peoples have of one another, whether the people or groups are ethnically, geographically, religiously, or otherwise defined, are commonly called stereotypes. They are not held to so tenaciously, are not seen to characterize the disparaged group's every member (or sometimes even its majority), and exist as part of a broader understanding of the plural aspects of other people and even, such distasteful aspects notwithstanding, of the commonality the prejudiced people share with the disparaged group. They are the kinds of overgeneralizations or false generalizations humans regularly make but are not all-defining of the group and are not central to their bearers' self-conception, existential state, or political thinking. They are putative attributes but not seen as *the essence* of the group and its members. Such intergroup views and the conflicts they sometimes cause are the stuff of different peoples or groups rubbing up against one another, and often competing for cultural space, economic well-being, social status, or political power. Such prejudices may not even be articulated so clearly or be much more than *I'm Italian, he's Spanish or Polish, and that's that.*

Such low-level prejudices are both common and insignificant in the grand scheme of society and politics. They are prejudices as they structure a person's expectations of another person before he ever meets him and, likely, his perceptions and reactions to that person as they interact, yet they do not create an insuperable boundary. They are attributes or circum-scribed essences, rather than all-defining essences, such as *Jewness,* because they do not construct the other group to be incapable of sociability.

But many prejudices do just that. Some prejudices deem groups of people to have essences lacking attributes fundamental to being fully human. People have commonly deemed other groups to congenitally lack the req-uisite intelligence. White Americans believed this about the Africans they enslaved and, well into the civil rights era, about blacks after Emancipa-tion. Colonizers, especially European or American colonizers of people of color, have believed this about the peoples whom they have conquered, oppressed, and dispossessed. Indeed, on every continent, whether the col-onizers were British, French, Spanish, Portuguese, German, or Ameri-can, they conceived of indigenous peoples to be lesser human beings or barely human at all, likening them to lower animals—especially in the case of black Africans, to primates. Such prejudices also characterized modern European racism, especially the prevalent German variant, which held that many European peoples also lacked essential human attributes. Many Germans believed, and it was a Nazi article of faith, that Slavs (Poles, Ukrainians, Russians) were inferior beings, fit only to be beasts of burden. The term they used, then a fixed part of the German lexicon, was *subhuman.* Prejudices that deny the full humanity of others vary enor-mously in content, but in general they conceive of people as being racially—what we would today more technically call genetically— inferior principally and most significantly in their mental capacities. This, a second type of prejudice, is properly called *dehumanization.*

A third class of prejudice defines groups or peoples as being incapable of sociability because of thoroughgoing malevolent essences. This view does not rob people of human capabilities. It sees the people as fully capable human beings but, for whatever reason, evil. This dimension of prejudice is *demonization*.

Dehumanization is a conception of other people that robs them of fundamental human capabilities and qualities.* Demonization is about their moral essence and intentions. Like dehumanization, the demonization of groups or peoples has been common both historically and today. Unlike dehumanization, which grounds its prejudice in the imputed race, biology, or genes of others, demonization grounds itself most frequently in their religious, cultural, or political beliefs. That is, the prejudiced hold them to be unsociable not because they are constitutionally inferior but because of their religion (they are Muslim or Christian) or political views (they are communist or capitalist). If the disparaged or feared people changed their views, by converting or changing their politics, then they would no longer be the objects of such prejudice. But if, as does occur in rare cases, a people's imputed malevolence is deemed to be part of their essence, biologically or genetically based, it becomes a reified, unchanging thing. Antisemites have done this to Jews. This thing is their *Jewness*.

Dehumanization, fundamentally a dimension of prejudice about other people's inferiority, their diminished capabilities, does not deem those people to be dangerous, except as uncontrollable animals might be. Demonization is fundamentally about the threat that other people pose, and rarely are the objects of such prejudice deemed to be inferior, in the sense of being less capable. Indeed, the demonized people are often considered to be capable, sometimes even highly capable, and therefore their danger is that much more acute. This is a reason that the two dimensions or kinds of prejudice are usually distinct and rarely appear together. People who are prejudiced against another group or

---

* One caveat: A constituent feature of prejudice is to reduce or limit the role set, namely the different attributes of individual or group identity or practice, that the prejudiced person accords the people against whom he is prejudiced. This could be seen as a mild form of dehumanization or, put differently, on a continuum with it. Still, it is qualitatively different from what I discuss here as dehumanization.

people—beyond the garden-variety intergroup prejudices that are not all that significant or acute—either dehumanize that group or people or demonize them but seldom do they do both at once. Only in rare instances do people simultaneously dehumanize and demonize a given group or people. In central Africa, in Rwanda and in Burundi, Hutu and Tutsi have done so to one another. Each group, in mirror-image ideologies, deemed the other to be biologically programmed, like poisonous snakes, to inflict harm upon the other. In each country, the dominant group has perpetrated eliminationist and exterminationist assaults against the other, the largest and best-known instance having been the Hutu's mass murder in 1994 of eight hundred thousand Tutsi.*

With this in mind, focusing on demonization and dehumanization can help us understand any number of these issues better, including the logic of antisemitic beliefs and animus and, crucially, their relationship to antisemitic actions and policies, as well as to the phenomenon as a whole. Demonization and dehumanization are kindred, as each results from prejudice and then further feeds prejudice in a powerful feedback loop. But even though they are typically conflated into one thing and subsumed, incorrectly, under the master rubric of dehumanization, they are conceptually and as a matter of fact distinct, and though they regularly do not appear together, at times they have. The most historically common and spectacular instance of the simultaneous dehumanization and demonization of a people has been on the part of antisemites, especially modern racist antisemites, centered in Germany but in existence in many European countries. Germans and others considered all Jews to be racially programmed beings bent upon the destruction of Germany

---

* To be sure, there are times when the people who hold different political (and sometimes religious) views are bent on doing harm to others. But more often they are not. And in either case, what makes the view of them prejudice, instead of justified wariness, is their reduction of the individuals who belong to those groups wholly or overwhelmingly to the single aspect of their identity—Christian or Muslim, communist or capitalist—and seeing them only or overwhelmingly through the prism of what that characteristic means to the beholder. Thus, when a prejudiced Muslim meets a person who is Christian, he defines and reduces him to being a Christian and furthermore might think of the Christian as a "crusader," bent upon the destruction of Islam, when in reality, the person being so described may not think of himself primarily or even centrally as a Christian, has no particular views for or against Islam, and certainly has no desire or intention or hope to destroy it or harm any of its adherents.

and all humanity. As Germans conceptualized it at the time, the Jews' perniciousness was borne by their blood — literally, their blood — which was not the blood of human beings but of inhuman beings, of a nonhuman race apart. Hitler, who in this way was articulating the commonsense view held by the vast majority of Germans, described the Jews' aspirations in the most apocalyptic terms and tone possible:

> The Jewish doctrine of Marxism rejects the aristocratic principle of Nature and replaces the eternal privilege of power and strength by the mass of numbers and their dead weight. Thus it denies the value of personality in man, contests the significance of nationality and race, and thereby withdraws from humanity the premise of its existence and its culture. As a foundation of the universe, this doctrine would bring about the end of any order intellectually conceivable to man. And as, in this greatest of all recognizable organisms, the result of an application of such a law could only be chaos, on earth it could only be destruction for the inhabitants of this planet.
>
> If, with the help of his Marxist creed, the Jew is victorious over the other peoples of the world, his crown will be the funeral wreath of humanity and this planet will, as it did thousands of years ago, move through the ether devoid of men.[16]

For Germans, and for Hitler, who was their leader and their most prominent spokesman, Jewness was a fearsome, self-explanatory account of biologically programmed monstrousness, defilement, and mortal danger.

It is no wonder that, animated by such views, Hitler enacted a program, and so many Germans willingly set out, to exterminate the entire Jewish people. What makes this prejudice against Jews so noteworthy during this period, and, as we will see, also on the part of many today, is that this rare instance of the simultaneous dehumanization and demonization of a people was and is taken to an even higher intensity than any widespread prejudice against any other people has been. Jews have not merely been likened to devils, as bad as that is. Antisemites have gone still further by conceiving of Jews as actual demons, as minions of the devil, actually in league with the devil, as devils themselves. About no other people can this be said to have occurred on any similar scale.

Grounded in the Christian bible (New Testament), theology, and teaching, the Christians' psychological logic was that if the people of Jesus—in other words, those who should have known him best and heard his word directly—rejected him, then they must be wayward; that only a being as powerful as the devil could have deafened the Jews to Jesus' beneficent ministry and offer of salvation. Therefore, Jews must be in league with the devil. During the Middle Ages, this identification of Jews with the devil was nearly universal in Christian countries, and it transmuted from Jews being but servants or minions of the devil to being devils themselves. Medieval Christian imagery routinely depicted Jews with devil horns and tails. As Christians put it in another way, Jews were *antichrists* (also discussed in the Christian bible), inhuman beings malevolent to the core seeking to destroy Christians and Christianity.

The fact that eliminationism follows from the long-reigning foundational antisemitic paradigm about Jews should not be surprising. Indeed, eliminationism, a by now well-known historical and contemporary mindset and political ideology that is at the root of genocide, is so tightly bound to the foundational antisemitic paradigm about Jews as to be hard to extricate from antisemites' and codified antisemitism's considerations of them. The Christian bible is, whatever its subsidiary pronouncement to the contrary, at its heart an eliminationist document, a codification of eliminationist antisemitism against Jews. Their evangelical calls for Jews to follow Jesus aside, the Gospels so deprecate the Jews' existing cultural core (namely the Jewish bible's laws and codes), implicitly and explicitly calling for an end to this people as Jews, and so demonize Jews in the process for putatively being Jesus' enemies and murderers, and so threaten them with violence and destruction, that it is hard to see this as anything but an eliminationist mindset, a blueprint for eliminationist politics, and, if only tacitly, a call to eliminationist action—and that is how it has been taken by Christians and others beholden to the foundational paradigm it grounded. And the Christian bible promised and celebrated such destruction, including in parables about how those, the Jews, who reject Jesus will be destroyed—"every tree that does not produce good fruit will be cut down and thrown into the fire"—and in telling of Jerusalem's coming destruction, "Jerusalem, Jerusalem, you who kill the prophets and stone those sent to you . . . your house will be abandoned, desolate."[17]

This eliminationist reading of the Christian bible is anything but idiosyncratic. It has been the predominant interpretation and teaching of Christian churches and people through the ages, and they have further codified it, created elaborate discourses around it, and often implemented it as policy and practice. Eliminationism, as troubling as this may be for many believing Christians, is not only tied to the foundational antisemitic paradigm, which Christian churches then spread throughout much of the world, but also—albeit not necessarily with violence—inherent to it. Under the influence of Christianity, it has manifested itself in all major European countries and, as a matter of fact, done so often with violence: in England, France, Germany, Italy, Poland, Russia, Spain, and elsewhere. For Christian churches and their followers, the wayward Jews, their religion now superseded, killers of Christ, symbols and actual minions of evil and the devil, had to stop existing, which implies or can imply that they needed to be eliminated.

This view of Jews as devils in human form persisted even when, owing to the Enlightenment, antisemitism's religious foundation withered and was, depending on the country and region, augmented or replaced by a racial understanding of Jews. In this view, Jews became secular devils in human form, programmed by their blood to seek to immiserate, enslave, and destroy non-Jews. Not merely human but anti-human, fundamentally not sociable, evil in heart and mind, indeed the source of much or most evil in the world, they had to be eliminated from society and ultimately from the world. Hence the Germans' program, helped by so many other Europeans, to do just that.

The continuation of Christianity-based antisemitism and antisemitism among Christians, including its devilish element, has been largely ignored in extent and underestimated in importance. Among racial (biological) antisemites, this demonic paradigm of Jews, with slight variations, continued to exert extreme power, and even in the Holocaust's aftermath, significant elements of it continue to fuel antisemitic thought, including though not only in the Islamic world and among political Islamists, who regularly denounce Israel and warn the faithful of its threat by calling it "Little Satan."

The simple fact is that there has been no prejudice historically—not grounded in an objective account of an armed, avowedly enemy people ready or potentially ready to undertake a military, eliminationist, or exterminationist campaign—that has held another people to be so heinous and dangerous as antisemitism has deemed Jews to be over the centuries. It is hard to think of any prejudice that holds the people to be as determined in their malevolence as antisemitism has ascribed to Jews. It is hard to think of any prejudice that has such an intensiveness, fantastical component, obsessive quality, let alone worldwide reach and character, as antisemitism has for Jews. If we were to construct an index of the threat that different prejudices ascribe to the groups or peoples they describe, which would consist of scores for the various dimensions that I have just enumerated—including the number of people who subscribe to the prejudice and its spread geographically—there can be no doubt that antisemitism would top the list, perhaps by several orders of magnitude beyond the second-place prejudice. This would be true whether we looked at the antisemitisms (whatever their other differences and fluctuations) of 1200, 1500, 1800, 1900, 1940, or 2013.

To anyone not familiar with antisemitism's history and contemporary manifestations, it is difficult to convey, and perhaps to believe, the unsurpassed defamatory and outright injurious character of the invective that has been routinely hurled at this small and, almost everywhere, weak and vulnerable people. Antisemites have accused Jews of the worst crimes and transgressions imaginable. Here are a few typical examples among the hundreds, even thousands, from different eras and different kinds of prominent antisemites hailing from the worlds of religion, philosophy, culture, and politics.

John Chrysostom, the most significant theologian of the Catholic Church after Christianity became the religion of the Roman Empire, delivered in 386–387 a series of eight homilies "Against the Jews" that became the most influential post-biblical text guiding Christianity's rendering of Jews. Among its pages and pages of antisemitic invective, it asserts that Jews are devils, and must be treated as such:

> Tell me this. If a man were to have slain your son, would you endure to look upon him, or accept his greeting? Would you not shun him as a wicked demon, as the devil himself? They slew the Son of your Lord; do you have the boldness to enter with them under the same roof? After he was slain he heaped such honor upon you that he made you his brother and coheir. But you dishonor him so much

that you pay honor to those who slew him on the cross, that you observe with them the fellowship of the festivals, that you go to their profane places, enter their unclean doors, and share in the tables of demons. For I am persuaded to call the fasting of the Jews a table of demons because they slew God. If the Jews are acting against God, must they not be serving the demons?

Chrysostom also explains the logic of binary opposition between the inveterately evil Jews and Christians:

Where Christ-killers gather, the cross is ridiculed, God blasphemed, the father unacknowledged, the son insulted, the grace of the Spirit rejected.... If the Jewish rites are holy and venerable, our way of life must be false. But if our way is true, as indeed it is theirs is fraudulent.... I am speaking of their present impiety and madness.

Here the slayers of Christ gather together, here the cross is driven out, here God is blasphemed, here the Father is ignored, here the Son is outraged, here the grace of the Spirit is rejected. Does not greater harm come from this place since the Jews themselves are demons?... If the Jewish ceremonies are venerable and great, ours are lies. But if ours are true, as they are true, theirs are filled with deceit.... I am talking about the ungodliness and present madness of the Jews.... Certainly it is the time for me to show that demons dwell in the synagogue, not only in the place itself but also in the souls of the Jews.[18]

Peter the Venerable of Cluny, a pivotal medieval Church leader, drawing on the by-then pan-European commonsense notion articulated earlier by Chrysostom that demons dwell "in the soul of the Jews," and the identification of the Jews with the devil, concluded that the Jews' resistance to Christianity bespoke their essential nature:

You, you Jews, I say, do I address; you, who till this very day, deny the Son of God. How long, poor wretches, will ye not believe the truth? Truly I doubt whether a Jew can be really human.... I lead out from its den a monstrous animal, and show it as a laughing stock in the amphitheater of the world, in the sight of all the people. I bring thee forward, thou Jew, thou brute beast, in the sight of all men.[19]

Geoffrey Chaucer's "Prioress Tale" from *The Canterbury Tales* centers on the Christian blood libel of a Jew's murder of a Christian child. The Jew is firmly identified with the devil, "our firste fo, the Serpent Sathanas, that hath in Jewes herte his waspes nest," who induces the Jew to kill the child.[20]

Leading and classical medieval Qur'anic commentator Baydawi, who died around 1316, in his important Qur'anic exegesis *Anwaar al-Tanziil Wa-Asraar al-Ta'wiil,* analyzes passage 2:61 of the Qur'an:

> The Jews are mostly humiliated and wretched either of their own accord, or out of coercion of the fear of having their *jizya* doubled.... Either they became deserving of His wrath [or]...the affliction of "humiliation and wretchedness" and the deserving wrath which preceded this....
>
> In addition [God] accuses them of following fantasy and love of this world, as he demonstrates in His saying [line 14] "this is for their transgression and sin" i.e. rebelliousness, contrariness, and hostility brought them into disbelief in the signs, and killing the prophets. Venal sins lead to serious sins, just as small bits of obedience lead to larger ones... God repeated this proof of what is *inveterate* [in the Jews], which is the reason for their unbelief and murder, and which is the cause of their committing sins and transgressing the bounds God set.[21]

Martin Luther, the founder of Protestant Christianity and the self-styled spreader of Jesus' ministry of love and salvation, discusses the contemporary manifestations of the Jews' essence and what is to be done with them, as they are "venomous, bitter, vindictive, tricky serpents, assassins, and children of the devil," and proposed, among other extraordinary acts of aggression, that they be forbidden to learn their religion, they be enslaved in agricultural labor, and that their "homes should likewise be broken down and destroyed," and that "their synagogues and churches should be set on fire" so that "you and we may be free of this insufferable devilish burden — the Jews."[22]

Voltaire, perhaps the leading Enlightenment philosopher and figure, and as much responsible for the intellectual break with Christianity as anyone, still did not depart from the foundational Christian antisemitic paradigm of Jews: "The Jew does not belong to any place except that place in which he makes money: would he not just as easily betray the king on behalf of the emperor as he would the emperor for the king?" The Jews are so anachronistic and at odds with the rest of humanity that one day the "catastrophe" of being eliminated will befall them: "When the society of man is perfected, when every people carries on its trade itself, no longer sharing the fruits of its work with these wandering brokers, the number of Jews will necessarily diminish. The rich among them are already beginning to detest their superstitions; there will be no more than the lot of a people without arts or laws, and who, no longer understanding their ancient corrupt jargon...will assimilate among the scum of the other peoples."[23]

Immanuel Kant, considered by many the greatest modern philosopher and proponent of a universalist and humanistic morality, saw a major exception in the Jews, who

> owe their not undeserved reputation for cheating (at least the majority of them) to their spirit of usury which has possessed them ever since their exile. Certainly it seems strange to conceive of a nation of cheats, but it is just as strange to conceive of a nation of traders, most of whom—tied by an ancient superstition—seek no civil honor from the state where they live, but rather restore their loss at the expense of those who grant them protection as well as from one another....Instead of vain plans to make this people moral...I prefer to give my opinion on the origin of this peculiar constitution of a nation of traders.

Kant declared Jews to be "vampires in society"; no wonder he concluded that "the euthanasia of Judaism, is the pure moral religion"![24]

The towering philosopher of the nineteenth century, Hegel, though working in a very different, indeed antagonistic, philosophical tradition to Voltaire's, nonetheless agreed with him on the issue of the Jews, seeing them as mired in an unnatural state owing to their essence defined by Judaism: "The subsequent condition of the Jewish people which continues up to the mean, abject, wretched circumstances in which they still find themselves today is all simply consequences and elaborations of their original fate. By this fate — an infinite power which they set over against themselves and have never conquered — they have been maltreated and will be maltreated continually until they appease it by the spirit of beauty and so annul it by reconciliation."[25]

Charles Fourier, the enormously influential French nineteenth-century utopian socialist thinker, cast Jews as the "incarnation of trade," which is the "source of all evil," so the Jews were responsible for all manner of parasitic and injurious practices. Never, according to Fourier, was there a "nation more despicable than the Hebrews."[26] Meanwhile, Pierre-Joseph Proudhon, another critical and influential early socialist thinker, declared, "The Jew is by temperament unproductive, neither agriculturalist nor industrialist, nor even a genuine trader. He is an intermediary, always fraudulent and parasitical, who operates in business as in philosophy, by forging, counterfeiting, sharp practices.... His economic policy is always negative; he is the evil element, Satan, Ahriman, incarnated in the race of Shem."[27]

Richard Wagner, the towering musical and cultural figure of the nineteenth century, cited by Hitler as his one true inspiration, wrote perhaps the most influential antisemitic essay of his time, "Jewry in Music," in which he described the Jews as an alien and corrosive element to music, which he deemed the incarnation of spiritual life. He opens his essay to "explain to ourselves the *involuntary repellence* possessed for us by the nature and personality of the Jews, so as to vindicate that instinctive dislike which we plainly recognize as stronger and more overpowering than our conscious zeal to rid ourselves thereof. Even today we only purposely fool ourselves when we think necessary to hold immoral and taboo all open proclamation of the natural repugnance against the Jewish nature." And their presence is alien and degenerative: "[All] is turned to money by the Jews. Who thinks of noticing that the guileless looking scrap of paper is slimy with the blood of countless generations? We have no need first to substantiate the Jewification of modern art. It springs to the eye.... If emancipation from the yoke of Judaism appears to us the greatest of necessities, we must hold it crucial above all to assemble our forces for this war of liberation."[28]

Marx, still different from the others in being the revolutionary leftist without peer, nevertheless used common antisemitism in private to describe his rivals and fundamentally saw eye to eye with the others about the Jews' essential nature. In his antisemitic polemic, "On the Jewish Question," he uses crass antisemitic tropes such as "huckstering" to describe the essence of Jews: "The Jew has emancipated himself in a Jewish manner, not only by acquiring the power of money, but also because *money* has become, through him and also apart from him, a world power, while the practical Jewish spirit has become the practical spirit of the Christian nations."[29]

T. S. Eliot, perhaps the most influential poet of the twentieth century, more pithily, befitting the poet, describes the Jew as a source of decay:

> *My house is a decayed house,*
> *and the jew squats on the window sill, the owner,*
> *Spawned in some estaminet of Antwerp,*
> *Blistered in Brussels, patched and peeled in London.*
> *The goat coughs at night in the field overhead;*
> *Rocks, moss, stonecrop, iron, merds.*

And:

> *The rats are underneath the piles.*
> *The jew is underneath the lot.*
> *Money in furs.*[30]

In a private letter, Eliot elaborates his antisemitic stance: "The population [of a community] should be homogeneous.... Reasons of race and religion combine to make any large number of free-thinking Jews undesirable.... And the spirit of excessive tolerance is to be deprecated."[31]

Adolf Hitler spoke openly and repeatedly to the German people about the evil of the Jews and what to do with them:

> ...we are animated with an inexorable resolve to seize the Evil [the Jews] by the roots and to exterminate it root and branch. To attain our aim we should stop at nothing, even if we must join forces with the Devil.[32]

Charles de Gaulle, the lionized president of France, thought nothing of speaking at a press conference in 1967 of "the Jewish people, self-confident and domineering."[33]

Sayyid Qutb, the leading political Islamic theorist, spiritual father of the Muslim Brotherhood, al Qaeda, and other political Islamic groups, and one of the most authoritative Qur'anic interpreters and Islamic thinkers of modern times, wrote in his programmatic and widely influential tract "Our Struggle with the Jews":

> The Qur'an spoke much about its Jews and elucidated their evil psychology. It is not mere chance that the Qur'an elaborates on this. For there is no other group whose history reveals the sort of merciless-ness, (moral) shirking and ungratefulness for divine guidance as does this one. Thus had they killed, butchered, and expelled many of their prophets. This is the most disgusting act that has come out of any community which had sincere preachers of the truth. The Jews perpetrated the worst sort of disobedience (against Allah), behaving in the most disgustingly aggressive manner and sinning in the ugliest way. Everywhere the Jews have been they have committed unprecedented abominations.
>
> From such creatures who kill, massacre, and defame prophets one can only expect the spilling of human blood and any dirty means which would further their machinations and evilness.[34]

Bishop Richard Williamson affirmed the authenticity on the Lefeb-vrist Society of St. Pius X (SSPX) of the Catholic Church in 2000: "God put into men's hands the Protocols of the Sages of Sion [the Protocols of the Elders of Zion]... if men want to know the truth, but few do."[35]

Sheikh 'Atiyyah Saqr, former head of Egypt's Al-Azhar Fatwa Committee, whose edicts hold sway for Sunni Muslims around the world, having previously issued a fatwa declaring Jews "apes and pigs," declaimed on the popular website for Islamic education Islam Online the twenty bad traits of Jews, including:

> They used to fabricate things and falsely ascribe them to Allah....
> They love to listen to lies....
> Rebelling against the Prophets and rejecting their guidance....
> Wishing evil for people and trying to mislead them....
> They feel pain to see others in happiness and are gleeful when others are afflicted with a calamity....

They are known for their arrogance and haughtiness....
Their rudeness and vulgarity is beyond description....
It is easy for them to slay people and kill innocents. Nothing in
the world is dearer to their hearts than shedding blood and murder-
ing human beings....
They are merciless and heartless....
They never keep their promises or fulfill their words....
They rush hurriedly to sin and compete in transgression....
Miserliness runs deep in their hearts....
Distorting Divine Revelation and Allah's Sacred Books.[36]

Yasser Arafat, the George Washington of the Palestinians, felt no
compunction about uttering such horrific calls to arms as "Continue to
press on, soldiers of freedom! We will not bend or fail until the blood of
every last Jew from the youngest child to the oldest elder is spilt to
redeem our land!"

These accounts of Jews and what should be done to them have come
not from the uneducated mob but from religious and political leaders,
the people who shape institutions, bodies of thought, followers' understanding and aspirations, and the policies that powerful institutions,
movements, and countries adopt and carry out. They are utterly typical
of legions of other intellectual, religious, and political leaders through
the ages and, to be sure, of endless numbers of lesser writers, polemicists, religious preachers, and local political leaders and rabble-rousers.
An effectively endless stream of such statements, with many variations,
including many damaging accusations and proposals, could be easily
proffered here. Furthermore, such statements are not solely the province
of the ad hoc utterances and writings of people of all stations throughout different societies. The underlying structure of antisemitism has
been encoded in official documents, from the religious scripture, said to
be God's word, of two major world religions, the two with the most
adherents in the world; official programs and charters of political parties; and church and national legislation.

The Christian bible contains four hundred fifty antisemitic verses just
in the four Gospels and the Acts of the Apostles, averaging more than two
per page. Just the Gospel According to Matthew has eighty, including

Jesus calling the Jews, here called Pharisees, "you brood of vipers, how can you say good things when you are evil?" The consequence of this, Jesus explains: "I say to you, the kingdom of God will be taken away from you [Jews] and given to a people that will produce its fruit [the Christians]." Matthew's Jesus later addresses the Jews more extensively:

> Thus you bear witness against yourselves that you are the children of those who murdered the prophets; now fill up what your ancestors measured out! You serpents, you brood of vipers, how can you flee from the judgment of Gehenna [hell]? Therefore, behold, I send to you prophets and wise men and scribes; some of them you will kill and crucify, some of them you will scourge in your synagogues, and pursue from town to town, so that there may come upon you all the righteous blood of Abel to the blood of Zechariah, the son of Barachiah, whom you murdered between the sanctuary and the altar.

For this and for rejecting him, Matthew's Jesus tells the Jews that they will be devastated: "your house will be abandoned, desolate."

In different places the Christian bible places the culpability for Jesus' death on the Jews. Matthew tells all Christians that the Jews themselves gladly acknowledged their principal role in his death and accepted the consequences of this greatest crime in human history as to be borne by Jews for all time: "And the whole [Jewish] people said in reply, 'His blood be upon us and upon our children.'" Why have the Jews murdered God's son, and why do they gladly accept the curse of doing so upon themselves and upon all Jews for all time? If you know from whom they are descended, it all makes sense. The Gospel According to John, among its approximately one hundred thirty antisemitic verses, has Jesus explaining while still alive that the Jews "do not belong to God" for they are trying to kill him, which leads Jesus himself to conclude that the Jews "belong to [their] father the devil."

For its part, the Qur'an is rife with the most damaging antisemitic passages and depictions of Jews:

> Do you see those that have befriended a people [the Jews] with whom Allah is angry?

They belong neither to you nor to them. They knowingly swear to falsehoods.

Allah has prepared for them a grievous scourge. Evil indeed is that which they have done.

They use their faith as a disguise and debar others from the path of Allah. A shameful scourge awaits them.

Neither their wealth nor their children shall in the least protect them from Allah. They are the heirs of Hell and there they shall abide forever.

On the day when Allah restores them all to life, they will swear to Him as they now swear to you, thinking their oaths will help them. Surely they are liars all.

Satan has gained possession of them and caused them to forget Allah's warning. They are the confederates of Satan; Satan's confederates assuredly will be lost.[37]

The Catholic Church's prayer book's "reproaches," some of which date from the ninth century, which are part of the Good Friday liturgy, and have been recited by Christians every year for centuries, take the form of Jesus admonishing the Jews for his death.

And then there is the *The Protocols of the Elders of Zion*, a fabricated account of the international conspiracy of Jewish elders purporting to be their own authentic account of their plans to dominate the world. It has become a modern-day bible of sorts for antisemites around the world, as it offers a litany of the Jews' evil and destructive goals, means being used, and effects already and soon to be felt within national borders and internationally. The supposed discoverer and translator of the Protocols, in a brief epilogue that is an integral part of the fabrication, summarizes the Jews' apocalyptic end lying in wait for humanity:

One can no longer doubt it, the triumphant reign of the King of Israel rises over our degenerate world as that of Satan, with his power and his terrors; the King born of the blood of Zion — the Antichrist — is about to mount the throne of universal empire.[38]

Hitler's *Mein Kampf* is full of comparable venom:

With satanic joy in his face, the black-haired Jewish youth lurks in wait for the unsuspecting girl whom he defiles with his blood, thus stealing her from her people. With every means he tries to destroy the racial foundations of the people he has set out to subjugate. Just as he himself systematically ruins women and girls, he does not shrink back from pulling down the blood barriers for others, even on a large scale. It was and it is Jews who bring the Negroes into the Rhineland, always with the same secret thought and clear aim of ruining the hated white race by the necessarily resulting bastardization, throwing it down from its cultural and political height, and himself rising to be its master....

In the political field he refuses the state the means for its self-preservation, destroys the foundations of all national self-maintenance and defense, destroys faith in the leadership, scoffs at its history and past, and drags everything that is truly great into the gutter....

Culturally, he contaminates art, literature, the theater, makes a mockery of natural feeling, overthrows all concepts of beauty and sublimity, of the noble and the good, and instead drags men down into the sphere of his own base nature....

Here he stops at nothing, and in his vileness he becomes so gigantic that no one need be surprised if among our people the personification of the devil as the symbol of all evil assumes the living shape of the Jew.[39]

Grounded in Hitler's views, Germany's Nuremberg Laws stated that because of their blood, "a Jew cannot be a citizen of the Reich. He has no right to vote in political affairs and he cannot occupy public office."[40]

In April 1942, Slovakia's Catholic bishops collectively issued a pastoral letter that priests read to parishioners all across the country during one Sunday's Mass justifying the Jews' deportation (to their deaths) as Christ-killers: "The greatest tragedy of the Jewish nation lies in the fact of not having recognized the Redeemer and of having prepared a terrible and ignominious death for Him on the cross." The bishops complemented this foundational antisemitic accusation with modern antisemitic ones: "The influence of the Jews [has] been pernicious. In a short time they have taken control of almost all the economic and financial life of the country to the detriment of our people. Not only economically, but also in the cultural and moral spheres, they have harmed our people. The Church cannot be opposed, therefore, if the state with legal regulations hinders the dangerous influence of the Jews."[41]

Once Israel came into being, the hatred of the Jews expanded to a generic tarring of both people and place. The United Nations' Zionism Is Racism resolution of 1975, which received massive worldwide media attention and became official United Nations doctrine, "most severely condemned zionism as a threat to world peace and security and called upon all countries to oppose this racist and imperialist ideology, [the United Nations thus] *Determines* that zionism is a form of racism and racial discrimination."[42]

Stéphane Hessel's book *Time for Outrage,* a French publishing phenomenon, sold more than 1.5 million copies in six months after publication in 2011. Translated into dozens of languages, it was ostensibly calling people to be outraged at the general state of the world, yet singled out only one country by name, Israel, to be outraged at, and stated boldly that "for Jews themselves to perpetuate war crimes is intolerable."[43] In a world of North Korea, Syria, the Democratic Republic of the Congo, and on and on—only Israel.

Hamas' charter, reaffirmed by Hamas to this day, casts Israel, Zionism, and Jews (used interchangeably), in addition to Jews perpetrating a long series of crimes against all peoples and against Islamic peoples in particular, as seeking "to demolish societies, to destroy values, to wreck answerableness, to totter virtues and to wipe out Islam." The only adequate measure is to destroy Israel. Thus the charter is a call to arms, telling the faithful, in its first paragraph, "Israel will rise and will remain erect until Islam eliminates it as it had eliminated its predecessors."[44]

What prejudice other than antisemitism has spawned so many bestsellers or been codified in law or explained in religious texts to millions over so many centuries? The Christian bible and the Qur'an are the two most widely printed and circulating books of all time, each with many hundreds of millions copies, perhaps billions. They are also by far the two most frequently read and reread, not to mention quoted and recited, books of all time and have served and continue to serve as the basis for weekly and even daily sermons, speeches, and talks, and quotes in country after country, community after community, for decades and centuries on end. By the end of World War II, *Mein Kampf* had sold twelve million copies in Germany alone, making it not only the principal text of Hitler's plans for Germany and the world, but one of the best-selling books of all time, and it has since sold countless more copies in a multiplicity of languages around the world. *The Protocols of the Elders of Zion* has been a hugely influential book historically and a bestseller especially today in countries across the Arab and Islamic world; has even sold, together with dozens of books based on it, millions of copies in Japan since the 1980s; and is likely the all-time leading book about international conspiracy. Antisemitism and eliminationism have been legally enshrined in Germany's Nuremberg Laws of 1935 and in other countries around mid-twentieth-century Europe, including France, Italy, Slovakia, Romania, Croatia, Bulgaria, and Hungary. Hamas' charter not only effectively guides the majority of Palestinians, but is the de facto guide regarding Jews for much of the Arab world. The United Nations antisemitic resolution has been promulgated the world over, its contents repeated again and again, with the imprimatur of the institution that is seen to govern the international order.

Antisemitism has been codified and given a legally binding status in country and after country, which, as with antisemitism's many other features, has no parallel. Thus, antisemitism is a prejudice animating not just common people or elaborated not just in vast bodies of literature or propagated not just by the politically, religiously, and culturally powerful, or used merely to mobilize people for social and political movements — though it has done all of these. It has also been codified in the world's most essential and guiding texts, and been formalized and legalized in political and religious movements, legislation, governance, and policy. It has produced robust communal, national, and transnational discourses with vast numbers of participants and stable, often sacralized, damaging discourses centered on evil.

From this small sampling of antisemitic positions, which have been historically and continue to be hugely influential in shaping so many people's views about Jews, we can see some of antisemitism's contours and central features.

Whatever the specific charges — Jews seek to destroy Christianity, poison the local wells, start wars, corrupt the race, throttle Islam — the power and malevolence that antisemites and codified antisemitism ascribe to Jews is routinely apocalyptic. Jews putatively threaten in the most fundamental senses the well-being of non-Jews, often their lives, all goodness, even God. And these charges have been made, in many variations, and in the contextually appropriate idiom, across time and place, country and culture. To be sure, milder forms of antisemitism exist, such as accusing Jews of being stingy or clannish, or underhanded in business, or unfairly dominating this or that profession. Such common kinds of intergroup prejudices are also widely believed and are, in themselves, not remarkable—though with regard to Jews they become remarkable because they are often integrated into far more damaging antisemitic bodies of thought and emotion, which they repeatedly activate.

These antisemitic discourses, which have been and continue to be wildly divorced from reality and real-world Jews, have nevertheless constructed people's understanding of the world. If an effective accusation against the Jews could be thought up, it likely would be leveled at them and incorporated into the antisemitic discourse, then repeated, amplified, and turned into assumed fact. It is as though the antisemites were describing and fashioning a mythical creature: *the Jew,* a being possessing supernatural, demonic powers. Antisemites have created and daily reinforced the notion of such a mythical creature.

Most people historically, and even most people today, have had no contact with Jews. The prejudicial frame and the animus that gave antisemitism's picture of the Jews' color were so extreme that the antisemitic speakers and listeners—partaking in an ongoing conversation about this malicious and dangerous people—could not see the actual person through all the distortions, let alone the people, let alone the plurality and diversity of the human beings. Instead—in their imaginings or standing before them or living behind the ghetto walls—they beheld creatures possessed by the demonic quality of *Jewness.* In its purest form, Jewness, like the Jews and the devil themselves, were the embodiment of all that offended and threatened the world. Hitler articulated this in visceral and cognitive terms: "Their whole existence is an embodied protest against the aesthetics of the Lord's image."[45] Especially in Germany but also across Europe, and today in many Arab and Islamic countries, the stand-alone term *the Jew* has conjured a range of foreboding meanings, associations, and symbols and a powerful revulsion, disgust, at this offending creature.

What does one do when facing such an apocalyptic danger, and even if the danger is not considered quite so extreme? Alert others in one's family, community, society, the world? For sure. Keep one's distance? For sure, if possible. Segregate them? For sure, if possible. Create many other kinds of disabilities for them, to reduce the danger? For sure, if possible. Expel them? For sure, if possible. Use violence to achieve any of these security and potentially life-saving measures? For sure, if possible. Kill them? Yes, even kill them, if possible. Kill them all? Yes, even kill them all, if possible. It is amazing how many tens of millions of people — especially, in the past, Europeans — at different historical moments would have said yes to each of these questions.

A striking feature of antisemites' agitation about Jews, when both spoken and written, is how frequently they advocate violence — pointedly, openly, unapologetically, and on a vast scale. Antisemites and codified antisemitism have been fundamentally eliminationist toward Jews, and one form of eliminationism that they have routinely considered, and almost as often proposed as part of the ordinary and normal antisemitic conversation is extermination. I have already quoted any number of major political and cultural leaders or texts through the ages that have called for the mass annihilation, even the complete extermination, of the Jews, and noted how striking it is that such calls have come from the leading theological and movement figures of the major Christian traditions. Catholicism's St. Augustine in his Confessions tells God: "How hateful to me are the enemies of your Scripture! How I wish that you would slay them (the Jews) with your two-edged sword, so that there should be none to oppose your word! Gladly would I have them die to themselves and live to you!" Luther, rebel extraordinaire against the Catholic Church, and cofounder of Protestantism, would burn their synagogues and hold up "the Turks and other heathen" as models for not tolerating what the Christians do endure, and wants Jews to be only "where there are no Christians." John Calvin, the other great Protestant founder, wants to dam up all empathy toward Jews, so that they be treated appropriately until they perish: "Their [the Jews'] rotten and unbending stiffneckedness deserves that they be oppressed unendingly and without measure or end and that they die in their misery without the pity of anyone."[46] As we shall see, such calls to action, once the common currency of leading Christian and European lights, both religious and secular, philosophical and political, are today the common currency of their Islamic and Arabic counterparts, though centuries apart. Indeed, for no other people have such calls come from such major political, religious, and cultural leaders and texts and discourses of different civilizations, different countries, different political orientations — from a transhistorical and international roster of genocidal dreamers. If a public figure were to call for the extermination of African Americans today, or to call for the extermination of the French, Germans, Koreans, Christians, or the people of any other ethnic group, we would be shocked and dumbfounded. Although such calls against other peoples would not even make sense, they do against Jews. That is as firm testimony as we could want about the singular and horrifying status of the antisemitic discourse and the prejudice it expresses.

# 4

# Fear and Trembling

ANTISEMITISM HAS NO parallel in prejudice's annals. No other widespread prejudice has characterized people as such cosmological threats, been so fantastical — indeed, hallucinatory — in character, or produced greater passion and hatred. No other prejudicial discourse has been so eliminationist or produced such regular calls for violence and extermination. And all this regarding a people with whom for centuries there was no acute, objective conflict over territory, resources, or political control or domination, and who has been numerically small, politically weak or powerless, and militarily utterly without capacities for most of the last two millennia.

Why?

Why has antisemitism been sui generis among prejudices — not only in one or two ways, but on a host of dimensions and in sum total — having no close or even distant parallel? Prejudice's annals contain hundreds, thousands — who knows how many prejudices. Within every country, local prejudices against local groups and peoples exist, as do local instances of common prejudices, such as gender prejudice, and local versions of prejudices among different Muslim sects, Christian sects, Hindu sects, Jews of different degrees of religiosity, or peoples of different locales or ethnicities against one another. Yet even if one or another prejudice resembles antisemitism in one of its aspects, none has come close to antisemitism's many distinctive and central features, to its vast geographic and time scale, all of which derive from the foundational antisemitic paradigm.

Context creates the acceptability of belief. In premodern, prescientific times, people easily believed that supernatural forces, including magical powers wielded by humans, were responsible for just about anything, from whether a child would be a boy or a girl, the sun would rise or rain would fall, a person would get sick or well, crops would grow or die, a battle would be won or lost, and on and on and on. We can use the term *plausibility structure* to help us see what will seem credible to us in light of our broader beliefs and understanding about the nature of the world, or human societies, or different groups, or human beings. The plausibility structure grounded in today's scientific understanding of the world invalidates premodern notions of supernatural causation. And indeed, today a small minority of people compared to the past would believe that it has not rained because the gods willed it or an earthquake happened because their neighbors lacked piety.

Plausibility structures' power to make some things seem believable and others not depends upon people's capacity, clearly innate, to assess what they see and hear against their understanding of reality—to reality test. This understanding of reality, such as of prescientific peoples, may be enormously faulty, but whether faulty or not, it is according to that understanding that they assess notions about the world for believability.

Reality testing and plausibility structures have constrained the prejudicial descriptions and charges (and also proposed actions) against non-Jews. This has been true of a wide array of prejudices, even of incredibly intense and enormously damaging ones—by men against women, by whites against blacks, between Catholics and Protestants, between the French and Germans, between northern and southern Italians, between Poles and Russians, by white Americans or Americans more generally against Latinos or even illegal immigrants from Mexico and elsewhere, by Europeans against nonethnic European immigrants, including Muslims, in their countries, and on and on. Who says that these groups have sought to conspiratorially take over or ruin an economy, destroy others, start wars, or betray their countries; who claims that they are in league with the devil or kill children to use their blood for ritualistic purposes? Thinking such things, let alone saying them publicly, let alone having such views be the basis on which you try to mobilize others politically, simply would not make sense because the victims of such prejudices are still considered to be people — not beings or creatures of a categorically different kind. Not even the most racist white segregationists asserted such things about blacks in 1960, nor did slaveholders say this about blacks in 1860. Certainly no American prejudiced against African Americans today, of which there are legions, would dare say such wild things in public (even if the odd crank might think it). Only the most lunatic would believe such claims plausible. And yet reality testing and plausibility structures have not similarly constrained antisemites regarding Jews. In fact, they have done the opposite, to such an extent that wild accusations of malevolence or threat come from past and present communal, religious, and national leaders and opinion makers, and are shared by vast numbers of ordinary people in country after country.

All this has been dependent on and derived from the foundational antisemitic paradigm of Jews, which has been set in place by the Christian bible. Grounded in the original Christian conflict and deprecation of Jews owing to the Jews' having opposed and supposedly killed Jesus, the foundational antisemitic paradigm created an understanding of Jews' putative evil that reified Jewness as the inimical opposite of Christianity and the inimical opposite of goodness — whether or not goodness was grounded in Christian thought. A vast demonology based on this developed and became deeply entrenched in Western culture and communities. Christian antisemites and subsequent non-Christian antisemites, exposed to the elaborated charges and ways of thinking about Jews, adopted them, believed in them, acted upon them, and continued to spread them.

The foundational antisemitic paradigm is the underlying conceptual structure or definition of Jews that remains when the particulars of the specific Christian account of or content about the Jews are removed. This conceptual structure of the foundational antisemitic paradigm constructs Jews in their *essence* as being:

- different from non-Jews
- noxious
- malevolent
- powerful (or potentially powerful)
- dangerous

The Jews' differences are fundamental, not incidental, and the understanding of the source of those differences and the paradigm's other features (religion, race, politics, et cetera) can vary. Their noxiousness, their harmfulness, can also vary in character and degree, but in any case, its degree is also not incidental or trivial. Their malevolence means that the harm they pose or do is willful, that it is something they seek. That they are powerful means they possess substantial capacity to act effectively on their malevolent designs. This all means that Jews, fundamentally different, harmful to others, willfully so, with substantial power (or potential power) to cause harm to others, are in their essence dangerous to non-Jews.*

What the particular understandings of Jews' essence, the character of their noxiousness or the harms that they do or would do, the precise extent of their malice, the source, extent, and scope of their power, and the nature of the danger they pose could and have all varied over time, from one society, culture, and locale to the next, changing in their higher-level elaborations more or less substantially as plausibility structures and social and political contexts have changed, and indeed can vary from group to group, from subculture to subculture, and even among individuals in a given religion, society, or country. The more specific content that fills out the foundational antisemitic paradigm in this way, namely the specific form that antisemitism takes in elaborating the character of the Jews' harmfulness and danger, et cetera, constitutes the Jews' Jewness. While the foundational antisemitic paradigm has remained constant over time, meaning the fundamental and under-

---

* It should be clear that the foundational antisemitic paradigm is a specific, historically long-lived, and potent form of the broader phenomenon of antisemitism. It is the foundation of the antisemitism (in its various permutations) that has been overwhelmingly of the most importance historically and today, and has been the cause of such long-enduring and intensive persecution of Jews—and it is *that* antisemitism which we are exploring here. In its most general form, antisemitism consists of unflattering views and/or distasteful emotions toward Jews in general, which hold Jews to have disagreeable or harmful qualities. Such views or emotions may be but common stereotypes, and the content of such prejudice may not be very, or comparatively, consequential. In explicating here the character and consequences of the foundational antisemitic paradigm, and the various forms of antisemitism that have emerged from it, though mindful of antisemitism in its less potent forms, such antisemitism is decidedly not the object of our focus.

lying conceptual structure of antisemitism (that is, not garden-variety stereotypes and prejudice, such as Jews are stingy) has been unchanging, the more concrete conception of what a Jew is and why and how he is noxious and dangerous, his Jewness, has evolved, changed, and varied considerably historically and from society to society, group to group.

The foundational antisemitic paradigm, together with antisemitism's contours and features, eventually took on their own life, and were, in form and substance, internalized by various peoples and movements, who then delivered their own inflections to and elaborations on them. Whatever the changes in how the foundational antisemitic paradigm was filled in with particulars, throughout, antisemitism retained its extraordinarily damaging content, its animus-inducing passions, its fantastical thinking and underpinnings, its unrestrained quality, its distinctiveness compared to other prejudices, its violent imaginings, threats, acts, and policies, and its tenacity in the face of countervailing evidence and the evolving nature of economy, society, and politics. Simply put, whether or not you believe in the story of Jesus as it is understood by Christians, if you subscribe to the foundational antisemitic paradigm, which amounts to thinking that the Jews are evil, then it is easy — it is hard not to do so — to make them into the enemy of Muhammad, or the nation, whether it be the German Volk or the Polish people, or the common people, or Arab unity, or the working class, or the downtrodden, or people of color, or humanity as whole. If you think that the Jews are evil, it is easy to project whatever noxious or threatening quality or deed you want onto their Jewness, the essence of Jews — the Jews you encounter, who live around you, or just those you imagine. It is easy to then think about what you and others must do to forestall or combat it. Then you encode this new understanding by grounding it in foundational notions, including ontological and religious ones, that accord with your understanding of the world and what constitutes good and evil.

Because of the foundational antisemitic paradigm, in society after society antisemitism became part of the natural order of things. Jews' existence, their Jewness, has been seen as unnatural. Jews' Jewness makes them uncanny beings, strange, not part of the ordinary family of humanity, or, for those who did not believe in peoples composing a common humanity, not even a part of the ordinary array of peoples and, moreover, an acute danger to others. The transmission of these ideas, and their societal consensus, made these ideas as natural as the notions that peoples fundamentally differ from one another, as men do from women, and races do from one another — as natural and sure as that of any other such fixed social and cultural notions, perhaps surer than many.

The existence of evil and the many specific harms and sufferings that ordinary people endure are hard to understand or accept in any age, particularly in a prescientific age, so Jews were said to be in league with the devil and responsible for them. During the Middle Ages, prior to medical understanding of illness and epidemiology, epidemics were regularly said to be the work of Jews, most notably the black plague that killed 40 to 50 percent of Europe's population, perhaps as many as two hundred million people, between 1348 and 1350. It was during this period, informed by the foundational antisemitic paradigm and its hallucinatory constructs, that Germans slaughtered the Jews of approximately three hundred fifty communities, nearly every sizable Jewish community. Around the turn of the twentieth century, with growing communication and ease of travel, Jews were said to plot international conspiracies to dominate and injure non-Jews. Today, antisemites, including those in the West, are upset that the United States supports Israel and claim that Jewish fifth columnists conspire and successfully manipulate and control successive American presidents and Congress like puppets.

In era after era, the foundational antisemitic paradigm led antisemites to know no bounds in considering so-called solutions to the so-called problem, the imputed colossal danger, of the Jews. All manner of treatment, including those that violated society's ordinary moral and legal conventions, were on the table, put forward, discussed and argued about, settled upon, and then codified, only to be discussed more, kept alive, be central to antisemitic discourses and influence or to lay the groundwork for plans, policies, programs. Following on the logic of the foundational antisemitic paradigm that the Christian bible laid down, such proposals and surrounding discourses have been eliminationist at their heart. Indeed, the foundational antisemitic paradigm strongly tends to be eliminationist. If you think a people to be essentially different, malevolent, powerful, and dangerous, then it follows, then it is logical and emotionally desirous, to get rid of them. It is an obvious and prudent measure of self-protection, of self-defense. Eliminationism, certainly not in its most violent forms, is *not* an inherent part of the prejudice against most groups and peoples, whether it be people of other regions, religions, or ethnicities. But it has been integral to antisemitism, so much so that it could be seen as being an element of the foundational antisemitic paradigm itself. Eliminationism is a mind-set, a discourse, an orientation, a kind of politics, and a program and set of policies.[1] Its principal forms are:

*transformation,* such as forced religious conversion, which entails changing the central qualities that the perpetrators see as noxious or dangerous in the victim group.

*repression,* which entails using violence or the threat of violence and other eliminationist measures to keep the victims or their putatively noxious or dangerous qualities in check.

*expulsion,* which means forcing people to leave their homes and regions. This can be either internal, within a country — this includes incarcerating people in concentration camps — or external, compelling people to flee beyond a country's borders.

*prevention of reproduction,* which can be done by various means, including sterilizing people or raping women en masse.

*extermination,* from selective though large-scale mass murder (such as of military-aged men) to total annihilation.

From the viewpoint of the perpetrators, these eliminationist measures are on a continuum and functionally equivalent. All contribute to the goal of getting rid of the unwanted or hated group or the essential qualities they deem noxious or dangerous. In most eliminationist assaults, especially on Jews, the perpetrators use a variety of means simultaneously. In the Spanish Inquisition, the antisemites used violent repression, forced tens of thousands of Jews to convert, expelled two hundred thousand, and murdered others. During the Nazi period, the Germans liberally used four eliminationist means — repression, expulsion, prevention of reproduction, and extermination—to rid themselves of Jews. (Believing the Jews' nature to be grounded in their blood, immutable, the Germans did not seek to transform the Jews.) Depending on the prevailing conception of Jewness, namely what the precise content is that fills out the foundational antisemitic paradigm and what the further higher-level elaborations of charges and accusations are against Jews, different eliminationist means will seem more or less effective and advisable.

Discussions of prejudice focus on people's unflattering views of others. But as the mere mention of the Holocaust and the Germans' differential eliminationist assaults against non-Jewish peoples against whom they were prejudiced, or of the Hutu's exterminationist assault on the Tutsi in Rwanda, suggest, a complex relationship exists between prejudiced peoples' beliefs and emotions, and what those people would like to or be willing to do to others. Because most prejudices neither dehumanize nor demonize, but consist of nonprofound, unflattering views of the people they characterize—as being perhaps slovenly, disorganized, too emotional, eating smelly foods, thinking themselves better than they are, and so on—most prejudices suggest no particular action program, except perhaps to teach the people better habits of various kinds, including hygienic, to "civilize" people, or to keep them an arm's length away. The prejudices that consist of more profoundly damaging beliefs about, and a powerful animus against, other people, especially dehumanizing or demonizing ones, often include suggestions if not explicit programs of the serious measures needed to deal with them. Everything from keeping them down or out, to fundamentally transforming them, to enslaving them, to curtailing in some fashion their imputed danger, to killing them have been implicit and often explicit components of prejudicial thinking and systems of prejudice, and indeed the correlates of conduct by the prejudiced people. Antisemitism, more than any other prejudice, has so regularly engendered explicit and open eliminationist programs.

Beliefs, whether prejudicial or not, political or not, are regularly assumed or asserted to produce a one-to-one correspondence with action. But this is mistaken. Instead, prejudicial beliefs suggest or are compatible with an orientation that is based on an ideal of how to govern the relationship with the disliked people, which itself is highly contingent and can vary from society to society. Also, the kinds of informal or formal programs of action that prejudicial beliefs engender depend on a host of contextual circumstances, opportunities, possibilities, and calculations which can vary as much as any other set of communal, social, and political circumstances vary that make other kinds of programs of action mutable and highly contingent. Many people hate other people, but, even though they would love to drive them away or do them some other injury, they do nothing at all because the circumstances, including the prospect of being arrested and punished, suggest to them that such action is unfeasible or self-defeating. Many groups of people — absent the constraints and restraints of economic self-interest, broader social and political relations, law enforcement or armed forces — would love to take some action against other groups, but do not for reasons of prudence and practicality. Thus, it is important to think about what antisemites — were such constraints nonexistent — would *ideally* like to do with or to Jews, to investigate the circumstances that suggest to them that the time to act might arrive, and to recognize that even though such action is not now being undertaken, its dangers lurk.

People can want, whatever their dislikes may be, to coexist with the people against whom they are prejudiced. They can want to reform them of their perceived disagreeable qualities, which is often done through planned acculturation or education. They can want to dominate them or, as the case may be, to escape their domination. Or they can want to eliminate them. Most people who are prejudiced fall into the coexistence and reform categories, for the simple reason that their prejudices are not so profound as to suggest to them that domination, let alone elimination, is necessary or desirable. Domination can be a complicated matter of keeping another people down, but falls short of eliminationism. Therefore, wanting to make sure that putative lesser beings "stay in their place," show obeisance to their ethnic or religious betters, do not get out of hand — whether done through discrimination, various formal and informal social practices, law, or politics — is a common orientation of the prejudiced to dominate those they disparage. Finally, there is eliminationism, the most extreme orientation of prejudiced people who would like to rid themselves of the problem, danger, or threat they deem others to pose. This too has been a common stance taken by prejudiced people and groups, and against no one more so than Jews.

Thus, prejudicial beliefs, though suggesting particular orientations about what would be ideal, and also suggesting particular courses of ideal action, or at least logically being compatible with them, have no one-to-one correspondence to specific actions. Instead we need to understand prejudice and specifically antisemitism as being multipotential for action, meaning compatible with a range of policies, initiatives, and practices, which can be acted upon when the circumstances allow and call for them. The two critical points here, though, are, first, that different prejudices have different multiple potentials. Not all prejudices are compatible with all actions — northern Italians are not going to embark on a violent eliminationist campaign against southern Italians. Second, just because a prejudice has not issued in its most extreme form of potential action does not mean that it won't. It is through politics, almost always spearheaded, organized, and implemented by states, that such desires are turned into practice. Indeed, the history of prejudice, especially of profound prejudice including antisemitism, shows how easy it is for political leaders and states to inflame prejudice and antisemitism in particular, and to move its bearers to adopt the more extreme and violent actions that its content suggests are appropriate for dealing with the people who purportedly harm or threaten to harm the prejudiced and their societies.

Antisemitism more than any other major prejudice historically and today has inhered an eliminationist orientation, meaning its depiction of Jews has been compatible with and has suggested that the proper and necessary way, indeed the ideal way, of dealing with Jews is through a politics of eliminationism. To be sure, milder forms of antisemitism, particularly since the Holocaust through today, have not been eliminationist in orientation. In part, having been sobered by the Holocaust, many people who harbor mild to moderate dislike for Jews or some of their alleged qualities in the United States, in Europe, and elsewhere nonetheless clearly have a nondemonized view of Jews and therefore are oriented, indeed unquestioningly, toward coexistence. The qualities they attribute to Jews — that they are clannish, smarmy, or too clever — are, like other mild if distasteful and offensive prejudices, in no sense compatible with more extreme orientations of what one should do with or to Jews. But sadly, such nondemonized conception and orientation toward Jews has been the minority historically. And their adherents are overshadowed today by the many people and powerful public discourses that continue to demonize and dehumanize Jews and that are eliminationist in orientation.

Identifying Jews with the devil, either as literal devils or in the devil's service, or metaphorically as devilish whether explicitly or tacitly through the adoption of devil imagery and tropes, suggests that Jews' existence within a community or society, and for many, in the world at all, is undesirable, even necessary to end. After all, if people genuinely believed, as farfetched as this may sound, that a person or a group of people were devils or served the devil, threatened to enslave, do incalculable injury to, even kill them, their families, and their people, would they not seek to neutralize, to banish, to expel, even, as a matter of necessary self-defense, kill those demons? The seeming unnaturalness of the Jews' existence, a foundation of millennia of Christian thought that held their disappearance after the appearance of Jesus and the advent of Christianity to be natural and necessary, which was subsequently taken over by adherents of secular and Islamic religious antisemitic streams (such is the power of paradigms), also, by definition, suggests the naturalness of eliminating Jews, of hastening a necessary process or of completing one that somehow went historically awry.

Antisemitism's eliminationist orientation has not been confined to beliefs, thoughts, hopes, ideals, or even intentions and plans. Antisemites have also *acted* singly and in concert against Jews. In doing so, they choose among the means compatible with a given orientation depending on broader social and political circumstances and factors that have little or nothing to do with antisemitism's character itself. This is not exceptional. It is true about social and political initiatives in every other realm of human existence — from educational programs, to economic initiatives, to social policy, to the treatment of minorities in general, to foreign policies, and more — which are never predetermined and always the product of complex considerations of power, opportunity, means, desirability, competing desires, and calculation. Antisemites, following on the logic of their beliefs, have proposed, decided upon, and enacted all principal forms of eliminationism. They have prevented Jews' reproduction, including through sterilization. They have violently repressed Jews. They have forced Jews to convert. They have expelled Jews from their midst, either in ghettos or camps within the borders of the antisemites' countries or domains, tightly regulating their conduct and social intercourse with non-Jews and thereby diminishing the Jews' putative danger, or beyond their borders into neighboring regions. They have slaughtered Jews. We have already seen the broad and repeated sweep of antisemites' ghettoizing, expelling, and mass murdering of Jews that spans eras, peoples, and countries across Europe through the Nazi period, which has no parallel or even close analogue in human history. Indeed, the scope of antisemites' eliminationist expulsions of Jews rivals the mass murdering itself and, like the frequency and extent of the mass murder of Jews, has no parallel or close second historically. Antisemites' ghettoization of Jews also has no parallel. And each has also taken place outside of Europe and the Christian world, as well as after the Nazi period. Indeed, in the wake of the Holocaust, Poles eliminated an untold number of Jews returning to their homes, driving many away and slaughtering perhaps fifteen hundred of them. Shortly thereafter, Arab and Islamic countries, including Algeria, Egypt, Iraq, Libya, Morocco, Syria, and Yemen, in what is undoubtedly the most broad-sweeping eliminationist coalition in human history resorting to expulsion, used the founding of Israel as the impetus for ridding themselves of close to a million Jews. In addition to this, Arab countries and peoples launched exterminatory war upon the Jews of Israel, and did so again in 1967, both times failing in their eliminationist objectives. The Soviets engaged in thorough eliminationist repression of Jews, who avoided a large-scale, more violent purge that was in the works only because Stalin died in 1953. As if the Germans ridding Poland of almost all its three million Jews was not good enough, the Poles expelled most of the remaining Jews, numbering perhaps twenty thousand in 1968, accompanied by an antisemitic campaign that accused the Jews of being Stalinists and Zionists! Most continuously of all, dedicated eliminationist and exterminationist enemies — states, movements, and groups — have besieged Israel and its Jews for all of Israel's history.

When we see any eliminationist thinking, proposals, or measures, it means that antisemites might also be considering other ones and may decide to act upon them. This is particularly the case for expulsions, which have so often gone hand in hand with mass murder. If people say that Jews have no right to live in their homes, whether their homes are in a majoritarian non-Jewish or majoritarian Jewish country, namely Israel, it is not a big step to say, in the world of nation-states where countries are the basic organizing principle and location of people's existence, that Jews have no right to exist. Eliminationist measures are on a continuum of least radical, namely violent repression, to most radical, namely mass annihilation. When people harbor eliminationist antisemitism, and especially when they begin agitation for and then implementing eliminationist measures, moving from one place on the continuum, having one policy measure morphing into or being augmented by others is easy and seemingly natural. After all, they all come from the same place and express the same desire.

Yet because eliminationist measures might be deemed impractical, unfeasible, or self-defeating, they often lay dormant. Today, no politician in Western Europe or the United States, even if he harbors eliminationist antisemitism, would dare propose, let alone try to enact, an eliminationist program against his country's Jews. Or if he harbored a less intensive but still profound antisemitism, he would also not dare propose, let alone seek to enact, any legal restrictions or a political campaign against his country's Jews. Any such eliminationist or even non-eliminationist program would be chimerical and politically suicidal.

This could be seen, as can many other features of antisemitism, in the revealing and — as many people expressed in 2002 when the tape recording was released — horrifying exchange between U.S. president Richard Nixon and the leading evangelist Christian leader in the United States and perhaps the world, Billy Graham. In 1972, in the White House's Oval Office, Nixon let forth a brief antisemitic rant about Jews' "total Jewish domination of the media," and what he characterized as their left-wing bias. The president of the United States, with unlimited access to the best sources of information about every aspect of his country, adopted the jargon of an ignorant antisemitic bigot when speaking about Jews in private. Such is the powerful, stupefying quality of this prejudice. Graham immediately agreed with Nixon regarding Jews' power and nefariousness. Taking the president's words as a green light for him to speak to a kindred spirit, Graham, elaborating his real views about Jews, went still further. "They're the ones putting out the pornographic stuff," he informed Nixon. And so severe is the danger the Jews pose that, Graham declared, their "stranglehold has got to be broken or the country's going down the drain." This in itself is a chilling, behind-the-scenes, candid exchange between the country's foremost political leader and leading religious leader. It conveys what we have already seen as well as anything, that much antisemitism lurks beneath the surface, including among political, religious, and other influential leaders—and by no means only in the United States—including among those who when speaking publicly give absolutely no reason to suspect they harbor such views. Billy Graham, after all, was publicly a great friend of Israel and had good relations with Jewish-American leaders. This exchange also conveys the fantastical nature of antisemites' views about Jews: "total domination," nutty notions about pornography, "stranglehold," and the acute threat Jews willfully pose to the United States of sending it "down the drain." The plausibility structure for *holding* such fantastical views existed (and about what other tiny group of—patriotic!—people can we imagine such a conversation among such powerful leaders taking place?), but the plausibility structure for *doing* something about the situation in 1970s America did not. Nevertheless, Graham, seemingly intoxicated by the opening Nixon gave him, ventured that dealing with the problem might be, after all, possible. He suggested his hope and thereby his encouragement that, should Nixon win reelection, "then we might be able to do something" about the Jews.

Graham, we see, confirmed that he had kept his antisemitism hidden from Jews (which means the public as well). He explained the lengths he went to do this.

"I go and I keep friends with Mr. Rosenthal at the *New York Times* and people of that sort, you know." (Rosenthal was the *New York Times'* executive editor.) "And all—I mean, not all the Jews, but a lot of the Jews are great friends of mine, they swarm around me and are friendly to me because they know that I'm friendly with Israel. But they don't know how I really feel about what they are doing to this country."

In his next sentence Graham reverts back to his ominous tones: "And I have no power, no way to handle them, but I would stand up if under proper circumstances." With this, Graham reveals his awareness of how changed circumstances—a changed plausibility structure, changed power relations, changed politics—would lead him to change his public tune and stance. He would "stand up" to and "handle" the Jews. Not surprisingly, as do so many antisemites who let their antisemitism slip out or who speak publicly in clearly coded antisemitic idioms, especially that of anti-Israelism, Graham, when his antisemitic rant was first disclosed by Nixon's chief of staff, H. R. Haldeman, in his memoir, but before the actual evidence from the recording was in the public domain, told the bald-faced lie: "I have never talked publicly or privately about the Jewish people, including conversations with President Nixon, except in the most positive terms."[2] In fact, the next year, this time on the phone with Nixon, Graham wondered aloud about the truth of the report he had read that Israel wanted to "expel all the Christians." Graham explained that Jews are "going right after the church." Drawing on the powerful Christian antisemitic paradigm and following the Christian bible's Book of Revelation, Graham openly spoke to the president of the United States of one of two kinds of Jews, as the "synagogue of Satan." Nixon, in turn, citing how Jews had — he implied owing to their own actions — provoked eliminationist assaults on themselves in Spain in 1492 and in Germany during the Nazi period, observed that "it's happening [again] — and now it's going to happen in American if these people don't start behaving. . . . It may be they have a death wish." They, the leading political and religious leaders of the United States, agreed — as they each knew about their own hidden animus toward Jews — that there was much more antisemitism in the United States than many suspected, with Graham saying that antisemitism is "right under the surface" and American Jews with their conduct would bring it "right to the top."[3] For Graham, the devil's Jewish brood was still alive.

Post-Holocaust liberal democratic societies simply do not permit antisemites who are public figures from speaking openly, let alone agitating for eliminationist measures against their own countries' Jews. Here in private, the president of the United States and perhaps the leading American religious leader sound like two members of an antisemitic conclave, conducting a hushed conversation about Jews that is divorced from reality. But imagine changed circumstances, which is not so hard to imagine, as they existed in Europe in the 1930s and 1940s. Some politician who today, like Nixon and the would-be power holder Graham, harbors eliminationist or noneliminationist views of Jews yet who conceals them, would have supported and indeed perhaps carried out a range of eliminationist, perhaps even exterminationist, initiatives. Because of contextual constraints, antisemites, even when wishing to eliminate Jews, often have had to live with inadequate half measures or no action at all. But this does not mean they would not be ready or eager to support far more radical policies and initiatives. People's rapid move from latent antisemitic beliefs (and this is true of other extreme prejudices) to supporting or implementing violent antisemitic action has occurred again and again historically, and well could occur again today under changed social and political circumstances. Such is the character and potential of the foundational antisemitic paradigm and of those beholden to it.

Antisemitism's singular status goes even deeper and is still more fundamental, in several discrete though also interrelated ways. The foundational antisemitic paradigm, and its development as an encoded prejudice and animus in a series of highly elaborated discourses, has been inscribed into the core of at least four civilizations, producing different discourses or streams of this prejudice.

For two millennia antisemitism has been at the core of Christian civilization, first in its European heartland and then, as it missionized, around the world. It is inscribed in its bible. The deprecation of Jews and the replacement theology, meaning that Jews ought to disappear, has historically been central to Christianity's and Christians' self-definition. Christianity's churches have until recently incessantly preached against Jews. Closely identifying Jews with evil, including the devil, organized Christianity's thinking and politics for centuries and had as a focal point the disposing of Jews.

Even with the eighteenth-century Enlightenment and Christianity's declining influence, antisemitism remained securely ensconced in Europe's broader cultures and institutions, persisting to become embedded in European (as distinct from Christian) civilization. The Christian religious elaboration of the noxious and dangerous nature of the Jews fell, for many, by the wayside, yet the animus and eliminationist orientation remained, even gained power, as it drew upon the Social Darwinian and racist conception of Jewness as being grounded in biology, race, or blood. The old Christian prejudice and animus maintained its firm hold in certain areas of Europe, such as Russia, Poland, and Ukraine. In others it competed with and was complemented by the new racial antisemitism, such as France. In still others, it was all but superseded by the racial conception of the Jews, such as in Germany. The putative Jewish Problem became central to European civilization, as it was central to the politics of country after country, where conceptions of the nation and the attempt to build nations focused on the alleged problem of the racially alien, dangerous Jews in their midst, and where political parties regularly campaigned on antisemitic and eliminationist platforms, culminating in the pan-European exterminationist assault on Jews, emanating from Germany, known as the Holocaust.

For more than thirteen hundred years, Islam has had enmity for Jews inscribed in the Qur'an, which Muslims deemed the infallible, literal, and unchanging word of God, as a prominent part of its teachings, especially in the Hadith (its oral tradition), and broadly disseminated among Muslims. Although antisemitism was not initially as central to organized Islam and to Muslims as it was to Christianity and Christians, Islam's foundational text sacralized and encoded a powerfully damaging account of Jews. Yet as demonizing as the Qur'an's account of Jews is, Jews do not play the central existential role in Muhammad's story or for the well-being of Islam as they do for Jesus' story and for Christianity. And unlike the Christians who in their rivalry with Jews sought custodianship of the Jewish bible as their own, Muslims wrote and adopted an entirely new sacred text, the Qur'an, which rendered the Jewish bible more or less moot. Hence, for various reasons, Muslims' more tempered attitude and less consistent and violently eliminationist stance and practice toward Jews.

Yet it is only by the horrific Christian standard that Islamic antisemitism and Muslims' antisemitism have been (wrongly) judged to be not all that bad historically. Islam cast Jews as the enemies of God's prophet Muhammad, alleging that they tried to kill him and casting them as stiff-necked holdouts of the old Judaic dispensation which Muhammad had brought word must be superseded and replaced by Islam. Muslims held Jews to be willful infidels who, owing to their wickedness — unlike the many innocents around the world — knowingly rejected Islam and God. Muslims also were moved by an eliminationist orientation toward Jews, who were to be always temporarily tolerated and pressured until they could be made to convert to Islam and their Jewness could be eliminated. Although at times, such as in Moorish Spain, Muslims and Jews coexisted tolerably well, Muslims across Islamic civilization were made well aware of the Jews' supposed perfidy and apostasy, were wary of them, and sought their eventual, and sometimes immediate and violent, elimination.

Antisemitism, and its centrality to Islamic civilization, has been ramped up by many orders of magnitude since the 1930s. It is now as ferocious as it has ever been and as central to Islamic civilization as it ever was to Christian civilization. Islamic civilization's understanding of Jews grounded in the foundational antisemitic paradigm, with fundamentals more or less the same as the one laid down by early Christianity, is now the norm in Arab and Islamic countries. The encoding of this antisemitism, and its basis in Islam's sacred texts and foundational writings, in new foundational texts — including but not restricted to Arab and Islamic political manifestos, charters, and programs — has been a widespread practice in the Arab and Islamic world. And the dissemination of antisemitism, indeed in the loudest and most strident of tones, is done by political leaders, religious leaders, opinion makers, governments, media, mothers and fathers, and local Imams at all times, including — regularly — at Friday prayers in mosques, to hundreds, thousands, indeed millions of Muslims at a time. Today, antisemitism, which is an amalgam of Islamic deprecation of, and Nazified notions about, Jews, is a constituent feature of Arab and Islamic civilization. Today, antisemitism is at the core of its most powerful transnational political movement, political Islam.

Antisemitism today is a prominent part of what exists for the first time in history, global civilization. Not sufficiently emphasized in the discussion of globalization is the global culture that has developed, its contours, and the many consequences for people's understanding of each other and the world that the existence of this new phenomenon produces. Global civilization has brought together the various antisemitisms that have existed in the last hundred years into a powerful new constellation that, whatever the many individual streams and differences among them, coalesce around the enduring foundational antisemitic paradigm. Using international institutions, transnational media — newspapers, radio, satellite TV, and the Internet — for spreading their ideas, antisemites have managed to band together in an informal and loose coalition, and to codify antisemitism in new institutions, such as the United Nations with its many subsidiary organizations, and in the ubiquitous Internet itself. Christian antisemites, Islamic antisemites, neo-Nazi antisemites, leftist antisemites, and European antisemites think, listen, shout, march, adopt symbols, and cheer under the same banner, even when each group's preferred consumption and production of antisemitism varies. They agree on the fundamentals: Jews, though some of them are careful to couch their speech around the Jews of Israel, are a breed apart, noxious, dangerous, responsible for many of the ills that afflict the world, and they—and their Jewness—must be hemmed in or eliminated. Global antisemitic culture's power leads leftist, gay, feminist, neo-Nazi, and Islamic activists—many of whom would otherwise gladly also assault, jail, or kill one another—to march arm-in-arm in antisemitic, sometimes ostensibly anti-Israel, rallies.

Antisemitism's distinctive place as the one ethnic prejudice that has been a part of and, more, at the core of several large and powerful civilizations encompassing hundreds of millions, indeed billions, of people indicates its scope and power. It has also been the only prejudice integral to a wide range of corporate and national identities: of Christians, of Europeans of many countries and peoples, including Germans, Ukrainians, and Poles, and of Muslims, Arabs, and Palestinians. These groups' and peoples' identities—some religious and some national, some national and some transnational, some in the stage of nation-formation, some beyond it, and some not interested in it—have formed around the notion that they are not-Jews, different from Jews, or against Jews. Even when a group's or people's conception of its collective identity evolves or transforms fundamentally, as it has for many Europeans and Christians since the Holocaust, so that today it is not true that European or German identity is defined significantly in relationship to Jews, the legacy of the previously powerful prejudice and identity paradigm still is pronounced.

# 5

# The Demonology and Its Consequences

GROUNDED IN THE fundamental antisemitic paradigm, as codified in the Christian bible and in Catholic Church teaching, medieval Christianity produced an elaborated antisemitism with a full-blown demonology that became pan-European, a property of churches, kings, and ordinary people alike. As we have seen, its fundamental conception of Jews was that they were devils, in league with the devil, real or de facto antichrists. This followed from people's overwhelmingly magical nature of understanding reality, which cast the world in religious terms, including the understanding of its physical existence, of society, of human beings, of their spiritual and to a great extent their material lives and fates, of the sources of disorder and suffering in the world, and of the nature of conflict. Thus, it is no surprise that the conception of Jews was religiously grounded, and that given the degree of their imputed perniciousness, they were identified in various ways with the devil, the source of evil in the world.

In Europe, the medieval period of antisemitism ended with the advent of modernity, but in the Arab and Islamic worlds medieval antisemitism lasted until the Nazi period when the new modern — in this case actually Nazi — antisemitism was exported to these countries and peoples.

Modern antisemitism and modern antisemites, with modern antisemitism's most developed and horrifying form being at Nazism's heart, fundamentally conceived of Jews as a race apart, biologically programmed to dominate, harm, or enslave humanity. This new conception of Jews never fully supplanted but instead developed in parallel to and augmented with new dimensions the demonizing medieval religious forms of antisemitism. Modern antisemitism derived from the new, modern conception of humanity and the world, which was no longer magical in the sense that the medieval one had been relying upon God's will and hand, but was essentially material and scientific, grounding humanity in an understanding of the world's physical processes — especially in the most powerful intellectual insurgency of perhaps all time, which finally and firmly broke religion's hold on people's conception of humanity and on the causes of human and environmental conditions and change, Charles Darwin's discovery and explication of evolution.

Evolution provided a revolutionary account, indeed a fundamental paradigm shift, in the understanding of (1) the origins of human beings (as evolved, and not made by God), (2) the constitution or ontology of the human being (fundamentally a material being, not a spiritual one, existing and being shaped by the environmental context), (3) relations among human beings (inherently competitive and conflictual), (4) the nature of group differences (hard and fast and biological, like those of species), and (5) by extension, the relations between groups (forever competitive and for survival), especially regarding groups' inherent conflictual nature and the illusion of intergroup cooperation and peace.

Antisemites quickly adopted this new paradigm and modernized antisemitism to accord with it. This shift from medieval antisemitism had already been under way for a good half century before Darwin. The Enlightenment's and the French Revolution's earlier challenges to religious beliefs as the foundation for understanding humanity and the world had already powerfully advanced; and in what was already a new nationalist age, where nations were beginning to coalesce as ever more the principal unit of social and political organization, antisemites had for a while been casting about for a new way to understand Jews and Jews' relationship to their own people.

This new nationalism and the change it produced in antisemites' conception of Jews cast antisemitism in more political terms than ever before and raised the issue of national purity in new ways. It also prepared the ground for antisemites to adopt the Darwinian revolution as the basis for a reconfigured antisemitism that easily harmonized with the nationalist orientation. The Jewish religion, as epitomized by the demonized text the Talmud and its alleged teachings, Jews' putative transgressions against Jesus, their rejection of Christianity and their alleged desire to destroy it—all these continued to be seen as problematic or part of the ledger of the Jews' malfeasance, but they were now seen not to be the fundamental issues. Instead these transgressions were but some of the most spectacular expressions of the Jews' underlying nature, which was a biological race that set out to dominate (and, in the view of some antisemites, destroy) other races, indeed all other races, meaning all humanity. Antisemites began to see and cast Jews as secularized devils, the source of much conflict and strife in the world, the principal cause of divisions within a nation, and the principal or at least a major generator of conflict among nations and threats to the people and the polity. To medieval antisemites Jews, of course, had always been dangerous, and especially dangerous because, like their master the devil, they could operate in insidious ways behind the scenes or in barely detectable manners. Now with a racial biological conception of the world and of Jews, and with it an almost immediate division of races according to a hierarchy of inherent abilities, other races deemed inferior but not satanic, this notion of the cunning Jew was tweaked, recasting the Jews into a highly able and intelligent foe with their very constitution, their *Jewness,* immutable as was their satanic threat.

The international danger that Jews posed was one of utter domination. It is during this period that the Russian secret police fabricated the *Protocols of the Elders of Zion,* which purported to be the minutes of the meeting of a powerful international Jewish conspiracy that sought to dominate the world. The *Protocols* both encoded and spread the notion of such a demonic and powerful international Jewish conspiracy, and mirrored the existing thinking that much of the Jews' power was international. This itself reflected the sense that the world was opening up and becoming smaller, with its growing communications, greater ease of transport, and far-flung empires. Nevertheless, the locus of the major battles was neither international nor, as it had been, predominantly local. Instead, antisemites understood that Jews had to be battled mainly on the national level and mainly in the realm of politics, which is the arena of the national par excellence. And thus the antisemites' fight against the Jews moved into politics as never before and antisemites sought solutions on the national level. It is stunning how thoroughly eliminationist the late-nineteenth-century and pre-Nazi twentieth-century public antisemitic discourse was in Germany and in Europe more broadly. In one country after another, a significant part of this powerful public discourse focused on the Jewish Problem—often with the assumption that Jews or Jewness needed to be eliminated, and with solutions of one kind or another to do so.

The Arab and Islamic worlds entered modernity much later than Europe. Such changes were retarded by many factors, including their lack of independence owing to Ottoman and European imperialism, which meant among other things that their politics did not develop, nation states did not commensurately emerge in the nineteenth or first half of the twentieth centuries, and their political cultures remained mired in medieval, magical orientations, with Islam being their core. Thus, while modern, racist antisemitism was evolving in Europe, the other religious civilization of antisemitism, the Islamic and Arabic one, had no parallel development. The degree of preoccupation with Jews among Arabs and Muslims was far less than in Europe until the British Balfour Declaration of 1917 promised Jews a homeland in British Mandate for Palestine, Jews' progressive migration to their people's ancient homeland, Arabs' murder of more than one hundred Jews in what became known as the "1929 riots," and the growing conflict between Jews and the local Arabs, who developed a national identity of Palestinians in opposition to the Jews' nationalism and modern Israel's creation in 1948. Owing to Arabs' exposure to and ready incorporation of Nazi views of Jews, the antisemitism of the Arab and Islamic worlds finally gathered a modern essentialist tenor, which Arabs and Muslims incorporated into their own notions of detestable and putatively dangerous Jewness.

Antisemitism thus saw uneven development, its two principal medieval forms modernizing at different rates and eventually in different ways. Even with Arab and Islamic antisemitic discourses—including and especially those of Egypt's Muslim Brotherhood, which spawned Hamas offshoots in other countries—incorporating almost unreflectively the gamut of the Nazis' specific antisemitic elaborations, visual images, calumnies, tropes, and prescriptions for what to do with Jews, it was but an overlay onto the still-existing foundational Islamic antisemitism that had remained in its fundamentals more or less unchanged from what it had been for centuries. As we will see, this amalgam, always further changing its formula as the context for it changes, continues to this day.

In Europe, antisemitism had within it an analogous variability. The extent to which the modern racial-biological antisemitism replaced the religious-based medieval antisemitism varied substantially from country to country and even within countries and cultures, and the partial ways in which the replacement occurred, often in one community along some dimensions but not others, also varied considerably. So, while in Germany the central tendency was for racist antisemitism to prevail, and to exist in its purest form in Nazism and among the Nazis' tens of millions of followers, there were still considerable pockets of more medieval antisemites. For example, the Catholic Church and Catholics continued to maintain that the Jews' evil resided in their rejection of Jesus, and that they, at least in principle, were able to be converted from Judaism and thereby from their evil ways—even if experience had shown that in practice little hope existed. Such antisemites, namely those seeing the source of Jews' unwholesomeness and danger to reside in their religion and not in their race, existed in larger numbers, probably in the majority in Lithuania, Poland, Ukraine, and other countries of the region. But many of them had adopted (as had so many holdout religious antisemites in Germany and the West) the modern racist antisemitic litany of charges against Jews and its general orientation to seeing the realm of danger to be at the national level and the way to meet that danger being through politics and political action, also at the national level, with the ultimate goal being eliminating the Jews, often through the use of violence. A map of antisemitism in Europe, which would be a map of antisemitisms in the plural, could identify places as harboring predominantly one of four kinds of antisemitism created by the two dimensions of what antisemites considered the source of the Jews' evil to be (religion or race) and what the antisemitic action orientation was (medieval, which means local and to manage the problem, or national and eliminationist). It would show a patchwork of the four types of antisemitisms, with the majority being certainly of the two kinds with a modern action orientation, the racist one being predominant in Germany and the religious one in Poland, and the distinct minority of the four being the religious-based medieval action orientation.

In the areas of Europe where modernity came later and where religion continued to maintain its sway on the public, modern racist antisemitism did not become the dominant antisemitic mode — its substantial inroads (mainly in its higher-level elaborations of Jews' perniciousness and its action orientation) aside — but existed side by side and commingled with Christian antisemitism. Indeed, the ways in which modern racist antisemitism has conventionally been cast as a replacement for and categorically different from medieval Christian antisemitism has been both overstated and too stylized. The changing contexts of European civilization — with pan-European developments in economy, society, culture, and politics, whatever the differences and unevenness of these developments — affected all antisemitisms, public and private antisemitic discourses, and antisemites. Christian antisemitism, perhaps most notably within its bastion of the Catholic Church, was not the same in 1935 as it had been in 1835, let alone 1735, even though the fundamental Christian account and beliefs about Jews grounded in the foundational antisemitic paradigm had not formally changed. A most significant change that did occur was the increase in the intensity of Christian and non-Christian antisemitism alike — as the topic of Jews' place within the nation and therefore the activation of antisemitism on a daily basis in the public sphere, often as a hot political issue — making antisemitism ever more manifest and the degree of perniciousness attributed to the Jews (and the action orientation that followed from it) the crucial aspect for understanding antisemitism during the latter part of the nineteenth century until the end of the Germans' and others' exterminationist assault with the close of World War II.

Students of antisemitism have been overly taken by the racial/religious distinction, even for understanding the modern period when the critical issue and realm for working out people's views about Jews and what to do with them had become politics with its broader horizons and orientation toward policies and actions. This was easy enough to see once the Germans began to implement their eliminationist program, including in its exterminationist phase. In region after region and country after country, in Latvia, Lithuania, Poland, Ukraine, Slovakia, and elsewhere, they found that a staggering number of Christian antisemites, and many clergy from Pope Pius XII on down within the Catholic Church itself, signed on to the eliminationist assault — for some, even or particularly in its exterminationist form. Many people of these different countries and religious institutions easily harmonized the new anti-Jewish program with their existing antisemitic beliefs, such long-standing beliefs having long prepared them for this kind of solution to their putative Jewish Problem. Even nonracist antisemites had been affected by the emergence of modernity, the context of which changed their antisemitism as well. With new communications and expanded transportation, they too had their horizons lengthened and expanded beyond the village or town or even city and perhaps the local area surrounding it, to the region or the nation, about which they now knew much more, understood its importance for their daily lives, and to which they were oriented politically in the new politics of national governance and national contestation. With this changed perspective, Christian antisemites, no less than their racist confreres, adopted a national and more present-oriented and action-oriented perspective, which rendered the Jews' putative danger greater than ever. Germans, French, Poles, and others — in this respect more like people with regional or local identities such as Bavarians, Burgundians, Galicians, or Munichers or Freilassingers and the local city dwellers and villagers of the other regions — had always faced local threats, including or especially from the people in the next town or village. Now with local conditions enormously more pacified, providing more general existential security, a new danger came into focus: the threat that the Jews posed to the nation, to the Volk, a danger that would never be stopped so long as the Jews existed among the nation or on the earth.

In a profound sense, modern racist antisemitism fit the intense passions of resentment, disgust, and hatred that Christian antisemites felt toward Jews. It fit this animus even better than the foundational Christian antisemitism it replaced or was becoming amalgamated with. It did so because modern racist antisemitism's unrestrained action orientation fulfilled the logic of those emotions and even, when stripped of the theological constraints on action, the logic of their beliefs. Certainly, despite the Church's and secular rulers' injunctions during medieval times against slaughtering Jews, ordinary Christians repeatedly erupted in spasms of murderous violence. There were many times when Christians slaughtered Jews during the medieval era of antisemitism because the Church's relatively tame prescriptions for action, which came from concerns other than its account of Jews—centering on the Jews' alleged horrifying deeds, malevolent nature, and day-to-day danger that they were—were inadequate to restrain ordinary people's antisemitic logic and emotional animus. This occurred on a grand scale during the First Crusade of 1096, when the warriors were marching to liberate the Holy Land from the grip of Muslims in the name of Christ. They slaughtered the Jews of one community after another in northern France and Germany, claiming ten thousand victims, as they made their way to Jerusalem, even though a reckoning of any kind with Jews was not part of their charge. It came naturally to them, as it did to later Crusaders, naturally in the sense that it comported with their beliefs about and animus toward Jews, which were that much more activated because they were crusaders in the name of God, at once defending and furthering Christianity. How could they let the defilers and opponents of Christianity live among them if they were going to march to faraway lands to vanquish Christianity's enemies there? Christians blamed the Black Death on Jews, so throwing Church restraints aside, from 1348 to 1350 they annihilated the Jews among them. Similarly, in the context of reestablishing Christian suzerainty over Muslim Spain, in 1391 Spaniards murdered Jews all over Spain, as they did during the final years of the Spanish Inquisition at the end of the 1400s.

This bursting of the constraints that Church and secular rulers placed upon antisemitic violence occurred on a small if repeated scale. It can best be seen in the annual frenzy that Christians across Europe would work themselves into during Passion Week, the week leading up to Easter when the story of Jesus' death is recounted in Church and often enacted in dramatic productions. Despite prophylactic preparations and warnings from church and local rulers meant to defuse this dynamic and to protect the Jews, the Jews knew that they would be lucky if they escaped this most murderous time of the year with but a few deaths and little damage.

Modern antisemitism's recasting antisemitism around the Jews' unbounded *contemporary* perniciousness, and away from a historical focus on alleged *past* deeds (however horrifying they were in the telling), its transfer of the locus of action to politics with a national perspective replacing a local one, and its action orientation calling for radical measures to solve the alleged Jewish Problem easily refocused even Christian antisemites and their institutions by bringing them in line with most of the social and political fundamentals of the age. It did the same, albeit in a different historical and contextual trajectory, with Arab and Islamic antisemitism.

At the time of Germany's defeat and the end of the continental wide exterminationist assault upon the Jews, antisemitism, in theory and practice, was at an all-time high. One of the many tenacious myths about this period is that the Germans were alone, or mainly alone, in persecuting Jews. As noted, across Europe, the foundational antisemitic paradigm, with various higher-level elaborations, had, independent of the Germans, shaped people's views of Jews or was at least powerfully present among a good part of many countries' peoples, and was central to the public discourse and politics. The Jewish Problem, grounded in that paradigm, was a pressing question. Especially once the Germans turned eliminationism into the public philosophy and practical program of Europe, in country after country, the majority or a significant percentage of the population was manifestly moved by an eliminationist orientation toward the Jews to support the Jews' segregation, expulsion, or extermination. The Germans therefore found abundant willing supporters, and willing executioners around Europe—from France to Ukraine, from Norway to Greece, even in countries such as Poland that the Germans were otherwise brutally subjugating—among both German allied political regimes and peoples, precisely because the foundational eliminationist paradigm was shared by vast swaths of the European populace, heirs, whether people were continuing religious heirs or secularized nationalized or racial biological ones, to the Christian foundational antisemitic paradigm and teachings about Jews. In any number of countries and regions, local governments and peoples—to be sure, in the context of the new German dispensation and with German encouragement—took local initiative to further the eliminationist and mass-murderous persecution of their Jews. This was the case in Vichy France, Mussolini's Italy, Slovakia, Ukraine, Lithuania, Croatia, and elsewhere. Local peoples, not everywhere but far more often than not, hounded and hunted Jews. Among the peoples of Western Europe, it was horrible for Jews. Among the peoples of Central Europe, it was horrible for Jews. Among the peoples of Eastern Europe, it was horrible for Jews. Even among the less antisemitic regions and among the less antisemitic people, few said that antisemitism, root and branch, was a lie.

Any number of people did oppose the mass murder as morally impermissible. Danes first stood by and then rescued their country's Jews, ferrying them to safety in Sweden just as the Germans were about to deport them to Auschwitz. Bulgarians resisted the Germans' deportation demands and preserved the Bulgarian Jews (but not non-Bulgarian Jews in Bulgaria!). Many Italians saw the mass murder of Jews as monstrous and sabotaged their deportation in the Italian-occupied part of Yugoslavia and in their own country. Individual Catholic bishops, priests, and nuns saved individual Jews, especially Jewish children, by hiding them in monasteries and schools. These and other exceptions are notable, and they are celebrated precisely because they were exceptions to the eliminationist antisemitic rule. They were exceptions according to how the peoples and governments (those that existed) of most countries by and large acted to further the persecution or even the mass murder. They were exceptions to how the majority of people in many countries was favorably oriented toward the Jews' persecution and often extermination. And they were exceptions to the supportive positions that institutions, including the Catholic Church and the Protestant churches of Germany, took toward the Jews' persecutions, not to mention the antisemitic orientations that their acts expressed and demonstrated. Many of those who helped Jews have testified to how isolated they were in a world teeming with antisemites, and the Jewish victims have regularly noted, often with wonder, how the people who dissented from the antisemitic norms were lone candles in the dark night.

# 6

# The Post–World War II
# Illusion

To MANY PEOPLE, antisemitism after the Holocaust seemed unthinkable: "If anyone had told me in 1945 that in Germany Jewish cemeteries would again be desecrated, synagogues set afire, foreigners hounded, I would have declared him to be mad. Shortly after the war the philosophers Horkheimer and Adorno wrote in their book *The Dialectics of the Enlightenment:* after Auschwitz antisemitism is no longer possible. At this, today, we are tempted to burst out laughing, bitterly....I experience here very much antisemitism and very much xenophobia."[1] Such was the distress of Paul Spiegel, leader of Germany's Jewish community, in 2002 over antisemitism's resurgence in his country. Since then, in one decade, things have changed so much that no Jewish leader or, for that matter, no ordinary Jew in Europe or in virtually any country of the world where there are Jews would utter such a naive statement about the new, firmly entrenched antisemitic reality with its violence and potential for violence. Except, perhaps, in the United States, where, happily, American exceptionalism remains, for now, the rule, at least regarding Jews.

Spiegel's cri de coeur is instructive because of what is right about it and what is wrong about it. Most significantly, it highlights the resurgence of antisemitic expression in the public sphere that was well under way, after decades of its relative absence—and how its upsurge was so sudden after decades of its public restraint. Nowhere was this change more noticeable, shocking, and significant than in Germany, for the reason that Spiegel intimated. And it was certainly most bracing there, and that is why Spiegel expressed his derision for the foolish assertion of Max Horkheimer and Paul Adorno, two of the post–World War II era's most influential yet miguided writers about antisemitism. The assertion that antisemitism would no longer be possible was as silly a statement as prominent public intellectuals have made in the last century—which is saying a lot.

This points to what was wrong about Spiegel's own retrospective prediction that the Holocaust, and its inoculating effects, would prevent future antisemitic acts. Powerful beliefs and emotions produced the Holocaust, which was, though spearheaded and principally carried out by Germans, implemented by an international genocidal coalition rooted broadly and deeply in cultures and institutions of antisemitism across Europe that went back hundreds of years.[2] It was extremely naive to think that such titanic antisemitism, capable of producing an assault unprecedented in its perpetrators' breadth, its geographic range, and its intent's comprehensiveness—total extermination of every woman, man, and child—would somehow cease to exist.

Spiegel's statement, with the issues it explicitly or implicitly raises in the context of today's resurgent antisemitism, thus suggests the complexity of antisemitism's trajectory since the Holocaust. Antisemitism's course in the initial decades after the Holocaust, the decline in its *public expression,* had been so steep as to be almost absolute, unnatural, and certainly unforeseen by anyone. Auschwitz soon became the central and most horrifying symbol both of the Holocaust and of what has come to be known as "man's inhumanity to man." A firm public identity formed between Auschwitz and the Germans' extermination of the Jews and all the death, destruction, and horrors that Germany and Nazism visited upon Europe and the civilized world. This identity symbiotically framed evil: the Nazis, (1) whose evil was indisputable as they had produced unprecedented death and destruction to the European peoples themselves with their conquest, plundering, and mass murdering across the continent, (2) were also or especially evil because they created the new, existentially previously unimaginable horror of *death factories,* and (3) the extermination of the Jews was evil because (4) the Nazis did it and because (5) they erected these death factories to do it in.

If the Germans had mass-murdered the 2.5 million Jews they gassed in the death factories in the more conventional ways they killed the 3.5 million other Jews (shooting, starvation, et cetera), then the annihilation might not have become synonymous with evil and so delegitimized everything, including antisemitism, that seemed related to it. After all, the mass murder of Jews itself, although widely known, did not so profoundly impress European and world civilization as it was taking place. Neither did the Germans' mass murder of non-Jewish victims, including three million Soviet POWs and millions of Russians, Poles, and others; nor did the millions the Japanese murdered in China, Korea, and elsewhere while the Germans were slaughtering Jews. Nor did the earlier, contemporaneous, or later mass murders of other peoples, from the millions of Congolese slaughtered by the Belgians at the turn of the twentieth century, to the Armenians exterminated by the Turks during World War I, to the many other peoples slain around the world in the decades after the Holocaust. The Holocaust did not attain its symbolic status and delegitimize antisemitism because the Jews were powerful. (That is another antisemitic myth.) Jews were as weak and uninfluential as could be—Europeans hated and slaughtered them, the British kept them down in Palestine, Stalin subsequently turned them into the victims of his antisemitism, and the American government, allegedly so beholden to Jews, did not lift a finger to combat the mass murder when it was happening.

Nevertheless, in 1945 there was reason to think that antisemitism would be publicly suppressed and thereby atrophy because the people of Europe and the world had instantly and rightly understood it to be the foundation for the mass murder, an evil incarnate, at the core of Nazism and most Germans' worldview. Moreover, the United States, the world superpower and savior and the new governor of the international system, was decidedly not a part of the eliminationist antisemitic alliance that had spanned most of Europe. The United States, whatever the substantial antisemitism that existed among its people and leaders, did not harbor, let alone propagate, the demonized and dehumanized view of Jews current in Germany and in much of Europe.

The United States had been by no means immune to antisemitism. After all, it too was from the start a Christian country animated by Christian notions about the world, including of Jews. And it remained deeply religious. But it differed from European countries in several important respects. As the United States had always been an immigrant country, defined itself as such, and opened citizenship from the beginning to people who had not been born Americans, it was always more tolerant of immigrants and minorities, always more willing and able to absorb them into American society, and always more tolerant of divergences from a less firmly conceived and stultifying national norm. This meant that the country (albeit with a hegemonic white Protestant model) was still always pluralistic, indeed what the United States was and what Americans as a people were was conceived in terms of pluralism. *E pluribus unum* — out of many, one — recognizes the rightful place and membership in the national community of the many. The country had its nativist moments, and two enormous and grotesque exceptions to all this were the whites' treatment of blacks, enslaving, Jim Crow-ing, and segregating them for centuries; and Americans' treatment of Native Americans. Yet, by and large, except for a few battle cries from the fringes, there was no call for or drive for or mobilization around, let alone programs for, the creation of a racially or nationally pure America, whatever that could possibly mean in the American social context. All this opened up social space for Jews and also pertained explicitly to Jews. No less a critical figure than George Washington, the first American president, in his letter to the Jews of Newport, Rhode Island, set the terms that would govern American public life vis-à-vis Jewish Americans.

> The Citizens of the United States of America have a right to applaud themselves for giving to Mankind examples of an enlarged and liberal policy: a policy worthy of imitation. All possess alike liberty of conscience and immunities of citizenship. It is now no more that toleration is spoken of, as if it was by the indulgence of one class of people that another enjoyed the exercise of their inherent natural rights. For happily the Government of the United States, which gives to bigotry no sanction, to persecution no assistance, requires only that they who live under its protection, should demean themselves as good citizens....
>
> May the Children of the Stock of Abraham, who dwell in this land, continue to merit and enjoy the good will of the other Inhabitants; while every one shall sit under his own vine and fig tree, and there shall be none to make him afraid.[3]

In the United States membership in the national community was defined politically by citizenship and not, as it was everywhere throughout Europe (even in France regarding Jews, its formal focus on citizenship notwithstanding), by ethnicity or race, by some notion of one people inextricably, organically grounded in a territory. Jews were citizens in the United States, just as non-Jews were. They therefore had every claim on their place within the country and in the society that anyone else did. This was not only constitutionally enshrined and protected, but it also formed the cognitive frame for Americans' national self-understanding, which (even when there was antisemitism) pertained to Jews as much as anyone else.

All this in itself would have likely made the United States considerably less antisemitic than European countries. Yet the United States possessed still additional powerful ameliorators of antisemitism. The formal legal separation between church and state, though imperfectly observed, benefited American society and politics generally and Jews in particular. It took religious conflicts out of the political sphere, which prevented them from escalating because they did not enter into that most important public arena for conflicts to intensify. So it depoliticized religious differences, turning them into affairs of civil society, to be negotiated well or not, as so many other nonpolitical conflicts are. This lowered the stakes in interfaith conflicts because neither could religions, churches, or religious groups capture the state to further their purposes, whether otherworldly or this worldly, nor would the state seek to suppress a religion, church, or religious group, or help one prevail over another.

Although this separation and all its benefits were never perfectly observed or accrued, more than not they were, and they set a tone and a set of expectations that religion was not going to be a political affair. This was critically important for Jews, and for the character of antisemitism, for three reasons: Until well into the twentieth century, Jews were almost always defined and understood in American society to be a religious group, so they were off limits as an object of politics. Second, when the basic contours and conflicts of politics came to be, with the emergence of modern politics during and after the American and French revolutions, because Jews were understood to be a religious group, their status did not become part of the foundational political questions of the United States even though it did in Europe. And third, everywhere but the United States antisemitism was highly political, and governments either enacted laws or programs against Jews or potentially could do so at any time, which meant in Europe, but not in the United States, contesting the status of Jews in public almost by definition also became a political issue and usually a hot button one.

Furthermore, all religious groups knew that trying to break down this church–state separation, which was a cherished part of the American compact, risked two things: bringing severe opprobrium down upon themselves, and, if successful, opening the door for the tables to be turned on them one day. This, together with the multiplicity of social groups (many ethnic groups, many religious denominations, many national, state-based, class collectivities, and so on), which made most every group a minority in American society's vast tableau, tempered intergroup conflicts in general. American society, it was understood, was safer and worked better for everyone if social and group conflict was kept within highly circumscribed bounds. Thus, even the Catholic Church, the leading antisemitic institution in the world in the nineteenth and arguably into the early part of the twentieth century, was not so vociferously antisemitic in the United States, where it, as a good American institution, was much more socially, culturally, and politically liberal than anywhere else, so much so that in the late 1890s Pope Leo XII formally declared the tolerant ways of the American Catholic Church to be a form of heresy called "Americanism"!

No matter that Henry Ford was as prominent an antisemite, also internationally, as there was. No matter that there was plenty of social discrimination against Jews. No matter that a rabidly antisemitic Catholic priest, Father Charles Coughlin, had a popular radio show in the 1930s and a substantial following for his anti-Jewish agitation. Jews always were and remained not just a fixed part of the motley American landscape's ethnic and religious mix, and not just firmly protected as unquestioned citizens of a country that fully enshrined religious tolerance, but also, whatever many others' unease, recognized members of the American people, of the national community. And with the end of World War II, indeed, with the American entry into the war, antisemitism also took a public and social nosedive in the United States. Father Coughlin, now identified with German and European antisemitism's horrors, was finished. Never again would the country see a hint of viru-lent public, let alone eliminationist, antisemitism or political mobiliza-tion around antisemitism within American society's mainstream. Antisemitism as a public discourse and political ideology was utterly finished, having died the death it so roundly came to be understood to deserve. All this produced the most critical difference in antisemitism's character and danger in the United States compared to Europe. In the United States there was no significant political mobilization around antisemitism. Never did any major American political parties try to win voters with antisemitic appeals. Never did they incorporate antisemitic planks in their platforms. Only once was there a major leader who was an open antisemite who made his antisemitism part of his public stance and politics. This was General Ulysses Grant, with his one-time expul-sion during the Civil War of the Jews in his military district comprising areas of Tennessee, Kentucky, and Mississippi for allegedly profiteering (drawing on the age-old Christian calumny of Jews' treacherously serv-ing money and betraying goodness). President Abraham Lincoln imme-diately rescinded Grant's order and it was never implemented, and the cry and repulsion against it was such that Grant, while president, had to repeatedly show that he was a nonantisemite, appointing many Jews to his administration and even becoming the first president to attend a syn-agogue dedication ceremony. If any other major political leaders would have liked to emulate Grant's one antisemitic initiative, they knew that their country would not stand for it. Indeed, Jews, whatever the preju-dice and discrimination, were an accepted part of the public American pluralist landscape—leading many in Europe, especially in Germany, to wrongly believe that Jews were enormously powerful in the United States. In Germany, it was often said that President Franklin Roosevelt was actually of Jewish ancestry.

Germany's destructiveness and its defeat together ushered in a new era also for Europe. The need to reconstruct it, and its division into west and east created in the West a new politics, not one of national self-pursuit, let alone of national or racial purity, but one dominated by three geopolitical concerns: how to keep democratic forces in, the Russians out, and (at least initially) the Germans down. The answers had nothing to do with the Jews and everything to do with a politics of domestic accommodation, international alliance, and collective interests and security, and with the

United States as the unquestioned political and cultural model. These priorities replaced the poisonous politics of class antagonism and ideological polarization around left (blamed on the Jews) and right (blaming the Jews), national striving (Jews have no place in the nation), national purification (Jews defile and corrupt), local and national hatreds (Jews always a ready and convenient target). Two new supranational institutions institutionalized the new politics: the European Coal and Steel Community in 1951 for economic cooperation, which would eventually grow into the European Union, and the North Atlantic Treaty Organization in 1949 for common security. Poisonous domestic politics and cultures, and national and racist enmity, including antisemitism, were out.

The United States as victor, guarantor, and model, together with the defeat of Nazi Germany and the emergence of a new world East-West order, were the principal causes for repressing antisemitism. A public legal and moral reckoning further contributed to this new dispensation: the Nuremberg Trials put leading Germans in the dock and, because the Germans' mass murder of the Jews was one of the prosecution's four principal charges, essentially put antisemitism on trial. It unveiled the world historical horrors that the Germans had perpetrated upon Jews, horrifying blow by blow, in unvarnished form, with overwhelming sympathy for the victims. This cool and bracing eye's perspective on these evils, with the American prosecutor Justice Robert Jackson aptly calling antisemitism the "spear head of terror" in his opening statement, was a wakeup call for Europe's and the world's antisemitic elites and publics, and for the world's nonantisemitic elites and publics to become extra vigilant because, as Jackson put it in his second sentence, "the wrongs which we seek to condemn and punish have been so calculated, so malignant, and so devastating, that civilization cannot tolerate their being ignored, because it cannot survive their being repeated."[4]

Of course, not every European, let alone every antisemite around the world, followed the trials, both the Trial of the Major War Criminals, which was the most famous and publicized one, and the many subsequent trials of different German institutions that carried out the eliminationist and exterminationist assault on the Jews—the Einsatzgruppen, the concentration camp administration, the armed forces, and so on. Yet the trials, conducted by the victorious allies in the symbolic heart of prostrate Germany, symbolized a fundamental change in

European culture and politics, and conveyed to European elites and publics alike the unmistakable message: the age of antisemitism's public culture, politics, and eliminationist practice is over.

Yet the changed *public* atmosphere regarding antisemitism was only a figurative half of the issue. There is a difference between understanding that antisemitism could no longer be politically *practiced* in the public sphere — except in religious institutions and teaching where it continued as it was embedded in creed, scripture, and liturgy — and believing that antisemitism's precepts and its practice are wrong. Such a profound set of beliefs as antisemitism, ingrained in such elaborated and powerful underlying cultures, discourses, and narratives, did not so easily dissipate. All the many tens of millions of antisemitic people, who had recently approvingly witnessed antisemitism's implementation in a continent-wide eliminationist and exterminationist assault, did not recant and utter mea culpas. The shock of the gas chambers and the United States' moral and political suzerainty gave many people cause to reconsider their antisemitism's rightness, with lasting positive effects, but many other antisemites, themselves recovering from war's ravages and occupation and struggling to reconstitute their lives and society, often just trying to feed themselves and their families, paid little heed to these transgressions and saw little need to cast off the beliefs and the underlying paradigm that formed their moral, social, and political axes' cardinal points.

Antisemitism and overt hostility to Jews continued. In some cases it increased in the war's immediate aftermath. The very developments that delegitimized antisemitism in the public sphere and compelled many people to reconsider its rightness also irritated many antisemites who blamed the Jews for miseries associated with the postwar dispensations, blamed the Jews once again — falsely, again — for getting special treatment for themselves, and blamed the Jews for the repeated reminders of what they would happily forget, namely that their countrymen, coreligionists, and fellow Europeans had so victimized the Jews. People's strong tendency to justify and legitimize their past stances and practices, their confirmation bias, further buttressed their prejudicial views, already strongly resistant to evidence and revision. Blaming the victim, especially by the perpetrators, is as time-practiced a human practice as there is, and one that antisemites have honed through the ages for

Jews. This practice continued to exert a powerful influence on antisemites' understanding of the Germans' and others' eliminationist and exterminationist assault on the Jews. *Yes, of course, the Jews shouldn't have been killed, but if they hadn't brought it on themselves by controlling the banks, by being communists, et cetera, then it wouldn't have happened. Yes, of course, the Germans shouldn't have killed the Jews, but we suffered so much as well, and look at how the Jews are now being favored.* As so many Europeans had been complicit, at the very least morally complicit owing to their approval or support for one or another aspect of the eliminationist project and assault on Jews, having to hear of the wrongs and suffering inflicted on the Jews stirred ever more hostility toward the already victimized people.

Many Jews emerging from the camps wanted nothing more in the Holocaust's aftermath than to return to their homes and retake what property, furniture, and belongings were left to them. Germans, Poles, Lithuanians, Ukrainians, the Dutch, the French, and others had expelled and driven Jews from their homes and had stolen their property. In every community where Jews had lived, non-Jews had, as an immediate by-product of the Germans' and often their own countrymen's eliminationist assault upon Jews, or in its aftermath, taken over the Jews' homes and lands, their communal buildings and businesses, their bank accounts and insurance policies, their furniture and belongings, dispossessing the Jews of their worldly belongings. Think of how many people in Germany, where more than a half million Jews had lived who were on the whole economically well-off, continued to engage in or profit from this criminality after the war. Think of how many people in Poland, which had been home to three million Jews, stole Jewish property. In France, in the Netherlands, in Austria, in Ukraine, in Romania, in country after country, the millions of people — who in any other contexts would be called criminals — with each passing day lived with their stolen goods knowing from whom the homes and goods had come. In every community many others knew of this theft — but it was from this deprecated and hated people — and tolerated or approved of it. The hostility this engendered with the Jews' return only reinforced the virulent antisemitism that had moved so many to work to eliminate and annihilate Jews during the war, and which still moved people to act similarly, even when the Holocaust's horrors had so profoundly disturbed nonantisemites, and even many antisemites, the world over. Poland saw many attacks on Jews from 1944 to 1946 in which Poles murdered one thousand to two thousand Jews. The most notorious one, a pogrom, occurred in July 1946 in Kielce when Poles marauded against and murdered Jews after the age-old Christian blood-libel rumor had spread, alleging that local Jews had kidnapped a Polish child (who was unharmed) and killed other children in order to use their blood in rituals. Postwar surveys of Polish peasants' views of Jews in the 1970s and 1980s revealed the depth of their antisemitism, including the peasants' explicit support for Poles' murder of Jews after the war, which also occurred by ones and twos in the peasants' own villages and around Poland as Jews returned to their homes to reclaim their lives. The surveys' author Alina Cała reports, "Even those who had severely condemned the Nazi persecutions judged the postwar murders very tolerantly or even justified them." She explains that, in addition to the persistent criminality of the Poles keeping Jews' property, the killers and their approving neighbors were fundamentally motivated by age-old antisemitism: "The immediate cause of most of the murders...was the accusation of drinking human blood."[5] Yet with the exception of a brief period of physical attacks on Jews in Poland and elsewhere after the war, all physical assaults upon Jews in Europe, especially in the West, came to an end, and the possibility of public political action against Jews, of political mobilization around the so-called Jewish Problem, of violence, let alone an eliminationist program, against Jews utterly ceased and was taken off the table.

That notion that Jews kill Christian children to use their blood was one of the most powerful calumnies to be found in pervasively antisemitic countries such as Poland prior to the end of World War II. And while, exceptional moments notwithstanding, the Polish public sphere and media in the postwar decades were practically devoid of classical antisemitism, the blood-libel accusation continued to live on, being propagated, reinforced, and passed on to new generations beneath the public sphere's radar. A group of researchers, including anthropologists and sociologists, have recently gone into communities to examine the prevalence of such beliefs after sixty years of public silence about them. One of the scholars, Joanna Tokarska-Bakir, explains: "The blood-libel myths include the belief that Jews used to kidnap and 'draw blood' from

Christian children. We wanted to check in the field whether any trace of these myths could still be found in the Sandomierz region, where paintings representing Jews 'drawing blood' from a Christian infant are still hanging on the Cathedral wall." They were looking for "traces," seemingly expecting nothing more than that. The reality of antisemitism is far different: "We were surprised to find how pervasive the myth was. It turned out to be in circulation on all cultural levels, among family, friends, and congregation. Astoundingly, it was recounted by members of the elite: clergymen, artists, teachers, conservators, the diocesan curia, regional historians."[6] For decades and decades, and through several generations, this fantastical and demonizing antisemitic accusation has been passed on from father and mother to son and daughter, from clergy to flock, and among friends and schoolmates. The power of communities within themselves to keep antisemitism alive and to give it new life, in Poland and as a rule elsewhere, is both powerful and enormously underappreciated.

Whatever antisemitism's public suppression, the foundational antisemitic paradigm, holding Jews to be different, noxious, and inimical to the well-being of others, was robustly carried on in communities, among families, in the religious guidance that so many received and from which they derived the fundamentals or at least central portions of their cultural and social worldviews and moral compasses. The post–World War II period saw no formal, let alone extensive, anti-antisemitic education or, put differently, no powerfully supported and disseminated, accurate image and account of Jews, no new anti-antisemitic discourses that would counteract and eventually replace the horrifying one that was so widespread and deeply embedded. The powerful foundational antisemitic paradigm, the elaborated antisemitic beliefs, the communal, national, and even international discourses, let alone the profound antisemitic animus that had formed and informed many of the major cultural and political currents of the European national and social landscapes, did not simply dry up merely owing its suppression in the public sphere or owing to some public condemnation or in the face of the World Council of Churches' announcement that antisemitism is incompatible with Christianity. Few people, assuming that they noticed, woke up one day and said to one another: *Oh, the World Council of Churches says antisemitism is bad, so that's a good enough reason for me to stop believing everything that I have believed about Jews. I will, with an act of will, banish all further thoughts, emotions, and feelings of suspicion, wariness, hostility, and enmity for Jews.* Cognition, including emotional response, does not work that way. Deeply embedded paradigms, cultural compass points, systems of belief and practice, emotions and hostilities, do not dissipate so quickly or completely unless an enormous amount of active and sustained work undermines them, educating people, and crucially substituting those notions with new, more compelling ones that can crowd them out and eventually replace them. None of this was done, even in Germany, where the need, and the opportunity, to do so was greatest.

Germans, even though they were perhaps placing themselves in jeopardy, still expressed enormous antisemitism. December 1946 marked a year and a half of American and Allied occupation of Germany. By then all Germans fully understood how thoroughly criminal were the eliminationist and exterminationist acts against Jews that had flowed from their antisemitism. They understood that the occupation authorities and the world thoroughly condemned antisemitism. They had already had a year and a half to begin to reconsider their views. Even then, fully 60 percent of Germans were willing to admit that they were unequivocal racists and antisemites.

Such admissions were made not in private but in face-to-face interviews with American occupation authorities. So convinced were so many Germans of their antisemitism's rectitude that they readily confessed to American officials that they were antisemites, and this was when denazification — a policy to do just that, denazify Germany, with a variety of measures from jailing Nazis to removing them from public positions, and more — was in full swing. Because of denazification's danger to ordinary Germans, the extraordinarily high findings of these surveys still enormously understate the extent, intensity, and eliminationist character of Germans' antisemitism. We know that such face-to-face interviews by an occupying power about such a disapproved topic as a mass-murderous prejudice is bound to grossly minimize the degree to which people hold such views, as they lie to make themselves look better and also, especially here, in order to avoid endangering themselves. Having until recently lived under a regime, Nazism, which infamously jailed or sent to a concentration camp people who voiced opposition to its cherished goals—though we now know that the degree to which Nazism did this had been for decades wildly overstated—Germans would have been that much more reluctant to express antisemitism to officials of the country that had just conquered them.

From 1945, when there was near-universal antisemitism, to the end of the 1980s, antisemitism in Germany, as in other parts of Europe, declined, its content was de-demonized (compared to the Nazi period), became less intense, and it was shorn from the public sphere. By one critical measure, whether Jews should be in Germany, a marked decline in antisemitism of roughly two-thirds, occurred during this period. In 1952 thirty-seven percent of Germans said there were too many Jews in Germany—an astonishing figure given that Germans had slaughtered or driven out almost their country's entire Jewish community, with only a few thousand remaining by then among the almost seventy million Germans. With the changed public discourse and generational replacement, by 1987 the number of Germans maintaining that too many Jews were in Germany, saying they should all go to Israel, declined to 13 percent. More generally, Germans went from overwhelmingly supporting eliminationist measures against the Jews during the early 1940s to more than 80 percent saying in 1987 that people involved in anti-Jewish activities in Germany should be prosecuted—almost a complete turnaround in belief and sensibility! It is crucial to emphasize what has been overlooked, that it is not only *attitudes* toward a targeted group that measure prejudice. Whatever the character may be of people's beliefs and emotions, their orientation toward social and political action is also a critical feature and indicator of prejudice's nature and power. In four decades, Germans went from nearly universally and wholeheartedly supporting eliminationist antisemitic policies to, by an overwhelming majority, wanting *any*—not only eliminationist, but any—anti-Jewish activities prosecuted. This sea change in antisemitism's character is a historic monumental decline.

Such progress notwithstanding, the naïveté, as captured by Spiegel, regarding the impossibility of continuing antisemitism after the Holocaust was even more acute than we have seen. Its Eurocentric view of the world ignored other regions that had their own antisemitic traditions and cultures.

In the decades after World War II, three major trends crisscrossed one another. In Western Europe and North America, antisemitism lessened. In Eastern Europe, antisemitism declined somewhat but also ossified. In much of the rest of the world, most significantly in Arab and Islamic countries, antisemitism spread and intensified. Within each region the changes occurred along five dimensions: antisemitism's quantity, content, quality, politicization, and programmatic impetus. In Europe the developments were on the whole positive.

*The quantity of antisemitism lessened and its content became tamer.* The percentage of people who harbored antisemitic views gradually and steadily declined from 1945 for the next several decades (though the absolute number, owing to population growth, perhaps increased). In Europe, until the defeat of Nazism and the defeat of the international genocidal coalition and, implicitly if not explicitly, all those who supported it and its underlying paradigm, antisemitism had been virtually universal in many countries, the common sense of the societies, integrally interwoven with still overwhelmingly dominant Christianity, interwoven with the racist understanding of humanity (the notion that different peoples constituted biologically different races, hierarchically arranged, with different attributes, in both morality and capability), interwoven with political culture, and an unavoidable — indeed usually uncontested — powerful part of the public discourse and of political life, mobilization, and action. In many of the countries, with the end of the war, much if not most of this decreased gradually or quickly, with some of it stopping overnight, such as the powerful public antisemitic discourse. Without the antisemitic public discourse (or even with, in some places, a far tamer one), with the destruction of the public racist view of humanity, and with the progressive delinking of Christianity and antisemitism — therefore without the constant and institutionally supported reinforcement — these wild views of human beings became less powerful, less believable. Younger generations, reared in new public discourses with new plausibility structures and taught in schools a nonantisemitic paradigm of the world, inevitably grew up less antisemitic, so antisemitism became less prevalent across Europe, especially in its antisemitic heart, Germany. The survey data substantiate that the effects of the decline of antisemitism in or delinking of it from the public sphere, cultural institutions and discourses, and politics had predictable ameliorating effects on people's beliefs: from the Holocaust until the late 1980s antisemitism diminished across Western countries, including in Germany, where an overall decline in levels of antisemitism occurred and successive postwar generations became less antisemitic than previous or older ones. In the United States, the percentage of people who said Jews have too much power dropped from 55 in 1946 to 18 in the late 1980s, a reduction of almost two-thirds, which is enormous. By a more general index of intensive antisemitism, it declined in the United States in the three decades from 1964 to 1992 by one-third. In France, the percentage of people doubting the loyalty of French Jews to their own country lessened from 1946 to 1978 by almost 80 percent, dropping from 43 percent to 9 percent. The percentage of Austrians who said that too many Jews are in their country diminished from 46 percent in 1946 (as in Germany, an astonishing number in a country whose people had eliminated and murdered almost all its Jews) to 15 percent in 1987, a reduction of two-thirds.[7]

*Antisemitism's content changed* profoundly. Jews were no longer demonized, meaning that whatever the other prejudicial beliefs and animus people held about Jews, they by and large stopped seeing Jews as devils in human form, or as Satanic minions (though Christians who saw them all guilty for the death of Jesus would still tend to associate them with the devil), or as inveterately malevolent and existentially dangerous. This is — aside from or perhaps coequal to denuding the public sphere of antisemitism — the single most important development during the post–World War II era, indeed, in history, regarding non-Jews' views of Jews. As long as non-Jews deem Jews unalterably demonic, they can have no real accommodation with Jews, and such views leave little or no room for people who hold such profoundly prejudicial beliefs and animus to reconsider and adjust those beliefs and temper those emotions in all the ways and for all the reasons that people continually question, negotiate, and adjust their views and feelings about other matters large and small. As long as non-Jews cast Jews principally as Christ-killers or a demonic race apart, they erected an insuperable barrier against engaging with Jews as human beings in all their complexity and individuality. This de-demonization of Jews, therefore, produced further progress, which continued to occur, on every dimension of antisemitism, including diminishing its absolute quantity.

*Antisemitism's quality changed.* Its intensity and the degree to which it preoccupied people declined in the decades after the war. Antisemitism, or even the topic *Jews,* let alone the so-called Jewish Problem, was no longer the hotbed of public discourse and no longer occupied a central place in the European public sphere. Antisemitism's intensity and urgency in communal and personal discussion, and in people's minds, also greatly diminished. The coded language that has so often been used to discuss Jews did not even appear much in public, as it would certainly have, had Jews' centrality to peoples' and their societies' lives not been so thoroughly repressed.

Antisemitism thus became latent in two senses. It was repressed from the public sphere so therefore subterranean, and it was less central to the lives of communities and individuals, which public discourses' content and character always powerfully affect and shape. This is different from being extinguished, or from going into ideational and emotional remission. Antisemitism's history, among other things, is a history of the ebbs and flows of its growth in centrality and intensity, and its upsurge into or submergence from the public life of societies. The reasons for this vary with place and time, but two things are sure: the oscillation has happened again and again, and public authorities have had a powerful, often determinative influence on its public activation or suppression. This is precisely what occurred after 1945 in the West. The American colossus — Western Europe's liberator, occupier, and guarantor — in so many ways conveyed the idea and demonstrated that antisemitic agitation had no place in democracy, while defeat of history's most antisemitic and murderous regime, and of its client regimes and parties throughout Europe, silenced those who preached and practiced antisemitic politics. Germany, by then the demonstration country for combating or rather suppressing antisemitism, criminalized antisemitic expression. Partly because of this clamping down from the top, antisemitism in Europe acquired a different feel, a lesser intensity, a lesser centrality, a less impassioned and mobilized constituency than it had had for decades, even for centuries. Political and public antisemitism was suddenly and simply off the table.

The postwar transformation's fourth dimension was *antisemitism's depoliticization.* For generations the place of Jews, the so-called Jewish Problem, and the demonization of Jews had been central not only to a discourse focused on Jews themselves, but also to broader ideational and social concerns, and cultural and political discourses about how society ought to be constituted and what its politics ought to be. The discourses of what it meant to be Polish, French, Austrian, Romanian, Hungarian, or German, or of what boundaries of society and social life should be, or of how professions should be organized, or of what having a democratic or nondemocratic politics would be like, or what a fascist or nonfascist politics would bring, or of communism's prospects, perils, or promise, or of what the societies' religious and moral, and even sexual, lives ought to be — all of these to a greater or lesser extent, and varying from country to country, had been for decades or centuries tied up, informed by, and, in some, conducted with more or less reference to the existence of Jews within those countries. In Germany, France, Austria, Poland, and elsewhere, political parties had mobilized people around and sought to persuade people that the theme of Jews was a central issue, almost always framed as a problem, with parties proposing threatening solutions, weaving them into their self-understanding, often at the core of their official stances and campaigning. Across Europe, political parties — many in Germany, France, Poland, Hungary, and elsewhere — proudly endorsed the foundational antisemitic paradigm and, more, explicitly declared themselves antisemitic by constitution and eliminationist in orientation.

After the war, however much such concerns continued to occupy people in their thinking and in their discussions in private circles, antisemitism's incorporation into broader public discourses and politics ceased in the West. Aside from the mass murder of the Jews itself, the major themes of post–World War II public thinking and discourse — reconstruction, economic organization, class relations, democracy, redrawing national borders and constituting national identity and the nation, justice and retribution, what to do with Germany, communism, East-West conflict, what had gone wrong in Europe and in Germany, not to mention philosophical, artistic, and literary discourses — were conducted without reference to Jews, let alone with the previous near-ubiquitous Jewish Problem clouding and confounding the issues.

Divorcing the theme of Jews from these broader discursive themes and the public discourses built upon them served further to temper antisemitism and to open up space for antisemitism's further reconsideration and decline. So long as people's thinking and the public discourse about Jews were interwoven with the critical cultural, social, economic, and political issues of the day and of a country's or people's fate, any discussion about Jews automatically gained a weight far beyond what would be good for any people's image — especially a people already governed in conception by the foundational antisemitic paradigm and further framed so prejudicially badly, and against whom such animus flowed. Such a public discourse's state of affairs also further ossified the prejudices people had about Jews, as those antisemitic notions were interwoven into more general worldviews, giving them an even broader and more impenetrable ideational armor. If you associate Jews with communism, or worse, hold communism to be a Jewish invention and weapon, every time the theme, let alone the threat, of communism, Marxism, revolution, or the Soviet Union comes up, it also conjures, reinforces, even deepens thinking prejudicially about Jews and the animus against Jews in one's country. Such regular, indeed daily, activation of antisemitism was common across Europe prior to the new post–World War II dispensation. Indeed, describing it as regular activation so understates the matter for Europeans east, central, and west. Antisemitism was not merely woven into the most crucial and many noncrucial themes of the day, to be brought up with greater or lesser frequency, it was an ever-present part of nonconscious thought and consciousness itself, part of the framing of experience and thinking, of hoping and fearing, hovering beneath and lurking within the sphere of one's attention, even if only dimly, at all times. This was (and continues to some extent to be) especially true of Christians, when, as they often did, they think of Jesus' death or many other of the Christian bible's aspects or passages. Nevertheless, after the war, the specifically religious antisemitic public discourse, aside from the relevant church services, also ceased being part of the broader public discourse. There was an added benefit of removing the theme of Jews from the public sphere and discourse accrued to non-Jews and to societies and cultures more generally: antisemitism no longer infiltrated and poisoned people's minds nearly as much, or the discourses and deliberations over these other themes of social and political life, which meant that they could be addressed more soberly and productively.

Fifth, *antisemitism stopped being a basis for programs, practices, and action,* and this was both the cause and then the further consequence of these other changes. The antisemitic practices and options, which were suddenly off the table, ranged from deprecating Jews in public, to protesting against Jewish businesses, to writing (or reading) antisemitic newspaper articles, tracts, or books, to working to exclude Jews from one's profession, to teaching children in school about the strangeness, dangers, racial differences, or inferiority of Jews, to giving or attending antisemitic speeches or rallies, to organizing politically against Jews, to openly discriminating against Jews, to physically attacking them, to supporting or initiating programs to exclude them legally or physically from one sphere of society or another, or from one's country as a whole, to killing them. None of these could any longer be done (except in the immediate post–World War II tumult), aside from teaching and preaching antisemitism under the cover of Christianity and in church institutions. This change in antisemitic practice and in the possibility of antisemitic practice was undoubtedly the most precipitous decline in antisemitic expression, in the manifestation of antisemitism, in the sum of antisemitism (remember, its practice, not just its notions, also constitutes the phenomenon) in the long history of this or, almost for certain, any other major prejudice. Absolutely foreclosing certain options inhibits their consideration, as people's minds naturally (this may be an evolutionary heritage) focus attention, emotion, and invention on what is possible, rather than persistently and counterproductively frittering away such precious resources in wasteful daydreaming. Thus the decline in considerations of antisemitic programs and action had the virtuous effect of reinforcing the shift of attention away from Jews, which, given the feedback loop of prejudice, further allowed people to be less cognitively and emotionally blinded. This in turn created further mental and emotional space for people to reconsider their views about Jews or merely to let the old, utterly untenable notions about them finally die their natural deaths.

Except for furtive and personal acts, such as keeping one's distance from Jews, antisemitic practice was the easiest aspect of antisemitism to send into decline, in many countries into oblivion. Yet accounts of antisemitism's post–World War II course have focused on Europe and often been wrongly treated as a stand-in for the story writ large. Although in the Holocaust's wake the predominant focus on antisemitism's decline in the West was, and to some extent still is, understandable, owing to its significance and its unprecedented character, it must be augmented by a consideration of what happened beyond Europe, namely in the developing world, particularly in Arab and Islamic countries.

In the Arab and Islamic world, the situation was both more straightforward and more alarming. Islam's and Muslims' vast regional, intensive conflict with Christianity and Christians over territory, suzerainty, souls, and the Holy Land, which endured for centuries, made their concern with Jews a less pressing matter. Yet with the Jews' arrival in sizable numbers in British Mandate Palestine, the area out of which Israel was to emerge, public antisemitic discourse grew ever more powerful, insistent, and inflammatory, and the animosity toward Jews became ever more central, threatening, and violent. After 1945, the Arab and Islamic iteration of the foundational antisemitic paradigm was therefore vibrant, more powerful than it had been for centuries. And it was, if at all, barely subject to the post-Holocaust ameliorating factors and influences that touched European countries and peoples. Indeed, with Israel's founding in 1948, the Arab and Islamic antisemitic stream and discourse were reinvigorated, ideationally and geostrategically, and in the subsequent years it continued to be fed by Arabs' and Muslims' growing obsession with Israel and Arab and Islamic countries' and peoples' ongoing attempts to destroy Israel and eliminate its Jews. Here the Holocaust — which led Jews and many non-Jews alike to see a Jewish country for Jews' security and political expression as necessary, as it is for other people — served not to ameliorate but to fuel a preexisting antisemitism. Indeed, the Holocaust offered a model, mass elimination, of what might or ought to be done to Jews.

This second, powerful world-historical stream of Arab and Islamic antisemitism, though known and acknowledged by some, seemed to the Eurocentric West of lesser, often of little, import. Arab and Islamic antisemitism's power and perniciousness were denied or minimized in their extent and importance because Arabs' and Muslims' treatment of Jews, while antisemitic to the core, had not been mass murderous or, even when it had been, was not nearly as brutal as the Europeans' unparalleled mass slaughter of Jews. As time has shown, Americans' and Europeans' overlooking and minimizing of Arab and Islamic antisemitism was naive. The antisemitism of the Arab and Islamic world, of its peoples, institutions, and politics in country after country, has with open pride supplanted the Christian and European world as this deadly prejudice's heartland.

Antisemitism's improvement in the West along five dimensions was not reproduced in the other civilization and region where antisemitism was also rife. In the post–World War II era in the Arab and Islamic worlds, along each of these dimensions of quantity, content, quality, politicization (including its place in the public sphere), and programmatic impetus, antisemitism was worsening as the Jewish community in Palestine agitated for statehood. This had several consequences that led Arabs and Muslims to respond with increasing and greatly intensifying antisemitism. It cemented in place and enormously exacerbated the already growing conflict over territory between Arabs and Jews, which produced ever more enmity, focusing Arabs and Muslims ever more on the country Israel and its Jews. Arabs and Muslims commandeered existing Islamic antisemitic tropes and narratives, and added to them new ones that had recently been gleaned, and would continue to infiltrate, from the Europeans. Second, these developments coincided with the rise of Arab and pan-Arab nationalism in the context of decolonization, as the spent colonial powers Britain and France retreated across the region. With the world losing its moorings and virtually everything up for grabs — from countries' contours, to governance, to economic spoils — Arabs and Muslims were politically and culturally seeking to make their way in individual countries and regions, and across the Arab world. Israel and its Jews suddenly became not only a focus of animosity as a non-Arab, non-Islamic state, and later a military power in the region, but soon the principal, if not the only, such one. Thus, Arab and Islamic resentment could be and was concentrated and focused on this one perceived alien body in the Arab and Islamic world — and not just anywhere but in its geographic and religious heart. Third, with the newfound national and cultural enmity that Arabs and Muslims developed for Israel and Jews, Arabs and Muslims refocused their attention on the Islamic tradition's antisemitic parts in the Qur'an, the Hadith, and the broader antisemitic political cultures and practices that had been built upon them. With this refocus came a renewed emphasis on those parts of Islamic and Arabic culture and politics that cast Jews in a bad and threatening light.

A prejudice that had been important but secondary to the core of

Islamic concerns became ever more interwoven into the religious and cultural and political narratives that oriented Arabs and Muslims, suggesting to them what was desirable and necessary regarding Jews, and what concrete social and political initiatives and programs should be pursued. These developments transformed antisemitism, which had been latent or peripheral to the concerns of the Islamic faithful, into a salient, eventually often *the* salient, cultural and political issue. Creating this sort of salience is always bad for Jews but is especially bad when it is integrated into politics and becomes the basis for political mobilization and policy making, and in this case—raised to the level of war and peace—seemingly of survival.

Antisemitism increased dramatically and transformed from a minor and episodic religious concern into a major and continuous religious, cultural, and political one in Arab and Islamic countries during the post–World War II decades. Starting in 1948, multiple Arab countries and armies and peoples fought a succession of wars (in 1948, 1956, 1967, 1973, 1982) and sponsored or witnessed continual terrorist assaults against Israel and its majoritarian people, the Jews. Even though the Arab countries lost each war, they never made formal or genuine peace with the Jews' continuing existence in their midst.

The character of the Arab and Islamic countries' and people's rhetorical, political, and eliminationist assaults on Israel, as well as the relationship between their fervent anti-Israel orientation and their fervent antisemitism, are taken up more extensively in later chapters. Here, we need note only that the qualitative change turned a profound, if secondary, prejudice into an obsessive, central one. The centuries-old foundational Islamic notion that Jews had been treacherous and murderous toward Muhammad, had been irredeemably hostile to Islam, and, employing cunning, had injured Muslims produced considerable animosity. Yet all this had also been overspread with Muslims' contempt for this weak and seemingly servile people who, in this view, remained stuck in their ancient ways which they should have repudiated for the enlightenment and truth that Islam offered. With the advent of Jews' political incorporation in Israel, and their ever-growing might, as seen in their repeated military, political, and socioeconomic victories, the Arab and Islamic political and religious discourse transformed their image of Jews without altering their antisemitic foundation. They began to cast Jews as overbearing and arrogant, to portray Jews as brutal marauders, a construct that supplanted the servility with which they had for centuries depicted Jews. After 1967, Jews — and this was unbearable to Muslims — were the de facto rulers of Islam's third-most-holy city, Jerusalem. Contempt was replaced by hatred and fear of Jews' multiple threats to Islamic holy sites, Arab peoples, and Arab lands, which became Arab and Islamic discourses' new dominant portrayal of and stances toward Jews.

Two overlapping, profound cultural and political trends most significantly powered the later developments that, in our global age, have seen antisemitisms from different eras and civilizations melding. The first was Arab and Islamic antisemitic public and political discourses' wholesale importation of modern racist and Nazi antisemitism, itself grounded in the foundational antisemitic paradigm. This provided a rich, varied, and devastating litany of images, tropes, and accusations of Jews' noxiousness, malfeasance, dastardly techniques, power. The second trend was Islam's growing centrality in the Arab world and in other Islamic majority countries, most notably Iran. This had begun already in the post–World War II decades, although it gathered ever more steam starting in the late 1970s, when pan-Arabism had clearly spent itself even as a compensatory and a persuasive regional ideological movement, not to mention as a viable political one. The Iranian Revolution of 1979, bringing political Islam to power in one of the largest, wealthiest, and most powerful Islamic countries and, in some ways even more, the founding of Hamas in 1987–88, formally, explicitly, and unabashedly dedicated to the single-minded destruction of Israel and Jews, ushered in the nearly full political Islamization of Arab and Islamic orientation toward Jews and their country, and made antisemitism — specifically and unequivocally prejudice against *Jews* — the glue that held together the anti-Israel stances and politics of these varied and various countries and their peoples. During this period, the distinctions, conceptually and as matters of fact, among Jews, Zionism, Israel, world Zionism, and world Jewry broke down. Arab and Islamic culture and thought supplanted them with antisemitism, a monolithic image in which these heterogeneous ethnic identities, religious beliefs, cultural practices, political ideologies, et cetera, were once again all rolled into an integrated and singular hatred of Jewness.

Hamas, a branch of Egypt's Muslim Brotherhood, ruler of Gaza, and the organization that represents the voices and votes of a majority of Palestinians, embraces and draws liberally on Nazi and modern racist antisemitic views about Jews, which Arab and Islamic discourses about Jews across the Middle East and beyond had by the time of Hamas' founding fully incorporated, including its notion of Jewness. Hamas expresses all this daily and on a permanent basis, as it is codified in the Hamas Charter of 1988, which it and its individual leaders affirm again and again. According to the charter, the Jews are an essential, implacable, and depraved enemy that mocks Islam with its conquests, shouting "Muhammad is dead, he left daughters behind," and therefore must be met by Muslims with titanic vigilance and a Herculean effort: "For our struggle against the Jews is extremely wide-ranging and grave, so much so that it will need all the loyal efforts we can wield, to be followed by further steps and reinforced by successive battalions from the multifarious Arab and Islamic world, until the enemies are defeated and Allah's victory prevails." This understanding of Jews—which Hamas treats as their essence, their Jewness—is also the essence of their country, Israel. Hamas has further grounded all this *in Islam itself,* and in a wildly antisemitic account of Jews' past crimes against Islam, Arab peoples, humanity, and God. "Zionism," which means Jews and Israel, does "not hesitate to take any road, or to pursue all despicable and repulsive means to fulfill its desires." And what are those desires? "To demolish societies, to destroy values, to wreck answerableness, to totter virtues and to wipe out Islam. It stands behind the diffusion of drugs and toxics of all kinds in order to facilitate its control and expansion." Hamas and other political Islamic movements thereby turned Israel's elimination into a religious duty. This is codified in the Hamas Charter. "Israel, by virtue of its being Jewish and of having a Jewish population, defies Islam and the Muslims."[8] The charter urges Muslims to mass-murder *Jews.* This eliminationism and exterminationism exists also in Hamas' daily words, initiatives, policies, and promise. The Hamas Charter reads to the nonantisemite like a college assignment to parody a merging of Islamic and Nazi antisemitism. But to the tens of millions of faithful, it reads like a message from God—"Allah" is mentioned more than seventy-five times in its introduction and thirty-six articles—as brought to them by God's political Islamic messengers. From various sources—including but not restricted to political Islamic Iran, Hamas, and the Muslim

Brotherhood—an understanding of Jews' and therefore Israel's nature, grounded in the otherwise unlikely coupling of Nazi antisemitism and Islam, became the wellspring of the post–World War II era's reformed and radicalized antisemitism in the Arab and Islamic worlds' public discourses and private passions.

As we have seen, in contrast to the Arab and Islamic world, in Europe antisemitism declined after World War II. In the 1930s and 1940s anti-semites, and that meant much of Europe, had considered Jews to be a, or the, major domestic and even sometimes international threat to their societies, cultures, and nations. Certainly by 1960, embedded in the new postwar European political and cultural and ideational realities, this had become but a minority view. There was no longer a fearsome defi-nition of Jews. There was no longer a Jewish Problem as a political issue, and certainly not as a burning issue of any kind in the public sphere. There was no eliminationist antisemitism as part of the public life of European countries regarding their own countries' Jews, who could no longer be seen as polluters of the race, defilers of purity, or, after the Holocaust and in the context of the superpower showdown, as the malevolent string pullers of the world. Christian churches had reori-ented and stopped assiduously promoting antisemitism, which became deemphasized in their worldviews, even if they (especially the Catholic Church) continued to preach and reinforce antisemitic elements from their bible and that were embedded deep in their traditions. Legal dis-crimination in the form of Nazi anti-Jewish laws, or less comprehensive though powerfully discriminatory laws such as in prewar Hungary and Italy, were unthinkable. The notion of legally prohibiting Jews from working in certain professions, from sharing social facilities with non-Jews, from occupying positions in the government, state bureaucracies, or the military, from being students or faculty at universities or schools, from living in certain areas, from freely practicing their worship, was off the table. Such notions could now not even be broached in public. More violent, and previously regularly proposed and practiced, elimina-tionist measures were, of course, also absolutely tabooed. Ghettoization, incarceration in camps, expulsion, and mass murder were no longer politically legitimate options in publicly discussing or treating Jews. Starting in May 1945, it was as if, regarding the burning hatred of Jews, the hothouse of European culture, society, and politics suddenly opened its roof and let the artificially stoked air and environment out, and suddenly the overheated people could breathe normally and, more or less, return to their senses.

Yet Jews as Jews were still, even in this period of antisemitic tempering and transformation, not considered by most of their broader societies to be members of the national communities in which they lived. To be sure, other minority groups are also not considered members of their national community, even though they too may be citizens of their countries. This is common across Europe and many other parts of the world for recent immigrants and sometimes even for their children, or for visible minorities dedicated to maintaining themselves apart or in opposition to the majority's norms and self-defining practices. But none of this characterizes Europe's Jews. French Jews have been in France, British Jews in Britain, German Jews (there are also new immigrants) in Germany, Polish Jews in Poland, Hungarian Jews in Hungary, Dutch Jews in the Netherlands, for generations, for hundreds of years, and continue to be considered not fully and loyally French, German, Polish, Hungarian, or Dutch. This manifests itself in various ways, which we will explore shortly. For now, let us recognize that if Jews speak out as Jews, should they take unpopular positions supporting Israel, many among their countrymen automatically deem them suspect in their loyalty to or their affiliation with their countries. How long should Jews have to be French or British or Poles or Germans before they stop being seen as not fully French, British, Polish, or German? In many of these countries secularism reigns, so the centuries-old religious argument about Jews' standing apart from or in opposition to Christianity is ever less germane and plausible.

How long? This question is important, aside from the obvious intolerance it reflects that exists in these contemporary democracies especially, rendered that much more grotesque with their histories of eliminationist and mass-murderous persecutions. It is important because it highlights *how powerful* the foundational antisemitic paradigm remains, holding Jews to be different and not members of their national communities.

These continuing distinctions and conceptual segregation acquired still greater force because antisemitism, whatever its decline and tempering, was independently sustained within local communities and the family. One who has spoken openly about it is Ayaan Hirsi Ali:

As a child growing up in Saudi Arabia, I remember my teachers, my mom and our neighbors telling us practically on a daily basis that Jews are evil, the sworn enemies of Muslims, and that their only goal was to destroy Islam. We were never informed about the Holocaust.

Later, as a teenager in Kenya, when Saudi and other Persian Gulf philanthropy reached us, I remember that the building of mosques and donations to hospitals and the poor went hand in hand with the cursing of Jews. Jews were said to be responsible for the deaths of babies and for epidemics such as AIDS, and they were believed to be the cause of wars. They were greedy and would do absolutely anything to kill us Muslims. If we ever wanted to know peace and stability, and if we didn't want to be wiped out, we would have to destroy the Jews. For those of us who were not in a position to take up arms against them, it was enough for us to cup our hands, raise our eyes heavenward and pray to Allah to destroy them.

Until the age of twenty-four when living in the Netherlands and finally being exposed to the truth about the Holocaust and antisemitism, Hirsi Ali had believed what she had grown up with regarding Jews, for that is all she knew about them. When she told her twenty-one-year-old sister that what they had learned from their family and community about Jews was false, her sister, still in the grip of their upbringing's unquestioned antisemitism, reacted badly: "It's a lie! Jews have a way of blinding people. They were not killed, gassed or massacred. But I pray to Allah that one day all the Jews in the world will be destroyed."[9]

Antisemitism's familial and social-communal transmission is often ignored precisely because it takes place out of view, in the home, the pub, the playground, where socially accepted strictures of polite society and discourse do not inhibit people. One young German, twenty-one in 2004, recalled how this continued in the mid-1990s: "In school, it was like this: In the classroom we sang songs in-between classes, like 'We shit on the Jews,' and 'We want to drink Jewish blood.' If someone didn't sing along, he got dirty looks, et cetera. Quite honestly, I have to say, when I was 14 or 15, I also went along with the others."[10] How else did these young people all learn these songs from the Nazi period, except from communal transmission — from grandfather to father to son, in the pub, from peer to peer, in the schoolhouse?

Such transmission occurred perhaps most strikingly in the countries of Europe that were behind the Iron Curtain.

During the period of communism and Soviet domination, the Eastern Bloc countries' public spheres, even if conducting a campaign, sometimes intensive, against Zionism with antisemitic overtones, were almost devoid of the overt religious or modern antisemitism, especially of the classic antisemitic canards, as the Eastern countries' public media, including the publishing industries, were governmentally controlled and therefore classical antisemitism was suppressed. Yet there was also little education directly combating the extensive existing antisemitism, so the factors in the West that diminished and tamed antisemitism barely existed in the East. The Holocaust received little attention and was often falsely presented as an assault on the peoples (as opposed to the Jews) of each country—an early and barely recognized form of Holocaust revisionism or denial. The teaching of democratic and liberal values did not take place. The powerful delegitimation of antisemitism by American cultural infiltration did not take place. The public repudiation of antisemitism by churches did not take place. In a world that was governed by communism's manifestly false and propagandistic accounts, and its systematic denial of critical parts of reality, no powerful assertion of reality regarding Jews, namely, that Jews were innocent people who had been victimized by those animated by a horrible prejudice, took place. While Eastern Europe effectively lived with a public near blackout on antisemitism, two of the notions that fed it, racism and nationalism, were condemned. Its peoples neither benefited from the teaching of antisemitism's perniciousness and falseness nor, with notable exceptions such as at the end of Stalin's life, did they suffer from antisemitism's further public reinforcement and dissemination. So what happened?

As in the West, in the countries of Eastern Europe, public antisemitism submerged, and seemingly went into remission, but unlike the West, its content was not tempered. As with hibernation, not being nourished by a public discourse, antisemitism lost some of its size and power, but it nevertheless was ready to be publicly and discursively reactivated as the same animal that it had been before it put its head down for the long, cold winter of communist rule. We know this because, with the lifting of communist rule in 1989, antisemitism burst forth in these previously subjugated satellite states.

Several things are significant about the return of antisemitism to these public spheres denuded of this prejudice for two generations, more than forty years. Why, in countries where Jews were not powerful and indeed barely present (except sometimes as prominent communist officials)—most of them had perished during the Holocaust (often killed with the help and support of many people in those very countries)—would people, at the lifting of the generally hated communism, with all the political, economic, and cultural shackles it had placed on people's freedom and ability to live in any kind of prosperity, begin attacking Jews? Where did the notions come from that the Jews possessed malevolent qualities and were doing harm and promised to do more injury to the peoples of these countries? Among the many bizarre aspects of antisemitism, this is another one. One might have thought that with substantial problems and projects facing them, and with culpability for their countries' and people's poor conditions unequivocally the responsibility of the communists and of the ideology they espoused, and looking to the decidedly publicly nonantisemitic West's culture and politics of democracy and universalism, the peoples of these countries would emerge from communism and from domination by the Soviets or Russians with a clear purpose and would not have reason to be antisemitic, or possess the antisemitic resources to draw upon to develop views that no longer existed in the public sphere. But no: antisemitism reemerged, and with substantial force. Poles, Ukrainians, Lithuanians, Hungarians, Russians themselves began to produce and articulate the same antisemitic tropes and images, the same canards and charges, with wide resonance among publics, that had been the common sense of these countries prior to 1945. They thrust Jews again into the roles as Christ-killers and devils, and of their secular incarnation of communists. They used age-old images and accusations—such as the blood libel—to convey the malevolence and threat of the Jews. Jews were exploiting the people, manipulating the economy, sucking the blood of the nation.

This all occurred without contemporary reference to or great concern with Israel's relations with the Palestinians (which, in any case, were improving during the hopeful Oslo years), as the former Soviet Bloc countries focused their attentions on reconstituting themselves domestically, and it took place after decades of little public classical antisemitic discourse or media. In the West, where an independent media and freedom of expression made antisemitism available at least to those who sought it out on the margins, it could be found in right-wing newspapers and magazines, in books, including in libraries. There were coded forms of antisemitism also expressed in the Western media, such as disparagingly references to "East Coast" American elites and media, which in Western European countries was understood to be dominated by Jews. Even the issue of the Holocaust, which was treated extensively in the Western public sphere and so kept the theme of Jews and their persecution alive, was all but absent in Central and Eastern European countries, where tacit or explicit Holocaust denial prevailed. (The topic of the Holocaust was simply ignored or the Jews were omitted or subsumed among others as the victims.)

So there was no public cultural, no material, no even tenuously rational reason for antisemitism to reemerge in the countries of the East, lands of dead or dying Jewish populations. Yet, after 1989, the same antisemitic tropes started to play, loudly, again, as if the tape of the public discourse had not been lost or destroyed, but just put on pause, and all the while for decades people had privately repeatedly played, discussed, and elaborated on its deeply ingrained and heartfelt content. When conditions changed to allow it, they hit the public *play* button again. Discourses in the public and private spheres were again in consonance with another.

In the countries of Central and Eastern Europe, the almost overnight reemergence of antisemitism in the public sphere in 1989, fully formed in the image of its past, was followed by a parallel though different return of antisemitism to the public sphere of Western Europe not long thereafter. The disintegration of the Soviet empire was a watershed moment for the politics of the world, which, not surprisingly, as antisemitism's fortunes and nature have typically been affected by large political and social changes and developments, was also a watershed moment for antisemitism. Suddenly, so much of the post–World War II social and political compact, within countries and internationally, was up for grabs, as the basic paradigm that had governed the Western alliance and Western countries no longer held. The East-West divide, and the need to face down communism, the coloring of national and international politics by these two basic facts, evaporated. Stable reference points, constraints on certain kinds of considerations, goals, policies, and discourses vanished or slowly dissipated. A new era began, and it was understood to be beginning not just in retrospect, but at the time — and by everyone.

This could be seen most acutely in the place around which so much of Europe's history for more than a century had been most critically made and, coincidentally or not, so much of antisemitism's history was made: Germany. Germany was soon reunified. A more assertive, which was nothing more than a normal, Germany reoriented. It mostly stopped being the paymaster of Europe as a way of buying off its neighbors and fellow European Union members, and, to the extent that such generosity continued, it was done so in exchange for, and as an expression of, power and acknowledged leadership. Many other changes took place within Germany, as they did within other European countries and around Europe, most notably the drive to expand (to the countries of the East) and deepen (create a single currency, among many other measures) the European Union, and thereby to democratize the former communist countries, many of which had adopted *Central Europe* to replace the Russified *Eastern Europe* as their geographic moniker. Cultural orientations also changed within Germany and around Europe. Even more than challenging their bonds of quasi-political and military dependence on the United States, they threw off the mental restraints of American cultural leadership, which Germans had never entirely comfortably worn. As much as Germans could be more honest about the past, and not write off all the terrible things their government did to the ever historically shrinking number of "bad Nazis" among them, they also could, and with much justice, say that the past was behind them, that the events of the 1930s and 1940s were no longer centrally relevant to considerations of contemporary German culture, society, or politics. Few feared a return of Nazism (that had long been apparent, certainly since the mid-1970s, to those who understood the by then firmly democratic Germany), and Germans no longer needed to censor themselves in their cultural products, their social arrangements, or their politics for fear of Nazified infiltration of one kind or another.

This substantially changed European paradigm of self and cultural understanding, and of politics, in turn transformed the underlying circumstances that had formed the foundation of antisemitism's expulsion from the public sphere and its submergence into the reservoir of civil society in the postwar period. The question existed about the extent to which this transformation in antisemitism, its diminution and tempering, was real and enduring, and to what extent it was an artifact of the moment, transitory, and hence illusory. In a sense, this description of the antisemitism of this period as being submerged, a reservoir, and latent in terms that make it sound to have been relatively quiescent, is both right and insufficient. It is right insofar as, during this almost half century, antisemitism, though existing in private life, was absent from the public sphere and dominant cultural discourses of the West. But that which is submerged can bob back up to the surface. A reservoir in its most literal sense can be drawn upon and, in its common metaphorical usage, contains a substance that can be easily tapped, used, or exploited. That which is latent can become manifest, when circumstances change or when it, for whatever reason, is to be called upon or activated. Yet while such metaphors convey much about antisemitism during this period, specifically its location (submerged into civil society), its size (the reservoir is vast), and its potential (latent things can be transformed), they fail to capture a critical aspect: the internal pressure within people and communities that antisemitism creates among its adherents to bring their views and passions into the public sphere; to express themselves openly and uninhibitedly. Because biting one's tongue about matters that are deeply felt and central to one's self-understanding or worldview causes people to chafe and to long for a time and circumstance when they, from their perspective, can *tell it like it is, speak the truth,* let their communities, countries, politicians, and the world know what they really think.

This was particularly true of Germany—which does not mean it was not also true of other European countries. In Germany professions of philosemitism, or at least solidarity with Jews and condemnation of the German past, had for decades after World War II been obligatory, compelling politicians and other public figures to speak and write in public, particularly at anniversaries and commemorations, in ways contrary to their beliefs, and compelling ordinary Germans, many of whom dissented from such views, to be exposed to such statements and spectacles on a fairly regular basis. The resentment this caused for many, though hardly everyone, is well established.

Finally, let us step back for a broader perspective on this period. To consider the strength and endurance of this prejudice, and the way in which the foundational antisemitic paradigm structures people's experience, perceptions, and thoughts and emotions (which our upcoming consideration of the survey data will further amplify), think of what the Germans did to Europe and Europeans, to France and the French, to the Netherlands and the Dutch, to Poland and the Poles, to Russia and the Russians, not to mention to the Jews. The Germans variously conquered and occupied their countries and peoples in a war of imperial aggression, destroyed their economies, dragooned and enslaved their peoples, destroyed their monuments, impoverished the people, committed mass murder, and turned them into subjects or slaves in the service of their German overlords. This naturally produced hatred of Germans throughout Europe, which continued and then lingered after the war. This is not remarkable. But for understanding antisemitism, it is noteworthy: How quickly this hatred against Germans dissipated, and how comparatively superficial it proved to be compared to the prejudice and animus against Jews.

Hatred for Germans never hardened into a prejudicial paradigm — and this despite the fact (and it is a fact) that what the Germans did to Europeans, the horrifying orientations and traits they displayed (exceptions notwithstanding, though in thinking about national groups most people do not pay attention to the exceptions anyway, such is the nature of the very phenomenon under discussion), were a hundred, a thousand, a million times, actually infinitely, worse than anything Jews had ever done to Germans, Poles, Ukrainians, the French, the Dutch, or anyone. Why is there no discernible, significant prejudice (of course there remains the garden-variety stereotypes about Germans' loving order and authority) in Europe, among Europeans, or even among Jews, against Germans, in light of the unbounded horrors they perpetrated on hundreds of millions, and in light of the fact that Germany has again become the heavyweight of Europe and in many ways, sometimes to the detriment of other national groups, exercises its power? Why has there been no perceived need to do regular surveys about the extent of anti-German prejudice in Europe, or studies as to its causes, and proposals about how to combat it — all of which are obviously necessary and being done regarding antisemitism? Anti-German sentiment around Europe, as profound and as deserved as it was during the Nazi years of conquest, plunder, immiseration, enslavement, and mass murder, never congealed in a powerful postwar public discourse and never became codified in foundational public texts, religions, or worldviews — democracy, liberty, and universal rights (including the Germans'), and the universalism and internationalism of communism (including for the Germans), were the core of the secular religion of the West and East respectively. So, the hatreds simmered, diminished, and gave way, especially with generational replacement, to more ordinary views and emotions.

That this happened as quickly as it did also shows how false the mantra-like explanations are for antisemitism, which variously hold that profound prejudice is natural when a people is seen as the "other," or when rivalry or antagonism exists over territory or resources, or when one people appears to outdo another economically, or when a people feels threatened by another, or when some injury to a people is done, or when a people is jealous of another people, or (as is often said about Israel) when a country or people is said to be treating another people unjustly. Even in 2013, with the revival of German domination of the European continent, its people's economic success, its attempts to dictate punishing fiscal and economic policies to other countries and peoples, its perceived haughty lecturing of them as if they were schoolchildren — all of this, whatever the anger, resentment, and denunciations, has not led to a return of previous hatreds. Prejudice of the kind against Jews — the foundational antisemitic paradigm, its higher-level elaborations, the very existence of an underlying and detested notion of Jewness — is simply not a natural response to anything. It is not even natural among prejudices. It is not natural in its causes, not in its content, not in its tenacity and endurance, not in its intensity, not in its malleability, not in its repeated activation in country after country after country.

# 7

# Getting to Global

ANTISEMITISM'S REPRESSION IN the post–World War II era was, to a great extent, artificial, even though it substantially diminished and tempered prejudice and hatred against Jews. The Holocaust's shock, and its intimate connection to antisemitism, making anti-Jewish expression out of bounds, was sure to wear off as years passed, memories faded, historical understanding got muddled by apologists and misguided interpreters, and the lives of people and the lives of societies moved on to new times with new foci, concerns, and sensibilities. When would the past horrors' constraints on the anti-Jewish imagination of the present weaken sufficiently to open space for antisemites to begin using the public sphere's information alleys, then streets, main streets, and eventually highways, and now cyberspaceways? Antisemitism's reservoir was vast, the supports and incentives for antisemitism to be resurgent forceful, the prejudice's power bracing, and the potent sources (in the Arab and Islamic worlds) far greater than had been reckoned.

Had the passage of time been the sole issue, perhaps the lid on antisemitic expression would have held longer or, if dislodged, then less fully. But other changes took place. As the post–World War II era came to a close, the social and political, and therefore discursive, terrain transformed and thereby more quickly and fully opened up new space in the public sphere for antisemitism. The character of expression it admitted, owing to the changed politics and plausibility structure, differed substantially from what existed and was permitted prior to 1945. Wild, race-based antisemitism, with Jews cast as potent devils, was definitely impermissible in the altered European-Unionized Europe. Yet there and elsewhere, the foundational antisemitic paradigm still provided the widespread fundamentals for people's stance toward Jews. The deep reservoir of antisemitic beliefs and passions was ready to be tapped and old animosities to be expressed. The recharged and emerging Arab and Islamic worlds were set to assume a more central place in the world's politics. What would the new plausibility structure allow and promote? What new political, cultural, and social developments would give shape to antisemitism's latest iterations?

There can be no doubt that Israel's enduring occupation of West Bank and Gaza, which began in 1967, was an ongoing and ever-intensifying impetus for criticism around the world, as it increasingly came to be understood as an unjust, even colonial occupation of victimized Palestinians. Criticism of Israel — fair or unfair — had been gradually mounting but remained comparatively muted and, though undoubtedly tapping into people's, notably Europeans', latent antisemitism, remained a minor chord in the political discourse of the Western world. But with the end of the East-West conflict, the discourse changed qualitatively and quantitatively.

The dissolution of the Soviet empire, in a historical instant, shuffled the European political and discursive landscape, deflated the Western left, swept away the foundation for much of the Western human-rights community that had arisen and worked against communism, and freed the developing world, especially the Arab and Islamic countries, from the East-West conflict's shackles. For varying reasons, each unleashed or promoted renewed antisemitic expression, which also had a natural outlet in the already existing anti-Israel discourse, which itself already had a fair amount of wind behind its critical sail. Europeans, whatever their political affiliations, again got to speak their verities and vent their resentments against Jews. Local hatreds of Arabs and Muslims got a full, ever more sympathetic hearing before the world. The political left latched on with new intensity to their existing antipathy to Jews and Israel (discussed in more depth in coming chapters) as a means to refocus aspects of their now-vacated program. The international human rights community, and its thousands of NGOs, sought a new cause that could be broadly legitimizing, and institutionally sustaining. Concurrently, the new international order of globalism, which touched virtually all spheres of life, emerged, creating a new foundation for many things, including antisemitism.

With the collapse of the disastrous communist regimes in the East, the Western political left, from academic Marxists to third world–oriented critics of the first world to the youthful left—even the many who had been anticommunist—lost any legitimacy to a claim that they had a convincing economic or political program for their societies' *domestic* lives. Casting about for a surrogate cause or set of causes, they turned their attention to the international realm, where they could make common cause with the anticommunist, until then predominantly liberal, human-rights movement and organizations, which themselves were pivoting from anticommunism to anti-Israelism, often termed anti-Zionism. This reorientation was symbolized by the name change of what has become the leading international human-rights NGO (nongovernmental organization), and perhaps the most influential anti-Israel crusading NGO. In 1988, as the days of the Soviet Union and its empire were numbered, Helsinki Watch, established in 1975 to fight for human rights in the Soviet bloc, repackaged itself in name and purpose as Human Rights Watch. Concurrently, the political left, having refocused their attention on the old nemeses of international capitalism and its champion the United States, simultaneously latched on to a new foe through which they could intensify their critique of the United States, recruit allies internationally and within their own countries, and make for a more than satisfying outlet for their political passion: the Jews, this time in the guise of the putatively predatory Jews in Israel.

The foundation was already there for the political left to take up the antisemitic, anti-Israel banner as a rallying cry, and its members across the Western world did so with eagerness. With Israel's military victory in 1967 and its occupation of the West Bank and Gaza, the political left began to switch sides, from championing the once-downtrodden and egalitarian-oriented Israelis—after all, they had socialist kibbutzim—to seeing the Israelis as oppressors. This new perspective steadily hardened—in some countries more quickly than others—and the view became an article of faith to most on the Marxian left that Israel and its supporters were imperialists who were throttling the lives of

Palestinians, no matter that Israel was under existential threat. That the Jews were seen as overly powerful in the United States, which was Israel's main benefactor (making Israel the main outpost of American "neocolonialism"), proved incredibly effective in mobilizing old and new adherents to the cause, fellow travelers, and other people whom they could just dupe. What capitalism had once been to the old left, and what, in the 1960s, the older generation conjoined to capitalism had been to the new left, Jews in the guise of Zionism or Israel, tethered to capitalism and the United States, became to the new new left.

Driving the discourse in the public sphere, and certainly among the young, especially at universities (whose graduates from the 1990s are now not so young), the political left's assault on Israel was quickly adopted and was paralleled by many other people in European countries who were nonleftists yet who found their own disdain for the United States, championing of human rights, and sympathies for the developing world, and their latent antisemitism to be compatible and mutually reinforcing passions. What was striking about the political orientation and expression of the 1990s was how rapidly it shifted in the West, aside from the United States, from being in the 1970s and 1980s predominantly sympathetic to Israel and its Jews to being overwhelmingly hostile to them. This occurred even though the geostrategic situation in the region had gotten *better,* and the Israelis and Palestinians had appeared to make great strides toward some kind of peaceful settlement starting with the Oslo Accords of 1993, and the several near settlements of the conflict, which the Palestinians three times walked away from, most notably PLO chairman Yasser Arafat's sudden retreat from the deal that American president Bill Clinton appeared to have brokered between him and Israeli prime minister Ehud Barak at Camp David and Taba in 2000 and 2001. It is hard to see how events on the ground themselves would have produced this period's sea change in public attitude toward Israel. Yet, the precipitously developed obsessiveness in Europe generally, among the political left, and around the world more broadly, with Israel's real and mainly imagined transgressions, and the expression of wild views and ungrounded hatreds of Israel and its supporters became ever more pronounced.

The spearheading of this developing, indeed exploding, discourse by the political left, including the human-rights community, substantially opened and legitimized the public space for antisemitism. As crucial as this development in breaking the antisemitic taboo was, however, it did not alone spur the rise in antisemitic expression and the public antisemitic discourse's resuscitation.

A particular psychological post–World War II reaction in Europe, most pronounced in Germany, was a broad-based phenomenon fueled by the political right as well as partly by the anti-Israel political left. Europeans developed resentment over having to hear about and pay the interpersonal and psychological price for what was increasingly seen as distant persecution and mass murder of the Jews. Germans in particular, because they or their relatives and countrymen had been the Holocaust's prime movers and principal perpetrators, not to mention the ones overwhelmingly identified with it, became ever more tired of and stridently critical about talk of the Holocaust, having to make amends for it, and having their country's image and self-image implicated in this unsurpassed horror. Increasingly with passing years and decades, they sought to relieve themselves of these various burdens. This was especially (and quite understandably) true for Germans born after the war, who themselves committed no transgression but bore the real and imagined national debts left to them from the Nazi period.

This provoked a new antipathy toward Jews, whom Germans held responsible for the Holocaust having become such a large theme in the cultures and information corridors of the world, especially of the West, even of Germany itself. Hence the temptation, too often given in to with alacrity, to paint contemporary Jews, especially in Israel, as transgressors; their victimhood being anything but pure; as being, in its most extreme and amazingly frequent formulation, like Nazis. This psychological and strategic move was also made on the part of people in other European countries known, at least historically, for their antisemitism, as a way to lift this stain's association from their national name. The added bump to this was the accusation, now repeated so often, by antisemites of many varying stripes — political Islamists, neo-Nazis, leftists, guardians of national honor, and run-of-the-mill contemporary antisemites — that the Jews exploit the Holocaust (or, in the case of the many people who denied that the Holocaust occurred, that the Jews invented the Holocaust to exploit it) in order variously to extract money, blacken the names of other peoples, bring pity upon themselves, win support for Israel. So, in the antisemitic mind and hence in its discourse, even the Holocaust's international coalition's genocidal assault on the Jews becomes reason to invent a new antisemitic calumny, as well as the basis for attacking Jews anew. This was, of course, exacerbated by the seemingly bizarre though quite explicable Holocaust denial movement, a province of hard-core antisemites and neofascists, especially German nationalists and neo-Nazis, who wanted to lift the burden of the past from German politics and national self-assertiveness, and whose profound antisemitism and hatred of Jews could not admit that Jews—always cast in antisemitic demonology as perpetrators—had been victims. We will explore this movement in greater depth below. Here its relevance is that it, as is so often the case, inverted the Jews' victimization into a calumny that the Jews were actually the victimizers, using the real, invented, or exaggerated Holocaust to gain sympathy, riches, and power—in the words of the well-known German antisemite and prominent literary figure Martin Walser, celebrated despite or because of his antisemitism, to "cudgel" the Germans and, more broadly, Europeans and extract wealth and support for Israel. Whether coming from right or left, claims such as Walser's resonated with the antisemitic predispositions and resentments of broad swaths of the public in Germany and elsewhere who complain, among other things, that Jews talk too frequently about the Holocaust (in 2012, 43 percent in Germany) and that they do so in order to extort money from Germans and others.

The Soviet Union's disintegration and the East-West conflict's end reshuffled not only European politics, orientations, and public discourses. It did the same for the Middle East. There had been no region in the world outside of Europe where the East-West conflict had so divided countries into identifiable blocs as in the Middle East, and where it had so overshadowed regional and local affairs. Centered on the Arab-Israeli conflict, with each side armed to the teeth by their respective patrons, the front-line Arab countries and organizations, such as the Palestine Liberation Organization (by and large now white-washed and forgotten as a Soviet client) and the relative latecomer Hamas, both had their politics defined by their hostility toward Jews' existence in the Middle East, and therefore their eliminationist, often openly annihilationist, antisemitism. Indeed. they exploited this conflict to help maintain their dictatorial rule over their peoples. Neither the

Soviets nor the Americans, nor the Europeans during this period, showed much concern at all for the almost universally oppressed peoples of Middle Eastern countries suffering under dictatorships, which ranged from brutal to genocidal. Western and Eastern European perceptions and judgments about this region and its people were funneled through the prism of the East-West conflict, and a fair amount of ignorance and probably prejudice to boot. With the end of the Soviet Union, two things occurred. The Arab countries that had been clients of the Soviet Union were no longer off-limits for Western support. While during the Cold War attacks on Israel were tantamount to supporting the Soviet Union in its ongoing strategic drive to undermine capitalist and democratic countries, now it was possible for people in the West to change their Middle East allegiances and, without inhibitions, launch rhetorical and political attacks on Israel, its Jews, and its (especially Jewish) supporters elsewhere.

But one might have thought that sympathy toward these Arab countries' political alliance against Israel would not increase markedly, as those countries, one after another, were dictatorships, ruled with the iron or mass-murderous fists of the likes of Hafez el Assad in Syria, Saddam Hussein in Iraq, Ali Hosseini Khamenei in Iran, and Muammar Gaddafi in Libya. Moreover, the countries and these leaders were an international coalition of dictatorships arrayed against the lone democratic country in the region, Israel, which had been under siege for more than four decades and had been even more threatened than Western Europe by the Soviet Union. Yet the reversal of sympathies did occur, propelled by the combination of the newfound welling up of antipathy for Israel and its people and the newfound support for the Palestinians as people, even though they were led by an openly murderous leadership that, under Arafat, had arguably invented and undoubtedly vastly expanded the practice of international terrorism, which itself was propelled forward by a new international politics in which Arab and Islamic countries became more prominent and vocal.

The Cold War was an all-consuming and defining feature of the post–World War II world, especially of European and North American civilization. The nuclear-armed facedown of superpowers championing incompatible social and political systems split the world into competing camps. That, and the paradigm of understanding about politics that the

Cold War created, warped the international arena, many individual countries' societies and politics, and, here particularly relevant, reigning perspectives on and understandings of the world. Political Islam — often called Islamic fundamentalism, radical Islam, Islamism, militant Islam — grew, spread, and deepened in Arab and Islamic countries, yet because it took place below the political surface of dictatorship and alliances embedded in the East-West conflict where all eyes focused, it escaped the view of those in the West. In the 1990s, political Islam's coming-out decade, giving birth or reinforcing the power and place of potent terror groups (Al Qaeda, Hamas), movements (Muslim Brotherhood), parties, insurgencies, and governing regimes (in Sudan), therefore took the world by surprise. And even where political Islam did not capture power or threaten to do so, the leaders and elites of Arab and Islamic countries changed their messages and politics in a more political Islamic direction in order to try to co-opt the appeal of such powerful movements. The new Arab and Islamic politics and discourse became unavoidably visible, of course coming into absolute focus with their most spectacular, though hardly most deadly, mass murders of 9/11.

Political Islam has many features that make it a threat to the people it rules and those it seeks to rule or overcome. It is highly aggressive, totalitarian in aspiration, violent, even mass murderous in means; it glorifies death and is eliminationist antisemitic at its heart. Its members espouse, relentlessly and obsessively, the most open and thorough eliminationist antisemitism the world has seen from a major political movement since Nazism. And as it, in this respect, by and large shares a view of Jews — their nature, their threat, and how to meet it — with the peoples and societies they rule, and those in Arab and Islamic countries they do not yet rule, their championing of eliminationist antisemitism has a broad resonance both within Arab and Islamic countries and also internationally. So, bursting on the international scene, and made visible to the rest of the world, most critically to Europeans, by the Cold War scales dropping from their eyes, was a powerful antisemitic discourse and politics with a consistent message: Israel is evil and must be eliminated; its people are committing the gravest crime in the world, which is to oppress and deny the legitimate rights of the Palestinian people; and its people are Jews, who everyone knows are powerful and evil. The drumbeat of these charges alone had a potent effect. Intersecting with homegrown antisemitism, and the latent antisemitism of many people in Europe and North America, this antisemitic incantation, here and there cloaked as anti-Zionism or anti-Israelism, though often open and unvarnished, opened the floodgates to antisemitic expression around the world.

The space opened up by the Cold War's end thus allowed Arab and Islamic countries and peoples to become more antisemitically assertive and more influential elsewhere. It led to various ways for them to offer and press their antisemitic notions upon others and liberated them to become more aggressive in these efforts. People in the West, out of genuine sympathy for the Palestinians and having the suddenly legitimate outlet for their repressed antisemitism, came to express over-the-top antipathies in varying degrees toward Israel, its Jews, and Jews more broadly.

The great influx of people from Arab and Islamic countries into Europe, forming sizable and ever more vocal minorities in most European countries, augmented the growing antisemitic discourse in Europe and in many ways coarsened its content and tone. This development created a powerful antisemitic insurgency that poisoned the public sphere. Ethnic Arabs and Muslims created a social antisemitic groundswell, keeping the theme of Israel and Jews on the front pages of the public's consciousness. They led to violent attacks upon and physical insecurity for Jews across the European landscape. They allowed European antisemites to show their faces and exercise their voices and create an alliance with antisemitic Muslims. And they cowed political authorities — often having either large constituencies among Muslims or large general populaces to appease — into not defending the public sphere against the expression of Muslims' antisemitism, let alone even sufficiently defending Jews from the physical attacks inspired by such unbridled hatred.

This Arab and Islamic antisemitic discourse, grounded on the foundational antisemitic paradigm and with its wild elaborations, was further intensified by a clever strategic move among Arab and Islamic political elites and movements, when speaking to the international community or more generally to non-Arabs and non-Muslims, to emphasize their antisemitism's so-called anti-Zionist aspect, generally ignoring or denying the rest of their antisemitic views. This strategy, a proven tactic to selectively emphasize their bigotry's aspects that appeal to a given audience, gave cover to governments, institutions, and people in the Arab and Islamic countries and around the world more generally, and bought them substantial immunity from outside criticism. Israelis looked like colonizers, and Israel's policies in West Bank and Gaza included occupation, guaranteed by force and its use. So, attacking Israel in multiple ways, as long as this occupation was its clear, or even loosely intimated, foundation, seemed legitimate. The Israelis' occupation of these territories, and their need to regularly defend themselves with weapons, therefore finally gave a seeming foundation in reality — after two thousand years — to central aspects of the elaborated charges and the animus against Jews that is antisemitism.

Despite the attempts at misdirection, without a doubt, what Israel's enemies were expressing was still antisemitism. It retained the classic hallmarks of prejudice in general, and of this peculiar prejudice — defining people according to, and reducing people to, one aspect of their identity, with myriad accusations that have nothing to do with reality, selectively applying criticism to them while ignoring the same or worse dispositions or acts by others — and relied on specific prejudicial tropes that had been used to characterize Jews for hundreds of years. Nevertheless, Jews were, for the first time since the Jewish diaspora began, in serious conflict with another people without being the powerless victims, and so for the first time there seemed a real foundation for a discursive assault on Jews, at least the Jews of Israel, which inevitably to antisemites the world over meant Jews more broadly. And, as we have seen, once people buy into the fundamentals of a prejudice, and they start to view a people through a framework as powerful as the foundational antisemitic paradigm, it predisposes them to believing ever more outlandish accusations about that people.

Arab and Islamic countries, finding natural sympathy among many developing countries as they successfully portrayed the Middle East conflict as a first world (Israel) versus developing world (Arabs and Palestinians) conflict over domination and liberation — the PLO was, after all, the Palestine *Liberation* Organization — easily garnered much international support for their assaults not only on Israel's policies but on Israel and its Jews themselves. As if this affinity were not powerful enough, the Arab and Islamic countries form a potent and, on this matter, unified anti-Israel bloc with a great deal of money (from the Saudis,

Iranians, and others) and a great number of votes in international institutions, particularly in the United Nations and its subsidiary organizations. With these economic and political resources, they influenced, cajoled, bought, pressured, and threatened many countries into supporting their anti-Israelism and antisemitism. And, thereby, and very significantly, they captured and transformed the international community's institutional infrastructure and much of its superstructure, most importantly and notably the United Nations, into (whatever the institutions' strident denials) de facto antisemitic entities, where a virtual calling card for membership or advancement is anti-Jewish agitation mostly in the form of anti-Israelism, or at least its indulgence. The Zionism Is Racism resolution in 1975 kicked off unremitting hostility and antisemitic agitation and other practices by the United Nations that has lasted now for more than three decades. For the first time, beyond the transnational institution of the Catholic Church, antisemitism has existed not just internationally but in the sinews of the international system itself.

# PART II

---

# GLOBAL
# ANTISEMITISM

# 8

# Learning to See

SINCE THE LATEST upsurge in antisemitism began, it has gained energy and rapidly broken existing bounds and constraints, achieving a reach and degree of normalcy with dizzying speed. It is at times hard to see this because we take antisemitism's existence, the expression of prejudicial beliefs and animus against Jews, so much for granted that its presence and its increase gain little notice (especially in the United States, where it is less prevalent and easier not to encounter). As with background noise, we habituate to it, barely notice it, and therefore scarcely pay attention.

Imagine though that out of nowhere a worldwide prejudice similar to antisemitism developed against the Irish or the Turks. Contemplating such widespread and intensive prejudice against these or, for that matter, any other people seems absurd. How, we might ask, would anyone, let alone tens upon tens of millions of people — spanning countries and continents, inflaming religions, churches, and their adherents — come to think the kinds of things or any of the loosely analogous things antisemites say about Jews, including that the Irish are a threat to the well-being of the people of country after country, let alone the world at large? How would anyone, let alone tens upon tens of millions of people, develop such an animus and invest that much prejudicial passion in the Irish?

The same questions could be asked about Turks, though with a moment's thought we would see that there are more similarities between

Turkey and Israel, and between Turks' and Jews' places in the world. A large Turkish minority of approximately nine million lives in Europe, with the largest population, six million, in Germany (compare that to the tiny minority of about one hundred thousand Jews among Germany's more than eighty million citizens). Notably, the Turks in Germany, almost half of whom are now German citizens, are not well assimilated into German society. Many live in Turkish-concentrated neighborhoods. They retain their distinctive religion, Islam, and religious and cultural practices, which include everything from speaking Turkish to eating Turkish food to their manner of dress to more traditional family practices (they have more children on average than ethnic European Germans), sexual roles (women can sometimes be seen walking several steps behind their husbands), and more. To many Germans, ethnic Turks appear mired in the nineteenth century. To be sure, non-Turkish-descended Germans harbor considerable prejudice against Turks, but it rises to nothing like the prejudice that exists against Jews, who are far more integrated into German society and culture, so much so that they, including their modes of dress, speaking, and conduct, are indistinguishable from non-Jewish Germans.

Beyond Europe, Turkey is a second-to-third-tier player with some political, strategic, and diplomatic visibility that initially rose considerably in the context of the Arab Spring. Turkey, as a NATO member and United States ally, has had more to do with furthering American policy in the world and in the Middle East specifically than Israel has. The United States and its allies used Turkey as a frontline garrison and nuclear missile base against the Soviet Union throughout the Cold War, and then as a staging ground for the war against Iraq in 1991, though not in 2003. It would have been easy for Arab and Islamic countries to see Turkey as an agent of Western imperialism, of American hegemony in the Middle East, as an outpost of the West, especially as Turkey has been longing and trying (so far unsuccessfully) to become a full-fledged member of the West by joining the European Union. Such a view would have been easier for Arabs to adopt in light of many Arabs' resentment toward Turks, as the Turkish Ottoman Empire and Turks (who are not Arabs and speak a non-Arabic language) ruled broad swaths of the Middle East, often brutally, in years past. And it would have been that much easier as Turkey, though predominantly Muslim, had been until

2003, with the avowedly Islamist Recep Erdoğan's election as prime minister, decidedly secular, keeping Islam down and in check, and often ruled by highly secular military or civilian leaders. Objectively speaking, Turkey could have been considered more of a threat to Middle Eastern countries geostrategically and culturally than Israel, or even if not more of a threat, then certainly a substantial one. Yet no great hatred or prejudice developed across the region for Turkey or Turks, let alone a widespread and fantastical prejudice paralleling or even giving a hint of antisemitism. In 2011, indeed, 78 percent of people across sixteen Arab countries expressed approval for Turkey and its policies.[1]

Turkey has a large minority of Kurds—estimated as between fourteen and twenty-five million—who have a distinct ethnic, linguistic, and national identity and national aspirations for independence that the Turks have denied, thwarted, and used violence to suppress in a campaign that has lasted now for decades. Over the last few decades, the Turkish government, supported by the vast majority of non-Kurdish Turks, has fought systematically to deny the Kurdish people's legitimate rights and aspirations to their own country in what is now southeastern Turkey, which is overwhelmingly Kurdish. As recently as the 1980s and 1990s, Turks slaughtered an estimated thirty thousand Kurds. They have depopulated much of the region by razing more than three thousand Kurdish villages and expelling three hundred thousand Kurds. Successive Turkish governments, military and civilian, secular and religious, with broad support of the Turkish people, have done this and more, including suppressing and persecuting Kurds for using the Kurdish language.

If all this sounds a bit like how the world considers the Israeli-Palestinian conflict, it should, although there are significant differences. Israel recognizes Palestinians as a separate people and acknowledges that the four million Palestinians in West Bank and Gaza should have their own state. Turkey does not do the same for its considerably more populous Kurds (who are also three to six times more numerous than the Palestinians of these regions), refusing to recognize them as an ethnic minority and fictitiously claiming that they are just Turks. Turkey has repressed the Kurds' national identity and aspirations, often with extreme violence, for almost one hundred years, far longer than the Palestinians have had a national movement. Israel is surrounded by countries, political leadership, and peoples—from neighboring Hezbollah-dominated Lebanon to farther away Iran—that openly declare their desire to destroy it and its people. One of the two major Palestinian governing bodies, Hamas, is openly dedicated to this, and the other, the Palestinian Authority, though formally not in this camp, has done many things over the years to suggest that this would be their ideal, if attainable, and is their ultimate, if deferred, goal. Turkey is under no such existential threat, or any external threat of any kind whatsoever. Israelis have not killed any number of Palestinians close to the number of Kurds the Turks have killed, let alone conducted a systematic eliminationist campaign against them, as the Turks have against the Kurds. Indeed, Israel has often taken great pains, including by notifying Palestinian civilians of impending attacks so that they could vacate areas, to minimize Palestinian civilian casualties during military operations. Israel has never forbidden Palestinians from speaking or being educated in Arabic, while Turkey had prohibited Kurdish from being spoken and the use of Kurdish in schools. In fact, Israel helped found or permitted universities for Palestinians in West Bank and Gaza that were bound to be incubators of Palestinian consciousness and support for Palestinian statehood. It is true that the PKK, the Kurdish liberation organization, has conducted guerrilla war and terrorist attacks against Turkey and Turks, but not to the extent that the Palestine Liberation Organization, Hamas, and Palestinians have against Israel. Any objective account of the respective conflicts—between the Israelis and Palestinians on the one hand, and between the Turks and Kurds on the other—or of the respective dominant powers' conduct in each of them would hold the Turks to have been far harsher and more deserving of condemnation than the Israelis. The Turks' repression of the Kurds' legitimate and rightful national aspirations continues to this day and shows no signs of abating, as does their violence to enforce this denial of Kurds' rights. Indeed, Turkey faces judgment after judgment by the European Court of Human Rights for its rampant human rights violations, far more than any other country in Europe. Yet the world has made and makes barely a peep about the Turks' treatment of the Kurds, which borders on or has crossed the line to being eliminationist—which cannot rightly be said of Israel's stance toward Palestinians.

In a rational world, the Turks' systemic and large-scale violence against and suppression of Kurds' legitimate rights and national aspirations, not to mention the Turks' genocide of the Armenians, and mass killings of Greeks and others, not to mention their invasion, dismembering, and occupation of half a sovereign country, Cyprus, in 1974, the occupation lasting now for almost forty years, might have brought upon Turkey the world's condemnation and generated in international organizations, including the United Nations, a preoccupation with its predations and the production of intensively negative beliefs and passions, including prejudice (if one believes, as all those who blame Jews and Israel for the existence of antisemitism believe, that prejudice is a reaction to a people's misdeeds) similar to and perhaps far exceeding that against Jews. But it has not—not even 1 percent as much.

We might ask similar questions about Palestinians themselves and their governing institutions. They have caused so much damage to so many countries and peoples, not just to Israel and Jews, but also to Lebanon and Lebanese (they virtually took over half the country in the 1970s and precipitated a civil war), to Jordan and Jordanians (another armed conflict owing to their attempt in 1970 to overthrow the country's ruler, King Hussein), to terrorism around the world, including on the biggest world stage at the Olympic Games in Munich in 1972, their outspoken glorification of murder (including of children) and of mass murder, and the brazenly eliminationist and exterminationist orientation toward Israel and Jews of a significant portion of Palestinians and of both their governing organizations until recently, with one, Hamas, continuing to advocate such eliminationism as a core political principle. Yasser Arafat, the PLO, and Palestinians did more to turn terrorism into a worldwide political instrument than any other organization of people did. It could be reasonably thought that Palestinians have done more to keep the Middle East embroiled in conflict than any other people (owing to their military adventurism, their terrorism, their long unwillingness to recognize Israel's right to exist and therefore an unwillingness to make peace with Israel and accept West Bank and Gaza as the location for Palestine). Why is there no widespread, let alone fantastical hatred and prejudice against Palestinians around the world? Why, for example, are there no surveys to uncover the extent and reasons for anti-Palestinian or, for that matter, anti-Turkish prejudice? There is so little of each around the world, as evidenced by how little either is part of the public discourse, let alone a widespread and impassioned public discourse, that the notion of doing worldwide survey research about anti-Palestinianism or about anti-Turkism would be absurd.

This discussion of Turkey and Turks, of Palestinians and their governing institutions, and the passing mention of the Irish is meant to highlight how inured we have become to antisemitism's expression. It is so much a part of the world's architecture and its furniture. It is, in part, because the foundational antisemitic paradigm has produced so much antisemitism through the ages and in the last years, and the antisemitic discourses built upon it are so commonplace that we, in some sense rightly, take it for granted. But we should not. Antisemitism should be no more natural than anti-Turkism, which as we see is not natural at all, and is (except in local conflicts) very difficult to engender, certainly as a general, cross-national, and acute prejudice. Indeed, as we have seen earlier, contrary to antisemitism's purveyors, apologists, and academic and media enablers, it is actually extremely difficult to provoke prejudice and animus of the kind that is directed at Israel and Jews, in all the countries, places, and among all the different kinds of peoples, and in all the issue areas, even in quantities far reduced from what exists. In fact, it is so difficult and so uncommon that prejudice on a par with antisemitism has come into existence only once historically, and exists today for only one people. This is so despite all the horrible things that countries and peoples have done historically and today all around the world and all the objective threats and problems that countries and other peoples (whether they are majority or minority populations) have posed and pose to their neighbors that have been far worse than anything Israel and its Jews do.

By seeing antisemitism's existence as natural and, in part because we take it as natural by remaining blind to how pervasive it is, we take it for granted. Let us, instead, treat antisemitism's existence as what it is — something unnatural — and let us also take its anti-Israel form as unnatural and set out to explain the character of this most bizarre and unjustified prejudice as it has existed and does exist in the world. Doing this begins by noticing it; noticing how much exists and how much it has increased. By thinking about how it has evolved in the last years and that evolution's significance. Most pointedly, by no longer pretending that there is not much of it or that in confronting it truthfully we are making much ado about nothing.

# 9

# The ABCs of Global Antisemitism

THE MOST FUNDAMENTAL new fact about antisemitism is that it is global. Never before could this be said about antisemitism. What that means and portends — just like globalization itself — is not obvious. Even so a great deal can be said about global antisemitism: more than that it is but another variation upon and elaboration of the foundational antisemitic paradigm, and more than the comparisons we can and will make between it and the two principal earlier eras and forms of antisemitism regarding their central dimensions and their elaborated understandings and passions about Jews.

The most disturbing fact about global antisemitism is that it is rising and intensifying, especially its expression in the public sphere. It is doing so in country after country. The enormous upsurge in antisemitism's verbal and written expression dating from the 1980s has taken place across all media. Without suggesting that spreading antisemitic notions and hatreds is not in itself a deeply damaging and disturbing assault, or that publicly accusing Jews of subverting or controlling a country's politics or publicly calling for the elimination of the Jews in Israel and in other places powerfully injures and threatens, nothing captures public attention and seems to alert people to danger more than physical threats and attacks.

The data on such threats and attacks are alarming. They in themselves show that antisemitism is enormously widespread. And they are trending upward, often steeply upward compared to 1980, 1990, and 2000, especially so in antisemitism's most intensive expression: actual physical attacks upon Jews or their institutions. Because these are crimes whose perpetrators are subject to imprisonment, the deterrent against committing them, unlike expressing coded or explicit antisemitic invective in the public sphere, is enormous. Their upsurge's significance for the state of antisemitism is unmistakable.

In 2000, the number of recorded major violent antisemitic incidents around the world — excluding Israel, West Bank, and Gaza — was 255. The institution reporting the data "stress[es] that the number of incidents presented in the various tables reflect only serious acts of antisemitic violence," which include major attacks, such as arson, firebombs, and shootings, and major violent incidents, such as desecration of synagogues, vandalism of Jewish properties and sites, and attacks on Jews that do not involve weapons. We should note that these figures grossly underreport such attacks, as only when violence has been deemed, often by reluctant local authorities, to be antisemitically motivated, which typically means that it has a clear, demonstrable antisemitic component (other than the mere fact that a synagogue, for example, is attacked), such as the perpetrators making antisemitic statements, are they registered as antisemitic. When such articulated antisemitic proof is absent, the police often minimize antisemitic attacks or write them off as being random violent acts. As B'nai Brith Canada, which compiles its own annual Audit of Antisemitic Incidents, despairingly comments, "we cannot simply stand by passively when death threats are dismissed as insignificant, when targeting Jewish homes is described as 'just kids acting out' and when physical assaults are subsequently boasted about on Facebook."[1] As with all crimes, particularly those that do not rise to the level of bodily harm, many antisemitic attacks are also never reported in the first place.

The number of major violent antisemitic attacks rose from 255 in 2000 to 686 in 2012. In a mere decade the annual number of such assaults more than doubled, an increase of 170 percent. This followed an even larger annual rise in major antisemitic violence from 1989 (the first year that such data were gathered) to 2000 of 225 percent. This means that from 1989 to 2012 the annual number of major violent antisemitic inci-

Antisemitism—Major Violent Manifestations Worldwide 1989–2012

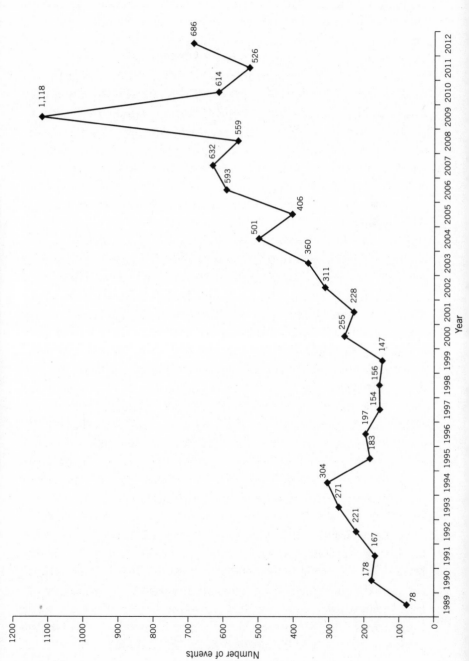

Number of events

Year

dents against Jews living outside Israel and Palestinian areas soared almost 800 percent. That is an astonishing rise in antisemitic expression, here in its most serious form, to have transpired in the historical blink of an eye of two decades. The graph on page 165 shows that these numbers are representative points in such assaults' steady climb. Except for the massive spike in 2009, which coincided with Israel's Operation Cast Lead, the incursion into Gaza to stem Hamas' continual rocket attacks on Israeli cities and towns, the major antisemitic assaults' distinct upward trajectory outside Israel and Palestinian areas is unmistakable, with the number in the last six years (excluding 2009) reaching a new average annual high of approximately six hundred, showing that 2012 was no aberration. The current level of such major antisemitic attacks is the new norm.[2]

These worldwide trends of *major* antisemitic violence are mirrored in country-level data regarding a broader range of—including nonmajor but still significant—antisemitic attacks and incidents. B'nai Brith Canada has been monitoring antisemitic incidents for three decades in Canada, a country with a substantial antisemitic past but one that is still far less powerful than those of European countries with their once thoroughgoing eliminationist orientations and policies. Yet in recent years, Canadian antisemitic expression has grown to unprecedented proportions. Proclaimed the B'nai Brith Canada report, "we continue to see rocks being thrown at synagogue and school windows, death threats being sent via social media, visible Jews being taunted and physically assaulted en route to their homes and places of worship and even a young Jewish girl's hair being set on fire." In 2011, "across Canada, 1,297 antisemitic incidents were reported . . . antisemitism targeting Canadian Jews remains at such all-time high levels. In the thirty years since the League began documenting antisemitism, incidents have increased more than twenty-fold." This striking increase becomes even that much more significant when the current levels are seen comparatively. More than 70 percent in 2009 and 55 percent in 2010 of all hate crimes committed against members of religious groups in Canada were perpetrated against Jews, even though they compose a mere 1 percent of the Canadian people! Muslims, whom the popular media present as the predominant religious group victimized by prejudice, are twice as numerous as Jews in Canada. Yet during these years Muslims were the victims of only 10 percent of hate crimes, one-sixth as many as the Jews. Even though Jews have been in Canada much longer and are far more culturally integrated into Canadian society and politics, they have been the victims of prejudicially motivated violence at a rate roughly twelve times that of Muslims.[3]

Jews experience ever more inhospitableness in their own countries and fear marking themselves in any visible way as Jews. Jews from many countries, most notably in Europe, started to report in the 1990s and ever more in the 2000s that it is too dangerous to wear signs of their identity — kippas, Stars of David — in public. Even rabbis — rabbis! — are publicly denuding themselves of signs of their Jewishness. Orthodox Rabbi Itzi Loewenthal, who despite the numerous attacks on other Jews in Copenhagen still walks there openly as a Jew, won't dare to in Odense, Denmark's third-largest city: "In Copenhagen I go with a kippah, but when I come to Odense, I remove all external signs that I'm a Jew. I just don't dare." Why? Because of his experience in Odense, "I waited for the train, which was late, when they approached and began to hit me. They could see I was a Jew because I had my kippah on. When one woman on the platform began to shout, they disappeared again."[4] The image of a rabbi inspecting himself, perhaps in the mirror, to ensure that all signs of his Jewishness are absent is remarkable and a sure sign of unbearable hostility and danger for Jews.

Jewish parents forbid their children from publicly wearing Jewish symbols, realizing the likelihood is high that sooner or later, and in many places very much sooner, their children will be attacked. In Malmö, Sweden, after a funeral in 2010, the son-in-law of the deceased had to inform people coming from elsewhere about the dangers of being openly Jewish there: "Take off your yarmulkes." Israeli author Barbara Sofer similarly recounts her and her husband's initial innocence when in Rome in August 2012. While they visited the Largo del Torre Argentina, the Roman forum from before Jesus' time, "a man comes up behind us and begins speaking softly in Italian-accented, fluent Hebrew. 'The hat,' he says. 'When you leave the ghetto [the Jewish area of Rome], you take off the kippa.'"[5] Amit Peer, an Israeli student at the University in Turin, explains that Italian Jews themselves heed this advice. "The

Jews here are hiding their own identity because they risk becoming a target."[6]

And this is a general condition in Europe. In a string of European countries, most notably in famously socially tolerant Northern Europe — Denmark, Germany, Sweden, Norway, and Finland — Jews have been explicitly warned either by their own communities or institutions or by their countries' governments and leaders not to display signs of their Jewishness. In Finland the message was crudely delivered that for safety Jews should not wear "Jew clothes." Speaking of the failure of governments and political leaders to protect them, or, in most cases, even to evince care, one young Jew in the Netherlands looks hopelessly for help: "I cannot go to public events dressed as a Jew, let alone go out on Saturday night. Which party do I have to vote for in order to live safely with the kippah on my head?"[7]

Aaron, a sixteen-year-old in 2011, knows that Jews being a target is the reality of everyday life in Germany's capital and most cosmopolitan city, Berlin. "I would not walk on the street with a David Star." Why not? "You must not be provocative." A schoolmate, Dalia, who is seventeen, tells of walking into a department store on the Ku'damm, one of Berlin's main shopping streets, with some friends, the boys wearing kippas and the girls with Israeli T-shirts: "It was shocking. They looked at us as if we were criminals." When they asked a sales clerk whether there was kosher food, the woman replied, "This is not Jew-land."[8] As unpleasant and indicative as this is, the consequences for not following the standard "take off your yarmulkes" practice can be much worse.

Rabbi Daniel Alter, walking the streets of Berlin, did not heed such advice, though he was surely aware of it. In August 2012 four teens spied his kippa, approached him, and asked him if he was a Jew. Then, in front of his daughter, they assaulted him with antisemitic insults and a beating, including to his head, sending him to the hospital. The assailants also threatened to kill the little girl. The president of the Jewish community of Berlin, Gideon Joffe, referring to high-visibility attacks elsewhere, conveys the generalized fear that antisemites have produced around Europe: "Following Sweden, France, and the Netherlands we are apparently now also here confronted with such a grave form of antisemitism that many Jews will seriously consider concealing their Jewishness. To beat up a 53-year-old father accompanying his small daughter is possible only if one does not see this person as a human being. The humanity of this person is denied because he is a Jew and lives openly as a Jew."[9] Alter, in a bitter irony, was in 2006 one of the first rabbis ordained in Germany since the Holocaust. And it is rabbis, who uphold religious law to cover their heads and who do not wish to hide their Jewishness, who are particularly vulnerable the world over, including in Argentina, the home of the largest Jewish community in South America, which owing to antisemitic pressure and danger has been severely diminishing in number. In 2011, in its capital and most cosmopolitan city, Buenos Aires, Rabbi Moshe Cohen, the director of an Orthodox Jewish school, was verbally assaulted, including "Jew, Jew.... Dirty Jew," and with nunchucks [a martial arts weapon] physically beaten on the head, causing serious head injury and hospitalization.[10]

Visible indicators of Jewishness have all but disappeared from public spheres in much of the world, and especially significantly from many European countries. And when they appear, as in Venice on New Year's Day 2013, in the person of an American yeshiva student vacationing with his family, they expose their bearers to shocking dangers, in this case a brutal beating into unconsciousness by a gang of about fifteen Arab youths.[11] In France, "anti-Semitism has become unbearable," attests one French émigré who settled in Israel. "Children are harassed on their way to school just because they're Jews." So threatening has Europe become that, aside from the many who have already emigrated, more and more Jews are considering leaving their homelands in Europe, which are often countries they otherwise deeply identify with and used to think of themselves as integral members of, to emigrate to Israel. These people, who only want to be themselves in peace, consider it safer to be in Israel, a country where rockets or bombs, or full-scale war, can engulf its people at any moment. As this French émigré attests about Israel, in daily life "it's much safer here than in France." A survey in 2004 found that one out of four of the half million French Jews is considering emigrating from France to Israel. By 2013 the conditions had gotten so bad, and not only in France, that 40 percent to 50 percent of Jews in France, Belgium, and Hungary reported that they might emigrate because their countries were not safe for them. Those are astonishingly high figures, especially for the French Jewish community that has been in place for centuries and feels itself deeply attached to being French. But it is not Israel's pull, not Zionism that causes Jews to move to Israel or to seriously think about doing so. It is France's push and its antisemitism's intolerable nature and threat. Daniel Ben-Simon, member of Israel's parliament and author of the book *French Bite,* explains: "Almost one in two French Jews maintains a residence in Israel. It's a sort of insurance policy, just in case the situation in France gets even worse."[12]

In two senses French Jews have for a couple of decades been leaving French society. Little used more than a decade ago, Jewish schools in France have increased enrollments to thirty thousand, filling them to beyond their capacity. And French Jews have departed the country, with one hundred thousand of them emigrating in recent years, and many others thinking of following suit having prepared apartments abroad just in case. And these dual responses, the self-protective trends toward inward and outward migration, are to a greater or lesser extent true in country after country.

Even in this context, or particularly in this context, we see how galvanizing one attack can be on an entire national community. Mohammed Merah's antisemitic murder of four Jews, including three children, at the Ozar Hatorah Jewish school in Toulouse in March 2012, riveted France. Merah, arriving on a scooter, stopped at the school's drop-off point at 8:00 a.m. and started shooting at anyone there, as adults and children alike scrambled for their lives. Before fleeing, he succeeded in murdering Jonathan Sandler (a teacher and a school parent), his five- and four-year-old sons Arieh and Gabriel, and seven-year-old Miriam Monsonego, whom Merah executed by putting a gun to her head and firing.

Coverage of the mass murder, images of it, news stories about it, including French President's Nicolas Sarkozy's arrival on the scene, and the subsequent funeral blanketed French media for days. The attack on the Jewish children of one school in one city in France, in our media-saturated and nationally and globally integrated age, was, as the antisemitic Merah undoubtedly knew, an attack on all French Jews, arguably even Jews everywhere. Since the mass murder, the fear has intensified further, as the attack, like public antisemitism in general—which typically brings out ever more public antisemitism—has only emboldened the antisemites. "Insults, spitting and violence happen on a daily basis," Rabbi Harold Weill of Toulouse explains. "I grew up in France and never thought I'd be so pessimistic and believe that there's no future here."[13]

*Through television, the murders affect Jews everywhere.*

*A Jewish child.*

172 • THE DEVIL THAT NEVER DIES

All over Europe, taking off kippas, checking to make sure that Stars of David are tucked away under shirts, and warning one's children not to exhibit any other indications of Jewishness in public are not precautions enough. In Denmark, a public school principal in Odense announced in 2009 that he would discourage Jewish children from attending because he could not guarantee their safety. His announcement was then joined by other like-minded Danish principals, indicating this problem to be widespread. Though each individual Jew might dwell in a personal ghetto of fear, leaving all markings of Jewishness behind as he or she steps out into the public sphere, if Jews are to participate in communal Jewish life they cannot know that they are safe from the ever more frequent attacks. In Malmö, a Jewish center was attacked and bombed in September 2012 — Toulouse in March, Berlin in August, Malmö in September.

In London as well. Well-known Israeli professor Benny Morris was assaulted there in 2011 by a group of Muslims while he was attending a conference. An expert on Israeli-Palestinian relations and no stranger to dangers that that conflict produces, Morris was nonetheless shaken by what happened and more generally by what he knows is taking place across Europe. "I felt like a Jew in Berlin in the twenties," he explained. "Israel is an absolute taboo in Europe. At Cambridge [University], my class was canceled after intimidation by Islamist groups. And I think that it will only get worse."[14]

In Germany, always one bellwether for Jews, the country's president Joachim Gauck wondered publicly in December 2012 at the dedication ceremony for a new synagogue in Ulm whether antisemitic conditions have become so bad for Jews that a future for them is possible in the country. His remarks there come after the months-long, blatantly antisemitic public debate over banning circumcision. "I know that in recent months concern and fear has arisen about whether Jewish life in Germany is still possible. The attacks on Jewish citizens were a cause for this concern, as was the circumcision debate, which was set off by a court ruling, but which very quickly adopted tones that also frightened me."[15] Antisemitic expression has become so bad that the president of Germany is frightened, and in a country where politicians of all stripes almost as a rule play down the extent of antisemitism among the people in order not to hurt Germany's standing in the world, he feels compelled to acknowledge its alarming character explicitly in public. The upsurge in antisemitic expression during this "debate" was so stunning not just to Gauck but also to the former leader of Germany's Jewish community, Charlotte Knobloch, that in September 2012 she wrote a stinging article in one of Germany's major newspapers and then gave interviews in which she wondered publicly whether she had been wrong for decades to defend Germany and the possibility of Jewish life there. In her article, she pointedly asked the country, "Do you still want us Jews?"[16]

Moshe Kantor, surveying the European landscape from his position as president of the European Jewish Congress, knows that the peril to Jews' existence as individuals and as a community is far more widespread than in Germany alone. In June 2013, a Europe-wide survey revealed that 26 percent of Jews have personally been the victims of antisemitic harassment over the previous year, and that in the previous five years, one out of every fourteen Jews was physically hurt or threatened. No wonder so many Jews feel that they are being driven from the continent. Already nearly a year before, in September 2012, Kantor summed up the dire social, political, and existential situation for Jews: "The explosion of Malmö follows an unprecedented wave of attacks against Jews and Jewish targets in recent months, since the murders in Toulouse. The Jewish community in Europe is under attack, there is a real threat to Jewish communal life in parts of Europe and not enough is being done to protect it. A threat to Jewish life in Europe is a threat to the foundations of Europe."[17]

As this initial look at an aspect of global antisemitism — major assaults on Jews — shows us, global antisemitism is real and it is violent — violent in its conception of Jewness, violent in its passions, violent in its logic, violent in its acts and consequences. The trend lines around the world are unmistakable both in the dangers Jews face just about wherever they are, and that the dangers are increasing. This is clear before we even address the by many orders of magnitude, still more widespread and intensive violent dreams, strivings, and acts of peoples and governments in the Arab and Islamic world. There are many other aspects to global antisemitism, and much of it is not violent in this way, but the violence and the danger inherent to it is widespread and real. In country after country, in *democratic* country after country no less, in what in now dated terms would have been called "civilized" country after country, Jews must hide their identity lest they be physically, not to mention verbally, assaulted. We speak here not of 1400, or of 1940, but of 2013, in the self-styled most "humane" and pacified region of the world, Europe. In country after country, indeed across the continent, Jews say they have no future. This is in addition to the other regions of the world containing Arab and Islamic countries, where Jews have no future, in part because they have already left or been driven out. What other people or ethnic group would say the same thing, that in country after country, they must hide their identity in order not to be physically assaulted, and that they have no future? None. Only the Jews. Such is one distinguishing and important feature of global antisemitism.

Before exploring global antisemitism, we should pause to take up, establish, or emphasize four critical points that are systematically, often wholly misrepresented in the treatment of today's antisemitism and that will contribute to the framework of our discussion of global antisemitism, as well as be further elaborated.

First, as discussed in previous chapters, after antisemitism's postwar decline, it has been on the upswing, certainly since the 1990s, in its absolute levels, its expression in the public sphere, and in its violence both in deed and in rhetoric and potential. Antisemitism's vigorous return to the Western world's public sphere and (in even more vitriolic form) Arab and Islamic countries' public discourses is broadcast via media of all kinds in the West, the Middle East, and beyond. Thus, antisemitism should not be treated—as those who minimize it, for political and often antisemitic purposes, do—as being either (1) not enormously widespread, (2) not increasing, (3) not potent, or (4) not dangerous to Jews.

Second, although the upsurge in antisemitism has been real, the increase in its *expression* in word and in deed has been far greater. This distinction between the extent of people's prejudicial belief and animus and the extent to which it is expressed in the public sphere, always critical to keep in mind, exposes as a falsehood the commonplace notion that if antisemitic attacks, whether verbal or physical, are not voluminous, then little antisemitism of consequence exists. We have already seen for the post–World War II period that although little antisemitic expression made it into Western countries' public spheres, antisemitism continued to exist as a powerful subterranean prejudice. We will see in our examination of the global period how immensely widespread and powerful antisemitism still is, and in some areas and ways even more powerful than before. This can be seen in the data cited above, with the rise in the attacks on Jews being meteoric compared to the steadier state of underlying antisemitism.

Third, and this relates to the second point, is a theme we have already encountered. External social and political stressors, including the most frequently (often reflexively) invoked one, of economic crises or problems, may contribute to an increase in the expression of antisemitism, but they do not cause antisemitism itself. The ongoing financial crisis, which, starting in 2008, has hit the world's economies hard, has not, according to general indexes of intensive antisemitism, appreciably increased the levels of antisemitism in European countries or in the United States (see next paragraph). It has not even increased the explicitly economic-related antisemitic notions that Jews have too much power in the business world and too much power in international financial markets — which were already extremely widespread in Europe. From 2007 to 2009 to 2012, such antisemitic notions about Jews' economic might remained amazingly constant in Germany, rose a bit in France and Spain, declined an equal amount in Austria, and stayed more or less the same in Italy, the Netherlands, Poland, and the United Kingdom. These levels remained stable even though a high percentage of Europeans, as we will see in Chapter 11, explicitly blamed Jews for the financial crisis itself, and even though the crisis led to an upsurge in antisemitic expression around economic issues.

Finally, and this is a theme we will consider in depth, the enormously widespread antisemitism today, as revealed in survey data and as manifested in the public sphere, is not a consequence of Israel's actions. Age-old antisemitic tropes that are still prevalent, as we will see, both precede Israel's founding and, in content, have nothing to do with anything Israel does or with the reality and terms of the conflict Jewish Israelis have with Palestinians and neighboring Arab countries, which has been principally over Israel's existence, as well as over territory and power. This disconnection is particularly obvious regarding the antisemitism that courses around Europe. What is more, it is easy to show that Israel's conduct does not affect the incidence of antisemitism in general, which is grounded in deep-seated and longstanding orientations, emotions, and beliefs. If it did, then when Israel engages in policies, say military operations, that are widely deemed objectionable, antisemitism would rise in some commensurate way. But it does not. Operation Cast Lead, Israel's insurgency into Gaza in 2009, demonstrates this dramatically. As we have seen, it led major violent antisemitic incidents outside of Israel and the Palestinian areas, mainly in Europe, to spike. This constitutes a sizable increase in antisemitic *expression,* which reflected the strong disapproval, justified or not, with which people in many countries regarded the military attack on Gaza. This disapproval was expressed also in a torrent of governmental criticism, media condemnation, public protests in capitals and major and minor cities around Europe and elsewhere, as well as in a ratcheting up of the terms of condemnation used for Israel, which frequently included such words as Nazi, extermination, genocide. Yet Israel's actions and even this outrage pouring out at Israel had virtually no effect on the general levels of antisemitism, namely the prejudicial beliefs that exist specifically for Jews, and even more that exist specifically for the Jews living in the countries of the people being surveyed (as distinct from the animus for Israel and its policies). To take one quick and reliable indicator, surveys of multiple European countries regarding antisemitism taken in 2007, 2009 (partly during the Gaza war), and in 2012 show no major change in antisemitic levels (some countries increased a bit, others declined a bit), and there was even no spike in the 2009 data, which, if Israel's actions were the *cause* of antisemitism, should have dramatically elevated the levels. According to the survey's composite index of antisemitism, for the four European countries for which there are data for the three years, France varied by a total of four percentage points during this period, Germany remained almost entirely constant, Poland barely changed, and Spain trended slightly upward.[18] In the United States, an even broader antisemitic index shows no appreciable change from 2007 to 2011, with the 2009 survey taken after the Gaza war even showing a small decline in antisemitism among Americans!

If condemnation of Israel and its policies were at the root of contemporary antisemitism, as so many claim, then Israel's 2009 attack on Gaza, the most universally and vitriolically condemned Israeli policy perhaps in the last two decades, would have produced an enormous increase in general antisemitism. It did not. That is only one spectacularly important piece of evidence among a wide range and enormous quantity of other evidence that antisemitism has little if anything inherently to do with Israel's actions (as it has always had almost nothing to do with Jews' actions), let alone with a non-antisemitically induced understanding or critical appraisal of those actions. And that antisemitism's levels did not increase even when this overwhelmingly covered and condemned attack coincided with the world financial crisis only further reinforces the conclusion that it is not Israel or external stressors of any kind (including economic) or in general that produce antisemitism.

Neither antisemitism itself nor even the overall trajectory in the number of attacks on Jews around the world, which is a form of antisemitic *expression,* is tied to the actions of Israel. During the 1990s, with the Oslo peace agreement and the establishment of the Palestinian Authority, when hopes for a final agreement between Palestinians and Israelis were highest and when genuine progress was being made in establishing Palestinian autonomy, the incidence of antisemitic attacks on Jews steadily rose. With the ever more apparent failure of the so-called peace process in the 2000s, starting with the Palestinian assault on Israel known as the Second Intifada in 2001, the incidence of antisemitic attacks on Jews also steadily rose. Looking to Israel and its conduct to explain antisemitism, or even antisemitism's public expression, around the world is akin to looking to some of the horrors perpetrated by some African countries to explain racism against African Americans (which also long predates many of those countries' existence as sovereign states) in the United States.

Global antisemitism is new in many ways, including in being global. Global antisemitism's relationship to the principal past eras and types of antisemitism is complex. It is not a break with past antisemitisms, let alone a radical break with them. It incorporates many elements of earlier forms of antisemitism, and it is held by many of the same groups who have been previously antisemitic, with clear lines of continuity between the current membership and their forebears. It is grounded in the same foundational antisemitic paradigm as medieval and modern antisemitism, indebted to them in its basic animus and structure: it would not exist without them, and from them it has evolved.

Yet in certain ways global antisemitism also differs from what came before on virtually every major dimension. It has new features. It casts old features in new ways. It has new molecular arrangements that reconfigure existing features to produce something novel. The global-ized world now constitutes the plausibility structure for antisemitism, and Jews' position has similarly undergone changes compared to all earlier eras. This forecloses as impractical (because they are seen as primitive or disreputable) certain ways of understanding and casting Jews. Talking about race and blood (or genes) no longer makes sense, and would only delegitimize antisemites and antisemitism even among many who accept the foundational antisemitic paradigm and the actual or potential thoughts, emotions, and proposals grounded in it. Global-ization also presents antisemites new features and opportunities for updating their antisemitic discourses and litanies of accusations.

Antisemitism's history and evolution can be discerned and told in the typical images of Jews of their eras. For antisemitism, and prejudice in general, visual imagery, including cartoons and caricatures, have power-fully and persuasively conveyed prejudicial and hate-filled notions. The images are arguably more powerful because they concretize in corporeal visual form and then in memory the internal qualities and even the external deeds the antisemitic litany imputes to Jews. They can be com-prehended and visually encoded in an instant and more easily recalled than a long disquisition on the Jews' evil. When people hear such accounts and accusations or more casual antisemitic remarks, they also recall the powerful images. For anyone who has been exposed to past or present antisemitic discourses' visual components, hearing or reading many vulgar, mean, or malevolent notions about Jews easily conjures up relevant visual images. From medieval times through today, antisemites have employed cartoons and caricatures liberally and effectively.

These cartoons as an ensemble convey the three major periods and types of antisemitism — medieval, modern, and global. Of course, char-acteristics of each can and do coincide with characteristics of the others, sometimes producing an amalgamation. Nevertheless, each of antisemi-tism's periods and types — the medieval and modern we have already explored — has a discernible and stable core that includes notions and images about Jews that can be mapped on the range of antisemitic dimensions and summarized in table form (see page 181).

Global antisemitism's deep affinities and continuities with antisemi-tism's two earlier dominant forms notwithstanding, global antisemitism differs more from them than they do from one another. While main-

*The Wandering Jew (1852), who was condemned for taunting Jesus to wander the earth until Jesus' second coming.*

*In 1939, the front page from popular Nazi newspaper* Der Stürmer *depicts German womanhood about to be destroyed by a Jewish snake. The snake, more than any other creature, combines and conveys stealth, deceit, and malevolence. The Jews are defiling and destroying the purity of the nation. The bottom headline reproduces the antisemitic rallying cry of the period: "Jews are our misfortune!"*

*In November 2012, Saudi Arabia's* Al-Iqtisqadiyya *shows Jews, as symbolized by Star of David eye patches, blinding the world and rendering it defenseless. The Jews are backed by American power perched as an Uncle Sam hat on top of the world so that they can gash the helpless world with a jagged knife.*

*In 2002* Arab News, *a moderate Saudi English-language newspaper, depicts Israel as Nazi Germany. Ariel Sharon uses a swastika-shaped ax to mercilessly butcher Palestinian children. The Jews' naked and brazen violence replaces the stealth of previous eras.*

| | Conception of Jews | Conception of World | Source of Perniciousness | International Threat | Principal Locus of Conflict | Main Means to Combat Jews/ Action Orientation |
|---|---|---|---|---|---|---|
| Medieval European | Antichrist/ Devil | Religious | Religion/ Devil | Threat to Christianity/ Christians | Local | Convert/ Contain Jews |
| Modern/ Nazi | Anti-race/ Enemy of humankind | Race/ Nation | Race/ Nation | Quest for International Domination | National | Expel or exterminate Jews |
| Global | Antistate/ People | Plural | Diffuse/ Identity/ Inherent in Jewness | Produce Conflict/Dis- order/Terror: Greatest threat to world peace | Interna- tional | Eliminate Jews' country and interna- tional power/ Partial and strong exter- minatory thrust |

taining the foundational antisemitic paradigm, it centers on an altered conception of the Jews' nature, holding them to be neither a religious group nor a race, and their noxiousness or danger to be not in their wayward dissent from and alleged enmity toward other religions, and not in their religious teachings, and also not programmed into their biology. Instead, it conceives of the Jews' nature and their problematic qualities' sources as more plural, more hazy. They are simply *Jews,* an ethnic identity that is, akin to so many other ethnic identities, socially as much defined by non–group members as by the group's members themselves.

An example of such a group, indeed overlapping groups, are Hispanics or Latinos in the United States. This group's members have varying national origins, skin tones, and native languages. They even have three noncongruent names (Chicanos, Hispanics, and Latinos) but often have little in common in the United States except that they are not defined as of white European descent (even though their ancestry may be Spanish or Portuguese), are from south of the American border, and now organize politically often as one demographic, and therefore ethnic and therefore political group. Hispanic or Latino is thus an ascribed identity based on an ill-defined notion of ethnicity, an ultimately amorphous social concept based in some idea of fundamental underlying shared qualities that becomes commonly accepted and the basis for perception, understanding, social action, and politics both by the people it characterizes and by the rest of society. The result is an also widely practiced basis for prejudice and its expression.

This has happened to Jews in the United States as well and, more important, around the world, especially among antisemites. Antisemites understand Jews to be Jews simply because they are Jews. This is not a tautological statement. For antisemites, the source of *Jewness,* of the noxious and undesirable qualities they ascribe to Jews, is the Jews' own adoption of their identity as Jews, their belongingness to their ethnicity, their practice of "Jewish" politics because, at a time when the principal arena for influence is understood to be politics, acting politically is what most constitutes the relevance of group life to others. This is particularly the case for antisemites' understanding of Jews, because the most burning issues for antisemites are international and political, as they see the Jews' greatest threat to reside in the political arena, particularly the international political arena. There are antisemites who still privilege the religious sources of Jewness. There are others who still adhere to classically racist notions about the source of Jews' perniciousness. But for most antisemites today, Jews are Jews also or principally because they act or are assumed to act politically as Jews and the quality that makes them this way is their essence of *Jewness.* Thus the source of the Jews' perniciousness today, whatever various other things different antisemites also consider it to be, is the Jews' political identity, which means their allegiance to Jewness' political goals, which is overwhelmingly defined by the repository of Jews' politics and greatest political capacity as much as it is the repository of much of Jewish life: Israel.

That Jews are defined by overlapping notions of ethnicity, identity, and politics — the first being an ascriptive notion of shared qualities, the second being a subjective sense of commonality, and the third being defined by goals and actions using resources and power in the public sphere — is entirely in keeping with our age. In our global age, characterized by pluralism of identities, crisscrossing allegiances, membership in different communities, and the decline of old notions of race's and religion's determining power, people come to be defined more and more by their ethnicities (often only ascribed to them by others), their own identities, and most of all their politics, which is a matter of who they stand with and what they work for in the public sphere—whether in actual fact or only in the minds and discourses of others. Whatever a person's individual identity—or, better put, assemblage of identities— whether according to skin color, ancestry, gender, age, religion, profession, or any number of other possibilities, politics more often defines her or him for others because this is the identity that governs what she aspires to, sometimes in a competitive sense. And that politics can be domestic within a person's country, or international on the global scene, where it is now rightly understood that so much of humanity's destiny is being forged.

For today's antisemites, the manifest source of Jews' perniciousness is their identity as Jews, based on their ethnicity and translated into and thereby constituted by their politics, which all becomes embodied in their underlying nature of, and then projected with dastardly qualities onto, their Jewness. Global antisemites understand Jews' perniciousness to be grounded not in their religious or other ideas or in their biology but in their politics. This does not mean that Jews actually have to politically support the perceived Jewish political agenda to be considered to be doing so, because antisemites generally assume that people self-identified as Jews are naturally defined by and will support and further Jews' political practices and goals and, most of all, Israel's political practices and goals.

Thus, global antisemites think of Jews not in crystalline terms, as medieval antisemites did holding them to be the Antichrist or devils (even with horns and tails), or as modern antisemites did holding them to be race-enemies, an anti-race, devils in human form, with biologically different blood. Actual religious beliefs are secondary or irrelevant. Instead, global antisemites conceive of Jews as something more diffuse or amorphous—which is in keeping with the widespread breakdown of conventional categories, ways of thinking, practices, sources of authority that has occurred with globalization—and as something equally essential, diabolical Jewness. Nazis said Jews fomented disorder and caused wars, understanding Jews to be biologically driven to do so. Today, Arab and Islamic antisemites say the Jews do the same but, like contemporary antisemites in the West and especially in Europe, understand Jews' motive power to be more amorphous, grounded in their self-constructed (as a group and singly) wants and antipathy to goodness. It is as if Jews, for whatever reason, form a criminal syndicate, coming together to pursue sinister aspirations more successfully, and do so by effectively capturing the political realm. In a globalized world, with all its pluralism, it is only this commonality of political ambition that unites people of otherwise diverse nationalities, identities, and allegiances.

Jews are to the global antisemites a political group brought together by their identity as Jews. The source of perniciousness is this common politics itself, grounded in their Jewness and corollary aspirations as Jews. The principal threat they pose is not to destroy Christianity or Islam (which they also in the minds of many, especially Islamic, antisemites want to do), and not international domination (which they also might want in the eyes of many), but to sow disorder and stand in the way of goodness and justice itself. In what can reasonably be seen only as a persisting fantastical stance (despite the post–World War II era's decrease in antisemitism's fantastical content), Europeans broadly, and even more so Arabs and Muslims, say that Israel poses *the* greatest threat to world peace. Yes, 59 percent of Europeans across fifteen countries asserted in 2011 that Israel — not nuclear saber-rattling North Korea; not Iran, seeking to export its political Islamic revolution and striving to build nuclear weapons against the combined efforts of the European Union, the United States, and the international community; not ever more belligerent and authoritarian Russia; not surging colossus China upsetting customary power and strategic arrangements throughout Asia and potentially beyond — is the world's greatest threat to peace. Remarkably, this poll was conducted in the context of the Arab Spring with conflicts taking place or threatening to break out in one Middle East country after the next, as dictatorships and political Islamists faced off for control of countries and of the region in general, and democratic Israel sitting quietly by, not involved in any of these conflicts. Asked in 2012 whether Iran, still driving for nuclear weapons and with its openly eliminationist political Islamic regime and president, or whether Israel, the explicit potential target of such weapons, is a greater danger to peace, twice as many Germans (48 percent to 22 percent) said Israel.

Antisemites view the principal locus for Jews' action and for combating Jews to be the international realm and over international goals. The political conflict with Jews is taking place *all over the world,* which is fantastical as an account of what the Jews are doing but has been self-fulfilling as that is how the antisemites are waging the discursive, institutional, and ultimately martial fight. This analytic and action orientation of today's antisemites is also grounded in and reinforced by the overwhelming focus of antisemites first on Israel, the Jews' sovereign country (even though roughly 20 percent of its citizens are Palestinians), which can be combated (except by Palestinians) only on international terrain, and second on the Jews in the United States, the world superpower that is present in most significant international arenas and many of their smaller corners and which, according to the antisemites, Jews have captured and use as their tool. The means to combat the Jews must be equal to the Jews' colossal power and threat.

As befitting the globalized world, the global antisemitic discourse about Jews is also more varied and more diffuse than the medieval Christian one or the modern racist one, with more strands that both overlap and do not, that harmonize easily in some ways but not in others. Thus it is harder to summarize and requires a more extensive treatment. For now, suffice it to say that a significant part of this far-flung discourse insists on the utter necessity of eliminating Jewish power, often Jews themselves, and, by one means or another, their country. The means of elimination that so many openly advocate — because it is the only way to eradicate Jewness — extermination, and sometimes in the case of Israel, destruction by less thoroughly violent but ultimately equally effective means, such as calling for it to cease to exist, either as a *Jewish* country or as a country at all. In past eras, owing to their respective conceptions of the source of the Jews' putative perniciousness, antisemites saw that Jews could stop being Jews by converting, or that they could not stop being Jews because they could not change their biologically governed stripes any more than a tiger could. Today the view is different. It is not the Jews' biology that governs them. So Jews, in principle, can change. But converting from Judaism to something else would not be sufficient because religion is not the source of most Jews' politics. After all, as many antisemites well know, a significant portion of Israel's Jews are thoroughly secular and in this sense have already converted away from Judaism. So they, and other Jewish converts, in the eyes of antisemites beholding the prospect of Jews converting, do not and would not stop being Jews until they exorcise their Jewness and stop practicing

Jewish politics as it is understood. Moreover, this discussion is a fanciful one in any case, as most antisemites do not even think of conversion as a real option—it appears barely, if at all, in the voluminous antisemitic discourse—for a solution to the perceived problem. They are not concerned with saving souls, let alone individual souls. Conversion of Jews en masse to Christianity or Islam—whether it be the six million Jews in Israel, the more than five million Jews in the United States, or the two and a half million Jews strewn about the world's other countries—is not feasible, not a practical goal, so, being outside the plausibility structure of the world, it is not even discussed. The antisemites are left, in their minds, with the option of fighting Jews where the fight is, politically, and to vanquish them one way or another, politically, to destroy their power, including but not only to destroy one of their two principal power bases, which is the country of Israel.

Much of this can be seen in the events of 2000–2001 when Israel was eager to sign a comprehensive settlement, which it had hammered out with the Palestinians' leadership, to create an independent Palestinian state and resolve the Israeli-Palestinian conflict. The agreement contained the fundamental elements of what the consensus view holds a final settlement to need, including land swaps, and indeed a more generous arrangement of shared sovereignty in Jerusalem than Palestinians might have reasonably hoped for. Yet the Palestinians spurned it. After the negotiations had reached a final stage with a detailed draft agreement, Yasser Arafat, despite the implorations of American president Bill Clinton, who was deeply involved in the process, refused to return to the table for further negotiations. Instead and peremptorily, the Palestinians unleashed a war of sorts, called the Second Intifada, against Israel. Yet Israel, despite its conduct compared to the Palestinians, despite its democratic constitution, and despite its deep desire for peace, was in 2003 (as it is to this day) widely considered in Europe and elsewhere to be the country that is the greatest threat to world peace. Such survey data then and now indicates three things about global antisemitism: how little the facts about Jews and their country penetrate the prejudice that broad publics around the world have against them; how powerful the public antisemitic discourse is—including its capacity to persuade people of its elements and awaken fears in people who otherwise would not hold much against Jews; and how hyperbolic are anti-semites' accounts of the Jews' and the Jews' country's perniciousness and danger to the world.

Antisemitism has seamlessly adapted itself to and modernized, really globalized itself according to globalization's main contours and features. Globalization is typically conceived of as having shrunk the world. Yet another side of globalization's metaphorical effect has been to *enlarge* the world. Peoples' social, cultural, and even political expanses are now far greater, far beyond what they were thirty, twenty, even ten years ago. Meanwhile, personal worlds, namely the worlds intimately accessed by individuals, have greatly expanded and plurified. So too have their mental and emotional worlds similarly enlarged. In medieval times, a person's world consisted overwhelmingly of his village and immediate physical environment and the few ideas (aside from religion) that penetrated it beyond village life's commonsense and folk wisdom. In modern times, it enlarged with expanded communications, transportation, and newspapers to a person's region and, with snippets of news, to the world and potential ideas beyond at least in the sense that he could be aware of its existence. With globalization, people jet all over the world in hours, minutes, or seconds by plane, with a television clicker, with a mouse click or a touch of a finger — and even if a person is trying to stay at home, the world, via such media and in other ways, comes to find her. Forget the Internet: the amount of information available today in one *New York Times* issue is said to equal the amount of information a person in rural eighteenth-century France would encounter in his entire life.

As a result, the world has become enormously more plural. More countries and their peoples affect other countries and peoples — economically, politically, socially, and culturally. More countries are heterogeneous in their populace and are more densely in contact with other countries and people, especially owing to ever expanding digital media and communication technologies, including the now ubiquitous and ever handy cell phone as portal to the Internet. As physical, social, and cultural locations become more fluid and indeterminate, what constitutes a person most is his or her chosen identity — that is, in the public sphere, what that person defines and acts upon politically. In this new context, antisemites conceive of the source of Jews' perniciousness to be in line with the character of this global world: residing in the Jews' identity — which is mainly an ethnic one shaped by Jews' underlying Jewness — and their politics.

Perhaps the best adjective to describe the globalized world's physical state is *denser*. There is more of it, its elements are packed closer together, its elements therefore interact more; the world is in a very real sense weightier. It has more people, who consume more and who produce more, including and especially words and images. Information is abundant and everywhere. All this is true of contemporary antisemitism: there is more of it, and it is closer — namely more readily available at any moment to people, both to the antisemites who can access its discourse at will and to Jews who find themselves exposed to it at any moment regardless of their will. It is everywhere, as it occupies virtually every corner and most of the nooks and crannies of the world, in a real physical sense that the antisemitic discourse and antisemites can be found all around the world, and in the real virtual sense that it courses and crisscrosses through world-enveloping cyberspace. And antisemitism is denser. Antisemites, owing to their vast number and owing to television and the web, are packed closer together, whatever the physical distance separating them. Antisemitic elements interact with each other far more frequently than in the past, with various streams of antisemitism being exposed to one another on a daily basis and new elements being steadily introduced into those streams, then carried along by them wherever they go. Antisemites themselves similarly interact with each other more readily and often.

This greater density of the global world and of global antisemitism has, and produces, other parallel features. With greater density comes greater power. Power means the capacity to transform, and there is much greater transformative capacity in the world today than there was in 1900, let alone in 1800 or 1000. States can do much more, as can individuals. The growth of economies, organizations, organizational know-how, knowledge about the world, and technology and its products in general means that enormously more of the world can be affected, shaped, controlled, built up, or destroyed than ever before — by states, by groups of people working in concert and in institutions, and even by individuals with their own more limited reach. People know this. Political leaders know it. Elites know it. States and institutions know it. Ordinary people know it. Because they know it, at every level and among institutions and groups of all kinds, they think of using this enormous capacity — indeed, desire to do so, to make plans and implement them. Antisemites also do this, knowing that they have far more power to affect themselves and their victims, the Jews. This is one of the reasons that many of them dream, and not just dream but actively hope and agitate for the Jews' elimination, even their extermination.

A rally takes place in Paris, as one did in 2003, in which signs and chants are brandished that call for the mass murder of Jews. The Jews of France — not just those who happened to walk by or may have heard by word of mouth an account, a rumor of the gathering — and many Jews beyond know that in the capital of one of the most seemingly civilized and pacified countries in the world, people are again openly calling for their mass murder. Local and far-flung antisemites learn of this too, emboldening them — as if they need to be further emboldened — to begin including such signs and chants in their rallies, so starting with a small rally in Paris, this most heinous call becomes a feature of antisemitic marches. The public antisemitic discourses also get augmented immediately with this Parisian rally's facts and elements. The power of this small antisemitic group in Paris to affect large numbers of Jews, who see that people in the heart of Europe's public sphere, literally physically in it, are once again openly calling for their extermination is more than to hear people utter some words that they do not like. It conjures up memories and knowledge of the Holocaust, of lost loved ones or of family one never got to know, and of how the world had turned on, hounded, and exterminated Jews. It, surely, makes many Jews feel less secure.

The power of these antisemites to influence and extend the antisemitic discourse is, owing to media and the Internet and the ready willingness of antisemites to learn from other antisemites the world over, similarly great. This small band of antisemites, their transformative capacity, was outsized. And as antisemites make clear, when they can, they want the injury not to be merely symbolic. At a Paris rally against the Iraq War in 2003, with which, it need hardly be said, Jews had no particular involvement, Noam Levy, a pro-Palestinian and antiwar Jew there to express his condemnation of "Bush's war," was assaulted by a group of men with metal pipes. Levy explains: "They were shouting

'Death to the Jews' and 'You and your kippah have no place here.' "[19] And so the verbal and physical attacks have continued and escalated, culminating for now with Merah's murder of four Jews in Toulouse and his symbolic murder of all Jews of France. The damage done was not confined even to the expansive community of the Jews of France. After the attack, European Jewish Congress president Kantor told of the despair among Jews across the continent: "Life in Europe after the murders in Toulouse continues as before, but for the Jewish community life is no longer as it was before."[20]

Such rallies, and signs and chants of death to the Jews, have become a commonplace of antisemitic, ostensibly anti-Israel, protests. In a sense, they received their legitimation at the United Nations antiracism conference in Durban, South Africa, in 2001, which, as we will see later, was planned and held as an antisemitic hatefest, and which further unleashed and intensified antisemitic poison in the world's public discourse. Calls for Israel's and Jews' liquidation, having gained the imprimatur and worldwide publicity of Durban, then, entering Europe's heart through Paris and other capitals, gradually become a fixture of public antisemitism.

On an even larger stage, Mahmoud Ahmadinejad, the world's most notorious antisemite and Iran's president from 2005 to 2013, stirs the pot. With his utterance of a word or two, again and again, most notoriously that Israel should be wiped off the map, the whole world watches, the whole world consumes it, the whole world talks about it. A sizable portion of the world applauds and is emboldened; others are appalled and condemn him. Regardless, Jews are put in antisemitism's uncomfortable limelight yet again, and so intensively. Ahmadinejad was such a political celebrity that Columbia University—a university with as close ties to Jews as any outside Israel because of its prominence in New York City, the unparalleled center of Jews' intellectual life in the United States—decided to host him in 2007 and to give him a public forum and public honor of the kind he has never had. No matter that Columbia's president Lee Bollinger justified the event with transparent nonsense that it would give people the opportunity to challenge Ahmadinejad, or as he put it, "to confront ideas—to understand the world as it is and as it might be."[21] Bollinger was affording the world's leading antisemite a prominent public platform that would never be given to a country's leader who spread the equivalent racist things about African Americans, such as American slavery never existed, or threatened the extinction of a country other than Israel. But the world has become so inured to antisemitism that Columbia honors, with its president delivering the fig leaf of tough criticism, and gives a megaphone that reaches across the United States to a man who does and would emulate Hitler. Or is it that those at Columbia responsible for the invitation and the event see that antisemitism is good theater and they want to put on a good show? After all, on the principle that any coverage is good coverage, Columbia reaped for itself a bonanza, even if some people there undoubtedly did not like the condemnation the university received. This event's effect — the controversy leading up to it, the event itself, and then the prominence and exposure it conferred on Ahmadinejad and his views — was significant, if nonetheless small compared to Ahmadinejad's efforts to give regular succor to his fellow Holocaust deniers, and causes regular concern if not fear among Jews as he threatens to "wipe Israel off the map" and spearheads Iran's drive to build nuclear weapons that if acquired would at best leave Jews and Israelis living with nuclear Armageddon hanging over their and their loved ones' heads, and at worst result in actually bringing about Armageddon.

The Western media and those who follow it pay much attention to only two of Ahmadinejad's many utterances and stances regarding Jews: his Holocaust denial and his threat to wipe Israel off the map. On these two issues a relative consensus exists that someone has crossed the line to the impermissible. For European elites, and obviously for American elites, saying that the Holocaust did not happen, or some lesser but obvious stripe of Holocaust denial, places a person outside the foundational moral consensus that the Holocaust was an unsurpassed evil. A person denying this gravely violates morality, and furthermore casts doubt on the person's sanity, judgment, or public fitness. Urging or threatening a Holocaust today also goes too far. So, calling for or even suggesting the nuclear annihilation of another country and its people is impermissible, even when directed at Israel and Jews. Most antisemites in the West know this and steer clear of articulating their animus for Jews in these two ways, no matter what they think. They know that at the very least, the veneer of not being antisemitic, which means not being rabidly against Jews and Jewness, must be maintained. Or perhaps

Europeans' and others' drawing the line against these two forms of anti-semitism is meant to generally inoculate them against the charge of antisemitism and thereby legitimize or allow other kinds of antisemitic expression that do not so glaringly offend the sensibilities of people of good will. That this is likely the case, which antisemites well under-stand, will be explored when we focus on Ahmadinejad's and many other Arab and Islamic political leaders' vast antisemitic outpouring, which goes virtually ignored by Western elites and media. Less venally, Europeans and others may just be inured to it, habituated to it, see such pronouncements as part of the natural social world. Many among them agree with it.

Consider the mass murder in 1999 at a Los Angeles Jewish Commu-nity Center, where a vicious antisemite opened fire with an automatic weapon, injuring five people, including three children among the 250 who were on the playground. This attack was extraordinarily atypical in the United States, so focusing on it might give the wrong impression. Yet it is worth discussing precisely because of its atypicality in this least antisemitic of Western countries. This is not to imply that attacks of this murderousness happen frequently in many other countries. But in other countries they likely do not happen because of the intensive security that exists for Jews' institutions, the security itself conveying how expected such attacks would otherwise be and how dangerous it is for Jews. Moreover, in other countries violent antisemitic attacks on Jews are far more common than in the United States, especially when one considers the United States' vastly greater number of Jews and their synagogues and community centers. France with fewer than one-tenth the number of Jews had more than three times the number of major violent inci-dents from 2010 to 2012, making the per capita incidence of antisemitic violence more than thirty times greater there than in the United States over those three years.[22] American Jews live under normal social and cultural conditions — meaning nothing more than that they expect to be assaulted verbally in the public sphere or physically no more than the members of other ethnic or religious groups, which is to say that the expectation is that they will not be attacked. This context rendered the Los Angeles attack all that much more shocking: one lone gunman had the power to rivet to attention in fear and in concern over the state of their lives and their community certainly a good part, if not the vast majority, of a group of people numbering more than five million, and also brought to antisemitic attention the rest of a country of three hundred million people. Such is the nature of modern global antisemitism and antisemites, whose ordinary people, terrorists, and political leaders modernity has so enormously empowered.

Bigness, ubiquity, commonality, and transformative capacity or power—these are some of the common elements of globalization and global antisemitism. There are still others that also show the novel nature of the form into which this ancient, medieval, and modern hatred has been transformed.

Antisemitism today has no fixed coordinates. This was not so before. In medieval times, antisemitism, though widespread, was contained to mainly two regions, Christian Europe and Muslim lands. Antisemitism left untouched or relatively untouched vast parts of the world where knowledge of Jews' existence was scant or none. Even during the modern period, with the increase in communications, the situation changed little. In Europe, throughout the medieval period and even into the modern period, there was an address one could visit to find the center of antisemitism, the Catholic Church headquartered in the Vatican, the spatial origin and social custodian of the foundational Christian antisemitic paradigm's spread. Today, there is no such center—not even close. There are in fact many such places, including seats of governments. But there are so many of them, and so many not related to governments at all, that it is more correct to say that there really are no such places, that antisemitism's fixed coordinates are today virtually every coordinate on the ever-turning globe. Whereas once antisemitism had mainly a static and rooted quality, today antisemitism is an enormously multiple and unceasingly moving target.

This is not to say that in previous eras antisemitism did not spread. Obviously it did; that is how it became as widespread as it was in medieval times, both around the European continent and in the Islamic world. Indeed, antisemitism's rapid, far-reaching colonization through Europe and then, outside of Islamic lands, beyond Europe, matched the march of Christianity and its churches with their particular if overlapping antisemitic messages, which accompanied imperial Europeans as they carved up and then fundamentally shaped the non-European worlds and their cultures. Similarly, as Islam conquered and colonized the Middle East and some areas beyond, it imbued its new adherents and their regions with its elaboration on the foundational antisemitic paradigm. Starting in the nineteenth century, modern racial antisemitism, and then even or particularly the Nazi variant, also rapidly spread to existing antisemitic regions, countries, and peoples, replacing, overlaying, or intermixing with the already regnant, often long ensconced forms of anti-Jewish belief and animus. The Nazi leadership self-consciously exported its lethal eliminationist antisemitism to the many conquered regions and, most significantly for today, did so with assiduousness to the Middle East, including, as best they could, to British Mandate Palestine and nearby regions. It is no small irony that the Nazis' antisemitic fundamentals, both their account of the source of Jews' alleged perniciousness, namely biology, and their elaborated demonology about the degree and type of that supposed unsurpassed perniciousness, all but died in Germany and Europe with Nazism but powerfully lives on, especially the Nazis' demonology about Jews, in two places: Arab and Islamic countries, and among the vast community of cyberspace antisemites.

Notwithstanding this geographic and human migration, colonization, and spreading infestation of antisemitism prior to our times, today antisemitism's flow fundamentally differs from what came before. In the past, antisemitism, as this account suggests, had a center-periphery relationship. It began in ancient Israel during the time of Jesus and migrated shortly thereafter to Greece. There it was codified in the context of early Christians' desires to appropriate the Jewish religious and messianic tradition, really Judaism revamped, for themselves. In Greece the Gospels were written, at best based on a long chain of hearsay, not until fifty to one hundred years after Jesus' death by people who never knew or saw Jesus or the events surrounding his life. Antisemitism then moved to and became entrenched in Rome, the center of the Western world, where Christianity and simultaneously antisemitism had its greatest conquest when Emperor Constantine adopted Christianity for himself and the Roman Empire in the early fourth century. As his empire spread to more European lands in particular, the secular and religious authorities brought the antisemitic gospel with them, which, after Rome's fall (which did not see the Church's fall), spread to all of Europe, so that dur-

ing the Middle Ages antisemitism, together with Christianity, had solidified itself as the one pan-European belief system, about which different
peoples, people of different classes and stations, different professions, and
eventually even different and warring forms of Christianity could agree
upon and coalesce. Then, with European and Christian colonization of
much of the world, antisemitism spread farther.

We see here a clear center-periphery relationship and pattern in the
diffusion of antisemitism prior to the age of globalization. Antisemitism
spread and was continually nourished from a center, or from its core,
which was ever expanding to peripheries. This is even true regarding
Islam's antisemitic dispersion with Islam's expansion, since, in a sense,
Islamic antisemitism itself is a manifestation of this center-periphery
relationship, for it mimicked then well-known Christian scriptural and
doctrinal antisemitism. Islam's adoption of antisemitism can even be
seen as a partial derivation of Christian antisemitism, which then took
on its own particular Islamic contours. Maps that traced antisemitism's
spread and the pattern of Jews' migration, which was quite peripatetic
over the centuries, would show that there was practically no overlap
temporally between the two. (This is yet another reason to conclude that
Jews' conduct or real-world characteristics have nothing fundamentally
to do with antisemitism's existence or content.) Jews' existence in a given
country or region, the number of Jews there (as we have seen, many
countries that were deeply antisemitic, such as England for several centuries, have had no Jews or virtually none), and the ebbs and flows in a
country's or region's Jewish population in no sense correspond to—
which also means they did not cause—local antisemitism's extent,
character, or intensity.

It is noteworthy that the postwar lull in antisemitism took place during the one period when the world's center—located in the unrivalled
economic, cultural, and political superpower of the United States—was
less antisemitic than the world in which it was dominant, and culturally
and politically was an active anti-antisemitic power. Antisemitism's
resurgence has similarly coincided with the United States' relative
decline as a cultural and political hegemon, Europe's full resuscitation,
and the Arab and Islamic countries' emergence as collectively powerful
actors on the world stage. In effect, this American decline (though

militarily it remains hegemonic) coincided with or ushered in the global age and the end of any center-periphery relationship to the world, whether economically, politically, culturally, or antisemitically.

Global antisemitism differs fundamentally from all earlier antisemitic times and forms in the character of its movement. Today, antisemitism does not spread from one place or region or people to another, being not in a certain place one day and then sometime later established there, where it remains relatively static. Instead, it flows in a constant stream from one place to another. It also does not move from the center to the periphery. Instead, it flows in many directions, flows from anywhere to everywhere. This is, to be sure, information's nature in the global age, with television and its images blanketing the world, and Al Jazeera inciting antisemitism against Israel and its Jews not only all over the Middle East but also with its English-language service in many countries around the world, notably but not only in Europe. The Internet, which we will explore in more depth, has of course made the global information age truly global, with a single posting potentially reaching hundreds of thousands, millions, or tens of millions in an instant, and then available indefinitely for all future and would-be antisemites, and innocents, including children, who stumble across it. Antisemites have been extremely strategic and adept at using the Internet for their ends.

This changed manner of how antisemitic notions move from place to place might be better described not in terms of flow or even in the plural *flows,* and certainly not as medieval antisemitism did, which was to spread and then stay relatively static, but as a tide. We are witnessing today the flows and sometimes ebbs of a global antisemitism that swirls and circles and reaches the entire world and then circles back again to touch everyone and anyone time after time.

Antisemitism's globalized multidimensional centerless properties notwithstanding, some areas or places or institutions still account for the bulk of today's antisemitic currents, incitement, and intensification. Yet global antisemitism's breakdown of the old center-periphery relationship has been so thoroughgoing that antisemitism's relative directional flow has been greatly, though not entirely, reversed. Antisemitic ideas and tropes that originated in Europe, whether initially of Christian origin or championed by the Nazis, and that had been incorporated into the Islamic and Arab antisemitic litany now flow back to Europe, also through the intermediary institutions of the United Nations and other international organizations. So, in case anyone in Europe had forgotten the once commonsense antisemitic notions about Jews, now mostly thanks to Arabs and Muslims, and especially their countries' governments, Europeans are being reminded of them.

Related to but also separate from antisemitism's global flows is the global flow of antisemites. Antisemitism, namely the beliefs, images, and the attached animus, has always traveled in the ways that ideas and images and their emotional implications do. In the body of churchmen and imams, preaching antisemitism's gospel, antisemites have spread their word effectively. Today, we have something different. Substantial antisemitism-bearing populaces have been migrating around the world, specifically from Arab and Islamic countries to Europe and elsewhere in a process of reverse colonization, at least with regard to this central prejudicial belief and animus that so many of them bear. With these flows they have replenished and emboldened the antisemitic human reservoir of many European countries, established new ones in countries where there had not been such a distinctive or powerful antisemitic presence, and resuscitated or created an unabashed antisemitic discourse that does all the harmful things such discourses do. The global age is one of increased flows of all kinds, including multiple and multidirectional human flows. The extent to which this has pumped up and spread antisemitism, nearly universalizing it — meaning that its bearers can at any moment of international travel be found just about anywhere — is considerable and bears further discussion.

The global and multiple flows of peoples have been accelerating, similar to the flows of money, goods, and services. The simple fact, not sufficiently paid attention to, is that an immense reservoir of antisemites — among the peoples of Arab and Islamic countries, and now Arab and Islamic immigrants and their descendants living abroad — is itself streaming around the world to populate it with deeply devout antisemites. This does not mean that all Arabs or all Muslims, either living in the countries of their ancestry or now in non-predominantly Arabic or Islamic counties are antisemitic, but an enormous number of them are, and they are a substantial population on the move. Tens of millions of people of Arabic descent live abroad. Nineteen million Muslims live in the European Union alone, seventeen times the 1.1 million Jews. In virtually every country of the world, including those with Jewish communities that are more than minuscule, Jews are greatly outnumbered by Muslims and by Arabs. (The two major exceptions are Israel and the United States—and Israel is, of course, surrounded by hundreds of millions of Muslims and Arabs.) Muslims and Arabs are aware of their numerical strength and conscious of their ability to spread their antisemitic beliefs and press for the adoption of their antisemitic politics, and they do so. No corner of the world is free of such an insurgency, meaning that no corner of the world is worry free for Jews, and much of the world where there are Jews (and probably where there are few of them) is dangerous for them owing to the actual or threatened violence perpetrated by Muslims and Arabs. Even during the Nazi period, when the threat facing Jews in the Germans' orbit was far more acute, and certainly the prospect of a German military victory mortally imperiled all Jews, in most of the world Jews did not have to walk around fearing physical assault. Global antisemitism—with the substantial exception of the United States—equals a global, if variable, physical threat.

Our age of global antisemitism, with broad-based antisemitic tides coursing around the world, being strengthened and accelerated on a regular basis, sometimes daily, and bringing many different kinds of antisemitic streams within them, offers antisemites—whether as large communities of antisemites, small groups of them, or individuals—a New York deli menu of antisemitic narratives, accounts, accusations, images, tropes, and degrees of passion from which to choose. Not only is this kind of plurification of antisemitism unprecedented historically, but today's antisemitic menu usually offers many appealing things to satisfy almost any grievance or aspiration, which individuals or groups can easily appropriate, incorporate into their worldviews, ideologies, and programs. For people casting about for explanations of the world, problems, suffering, shortcomings, even bad luck, the availability and allure, the power of suggestion, the psychic satisfaction of an antisemitic emotional and cognitive fix, not to mention of a potential antisemitic action program to right the wrong, can be, and for many obviously is, substantial. If a person lives in a country experiencing a serious economic downturn, or even an implosion, as many economies were during the great recession starting in 2008, or if a person is personally having tough times economically, it is easy enough to blame the Jews for the general financial crisis or even for his or her personal situation. Notions of Jews' economic malfeasance course through and around the Internet and are already as well known in many countries as any other antisemitic set of accusations, save perhaps Jews' alleged role and guilt in causing Jesus' death, and Israel's and Jews' alleged predations against the Palestinians and goodness. If a person's country has suffered terrorist attacks by political Islamists or faces terrorism dangers, or if he or she is worried about terrorism, given that terrorism is repeatedly said to be caused by the instability in the Middle East chiefly owing to Israel and its treatment of the Palestinians, nothing could be easier than holding the Jews — in Israel and elsewhere — responsible, including the supposedly all-powerful Jews in the United States and the Jews in that person's own country, for their real or alleged support for their brethren in Israel, or just because they choose to share what is, owing to terrorism, now considered a noxious identity. If a person feels abandoned by God, or does not understand why his or her lot in life is so hard, nothing could be easier than feeling animus for Jews for having allegedly murdered Jesus, especially as that person sits in Church thinking of his condition and his relationship to the deity who gave his life for him — or, rather, had his life taken by the Jews. If a person holds that there is no political and social justice in the world and is looking for a cause that will crystallize his dissatisfactions or around which he can easily rally with like-minded people, and therefore find the fellowship that so many seek in collective movements, political groups, communities of fellowship or of shared causes, then a most readily available movement, political grouping, and community is one dedicated to imprecations, agitation, protest against Israel and its political supporters, which means Jews. He or she might actively join them, or just take satisfaction and gain succor by regularly reading or consuming their antisemitic words and narratives, cartoons and videos on the Internet, all the time deepening his antipathies for Jews and knowingly or unknowingly preparing himself to support further antisemitic action, of words or deeds.

In country after country, all these notions are more than easy to find. Indeed they are actually hard to avoid, as they are part of the broad public discourses, sanctioned by governments and visible and influential political leaders, present in prominent institutions, widely in the media, and actively, sometimes aggressively promoted by propagandists, marketers, and branders—who are either open and seemingly earnest in what they peddle, or are camouflaging their messages by using seemingly legitimate front men so that their messages will be more appealing and persuasive, or are mixing their messages with other messages, known to be appealing to certain groups or subgroups. There may be no better and larger-scale example of this than the impassioned support that neo-Nazi and other right-wing antisemites give to Palestinians, for whom they would ordinarily have no particular sympathy, or more, would in all likelihood hold in contempt or worse. But because the Palestinians' cause is extremely popular and evokes a great deal of passion among peoples of many countries, communities, classes, and sensibilities, such dedicated antisemites join the cause in order to infuse it with ever more antisemitic content and thereby increase the flow and adoption of their notions about and animus toward Jews, get a hearing for their broader causes, make allies, and even just seem more respectable, more part of the legitimate public discourse. Once a critical mass—and that critical mass can be a notable minority—coalesces around an antisemitic notion, theme, or cause, such as the antisemitic anti-Israel movement, the combined appeal of belief and emotional satisfaction on the one hand and of fellowship that can be physical and proximate (a club) or distant and virtual (the Internet) on the other brings ever more people into that particular community of antisemitism.

Antisemitism affords people many different opportunities: self-expression, self-justification, emotional focus and discharge, fellowship, something to do, psychological compensation for life's shortcomings, a search for truth, a program of action, a way of tying together disparate aspects of the world into a coherent whole, a way to see more deeply behind the falseness of appearances, a diversion from problems, an outlet for aggression, an opportunity for retribution, a program of action, a way to dream, a way to serve God, a path to heaven, and for the Jews a path to hell. Today many sources suggest that the Jews are noxious or dangerous and offer people ways to prejudicially think about Jews. People have many motives, conscious or not, for adopting an antisemitic stance toward Jews. (I am referring here to people who do not grow up in uncontested cultures of antisemitism that exist in many Arab and Islamic countries.) They have many more reasons for doing so and choices in how they do so that are available than ever before. Antisemitism, like globalism, is not just plurified in its content more than ever, which it is, creating choices and making it appealing for so many, it also, in our global age of information flows and instantaneous mobility, is plurified in the satisfactions and functions it affords people to have, and in ways it had never been before. All this contributes to the power of the antisemitic tide, and all this further strengthens it.

Given the globalized world's substantially changed nature, with societies and politics more penetrated by countries, institutions, and flows from outside their countries, and with an international politics that is far more present and on people's minds, it would be surprising if global antisemitism's orientation and message did not reflect this. It decidedly does. Global antisemitism has a markedly changed orientation and content compared to antisemitism's earlier forms. It is much more oriented toward the international arena than it ever has been, and new tropes, images, and tones deliver its message.

The dominant conception of Jews in medieval times, whether in Christian or Muslim lands, reflected the weak, abject state of Jewish communities living within hostile majoritarian non-Jewish societies. So Christians and Muslims believed that Jews, using their cunning, resorted to stealth — acting behind the scenes or in the dark or using the mediating tool of money — to carry out their malevolent intentions. Muslims had their own widespread beliefs in Jews' sneakiness, yet this was particularly so in the Christian world, where the alliance and similarities between the Jews and the devil was, though variously specified, fast and absolute. The devil works his evil in the stealthiest of ways. He does not reveal himself. He does not materialize in the town square, with his devil ears, tail, and most of all face dripping with devilish lust and malice. This would undermine his effectiveness. It would rouse the good Christians in their own defense of their God and their souls. No, the devil works behind the scenes, seeking out the vulnerable and corrupting them. So too with the Jews. Sly, they seek out the vulnerable — the financially needy, the weak, women, or children. They try to get their clutches in people, whether literally in the case of women (sexually) and children (whose blood they allegedly used in making matzos), or figuratively with their money and manipulative power. They even conceal their true nature, never appearing in public with the literal or figurative horns and tails many Christians thought Jews possessed. The Jews posed an amorphous danger, like the devil spreading evil, and that is why it was best to restrict contact with them, why Christians had to avoid them or reduce their presence, why Christians expelled Jews from their cities and regions, and why, when allowing Jews to live among them, they frequently forced them to live in ghettos, locking the gates at night, the most fearsome time, when Jews' movements could be least monitored and their stealth would be most effective. Although the accusations that the dominant antisemitic discourse prior to globalization leveled at Jews were multiple, including of course the paradigm foundational one that they were Christ-killers, the dominant image of Jews operating within society was that of Shakespeare's Shylock. Cunning, manipulative, outwardly obsequious, all malevolence inside. Jews were not what they seem to be. They may look weak. They may look pliant. They may look unthreatening. But the true image, absent the camouflage, was of a lascivious, avaricious, amoral being and moral corrupter — a devilish and bedeviling creature. Although Jews work in concert, each Jew posed a personal threat to individual Christians, body and soul.

In the nineteenth and twentieth centuries, modern racial antisemites updated this image. Jews remained cunning and stealthy, operating behind the scenes. They continued to conceal their true selves, but with changing times in a strategically new fashion. No longer — particularly in the West, the bastion of modernity and of this racial antisemitism, and where Jews were most successfully integrating — did Jews don traditional clothing, wear beards, and present themselves as classically recognizable Jews, but they insinuated their way into the Christian populace by mimicking their dress and ways, speaking their languages, blending in so that they were not easily identifiable as Jews and therefore as the danger that they were.

With religion's accelerating decline and science's progressive ascent, the world became disenchanted. Jews no longer had to conceal their horns and tails, which they were no longer presented as having, and the biological marker, indeed the biological basis of their evil, which was their blood, was already concealed, enhancing their capacity to cloak their malevolence in normality's visage. With the Jews' emergence from the ghettos starting in the eighteenth century's latter part, and with more professions opening up to them, the Jews' opportunities to mix in Christian society, to worm their way into power and influence, to seduce Christians with their deceptions and Christian women with their wiles, increased commensurately. Hence antisemites developed a new set of calumnies and an intensified set of accusations against Jews. Most of all, in light of politics and society's new developments, particularly three large-scale developments in the nineteenth century, antisemitic fire was directed less at individual Jews and their danger to individual Christians and their souls and more toward Jews' alleged role in, first, the newly created public sphere; second, the national economy; and, third, a country's politics.

The public sphere, namely a place where a conversation or discourse occurs about the common or shared or competing needs or concerns of a society's people, did not exist until it began to form at the end of the eighteenth and then in the nineteenth century. Many developments contributed to its emergence, including crucially the advent of broad-circulation media, books, pamphlets, and especially newspapers. As Jews came out of the ghettos and the restrictions on their activities were lifted, antisemites came to see the Jews threatening the public allegedly by shaping the public sphere's character, being overly influential, and controlling the media. During this same period, particularly with the enormous changes wrought by industrialization and the vast increase in commerce, awareness of the existence of a national economy developed — which was a response to its real emergence and also to increased transportation and communication — replacing the previously localized notion of economics, of the town or city and the nearby surrounding region. Antisemites came to see Jews as systemically controlling and undermining national economies, particularly owing to their alleged outsized financial influence, through their alleged control of banking. And as people became mobilized into politics, whether democratic or nondemocratic politics (which was the third major development of this era), and political parties began advocating revolutions to topple existing orders, antisemites accused Jews ever more with fomenting discord and, behind the scenes, threatening their countries' body politic, most notably with their alleged creation of Marxism, later to be termed Bolshevism and communism.

The dominant antisemitic focus on and image of Jews was not so much centered on the individual Jew and perhaps his immediate environment but instead treated the individual Jew as a stand-in for the collectivity, and then often integrally connected to or visually attached to a symbol for one or another of these larger systems of the public sphere and society, economy, or politics. Perhaps the foremost figure and image of this era was the Jewish banker, and specifically the banking Rothschild family, whom antisemites held as an article of faith to be nefariously controlling governments, economies, and countries, particularly as branches of the family and its banks were in London, Paris, Vienna, and Milan. From the sly local money-lender of medieval times emerged the manipulative behind-the-scenes national and even international Jewish financier, epitomized in the person, imbued with mythological powers and deeds, of Rothschild.

In the global age, the cunning Jew of modernity concentrating on the larger systems of countries comes out from behind the curtain to take his predatory place boldly, beyond the domestic concerns of economy, society, and politics on the international stage. To be sure, one article of faith remains: that Jews control the media, a staple of antisemites the world over, and another article of faith for a sizable percentage of antisemites remains the medieval calumny that Jews are implicated in the murder of God or their failed murderous attempt against his greatest emissary Muhammad. But neither of them — nor the many other accusations, some holdovers from the past, some new — is as prominent as or more paradigmatic of global antisemitism than that of the armed, powerful, predatory, nakedly bloodthirsty Jew and Jewry crushing others, especially Palestinians, under the boot.

The fundamental shift that antisemites have made that now undergirds and shapes the global antisemitic discourse is threefold. Jews no longer appear to be what they are not, which was a meek obsequious people, when all along they had been cunning and dangerous sources of evil. Today, they are depicted as being brazenly open about their predations, asserting without shame that it is their right to use their power for their nefarious ends, and willfully defying others when they do. Jews are seen to exist and operate most significantly not next door in a nation's capital but mainly in the international arena, thereby targeting and disrupting many countries, the entire Middle East, and the world community itself. Finally, while Jews in the past all but exclusively used covert means to execute their plans, they now augment their even more powerful hidden conspiracy, which is fully internationalized, with an openly powerful and militarized side and are said to think nothing of perpetrating violence and openly seeking domination and dominion.

The antisemites' shift in focus to the international scene is highly significant. The antisemitic discourse has always had domestic and international components. Antisemites who prior to global antisemitism, and this cannot be said too frequently, used to be the vast majority of Europeans, first as Christian antisemites and then as modern antisemites, and used to be the vast majority of Muslims, had always considered Jews living within their communities to pose danger. They were also concerned with Jews beyond their borders because antisemites understood Jews to be colluding, aiding, and plotting with each other. Partly this reflected Jews' dispersed existence around the world, living wherever they could in a diaspora not of their own making, and in iterative and local diasporas not of their own making as Christians in particular expelled them from their homes, cities, and regions time and again. But also it bespoke the conception of Jews as an enemy people living among the nations, and among the Christian or Muslim nations, and, especially in Christian antisemitic demonology, their service to the devil who worked his evil the world over. As a force for cosmic evil, the Jews endangered others everywhere and from everywhere. In modern times, this dual focus of domestic concerns and international concerns continued to be evident in the antisemitic discourse and among antisemites. Rothschilds and other Jewish bankers worked internationally, and the *Protocols of the Elders of Zion* was concocted and became a sensation during this period, precisely because it seemed to reveal for the first time the inner workings of the alleged international Jewish conspiracy. All this being so, aside from the leadership of the transnational institution of the Catholic Church situated in the Vatican, which has always been concerned with the international dimension of its one-sided struggle against Jews, the concern of antisemites historically has always been principally with antisemitism's domestic component, with local, regional, and national Jews. In medieval and in modern times, Polish antisemites have been overwhelmingly concerned with Polish Jews. French antisemites with French Jews. Italian antisemites with Italian Jews. Russian antisemites with Russian Jews. Persian antisemites with Persian Jews. Egyptian antisemites with Egyptian Jews. Antisemites everywhere focused overwhelmingly on the Jews next door, who might be cheating them, poisoning the wells, defiling the host (the wafer or bread that symbolizes and is treated as if it is Jesus' body), violating the village's women, and threatening to kidnap its children for their blood. As people's orientation broadened with modernity's advent to include a strong regional and national consciousness, antisemites' concerns remained mainly domestic though expansively so, leading them to worry about how Jews were compromising and harming a country's or a people's social and cultural purity, its economy, its public discourse, and its national security.

This overwhelmingly domestic orientation also characterized German antisemites during medieval times and into the modern era. Interestingly, among Germans, and principally among them, a shift began to be made, especially after World War I with the Nazis' focus on the international arena. The twofold reason for this altered orientation is clear: the Germans had suffered a crushing defeat at the hands of an international coalition in World War I, and an even more crushing peace at Versailles, crippling the German economy, hemming in its power, and humiliating its people as the people of no other great power had ever been treated. So German antisemites' gaze widened to include critically the international realm as part of their own. But it was not just that the effect of the international arena was so acutely felt in Germany, it was also that Germans under the Nazis knew that they stood against the world's major powers while they aspired to establish their own European, if not world, domination. So Germans' concern with the Jews' alleged threat took on greater international dimensions. This concern also reflected the cosmic vision that was especially strong in the German antisemitic discourse that held the Jews to be intent on destroying or subjugating humanity, not to mention the German people, which Germans considered to be humanity's flower and thus making them the special target of Jews everywhere.

Global antisemitism has shifted the domestic-international balance. As a result, the so-called Jewish Problem as a domestic national issue is all but dead among one once domestically obsessed antisemitic people after another. It is even all but absent in countries today that continue to be imbued with many antisemites, many of whom remain obsessed with fantastical tales of nefarious Jews, their power, and their predations. This includes a bevy of countries that had once been consumed by the so-called Jewish Problem. The notion today that French Jews or German Jews or Polish Jews or, for that matter, Moroccan Jews or Syrian Jews are cheating their neighbors, poisoning the wells, defiling the host, violating local women, and threatening to kidnap children for their blood, or that they are wrecking local economies, destroying the mores of a country's citizens, or threatening to undermine let alone weaken or destroy a country's people, its identity, or purity or any updated equivalents of these (Hungarians notwithstanding) is barely discernible or certainly not powerful even among antisemites. The danger not only comes from without but takes place beyond the borders of people's own countries. In fact, making such age-old accusations about the domestic predations of one's own country's Jews is all but taboo in many countries and all but absent from the public sphere and certainly from its discourse about Jews, and not merely because it is a taboo. Antisemites in most countries, Hungary being an exception, simply do not have such concerns about the supposed domestic predations of their countries' Jews — certainly not in any considerable way. French Jews are off limits in France. German Jews are off limits in Germany. Polish Jews are off limits in Poland. Danish Jews are off limits in Denmark. Even, few as they are, Moroccan Jews and Syrian Jews are off limits in Morocco and Syria. As the world has become globalized, so too has the focus of the antisemitic discourse and of antisemites themselves.

This shift has been no doubt facilitated in Europe by the Holocaust's horrors, so that people leveling in public medieval or modern antisemitic accusations at their own country's Jews would cast the tint and the taint of Nazism and its horrors upon themselves, but more is behind this transformation than that. Such accusations simply are in most places not plausible today, given these countries' democratic dispensation, the vastly better understanding people have about the workings of society, economy, and politics, the transparency created by intensively focused and ubiquitous, and even pluralistic media, and their peoples' reeducation. Yes, the animus toward Jews remains and the foundational antisemitic paradigm remains, including the belief in the Jews' malignant character, so in order to find an outlet antisemitism has shifted to the international scene. There it finds a far more plausible context and principal object for its attention — Israel — and for constructing a largely novel public discourse with a new, satisfying, and believed-in litany of accusations against Israel, its Jews, and by extension Jews around the world. The Jew, in the antisemitic imagination, has been reconstituted yet again, this time with the dominant image of a machine-gun-wielding killer.

Shylock, through Rothschild, has morphed into Rambo.

Global antisemitism is an amalgam of new elements and old ones, sometimes in their age-old forms and sometimes in transformed, modernized, or globalized forms. The *Protocols of the Elders of Zion,* the turn-of-the-nineteenth-to-twentieth-centuries' fabricated minutes of the meetings of an international Jewish conspiracy, which was concocted by agents of the Russian Czarist secret police living in Paris, details the plans and activities of the unnamed shadowy "elders of Zion," minions of the Antichrist who seek, among other evils, to subvert the morals of gentiles, weaken their societies, subvert their economies, control the media, foment religious conflict, in sum to subjugate and rule over humanity. Its twenty-four chapters include "The Destruction of Religion as a Prelude to the Rise of the Jewish God," "The Kingdom of the Press and Control," "Economic War and Disorganization Lead to International Government," "Methods of Conquest," and the final chapter, "The Jewish Ruler."[23]

The *Protocols,* despite having been proven to be a fabrication almost one hundred years ago, lives on in a transmogrified global form. Actually, the *Protocols* does not merely live on but has been resurrected almost from the dead, and pumped up to monstrous proportions far outstripping its reach and stature during its initial heyday. Its transformation and significance today both express much about the nature of global antisemitism and constitute one of its essential elements.

In recent decades, the *Protocols* has been published and republished in countless languages and editions around the world. Its accusations have become standard fare of antisemitic discourses the world over and have been endorsed or had their arguments appropriated by major political, religious, and opinion leaders in all parts of the world.

The *Protocols* has become a bestseller in country after country and has been prominently displayed together with a panoply of antisemitic books at the Iranian booth at the world-leading Frankfurt Book Fair. It has been available as apps from the Apple Store and Google Play. It has inspired works in various media—books, magazines, television series,

*Six versions of* The Protocols: *Egyptian, 1951 and 2003; Syrian, 2005; Japanese; Russian, 1992; and English, 2011.*

film, video, and, of course, the Internet, including on YouTube — that are directly based on it. Egyptian television and stations throughout the Middle East have repeatedly aired *Horseman Without A Horse,* a forty-part antisemitic television series based on the *Protocols.* Iranian TV has broadcast its documentary *The Secret of Armageddon,* which repeatedly grounds its account in the *Protocols.* It closes by telling the public that "There is a genocidal Zionist Jewish plan for the genocide of humanity at the hand of the Zionist Jew-boys. Even though the Jew-boys sometimes talk about a 'Greater Israel,' their real goal is world domination," and earlier explains, "What is known worldwide today as *The Protocols of the Elders of Zion* contains the plans and policies of the elders of this sect to conquer the world and establish a global Jewish government, the *Protocols* as the basis for this plan."[24]

The *Protocols'* reach in numbers and influence today, in the demonology it promotes and sustains, far outstrips that of the past. Although there are no hard figures, it may be the case that the *Protocols* is one of the world's all-time leading bestsellers. In today's demonology, the *Protocols* has probably, almost certainly supplanted the Talmud, for centuries the leading textual target of antisemites, as the allegedly demonic text of choice that reveals the essence of Jews and Jewness, their malevolent intentions, and the threat they pose to others.

Why has such a rank fabrication come to take on international antisemitic totemic status? Given global antisemitism's international focus, it is the emblematic and by far best-known document that antisemites can point to that is international in focus. It is the emblematic and by far the best-known document, international in focus, that is also political in orientation. It supposedly reveals a devilish international conspiracy on the part of international Jewry that threatens the entire world, that taps into the notion that Zionism and Israel are sinister, global menaces. It helps make sense of how Israel and American Jews, and the Jews of other countries, have been able to work behind the scenes to garner the American superpower's seemingly slavish support for Israel, and how tiny Israel has managed to overcome the collective efforts of the vast Arab and Islamic world, in a manner that lessens the otherwise humiliating commentary on the state of the Arab and Islamic countries and peoples. In the Arab and Islamic world, it plays into and feeds the myriad conspiracy theories that exist about Jews and Israel, which run the gamut of plans from the macro to the micro and everything in between, from destroying Islam to blowing up the Al Aqsa Mosque in Jerusalem to secretly controlling the United States and other Western powers to being responsible for 9/11 to killing Arab men's sperm with hormone-laden fruit. For people who cannot understand how this supposedly servile and weak people, the Jews, have prevailed in establishing and maintaining their Israel in the heart of the Arab and Islamic world, or for people who do not want to face the facts that make this actually easy to understand, a penchant for seeking explanations in hidden forces and nefarious networks is not surprising. And when a blue-chip document in the words of the evildoers themselves lays out the foundation of such a conspiracy, indeed of the mother of all such conspiracies, and explains, building upon the foundational antisemitic paradigm, how the enemy

Jews orchestrate it all, it is no surprise that that document has become an antisemitic greatest hit, a go-to text that has gained more currency than any other modern or contemporary one.

A Spanish edition of the *Protocols* visually conveys the usefulness of its demonology to contemporary antisemites, who, focusing on the international and multifarious character of the shape-shifting Jews, can read into it anything and everything they want: Symbolically, it presents the immense power of the Jews, with global finance, Christianity, Nazism, communism, and the Freemasons (who stand in also for atheism) each a finger of the hand controlled by the David Star.

The *Protocols* is explicitly cited in Hamas' charter, perhaps the leading contemporary antisemitic Arab and Islamic statement of the widespread desire and intent to eliminate Israel and kill Jews: "Today it is Palestine and tomorrow it may be another country or other countries. For Zionist scheming has no end, and after Palestine they will covet expansion from the Nile to the Euphrates. Only when they have completed digesting the area on which they will have laid their hand, they will look forward to more expansion, etc. Their scheme has been laid out in the Protocols of the Elders of Zion, and their present [conduct] is the best proof of what is said there."[25] As with Hamas, for Arab and

*Spanish edition of* The Protocols, *2005.*

Islamic discourses, while the Qur'an and Hadith supply the foundational antisemitic paradigm and explain the essential nature of Jews, as well as lay out the religious justification and mandate for slaughtering Jews, the *Protocols* is the master document of the Jews' deviltry, their general and specific intentions and the means that they employ to achieve them. The *Protocols,* building upon and reinforcing the foundational antisemitic paradigm, creates an elaborate framework for understanding the Jews' assault on Arabs and Muslims, their countries, and their Islam.

With regard to the *Protocols,* Hamas' bitter rival, the Palestinian Authority, typically characterized as more moderate, is not to be outdone in its antisemitism. The Palestinian Authority explicitly and implicitly refers to the *Protocols* in its accounts and explanations of Israel's and the Jews' nature and deeds, both in Israel's and the Jews' overall agendas and in explaining particulars, Israel and Jews forming in such distinctions a unity. Because the *Protocols* provides the template to justify any kind of conspiratorial act, to believe that with regard to Israel and Jews all appearances can be deceptive, and that the reach and cleverness of Jews' sinister machinations is boundless, the Palestinian authority, its leaders, and ordinary Palestinians can and do regularly understand Israel's initiatives and deeds in the light that the *Protocols* seems to cast on them.

In 2001, the Palestinian Authority's largest newspaper, *Al-Quds,* explained how the Jews were implementing the long-term strategic plan laid down in the *Protocols* with an astonishingly extensive time horizon and military-like precision:

Remember history, Oh Arabs!
1. In 1897 the first Zionist Congress was held in Basel.
2. In 1907 the actual immigration operation began.
3. In 1917 the woeful declaration of Balfour was made.
4. In 1977 the visit which shocked the Arab Nation occurred, the President of Egypt visited Israel.
Every 10 years, a vital aim is achieved. These are *The Protocols of the Elders of Zion,* of a century, from 1897 till 1997. They have planned and accomplished. Every 10 years, another aim was achieved, proving their continuity and their power.

In 2013, the Palestinian Ma'an news agency carried a piece by the director of the Palestinian Center for Research and Cultural Dialogue that explained that the depravity laid out in the *Protocols* extends well beyond its local catastrophic effects for Palestinians and Arabs:

> The Protocols of the Elders of Zion are a kind of plan formulated by the Jews to infiltrate the world and take it over. While many Jewish leaders claim that they (the Protocols) are a forgery and one of the greatest political fabrications of the modern era, others confirm that they are true and that they are the most dangerous plot of global domination that history has ever known. The first protocol calls for the spread of anarchy and wars. The second protocol calls for a takeover of government, education, and the press. The fourth protocol calls for a takeover of trade and the destruction of religion — especially Christianity. While the seventh protocol calls to instigate global wars, the ninth lays out plans to destroy moral values and dispatch agents.
>
> Now, after this quick review of a few of these protocols, one wonders if the Jews belong to some other kind of human species, different from other nations. From where does all this evil and destructive energy derive? Do all the other nations deserve all this evil and hostility, just so that Jews may control them? Do all nations other than Jews really have clouded minds? Have most of the things that appear in the Protocols been implemented in the West and in the East? Did the idea of a Jewish world government begin to be carried out towards the end of the last century? And does the US rule the world today in the name of the new world order for the benefit of the Jews, in accordance with these Protocols? Are we on the brink of the establishment of an evident Jewish world government? Until we have answers to these questions and ponderings — as well as others — we say, "May Allah help us, we the children of Palestine."

Dehumanization ("some other kind of human species"), demonization, unmatched power and threat, all woven into a discussion of the *Protocols,* which is "true."

These are the sorts of views that issue from Palestinian Authority leaders and in the newspapers and television that they control. Such statements invoke and allude to the *Protocols,* which is a well-known

Palestinian, Arab, and Islamic cultural reference point, to instruct and explain, to intensify and spread antisemitism, and to justify any and all resistance to Israel and to Jews. And not just in the present moment but for future generations. In 2004, the Palestinian Ministry of Education published a high school textbook that unlocks the foundational secret of Zionism that Jews established at the First Zionist Congress in 1897: "There is a group of confidential resolutions adopted by the [First Zionist] Congress and known by the name 'The Protocols of the Elders of Zion,' the goal of which was world domination."[26]

In addition to the continuous stream of references to the *Protocols,* the regular invocation of its real or alleged contents in speeches, sermons, and writings in the Arab and Islamic worlds, which has exposed and continues to expose hundreds of millions of people to its contents again and again, in explicit and coded form, it is endorsed or appropriated or followed in open or disguised form the world over. The longtime prime minister of Malaysia, Mahathir Mohamad, endorsed and distributed it. Bishop Richard Williamson, the notorious and influential Catholic antisemite, rehabilitated by Pope Benedict XVI, who has accused Jews of devil worship and of seeking world domination "to prepare the Anti-Christ's throne in Jerusalem," in 2000 declared, "God put into men's hands the Protocols of the Sages of Sion, if men want to know the truth, but few do." Perhaps the leading leftist peace advocate in the world, Johan Galtung has championed the *Protocols,* holding an open forum on it at the University of Oslo. In China huge bestsellers, called *The Currency Wars* and two sequels, which have sold millions of copies, are based on the *Protocols.* They cast the Jews as responsible for the Western financial crisis of 2008 as well as many other financial and economic crises, especially in Asia. Japan, already beginning in the 1980s, has seen a spate of *Protocols* bestsellers, including *The Jewish Plot to Control the World, The Expert Way of Reading the Jewish Protocols,* and *The Secret of Jewish Power That Moves the World,* written by eminent people, including one member of parliament. Japanese also receive specific warnings about the Jews' predations, including when the large circulation mainstream magazine *Weekly Post* explained that the recent decline in the Japanese stock market was the work of "the Jews" who were "poised to destroy the Japanese economy whenever they desire." In the United States, *The Israel Lobby* and many less respectable screeds either echo its antisemitic tropes or openly adopt them.[27] From the religious right to the secular left to political Islamists across the Middle East and beyond, from rising power China to the established powers of Japan and the United States, the *Protocols* are used as a guide to the Jews' sinister nature, plans and actions for global domination, and danger. In the internationalized world of global antisemitism, what was once a minor theme in the antisemitic guidebook, the international dimension of the Jewish threat, has become its principal focus. The *Protocols'* growth in centrality and its having spread from its initial reach in parts of Europe to the entire globe today, making it more central now to the world's antisemitism than it ever was, provides a template and rich content for a good part of global antisemitism.

Global antisemitism has brought together from antisemitism's three eras and incarnations each of the major elements of *where* and *how* the Jews operate. It casts Jews in each of the two oppositional roles and locales and also conjoins them to a seamless and deadly image of the Jews' conduct and threat. Jews are, mainly in the United States and also in Britain, string pullers and puppeteers *and* they are, in Israel, the executioners. Jews in Israel and around the world are the authors of evil *and,* in Israel, are the agents of others, namely the West. Jews, in those few places where national policy is supportive of Israel, principally in the United States, operate domestically to corrupt and capture the politics and undermine the well-being of the nation, and they cause suffering and misery in the international arena, on the world stage. There has long been an explicit or implicit notion among antisemites that the Jews operate effectively because, among other reasons, a division of malfeasant labor exists among them. Nazism held and many Germans believed that the Jews both created and controlled Bolshevism and therefore ruled the Soviet Union and simultaneously pulled the levers of capitalism, especially in the United States. In the antisemites' minds these two seemingly antagonistic ideologies, regimes, and countries were not antagonistic at all when one understood, as German antisemites did, that these were but two faces of the same attempt to undermine, enslave, and destroy the German people and, by extension, humanity. Jews used Bolshevism to produce revolution from below. They used capitalism to undermine the wholesomeness and independence of the German people from above. And politically and geostrategically, the Jews would use these two countries as a pincer movement against Germany, situated between them. Antisemites, supple in their mental and emotional gymnastics, the latter contributing to the former, have demonstrated through the ages a remarkable flexibility in making oppositions and seeming contradictions disappear when it comes to Jews. One might have objected to the Nazified antisemite in 1938 by saying: "Jews can't be both behind Bolshevism and supposedly destructive capitalism, for these two systems are mortal enemies. The claim makes no sense." The antisemite would reply: "Yes, they can, and you can see it once you understand the essence of Jewness and how Jewry works. Whatever the superficial appearances and the theater of opposition the Jews stage, both systems are evil, and both are tools to subjugate, enslave, or destroy peoples and humanity. They are simply different means—all the cleverer and more effective in their seeming antagonism with one another—that the Jews have created to achieve the same goals." Today's antisemites, particularly those in the Arab and Islamic worlds, have no difficulties holding similar oppositions and contradictions in mind, especially because the Jews, always cunning and flexible, are capable of pursuing different strategies at once and morphing, as needed, from one form to another and one technique to another. Malaysia's Prime Minister Mohamad, who holds the Jews of Israel to be vicious and murderous themselves, is impressed also with their behind-the-scenes cunning. As he declared to the assembled leaders of many of the world's countries at the Organization of the Islamic Conference summit in 2003, "The Europeans killed 6m Jews out of 12m, but today the Jews rule the world by proxy. They get others to fight and die for them." Imagine a country's prime minister saying this about any other group—and implying as he did that Jews are trying to "wipe out" 1.3 billion Muslims—at a summit of world leaders.[28]

Deeming the Jews openly murderous and stealthily manipulating others to perpetrate great crimes is, of course, a classic case of projection, as the only people showing such flexibility of mind and tactics are the antisemites, in their seemingly limitless capacity to alter and augment their conception of and accusations against Jews and in their willingness to use the range of means available, from defamation to destruction, in order to combat, curtail, or eliminate them. And the more global the stage, the more arenas that the Jews are seen to affect, the more people of different countries, subcultures and groups, differing politics and orientations, different religions, different kinds of institutional affiliations, and different media and means of expression coalesce loosely or in a coordinated fashion, the more that this flexibility on top of the fundamental coherence is in evidence regarding antisemites' beliefs, passions, and intentions regarding Jews.

Global antisemitism is something radically new *and* is something deeply rooted in past antisemitisms. Its new features are distinctive, both in that some of them never existed before and in that the weight of others of them is magnified beyond anything in the past. It has multifarious and seemingly contradictory features, *and* it is stable and structured in its core, overcoming or lending an underlying unity to those contradictions. Global antisemitism is many streams and varieties of antisemitism, *and* it is one thing that adheres, in an updated version, to the foundational antisemitic paradigm that the ancient Christians forged but that has long been independent of its Christian roots: Jews are (1) different, (2) noxious and malevolent, a threat to goodness, so (3) they must be combated, curtailed, and defeated, and (4) the source of their danger being their Jewness must (5) ultimately be eliminated, and for many that means, (6) the Jews themselves.

# 10

# Today's Demonology

GLOBAL ANTISEMITISM IS new and distinctive. Its real nature and its many features have been barely discerned, and poorly if at all understood. It is antisemitism's third major type. We have seen how and why it has come to be. How it is, as antisemitism always is, embedded in its social, cultural, and political context, namely that of a globalized world. What its essential features are. And how they and antisemitism generally relate to antisemitism's previous forms. Having now acquired this foundation, we can begin a more extensive treatment of global antisemitism's nature, spread, variants, and power. Beyond these, we can explore global antisemitism's cultural, institutional, and political sources, the purposes it serves for various peoples and groups, how antisemites spread their beliefs and animus to larger publics the world over, and global antisemitism's ideals, intentions, and programs.

Global antisemitism is built upon the foundational antisemitic paradigm, with various kinds, or worlds, of antisemitism embedded in and shaped by its global contours, and with these various worlds of antisemitism in substantial part continuing their previous antisemitic lives while also being continually altered as they intermesh and include new antisemitic features, which have emerged as a response to our global world's changed nature. I take up each of the worlds of global antisemitism in turn, devoting different amounts of space to them, depending on their size, complexity, and centrality.

Arab and Islamic antisemitism is the juggernaut among the worlds of antisemitism that compose today's global scourge. I use the dual terms Arab and Islamic because they overlap greatly without being congruent. Most *Arab* antisemites are Muslims and are informed by Islamic thought on this and related subjects. Yet some have been secular, notably Palestinians; some are Christians, such as Copts in Egypt, Lebanese Christians, and Syrian Orthodox. The core of, though probably not most, *Islamic* antisemites are Arabs and live in Arab countries. Certainly the hotbed, the impassioned and devoted heart of Islamic antisemitism is in the Arab world. Many Islamic antisemites are not Arabs, most notably Iranians who are mainly Persians, though this is also true of other Muslims around the world, from Pakistanis to Turks to Indonesians to Americans. Because of this intertwining, I use a hybrid category of *Arab and Islamic* to describe antisemitism and antisemites, which should always be understood *not* to encompass all Arabs or all Muslims, and *not* to imply that their overlap is complete.

Many of the Arab and Islamic governments and movements that espouse antisemitism are politically Islamic. It should be clear that when I discuss political Islam I refer not to Islam itself or to the bringing of ethical values grounded in Islam into politics, unless I explicitly say otherwise. Political Islam is a *political* movement that grounds itself in an orthodox reading of Islam, much of it encapsulated by the Islamic law Sharia. Political Islamists seek political power and have gained power in many predominantly Islamic countries. They are devoted above all to collapsing the distinction between politics and the Muslim religion. They want their movements, parties, countries, and ultimately the world to be governed — politically, legally, socially, culturally, and morally — according to a strict or fundamentalist reading of Islam. And they consecrate their politics as being Allah's will, to which slavish, indeed mindless, devotion is due. They are totalitarian in organization and aspiration, seeking to compel Muslims to live, in public and in private, according to their uncompromising understanding of Islam. Augmenting these defining qualities of political Islam are several other features that can be found in political Islamic movements to a greater or lesser degree: political Islam and its adherents are highly aggressive. They espouse using violence to attain their ends even when downplaying or denying this for tactical electoral reasons. (As the Muslim

Brotherhood, the longtime political Islamic movement and now powerful political party in Egypt, with branches across the Middle East, declares emphatically and without equivocation: "The *Jihad* is our way and death for Allah is our most lofty wish.") Political Islamists are often animated by a culture of death, glorifying killing people in large numbers, reveling in imagining how they will do it and the suffering of their victims, and glorifying also dying for the cause. Political Islam and political Islamists—including the aforementioned Muslim Brotherhood in Egypt, Hamas, the Palestinian Authority, Hezbollah, the powerful Saudi clerics and their followers, Ahmadinejad and the clerics who run Iran, and many others in Islamic countries around the world— are centrally animated by a demonized account of the Jews that holds them to be one of the political Islamists' principal enemies and impediments to realizing their goals. The coarseness and violence of such annihilative movements undoubtedly loosens inhibitions regarding Jews. This is amplified by a prospective triumphalism of killing and dying encapsulated by the political Islamists' oft-repeated notion that the Jews will be defeated and destroyed because *Jews do not love death, but we love death* — that is, that Jews are too cowardly to commit the necessary sacrifice. The violence of political Islamists' antisemitism surely reinforces the movements' general culture of death.

The resources within Islam itself to think badly of Jews, regardless of a Muslim's broader politics, are extensive. It has become a commonplace of the Islamic tradition and contemporary Islamic thinking, intoned repeatedly, that Allah, as punishment for their transgressions, turned Jews into pigs and apes, which thereby presents Jews as not being human beings. Why would such a dehumanizing notion become so widespread? Because it says so in the Qur'an, the literal and infallible word of Allah. It asserts this there not just once but, so that there is no mistaking it, in three separate sections. The prophet Muhammad, speaking of the Jews, tells all Muslims: "Shall I tell you who deserves a worse punishment from God than [the one you wish upon] us? Those God distanced from Himself, was angry with, and condemned as apes and pigs, and those who worship idols: they are worse in rank and have strayed further from the right path." Later in the Qur'an, Muhammad goes beyond explaining the Jews' immediate fate for their supposed disobedience against Allah to decree what Allah wills be done to them: "When, in their arrogance, they [the Jews] persisted in doing what they had been forbidden to do, We said to them, 'Be like apes! Be outcasts!' And then your Lord declared that, until the Day of Resurrection, He would send people against them to inflict terrible suffering on them."[1] Muhammad is clear: Allah's emissaries will make Jews on this earth suffer. And who but Muslims are his emissaries? Who but Muslims are to carry out his will?

We should pause and dwell on this. Consider that this world religion's sacred scripture, which on more than one occasion refers to Jews as being or being turned into pigs or apes, is steadily asserted or interpreted to say that Jews today actually *are* the offspring of pigs and apes. Then realize that certainly hundreds of millions of the 1.3 billion Muslims in the world actually believe that the Qur'an is the word of God and true in its every word. And then realize that this passage about Jews not being human beings is quoted again and again, is elaborated upon again and again in Islamic religious and political discourse, so much so that it becomes a standard trope, even more a cardinal point of discourse, and is turned into a touchstone of dehumanizing and eliminationist polemics against Jews again and again, seemingly continuously, in the public denunciations of Jews in mosques by Muslim leaders and preachers, in written and oral interpretations of sacred texts and traditions, and in the hortatory words of contemporary religious and political guides to the social world and politics. The Imam of the Al-Haram mosque in Mecca, Sheikh Abd Al-Rahman Al-Sudayis, explained in a 2001 sermon what the Qur'an and the Islamic tradition teach Muslims:

> Brothers in faith, what do our *Qur'an* and our Sunna [Hadith] say? What does our belief say? What does our history prove...? They show clearly that the conflict between us and the Jews is one of belief, identity, and existence...
>
> Read history and you will understand that the Jews of yesterday are the evil forefathers of the even more evil Jews of today: infidels, falsifiers of words, calf worshippers, prophet murderers, deniers of prophecies...the scum of the human race, accursed by Allah, who turned them into apes and pigs...These are the Jews—an ongoing continuum of deceit, obstinacy, licentiousness, evil, and corruption."[2]

Jews being apes and pigs, or their descendants or their brothers, is Islamic public discourse's staple. It is the Jews' Jewness that makes them the enemies of Islam. It is the Jews' *belief,* so what they profess. It is also their *identity,* so what they choose to be. And it is their *existence,* so their very life on earth. All are wrapped into one ball of evil, their Jewness. In Arab and Islamic public discourse, such notions are regularly conveyed, proclaimed, sermonized, broadcast, and exhorted. At Friday prayers. In books, pamphlets, and newspapers. On television. On the Internet. By political leaders. By religious leaders. By political religious leaders and movements.

As Al-Sudayis elaborates in a manner that is extremely common and the norm in the Arab and Islamic worlds, the Qur'an also casts the Jews as an evil danger. The Qur'an and Islamic tradition presents Jews as Muhammad's fearful enemy, asserting that they sought several times to kill Muhammad (including by poisoning him) and repeatedly asserting that the Jews killed Allah's prophets. Jews, according to the Qur'an, are not just enemies but treacherous ones. They betrayed their alliance with Muhammad. They killed Allah's prophets who were sent to them in good faith. They lie. They reject the truth. They are untrustworthy. The Qur'an explains about the Jews: "Disbelievers have ended up with wrath upon wrath, and a humiliating torment awaits them. When it is said to them, 'Believe in God's revelations,' they reply, 'We believe in what was revealed to us,' but they do not believe in what came afterwards, though it is the truth confirming what they already have. Say [Muhammad](*sic*), 'Why did you kill God's prophets in the past if you were true believers?'"[3] This passage and its account of Jews is picked up and embellished upon also by religious and political leaders and in the same places and media, over and over again: the Jews are the murderers of God's prophets.

The Qur'an both powerfully dehumanizes Jews and powerfully demonizes Jews, which is evident in Al-Sudayis' religious sermon to the faithful, which is typical, indeed run-of-the-mill, for the Islamic world. Such simultaneous demonization and dehumanization is a rare combination in prejudice's history that I have shown in my previous book *Worse Than War* to be a dangerously eliminationist—exterminationist and genocidal in potential—complex of beliefs with the associated passions that accompany them.[4] In a central moment in the Qur'an's story of Muhammad, Muhammad is the target of an alleged assassination plot on the part of *only a few Jews* who by their acts reveal what is concluded to be the essence of Jewness. In response, Muhammad punishes not only those Jews but—as the essence of Jewness had been determined—also eliminates from his realm, through expulsion, two entire tribes of Jews, and sells the women and children of a third tribe of Jews into slavery while mass murdering its men. He thereby sets an eliminationist and mass-murderous example that is both hardly lost on contemporary Arab and Islamic antisemites and, as are all Muhammad's deeds, seen as a model to emulate. Indeed, regarding Jews one of the most quoted elements today of the Islamic interpretive tradition is the commandment to kill Jews, grounded in the Hadithic account of Jews: "The Day of Judgment will not come about until Muslims fight the Jews (killing the Jews), when the Jew will hide behind stones and trees. The stones and trees will say O Muslims, O Abdulla, there is a Jew behind me, come and kill him. Only the Gharkad tree would not do that because it is one of the trees of the Jews." Thus Islam's scripture and sacred texts, and its sacred Hadithic tradition, prominently contain notions about Jews that close the eliminationist and exterminationist circle: (1) an account of their nonhuman nature; (2) an alarming account of their demonic perniciousness and potential threat; (3) the exhortation to fulfill Allah's wish that the campaign against the Jews, including to make them suffer, never stops; (4) an eliminationist program for solving the putative problem of the Jews; with (5) a powerful example and model of Islam's holiest person, the Prophet, having put into practice, with righteousness, such an eliminationist and annihilationist program; and thereby (6) a model showing the way for Allah's and Muhammad's faithful today.

The Qur'an's and Hadith's treatment of Jews is horrifying, grounded in the foundational antisemitic paradigm, and provides the foundation for the Arab and Islamic world's profound antisemitism. Nevertheless, the Qur'an's stance toward Jews—as bad as it is—is not in any reasonable sense equivalent to the Christian bible's casting of Jews as the central villains in the story of Jesus' life, mission, attempt to save humanity, and death. The Qur'an neither accords the Jews such a place nor turns them into the villainous fulcrum for Islam around which for Christianity much of the Jesus story turns nor makes them responsible for humanity's greatest loss, that of Jesus' life on earth. Although it would be hard for a Christian who takes the gospels as God's word, or who simply believes their content's essential truth, to come away from the Christian bible with anything less than at least a highly prejudicial image of Jews of the time, if not of all time, the place of Jews in the Qur'an and the far less frequent and far less intensive and damning (in sum) treatment of them makes such a prejudicial outcome not as likely for the Qur'an's readers. Also, the Qur'an is not devoid of positive statements about Jews and Allah's and Muslims' attitudes toward them, such as that the Jews are also the people of the book, and if they follow God they too can be rewarded by God. And Islam did offer Jews a legal protective status that Christianity decidedly did not, which helps explain Muslims' overall comparatively better treatment of Jews over the centuries. But in sum, the Qur'an's and the Hadith's account of Jews remains damning and, more relevant to today's antisemitism, provides the resources for Qur'anic and Hadithic, meaning Godly, consecration of a dehumanizing and demonizing view of, and consecration of antisemitic assaults on, Jews, whether verbal or physical. Piecing its pieces together, as many Muslim leaders, clerics, and media have done, the following logic can be, and is often, smoothly laid out.

Jews knew Allah. They, because of their stubborn, arrogant, deceitful, and mendacious character, rejected him. Jews are cursed for doing so. Knowing this, they persist in their rejection of him. Jews betrayed and fought Muhammad and injured and killed God's emissaries, his apostles. As a consequence, Jews will be banished from heaven. Jews may be or should be expelled from Muslim lands. Jews are to be killed. That they are apes' and pigs' children or relations both encourages such an outcome and lifts ordinary inhibitions against such radical treatment. Some of this is in the Qur'an, taken as God's literal words. Some of it is in the Islamic tradition. It has a formal body of written thought — in the Hadith, the early biographies of Muhammad called the Sira, and early Muslim jurists, theologians, and scholars — with a firm status, making it almost as influential as the Qur'an itself. This is augmented by additional defaming and incendiary material about Jews, including the early narrative and putatively historical accounts of Muhammad's life (and others), which recount a more elaborate narrative of the Jews' transgressions and malevolence and which powerfully fuel, with their additional and often still better resources, this antisemitic—indeed, eliminationist—orientation toward Jews. These are laced with additional damaging and demonizing constructs of Jews, including the Jews' intimate connection to the Dajjâl, the Muslims' Antichrist. The Dajjâl, in the days before the resurrection and last judgment, will appear accompanied by seventy thousand armed Jews who stand ready as his soldiers of evil. The Dajjâl himself is sometimes described as Jewish, but, no matter his origins, when he is defeated on the battlefield Allah's faithful will exterminate his Jewish minions.[5]

Political Islamic antisemites and Islamic antisemites alike draw upon these antisemitic notions and resources within Islam almost reflexively and as standard fare. Thus, antisemitism liberally exists within and structures both the general Arab and Islamic public discourses about Jews as well as the more particular political Islamic ones. These two discourses also overlap and in some places are all but one and the same; indeed political Islamists are aware that it is on this issue of the Jews' perniciousness, and with the mobilization of antisemitic sentiment, that they can win over additional Muslims to their larger political cause. And it is not only political Islamists who have mobilized and who continue to mobilize in such a manner. Leaders of Arab countries and political movements, and the leaders of many non-Arabic Islamic countries and movements—including the most cynical secular dictators, such as Saddam Hussein and Hafez al-Assad—have done so, precisely because antisemitism is so widespread among their peoples that using it politically is a winning formula for keeping power, and not doing so is dangerous, as the antisemitic sentiment and its adherents will be left as a powerful political resource for others, rivals and enemies, to mobilize.

Arab and Islamic antisemitism extends over a vast terrain and is the property of numerous peoples. Many of the people are political Islamists. Many are not. Its essence, nevertheless, is clear, and it has elements grounded in the foundational antisemitic paradigm that structure the prejudice and govern the discourse or discourses.

- The Jews are not a religious, but a corporate group. (Many Arab and Islamic antisemites know that a large percentage of Israel's Jews are secular.) Jews are defined by their identity as Jews, their Jewness, their civilization.

- The Jews are the prophet Muhammad's inveterate enemies.
- The Jews are the vanguard of the West's infiltration of the Arab and Islamic world.
- The Jews occupy holy land (even the enemy Christians cannot muster that).
- Jews are malevolent as a group and as individuals. The Jews are malevolent as Islam's enemies. The Jews are malevolent as the West's vanguard against Islam.
- The Jews seek to destroy Islam.
- The Jews have become militarily powerful and politically powerful. Because they are powerful, the Jews, once deemed merely contemptible for their inherent deceitfulness and treachery, are now extremely pernicious and dangerous.
- Israel (the state) is a confluence of the Jews, the West, and all its putative moral corruption; the weakness of Islam; the perceived occupation of the holy place of Jerusalem and the land around it, which is and should be at the geographic heart of the once and future unbroken Islamic caliphate. Israel thus embodies territorially, socially, in human terms, politically, and militarily so much of what Arabs and Muslims despise.
- Because Israel embodies these diverse and vast elements, which are so resented, despised, and deemed threatening, Arab and Islamic antisemites, and antisemites in the West and elsewhere around the world, can project onto it almost anything that is negative, hateful, or injurious.
- The upshot for many Arab and Islamic antisemites, and practically an article of religious and secular faith among them, is that Israel and its Jews—or among more "moderate" factions, at least the power of the Jews (which would be maintained in a two-state but eventually not in a one-state solution)—must be eliminated.

These notions, and the ways they are interrelated, are elaborated in a host of substantial variations in different Arab and Islamic countries and groups, and within the different streams of the political Islamic and general Islamic discourses that exist in these countries. Given the vast outpouring and the enormous range of antisemitic institutions, organs, groups, and people and their diverse social and political and cultural positioning, not to mention their often differing broader political stances and goals, this is no surprise. But all of them, whatever the diversity of their specific emphases, tropes, and accusations regarding Jews' or Israel's perniciousness, and regarding the nature of Jewness and the need to eliminate it, rest their antisemitism within the discursive paradigm.

Arab and Islamic antisemitism exists in one of its purest forms in Hamas, the popularly elected governing party and political movement in Gaza. Hamas is particularly interesting and instructive because it is Arab, politically Islamic, and at the forefront of conflict with Israel and is populated by, is enormously supported by, and governs people who actually know Israel and Jews. For Hamas and those under its authority, Jews are not the pure phantasms that animate the antisemitic minds and hearts of most of the Arab and Islamic world. Hence, Hamas' opportunity, both institutionally and on the part of its members and supporters, for reality testing might suggest that its understanding of Jews, however antagonistic and hate-filled, would be more reflective not of incantatory antisemitic tropes or a dehumanized and demonized account of Jews and Jewness but of the real human beings they have encountered and even dealt with, often as workers in Israel's economy.

But antisemitism's power is so great that this is not so. Indeed, it is anything but the case. In 2010, speaking to all Palestinians on Al Aqsa TV, the Hamas government's official television station that is thus the main station of Gaza, Hamas' Deputy Minister of Religious Affairs, Abdallah Jarbu', reiterated the reigning understanding of Jews:

> [The Jews] suffer from a mental disorder, because they are thieves and aggressors They want to present themselves to the world as if they have rights, but, in fact, they are foreign bacteria—a microbe unparalleled in the world. It's not me who says this. The Qur'an itself says that they have no parallel: "You shall find the strongest men in enmity to the believers [Muslims] to be the Jews."
>
> May He [Allah] annihilate this filthy people who have neither religion nor conscience. I condemn whoever believes in normalizing relations with them, whoever supports sitting down with them, and whoever believes that they are human beings. They are not human beings. They are not people. They have no religion, no conscience, and no moral values.[6]

In two brief passages, this leading Hamas political figure and official invokes a remarkable density of antisemitic and just plain horrifying tropes and images. He and Hamas (both the government and the social movement for which he speaks) make the Jews malevolent: criminals. Beyond reason and reform: mentally ill. Deceivers: They falsely present themselves to the world, "as if they have rights." Not human beings: foreign bacteria. Singularly dangerous: microbes that are unparalleled in human history. Casts the halo of God over this view of the Jews: the Qur'an says what the Hamas spokesman and religious authority says. Makes them the explicit enemies of Islam and therefore of Allah: Jews are the strongest men in enmity.

Note that the Hamas spokesman does not refrain from drawing the logical conclusions about what Muslims ought to do with the Jews. If a person believes what the first paragraph says about the Jews' nature and menace, then what follows in the second paragraph not only makes sense but seems necessary, normative, and laudatory. For Islamic and Arab antisemites, including their political and religious leaders, this account of and statement about Jews is rather ordinary, unremarkable in its content. It has in its essence and with variations been repeated a figurative million times. I dwell on it to provide a sense of what passes for normal public discourse and policy thinking in Arab and Islamic communities, including and especially among Palestinians in Gaza and the Palestinian Authority regarding Jews. Here is an analogous exhortation offered in Friday prayer by a member of the Palestinian Authority's official Fatwa Council, Sheikh Ahmad Abu Halabiya, who is also the former acting rector of the Islamic University in Gaza. Official Palestinian Authority television broadcast this in October 2001 for all Palestinians to see:

> Have no mercy on the Jews, no matter where they are, in any coun-
> try. Fight them, wherever you are. Wherever you meet them, kill
> them. Wherever you are, kill those Jews and those Americans who
> are like them—and those who stand by them—they are all in one
> trench, against the Arabs and the Muslims—because they estab-
> lished Israel here, in the beating heart of the Arab world, in Pales-
> tine. They created it to be the outpost of their civilization—and the
> vanguard of their army, and to be the sword of the West and of the
> Crusaders, hanging over the necks of the monotheists, the Muslims

in these lands. They wanted the Jews to be their spearhead...Allah, deal with the Jews, your enemies and the enemies of Islam. Deal with the crusaders, and America, and Europe behind them, O Lord of the worlds.[7]

Aside from the common logic of Jews and Jewness being evil, so they must be annihilated, which the Palestinian Authority's Halabiya shares with the authoritative Hamas representative, and with so many other Islamic political and religious leaders, four additional things are worth noting here. This religious and educational luminary inverts the presentational order. He starts with the need to slaughter Jews, which he then grounds by citing their gravest transgressions. Second, he speaks of Jews in general, and everywhere, not merely the Jews of Israel. Third, their principal transgression, aside from being the inveterate enemies of God and Islam, is not that they occupy Palestinian lands but that they "established Israel here, in the beating heart of the Arab world." It is the Jews' very existence, not Israel's policies that, as Palestinian Authority television broadcasts again and again, must be combated. And fourth, whereas the Hamas leader's statement speaks more generally about Allah's will that Jews be destroyed, this Palestinian Authority's leading figure's exhortation is more focused on explicitly mobilizing individual Palestinians and Muslims themselves to kill Jews. This he surely did mean, and surely his words were not understood as idle. Halabiya spoke them in the consecrated setting of Friday prayers, and Palestinian Authority television broadcast them, to mark the one-year anniversary of a mob of Palestinians in Ramallah having lynched two Israeli reservists, mutilated their bodies, and cheered the deeds with celebratory gusto, captured on video. (British photographer Mark Seager, who came upon the scene, recounted, "To my horror, I saw that it was a body, a man they were dragging by the feet. The lower part of his body was on fire and the upper part had been shot at, and the head beaten so badly that it was a pulp, like a red jelly.")[8] Halabiya knew that his audience would be receptive when he urged, "Have no mercy on the Jews"!

Such *is* the normal public discourse and policy thinking in Arab and Islamic communities regarding Jews. We could easily quote and quote ad nauseam political leaders and religious leaders and ordinary speakers and media of all kinds, statement after statement, speech after speech, broadcast after broadcast, of antisemitism of this ardently held, fantastical, threatening, and eliminationist sort.

This raises the problem of conveying antisemitism's real nature. To provide even the slightest flavor of the antisemitic drumbeat and quality in Arab and Islamic countries, I would have to present paragraph after paragraph, page after page, chapter after chapter, volume after volume, room after room, library after library, of their antisemitic worlds, with all their antisemitic tropes, images, passions, accusations, calls to action, urgings of eliminationist violence—but even such repetition would not be close to enough to convey what courses through the hearts, minds, and societies of Arab and Islamic countries. A few representative quotations with copious supporting statistics (in the next chapter) do not begin to convey, do not begin to make the necessary impression, about the sheer volume of antisemitism and do even less well in conveying its virulence. Blood-curdling caricatures. Posters and graffiti on walls. Slogans that get drummed into and reverberate in antisemites' minds. Inflammatory photos of real or invented (photos can be doctored or depict staged scenes) suffering of Arabs at Jews' hands. Video, namely moving images, of the same. Antisemitic songs with incantatory, catchy lyrics, which circulate particularly among the radical right in the West. Antisemitic jokes' telling and often lurid punch lines. Videogames, with all their lurid visuals and sounds, in which the purpose is to slaughter, often gas Jews. And the brief descriptions here fail to suffice for still other reasons, for they cannot capture the speakers' tone, intensity, facial expressions, the ways they convey—and therefore the ways they are persuasive—that raising consciousness about the specter of Jews, the essence of Jewness, and doing what is necessary to defeat this putatively unparalleled enemy is a necessary and historical, indeed existential task—a jihad.

With all this in mind, here are some representative statements by significant political and religious leaders, and from exemplary children, from across the Islamic and Arab world:

From *Gaza:* Mahmoud Al-Zahhar, Hamas' leader, after giving his history of Europeans' expulsions and killings of Jews in November 2010:

> The series of expulsions continues to this day. Blood continues to be
> shed, martyrs continue to fall, our sons continue to hoist the banner

high, and Allah willing, their [the Jews'] expulsion from Palestine in its entirety is certain to come. We are no weaker or less honorable than the peoples that expelled and annihilated the Jews. The day we expel them is drawing near. [...]

The nation that opens up its doors, its hearts, and its homes to the [Jews] who were expelled from all corners of the earth was the Islamic nation. [...]

We extended our hands to feed these hungry dogs and wild beasts, and they devoured our fingers. We have learned the lesson — there is no place for you among us, and you have no future among the nations of the world. You are headed to annihilation.[9]

From *Lebanon:* Former Lebanese defense minister Mohsen Dalloul on ANB TV in September 2011:

> In a very important speech, George Washington called not to trust the Jews, saying that the Jews are blood-suckers. In the constitutional convention, Benjamin Franklin, one of the founding fathers, stood up and said — and I quote — "Gentlemen, let me warn you that the Jews might gather on American soil. They are bad seed, and so on and so forth. I propose adding an article to the constitution preventing the entry of Jews into the US." He was a president and one of the founding fathers. [10]

From *Syria:* Bishop George Saliba of the Syrian Orthodox Church in an interview on Al-Dunya TV in July 2011:

> **George Saliba:** The source that finances and incites all these international organizations, in the East and West, and especially in the Arab world... They are led by a single, evil organization, known as Zionism. It is behind all these movements, all these civil wars, and all these evils, using the people of the West — whether in the US, in Europe, or their followers. [...]
>
> What is happening is only natural. Jesus Christ healed the sick among the Jews. He gave sight to the blind, cleansed the lepers, and resurrected their dead.

**Interviewer:** How did they repay him?
**George Saliba:** They strived to crucify him until he died. [...]
Do the people of the opposition, with their notions and their deeds, belong to Christianity or to Islam? No. They are deeply rooted in Judaism and in Zionism, which does not wish well on any nation, people, or country. [...]
Any intelligent person who reads *The Protocols of the Elders of Zion* will see the extent of its influence on the politics of our region and the world. [11]

From *Iran:* Ayatollah Ruhollah Khomeini, the founding father and unquestioned spiritual leader of the Iranian Revolution and political Islamic Iran:

Regardless of [the] occupation of Palestine, it is crystal clear and never has been denied by the heads of the fake regime of Israel that they want to gain control of other Muslim countries, and want to expand their occupied territory to include other parts of [the] Islamic entity between [the] Nile River [and the] Euphrates. Every day they plan how to achieve this evil goal. It is a must [for all Muslims] to defend the Islamic countries with all means.

This, and Khomeini's other antisemitic pronouncements—still enormously influential—and calls to lethal jihad have been echoed repeatedly by subsequent Iranian leaders, including those today, such as Alireza Forghani, a confidant and strategist of Iran's Supreme Leader Ali Khameini, who in 2012 cited this statement by Khomeini as justification for asserting his own parallel version and in further maintaining that Iran had to "annihilate" Israel:

Israel on the land of the Palestinian people is a cancerous growth that is hatching schemes within the kingdom of Islam, and the fear is that it will take over [additional] Islamic lands. Therefore, it is incumbent upon all the Muslims to foil its schemes by all means available, and to prevent the spread of Israeli influence.[12]

From *Egypt:* Faraeen TV owner and Egyptian presidential candidate Tawfiq Okasha, on Al-Rahma TV during the Arab Spring in July 2011:

**Tawfiq Okasha:** The Jews believe in a divine doctrine that they must be the masters and owners of this world. In their view, their ownership of this world will not be consolidated, and will not take the form of a man sitting back in his armchair, all smug, unless their throne council is set here in Egypt. If the throne council is set here in Egypt, the entire world will submit to the ownership of the Jews.

There are 16–18 million Jews in the world, while there are more than half a billion [*sic*] people in the world. How can these 16 or 18 million rule half a billion people? Through schemes, intrigues, civil strife, and so on.

**Interviewer:** And that is happening today.

**Tawfiq Okasha:** That is what is happening today in Egypt.[13]

About a textbook: Interview with Egyptian cleric Miqdam Al-Khadhari, on Egyptian Al-Rahma/Al-Rawdha TV in December 2010:

**Miqdam Al-Khadhari:** This is a very important book, a textbook reader, which is an important school subject at Al-Azhar. In the general education system, it is known as the reading subject. Through it, the student is educated, he reads, and listens to the sheik. Let's see what Al-Azhar is teaching our sons in this subject.

**Interviewer:** Let's take, for example, the 11th grade.

**Miqdam Al-Khadhari:** We'll take 11th grade because it is the most important grade, in which the youths are at a crucial stage of their lives. Let's see what they are being taught at Al-Azhar. This is the 2007–2008 reader for the 11th grade.

[...]

After four or five chapters, the book moves to a topic with a large title, as clear as day: "The Treachery of the Jews."

**Interviewer:** Let's show it to the viewers.

**Miqdam Al-Khadhari:** It's the main title, not just a subhead—"The Treachery of the Jews." This title shows what the student is about to learn. It is not talking about something marginal. It's an important topic. I haven't seen any curriculum that presents this subject so explicitly. This is the curriculum of 2008. I'm not talking about something ancient. This is now! It's a textbook from this year or last year. It reads: "The Jews thought that they were the Chosen People." It presents things very clearly.

**Interviewer:** That's the reader.

**Miqdam Al-Khadhari:** Right after "The Treachery of the Jews" — which takes up many pages, not just a word or two. It takes up six pages. The next title, right after "The Treachery of the Jews" — I think that the camera can show the title. I'd like you to read it, dear brothers. "Islamic Jihad and Its Various Forms." Right after "The Treachery of the Jews." You should know that the textbook of jurisprudence also teaches these topics, and so does the textbook on the *Hadith*.

They teach these topics so that the student will be militarized when he graduates. After the 11th grade, he can move from Al-Azhar to a military academy. The young man graduates with this in his blood. "Islamic Jihad and Its Various Forms." I hope the camera can show it clearly.[14]

From a *child:* On Al-Hayat TV, a Christian Arabic television station originating in Egypt that is broadcast to many countries in the Middle East and around the world:

**Interviewer:** Muhammad Gamal is a young boy who has not yet turned twelve. Muhammad is a poet, who writes poetry, not only recites it. Muhammad, how are you?

**Muhammad Gamal:** Fine, Allah be praised.

**Interviewer:** Muhammad, when did you start to write poetry?

**Muhammad Gamal:** In third grade.

**Interviewer:** How did this happen? Would you read poetry, did your father teach you, or what?

**Muhammad Gamal:** I don't know where I got it from. I wrote a poem called "A Call to Jerusalem." I wrote it in third grade, when the Jews were thinking of destroying Jerusalem, in order to build the temple...

**Interviewer:** The Al-Aqsa Mosque.

**Muhammad Gamal:** Yes, they wanted to destroy the Al-Aqsa Mosque in order to build the temple. So I wrote this poem, I don't know how it came to me.

**Interviewer:** Let's hear this poem.

**Muhammad Gamal:** The poem is called "A Call to Jerusalem."

*Oh Jerusalem, oh Jerusalem,*
*Your name is in the hearts of millions.*
*We have worked hard for you,*
*And will continue to do so for days and years.*
*If I could embrace you, I would, no matter what—*
*Regardless of those who wish to destroy you, but cannot,*
*Because the Lord protects you.*
*Oh Jerusalem, oh Jerusalem,*
*Your name is in the hearts of millions.*
*I would like to pray within you, behind the righteous prophets.*
*Oh my beloved Jerusalem, which is in Palestine—*
*You will continue to belong to the Muslims.*
*If we unite, we will regain you,*
*Just like Saladin.*
*You will remain in the hearts of the believers.*
*Oh Jerusalem, oh Jerusalem,*
*Your name is in the hearts of millions.*
*We will take you from the accursed Jews,*
*Who killed and massacred many people,*
*Many poor children, women, and the elderly,*
*And before them, they killed the prophets and messengers.*
*Nevertheless, you will continue to belong to the Arabs and Muslims.*
*Oh Jerusalem, oh Jerusalem,*
*Your name is in my heart and the hearts of millions.*

**Interviewer:** Well done, Muhammad. That was beautiful.

Egyptian Child Preacher Ibrahim Adham, Al-Rahma TV in Egypt, November 16, 2012:

Oh Zionists, we love death for the sake of Allah, just as much as you love life for the sake of Satan. We long for martyrdom for the sake of Allah, just as much as you hate death, oh enemies of Allah. I am just a small child, but nevertheless, I pray that Allah will allow me to lead the prayer in the Al-Aqsa Mosque....If it were up to me, I would come to you [Palestinians], and I would fight alongside you in the battlefield, even if I am killed a hundred—nay, a thousand—times.[15]

Sheikh Futouh 'Abd Al-Nabi Mansour, head of Egypt's Islamic Endowment in Marsa Matrouh at Friday services in the Al-Tana'im Mosque in October 2012. According to a journalist writing about the event, he concluded his sermon with "the following supplication."

Oh Allah, absolve us of our sins, strengthen us, and grant us victory over the infidels. Oh Allah, deal with the Jews and their supporters. Oh Allah, disperse them, rend them asunder. Oh Allah, demonstrate Your might and greatness upon them. Show us Your omnipotence, oh Lord.

This last supplication is in itself unremarkable: the run-of-the-mill eliminationist antisemitism found all over Egypt and the Arab and Islamic world. What makes it remarkable is the camera catching Egypt's then president, Mohamed Morsi, in the front row, eyes closed, hands outstretched in front of him, palms upward in supplication. The journalist explains what the video reveals: "Of course, Mursi nodded his head, mumbling 'amen' along with the congregants after each supplication [against the Jews]."[16] It is taken as a commonplace—"of course"—that Egypt's president Morsi would agree and that he would express his agreement. And it was beamed, with Morsi's obvious approval, to the entire nation on Egypt's Channel 1.

This should have come as no surprise because such an antisemitic outlook is so deeply entrenched in the orientation of Arab and Islamic leaders and their followers across the Middle East, within political movements, throughout governments, and most notably among political leaders, including the supposedly moderate political Islamic leader Morsi of the supposedly moderate political Islamic Muslim Brother-

*October 19, 2012, President Mohamed Morsi (front center) engaged in antisemitic prayer. (Provided by The Middle East Media Research Institute)*

hood. Morsi, when he felt unfettered by the need to present the Western world a plausible deniability that he is a powerful eliminationist antisemite, explicitly articulated his agreement with the dominant antisemitic views of his dyed-in-the-wool antisemitic Muslim Brotherhood, which he, even though in the international public eye, could not restrain himself from saying amen to while sitting as Egypt's president in this mosque. In January 2010 he explained to Egyptians on camera, posting this on the Internet for further viewing, their duty to teach antisemitism to their children, and for generations to come: "Dear brothers, we must not forget to nurse our children and grandchildren on hatred towards those Zionists and Jews, and all those who support them. They must be nursed on hatred. The hatred must continue." And what, more explicitly, should Arabs and Muslims teach about Jews so that this hatred will be continuously fed? Morsi explained, again on camera, a few months later for all his and the Muslim Brotherhood's followers and for Egyptians to see. There cannot be any accommodation with Israel and its Jews, because "Either [you accept] the Zionists and everything they want, or else it is war." Why? Because, according to Morsi, "this is what these occupiers of the land of Palestine know." And why are they this way, because they are "these blood-suckers, who attack the Palestinians, these warmongers, the descendants of apes and pigs." The president of Egypt held and has spread an utterly dehumanized, animalic conception of Jews, drawing on the continuously intoned and perhaps the single most common antisemitic Islamic trope known to every Muslim in the Arab world. The president of Egypt held and has spread an utterly demonized image of Jews as "blood-suckers" and inveterate "warmongers" with whom it is impossible and also impermissible to make peace. As Morsi understands it, the essence of Jewness comprises these things, and he explains that Jews have always acted in this way, "they have been fanning the flames of civil strife wherever they were throughout history. They are hostile by nature." *By nature.* The result of such beliefs is logical. Morsi's construction of Jews, unremarkable for the Arab and Islamic world, even though it is openly eliminationist, is that Jews have no right to their country, not a single square inch of it, or even to live there: "The Zionists have no right to the land of Palestine. There is no place for them on the land of Palestine. What they took before 1947–8 [even *before* the establishment of Israel] constitutes plundering, and what they are doing now is a continuation of this plundering. By no means do we recognize their Green Line. The land of Palestine belongs to the Palestinians, not to the Zionists" — by which Morsi can, in this formulation, mean only the Jews, for whom he uses interchangeably the term Zionists, which he makes clear with his call to nurse hatred equally for "Zionists and Jews." When Morsi, as president, recently repeatedly assented with "amen," it was explicitly "the Jews," whom Sheikh Mansour prayed that Allah would rip to pieces, or, in the more highfalutin language of prayer, "rend them asunder."[17]

People not steeped in Arab and Islamic antisemitism, or even the antisemitism of just Hamas, one albeit very important such antisemitic movement, cannot be aware of the frequency and volume of such antisemitic expression, diatribes, assaults — which are typically delivered *by the most prominent Arab and Islamic politicians, religious leaders, and cultural figures,* often as religious truths in mosques as part of the Friday sermon and on national television and radio stations or in national print media, including the various countries' most prominent and respected newspapers. I have especially noted a range of ones from Egypt, the country that has had a peace treaty with Israel for more than thirty years and that has, prior to the Arab Spring, had a working and peaceful foreign policy relationship with Israel, which shows how widespread, deeply rooted, and pernicious such antisemitism is, even in "moderate"

Egypt. Anyone interested in getting a better sense of the antisemitic hatred promulgated by these countries' and communities' most prominent men should spend an hour viewing clips posted on MEMRI TV's (The Middle East Media Research Institute TV Monitor Project) "Anti-Semitism Documentation Project" http://www.memritv.org/subject /en/64.htm, which monitors Arab and Islamic media's antisemitic broadcasts. You might be too disgusted by the horrifying remarks to last even half an hour. You might think you are watching madmen, or perhaps actors playing madmen. (Whether or not you do, you might recall the rants and the deeds based on similar notions of Hitler, Goebbels, or run-of-the-mill Nazi leaders.) But the speakers are real, sane, and often intelligent men and women possessed of our time's most profound widespread hatred. (Sometimes they are but children who innocently speak the heartfelt antisemitic notions on which they are nursed and reared, which are the sinews of culture, and which swirl around them as an ever-present discourse in Arab and Islamic communities.) Hundreds of millions of Arabs and Muslims take these antisemitic words as true and as inspiring. Not only that, but think of the great percentage of people in the West and elsewhere outside of Arab and Islamic countries and communities who have been exposed to such words about Jews in written, spoken, or video form, and yet they still sign on to these movements and their goals and support them, often fervently. Anyone who claims that the antipathy of the region, or of the world at large, is only for Israel because of its policies, and not toward Jews in general because of their Jewness, or who claims that such people's intent is anything but eliminationist toward Israel the country and toward Jews in general because of their Jewness, is being duped or seeking to dupe others.

The various spheres of Arab and Islamic worlds work synergistically to produce and reproduce among their inhabitants the demonizing beliefs and volcanic hatred against Jews and the concomitant drive to act logically and murderously upon them. From the top down, states, political leaders, and media spread the word to millions at a time. In the greater intimacy of communities, particularly but not only religious communities, the word is disseminated, elaborated upon, and shared more horizontally. And from the bottom up, in family life, it is inculcated from parent into child and then percolates upward to the other spheres. Abdelkader Merah pinpoints the complementary and mutually reinforcing qualities of the spheres usually more hidden from the Western publics' view in explaining how his brother Mohamed Merah, the Toulouse mass murderer of Jews, came to his beliefs. It starts with the family. "I will explain how my parents raised you in an atmosphere of racism and hate," and then the religious leaders reinforced and gave social and cultural context and buttressing to it, as Abdelkader continues, "before the Salafis could douse you in religious extremism." And the extremism, the racism, the hate continues to be drummed into the children until it beats within them as do their hearts. "My mother always said, 'We, the Arabs, we were born to hate Jews.' This speech, I heard it all throughout my childhood."[18]

Of the tens or hundreds of millions of Arabs and Muslims who support this eliminationism, a number of them choose freely to devote and even give their lives to pursue their destructive antisemitic dream. Suicide (better conceived of as genocide) bomber Adham Ahmad Abu Jandal, in his farewell video posted on the Hamas website for all Palestinians and all the world to see, might have drawn a straight line from the words of Arab and Islamic leaders to his own beliefs to his genocidal act: "My message to the loathed Jews: There is no God but Allah, we will chase you everywhere. We are a nation that drinks blood. We know that there is no better blood than the blood of Jews. We won't leave you alone until we have quenched our thirst with your blood, and our children's thirst with your blood. We will not rest until you leave the Muslim countries."[19]

Christian religious antisemitism is much more subdued and much more circumscribed. Antipathy toward Jews within Christian traditions remains fundamental, yet it is understood as having little or nothing to do with society's or politics' contemporary organization. In the West there is no viable political Christianity movement, no Christian analogue of political Islam, seeking to govern countries according to an orthodox reading of the Christian bible, seeking to collapse the distinction between religion and politics, and seeking to treat Jews in accordance with the most eliminationist, indeed violent eliminationist, possible reading of the Christian bible's precepts — which is a contrast to how many Christians had for centuries approached society and politics, especially regarding Jews.

Of course, Christian antisemitism's effects are real and remain a profound and persistent source of antisemitism, as is evidenced by the hundreds of millions of Christians around the world who believe that Jews today are guilty or cursed for Jesus' death. If this were the only part of the Christian religious discourse that is antisemitic, we could lament it, truly lament it, and move on. But grafted upon it is an ongoing, more elaborated account of Jews' malfeasance that further promotes suspicion of, passions against, and views about Jews that render them noxious, pernicious, and threatening.

Certainly the Catholic Church, despite its publicly stated and championed position, has failed to excise antisemitism from its teaching and liturgy, and this is the case even in Europe and North America, where it has done better than elsewhere. In the developing world, the less than fully systematic evidence nonetheless leaves no doubt that the age-old imprecations and denunciations and demonization of Jews remain widespread. The liturgy, which unlike the Christian bible itself is easily changeable, still contains many antisemitic portions, the most notorious of which is perhaps the "reproaches" said during passion week, which has Jesus himself blaming the Jews for killing him. "My people," asks Jesus, "what have I done to you? How have I offended you? Answer me! I led you out of Egypt, from slavery to freedom, but you led your Savior to the cross."[20] The enactment, really the yearly reenactment of the passion itself, in church and in productions, is at best a time of quiet though explicit antisemitic discursive reinforcement and indeed incitement. The Church has done little, and in many places nothing, to stop spreading antisemitism during the Christian calendar's most sacred time and in the Jesus story as it is portrayed. The Church has implicitly acknowledged its failure, at least within Catholicism's highly progressive (it is fair to say cutting-edge) portion, the American Catholic Church, with its need to publish its "guidelines on the presentation of Jews and Judaism in Catholic preaching," where it states about the passion, "Because of the tragic history of the 'Christ-killer' charge as providing a rallying cry for anti-Semites over the centuries, a strong and careful homiletic stance is necessary to combat its lingering effects today. Homilists and catechists should seek to provide a proper context for the proclamation of the passion narratives." This was accompanied by an expanded publication of guidelines devoted specifically for presenting the passion in a non-antisemitic way, containing *dos* and *don'ts,* including:

Jews should not be portrayed as avaricious (e.g., in Temple money-changer scenes); blood thirsty (e.g., in certain depictions of Jesus' appearances before the Temple priesthood or before Pilate); or implacable enemies of Christ (e.g., by changing the small "crowd" at the governor's palace into a teeming mob). Such depictions, with their obvious "collective guilt" implications, eliminate those parts of the gospels that show that the secrecy surrounding Jesus' "trial" was motivated by the large following he had in Jerusalem and that the Jewish populace, far from wishing his death, would have opposed it had they known and, in fact, mourned his death by Roman execution (cf. Lk 23:27).[21]

This publication's more than twenty major provisions, and what they say or imply about the passion's inveterate antisemitism, indicate only that this liturgy is antisemitic incitement to hate Jews. (And that Mel Gibson's rendition of it in *The Passion of the Christ* seemingly used the *do nots* of this publication as a guideline for the *dos*.) That the American Catholic Church's documents and other forthright ones from the Vatican, furthermore, are dishonored in their regular breach when the passion is enacted is the more important news sociologically than the good work that they are and the good intentions that they embody and that helped produce them.

Even though the Catholic hierarchy has finally come to understand that it has won its age-old, one-sided enmity over the custodianship worldwide of the Jewish bible and tradition, and that Jews neither pose a threat to the Church, to lead its flock astray, nor even care very much about what the Church does aside from its stance and teaching about Jews, old suspicions and old habits of reflexive suspicion and castigation of Jews remain powerfully present and serve as a forceful undertone in the Church's teachings about Jews. When the extent of Catholic priests' raping of children began to get public exposure, and the extent of the Church's systematic complicity and enabling, its effective conspiracy to allow the perpetrators to continue their sexual predations against children, also began to become clear, the Church's reflex behind the scenes was to blame the Jews, a view that was publicly articulated in 2010 by Bishop Giacomo Babini, who said that a "Zionist attack" was behind the criticism of the Pope over the sex abuse scandal, seeing as its character was "powerful and refined." Jews, Babini explained, "do not want the Church, they are its natural enemies." He added: "Deep down, historically speaking, the Jews are God killers."[22] Of course, the Church's formal public stance was to deny and repudiate this Italian bishop's public statements.

Whatever progress has been made in the Catholic Church's official bearing toward Jews in the nearly fifty years since Vatican II, and its implementation of its rethought public bearing toward Jews in the West—and it has been considerable, as I have discussed in *A Moral Reckoning*—its penetration has been inadequate to ordinary Catholics throughout the world, and especially in the developing world, where Catholicism is in a medieval state regarding its presentation of Jews. Few if any systematic initiatives have been undertaken to educate clergy and laity, so that Father Reinhard Neudecker began his essay on the state of the Church and the Jews with the basic facts. Why? He explains: "The text of [Vatican II's] *Nostra aetate* and of the two later documents of the Commission for Religious Relations with the Jews [from 1974 and 1985] must be explained here in some detail, since surveys have shown that many of the readers to which these writings are addressed have little, if any, knowledge of them." Neudecker was saying here that even the clergy, the ones who are creating the frame of understanding for these issues for Catholics, are ignorant of the changes wrought by Vatican II and since then. Despite my book's clear acknowledgment of the archaic state of the Church's teachings about Jews in the developing world in particular, I was repeatedly told by Catholics, including priests, who appreciated a forthright book on the Church and antisemitism, that the state of affairs is even much worse than they understood me to be saying. In Central and Eastern Europe priests are preaching traditional antisemitism, and across the developing world, which is where most Catholics live, the Church's teachings about Jews are in a pre–Vatican II state.[23] Survey data show that Hispanic Americans born outside the United States, not having had the benefit of a more Vatican II–shaped church upbringing, are significantly more antisemitic than Hispanic Americans born in the United States.[24]

Regarding Israel, the Catholic Church remains hostile, and explicitly and tacitly supports those who would de-Jewify the country. That fundamental hostility has been evidenced by its refusal to recognize Israel's existence for more than its first forty years—pope after pope, including the relatively forward-thinking John XXIII, who set Vatican II in motion, simply would not accept that the Jews were entitled to a country, had reestablished their country in the land of ancient Israel, called by many, including Catholics, the Holy Land. This aspect of the Church's antisemitic and eliminationist stance came formally to an end when, after the Soviet empire's disintegration and the former Soviet Bloc countries' ensuing rapid recognition of Israel, the only countries that no longer recognized Israel were a few of the most rabidly antisemitic Arab and Islamic ones in the world. With that, it had simply become too embarrassing for the Church to continue to withhold its recognition. Not surprisingly, the Church has continued to be extraordinarily critical of Israel while overlooking the wholesale repressions and transgressions of, and of even supporting, Israel's openly antisemitic enemies who seek to destroy it.

The Protestant world is more complicated, as no overarching institution unifies it, which in the case of Catholicism is also organized hierarchically, like the military, albeit without the military's firm command and control structure and discipline. Protestants tend to be more theologically liberal and more theologically literal or fundamentalist than Catholics. Many are liberal because they are not members of a church, such as the Catholic Church, whose absolute authority over doctrinal issues they accept as their membership's condition. Even though many Catholics de facto diverge from this position, the Church remains an authoritative institution over many matters, and for many Catholics that includes the woeful image of Jews that the Church presents in its scripture, liturgy, and teachings. Liberal Protestants, relying on their formal individual interpretive powers, as they understand themselves to have an unmediated relationship to Jesus and God, have broken away much more from traditional Christian theologies, including about Jews. As a result, many Protestants have a much less fraught relationship with Jews, taking the Christian bible stories not as a guide to actual history but as suggestive tales from which they pick and choose appealing moral lessons and principles. Yet many other Protestants are fundamentalists, literalists, in their reading of the Christian bible.

Thus, Protestants break down into different camps and can have complex views about Jews and Israel, depending on how backward- or forward-looking they are. Many fundamentalist Protestants, without the Catholic Church's somewhat tempering influence on conceptions of Jews, have an uncompromising and literal transfer of Christian biblical accounts of Jews onto Jews today. This includes a profound suspicion of Jews, a belief in their fundamental opposition to Christianity, and a belief that they murdered Jesus, which renders all Jews guilty and cursed for all time. Many further fervently believe in the devil (who looms prominently in much Protestant theology and more so than in today's Catholicism) and that Jews are in league with him. But this is only one of the two principal dimensions by which Protestants evaluate Jews. The other concerns Israel. Some Protestant churches, not constrained by the suspicions of antisemitism or by the internal inhibitions within the Catholic Church, have no difficulty in the name of Jesus of claiming to identify with the Palestinian cause out of religious and humanitarian motives, and heaping scorn, often cast in antisemitic terms, upon Israel. This certainly characterizes the Episcopal church, as well as leading Protestant churches in many Western countries, which over the last several years have taken more concerted initiative to explicitly sway their followers and the general public more forcefully against Israel and Jews. It is also an underappreciated problem, as many people, Christians and Jews, prefer not to discuss the continuing power of Christian supersessionism (or replacement theology) with its notion that Judaism and Jews ought to disappear — and not only because they killed Jesus — to generate antisemitic beliefs and animus. Reverend Paul Wilkinson in the United Kingdom, familiar with mainline Protestant denominations in general, does not shy away from pinpointing the problem. "I believe we'd be fooling ourselves if we believed that we can overturn and change what I perceive to be a Goliath of theology in the church. The Goliath we face is the Goliath of replacement theology." This, not other factors, is the root of the hostility to Israel and Jews. "That Goliath cannot be felled with a stone and a sling as in the days of King David, because the problem isn't political, the problem isn't sociological, the problem isn't about lack of education or lack of dialogue," Wilkinson explains. "The problem is a spiritual one."[25]

Other Protestants, especially fundamentalist and evangelical ones, focus on the Christian biblical prophecy about the end of days, which is to come only when the Jews are all gathered again in Israel. This identification of the country of Israel with Christian deliverance of humanity has produced among fundamentalist and especially evangelical Protestants widespread messianic support, both in the figurative and literal senses, for Israel and for Jews. Such support can exist among people who are otherwise antisemitic, as the messianism of the future comes to outweigh and, in a practical and political manner of acting in this world, trump the messianic problems of the past. Some commentators have interpreted fundamentalist Protestants' pro-Israel stance and philosemitism being but antisemitism's flip side, seeing the Jews as fundamentally different and investing in them certain eschatological qualities. Whether one wants, conceptually and theoretically, to understand it this way does not alter the most fundamental difference between the holders of such views and antisemites: they thereby express no animus for Jews. They look favorably upon Jews' collective and political existence. They actively support Jews and Israel.

The antisemitism of the political left and of the international human rights and NGO communities has the most openly global cast. The left's antisemitism has merged its long-standing identification of Jews with the predations of capitalism or, in today's terms, the world economic order with its newfound relentless international orientation. The resulting contours, akin to those of the international human rights stream, map best the overall contours of global antisemitism. The left and the international human rights communities tend to shy away from, even reject, many of the other classical antisemitic accusations, whether the religiously grounded ones of Christianity and Islam, the racist ones of Nazism and associated movements, and the more fantastical ones of current Islamic antisemitism. They are the most overwhelmingly political, as they are secular and entirely or almost entirely grounded in politics. It is the most relentlessly international, as that is its principal area of focus.

As much as bad faith courses through politically left antisemitism in general and through its various components, it is the most "innocent" of the major contemporary antisemitic streams in that many of its adherents vehemently deny—and believe their denial—that they are antisemites or have anything at all against Jews. Arab and Islamic antisemites know that they think Jews are evil and hate them and are often, indeed usually, open about it. Christian antisemites, while denying that the term antisemitism has anything to do with their creed, know that they harbor animus toward Jews. How could they not? They hold Jews guilty for killing their savior or, even if not that anymore, accept the biblical accounts of their nature and deeds, and the foundational antisemitic paradigm that it so forcefully constructs and lays out. Modern racist antisemites, it goes without saying, know what they are up to and are proud of it. Yet political left and international human rights antisemites, at least some of them — and among them are any number of Jews — genuinely believe that they are upholding universal and humanitarian principles as they fight for international justice and a better international order. This is particularly true of the broader international human rights community, of which the left forms only one part. Many of the left and the human rights community maintain plausible deniability when facing criticism that they are antisemites, and when they are looking in the mirror, by a combination of self-deluding biases, of focusing on their principles and what is laudable in them, and by willfully ignoring the undeniably seamy side of some of the antisemitism that courses through their movement or its Arab and Islamic allies against Israel. By being able to utter the words Israel and anti-Israelism, Zionism and anti-Zionism, and thereby being able to avoid the words Jews and antisemitism, they have their own powerful cover story — for public consumption, for self-deception, and for maintaining the veneer or more of respectability. And many of them really believe that they do not think ill of their Jewish neighbors or Jews in general, holding against them only that they support Israel and because of that distort the politics of the United States and the world. If Jews would cease such support, so the political leftist and human rights antisemites have persuaded themselves (and for some of them, it is undoubtedly true), they would have nothing at all against Jews. It is because of their overwhelming focus on politics and the conflict in the Middle East that many of them are likely not even aware of how much they have accepted the foundational antisemitic paradigm, of how much it drives what they think, and of how much it blinds them to evidence that falsifies their views or shows how selective they are in their application of principles, a principal hallmark of antisemitism, and especially of its political left and human rights streams.

Racist antisemites, having receded in public prominence and respectability since their delegitimization owing to Nazism's defeat, compose the one major stream of antisemitism that still has trouble speaking its views in polite company. Racist antisemites' adherence to the foundational antisemitic paradigm is absolute and their feeding of it as well (as higher-level elaborations) remains important and influential in the vast realm of the Internet, where so many innocent and not so innocent would-be and actual antisemites move around and devote their time. But they continue to be seen as dangerous cranks, Nazis or neo-Nazis themselves, Nazi celebrants, or somewhat more circumspect Nazi fellow-travelers, and thus such political poison that other antisemites cannot or genuinely do not wish to make common cause with them, at least not publicly. As a result, they remain somewhat marginalized, even if they embody and symbolize as pure and powerful a form of antisemitism as exists today. It is their purity and their inability to remain respectable given today's plausibility structure for antisemitism and for political and ideological thought in general—explicit racism and Nazism are tabooed—that have diminished their public standing.

Yet racist antisemites' influence remains considerable. It exists broadly on the Internet, where it fuels the hate-filled notions and imaginations of its adherents. There it finds converts among the innocent and those seeking meaning and explanations for the complexities and difficulties of the world, whether personal, social, or political. There it also contributes as a complement or as a synergistic component to the substructure of antisemitism that undergirds and feeds the crisscrossing beliefs and hatreds, grounded in the foundational antisemitic paradigm. It also exists more powerfully locally in places with active and prominent—in other words not merely completely marginal—neo-Nazi movements, especially Germany. Indeed, in a number of regions of Germany, mainly the former East Germany, but also in some areas of the west, neo-Nazis are quite powerful, especially among the young, and, though denied publicly by the political establishment, worrisome. Modern racist antisemitism exists there in its purist form, as Nazi-like, unabashed, open, and politically mobilizing, with many full-throttled adherents and a wider circle of less ardent, less activated like-minded and sympathetic people. Beyond the local social and political importance of racist antisemitism in Germany, and elsewhere in northern Europe, it has a more powerful political presence, though less openly, in the Arab and Islamic worlds. There its notions have been incorporated, often in naked form, into the Arab and Islamic antisemitic stream, with Jews often treated as inveterately evil and with Nazi-like fantastical constructs of Jews, accusations of Jews' malignancy, and programmatic responses to their predations and ongoing threat having become central to the public discourses. The belief that Jews are responsible for many of the calamities that have befallen humanity, such as being the instigators of one major revolution and war after another, which is encoded in Hamas' charter, has been imported into Arab and Islamic antisemitism straight from modern racist and Nazi antisemitism and has by now a fixed and central place in that discourse.

In a sense, the success of the modern racist antisemitic stream has rendered its own importance secondary. Its notions are most influential not among its own dedicated adherents but among Arab and Islamic antisemites, as they have merged and subsumed it into their own powerful and, in much of the world, hegemonic antisemitic stream. Its failure to be more widespread and more accepted — for what it is — in the world's general public discourse is, as Arab and Islamic antisemitism shows, not a consequence of its content's outlandishness or fantastical, obsessively hate-filled nature. Instead, it is racist antisemitism's absence of a fig-leaf, however small, that permits others to pretend that it is not just naked antisemitism — or if it is, then it is at least motivated, however mistakenly, by legitimate grievances. So long as antisemitism can be dressed up in the concealing garb of religious belief, or in the respectable or at least semi-respectable clothing of anti-Israelism, anti-imperialism, or social or political principles, however much the bad faith behind them is apparent, or in the suffering of those whom Israel has wronged or said to have wronged, or whom Israel oppresses or is said to oppress today, antisemitic belief and animus can be and is widely deemed respectable, gets a hearing, takes an honored place in the public discourses and institutions and politics of our time. Nazi notions, at least some of them, are okay, but not in naked, obsessive form.

The various kinds of antisemitism have an emphasis that defines them and differentiates them from one another, even though they share many overlapping elements or themes, which I discuss further below. Arab and Islamic antisemitism focuses on Jews as much as Israel, their putative threat to Islam and the Arab world, and is openly elimination-ist and even exterminationist. Christian antisemitism draws overwhelmingly on age-old Christian tropes about Jews' perfidy and culpability in Jesus' death. Modern and Nazi racist antisemitism, secular in cast, emphasize the Jews' racist constitution and consciousness and their organized power and malevolence to do harm. Leftist antisemitism fixates on Jews' alleged capitalist financial depredations and, together with human rights antisemitism, neocolonial ambitions and practices. Additionally, genteel or social antisemitism (though little discussed here), much in evidence in the polite circles of the West, concerns itself with the social and cultural stereotypes about Jews that make them distasteful but not much with notions of Jews' power or malevolence. Anti-Israel–focused antisemitism — to which the assorted strains variously contribute — is overwhelmingly, relentlessly, indeed often obsessively fixated (at least in its manifest rhetoric) on Israel's alleged transgressions, which are cast as world historical outrages and therefore disqualify Israel and its Jews from membership in the community of nations.

In thinking about global antisemitism, and what is distinctive, new, and ultimately qualitatively different from earlier antisemitisms, whatever global antisemitism's continuities, affinities, commonalities, and overlap with them, its most fundamental distinguishing feature — aside from its globalism — is that it has become an essential part of the world's substructure of prejudice. It has powerful Christian sources. It has powerful Islamic sources. It still has, though in decline, a racist source. It is fueled by the residue, hardly now but a residue in quantity, of Nazified antisemitism that thrives in Arab and Islamic countries and among their peoples. It feeds on a constant flow of news it can latch on to, or which it can manufacture, in order to keep it current, on people's minds, and to inflame people's passions, in the informational and image stream of the conflict between Israel and the Palestinians and the other countries, groups, and peoples who would eliminate Israel. It is also regularly further given voice by regular doses of antisemitic (some more open, some more subtle) agitation in the form of antisemitic or antisemitic-inflected and withering criticism of Israel and Jews, in the media and then even the controversies over such criticism. All this and more, including much that gets said and done in civil society but that does not make it into the national or international media, has produced the multiple antisemitic nodes, hubs, flows, and tides that dot, crisscross, and swirl around the world. There is also the Internet, which both houses and furthers all this and contributes enormously more to the antisemitic flows, the inundation, of invective that, devastatingly prejudicially, washes over the conception, image, and standing of Israel and Jews in Israel, and Jews more generally, rendering them into the demonic entities or characters of the most hypertrophied antisemitic imaginings.

These multiple sources and flows, including and particularly through the Internet, have made global antisemitism a thing unto itself with so many dimensions and facets that it is truly global in the sense that it is available to everyone and anyone everywhere and can be easily appropriated, adopted, incorporated, exploited for virtually any purpose — whether to mobilize hatred, explain misfortune and suffering, make allies, create seeming sense out of the world, vent hatreds, or find satisfying targets — no matter whether it is attached to or divorced from any of its original sources. It is truly the one global prejudice — no other prejudice is remotely like it — that is signed onto by people nearly everywhere, and it can be signed onto by people for virtually any reason. If one opposes wealth, power, poverty, injustice, the media, liberals, leftists, sickness, AIDS, illegal drugs, Israel, rightists, neoconservatives, United States, the truth about 9/11, oppression, colonialism, war, the devil, the past, the present, or the future, one is given reason, if one accepts what is commonly said and commonly available about Jews, to hold the Jews responsible, to think ill and deeply prejudicially about Jews, to develop an animus toward them, to see them as a danger, to subscribe to the foundational antisemitic paradigm, to become an antisemite. It is no longer just the Jews' religion that putatively makes them noxious, and one must no longer sign onto the idea of race and therefore to racial-biological determinism to be an antisemite. Today it is the Jews' identity as Jews, their freely chosen — for whatever reason — affiliation with Jewness that makes them noxious and willfully malevolent. This means that it is Jewness itself, whatever that means to a given person — Jew or antisemite — that antisemites oppose, whether it is a Jew, the human being, or some institution, country, position, or thing that is deemed animated by or expressive of Jewness.

Thus, and this is the final aspect of global antisemitism's character that needs to be discussed here, Jews have continued, in keeping with the foundational antisemitic paradigm that Christianity laid down (but that has spread and persisted independent of Christianity), to be demonized, to be seen as being so pernicious as to be a threat to just about anything that someone else might think is goodness. In one critical respect, Jews are more demonized than ever, as antisemitism's free-floating nature means that Jews can be seen to be defiling or endangering just about anything in the world. Earlier, when antisemites identified Jews with the devil, the Jews in principle were seen to be able to affect or do anything, but as a matter of fact the kinds of accusations that antisemites leveled at Jews, as horrific as they were, were limited. Although this expanded during the period of modern antisemitism, and expanded in particular under the Nazis, it was still restricted compared to the effectively unlimited number and types of accusations that antisemites hurl at Jews today. The demonic quality of Jews, in this important sense, augmenting the specific demonic evil they are said to perform, is greater in antisemitism's global form than ever before.

The passions global antisemites unleash in their individual and collective denunciations of Jews and in their campaign to counteract and curtail the Jews are immense. For antisemites the conclusion follows, as the means to combat the Jews must be adequate to the challenge, that the Jews must be fought politically, the fight must continue until the Jews stop practicing their politics, and so long as they are firmly entrenched in the regional superpower Israel and the world's superpower the United States, the danger will not subside. The Jews' real or imagined power in each of the two countries must be destroyed, and the only way to do that regarding the regional power Israel is for it to cease to exist. Global antisemitism, similar to, though specified somewhat differently from, the two earlier forms of antisemitism, is powerfully eliminationist, which includes a powerful logic of extermination, which very many, though not all, of its adherents practice or support.

# 11

# Millions Upon Millions of Antisemites

LOOKING AROUND THE world to assess antisemitism's extent and intensity, the picture is extremely disturbing. The sheer number of antisemites, the global prevalence of the foundational antisemitic paradigm, the many public discourses, the character of the antisemitism that people are readily exposed to and that is available for people, including the young, to latch on to, and the more explicit agitation for action against Jews compose constellations of prejudice that, individually in country after country and in sum around the world, have no equal. Then there is the digital media of satellite and cable television and radio, and especially of the Internet. The Internet in particular is available to everyone all the time anywhere, with the power of fueling and sustaining prejudice that is vast, new, in this respect revolutionary, and continuing only to increase in scope and intensity.

Let us begin our exploration of global antisemitism's extent by speaking plainly about antisemitism's constitution, which means first establishing an appropriate baseline for identifying it and for identifying those who harbor it. What would you think if you overheard someone say: *Blacks are lazy?* What would you say about someone who says: *Hispanics are not good Americans?* What would you think about a college admissions officer who commented: *Asians are sneaky?* Would you call them prejudiced or racist?

What else would you think of such people? Would you expect that they hold other prejudicial or racist notions about the groups they so describe with their single remarks? Would you be confident that such people could impartially judge and treat fairly people who fall into the groups they describe with such disdain or suspicion? Would you expect that such people might be hostile toward the people whom they have described in such ways and be receptive to believing other prejudicial or racist things about them?

All this would be many people's reaction, probably including yours, to hearing such single remarks. And in prejudice and racism's annals, being dubbed lazy, not an authentic American, and sneaky are hardly the worst things that prejudiced people have widely said and believed. Imagine hearing more damaging accusations, such as blacks are criminals, or Hispanics are drug dealers, or Asians unfairly make it impossible for others to advance educationally and professionally. Would you say that people who characterize entire groups in these ways are prejudiced, bigoted, or racist?

Why then do many people write off analogous or even more damaging views about Jews as not so consequential or indicative? The world is awash in the most damning views about and hostility toward Jews, embedded in widespread, elaborate prejudicial and hate-filled narratives and discourses, and yet so many people deny, often vehemently, that there is much antisemitism! Some people are so used to prejudice against Jews that the views barely register. Others find the truth too disturbing to acknowledge. Still others think there is validity to such views about Jews, so they do not want to admit the comments' real antisemitic nature. And others, usually the most vehement and aggressive such deniers, are themselves antisemites, often active antisemites, who seek cover and respectability for their own hateful notions by inoculating their views against exposure for the antisemitism they really are.

For blacks, Hispanics, Asians, or other groups, if a person holds *one* clearly prejudicial or racist view, we consider such views to be prejudiced or racist and we consider him or her—and we are right to do so—prejudiced or racist. Such should be the standard for assessing antisemitism. It is important to establish this explicitly for two reasons. First, people often explain away antisemitic remarks or positions as not being what they are, or not being all that significant, or, as we saw, with casuistic justifications about how the problem is really Israel, or Jews, or anything except for the views and the people who hold such views themselves. Think of how your head would whip around (at least figuratively) if while sitting in a business meeting or standing in a bus you heard someone say, especially with resentment or hatred, that blacks have too much power in this country. The same standard must be used for antisemitism. Second, the things people routinely say about Jews are typically far more damaging and prejudicial than the common remarks first mentioned here about blacks, Hispanics, or Asians. The views about Jews follow more along the lines (or worse) of those positing blacks, Hispanics, or Asians to be dangerous criminals in general, drug dealers in particular, or injuring the prospects of others. The prejudicial things people in large numbers hold and say about Jews regard Jews' alleged power, responsibility for colossal injuries, malevolence, or active threat or danger and can also include proposed responses that are prejudicial, violent, and eliminationist.

In assessing here antisemitism's extent, we thus adopt the conventional standard we use for other prejudices, which means: an antisemitic view constitutes (1) an antisemitic view, (2) antisemitism, and (3) on the part of the person who holds it, an antisemitic person.

Survey research helps enormously in assessing antisemitism's extent. The surveys, as we will shortly see, show that tens of millions, indeed hundreds of millions of people on different continents are antisemitic.

As if these numbers are not alarming enough (and also alarming and significant in that these colossal figures are not widely known), they substantially *understate* antisemitism. The surveys ask only a few questions, not even tapping into crucial antisemitic dimensions, let alone many common antisemitic notions and tropes. A person may well be antisemitic without these surveys registering this. The European and American surveys ask only one question (regarding responsibility for Jesus' death) to detect Christian antisemitic notions. Yet many Christian antisemites may accept the Vatican II or other Protestant churches' lifting of the intergenerational and eternal curse against Jews for their once-church-alleged guilt in Jesus' death yet continue to believe that Jews are Christians' inveterate enemies. Or are wayward. Or are in league with the devil. Or are beholden to a religion of vengeance (once a premise of a conversation at a dinner party I attended with other

Harvard faculty). Or that they are an arrogant and stiff-necked people. Or many more long-standing Christian antisemitic accusations and tropes. These same surveys ask no questions at all that would identify people who share antisemitic notions from the Islamic or Arab traditions, such as: Are Jews Allah's or Islam's enemies? Are Jews the sons and daughters of pigs and apes? Are Jews forever cursed for rejecting Islam? Or whether the statement from the Hadith that suggests Jews should be killed is divinely ordained or in principle correct?

These surveys fail to explore many other dimensions and aspects of antisemitism, indeed most of those including virtually all notions about Jews harboring ill intentions toward non-Jews, undermining their own societies' well-being (aside from through financial power), being a separate race, and many more. They do not tap many aspects of the litany of accusations about Jews' media or political power, including whether those who think Israel or the United States has committed transgressions against the Palestinians or against other peoples, say in Iraq or Iran, also hold Jews outside Israel responsible for perpetrating them.

Existing surveys also grossly underexplore the intensity of people's antisemitism. If, for example, the surveys would ask whether it is right to use violence against Jews in general (because of Jews' nature or deeds, or because of Israel's actions), or got people to scale their beliefs in Jews' malevolence or danger, surveys would reveal a great deal more than they do about the quality and intensity (and not just the existence) of people's antisemitism.

More generally, surveys are well known to underreport people's prejudice because people are reluctant to express their prejudicial views when such views are not sanctioned in the public sphere, and such views might get them dubbed racists or antisemites, especially as the latter might be seen to link them to Hitler and the gas chambers. This underreporting becomes that much more obvious when we see what surveys, for all their failings, do reveal about the discrepancy between how enormously prejudiced people are in their personal beliefs and attitudes and how comparatively little these views are expressed in the public spheres of, say, Western countries, even if, regarding antisemitism, there is a flood.

An extraordinarily telling exemplar of this all-too-common phenomenon of people consciously and often with great effort preventing themselves from expressing their deeply felt and profound antisemitism in public is the renowned anti-Nazi, German Protestant theologian Karl Barth, regarded by many as the greatest and most personally exemplary Christian theologian of the twentieth century. He wrote prolifically (so far forty-seven volumes of his collected works have been published), including famously propounding a "doctrine of Israel," and gave people no reason to suspect that he, a man of conscience, harbored antisemitic thoughts or sentiments. Yet in a letter of appreciation to Friedrich-Wilhelm Marquardt, a scholar who wrote a book on Barth's thought about Israel, Barth, in a confessional moment in 1967 at the very end of his life (meant privately only for Marquardt his exegete, who otherwise, according to Barth, understood his thought brilliantly), protests that he does not like Jews or want his regard for ancient Israel to be confused with any fondness for Jews. Barth is clear:

> I am decidedly not a philosemite, in that in personal encounters with living Jews (even Jewish Christians) I have always, so long as I can remember, had to suppress a totally irrational aversion, naturally suppressing it at once on the basis of all my presuppositions, and concealing it totally in my statements, yet still having to suppress and conceal it. Pfui! is all that I can say to this in some sense allergic reaction of mine. But this is how it was and is. A good thing that this reprehensible instinct is totally alien to my sons and other better people than myself (including you). But it could have had a retrogressive effect on my doctrine of Israel.[1]

Barth, having witnessed the horrors of Nazism, understood the danger of this "reprehensible instinct" of his, yet it was so deep within him that he experienced it as an allergic reaction over which he could not, whatever his efforts, prevent, including or especially when he came into contact with Jews, even those who had converted to Christianity—suggesting that, like the Nazis themselves, he considered the Jews to be constituted by their biology, their race. Aside from the depth of antisemitism in this celebrated anti-Nazi and otherwise progressive theological hero of many, what is most significant to note is how Barth "concealed" his antisemitism "totally" in his public "statements," and had to work so hard to "suppress" it. And why? Barth does not say, yet he certainly knew how devastating the public reaction would be and how his standing as a great Christian theologian would be undermined. And whatever the motive, conceal his "reprehensible" prejudice is what he did.

The disparity between the public antisemitism expressed in Western societies and the extent to which it is privately held is a gulf perhaps not as wide as in Barth's case, who in his writings could be mistaken for a "philosemite." But it is not far off. To believe that the surveys tap all of people's aversions and "allergic reactions" to Jews, all of people's prejudice or antisemitism, we would have to believe that every single bit of a person's self-censoring that prevents him or her from saying loudly in parliament, in a restaurant, or at work that Jews are responsible for the financial crisis of 2008 and beyond, or that Jews deserve to be attacked and killed because of Israel's actions, or that Jews are all guilty for Jesus' death, or that Jews are not loyal citizens of their own countries, that every such antisemitic thought and emotion falls by the wayside when being asked by a stranger in a survey — conducted as a telephone interview! — about these and other such alleged pernicious or noxious qualities of Jews. And we would have to believe this not only in general, but also in countries, as is the case of many European countries, including France and Germany, where antisemitic or racist public expression can be a punishable criminal act. If people underreport their antisemitism by only 10 percent, let alone by 50 percent, which is entirely likely, then antisemitism is that much greater than the vast amount the surveys already register.

Surveys also do not explore antisemitism's centrality to the broader thought, belief, and emotion that are important for people's understanding of themselves and the world. If antisemitism is embedded in a person's general understanding of God or sacred scripture, or interwoven into his understanding about the nature of humanity, namely that it is constituted of warring races, or essential to his understanding of his left, right, or centrist politics, then his antisemitism is likely to be profound and especially resistant to change. This has all sorts of consequences for his bearing toward Jews, including a much greater proclivity to believing new and more intensively pernicious things about them.

All this notwithstanding, existing surveys reveal that antisemitism in Europe, in the Arab and Islamic world, and elsewhere is rampant.[2]

As discussed, the most damaging antisemitic canard ever is that all Jews, at the time and for all time, are guilty in the death of Jesus, whom Christians believe to be the son of God. Indeed, many Christians through the ages believed that the Jews murdered him — even though, according to the Christian bible, the Romans killed him by crucifying him with great cruelty — and that all Jews are both guilty and cursed for this greatest crime and sin in human history. In Europe, all over Europe, they still do. In the United Kingdom, more than eleven million people consider Jews responsible for Jesus' death. In Germany also about eleven million people share this view. In France nine million people agree that this charge is true. In Spain, the number is almost ten million. In Poland, almost half the people, close to eighteen million, believe that Jews are responsible in Jesus' death. Surveys of European countries taken over the last decades consistently show that the European-wide average of those countries (the surveys range from between five and twelve countries, regularly including the largest ones) is that between 20 and 23 percent of the people believe this most damaging antisemitic charge of all time. In a survey done in 2012 of twelve European countries, including the six largest ones in the European Union, comprising roughly 80 percent of the EU's population, around eighty million people were revealed to believe this most prejudicial and damaging antisemitic belief and accusation. If this average held over the entire EU, with a population of five hundred million in 2012, which, given the diversity and size of the countries surveyed, is a safe projection, the number for these countries who are deeply prejudiced against Jews — in this at once age-old and very contemporary way — is around one hundred million.

In a more expansive notion of Europe, the number is still much higher, as the European Union does not include many of the European countries of the former Soviet Union, including Ukraine and Russia itself, both of which have historically been deeply antisemitic, indeed at least as antisemitic as their Western neighbors. They are therefore unlikely, being also deeply religious (indeed much more religious than the European average) — 75 percent of Ukrainians profess believing in God — to have a smaller part of their populations believing that Jews are guilty for murdering Jesus than in the European Union as a whole. Without reliable surveys, we cannot say how many people in these countries believe in the intergenerational guilt and cursedness of Jews for their forebears' alleged role in Jesus' death, but of the two hundred million people in Russia and Ukraine, the number is certainly in the tens of millions. If only 20 percent of Russians and Ukrainians hold such views, which is likely well below the actual figure that would be consistent with Europe more generally, that would add another forty million, bringing the European total to 140 million dyed-in-the-wool antisemites.

These numbers become magnified in significance when we realize that Europe has become an ever more secularized region, with traditional churches having ever less doctrinal authority, and with Western Europe in particular being the world's most secularized region. This means that the age-old Christian charges and animus against Jews should have as little hold in these countries today as they do in any part of the Christian world. The percentage believing in God in these countries is above 50 percent in Poland (80 percent), Ukraine (75 percent), Italy (74 percent), Spain (59 percent), and Austria (54 percent). In Germany (47 percent) and eighteen other European countries the number is below 50 percent, often well below. In the UK it is 38 percent, France 34 percent, the Netherlands also 34 percent, with Sweden at 23 percent and the Czech Republic at 19 percent.[3] When we realize that these numbers are bolstered in many countries by a considerable, believing, Muslim population, their percentage of people who believe in a Christian God is that much lower. Thus when tens of millions of people deem Jews responsible for Jesus' death, it is a very high percentage of the believing Christians in these countries, which shows the enormous tenacity of this belief — and likely of antisemitism more generally. This antisemitism remains so powerful, and this despite the Catholic and Protestant churches' explicit declarations to the contrary regarding Jews and Jesus' death. Old prejudices die hard. In this case, when the plausibility structure — the Christian one — is maintained, it dies hardly at all.

People's belief in all Jews' responsibility or cursedness for Jesus' death is but a continuation of age-old antisemitism. Such belief, in such numbers of people, is not in any way explicable by pointing to contemporary social or political conditions, the state of the economy, the real or alleged power of Jews, or the country of Israel's existence or its policies or its believed-in transgressions. It is worth noting again that anyone who believes that Jews are guilty for Jesus' death is, almost categorically, predisposed to believing other antisemitic notions and accepting other antisemitic accusations against Jews, even more than prejudice in general prepares the prejudiced person to be generally open to additional prejudicial notions about the group thought to be noxious or dangerous.

Because those people, in this case the Jews, who would murder the son of God, in order to want and to be able to do such a thing, must be both the incarnation of evil and extremely powerful, capable and desirous of perpetrating any injury that human beings, or perhaps in the Jews' case inhuman or devilish beings, could dream up. That on the order of one hundred million people in Europe (west of Russia and Ukraine) believe that Jews are responsible for Jesus' death means that as a definitional matter a vast and critical mass of European antisemites exists—which has nothing to do with Israel and in itself shows that blaming Israel's actions for the existence of widespread and profound antisemitism is nonsense—and that a vast and critical mass of European antisemites exists ready to keep antisemitism alive by being receptive to, and thereby creating demand for, antisemitic views, and by sharing their prejudices with others, sustaining a vibrant antipathy toward and discourse about Jews. All this being the case, and as bad as it is for antisemitism's constitution in Europe and for Jews' standing and state there, it still constitutes only a small fraction—and hardly the worst or most antisemitic part—of the contemporary European antisemitic complex.

Another classic survey question has been repeatedly put to Europeans: Do Jews have too much power in the business world? This question is meant to tap another long-standing (though not quite as long) and core antisemitic belief. Before we explore the broader significance of this question, which is typically ignored, here are the numbers:

In the United Kingdom, thirteen million people say it is probably the case that Jews are too powerful in business. In Germany, eighteen million people agree. In France, twenty-three million see Jews as too powerful in this respect. In Poland, 54 percent of the populace, almost twenty-one million people, see the Jews as too economically powerful. In Spain the numbers are 60 percent and more than twenty-seven million people. And in Hungary, three out of every four people, more than seven million of the ten million Hungarians, consider the Jews too powerful. Surveys of the last several years have found that between 30 and 40 percent of Europeans (again, not including Ukraine or Russia) consider that Jews hold too much power in business. This means that at least 150–200 million Europeans believe in Jews' overbearing power in business and are therefore antisemitic. Add in a likely commensurate percentage for Ukraine and Russia, and the number rises to 210–280 million people.

This widely existing antisemitic trope takes various forms regarding Jews and money, in this case Jews having too much power in business. As much as the surveys reveal about the vast number of antisemites in Europe, we should not move on from this antisemitic canard without further consideration. As a sign of how much the antisemitic mindset is taken for granted, the deeper meaning of questions about Jews' power or malfeasance remains reflexively uninvestigated. There are three aspects in which this question, taken at face value, conceals an even far more disturbing reality than the already extraordinarily troubling fact that perhaps two to three hundred million Europeans believe in its anti-semitic content.

Being asked a question about Jews' excessive business power actually makes sense to those being asked. This in itself is astonishing. To them we should ask: What does the aspect of people's identity — among the many other aspects of their identity — that happens to be *Jewish* have to do with them being businessmen or businesswomen? On the face of it: nothing. Yet that is how they are identified by the majoritarian popula-tion of their countries. What is *Jewish* about an Italian businessman or banker, and what is *Jewish* about his pursuit of sales, products, profits, or earnings? To ask the question is to make it obvious that any answer, except *nothing,* is an antisemitic answer. So the very identification of people's defining identity when they are in business as Jews — instead of as just being Italian or French or German businessmen or, for that mat-ter, just businessmen and -women operating in a market economy — is in itself marking Jews as fundamentally different, which is the founda-tional antisemitic paradigm's first element.

The second aspect of this question, which should not be treated as unproblematic, or rather not be seen as not being an utter nonissue, is that those business people wrongly categorized primarily as Jews are seen as having "too much power." What could this mean? It is not that they have too much money, whatever complaint that might produce. It is that they have too much *power.* Whatever exactly the people agreeing with this notion mean, it is nonetheless clear — because the alleged *power* is deemed too much — that Jews having such power in business is a problem, is threatening, is seen as a resource that they misuse or poten-tially misuse. Power is always potentially dangerous. Otherwise no one would talk about power or certainly about Jews having too much of it.

Because if it were not dangerous or at least problematic in some substantial if ill-defined way, then it would make no sense to say that Jews possess too much of it. Jews' power and the danger that they inherently pose are a hallmark of the fundamental antisemitic paradigm.

This antisemitic accusation's third aspect that bears investigation is its fantastical quality. The number of each of the European countries' Jews is between tiny and minuscule. The notion that a statement such as "Jews have too much power in the business world" could possibly make sense stretches any credulity and actually does make sense only to the antisemitically inflamed mind and its possessor, the antisemite. Here are some figures. The largest percentage that Jews compose of *any* of the European Union's large countries is in France. How big? Less than 1 percent. The number is seven-tenths of 1 percent. Yet twenty-two million French are preoccupied enough with alleged Jewish power in business that they are concerned this tiny minority has too much power. The UK, having the large EU countries' second highest percentage, has Jews comprising one-half of 1 percent of the population. After France and the UK, the numbers become truly infinitesimal. In Germany Jews comprise one-tenth of 1 percent of the people. Yet eighteen million Germans think they have too much power. In Italy, there are only twenty-eight thousand Jews in the country, comprising four one-hundredths of 1 percent of the Italian people. Sixty percent of Spaniards think that one one-hundredth of 1 percent of their country's people — Jews — have too much power. In Poland, 54 percent of the people have a similar worry. If so many people are concerned about such a serious matter, then a person might think that there is something to it. Yet Poland, a country of more than thirty-eight million people, has only three thousand Jews. That's right, only three thousand, comprising *one-hundredth of 1 percent* of the country's population, or one Jew among every ten thousand Poles. And most of them are elderly. In smaller European countries, the figures are comparable. In the economic powerhouse of Switzerland, a country now infamous for its shady and criminal business practices regarding Jews' assets during the Holocaust, not to mention sheltering the fortunes stolen from their people by the world's criminal political leaders in secret accounts, and where Jews are only one-tenth of 1 percent of the population, 40 percent of the people are concerned about Jews' alleged excessive power in business. Given that the extent of such beliefs in Jews' business power is so well and repeatedly documented, in one European country after another, we might be justified in thinking that a couple of hundred million Europeans are crazy or hallucinatory. But they are not: they are merely antisemitic, and the character of their fantastical antisemitism, which is so common, is "normal." This fantastical quality is a further characteristic of the foundational antisemitic paradigm that predisposes people, as virtually no other prejudice does, to believing any charge against Jews, no matter how outlandish it may be.

If the Francophone Walloons populating mainly eastern Belgium said in response to a survey question that the Dutch-speaking Flemish populating western Belgium had too much power in business, then that would at least make sense and be in principle defensible as a general statement. The Flemish are a large group. There is an ongoing social and political conflict between the two groups over the constitution and governance of Belgium. Each group identifies itself, including publicly, primarily as members of their ethnic group, which is also differentiated linguistically. The Flemish are more prosperous, and conflict over economic productivity and the economic distribution of the country's wealth has been considerable. But as we have seen, no such conditions apply *in any European country* to Jews. Jews simply do not form the critical mass to be in such a position.

The significance of these infinitesimal numbers of Jews in European countries pertains to understanding the character and power of many other antisemitic notions and accusations that course through European countries. One of the classic antisemitic accusations is that Jews are traitors to their own countries because they care about fellow Jews who, it is worth emphasizing, are utter strangers, who live in other countries and hundreds or thousands of miles away, more than they care about the people of the communities they grew up in and the countries that are their homes. This is known as the dual loyalty charge. In reality it is an accusation that Jews are treasonous in their political orientation. (That this is so, and that it taps into notions of Jews' asociability because they care only about Jews, is revealed by on the order of 190 million Europeans agreeing that "Jews in general do not care about anything or anyone but their own kind." *Anything* or *Anyone!*) The most notorious instance of the many times and places that such an accusation has been made about Jews' putative absence of loyalty and their political treason is the "stab-in-the-back" myth that became a fixed part of the German national and political landscape after World War I, when it became the common sense of German society that Germany had lost the war because its Jews had betrayed the nation. How and why exactly Jews, this weak minority at the time composing less than 1 percent of the population, utterly devoted to the well-being of their homeland, Germany, were supposed to have stabbed that homeland and Germans (meaning non-Jewish Germans) in the back with such telling effect as to make the country lose this war with all the disastrous consequences that followed was never sensibly articulated and is on the face of it fantastical. The German authorities, in keeping with the drumbeat of accusations during the war that Jews were not serving on the front, did a very public and humiliating census of Jews' service in the armed forces in 1916 (think of what carrying out the investigation said to the German public), which actually showed that Jews were indeed patriotically serving their country. But given such unwelcome findings, the authorities kept the results secret. The Jewish community also published its own statistical refutations of the antisemitic charges, yet the facts made no difference to the profoundly antisemitic German population. This devastating *stab in the back* canard became a powerfully effective antisemitic rallying cry during Weimar and the Nazi period and a powerful explanation to Germans for why Germans needed to eliminate the Jews, lest the same thing happen in any current or future conflict, such as World War II. In light of this history and the relationship of this canard to the Germans' eliminationist and exterminationist persecution of the Jews across an entire continent (with the help of so many other Europeans), that Germans (and other Europeans) today could charge Jews with disloyalty is an indication of either how scant historical knowledge is on the part of some, how deeply rooted such antisemitism is, or the considerable stock of chutzpah Germans (and others) are willing to draw upon in the expression of their antipathies toward Jews.

Today, this dimension is tapped by the survey question, Are "Jews more loyal to Israel than to their own country?" In light of the tiny number of Jews in most of these European countries, we might step back to first ask a prior question: Why would anyone care about the so-called loyalty of such a tiny percentage of their country's people in the first place? We might further wonder how anyone could care enough to see

Jews as not being "loyal," especially in light of the history of Jews in those countries, which is one of vile and violent and, indeed often, mass-murderous persecution. In most European countries, the larger populaces were deeply and openly antisemitic through the end of the Nazi period, with many people contributing to the Germans' exterminationist assault, and many more looking on in support of it. Anyway, what does the loyalty issue mean? That the tiny number of Jews of such countries—themselves in France to be French, in England to be English, in Netherlands to be Dutch, in Italy to be Italian, and so on—are merely well disposed toward Israel? Hardly. The survey question itself reflects an antisemitic charge of treason that is repeatedly aired, a suspicion that floats about the countries of Europe and elsewhere, an accusation that was once one of the central ones leveled at Jews during the heyday of modern antisemitism in the nineteenth and first half of the twentieth centuries. Today, consistently across European countries, around half the people say it is probably true that Jews are more loyal to Israel than to their own countries, where they choose to be citizens, choose to live, choose to make their homes, choose to work, choose to have friends, choose to bear and raise children, choose to be patriotic. Just to put this in perspective, in Spain three out of four people (72 percent) deem the one one-hundredth of 1 percent of the Spanish people who happen to be Jews to be disloyal! In Switzerland 44 percent of the people similarly think about the one-tenth of 1 percent of the Swiss who are Jews. Germany is the country, more than any other and more damagingly than any other, that articulated this disloyalty charge memorably. Today, more than forty-two million Germans continue to maintain that the one-tenth of 1 percent of the German populace that are Jews are disloyal. And in the United Kingdom the figure is 48 percent of what is by European standards a robust Jewish community of one-half of 1 percent of the country's population. All in all, 55 percent of Europeans, on the order of 275 million people (not including Ukrainians and Russians), think that the two one-thousandths of 1 percent of the populace of Europe that are Jews are disloyal. How could anyone even care enough about such a tiny and insignificant minority to have given this topic a second's thought, let alone not to have dismissed the topic as utterly trivial, not worthy of being cared about, let alone in light of the Holocaust—which was grounded in, among many other antisemitic notions, precisely this one, namely that

Jews are disloyal aliens — not be grossly offended by this grotesque question? More colloquially: Is this nuts?

Of course, small groups can have large impacts. But the dual loyalty accusation that Europeans and others so commonly level at Jews likely covers a host of prejudicial and antipathetic sentiments that the people harbor toward Jews. Beyond the mere accusation of disloyalty, the thoroughgoing rejection of Jews as members of the national community can be seen where the question has been put more directly. In Ireland, only two thousand Jews live among 4.5 million people, yet antisemitism is intense. In 2011, twenty-two percent said that Ireland should forbid Israelis who wanted to become naturalized Irish citizens from doing so, and one of ten Irish (11.5 percent) wanted to bar all Jews from becoming citizens. Jews, by dint of their Jewness, are in the eyes of many Irish unfit to live in Ireland.[4]

Returning to economic issues, dovetailing with Europeans' fantastical belief that Jews have too much power in business in their own countries is the international dimension of this age-old antisemitic canard, namely that "Jews have too much power in international financial markets." Again, the statement begs the question of why international bankers and currency traders who happen to be Jews would be defined as *Jews*, why such Jews' having such *power* (whatever that means) let alone *too much* power would be bad — for what evil are the supposed Jews supposedly using such power? In 2007, nearly 40 percent of the people in ten European countries held Jews to be too powerful in international finance, so about two hundred million people in the European Union (not including Ukraine and Russia) saw Jews as ominously powerful in world finance.

This general antisemitic orientation, and general unease with Jews' alleged power, became that much more relevant with the financial crisis that struck country after country, Europe as a whole, and indeed the entire world in 2008 and that has retained its common danger and has taken on various forms and stages depending on the country and region of the world. The crisis was caused by huge speculative housing bubbles bursting across North America and Europe; incredibly poor governmental regulation and oversight of mortgage companies, insurance companies, and banks across the industrialized world, producing crippling unsecured debt on the part of banks and other financial institutions just about everywhere; the virtual implosion of the financial systems of many countries, and the actual bankruptcy of some banking systems and countries; enormous debt overhang in tens of millions of households and in countries' economies in general; and finally sovereign debt crises in a stunning array of European countries, with devastating spillover for the financial systems, already weakened or tottering. This massive local, national, regional, and international financial and economic crisis had millions upon millions of contributors, vast financial institutional complicity, and extensive and varied governmental mismanagement or worse to bring it about, and then once it got kicked off, to prolong and deepen it (even as governments brought national and international economies back from the edge of the abyss, and even immediately shored up banking systems). So shortly after the crisis began — perhaps as reflex, perhaps as subjective considered judgment — who did vast numbers of Europeans turn to in order to blame for the "current global economic crisis"? Roughly 30 percent of Europeans in seven countries surveyed in 2009 specifically accused Jews to a greater or lesser extent for the considerable misery and injury caused by, and further threatened by, the global economic and financial crisis. This is, simply, an astonishing instance of fantastical prejudice. After all, this was not the seventeenth century or nineteenth century or even the first part of the twentieth century, when people had little grasp and meager information about the workings of regional and national economies and so they naturally relied upon their antisemitic notions of Jewish power and malfeasance, of Jewish power and economic malfeasance, to explain economic disruptions large and small. About the financial crisis that began in 2008 there was an immediate and continuing flood of reports and analyses across all media that accurately (or even inaccurately) discussed the many economic and political factors that had absolutely nothing to do with Jews that had contributed to or caused the crisis, in its overall contours and in its many particulars. Yet tens upon tens of millions of Europeans, despite this, still blamed the Jews.

Germany in this context, as for so many, is particularly instructive. That, after all the decades of formal and informal education in Germany, when Germans have been assiduously taught and been exposed to the perniciousness of such views, 30 percent or twenty-four million Germans hold such a Nazi-like view of Jews that they would see them as responsible for the financial crisis tells us of antisemitism's depth and breadth in European and German culture, of antisemitism's tenacity, and of the difficulty of dislodging antisemitism from its adherents' minds and hearts. It, as much of the survey data reveal, also shows the enormous disjunction between the private beliefs of people and what is being said, openly or in whispers in their communities and families on the one hand, and what on the other hand is expressed in the public sphere, including or especially in the media, where such views in Germany and across Europe barely, if at all, make it into a *public* discourse.

The extent of such antisemitism does not bode well for the future, because it is unlikely that formal and informal anti-antisemitic education anywhere in Europe or elsewhere in the coming years will be as intensive as it has been in Germany in the decades since World War II. If the numbers for these seven countries, including four of the largest six, held for the European Union in general — and given the consistency of such numbers across the European landscape, it would be unlikely if they did not — then one hundred fifty million Europeans have been holding Jews responsible for such a colossal injury done, a stance bound to provoke, broaden, and intensify antisemitism and its associated animus toward Jews. It is also noteworthy that this is a pure projection of many Europeans' fundamental belief that Jews have too much power in business and that Jews use such alleged power to the detriment of non-Jews. It could be nothing else, as, as if this needs to be said, there is no tangible evidence that Jews were responsible — or more precisely just government officials, businessmen, bankers, mortgage lenders who happen also to be Jewish — for the financial crisis.

Such a large number of Europeans projecting such culpability upon Jews is a clear instance of how a general antisemitic belief or orientation leads people to be ready to accept new accusations and specific accusations of Jews' supposed malfeasance as being true, and of how accepting the foundational antisemitic paradigm predisposes people to expand and intensify their antisemitism in all kinds of circumstances, ones that have something to do with Jews and ones that do not. With the intensifying sovereign debt crisis of Greece, Spain, Italy, and Ireland in 2011–2013, the absurdity of the beliefs that such minuscule numbers of ordinary people in country after country, known as Jews, are responsible for their countries' and Europe's financial problems become, if that is possible, that much more absurd.

Believing any of these classical antisemitic notions makes a person an antisemite. Such views of Jews cannot be explained away, rationalized, or — try as antisemites would — justified as being true. (A person trying to justify them, in other words, to say that they are either true or believable enough, succeeds only in revealing that he or she is antisemitic.) The same logic outlined earlier follows here, too: if any such statements, merely any single one of them, were made about other minorities, African Americans, Latinos, Germans of Polish ancestry, Protestants in France, especially about any minuscule and powerless minority that had almost been entirely exterminated in the recent histories of those countries, we would unhesitatingly call it prejudice or racism, see the person as prejudiced or racist, and deem the statement and the person who holds it incredibly damaging or potentially dangerous, a bigot, a racist, so in this case, an antisemite. By this measure at least half the people in the European Union, two hundred fifty million, are definitively and profoundly antisemitic.

And again: everything we know about antisemitism and prejudice more broadly teaches us, people who believe one prejudicial, namely antisemitic, thing about Jews are prone to accepting others. Not surprisingly, Europeans today bear this out. Nearly one out of three Europeans (31 percent) in ten European countries agree with at least three of four antisemitic statements that were asked of them — statements that are, significantly, about different kinds of allegedly noxious or dangerous qualities of Jews. One, the dual loyalty charge, falls on the political dimension, tapping Jews' putative sociability and fitness to be members of the national community or just citizens in their own country. The second, about Jews' allegedly excessive power in the business world, explores the threat posed by Jews on the economic dimension domestically. A third, about Jews' supposed excessive power in international financial markets, relates to the international dimension of antisemitism. The fourth, about whether Jews talk too much about their victimization during the Holocaust, gets at a post-Holocaust dimension of antisemitism called secondary antisemitism. This is another bizarre aspect of antisemitism that has few if any parallels: people blame the Jews themselves in various ways for having been the victims of eliminationist and exterminationist persecution, including at the hands of the countrymen of the people doing the blaming, maintaining that the Jews are deviously trying to gain advantage from their collective victimization. That this dimension is real has been ascertained in different surveys that revealed that a consistent two hundred million people (41 percent) in the European Union maintain each of the following, that "Jews still talk too much about what happened to them in the Holocaust" and that "Jews try to take advantage of having been victims during the Nazi era."

Six million Hungarians, fully three out of five Hungarian people, sixteen million French, seventeen million Germans, eighteen million Poles, twenty-four million Spaniards, and millions in country after country, have *multiple antisemitic views on a range of dimensions.* If the percentage of Europeans holding such views pertained for the whole European Union as they do in these ten countries totaling ninety million antisemites, then the number of people in the EU with demonstrable *multiple and mutually reinforcing, powerfully antisemitic* views is on the order of 150 million! And this certainly grossly understates the number of people who are animated by such interlocking antisemitic complexes, because the four questions asked of Europeans in these surveys tap and aggregate only the small subset of these four antisemitic beliefs from among all the many antisemitic notions that exist. There is every reason to believe that if other dimensions and views were added, including the large number of Europeans who hold Jews responsible for the death of Jesus, then still many more Europeans would reveal themselves to hold extensive complexes of antisemitic notions and passions and that these antisemitic complexes would also have more interlocking elements and more aggregate depth and power.

These data, and the reality they reflect and reveal, have nothing to do with Israel's policies or its people's conduct. They have nothing to do with Israel's alleged transgressions. They have nothing to do with the Middle East conflict. They demonstrate beyond any doubt that in Europe antisemitism at its heart has nothing to do with what it is written off to: Israel. Instead, European antisemitism remains extremely widespread, is a massive problem, and is grounded in long-existing antisemitic tropes, from seeing Jews as guilty and cursed for Jesus' death to seeing them as politically disloyal, dangerously powerful in business, internationally responsible for predations, responsible for grave (financial) harm, exploitive of non-Jews. Anyone who claims that antisemitism — as opposed to mere anti-Israelism — is not the problem is simply willfully ignoring the evidence or flat-out lying. (The latter is particularly likely for those insistent antisemites and anti-Israel ideologues, whether they are in the academy or not, who actually do pay attention to what is going on regarding antisemitism and regarding Israel.) These are *all* classically and classical antisemitic notions, notions that are so powerful that 250 million Europeans hold on to any number of them, and 150 million Europeans hold on to multiple ones of them. And they do so after the Holocaust. These data further show, which is another way of saying the Europeans themselves further show, that the foundational antisemitic paradigm is deeply and broadly entrenched in European culture and among European peoples, in country after country.

Turning to what Europeans believe about Israel, there can be no doubt that these classical antisemitic prejudices, so widespread in Europe, feed the animus against Israel and also are used to make plausible and reinforce accusations of Jewish Israelis' malevolence or misconduct. The Christ-killing trope, and its activation of the foundational antisemitic paradigm, remains powerful, so powerful that it is regularly employed in Europe, including in the cartoon below by one of the mainline Italian newspapers. When looking at what Europeans believe about Israel, this prejudice's power and the fantastical extremes to which it takes its adherents becomes even clearer. Two antisemitic notions that enormous numbers of Europeans have adopted reveal the power of this animus when directed at the country that is the home to a few million Jews and that is overwhelmingly the place of Jews' political expression and self-determination as a people. In seven countries alone, 127 million Europeans assert that "Israel is conducting a war of extermination against the

La Stampa, *Italy, April 3, 2002. A menacing tank with a David Star bearing down on him, the fearful baby Jesus on the left says: "Surely they don't want to kill me again?!"*

Palestinians." If the same proportion of the European populace as a whole (not including Ukraine and Russia) shares this view, which it likely does, as these seven countries from all parts of Europe comprise already 55 percent of the European populace, then on the order of 225 million Europeans today hold the fantastical belief that Israelis are committing genocide against the Palestinians. The percentage of the populace that clings to this out-and-out antisemitic view varies from a hardly comforting low of almost two out of every five people (37.5 percent) in Italy to almost two out of every three people (63.3 percent) in Poland. That constitutes twenty-three million Italians and twenty-four million Poles. Perhaps, but only perhaps, the most surprising number of people who hold this antisemitic view is in Germany, where there can be no doubt that saying that "Israel is waging a war of extermination against the Palestinians" is essentially equating Israel with Nazi Germany and the practices of Israelis with Nazis and essentially saying that what Germans once did to Jews, Jews are now doing to Palestinians. After all the education Germans have had about the horrors of Nazism and the Holocaust, about the creation of gas chambers and death factories, forty-seven million Germans, more than half the country's population (57 percent), have such an antisemitically clouded view of Israel and fantastical view of Jews that they say that Israel's occupation of West Bank and responses to incessant rocket attacks by Hamas in Gaza constitutes a war of extermination. These figures and what they reveal are nothing short of extraordinary.

Jewish Israelis' conflict with Palestinians has included an occupation that has lasted more than forty years. During this time—as it has been for its entire sixty-five-year history—Israel has been existentially threatened and in an unwanted state of war. For most of its history it has often been under attack, from surrounding Arab states, from rockets, genocide bombings (more conventionally called "suicide bombing"), and terror warfare, or from two uprisings called Intifada, in which Israeli soldiers and civilians were under constant attack or its threat. During the last ten years, the period most relevant for people's current understanding of this conflict and their assessment of the Israelis' conduct and intentions, Israelis have killed almost 6,500 Palestinians. Almost all of these fatalities occurred in conflict situations, either military operations against armed Palestinians or during the Second Intifada, when Palestinians, mainly youths, regularly assaulted Israel's security personnel with hails of stones and against which the Israelis had to defend themselves. Palestinians, in turn, killed more than a thousand Israelis. Palestinians also killed more than six hundred Palestinians.

However critical someone might reasonably be of Israel's security and operational doctrines, including the proportionality of its responses to Palestinians' attacks, there is no non-antisemitic way to think or say that Israel is carrying out genocide against the Palestinians. The Palestinian population of West Bank and Gaza totals almost four million, and of those areas together with Israel itself, more than five million. (The Jewish population of Israel is equivalent, around six million.) In the ten years before 2008, Palestinian population growth in Gaza and West Bank was one of the highest rates in the world, at 30 percent. From 1990 to 2008, the Palestinian population under Israel's occupation more than doubled! These numbers demonstrate that Israel, a militarily potent and effective country, could not possibly be trying to *exterminate* the Palestinians. Only deeply prejudiced people, either cynically lying or out of touch with Middle Eastern reality, could say that Israel is conducting a war of extermination against Palestinians.

The virtually obsessive attention, outrage, and wild exaggerations that characterize Europeans' (and non-Europeans') stances toward Israel's treatment of Palestinians is selective and shows bad faith not just in the sense we have seen — namely, that other beleaguered peoples, such as Kurds, who are suffering victimization equal to or greater than Palestinians do at the hands of the Israelis, and those who are victimizing other peoples, such as Turks, receive barely any attention — but also in another sense: when people other than Jewish Israelis are victimizing Palestinians, the world cares little at all. Among the many instances when this has been clear was, in 1991 after the first Gulf War, Kuwaitis' wholesale assault on the sizable Palestinian community for having allegedly collaborated with the occupying Iraqis. Despite the mass arrests, beatings and torture, expulsions, and killings by Kuwaitis themselves and more systematically by state security forces, the world barely took notice. Such neglect when Palestinians are the victims of non-Israelis could be seen, most recently, during the Syrian civil war. As of May 2013, Palestinian sources and the United Nations reported that various

Syrian forces have killed more than two thousand Palestinians and driven close to three hundred thousand from their homes. Yet about this real murderous and eliminationist onslaught against the Palestinians, there has barely been a peep from the Europeans or the international community.[5] Indeed, as there have been around half a million Palestinians living in Syria, this means that perhaps 60 percent of all Palestinians in the country have been victims of a mass eliminationist assault — proportionally it would be as if Israel were to expel two and a half million Palestinians from West Bank and Gaza! During the Syrian conflict's two years, the Palestinians have suffered a yearly casualty rate that is approximately *twelve times higher* than the yearly casualty rate of Palestinians living in West Bank and Gaza have averaged over the last ten years! That such enormously elevated levels of displacement and death is not a natural result of the general fighting in Syria is obvious, as the rates of elimination of Palestinians dwarf those of the more general Syrian population. Just from the numbers, and augmented by reports on the ground, it is obvious that Syrian forces (perhaps on both sides) are targeting, eliminating, and killing Palestinians. But as long as Jewish Israelis are not doing it, neither the Europeans nor the world seems to care very much. Hence the silence.

That such fantasies of Jews perpetrating genocide would occur to Europeans, and to Europeans in country after country in such overwhelmingly enormous numbers, is both further definitive evidence about the extent of antisemitism, definitive evidence about that antisemitism's demonizing quality, and powerful evidence that the hostility toward Israel, and the criticism of Israel, is not a result, certainly not merely or overwhelmingly a result, of Israel's policies or actions or even of principled concern for the Palestinians. If it were, then, even if exaggerated, the criticism would be grounded in Israel's actual conduct, and not be so categorically at odds with reality. Many regimes, conflicts, or governmental programs are condemned by other countries or peoples with the harsh criticism staying within the bounds of reality, and without such fantastical, out-of-this-world charges of the sort routinely directed at Israel. This sort of antisemitic stance on the part of tens upon tens of millions of Europeans in country after country is just one instance of the broader and profound antisemitic thrust that demonizes Israel and Jews, which we will explore more fully in the next chapter. This demonization is not even somewhat coded, as we might understand it to be when Europeans characterize Israel's conduct as genocidal. It is explicit. The assertion that Israel is like Nazi Germany is common in the European public sphere and also widely believed to be true by ordinary Europeans. In 2004, nearly 40 percent of Italians agreed that "the Israeli government is perpetrating a full-fledged genocide and is acting with the Palestinians the way the Nazis did with the Jews." In four surveys from 2004 and 2008, between 40 and 50 percent of Germans asserted that Israel's treatment of Palestinians "is in principle not different" from what "the Nazis did to the Jews." There is no quicker and more effective way to demonize a person, people, and country than by falsely using the *Nazi* label for them, which antisemites in Europe and elsewhere regularly do for Israel.* If these numbers, as other antisemitic prejudices do, held constant across the continent, then perhaps 200 million Europeans see Jewish Israelis as being Nazi-like. Fantastical as it is, it is significant that Europeans brand the Jews abroad, namely in Israel, Nazi-like in their conduct without explicitly publicly attacking Jews at home as Nazi-like, even though they assume the Jews living in their communities to be reflexive supporters of Israel and its policies.

The study that determined this extraordinarily high rate of Europeans demonizing Israel sought also to uncover whether the people confine such deeply antisemitic and fantastical views to Israel, or Jewish Israelis, or whether they also see the demonizing animus as applicable to Jews in general. For every five people who made the accusation that Israel is committing genocide, four say that Israel's policies understandably affect people's view of Jews in general. Almost two in five Europeans (37.4 percent), which across the European Union would amount to 185 million people, assert that "considering Israel's policies, I can well understand that people do not like Jews."[6] More tellingly, that those accusing Israel of conducting a war of extermination against Palestinians tend to implicate

---

* This does not mean that when a Nazi comparison is *appropriate* that we should not use it, such as when people explicitly employ Nazi-inspired or Nazi-like antisemitic accusations against Jews or Israel, celebrate the Nazis' eliminationist assault or mass murder of the Jews, or urge or seek to enact a new eliminationist or exterminationist program against Jews. In fact, in such cases, we would be remiss if we did not accurately characterize them as Nazi or Nazi-like.

Dagbladet, *Norway, July 10, 2006. "Olmert the Nazi." Israel's Prime Minister Ehud Olmert depicted as a concentration camp commandant.*

Jews living outside Israel, who are not Israeli citizens, in this alleged crime, also is not a conventional reaction to a country's real or alleged transgressions. Who would blame Italian Americans or Chinese Americans for transgressions by Italy or China respectively?

Indeed, antisemitism and condemnation of Israel has a recursive quality. Antisemitism frames and influences many people's perception of and reactions to Israel's conflict with Palestinians in a manner that demonizes Israel, which then, owing to another aspect of antisemitism that implicates all Jews in some Jews' putative transgressions, exacerbates or activates hostility toward Jews in general, which then further predisposes those same people and their society more generally to believe antisemitic things about Israel, and so on. Differently conceived, antisemites find the source of Israel's and its Jews' supposed Nazi-like quality in their Jewness, which is a quality shared by Jews in general, which leads them to transfer their animus for Israel to Jews in general at an enormously high rate.

The vast number of Europeans who concede in surveys that they hold views that, on so many different levels and dimensions, are effectively deeply antisemitic and that are often wild accounts of reality establishes that (1) the age-old animus is still powerful and widespread, (2) it is an enormous problem, (3) it has nothing to do with Israel or "anti-Israelism," and (4) we should stop pretending otherwise about all these. These results, showing the rampant antisemitism of Europeans, are not based on the findings of an isolated survey but are highly robust and reliable, grounded in repeated surveys. The numbers of Europeans responding antisemitically, waxing and waning a bit over the years, have remained during the last two decades essentially consistent, with each survey confirming the validity and reliability of the others. Nevertheless, because they are surveys of only a few (well-chosen) questions, they tap only a few aspects of antisemitism, and they do not convey the flavor or elaborated content of the the various antisemitic discourses that have been constructed on the foundational antisemitic paradigm's rock-solid and continent-wide foundation. They also do not flesh out the character of the antisemitic environment's social and physical atmosphere.

Global antisemitism's discourse is worldwide. Its various constitutive discourses in the public sphere and at various levels of civil society are continental, regional across countries, civilization-wide, national, sub-national, local, private. The global antisemitic discourse takes place in the age-old media of newspapers and books and images drawn on walls, twentieth-century media of television and radio, twenty-first-century social media of the Internet, Facebook, websites, chat rooms, YouTube, and Twitter. It takes place face-to-face in schools and at universities, in liturgy and sermons in Christian and Islamic houses of worship, in rallies and demonstrations, in restaurants and pubs, over the dinner table. It is composed of words, sometimes of slogans, sometimes of pseudo-learned disquisitions. It is composed of images, from cartoons to photographs to video. It is backward looking, grounds itself in the present, and is future oriented. It presents itself as fact, as reportage or documentary or news, as sociological, psychological, or political analysis that supposedly plumbs broader patterns, deeper reasons, and ultimate significance. It presents itself as imaginative works, whether poetry or fiction, or in film, theater, television series, or video games. It pretends to educate soberly or seeks to inflame passions, raise alarms, rouse people for action. It proposes remedies and policies, crafts strategies and tactics, and suggests courses of action that are social, economic, and political, that urge people to use words and gestures, policy instruments, both nonviolent and violent. It seeks to diagnose, prognosticate about, and solve the global Jewish Problem (even if it does not use this term), the global problem that Jewness poses.

As this suggests, a thorough account of this discourse's many and vast European components, let alone its character around the world in all its millions of nodes and its that-much-vaster number of words and images, would consume volumes.

In the face of this endless barrage, it is not surprising that antisemitic reporting agencies and roundups, while being of enormous importance, focus on only selected elements of the global antisemitic complex: they consist mainly of the physical attacks upon Jews and their institutions and property, surveys that investigate a few valid and highly revealing themes about people's views but which are superficial in that they leave out many other important themes and fail to dig deeper into people's attitudes, and accounts of opinion leaders' public statements and writings. Such reports and roundups are important and valuable. Yet they hardly provide an integrated account of antisemitism, including its conceptual underpinnings, an analytical account and workings of its discourses, or its potential, grounded in people's belief and emotion, for political mobilization and further injurious action. It is particularly worth emphasizing that because antisemitism today, in this global age of cross-national and cross-communal fertilization of ideas and notions, constitutes a discourse that recognizes no national boundaries, antisemitism also creates an international community or a series of communities of shared sentiment, which is insufficiently captured in the country-by-country orientation typical of reports about it. Antisemitism's broader coherence and power as a *global movement* is missing.

The overused metaphor of the tip of the iceberg is here apt. Most of the world's and overwhelmingly most of Europe's antisemitism remains submerged and hidden, with only a small portion of it breaking the surface for the eye to see. Some widely held antisemitic accusations hardly find a public airing of any kind, such as that Jews have too much power in business—even though 150 million people in the European Union believe it. Other deeply held antisemitic beliefs are expressed in public but not to any extent that would indicate how many tens of millions of people in country after country believe them. The vast and barely publicly detectable subterranean existence of prejudice is true of many prejudices that exist in societies where public norms provide powerful disincentives for their direct and clear expression. So most private views and passions do not get expressed publicly, or if expressed are often in coded forms that allow for plausible deniability that the antisemitism is actually antisemitism. Public taboos lead to a wildly understated and distorted public record of existing sentiments. And yet it is the public expression that overwhelmingly forms the public record and, more significantly, the assessments of what actually exists among the various portions of the populace. Nowhere has this disjunction been more obvious than in democratic Germany, which criminalized antisemitic expression after the Holocaust, so that the vast amounts of intensive and demonological antisemitism — which undoubtedly existed — suddenly, overnight, disappeared from the public sphere, finding almost no public expression for decades. If one had judged German society by antisemitic expression in public, including in books, newspapers, speeches, public rallies, and radio and television broadcasts, one would have had to conclude that the country that was the most antisemitic and most dangerously genocidal antisemitic in the world in 1944 was, five years later, after regaining its sovereignty, one of the least antisemitic countries in the world. That this disjunction between today's more considerable public expression, even if coded, of antisemitism and the vastly greater extent of antisemitism among the Germans that finds no public expression remains true even after the substantial reduction and tempering of Germans' antisemitism, owing to decades of democratic education and reality testing, was attested to in 2002 by the head of the German Catholic Church, Cardinal Karl Lehman, who while lamenting that "now as before there is an antisemitic sediment in the people," confessed what is the experience of religious leaders, politicians, and newspaper editors, "when I say something conciliatory with regard to the Jews, I still receive many dubious reactions, most of which are anonymous and antisemitic."[7]

Antisemitism in the United States differs in quantity, character, and intensity from that of Europe. It differs in what people believe and feel about Jews, what is said publicly, so what the public discourse is like, how people treat Jews, the level of violence and threat directed at Jews. In sum, it differs markedly on every critical dimension. American antisemitism differs not only when examined in isolation but much more when considered in the social, cultural, and political context, which includes a substantially — by many orders of magnitude — larger, more vigorous, more politically active, and more influential Jewish community.

Because we have explored the significance of the survey research's results, and the underlying meaning of those results, when looking at Europe, here we look at the numbers more quickly and with less explicit interpretation, while keeping a steady eye on comparison to Europe.

Almost one in three Americans (31 percent), ninety million people, believe the most damaging antisemitic canard of all time, that "Jews were responsible for the death of Christ." This is a huge number of people who accept the foundational antisemitic paradigm. The power of Christian antisemitism is much greater in the far more religious, and more deeply religious, United States than in more secularized Europe, making this the one area that the United States, especially its leading churches, Catholic and Protestant, needs to work on especially assiduously regarding antisemitism. On antisemitism's other dimensions, approximately sixty million Americans, one out of five (19 percent), believe that Jews have "too much power in the business world." This, of course, is an enormous number of antisemitic people, believing that Jews possess not only *power,* whatever that is, but too much of it — whatever that is. But the proportion of Americans who think this is considerably less than Europeans, where the percentage is roughly double. Similarly, one out of five Americans believe that Jews have "too much control/influence on Wall Street," a question that taps the antisemitic views of Jews in finance, and so is a rough equivalent to the question posed to Europeans about Jews' power in international finance, which in Europe is a code word for Wall Street. The European percentage, which is forty, is double that of the United States. One hundred million Americans, or one in three (30 percent), hold Jews to be "more loyal to Israel than America," which, though an indication of the degree to which this powerful dual loyalty charge still persists, remains much better than in Europe, where the proportion of people who believe this is two-thirds greater than in the United States, so fully 50 percent of the European public. Finally, many fewer Americans than Europeans deem Jews to be fundamentally asociable, with about one in seven saying Jews "don't care about anyone but their own kind." On the critical questions of seeing Jews as a threat (too much power, too much power in business, too much power on Wall Street, willing to use shady practices, dishonesty, not caring about others), the percentage of Americans who hold antisemitic views is remarkably consistent at between 14 and 20 percent. This means at once that a disturbing number of Americans, between about forty-five and sixty million, hold profoundly antisemitic views of Jews, and that the situation in the United States is heartening compared to Europe, where the percentage of antisemites is far greater, double or more. This fundamental difference between the United States and Europe is systematic. It can be seen in the substantially greater incidence of the dual loyalty accusation in Europe. On the measure of secondary antisemitism, namely whether Jews talk too much about the Holocaust, one in four Americans (26 percent) say that Jews do, compared to two in five Europeans (41 percent). The number of people who hold not only one antisemitic view but multiple and interlocking antisemitic ones is also twice as high in Europe, at more than 30 percent. In the United States it is 15 percent.

Three aspects of the antisemitism in the United States, and their relationship to one another, are worth noting. The country has seen a marked decline in antisemitism in the last four decades. The number of people who held multiple and interlocking antisemitic notions in 1964 was about one in three (30 percent). Today it is one in seven (15 percent). Indeed, it is fair to say that Americans and the character of the public culture and politics they have forged have brought this improvement about. This is indicated by a second aspect that helps explain antisemitism's current character, namely that Hispanic Americans born in the United States, having been fully reared and socialized in American society and exposed to the American public discourse, are deeply antisemitic at half the rate of Hispanic Americans born outside the United States. The third aspect of antisemitism relevant here is its variance according to educational achievement. Education, which in the United States decidedly teaches people anti-prejudicial views and integrates them much more broadly into society's public discourse, profoundly lessens antisemitism. Americans with a high school education or less are deeply antisemitic at a rate of one in five (22 percent). Those with some college education at a rate of one in eight (13 percent), and college graduates at less than half the rate of the first group, one in ten (9 percent).

Interestingly, the ethnic groups that experience the most overt discrimination in the United States, Hispanics and African Americans, are far more antisemitic than whites. Only one in ten whites is deeply antisemitic, compared to one in five Hispanic Americans born in the United States, with the proportion of Hispanic Americans born outside the United States double that, and compared to almost one in three African Americans. Thus American-born Hispanic Americans are deeply antisemitic at twice, and African Americans at three times, the rate of whites. The significance of this is twofold. As minorities who are set apart — whether by discrimination of various kinds, less access to education, or by communal and subcultural choices — they are not as much a part of the dominant American discourse. And as economically and socially disadvantaged groups, they naturally cast about for factors that help explain their individual and communal condition, and antisemitism, with a core component focusing on Jews' alleged excessive business power and exploitive practices, readily provides one. That these communities tend to be more religious means the age-old Christ-killer canard also has a powerful appeal.

Especially significant about antisemitism in the United States is the context, or rather the many contextual features of the country, for evaluating it. The American economy had recently suffered its meltdown of 2008 and by then settled into an undeniably deep and enduring slump with a president and Congress that were, in nearly everyone's view, jointly incapable of addressing the country's needs. The country's condition rightly caused people to despair. This was seen in what the American people were saying about the economy and the government, and what specifically the Americans surveyed about Jews thought, not about Jews, but about their country generally. Three-quarters of them believed that the United States was heading in the wrong direction, and 50 percent attested to being worse off financially than five years earlier. Both numbers were gloomier than the general numbers, especially regarding people's personal situations, which had been generally improving for decades. It is indisputable that during times of economic and political stress, antisemitism surges, in three senses: in the susceptibility of people to latch on to antisemitic explanations for the country's or their own condition, the degree to which people in their social circles focus on the Jews' alleged predations, and in antisemitism's public expression. As antisemitism's public discourse expands, it further reinforces and spreads antisemitism in society. This context of the acute state of the financial crisis reveals antisemitism's *relatively low* incidence in the United States to be that much more noteworthy. That during this time of hardship, crisis, and financial and political peril, antisemitism remained essentially at an all-time low and did not pick up steam in any of these three areas also shows that, at least for now, Americans are not that much more susceptible to antisemitic appeals and notions than the current levels indicate.

Three other specific features of American society might ordinarily explicitly feed and incite antisemitic notions and fantasies. The first regards security. September 11, terrorism, and many people's blaming of Israel for the enmity that political Islamists (who are the terrorists) have for the United States could possibly feed the antisemitic charge that Jews are more loyal to Israel than to their own country, especially since the agitation by antisemitic polemicists led by Mearsheimer and Walt along these lines has intensified, also in the mainstream media, since the beginning of the Iraq war. The second concerns economics. Regarding the economic crisis, 80 percent of the Americans surveyed say that "Wall Street and major banking institutions in our country operate in their own selfish interest and not in the interest of the American economy." As Jews are commonly associated with Wall Street and banking, and one of the standard questions in surveys about antisemitism focuses specifically on Wall Street, it is extraordinarily significant that there has been no upsurge in this accusation about Jews. The third concerns politics. As Jews are considered, in antisemitic lore, to be behind-the-scenes string-pullers extraordinaire, it is also significant that, though close to three in five Americans (57 percent) believed that a cabal in Washington was working for its members' own narrow interests — this is an extraordinarily high number — such a conspiratorial view of American politics and economy has not implicated Jews or affected people's conception of Jews to any sizable degree.

A final relevant American context highlights again how different the United States is from Europe, where the rampant antisemitism appears that much more stunning given how insignificant in number and influence Jews are in individual European countries and the continent as a whole. When we consider how much more prominent American Jews are—by any and every measure of prominence—antisemitism's comparatively low levels in the United States takes on even considerably more significance, as do antisemitism's comparatively high levels in Europe. American Jews are highly visible, being in fact the dominant ethnic group in the greatest metropolis, the financial and economic center, and in many ways the cultural center of the United States, New York City. They are prominent in business and finance, politics, culture, and the media. They are well represented in the highest reaches of power, the House of Representatives, the Senate, the Supreme Court, and as prominent members of successive American administrations. They actively and self-confidently, as individuals and as a community, promote their interests and their understanding of the United States' interests, including support of the besieged, sole genuinely democratic country in the Middle East, Israel. Although it is a far cry from the bogeyman of the fictional, octopus-like Israel Lobby, the American Israel Public Affairs Committee, known as AIPAC, as but one indication, is an influential pro-Israel organization in Washington. In such senses, American Jews could not be more different from Jews in much of the Western world.

If it were correct that real stresses, economic and political, are the fundamental causes of antisemitism, which, we have already seen, cannot begin to account for antisemitism in myriad ways, then we would expect to see a profound worsening of Americans' views regarding Jews during the current economic crisis and the American political system's failure to redress it and the many other ills afflicting American society and, in the eyes of Americans, its prospects. Yet we do not. If it were correct that the real actions of Jews, whether Jews in general, or the Jews of Israel in particular, is what promotes antisemitism, then the American Jews' prominence, vigorousness, open and powerful support for Israel, their centrality in the financial hub of New York, and in the financial center of the United States in New York on Wall Street, not to mention the many Jewish members of presidents' inner circles and of Congress, should be exciting considerable antisemitism compared to other countries and, during this period, a considerable increase in antisemitism. Neither has occurred, which only confirms what we already know, that it is not the Jews' real world actions or qualities that provoke or promote antisemitism. It is the antisemites, their hatreds, and their fantasies themselves that do it, as the antisemites create, partake in, and consume the antisemitic discourses of their societies and communities, of their cultures and subcultures.

Nevertheless, the state of antisemitism in the United States is complicated. On the one hand, if we started from the baseline that prejudice is bad, fantastical prejudice is that much worse, and when millions of people harbor profound prejudices, it is alarming, then the United States has a substantial problem of antisemitism, and the situation for Jews is bad. On the other hand, the decline of antisemitism in the United States over the last four decades, and the comparatively low numbers of antisemites among those with more education, is extremely heartening. Furthermore, if we compare the United States to Europe, then the situation looks remarkably still less bad, even good. If we additionally evaluate the comparative antisemitic figures in the context of American society where, compared to European countries and Europe as a whole, the American Jewish community is larger, enormously more visible, enormously more publicly identified as Jews, and enormously more openly self-assertive, then the American numbers look very good. And it further shows something at once crucial and not appreciated: when a powerful antisemitism and antisemitic discourse do not exist, Jews, like all other citizens, can be open and assertive about the Jewish aspect of their ethnicity, and can just be open about it, wearing kippas and Stars of David no differently from Christians wearing crosses. However, if we see the American public discourse's changed tenor in the last decade or so, and the rise of antisemitic expression in the guise of anti-Israel agitation, which, for the first time in more than half a century, is treated by the mainstream as respectable, then things could seem worrisome — even if the overall public antisemitic discourse is still not that bad as and, by several orders of magnitude, better than in Europe. Most of all, if we assess Jews' social, cultural, and political situation, their communities' public vibrancy, and the minimal physical threat facing them, then the United States is a virtual paradise compared to Europe. Jews, unlike in Europe, are fully integrated into American society, and in multiple ways absent from Europe: as Jews, as Americans, and as unquestioned members of the national community.

These are people's individual beliefs about Jews. They exist in familial, social, and communal discourses, though not necessarily in the public sphere, where in Europe some are well represented and others are not. In European countries, these fundamental antisemitic beliefs retain a remarkable consistency west to east and north to south—a fact that goes unnoted—and such beliefs differ considerably from Americans' views about Jews. Yet, it must be said, in a fundamental sense Europe and the United States do not differ: the foundational antisemitic paradigm still exists, it proves itself powerful, the number of people who are antisemitic is enormously large—being, according to surveys that tap only a few of many possible antisemitic themes, *only* 150 million in the European Union and *only* forty-five million in the United States who hold multiple interlocking antisemitic views of Jews—and thus the reservoir for the expansion of antisemitic discourse and other anti-Jewish manifestations is considerable, disturbingly so. Yet when we move from the personal and communal beliefs people have on each continent to the extent and character of antisemitism in the public sphere, Europe and the United States are like two different worlds.

European countries see a barrage of public antisemitic invective, usually though not always cloaked in one of the guises that most mainstream people have tacitly agreed to pretend is not quite or not exactly antisemitic, or is indeed legitimate, such as the antisemitic demonization of Israel or the coded or not-so-coded view that Jews manipulate governments, especially the American government to support Israel. This happened in spades during the time leading up to and during the Iraq War of 2003. Tam Dalyell, at the time the longest-serving member of the British Parliament, saw the conspiratorial power of the Jews to be so extensive and apparently well-coordinated that Jews managed to dupe and goad not only the American president George Bush but also the British prime minister Tony Blair to launch a war they would otherwise not have initiated. Fantastically, he declared, echoing the *Protocols of the Elders of Zion* and contemporary globalized antisemitic notions about Jews' international power and nefariousness, that a "Jewish cabal" had "taken over the government of the United States," and that Blair had been "unduly influenced by a cabal of Jewish advisers." Given the simultaneous silliness and outrageousness of such accusations, it is hardly worth noting that the people to whom he attributes such fantastical capacities are presumed by him in an antisemitic way, which he presents to the public as undoubtedly true, to be driven by their identity

as Jews, and not because of their regard for principles, politics, and policies that they judge to be in the best interests of their own countries.
One of the three named culprits supposedly manipulating Blair, Blair's
Middle East envoy Peter Mandelson, is not even Jewish. To the antisemitically inflamed mind that he is of Jewish descent is good enough to
land him in the conspiracy. Such antisemitic outbursts and considered
statements abound from across the continent. The newspapers, magazines, and airwaves—not to mention the Internet—offer regular dos-
ages of open and thinly veiled antisemitic notions and tropes about Jews
that sometimes come even from prominent national and local political
figures and opinion leaders, such as Dalyell.

A person no less than Karel de Gucht, formerly Belgium's minister of
foreign affairs and deputy prime minister and in 2013 the European
Union's commissioner for trade, was a bit more expansive than Dalyell
when he spoke in conspiratorial tones and in more classically antisemitic
ways. In 2010, he declared: "Do not underestimate the Jewish lobby on

*A 2012 variant on the Dalyell charge. Here, in the prominent British newspaper
the* Guardian, *Israeli prime minister Benjamin Netanyahu manipulates his puppets, a grotesque Tony Blair and the British foreign minister, to support Israel in its
military operation in November against Hamas to stop rocket attacks into Israel.*

Capitol Hill. That is the best organised lobby, you shouldn't underestimate the grip it has on American politics—no matter whether it's Republicans or Democrats." This in itself is unremarkable fare for European politicians and media. But de Gucht took the extra step to expose himself as a rank antisemite and his view of Jewish power's "grip on American politics"—note that its vise has all of American politics in its grasp, and not just the usual suspect of American policy toward Israel—as being embedded in that antisemitism: "Don't underestimate the opinion...of the average Jew outside Israel," he warned. "There is indeed a belief—it's difficult to describe it otherwise—among most Jews that they are right. And a belief is something that's difficult to counter with rational arguments. And it's not so much whether these are religious Jews or not. Lay Jews also share the same belief that they are right. So it is not easy to have, even with moderate Jews, a rational discussion about what is actually happening in the Middle East."[8] It is not too much to note the self-condemning irony of the antisemite saying that "a belief is something that's difficult to counter with rational arguments." De Gucht did not have to resign his important European Union position. His antisemitism, after a minor flap, was deemed fine for holding his office.

The notion of Jews' nefarious control of American politics is common among European political and media elites, including in Finland, where the vice chairman of that country's Foreign Affairs Committee, who in discussing the United Nations vote to grant the Palestinian Authority nonmember observer status, explained on Finnish national television the United States' support for Israel is because it has "a large Jewish population who have a significant control of the money and the media."[9] The facts are, of course, that these are all old antisemitic tropes—about Jews and money and the media and warping the will and politics of the people—dressed up for our new global age. The Jewish population of the United States is small, less than 2 percent of the country; they, though a wealthy community, do not have "significant control of the money"; and the vast and diverse media, much of which is highly critical of Israel and supportive of the Palestinians, are owned and operated overwhelmingly by non-Jews.

Then there is the rank antisemitism of Daniel Bernard, the French ambassador to Britain, which he articulated when he thought it would not be reported, saying, now infamously, that, "All the current troubles in the world are because of that shitty little country Israel." Bernard added, "Why should the world be in danger of World War III because of those people?"[10] Even at the height of the Cold War you would have been hard pressed to find people in the West who would have said that *"all* the troubles in the world" are because of the colossally more troublesome and powerful Soviet Union. But about Israel such wild hyperbole rolls off the antisemite's tongue. "Those people" and "that shitty little country"—again, it is hard to think of other countries—and is Israel such a shitty little place, being a prosperous democracy as it is?—that a prominent country's ambassador would characterize in such globally prejudicial and offensive terms. Cause *World War III?* Who would be fighting in this supposed world war, and how—and why?—would Israel dupe the world's powers to fight each other? France's Bernard, like de Gucht for Europe, was deemed fit, his wild antisemitism notwithstanding, to continue to represent his country.

As we have seen, the Jews of Malmö, Sweden, are under siege, physically assaulted in the streets or in their stores, verbally harassed if they display signs of Jewishness, confronted with organized antisemitic campaigns against Israel, and demeaned and insulted, and most of all blamed, by authorities for being the objects of such attacks. Malmö's mayor Ilmar Reepalu responds to the systematic attacks on the Jewish community not as a Swedish mayor would respond to attacks on any other group of Swedes, namely with solidarity, determination, and tangible aid and protection, but instead with antisemitism that only emboldens antisemites, in this case members of Malmö's large community of people of Arab descent, to continue their attacks. Jews, comprising a mere fifteen hundred people out of Malmö's three hundred thousand residents, so half of 1 percent, have been subjected to assaults since the turn of the millennium, reporting sixty hate crimes in 2009 alone—and that is just the number they reported to the authorities. An Orthodox rabbi, who estimated to a reporter that he himself had been the victim of one hundred incidents in the previous few years, described one attack on Malmö's Jews among many:

> The store window had been smashed many times before. The shoe-repair shop is located in one of the rougher parts of Malmö, Sweden, and the Jewish owner, a native of the city, had gotten used to this

sort of vandalism. But in the spring of 2004, a group of immigrants just under the age of 15 — too young to be prosecuted by Swedish law — walked into the store yelling about "damn Jews." The owner was hit in the face by one of the boys. Yasha, an 85-year-old customer and relative of mine, was struck in the back of his head. The doctor who received him at the emergency room concluded that he must have been hit with a blunt object. "I left Poland to get away from anti-Semitism," he later told the police. "But at least there I never experienced any violence. That only happened to me here, in Sweden."

The significance of Malmö's degeneration into an unlivable place for Jews is multiple: Jews, as under the Nazis prior to Kristallnacht, are being beaten and intimidated, and hounded from their homes and city, with the authorities' acquiescence. The highest local authority adamantly and publicly blames the Jews, who are the victims, for the disturbances. He invokes classical Nazi techniques and is vying to become a leading Western practitioner of global antisemitism. He blames international Jews (he claims it is "the Israeli Lobby" that organizes criticism of him) and the neo-Nazis (who have "infiltrated" the Jewish community) for corrupting domestic Jews. He says that the victims are the perpetrators, all the while tolerating and tacitly encouraging those who hate the Jews, in order to reduce their troublesome numbers in his city. He seems to justify it all by saying that Israel is committing "genocide" in Gaza. The Malmö situation, including the mayor's assertions and accusations, has been much in the news. Swedes seem fine with it. There is hardly an outcry — and this is in tolerant, humanitarian Sweden! Unpressured, the mayor's response to the assaults is to turn the Jews into liars and to wish them good riddance: "There have been no attacks against Jews, and if Jews want to leave for Israel that is not a concern for Malmö."[11]

The chronicle of antisemitic attacks physical and verbal could go on and on. On the anniversary of German unification, a German member of parliament, Martin Hohmann, calls Jews, adopting a Nazi idiom and a Nazi notion, a "nation of perpetrators" with the calumny that they were responsible for the Russian Revolution and its predations, which he likened to the Holocaust.[12] In Germany, a Nobel Prize winner, Günther Grass, publishes a poem in a leading German newspaper telling of a conspiracy of silence to cover up Israel's nuclear weapons, which threaten "world peace," and that he, brave as he must be, is breaking the taboo to speak about it. Leave aside that Israel's nuclear arsenal is common knowledge and written about in Germany and elsewhere as an indisputable fact, so that there is no silence, and certainly no conspiracy to enforce a taboo on discussing it, and leave aside that it is part of the sophisticated and unsophisticated discourses alike in Germany that Israel threatens world peace, Grass' poem did nothing except serve as a vehicle for him to express his antisemitism and to reinforce that of Germans, who gain confirmation for their like-minded views from this most esteemed man of thought and distinction. Surveys, in the ensuing controversy over the rank antisemitism of his poem, revealed what should have been expected: most Germans sided with Grass. As if all this is not bad enough, Thilo Sarrazin, a member of the German Federal Reserve's governing board, in an interview to one of Germany's leading national papers tells Germans, whether he meant it in an antisemitic way (as most people understood) or not, something that only reinforced the widespread belief in the alienness of Jews owing to their Jewness: "All Jews share a particular gene...that makes them different from other people."[13]

On the other side of the continent, Greek composer Mikis Theodorakis, the renowned UNESCO International Music Prize recipient, says publicly in 2011: "Everything that happens today in the world has to do with the Zionists...American Jews are behind the world economic crisis that has hit Greece also."[14] (At least he admits the obvious, powerful, and near ubiquitous link that so many others are too ashamed to admit, that he is "anti-Israel and antisemitic.") This cultural opinion leader's views dovetail well with those expressed in the Greek parliament, where one of its members, Ilias Kasidiaris, a spokesperson for the neofascist political party Golden Dawn, in October 2012 addressed the parliament while it was in session by reading from the *Protocols of the Elders of Zion:* "In order to destroy the prestige of heroism we shall send them for trial in the category of theft, murder and every kind of abominable and filthy crime." The parliamentarians present did not object and the parliament as a body has not censured him.[15]

These members of the political and cultural elite express the views common among European elites and ordinary people alike, as many people who report candidly about private dinnertime conversation and beer hall conversation confidentially attest. Privately, such utterances are rampant, as testified to in Germany by many, including Tuvia Tenenbaum, who, without revealing his Jewishness, traveled around Germany and published the profuse antisemitism that Germans expressed to him in a book pointedly titled *I Sleep in Hitler's Room*.[16] And when members of the elite break with decorum by uttering such hateful notions in public, they often meet some criticism because one is not supposed to flout the taboo of being too openly antisemitic, even while their declarations reinforce the antisemitic views that widely course through their societies. These views, and more, are reflected and paraded in European media, sometimes in more coded form, as when the "east coast" establishment or elites stand in for Zionists or for manipulative Jews, and sometimes in less coded form, such as with the frequent likening of Israel to Nazism and Israel's policies to genocide. The European public sphere and discourse, just two decades ago cleansed of the powerful socially existing antisemitism, and further dampening antisemitism merely by not reinforcing and fueling it, now teems with antisemitism, which further buttresses and spreads it among the receptive European publics.

In the Arab and Islamic worlds, the reigning beliefs about Jews are still much more nakedly hateful and brazen, as deeply antisemitic as we might imagine people can be in the modern world, with rationality's supposed triumph, people's widespread education, the information available through multiple sources, people's increasing travel and general cosmopolitanism, including exposure to a variety of sources and perspectives about economics, society, and politics that take issue with and call into question manifestly erroneous views of the world. All of this has since advanced and particularly accelerated remarkably during the last two decades. Yet in the Arab and Islamic world there has been a time warp regarding Jews, with such processes little in evidence. Indeed, if anything, some of these processes that usually augur progress and enlightenment (and which many people reflexively and wrongly assume must do so) have been employed for exactly the opposite purposes, and employed with stunningly harmful results for the image of Jews, for the minds of Arabs and Muslims, and for truth and human understanding. Education, a proliferation of information sources, especially the media, and the increasing density of contact between peoples and cultures have all been put to use to update, spread, make more convincing, and deepen the antisemitic message and beliefs among Arabs and Muslims. This has been the consequence of the foundational antisemitic paradigm's ever more entrenched power in these countries and their public discourses, and in particular of the general antimodern, antirational, antienlightenment force of Islam as is practiced in many places where Islam forms both the fundamental paradigm of understanding in general and governs the higher-level antisemitic elaborations that constitute the overwhelming majority of the public discourses and of people's private understandings regarding Jews.

In Arab and Islamic countries, the result has been a further demonization of Jews, not just of Israel and its policies but of Jews both inside and outside Israel. Until roughly 1967, in the Islamic and Arab public discourses a distinction existed between Israel the country and its policies, and Jews as people or as adherents of the Jewish religion. In the past several decades, political and religious leaders assiduously sought to collapse the distinction. Ever more, and certainly as an all but ironclad view today, the Arab and Islamic public discourse and private beliefs have unified the two separate elements into one. Israel is identified with Jews, and Jews—no matter where they live—with Israel. The standard Arab and Islamic term used in discourse about the people of Israel in the Middle East conflict is not Israelis or Zionists, but *Jews*. It is clearly *Jewness*—not the political country of Israel, which from its founding Arabs also sought to destroy—that has become Arab and Islamic peoples' central bête noir, a quality that they see as alien and expansive, ripping a hole in the Islamic caliphate's fabric, occupying and threatening holy Jerusalem's holy shrines, humiliating and weakening Islamic and Arab peoples, offending God, the prophet Muhammad, and their people, and committing grave crimes against them, most notably in the body and persons of the Palestinians, but also in the Jews' putative aspirations for expanding empire and dominance.

Essentializing Jews into Jewness with manifold vile, threatening, and indeed God-offending qualities has for decades characterized the public sphere and public discourses of Middle Eastern Islamic and Arab countries. Two features of this public portrayal of Jews and Jewness have been particularly damaging: the message has been near uniform and near incessant. Aside from the need to follow Allah and be true to Islam, and what that means, it has arguably been topic number one.

Indeed, the call to Allah and the antisemitic content of the public discourse have been so linked together that a near iron-clad identity has been created between being a good Muslim *and* opposing, curtailing, and eliminating the Jews and their country. Given the uniform public adherence to the foundational antisemitic paradigm, and in a drumbeat of antisemitic elaborations and accusations grounded in the Islamic scripture, traditions, thought, and teachings, and given the delivery of this extremely coherent, attention-grabbing, and powerful antisemitism by everyone and anyone from the highest political and religious leaders to the local Imam, from television news to talk shows to dramatic series, from learned scholars to the man on the street, and on holidays and days of celebration or commemoration, and from the houses of governance to the houses of worship, especially at Friday prayers, it would be taken as a given that the vast majority of Arab and Islamic peoples in such countries would be profoundly antisemitic. What is notable in the era of global antisemitism is that such views of Jews not only conform to what we hear from Mahmoud Ahmadinejad and coursing through the Iranian public sphere, Hassan Nasrallah and Hezbollah in Lebanon, Khaled Mashal, the Palestinian leaderships, and the organs of Hamas, the Palestinian Authority, throughout Gaza and West Bank, and the Muslim Brotherhood and in Egypt's public discourse, but also that Arab and Islamic peoples' encounter with the larger world, digitally and physically, has had effectively no liberalizing effect.

What Arabs and Muslims say to surveys additionally and definitively confirms and fleshes out the frightening intensity of Arabs' and Muslims' views of Jews. Survey data from 2008 reveal that Arabs' and Muslims' views of Jews—not of Israelis, mind you, but of Jews—is shockingly and alarmingly antisemitic. The survey posed the simple question of whether a person has "a very favorable, somewhat favorable, somewhat unfavorable, or very unfavorable opinion of Jews." In Lebanon 97 percent of the people say that they have an "unfavorable" view of Jews. In Jordan, a country that has had relatively good governmental relations with Israel, the percentage is ninety-six! In Egypt, which has had a peace treaty with Israel for more than thirty years, and which is the most populous Arab country, the number is a stunning 95 percent. The total number of antisemites in these three countries, 90 percent of whom are in Egypt, total almost ninety million. The degree of uniform prejudice in the three countries toward Jews is stunning. Even when substantial tensions exist between peoples, surveys yielding such near unanimity of prejudice are almost unheard of. What's more, the scale was not a dichotomous, favorable/unfavorable rating: two distinct unfavorable options were presented to the people surveyed: *somewhat unfavorable* and *very unfavorable*. Almost all of the people stating unfavorable ratings in each of these three countries used the more extremely prejudiced *very unfavorable* category. In Lebanon it was 89 percent of the people. In Jordan 94 percent. And in Egypt 92 percent. Again, just stunning numbers.

The degree of this prejudice and hostility is singular. The survey elicited views of Jews, Christians, and Muslims in twenty-four countries around the world, and in no other country for no group other than Jews were the *unfavorable* results anywhere close to what they were in these and other countries for Jews. This degree of near uniform antisemitism, moreover, was no fluke of the survey's timing. Surveys from 2005 and 2006 yielded similar, sometimes even slightly more prejudicial results. Notable in its own right and also for understanding the significance of the near universal antisemitism in these countries are the people's attitudes toward Christians. In Egypt, 46 percent are unfavorably disposed toward Christians. Only 18 percent of Egyptians have *very unfavorable* views of Christians compared to 92 percent who have a *very unfavorable* view of Jews. Five hundred percent more Egyptians view Jews *very unfavorably* than view Christians that way. In Jordan, the percentage with a *very unfavorable* view of Christians is eight and in Lebanon it is a minuscule two! And in these countries, many people have an affirmatively favorable view of Christians (they could have chosen not to answer the question, in addition to giving favorable or unfavorable evaluations). Fifty-two percent in Egypt state positive views of Christians. Seventy-three percent of people in Jordan do. And 85 percent do in Lebanon. In stark contrast, the average for the three countries' favorable rating for Jews is *less than 3 percent*.[17]

The blanket dislike of Jews in the Muslim world is, then, not a consequence of a *general hostility* to outsiders or to non-Muslims, but of a particular hostility to Jews. And such general hostility toward Jews is not a result of *conflict*, because much of the Arab and Muslim world had historically recently been colonized by Christian countries with whom there was much conflict, and sometimes great casualties, which was in itself but the latest installment of Islam's long conflict with Christianity — the "Crusaders" being standard villains in Muslim rhetoric — and which has as its domestic legacy sizable Christian minorities in various Arab countries whom the Muslim majorities oppress and with whom there is conflict. Such general hostility toward Jews is not a result even of *very intensive conflict.* Next-door to Israel, in Lebanon an extraordinarily destructive and consuming conflict between Muslims and Christians, which redrew the internal map of Lebanon and still defines the country's politics, has gone on for decades. It included sectarian divisions and violence and even a civil war lasting *fifteen years* (that ended in 1990), sizable massacres, and immense physical destruction to the country, especially the capital city, Beirut. The violence afflicted virtually everyone in the country, who, if they themselves were not wounded, lost relatives, friends, or acquaintances. The death toll was colossal: 100,000–150,000, with a million injured, in a country of only three million people at the end of the civil war — enormously more casualties than Israel has inflicted on its adversaries during its entire history. (Many of the Muslim and Arab countries animated by profound hostility to Jews have suffered no casualties whatsoever from Israel, let alone from Jews in general.) More than half a million people fled or were expelled. Yet in Lebanon only 17 percent of Shiite and 14 percent of Sunni express an unfavorably prejudicial view of Christians. No, it is not general hostility to outsiders or even conflict or even intensive conflict that produces hostility toward Jews in these countries: it is antisemitism.

American student Eric Justin reported in 2011 on his extensive experience over several summers in two of the countries discussed here, Jordan and Egypt. His piece powerfully captures the character of Arabs' beliefs about Jews:

> "When someone is acting heartlessly, we say, 'Your blood is blue.' And then we normally add, 'Like the Jews.'" The other students chuckled and some glanced in my direction, waiting for my response or perhaps my permission. I laughed. After all, this language lesson's bigotry was very tame compared to other conversations I had had in Jordan. One of my parents is Jewish, and my Jewish identity has always been light, but for those Americans and Arabs I discussed

my heritage with, I might as well have been wearing payots, tzitzis, and a star of David skullcap.

After all, I was a demon, of sorts. Belief of my damning existence was everywhere, but I was definitely not supposed to actually be there. In Jordan, every day and nearly every facet of society was a reminder that I was dirty—the very embodiment of an "Other." A whole genre of anti-Semitic "history" and literature mocked me in every bookshop, a whole field of anti-Semitic media from historical documentaries to music videos followed me on every television, and an interpretation of Islam that demonizes Judaism frequently bewildered me in conversations.

I heard and overheard countless anti-Semitic remarks in the summers I have spent in Egypt and Jordan. In my experience, arguments about politics almost inevitably turned to "those Jews," and conspiracy theories wafted comfortably through a room like cigarette smoke. It was suffocating.

I anticipated encountering anti-Semitism, but I expected it to be avoidable. I could not anticipate, nor could I have truly imagined, its systemic nature.[18]

Blanket antisemitic public discourse. Its systemic nature. The public discourse's tropes reflected absolutely in people's individual views. The obsessive nature of conjuring up in political discussions "those Jews" as sources of problems and danger. The essentializing of this lightly Jewish-identified man as a Jew. The utter demonizing, note here not of Israel, but of Jews. Here we see the many features of the public discourse, cultural and political pervasiveness, and powerful private beliefs of antisemitism in Jordan and Egypt, where there are essentially no Jews (perhaps one hundred in Egypt), centered around a notion of *Jewness* that comes into focus, and that is reflected, almost without exception, in the *unfavorable* and in the *very unfavorable* view of Jews that their people demonstrably express in surveys.

In predominantly Islamic countries further removed from the self-understood Islamic-Jewish conflict's epicenter, the degree of antisemitism is less, reflecting the less antisemitically obsessed public discourses, but it is still both in absolute and in comparative terms astronomical. In Turkey 74 percent of the people express an unfavorable view of Jews. In

Indonesia, it is 66 percent. And in Pakistan it is 76 percent. These are Muslim countries, but not Arab countries, that have little contact with Israel and virtually no Jews or contact with Jews among populations totaling 75 million, 235 million, and 180 million respectively. Yet, even if they are less intently focused and homogenized in their antisemitism, it does not mean that their public discourse regarding Jews is not intensely antisemitic. Journalist Michael Kamber recounted his experiences in Pakistan, from which he returned to the United States shortly after *Wall Street Journal* reporter Daniel Pearl was ceremonially beheaded for being a Jew. Kamber explained that the people suspected at the time of being Pearl's killers

> are identified as members of "a fiercely anti-Semitic Islamic terrorist group called Jaish-e-Mohammed." I can only wonder about what qualifies as "fiercely anti-Semitic" in Pakistan, where anti-Semitism flows as easily as water. For several months following 9-11, the country's newspapers published frequent editorials calling for an investigation into Jewish involvement in the World Trade Center bombing. In interviews conducted while I was there, government officials would occasionally veer off into long diatribes about the Jews; fundamentalist religious leaders, who educate hundreds of thousands of children in the country's *madrassas,* spoke of little else.

From government officials, religious leaders, and people on the street, the antisemitism is spontaneous and free flowing. And what do Pakistanis say? Whether the Pakistanis are more or less radical, their antisemitism is demonological, with Jews duping the world, perpetrating mass murder, and fomenting hatred and conflict. Kamber continued:

> In Islamabad, Syed Ubad Ulah Shah, an elderly mullah responsible for the education of hundreds of youngsters, said, "To me, [the bombing of the World Trade Center] seems the design of the Jewish lobby. The Jewish lobby wants to pit Islam against Christianity." Seeking out more moderate voices, I introduced myself to a religious leader from Pakistan's much persecuted Shia community. He was a gentle, educated man, the keeper of a holy shrine outside the city. After we had spent some time together and I had met his family, he

asked me, "So can you explain to me, why is it that America lets the Jews run everything? They run the government, the newspapers, they turn the American people against us. Why do you let the Jews spoil things between us."[19]

The total number of antisemites in Turkey, Indonesia, and Pakistan is more than 350 million. Virtually all that their people know about Jews is what they are exposed to in the secular and Islamic public discourses which, in keeping with much of the Islamic world, are overwhelmingly antisemitic.

It is both somewhat more difficult and somewhat easier to extrapolate from these numbers to Arabs and Muslims more generally than it is from the more plentiful and varied European survey data to Europeans. The European surveys cover many more countries and a higher percentage of the European populace, which makes the conclusions about Europeans' antisemitism more robust. Yet in Arab countries the public discourse's uniformity about Jews is far greater, and the extreme prejudice and hostility to Jews is so uniform in the countries for which we have data. This leaves little doubt that the conclusions presented here about Arabs' and Muslims' antisemitism are extremely reliable.

More plentiful data are available about Palestinians in West Bank and Gaza, who are far more exposed to countervailing images of Jews, as Palestinians consume Israeli media and have had contact with many Jews, including by working in Israel's economy and of course with Israeli security forces. That Palestinians would be antisemitic, in light of the public Palestinian and Arab and Islamic discourses that dehumanize and demonize Jews (and not merely Israel or Jewish Israelis) incessantly and in light of the acute conflict they have with Israel over territory, the occupation they live or have lived under, and the violence that Jewish Israelis have often used against them, is not surprising. Under such circumstances, prejudice would be expected, and indeed, overall 97 percent of Palestinians in West Bank and Gaza have an "unfavorable" view of Jews. Thus, they differ from other Arabs not at all in their overall degree of antisemitism, which, amazing as it may be, means that neither Palestinians' much greater knowledge of and actual familiarity with real, living Jews, which ordinarily decreases prejudice, nor their conflict's greater intensity with Jewish Israelis, which ordinarily increases prejudice, has any appreciable effect on the level of their antisemitism compared to the people of nearby Arab and Islamic countries. The power and ubiquity of the antisemitic public discourse and blanketing of their communities is so great that it cancels out these other factors of real-world experience. But then, there is also little room for antisemitism to be much greater than the 95 or higher percent it is in Egypt, Jordan, and Lebanon. Palestinians' stated views of Jews and of Israel tell us the devastating character and power of the antisemitism that animates Arab and Islamic countries' public discourses. When Palestinians state what they would like to do to Jews or Israel or what they see as an ideal way of dealing with Jews or Israel, we see how the foundational antisemitic paradigm's implications, when elaborated in (political) Islam's demonizing and eliminationist argot, propels an enormous number of people to idealize and favor the most radical, even lethal treatment of Jews.

Regarding the country of Israel, an incredibly high percentage of Palestinians do not seek independence or the mere establishment of a Palestinian country, but rather Israel's destruction. In response to three questions, Palestinians make it clear that they seek to utterly eliminate Israel. Ninety percent say that Jerusalem should be the capital only of Palestine, which is another way of saying that Jews have no claim to Jerusalem (particularly as the Israelis have more than once offered shared sovereignty). Sixty-two percent, three out of five Palestinians, say that jihad against non-Muslims who control Islamic lands is a binding duty to Allah. Sixty-one percent reject the "concept" of a two-country solution, which, because it is understood that establishing one country for Jews and Palestinians to share means that the Jews will become a minority amid a hostile Palestinian majority, is another way of saying Israel ought not to exist. Among Palestinians who accept the two-country solution, most of them see it as an eliminationist maneuver, as only a strategic stepping-stone to Israel's destruction. Two out of three Palestinians say this explicitly, affirming that their real goal is to start with two countries and move "to it all being one Palestinian State." Knowing the dedication among their people and among the neighboring Arabs and Muslims to eliminating Israel, 56 percent of Palestinians think that the goal of destroying Israel is achievable or will be achieved, saying that they are not certain that Israel will exist in twenty-five years.

Such notions are not surprising, as they are conveyed and reinforced again and again by Palestinians' highest political leaders, including in the supposedly *moderate* Palestinian Authority. What the Palestinian Authority's officials say in English or to Western media and audiences about being satisfied with a two-country solution and living side by side in peace with a secure Israel is at odds with what they routinely say and convey, explicitly and by implication, when speaking in Arabic to their own people. Thus Palestinian TV, the official station of the Palestinian Authority, broadcast the Friday sermon of its minister of religious affairs, Mahmoud Al-Habbash, on June 29, 2012, with President Mahmoud Abbas in attendance. He spoke of Israel's eventual destruction: "Al-Aqsa [Mosque in Jerusalem] will be Al-Aqsa only, and Palestine will belong only to its people. That's the end of the road. That's what we must be certain of, to believe in...[Even if] they (i.e., Israel) burn our fields, cut down our trees, burn our mosques, destroy our homes, arrest, kill—we remain here, and they will depart; they will leave. Upon this land there shall remain only that which is useful to people, while the chaff passes with the wind." In addition to the repeated pronouncements of the Palestinian Authority's leading officials, visually, the destruction of Israel is also a commonplace, as the official widely visible Palestinian Authority map conveys.[20] The goal of destroying Israel is what Palestinian leaders and public discourse have for years focused on, what Al-Habbash here calls "the end of the road." Yasser Arafat, whom Palestinians conceive of as their George Washington, was adamant about this for decades after starting the Palestine Liberation Organization as an openly eliminationist and mass-murderous organization in 1964. In 1980, as a response to Egypt's peace treaty with Israel, Arafat remained clear about what "peace" meant for him and the Palestinians: "Peace for us means the destruction of Israel. We are preparing for an all-out war, a war which will last for generations...We shall not rest until the day when we return to our home, and until we destroy Israel." Annihilating Israel remained for them a cardinal truth, even after Oslo and during the peace process between Palestinians and Israel. In 1996, speaking to Arab diplomats in Stockholm, Arafat made clear that he would never waver from the final eliminationist goal, whatever the first or even second step might look like: "The PLO will now concentrate on splitting Israel psychologically into two camps. We plan to eliminate the State of Israel and establish a Palestinian state. We will make life unbearable for Jews by psychological

*This map, taken from the Palestinian Media Watch website, includes both the PA areas and all of Israel (excluding the Golan Heights) wrapped in the Palestinian flag—a symbol of Palestinian sovereignty over the whole area—with a key through it, symbolizing ownership. Similar maps presenting all of Israel as "Palestine" appear in Palestinian schoolbooks and are shown regularly on PA TV.*

warfare and population explosion. Jews will not want to live among Arabs. I have no use for Jews. They are and remain Jews." Arafat's destructionist vision is today generally even more unabashedly articulated by Gaza's Hamas leadership than the Palestinian Authority's. On December 7, 2012, one of Hamas' founders and leaders, Mahmoud Al-Zahar, gave a speech at a Hamas conference declaring that his regime will not stop "until all of Palestine is liberated," which, he explained addressing the Israelis, means that "it is we who will annihilate your existence." As if to elaborate on how this would be done, one week later on December 14, Hamas prime minister Ismail Haniyeh explained on Hamas' official Al-Aqsa TV that: "These principles are absolute and cannot be disputed: Palestine—all of Palestine—is from the sea to the river. We won't relinquish one inch of the land of Palestine. The involvement of Hamas at any stage with the interim objective of liberation of [only] Gaza, the West Bank, or Jerusalem, does not replace its strategic view concerning Palestine and the land of Palestine."[21]

Some might say that Palestinians' eliminationist orientation toward Israel is, if lamentable, natural and understandable. But it is not. Many national conflicts populate the globe, yet one people maintaining that the opposing people or country have no right to exist politically, let alone actively striving to annihilate them, is not at all the norm. Indeed it is exceedingly rare. Kurds, for all their suffering and loss of life, for all their homes and villages destroyed at the hands of Turks, do not say this about Turks and Turkey. Moreover, Palestinians' antisemitism is hardly confined to such a mere political "solution" of eliminating the political entity that stands in the way of their national aspirations and of having their own country.

As the statements we see here from Palestinian leaders, which are representative of a virtually endless stream of similar ones, show, Palestinians' prejudice and animus focuses on Jews themselves and includes the desire to eliminate not just Israel but Jews. As Arafat so cogently said during the most promising period of the peace process, "I have no use for Jews. They are and remain Jews." Fifty-two percent of Palestinians affirm that schools should teach Palestinian children to "hate" Jews. This is a stunning state of affairs, the likes of which would be hard to find people of any ethnic group endorsing against any other ethnic group, save against Jews. They *want* schools to teach their children to "hate" another people. They say so explicitly. When asked a question that goes to the heart of the importance of symbolizing their deepest desires, 61 percent of Palestinians say that Palestinian streets should be named after genocide bombers, conventionally called suicide bombers. The majority of Palestinians wish to celebrate the people who have murdered Jews and who symbolize the genocidal killing of Jewish men, women, and children. This is not surprising, as Palestinians overwhelmingly, four out of five, or 80 percent, say that the struggle with Jews is wide-ranging and grave and that defeating them is a moral commandment because Jews are Allah's enemies. When asked about their support for the mass murders that individual Palestinians, such as genocide bombers, manage to perpetrate against the Jews of Israel, Palestinians declare their overwhelming support. In 2003, seventy-five percent of Palestinians expressed their approval for an Islamic jihad genocide bombing of a restaurant in Haifa, killing twenty-one Israelis, including families and children, and injuring fifty more. When asked in 2008 for their views of the shooting and killing of eight students of a Jewish religious school in West Jerusalem (the part of Jerusalem that has always been a part of Israel) by a Palestinian gunman, 84 percent applauded the massacre.[22]

The implication of all this antisemitism — which the endorsement of genocide bombers, the invocation of Jews as Allah's enemies, the notion that Jews have ripped a hole in the Islamic caliphate, the desire to destroy Israel all suggest — is born out in Palestinians' eliminationist, indeed annihilationist orientation toward *Jews.* The Palestinian Authority's Mufti of Jerusalem and the Palestinian Territories, Sheik Muhammad Hussein, speaks of the religious injunction to kill not Israelis but Jews in general. Doing so is the only way to bring about the "Hour of Resurrection." In 2012, he, invoking the continually repeated Hadithic trope of the stones and the trees calling out for Muslims to kill Jews, explained on the official Palestinian Authority television station for all Palestinians to hear: "Palestine in its entirety is a revolution . . . continuing today, and until the End of Days. The reliable Hadith . . . says: 'The Hour [of Resurrection] will not come until you fight the Jews. The Jew will hide behind stones or trees. Then the stones or trees will call: "Oh Muslim, servant of Allah, there is a Jew behind me, come and kill him."'" Such views are the common currency not only of Palestinian leaders but also of ordinary Palestinians. When asked in 2011 whether they agree with the Hamas Charter — which is grounded in Islam's Hadith and which in the Palestinian Authority as well as Gaza is preached and repeated incessantly — that it is a Muslim's duty to exterminate Jews, Palestinians overwhelmingly said *yes.* The statement read to Palestinians and explicitly identified as coming from the "Hamas Charter," followed by the request that each person "state whether you believe it or do not believe it," was: "The Day of Judgment will not come about until Muslims fight the Jews, when the Jew will hide behind stones and trees. The stones and trees will say O Muslims, O Abdulla, there is a Jew behind me, come and kill him. Only the Gharkad tree would not do that because it is one of the trees of the Jews." This well-known passage, interpreted repeatedly to mean that the Jews must be annihilated, and also as central to the well-known Hamas Charter that accords with Hamas' stated orientation that Palestinians and Muslims must eliminate Jews, elicits explicit support among 73 percent, almost three out of every four, Palestinians.[23] Such are the eliminationist, even exterminationist antisemitic ideals, ideals in line with the public discourses, grounded in but not restricted to Islam, that animate Arab and Islamic peoples.

This widespread Palestinian, Arab, and Islamic hostility and enmity toward *Jews in general* — independent of Israel — and its grounding in the Islamic tradition has been and continues to be drummed into the people's heads by many political and religious leaders, including the bearded, genial-looking, and seemingly thoughtful cleric Muhammad

Hussein Ya'qoub, popular for his antisemitic disquisitions about Jews. He broadcast a powerful and clear statement of this on Egyptian television in 2009:

> If the Jews left Palestine to us, would we start loving them? Of course not. We will never love them. Absolutely not. The Jews are infidels — not because I say so, and not because they are killing Muslims, but because... It is Allah who said that they are infidels.
>
> Your belief regarding the Jews should be, first, that they are infidels, and second, that they are enemies. They are enemies not because they occupied Palestine. They would have been enemies even if they did not occupy a thing. Allah said: "You shall find the strongest men in enmity to the disbelievers [*sic*] to be the Jews and the polytheists."
>
> Third, you must believe that the Jews will never stop fighting and killing us. They [fight] not for the sake of land and security, as they claim, but for the sake of their religion: "And they will not cease fighting you until they turn you back you're your religion [*sic*], if they can."
>
> This is it. We must believe that our fighting with the Jews is eternal, and it will not end until the final battle — and this is the fourth point. You must believe that we will fight, defeat, and annihilate them, until not a single Jew remains on the face of the Earth.
>
> It is not me who says so. The Prophet said: "Judgment Day will not come until you fight the Jews and kill them. The Jews will hide behind stones and trees, and the stones and tree [*sic*] will call: Oh Muslim, oh servant of Allah, there is a Jew behind me, come and kill him — except for the Gharqad tree, which is the tree of the Jews." I have heard that they are planting many of these trees now....
>
> As for you Jews — the curse of Allah upon you. The curse of Allah upon you, whose ancestors were apes and pigs. You Jews have sown hatred in our hearts, and we have bequeathed it to our children and grandchildren. You will not survive as long as a single one of us remains....
>
> Oh Jews, may the curse of Allah be upon you. Oh Jews. Oh Allah, bring Your wrath, punishment, and torment down upon them.

Allah, we pray that you transform them again, and make the Muslims rejoice again in seeing them as apes and pigs. You pigs of the earth! You pigs of the earth! You kill the Muslims with that cold pig [blood] of yours.[24]

The power of Arab and Islamic countries and peoples' mercilessly antisemitic public discourses to create near universally antisemitic beliefs and animus, with demonic views of Israel *and* dehumanized and demonic views of Jews, is at once shocking and, given what we know about antisemitism—which has a near historical parallel in Germany before and during the Nazi period—and cultural views and prejudices' dissemination more broadly, also not surprising. We have seen that it is these powerful prejudicial discourses grounded in the foundational antisemitic paradigm and elaborated with the amalgam of contemporary Arab and Islamic antisemitism that produces this mind-boggling degree and intensity of simultaneously dehumanizing and demonizing antisemitism, and that Arabs' and Muslims' hatred of Jews, let alone the hatred's extent and intensity, is not national or ethnic conflict's natural result. Survey data from Palestinians further confirm this conclusion.

Palestinians living in Israel are a party to this national and ethnic conflict. Many, probably most, Palestinian Israelis have relatives in West Bank or Gaza. Palestinian Israelis are also exposed to a very different public discourse about Israel and Jews and have vast and intimate experience with Jewish Israelis that includes, presumably, the full range of human types among the Jews and the full range of differentiated experiences and treatment typical of living in a complex society, with an added dose of the discrimination that comes with being a discriminated-against minority. As a result of this different public discourse—so at odds with those of the Arab and Islamic world generally—and of the density and reality and differentiated quality of Palestinian Israelis' experience with Jews, *enormously fewer Palestinian Israelis say that they view Jews unfavorably*. The number is 35 percent compared to 97 percent of the Palestinians and other Arabs immersed in the profoundly antisemitic public discourses of West Bank, Gaza, Egypt, Lebanon, and Jordan. The actual experience of most Palestinian Israelis in shaping their views of Jews is probably less powerful than the different public discourse that constitutes their information world, which is at odds with the overwhelmingly uniform demonizing public discourse in the surrounding Palestinian, Arab, and Islamic world generally.

Palestinians in West Bank and Gaza who have suffered much more at the hands not of Jews, but of Jewish Israelis, and other Arabs in nearby countries who have suffered not at all from the actions of Israel, let alone of Jews, have the same nearly universal antisemitic views of Jews. And we should not overlook that 35 percent of Palestinian Israelis being antisemitic is considerable. But given the regional norm of close to 100 percent antisemitism, this *relatively* low incidence of Palestinian Israelis' unfavorable attitude toward Jews is astonishing, a testament to public discourse's power to demonize or not to demonize, depending on its content. Of the people living immersed in the nearly totally demonizing antisemitic discourses of Arab and Islamic territories and countries, only minuscule minorities, less than 3 percent, view Jews favorably. The percentage of Palestinians in Israel, by contrast, who actually view Jews favorably is 56, so more than half the population. Put differently, Palestinian Israelis view Jews favorably at almost twenty times the rate of other Arabs.

Perhaps we might expect today a degree of antisemitism in Europe, North America, and the Arab and Islamic world. After all, Jews have been an active presence in all three regions (though not in Indonesia, Pakistan, and many other Asian Islamic countries), and all three have a long history of antisemitism that, we might have supposed, would have ensured that antisemitism would not have disappeared overnight. We might further think that the acute Middle Eastern conflicts in which Israel has been embroiled, and the United States' role as Israel's staunch supporter, additionally boosts antisemitism in these regions. Yet we have seen that such thinking errs in that it takes antisemitism for granted rather than as an unnatural prejudice that needs to be explained. We have also seen that such so-called natural processes that supposedly explain antisemitism hopelessly fail to account for antisemitism's extent, demonology, power, peculiar and singular features or place in the array of prejudices. Still, all these truths notwithstanding, that antisemitism exists in these regions is not surprising, even if we need to account for and explain its nature and power.

Someone unfamiliar with antisemitism's extent and character in the world today would, however, be surprised by its existence, not to mention its scope, in the rest of the world, where virtually no Jews live or ever have. Why would people in most of Asia or Africa or Latin America, in say Japan, China, Tanzania, or Brazil, have any particular views of Jews, let alone antisemitic ones? I daresay they do not of Kurds. Actually, we do not know what people think of the Kurds throughout the world because no one—and this is in itself significant—has seen the relevance, let alone the need to ask or do surveys to find out. On its face, widespread antisemitism's very existence in these regions would be perplexing, and it belies the prevailing notions about what produces antisemitism—namely Jews' conduct, economic jealousy, social or cultural conflict, particular characteristics of Jews, such as their alleged clannishness. But antisemitism does exist in these countries, often among large percentages of their peoples.

The percentage of antisemitic people in South Korea, as indicated by their stated *unfavorable view* of Jews, is forty-one. In Japan it is forty-four. In China it is an astonishing 55 percent—almost 750 million people! In India it is 32 percent of the population. In Latin America, exactly half the Brazilians, a third of the Argentineans (32 percent), and almost half the Mexicans (46 percent) are antisemitic. In Nigeria (43 percent), Tanzania (39 percent), and South Africa (46 percent) roughly two out of five people are antisemitic.[25] Totaling up the number of antisemites in just these countries yields an astonishing total of 1.5 billion. There is no reason to believe that the percentage of antisemites differs fundamentally in other (non-Arabic or Islamic) African, Asian, and Latin American countries.

And once again this is the case even though Jews make up an infinitesimal portion of each country's population. One hundred thousand Jews in Brazil total five one-hundredths of 1 percent of the population. In Argentina Jews compose one-half of 1 percent of the population. In Mexico the number and percentage of Jews are about the same as in Brazil. These are minuscule numbers, worth noting in this context because most of the other countries mentioned have essentially no Jews. One thousand five hundred Jews in all of China. Four thousand five hundred among 125 million Japanese. One hundred Jews, total, can be found in South Korea. The overwhelming majority of people in these countries have had absolutely no contact with Jews, and the Jews among them do not in any appreciable way affect their countries' or peoples' politics, character, or fortunes. But their peoples in large numbers have nonetheless developed unfavorable views of Jews.

This in a different way also shows the global antisemitic discourse's power, which reaches and substantially influences countries and people for whom, by any general measure, Jews are irrelevant. We have seen that such discourses powerfully exist, centering on home-grown versions of the *Protocols of the Elders of Zion,* in China and Japan. Still, we can safely assume that antisemitism's intensity among these peoples is far less than in Europe, not to mention than in Arab and Islamic countries. Most of the unfavorable views that these peoples express are in the *unfavorable,* not in the *very unfavorable,* category. We can also safely assume that their prejudicial views against Jews are far less central to their dominant concerns, far less grounded in powerful antisemitic tropes, and less integrated into their understanding of the world (the probable exception being the many whose antisemitism derives substantially if not wholly from Christianity). Nevertheless, their prejudicial views against Jews, however superficial or central, however mild or intense, remain antisemitic, predispose them to believing more calumnies from the antisemitic litany, and influences how they will react to current and future encounters with Jews, whether in the flesh, in reaction to news about Jews or Israel, or in supporting or opposing policies that could affect Jews in or outside of Israel.

Things are probably still considerably worse than this survey suggests. In Argentina, where more in-depth data exist, we see that this simple favorable/unfavorable survey, which yielded a 32 percent unfavorable view of Jews, enormously *understates* antisemitism's extent and character.[26] Many more Argentineans, more than half, deem Jews "more loyal to Israel than to this country." Still more, two out of three, Argentineans subscribe to the antisemitic notion of Jews' power, holding Jews to have too much power in business (68 percent) and in the international financial markets (65 percent). Forty-one percent, two out of five, hold the fantastical view that Jews are responsible for the global economic crisis. Twenty-two percent believe the all-time most damaging antisemitic accusation, namely that Jews are responsible for Jesus' death. And half blame Jews for talking too much about the Holocaust. These numbers are very much in line with the levels and character of European antisemitism and far more disturbing than the mere 32 percent who in the multi-country favorable/unfavorable survey said they view Jews unfavorably. The Argentinean situation shows that when we go deeper than only scratching the surface, which is all that the multi-country survey did, the vast amount of antisemitism that even that superficial survey uncovered around the world is still considerably more extensive and more profound—in the case of Argentina, twice as widespread and with seriously damaging antisemitic views, not merely some vague "unfavorable" attitude. Significantly enough, Argentineans, the clear majority of whom are antisemitic, also expose the alibi and excuse-making that it is unprejudiced peoples' disapproval of Israel's actions that lead them to want to perpetrate violence against Jews. Sixty-six percent, so two out of every three Argentineans, say that "anti-Jewish sentiment" motivates violent acts against Jews, with only 21 percent saying "anti-Israel sentiment" is the motive.

Like the other surveys we have explored, these numbers almost surely considerably understate antisemitism's extent and intensity in the Arab and Islamic worlds (beyond the arc of countries with nearly 100 percent of the populace antisemitic), and in the rest of the world. Where more in-depth surveys have been conducted, we see that this is the case. For example, the figures from this "favorable/unfavorable" survey substantially fail to convey antisemitism's still more enormous extent in Argentina and, as repeated more in-depth and detailed surveys of European countries show, also across Europe.

The prejudice against this minuscule group of people called Jews that exists around the world is staggering. After the Germans slaughtered most of Poland's three million Jews, and Poles persecuted and hounded most of the remaining Jews out of the country, Poland was left with a tiny remnant of mainly elderly, powerless Jews numbering three thousand scattered among a population of close to forty million, fewer than one, usually elderly, Jew for every ten thousand Poles. Yet the antisemitism in Poland remains so profound, widespread, and fantastical that 40 percent of the Poles in 2004 professed believing that Jews ruled their country![27] Aside from Jews, there is no other group of people of such small size, whether defined by ethnicity, religion, nationality, or any other salient group affiliation—there is probably no other group of any size—against whom so many people not only in Poland and Europe, and not only in the Arab and Islamic world, but also all around the world are prejudiced, and so intensely so. If such widespread antisemitism did not exist, in other words if there were no Jews or only an ordinary amount and quality of prejudice against them, then it would be hard to persuade people that against such a tiny people such a profound and bountiful prejudice could possibly exist, spanning the globe, being the property of hundreds of millions of people who believe the *worst* sorts of antisemitic things about Jews, and billions more who at the very least are antisemitic, with perhaps a large if unknown number of these antisemites also believing the *worst* things, such as that Jews are responsible for killing God's son, are today's Nazis, are engaged in hidden worldwide conspiracies to dominate the world, cause international and national financial crises, carry out an exterminatory war against a wholly innocent people.

And as we've seen, this should not be taken for granted. Imagine how ridiculous it would be to survey the countries and peoples of the world about their views of other religious groups numerically on a par with Jews. Of people who are Sikhs? Or Shinto? Or how about Jains? Or Baha'i? Some of these or other such groups are larger than Jews. Sikhs are on the order of twice as numerous, with 24–28 million adherents. They have been embroiled in conflict lasting since 1947 in their home territory of Punjab, first as a major battleground in India and Pakistan's partition and then as part of an ongoing conflict with India for Sikh autonomy, which has included the Indian government's imposition of dictatorship in Punjab, Sikh bodyguards assassinating India's prime minister Indira Gandhi, and Sikhs perpetrating terrorist attacks over decades. And Sikhs mark themselves publicly as different, with the men wearing their trademark turbans and carrying their obligatory daggers. Shinto are between two and five times more populous than Jews. Baha'i, as Jews once were, are a people living almost totally in a diaspora, having been hounded by political Islamists from their home base of Iran. No one would think of canvassing the countries and peoples of the world about their prejudicial views of these peoples, or of Kurds. If such surveys were undertaken, they would be met with many blank stares and questions of who or what is a Baha'i, or a Jain, or a Sikh, or a Shinto?

But Jews are in play. Everywhere. Problematized everywhere. Seemingly disliked or hated just about everywhere. And this is from millions and billions of people who have never met Jews, and know only that figmental creature, grounded in the foundational antisemitic paradigm, grounded in the various antisemitic discourses, known as the Jew, whose essential quality of Jewness is something better steered clear of or, better yet in the eyes of many, something best combated and eliminated.

# 12

# The Nazified Fantasy

As we see, the beliefs and animus that hundreds upon hundreds of millions of people have about Jews are erroneous and ungrounded, indeed absurd—including all kinds of false, wildly false accusations about the Jews' malignant qualities, intent, and deeds, not anchored in reality, often fantastical—and comprise a continuation, albeit with new elements, of an age-old prejudice called antisemitism. Yet when the same or other people level accusations of malfeasance, many of which are similar, against Israel, the prevailing view is that we are supposed to believe that their purveyors are unmotivated by antisemitism and that these attacks are coolly derived and reasoned conclusions born of a defensible morality and unadulterated ethical concern for the well-being of humanity, especially the parts of which Israel is said to directly and unjustly injure, abrogate rights, or threaten. Only a willfully naive or a venal person would maintain such an indefensible view, especially after global antisemitism's extent and character has been exposed and explored, as we have seen here.

Whatever antisemites conceive as being the source of Israel's and its Jews' perniciousness, and however they think of Jewness, the litany of accusations against Israel and its Jews is bountiful and extremely widespread, to be found in an immense variety of writings, media, speeches, and sermons, and shared by antisemites of many stripes, Arab and Islamic, Christian, secular Europeans, leftists and human rights internationalists, and rightists (though not each one by all). A distillation of them includes:

- Israel and its Jews as source of disorder for the immediate neighboring countries
- Israel and its Jews as source of disorder for entire Middle East
- Israel as cause of dictatorships ruling Arab and Muslim regimes
- Israel and its Jews as greatest threat to world peace
- Israel and its Jews as the contemporary Nazis
- Israel and its Jews as responsible for terrorism
- Israel and its Jews as having committed attacks against the United States of 9/11
- Israel and its Jews as responsible for Bin Laden and Al Qaeda perpetrating 9/11
- Israel and its Jews as responsible for United States and United Kingdom waging war against Iraq
- Israel and American Jews as responsible for controlling American politics, especially its foreign policy
- Israel and American Jews as harming or betraying the interests and well-being of the United States and its people
- Israel and American Jews as responsible for stoking much of the enmity for the United States that exists around the world
- Israel and Jews as controlling the Western and much of the world's media
- Israel and its Jews as committing genocide against Palestinians
- Israel and its Jews as seeking to destroy Al Aqsa Mosque (Islam's holiest mosque in Jerusalem)
- Israel and its Jews as systematically spreading drugs in order to addict Palestinians
- Israel and its Jews and the world's Jews as part of vast international conspiracy to subjugate humanity
- Israel and its Jews as vanguard of West to destroy Islam
- Israel and its Jews as willfully murdering the Palestinians, including Palestinian children who die in conflict

The list of such major, fantastical accusations goes on and on. And the list of specific antisemitic calumnies against Israel, its Jews, and Jews as associated with Israel, almost all being fantastical—including Israel and its Jews destroying Palestinian men's sperm and systematically harvesting the internal organs of Palestinians—is figuratively endless. Some of these wild accusations and reveries are more common in Europe and North America. Some of them are the province overwhelmingly of Arab and Islamic antisemites (a number of such accusations, such as Israel and Israelis being the West's vanguard, many Western antisemites would disown). Most of these accusations are staple motifs, indeed central or core parts of the antisemitic discourse that circles the globe, and are extremely prominent in various more geographically or culturally localized antisemitic discourses.

Antisemites, drawing on the foundational antisemitic paradigm and on a notion of Jewness as essentially evil, have succeeded in branding Israel, in the eyes of many hundreds of millions, a criminal, indeed a genocidal country, with its people, namely its Jews, full participants and supporters of Israel's essential nature and deeds. This branding of Israel and its Jews has, to be sure, been that much more effective, indeed almost universal, in Arab and Islamic countries, where it has been gaining steam ever since Israel's inception in 1948, although it has also become amazingly widespread in Europe and around the world more generally. (Because this has by and large not happened in the United States, even if it is increasing, alarm bells have not gone off there, even among many American Jews, about this state of affairs.) The drumbeat of antisemitic defamation of Israel and its people circles the globe and is incessant.

This antisemitic defamation, moreover, takes place on many levels, each reinforcing the others. Israel the country is explicitly and regularly defined, often with argumentation and justification, often in passing as though it were obvious and understood (which it typically is by the discourse's participants) as a criminal, mass-murderous, genocidal country. Israel's general policies are analyzed not just in the worst light but often cast in the glow of eerily distorting tones. Israel's specific acts, real or utterly invented, are presented in the most damning ways, often with inflammatory images played over and over again on television. Any and seemingly every blemish, whether about Israeli society and politics within the country or its policies and conduct toward the Palestinians or others outside the country, can be focused upon and magnified, making even the innocuous ominous, and the lamentable or transgressive world historically or quintessentially evil.

No country and no people would look well under constant, biased scrutiny on the lookout for every transgression, even if that scrutiny did not include sheer invention, as it regularly does regarding Israel. This is one of the antisemites' many nonunderstood triumphs: putting Israel under a magnifying glass that is applied internationally to no other country, enlarging Israel's every questionable act or false step or actual transgression, like a pimple or simply a pore, into the grotesque. Again, this is without even the embellishments, fabrications, and antisemitic interpretations that antisemites and those duped by them graft on top.

When tens of millions or hundreds of millions of people are deeply prejudiced against another people, and when the deeply prejudiced peoples' public discourses characterize in similarly prejudicial, even apocalyptic terms that second people's country, it seems obvious that they are motivated and influenced to attack that country by their preexisting deep animus and profoundly distorted views of that people. To say this about virtually any such circumstance would ordinarily be unremarkable. In nearly every walk of life, such a conclusion would be rightly assumed. But not in discussions of Israel. When it comes to Israel this is hotly and roundly denied, and people who assert that we should heed the prima facie evidence and obvious conclusions about the pivotal role of prejudice, in this case antisemitism, are dismissed or attacked as hysterical or malevolently motivated. This inversion of reality regarding Israel is yet another of antisemitism's unusual, if not singular, features.

Imagine that American Ku Klux Klansmen mounted a systematic and sustained years-long attack upon an African country and its people. What would we conclude about their motivation? That it was ethically grounded owing to that country's alleged misconduct? That they were not moved by their antiblack white supremacism? True, not all antisemites are Klansman equivalents—many antisemites are much worse. Still, imagine that white racists in Mississippi and Alabama mounted such an attack? What would people conclude about their motivation? We would, almost to a person, assume that their racism gave birth to and governed their actions.

The need to spell out that antisemitism is the obsessive anti-Israel animus' root cause and that this animus does not result from dispassionate analysis and ethically grounded critique shows how powerful the global antisemitic discourse has become, both in its assaults on Israel and in its capacity to falsely portray itself convincingly to masses of people as being a discourse that results from one of the world's most important moral causes and courageous stances. This is not surprising that given anti-semites' sway over the public discourse about Jews—indeed antisemites have almost always created, framed, and dominated such discourses—they have managed to make their position vis-à-vis Israel, grounded in the foundational antisemitic paradigm, persuasive to people of good faith who might not harbor other significant or insignificant antisemitic sentiments. By now, antisemites' demonization of Israel has become so thoroughgoing in many parts of the world that it has become infused with the elaborated and false core that it is actually Israel that produces antisemitism—instead of the real relationship, which is that it is anti-semitism that produces anti-Israelism. But it is antisemitism that is the foundation of the anti-Israel animus, as *Eleftherotypia,* one of the most popular newspapers in Greece, illustrated in this cartoon it published in 2004 after Israel killed the Hamas founder and spiritual leader Sheikh Ahmad Yassin. The woman asks: "Why did the Jewish government kill a religious leader?" The man answers, "They are practicing for Easter."[1] The foundational antisemitic paradigm is used to turn Yassin and the Palestinians into Jesus-like figures and is published with the full

understanding that such references will broadly resonate among the Greek public. Antisemitism that could otherwise not be so explicitly expressed—say, in a mainstream newspaper in an article about Jews, the assertion that the Jews murdered Jesus and Jews today somehow celebrate this—finds a "legitimate" outlet in anti-Israel animus and demonization.

The discussion of so-called anti-Israelism could and perhaps should end here, because at root it is manifestly just another, if a distinctive and special, version of antisemitism. That we should have to make the ritualistic nod to all the ways that we might legitimately criticize Israel's policies and conduct, and Israelis' actions individually and collectively, over the years and today, and to then say that it is (okay, everybody, all together now) *of course,* not antisemitic to articulate such criticisms" is as distasteful—and already a significant victory for the antisemites—as we might presume it is necessary. But we do not need to provide a line-item accounting of Israel's policies and conduct any more than we need to discuss and analyze (and when appropriate, show the accusations' fallaciousness regarding) Jews' conduct, let alone including transgressions, over the years. We need not because it is *not relevant* to discussing and analyzing antisemitism, including defining and identifying it. To discuss what this or that Jew or this or that community of Jews may have done is to concede the terrain to the antisemites by miscasting the discussion, which ought to be rightly about the *antisemites,* their beliefs' and animus' character, their motives, and their prejudicial agitation's effects, into a discussion about how bad this or that action of a Jew or the Jews is. Examining and criticizing Israel's policies and conduct—both its larger policy initiatives, including its occupation of territories captured during the 1967 war and its day-to-day operations—has a place, indeed many such places, and for the sake of Israel and for the region, for Jews and for Palestinians and others, such evaluations are necessary and often urgent. But an investigation of the antisemitic assault on Israel is not such a place.

Having said this, we will not end the discussion of anti-Israel antisemitism with the peremptory, punctuating period that it deserves and then move on. Anti-Israel antisemitism is inextricably linked to, and fundamentally grounded in, antisemitism and the foundational antisemitic paradigm, as an extensive study of tens of thousands of German media articles, commentaries, and postings, including fourteen thousand letters to the Central Council of Jews in Germany and the Israeli embassy in Berlin, further demonstrates. One of its authors, Monika Schwarz-Friesel, explains that "more than ninety percent of the texts blend anti-Israel and antisemitic themes," being replete with antisemitic conspiracy theories and age-old antisemitic clichés and images (which have nothing to do with actual Jews, let alone Israelis), including "moneymen," "cunning Jews," "Jewified media." As such antisemitic notions have in Germany always been the province of ordinary Germans, so they are today: around 70 percent of those writing to the Central Council of Jews and the Israeli embassy belong to the respectable core of society, including doctors, lawyers, and teachers.[2]

Anti-Israel antisemitism is thus a particular, special, and highly significant instance of antisemitism, and therefore deserves consideration and analysis no less than Islamic-grounded antisemitism does. Antisemites and their discourse focus so much on Israel, which thereby influences the general understanding, discussion of, and stances toward that country, so it is especially important to dissect its features and to demonstrate how thoroughly antisemitic the antisemitism is. And anti-Israel antisemitism is, in its crudest and more sophisticated forms and everything in-between, intertwined with other aspects of contemporary antisemitism, so understanding this variant of antisemitism is crucial for understanding global antisemitism in general.

We will examine Israel briefly, paralleling our discussion of "the Jews" of Chapter 2, not to evaluate Israel's achievements or its faults and misdeeds but to bring out some elements that appropriately backdrop analyzing the prejudiced, hate-filled, and intensive assault on Israel. Established in 1948, Israel is one of the world's longest-existing uninterrupted democracies. By decades and several generations, its democracy is older than that of any Arab or Islamic majority country. As a country, Israel is older than any other Asian democracy, and even than most of the Asian countries as sovereign countries. It is older than any African democracy, and most of the African countries. That Asian and African nationhood is shorter-lived owing to European imperialism does not change the fact that as a country, as a sovereign member of the international state system, Israel has existed longer. Israel's democracy is longer, uninterruptedly lived, than those of the vast majority of European countries—longer than Spain, longer than France, longer than Germany. And Israel's democracy is vibrant and robust: Israelis have maintained it—indeed, despite the most acute stresses, its existence has never so much as suffered a whisper of an *internal* threat—something that France, for example, was not able to do in 1958 during the Algerian War, when Charles de Gaulle engineered a coup d'état to assume quasi-dictatorial power. As a country, Israel was the United Nations' fifty-seventh member—before Jordan, Spain, Italy, Germany—preceding almost three-quarters of the world's countries, most of which did not even exist upon Israel's founding and entry into the United Nations.

Yet despite its creation and recognition by the United Nations and the international community, Israel has been under a state of siege and existentially threatened for *every moment of its existence,* with neighboring countries and peoples both formally dedicated to its annihilation and actively working to destroy it. Upon its establishment, neighboring countries' armies invaded with the expressed purpose of killing it off. In multiple wars, Israel has had to fight off attempts to annihilate it. It has faced, starting in the 1960s, constant terrorist threats and continual attacks that, in sum, have taken the lives of ten thousand people, which (in terms of today's population for each country) would be the equivalent of roughly one hundred thousand Germans, eighty thousand Britons, or four hundred thousand Americans. All told Israel, in defending itself from all these existential assaults, has lost thirty thousand of its people, with another seventy thousand wounded, and with one hundred thousand disabled. That death toll alone, as a percentage of the population, would translate to roughly three hundred thousand Germans, 250,000 Britons, and 1.2 million Americans.[3] Israel has had to absorb a colossal number of refugees, people who were by and large expelled from their homes and countries, doubling its population in *less than three years* from 1948 to 1950. (As a consequence of the exterminationist war that the Arab countries and peoples started against Israel, roughly an equivalent number of Palestinians fled their homes or were expelled by the Israelis.) Israel has maintained its democracy throughout, which it has done admirably, all the while containing a sizable Palestinian minority, which, to a great extent, did not accept the country's legitimacy, and with whom the Jewish majority has had an uneasy if tolerable working and living relationship. Israel and Jewish Israelis have subjected the minority Palestinian Israelis to considerable discrimination and have never integrated Palestinians into the country as first-class citizens, but for all Israel's internal and external stresses, and given the real world's character, Palestinians' situation within Israel's democratic dispensation has been tolerably good—certainly much better than many minorities around the world, including in the Arab and Islamic world, such as the previously mentioned Kurds in Turkey, Iraq, and Syria, the Baha'i in Iran, the Copts in Egypt, and many in other democratic countries, such as native Americans in much of North and South America.

There has been no moment in its more than sixty-year history when Israel would not have made peace with the surrounding countries, and with the Palestinians, had genuine peace been offered or possible. From the moment it became likely that Israel would come into existence as a country that would have Jews as its majority, in what was planned by Britain to be two slivers of territory much smaller than what emerged after the 1948 war, which the Arab countries launched to annihilate Israel and its Jews, the Arabs of the region, including the neighboring countries, were devoted to Israel's destruction. This had nothing to do with 1967 and Israel's ensuing occupation of West Bank and Gaza, let alone with Israel's conduct in general. As Saudi Arabia's King Saud explained in 1954, "Israel, to the Arab world, is like a cancer to the human body, and the only way of remedy is to uproot it just like a cancer."[4] Plain and simple, the objection was that Israel was a country that was a home for Jews. Until 1979, no Arab country would make peace or even say publicly that it wanted to make peace with Israel, with the surrounding countries refusing to recognize Israel's existence and remaining openly dedicated to Israel's destruction. In the wake of the Six Day War of June 1967, Israel's willingness to negotiate a return of the territories it had won in exchange for peace was foreclosed by the Arab countries guided by their infamous three *no's* of the unanimous Arab League Khartoum Resolution in September 1967: "no peace with Israel, no recognition of Israel, no negotiations with it." When Egypt under Anwar Al Sadat, only after initiating and being soundly defeated in another full-scale war in 1973, finally offered peace, Israel readily relinquished *all the territory* it had won from Egypt in 1967 (save the Palestinian-populated Gaza Strip, which Egypt did not want), which included oil fields that had provided prized energy self-sufficiency for otherwise energy-starved Israel. Israel did all this for only the promise of peace. When Yasser Arafat agreed to recognize Israel at Oslo in fall 1993, Israel committed itself to establishing Palestinian authority in West Bank and Gaza, which, if the Palestinians would honor the peace, and through negotiations, would lead to a Palestinian state.

Israel and Israelis have had to forge their democracy surrounded by tyrannical and mass-murderous regimes. Egypt has been a military dictatorship of one kind or another for Israel's entire existence, until elections brought about the political Islamic ascent of Mohamed Morsi in 2012 in the Arab Spring's wake. Syria has been a brutal and mass-murderous dictatorship, which under Hafez al-Assad committed a genocidal and eliminationist assault on Hama's people in 1982, slaughtering between twenty thousand and forty thousand men, women, and children, and under his son Bashar al-Assad slaughtering unknown thousands more during the Arab Spring's Syrian installment, which is taking place as I write this. The Palestine Liberation Organization essentially invented international terrorism, of which Israel has been overwhelmingly the number one target and victim. Other countries and regimes dedicated to Israel's destruction and which have attacked it, sponsored others to attack it, or threaten to do so, include Hamas in Gaza, with its charter calling for Israel's destruction and Jews' mass murder; Iraq under Saddam Hussein, one of our time's worst genocidal killers; and Iran under its political Islamic regime, which regularly threatens Israel, sponsors Hezbollah terrorism, and is devotedly working at massive costs to acquire nuclear weapons that could make real its repeated threats to destroy Israel.

By objective measures, the contrast between Israel and the surrounding countries and regimes could not be starker and could not be more in Israel's favor. Freedom House, the most authoritative guide to democracy and political freedoms around the world, scores every country, after in-depth investigation and analysis, on two dimensions, political rights (how democratic a country is) and civil liberties. Its scale is 1, for the most free, to 7, for the least free, with an overall status rating of *free, partly free,* or *not free.* Israel's neighbors and leading antagonists immediately prior to the Arab Spring's upheavals starting in 2010–2011, which is what had characterized them for decades:

- Jordan: Political Rights: 6
  Civil Liberties: 5
  Status: *Not Free*

- Egypt: Political Rights: 6
  Civil Liberties: 5
  Status: *Not Free*

- Lebanon: Political Rights: 5
  Civil Liberties: 3
  Status: *Partly Free*

- Syria: Political Rights: 7
  Civil Liberties: 6
  Status: *Not Free*

- Iraq (under Saddam, 2002): Political Rights: 7
  Civil Liberties: 7
  Status: *Not Free*

- Iran: Political Rights: 6
  Civil Liberties: 6
  Status: *Not Free*

- Saudi Arabia: Political Rights: 7
  Civil Liberties: 6
  Status: *Not Free*

- Gaza: Political Rights: 6
  Civil Liberties: 6
  Status: *Not Free*

- West Bank: Political Rights: 6
  Civil Liberties: 5
  Status: *Not Free*

Compared to Israel's major antagonists and neighbors, which consistently had among the worst indices of political rights and civil rights—of freedom—of countries around the world, Freedom House assesses Israel as a 1, its best score, for political rights and as a 2, its second-best score, for civil liberties, giving Israel, taking fully into account Palestinian Israelis' status and life, Freedom House's best overall status rating of *Free*—the same as the United States, France, Germany, Japan, Sweden, and the United Kingdom, and much better than *Not Free* China (political rights 7, civil liberties 6) and Russia (political rights 6, civil liberties 5).

Despite these sober and sobering ratings of those that declare Israel their implacable enemies, and the reality and vast underlying facts of their all but total abrogation of political rights and civil liberties—otherwise known as freedom—often backed up by extreme and sometimes eliminationist violence, which the ratings reflect, much of the world has demonized democratic Israel, its government, and its people. The same antisemites who have so assiduously, indeed obsessively, worked to persuade the world of Israel's and its Jews' evil, had for decades hardly, if ever, criticized the rampant human rights violations, wholesale denial of democratic rights, widespread use of violence, mass murdering, and the eliminationist orientation and strivings by these many brutal dictatorships that also surrounded Israel and have been its principal foes. (That is, until it became fashionable and politically expedient to suddenly champion the Arab peoples during the Arab Spring, which has still been done only very selectively and expediently, and which still does not target the fervently anti-Israel political Islamic dictatorships, such as those in Gaza and Iran.) This selectively alone, in itself, is prima facie evidence that prejudice and bad faith, in this case antisemitism, drives the vehement, in many circles obsessive, rhetorical assault on Israel and Jewish Israelis.

As we have seen, it is not only this selectivity and the bad faith it reveals, which so thoroughly characterizes the international antisemitic depiction of and orientation toward Israel, it is also antisemitism's wildness, its fantastical quality, people's preparedness to believe every imagined transgression, and magnify real or invented ones, by Israel into something heinous. The ongoing Syrian civil war provides additional evidence about and insight into this.

The antisemitic discourses about Israel and its Jews routinely depict them as monstrous, yet the best that antisemites can do to substantiate this is to invent lurid tales, such as the one about Jewish Israelis harvesting human organs. Contrast this to the real character of how Israel's neighbors and antagonists conduct themselves in conflicts both with Jews (recall Palestinians' lynching and mutilations of Jews in Ramallah) and among themselves. In May 2013, the *New York Times* reported about the atrocities that the combatants in Syria are perpetrating against one another:

> After dragging 46 bodies from the streets near his hometown on the Syrian coast, Omar lost count. For four days, he said, he could not eat, remembering the burned body of a baby just a few months old; a fetus ripped from a woman's belly; a friend lying dead, his dog still standing guard.

That mass killing this month was one in a series of sectarian-tinged attacks that Syrians on both sides have seized on to demonize each other. Government and rebel fighters have filmed themselves committing atrocities for the world to see.

Footage routinely shows pro-government fighters beating, killing, and mutilating Sunni rebel detainees, forcing them to refer to President Bashar al-Assad as God. One rebel commander recently filmed himself cutting out an organ of a dead pro-government fighter, biting it, and promising the same fate to Alawites, members of Mr. Assad's Shiite Muslim sect.[5]

Palestinians and other Arabs and Muslims credibly threaten the Jewish Israelis with similar fates. Hamas' leader Mashal affirmed after Hamas' election victory in 2006 leading to their takeover of Gaza that Hamas has an unalterable plan to destroy Israel. Mashal said this in a long, chilling address after the Friday sermon at a Damascus mosque aired throughout the Islamic world on Al Jazeera television, which lays out Hamas' fanatical political Islamic vision to conquer and slay its enemies. After his speech moved his audience of religious worshipers to interrupt him with the chant "Death to Israel. Death to Israel. Death to America," Mashal lapsed into blood-curdling reverie: "Before Israel dies, it must be humiliated and degraded. Allah willing, before they die, they will experience humiliation and degradation every day.... Allah willing, we will make them lose their eyesight, we will make them lose their brains." And shortly therafter, its official website began to carry two Hamas genocide bombers' video testaments, one of which included: "My message to the loathed Jews is that there is no god but Allah, we will chase you everywhere! We are a nation that drinks blood, and we know that there is no blood better than the blood of Jews. We will not leave you alone until we have quenched our thirst with your blood, and our children's thirst with your blood." From the "high" Mashal to the "low" mass-murdering bomber, when speaking among themselves the bloodlust, the dreams of being able to engage in such cruelty toward Jews all sounds the same—and just like Hamas' blueprint, its genocidal antisemitic charter.[6]

Jewish Israelis themselves, in all the conflicts with the Palestinians and wars with neighboring countries, neither do these sorts of things, let alone on the grand scale that Syrian forces on *both sides* appear to be doing, nor do they threaten, let alone act upon such threats, as Mashal and ordinary Palestinians do against Jews. Yet it is the Jews of Israel who are obsessively portrayed in images (especially cartoons) and words as the monsters of the Middle East and of the world!

As this preliminary treatment already suggests, the four criteria by which prejudice is identified—obsessive condemnatory focus on the object of prejudice, selectivity of the application of principles, resistance to information that falsifies prejudicial assertions, and systematic and gross errors in the accusations—is each the stock-in-trade of the people propelling and partaking in the global anti-Israel discourse. The ensuing discussion, which further demonstrates this, focuses, however, far less on an explicit chapter-and-verse account of why the rhetorical assaults and other actions aimed at Israel, its people, and its supporters are antisemitic, which they on the face of it are, and more on the antisemitism's content and techniques.

The post–World War II period, which for antisemites can be conceived of as the post-Holocaust period, frustrated antisemites. Western political and social leaders and post-genocidal mores, overnight, closed off antisemites' access, certainly in the West, to the public sphere and to shaping its discourse, and cleansed their countries' public discourses of the antisemites' cherished hatred, which was central to their world-views, programs, and for many, their beings. Imagine their distemper and anger at having to bottle up their anti-Jewish animus, which in so many places had until then flowed freely, informed and sometimes dominated public discourses, and been assented to readily by others. Imagine the distemper's intensification for many of them as they had to live with and contemplate the significance of American world domina-tion (minus the circumscribed Soviet empire), which, as welcome as it was to many given the Soviet alternative, was a country conceived by antisemites to be under the sway of, if not run by, Jews. How much worse it all must have seemed to the antisemites that the Jews—finally nearly eliminated altogether—also established a permanent base for the first time in two thousand years—their own country, Israel. And furthermore that, for the same reason that the antisemites were being publicly muzzled and had to exercise enormous self-censorship in the post-Holocaust period, criticism of Israel, which was understood to rise out of the Holocaust's embers, was, and had to be, initially similarly muted. And for another reason. In the Cold War's all-consuming and near all-defining context, Israel became the West's central Middle East-ern ally, the vanguard there against further Soviet encroachment.

All this changed with the Soviet empire's dissolution, and the oppor-tunity opened up in two ways for antisemites using antisemitism to start a concerted public discursive assault on Israel. With the end of the Soviet-supported siege, which began to crumble when Sadat's Egypt opted for peace with Israel in 1979, Israel was no longer the beleaguered underdog but could be fully and rightly cast as the region's military heavyweight supporting its ever more perceived neocolonial occupation of Palestinian lands and people. Also, the Palestinians, having lost their Soviet patron, decided that they must come to the negotiating table, for-mally renounce terrorism (while continuing to practice it), and formally recognize Israel, which now made the rest of the world's casting the Pal-estinians solely as the victims and Israel and its Jews as the aggressors possible and which, furthermore, would resonate with the hundreds of millions predisposed to thinking ill of Jews. This shift had already

occurred in the Soviet bloc, which certainly after 1967 began to ferociously use anti-Zionism spiced with thinly veiled crude deployment of
classic antisemitic motifs and tropes as an international anti-Israel and
anti-imperialist rallying cry with which they sought strategically to gain
allies among Arab countries and in the developing world more generally. This first anti-Israel strategic use of politics on more than a local
Middle Eastern scale was by and large successful. It led to the developing world's shift to seeing Israel and Jews as the only aggressors and
malefactors in the conflicts in which Israel was embroiled. This transformation was powerfully facilitated, and indeed the anti-Israel international alliance was given firm shape, in the 1970s by the emergence of
newfound political and economic might of the oil-producing behe-
moths, which founded OPEC, produced the anti-Israel boycott, and
using their economic and political muscle influenced many countries
and peoples to join the anti-Israel movement. The moment when the
developing world, supported by the Soviet bloc, which had under the
thin disguise of "anti-Zionism" long been vocally anti-Israel and antisemitic, and which had as early as 1965 tried to brand Zionism as racism
and imperialism in the United Nations, marked and celebrated the
completion of this anti-Israel pivot and steadfast alliance was with the
Zionism Is Racism United Nations General Assembly resolution of
1975. But in the West, the growing rhetorical assault on Israel, which
particularly among the left after 1967 did find echoes and gradually
grow, did not forcefully begin its reshaping and takeover of the public
discourse until the 1990s, which has gathered steam and been almost
entirely successful in the 2000s.

As a result, it became open season on Israel, and has been for a decade
or two. Antisemites in the West have turned Israel into their teeming
animus' pointed object, which has been that much more inflamed by
the simple fact that Israel is a highly successful society where Jews have
produced—in the midst of a region of authoritarianism, economic
basket-cases, illiberal societies, and antimodern cultures—a vibrant
Western democracy that, if people would look, would be seen, for all its
many flaws, as admirable and actually would serve as a model for many
countries. That the Jews of Israel have managed to do this is something
that antisemites desperately want to conceal, and there is no better way
to do so than to deny that any of this is the primary reality or the rele-

vant criteria by which Israel should be viewed and judged, and then by demonizing the country and its Jews to a degree that renders these admirable achievements and traits (assuming knowledge of them percolates outward) tertiary if not irrelevant.

Antisemites in Europe and North America still must be careful in how they attack Jews, especially of their own countries, publicly. The taboos on the manner of many aspects of antisemitic expression, despite consistent erosion, still hold. But restraints against Israel, the Jewish Israelis, and explicitly or implicitly the Jews outside Israel who actually or are imputed to support Israel have fallen. The powerful, incessant, and utterly licentious assault upon Israel and Jews that dominates the global antisemitic discourse and shapes public discourse's contours about Israel, its situation, policies, and prospects has hastened and immensely strengthened this process of eroding the general discourse's restraints in these matters, and also constantly strengthens the new antisemitic anti-Israel dispensation.

Clearly, Israel is now the obsessive center of antisemites' assaults, and the United States is a central part of that obsessiveness. Antisemites have worked hard and mainly succeeded in creating the global antisemitic account of Israel and of Jews' relationship to American power, and in shaping public understanding of each — that is, in inverting Israel's real nature and perverting the understanding of American support for Israel.

Israel, this democracy, under siege, with whom there is no willing partner to make genuine and lasting peace and to put an end to the region's conflicts, is now routinely portrayed as the world's most criminal country. If any major international political situation has given credence to Hitler's insight about the power of the big lie, the bigger the better, then the way antisemites have cast Israel is it. Contrast the way Jewish Israelis are routinely and fantastically depicted as bloodthirsty monsters in cartoons (see the cartoon of Sharon on page 341), while Arabs' and Islamists' real-world deeds and their explicit blood-curdling threats against Israel are all but ignored, let alone not translated into general accounts and images of the perpetrators and their peoples. Indeed, the lies about Israel are unsurpassed, repeated, figuratively shouted, unremittingly, and they have been extraordinarily effective in persuading people, and thereby in producing and reinforcing antisemitism. But this should not be a surprise, because Hitler's biggest lie (though he, like antisemites today with their lies, actually believed it) was about Jews. That the antisemites leading the anti-Israel assault are, in this sense, also the heirs of Hitler should surprise no one.

This is not a hyperbolic account. It finds extensive support in the survey research we just examined, including that almost half the Europeans fantastically say that Israel is conducting a war of extermination against Palestinians. These, moreover, are only some of the summary positions that are the stock-in-trade of the West's antisemites and that are the common sense of the Arab and Islamic world, its governments, discourses, and people. As we have seen with similar data, these summaries do not begin to convey the intensity and demonizing quality of the discursive barrage against Israel, which goes on and on and on.

The centrality of Israel comes ever clearer into focus as the rhetorical linchpin of resurgent antisemitism in which its perverse and perverting relationship to American power has become an ever-present theme. Especially in the Arab and Islamic world, where this complex of demonization and hatred began even before Israel's founding, and then after 1948 became a consistent, powerful, and ever intensifying theme, Jewness and Israel — which includes Jews, Judaism, and Jews' political expression as some interchangeable or mutually interdependent whole monolithic — are held responsible for the Middle East conflict and, beyond that, extensive disorders and problems in the region and far beyond, much of which has to do with Israel's and Jews' hold over the United States.

Indeed, there is a sense in which antisemitism has come full circle, harkening back to the Christian biblical, mythological, and demonological treatment of Jews that gave birth to the foundational antisemitic paradigm. As it goes, the Jews agitated openly for the murder of Jesus, going so far as to stand in unison, the *entire* Jewish people, shouting for the Romans to murder him in what would surely be a cruel and horrifyingly painful manner, crucifixion. The reciprocal relationship among the Romans and the Jews is also noteworthy. It is the Jews who conspire to defame Jesus so as to force the Romans' hands in moving against him, and the Romans, brandishing this worldly power in the form of the sword and the stake, delegate the final say over life and death to the Jews, who in the end are, in the denotative content and the connotative force of this narrative, responsible for his death. So the Jews are both instigators and principal moral agents of the Romans, who ultimately wield the formal and actual material power.

In today's global antisemitism Israel and its Jews are the predators who crush the Palestinians, and in the eyes of many have even more territorial aspirations of domination and destruction. The United States, in the role of Rome, with all its might and resources, backs the Jews and uses the Jews as its principal agent, granting them the final say in what is to be done with the meddlesome Palestinians. And then the United States, though often more subtly than the Romans, does the Jews' bidding. Indeed, the more powerful Jews today have, contrary to the mythmaking surrounding Jesus and the Jews, more sway over the imperial power. Even the antisemites who forged the Christian bible, animated by a demonological conception of Jews, could not, or dared not, claim that the Jews *controlled* all-powerful Rome. But today's antisemites say precisely that about the Jews' control of the United States, especially in its policies regarding Israel. Unlike in Roman times, today Jews have stacked the deck by their own masterful insinuation within the imperial power. At the same time, the Jews are seen as the agents of an American

*The colossus Obama prevents the incensed world from stopping Israel from stomping out the lifeblood of Gaza.*

and Western insurgency in the Arab and Islamic world, having established in the country of Israel, strategically and even spiritually, at the heart of the Middle East, a nascent colony for the bigger one to come, with the purpose of dominating Arabs and Muslims and of destroying their religion and way to God. The Jews are happy to do this, all the while pursuing their own, though complementary, self-interested ends.

In this internationalized, globalized account of Jews and their power and their predations, the antisemites have integrated the essential elements of the various antisemitisms, focusing sometimes on Israel and sometimes on the United States, and always aware of the two countries' and their two peoples' reciprocal and complementary, namely mutually reinforcing relationship, where each in its own way helps the other as it helps itself. Hence the aptness from the Iranians' and others' perspective of the monikers of the Great Satan and the Little Satan. This should not be dismissed as only a convenient expression of demonization that reflects the relative size and reach of each country's power. Its metaphorical implications and reflection of the underlying thought goes considerably further. The Great Satan and Little Satan form a family. As a family, each supports the other in their mutual and individual goals, which are mainly harmonious with one another. Of course, the Great Satan nurtures the Little Satan, but the Little Satan steadily grows in

*Bush and Sharon, mutually using each other.*

strength and has the power of its well-being to wield over the Great Satan. Each wants to make the other well. Each understands the other. Whatever their conflicts, it is all within the family, and toward the rest of the world they close ranks, standing and striving, in this case for their Satanic ends, locked arm in arm.

The demonology about Israel and its relationship to the United States, conceived of variously as Israel's master, brother-in-arms, or duped minion, has produced major lines of attack and the major strategies that antisemites use against Israel, its people, and its Jewish supporters outside the country, strategies that are multiple and interlocking, consisting of systematic omission of truthful information about them, their situation, or their enemies, gross factual distortion, and defamatory fabrications. As the common antisemitic lines of attack are so numerous, we focus here on only the major ones by starting with the prejudice's core elements:

Different kinds of antisemites specify the source of Israel's wickedness and perniciousness variously: Israel's perniciousness resides in its character as a Jewish state, namely a country of Jews, because even though many if not most countries in the world are conceived of as belonging to or expressing the political nationhood of a people, antisemites do not allow that Jews may do the same, routinely maintaining that to call Israel a "Jewish" state, even though the overwhelming majority of the population is Jewish, is "racist." Other antisemites hold Israel's perniciousness not to be that it is the country of Jews per se, but that its policies are shaped by and express the Jews' essential character, their Jewness, which is to wish and plot harm to others, to be predatory. The Catholic Church deemed the Jews unworthy of their country until 1991 for a very specific reason, namely that they have no right to have that territory be their country, as it belongs to Christians. Arab and Islamic antisemites also do not believe that the Jews have a right to their country because the Jews are Jews and because the country is located in the heart of the Arab and Islamic world. (Although these two positions have been formally the same, I do not mean, strictly speaking to equate them, for the dominant Arab and Islamic antisemitic position is that, using violence if necessary, the country ought to be destroyed along with, in many of these antisemites' eyes, many if not all its people. The Catholic Church's hierarchy obviously does not share such a position.) For still others, the source of

Israel's alleged malfeasance and predatory nature is its very existence on land that they deem not to belong to Israel. Because the Jews putatively stole the land from those who should rightfully have it, the Palestinians, Israel must continue to engage in criminal policies to keep what it has stolen and maintain itself against just claims for its dissolution. Still others do not much think about the sources of Israel's unfitness, taking at seeming face value that its policies toward the Palestinians and toward Arab countries and peoples are criminal—because that is what Israel and Israelis have chosen for themselves—and that their practices will not change, or unless they radically change, which is unlikely, the Jews in Israel forfeit all claims to having their own country.

Although different views of the source of Israel's supposed malignant and predatory nature or conduct matter in a variety of ways, fundamentally they boil down to a common de facto view: Jews, because of their Jewness, and unlike other peoples, including all other peoples with countries, alone among peoples inhabit a country that is self-invalidating, whether the form of invalidation merely renders it criminal, augurs its elimination, or produces the need to exterminate its people. Antisemites view Jewness, however they conceive of it, as the essential quality of asociability and danger to others. They view Jewish civilization, the civilization built upon Jewness—if civilization includes political power that may extend, and in the case of Israel does extend, to political sovereignty—as malignant, pernicious, and invalid or, at the very least, so suspect that when Jews exercise it, it gets focused on, dissected, criticized in ways that are not applied to non-Jews, in other words prejudicially, in other words antisemitically.

This is, of course, the conclusion, the logical conclusion of the antisemites' conception of Israel and the Jews of Israel, and of Jews outside Israel. It is highly significant and revealing that what consistently agitates antisemites more than other putative noxious qualities of Jews is the notion that Jews have power (whether or how much such notions are grounded in reality or imagined). This draws on two age-old antisemitic notions, at least in the Western world, about Jews. The first, of course, is that they are malevolent, so the whiff of them possessing power is disturbing. Malevolence is bad enough, and when it harnesses itself to power, it becomes deeply threatening. The second is the Christian antisemitic notion that Jews are to live in an abject and therefore servile state, as befitting the condition of those who willfully reject Jesus. This has been an antisemitic theme through the ages that Jews, stiff-necked, are unwilling to bend to truth and to their betters, who know the truth. This notion has a parallel within the Islamic tradition, namely that Jews (in this respect similar to certain other non-Muslims) are, at best, Dhimmi and, when tolerated, ought to live in a subject state. Thus antisemites become highly disturbed in the face of Jews possessing real or alleged power because it means that Jews will not bend and not be servile, that they are turning the tables on their supposed betters and would-be masters, that they are upsetting and threaten to upset ever more the antisemites' conceived natural order of things. The world is upside down. Israel, which, on top of everything else, is a regional military colossus, is the incarnation of Jews' power par excellence.

A young Egyptian American who grew up mainly in Egypt once explained to me that it was not only Muslims in Egypt who think of Israel as a criminal state, indeed the worst country in the world, and of Israelis as a criminal people. Christians in Egypt, of which there were ten million, think the same. The nightly news, he informed me, began "every night" with Israel's maltreatment of the Palestinians. This could be the motto of the antisemites' strategies and triumphs, to which so many, including the otherwise not ill-intentioned but merely naive media in the West, fall prey. Repeat something enough, even without added invention or fabrication, and that something appears, and therefore becomes, so much greater in significance, so much worse if it is considered bad, so much more causally relevant to things to which it might be related, so much more ominous if one thinks it bodes future harm. My interlocutor took this portrayal of Israel and Israelis at face value, namely that their malfeasance, and all the suffering and destruction they were putatively causing Palestinians, would not be leading the nightly news so frequently if it did not deserve to do so. The folk wisdom of *if there's smoke, there's fire* is very powerful. Such is the self-validating effect and logic of a powerful public discourse, especially one that forms a chorus with a clear unifying message: someone or something is bad.

This was during the 2000s of Hosni Mubarak's reign, when Egypt was one of the least, arguably the least, hostile frontline Arab country toward Israel. My interlocutor was discussing the effect of the nightly news alone, which composed but one part of the far denser multi-vocal antisemitic discourse. During this period, Egyptian television (and stations across the Middle East) again and again, beginning in 2002, broadcast *Horseman Without a Horse,* a forty-part antisemitic television series based on the *Protocols of the Elders of Zion.* The Arab Spring brought no end to this, as its airing on Egyptian television during March 2012 shows. And it is but one in a continuing string of such antisemitic television programs, demonizing Israel and Jews.

The individual accusations (some illustrated below), such as Jewish Israelis are planning to blow up the Al Aqsa Mosque in Jerusalem, are so numerous that it would take an enormous amount of space to catalogue and explicate them. Take just this one common accusation and change the terms only slightly. Imagine that in Italy and throughout Catholicism it were widely broadcast, and widely believed, that German Protestants were planning to blow up St. Peter's. It is a ridiculous scenario, or that Italian atheists in Rome were plotting such a destructive attack. Anyone who believed it would have to be mad or in the grip of a hallucinatory prejudice, you might say. And if it were indeed widely believed, then we could conclude only that a dangerous belief system about German Protestants or Italian atheists existed among Catholics that they could think such a fantastical notion true, and we would certainly say that they were prejudiced. If we changed the scenario to another fanciful one, namely that Jews planned to blow up St. Peter's, then we would say the same. And if we changed the scenario to one that actually exists, that the Jews are planning to blow up Al Aqsa, we should all just as quickly and assuredly say the same.

Any single one of the many such inflammatory notions and accusations that course through Islamic and Arab countries, let alone many of them, let alone all of them together, if widely believed and part of a broad-based discourse, would be considered a severe and dangerous form of prejudice. The individual accusations, because they are grave, merit considered and extensive exposition and analysis. Yet they also coalesce into the most fearsome kind of clear antisemitic message and powerful discourse about Israel and its Jews, which is even more important to explicate. This message and discourse has five core elements, four of which we can discern in this one antisemitic calumny about the Al Aqsa Mosque:

The Al Aqsa Mosque, situated on the Temple Mount in the Old City of Jerusalem, which is also the area holiest to Jews as the erstwhile site of

David's and then Solomon's temples, is one of Islam's most sacred shrines, the place Muslims hold from which Muhammad ascended to heaven in 621 (the Al Aqsa Mosque was first constructed there in 705 and the present reconstructed Al Aqsa dates from 1033). Anyone who would seek to blow up the Al Aqsa Mosque is, by definition, malevolent, colossally malevolent, indeed *demonic,* because, in the eyes of Muslims, to want to destroy one of Allah's holiest sites on earth is to want to perpetrate virtually unsurpassable evil. For one people to readily and easily accept such an outlandish notion about another people is already to have a view of them that makes such evil on their part plausible, a view that already holds them to be demonic. Such a calumny, moreover, casts the would-be perpetrators not merely as demonic, meaning evil in intent, but also *dangerous,* namely evil in capacity. For political leaders to spread this accusation, and to do so as an accepted article of faith, including among their peoples, conveys powerfully their prejudicial and incendiary mindset. The political leaders of the more *moderate* Palestinian government, that of the Palestinian Authority, have intoned the Al Aqsa calumny repeatedly, together with the notion that the Jews' temple did not exist, affixing the term "alleged" to it, by one count, at least ninety-seven times in official Palestinian press reports of its leaders' pronouncements over two years, which is but a small percentage of all such leaders' and others' such statements.* Regarding the fantastical anti–Al

---

\* Palestinian Media Watch has compiled a partial list of Palestinian Authority officials, institutions, and luminaries cited in the Palestinian Authority's media who in 2011 and 2012 used the term "alleged temple," often many times, to refer to Solomon's Temple:

Mahmoud Abbas, PA Chairman
Ahmad Al-Ruweidi, Advisor to PA Chairman Mahmoud Abbas
Muhammad Hussein, PA Mufti
Mahmoud Al-Habbash, PA Minister of Religious Affairs
Ahmad Qurei (Abu Alaa), former PA Prime Minister, head of PLO Jerusalem Dept.
Tayseer Tamimi, former PA Chief Justice of Religious Court
Salim Al-Za'anoun, Chairman of the Palestinian National Council
Sheikh Yusuf Ida'is, Chairman of the Supreme Council of Islamic Law
Yusuf Salameh, speaker at the Al Aqsa Mosque and former Minister of Religious Affairs
Mahmoud Al-Aloul, member of the Fatah Central Committee
Dmitry Dliani, member of the Fatah Revolutionary Council
Kamal Al-Khatib, Deputy Chairman of the Islamic Movement in Israel
Sheikh Ishaq Feleifel, columnist in the religion section of the official PA daily

Aqsa conspiracy and threat, no less than the Palestinians' president Mahmoud Abbas raised the alarm about it in 2012: "[The] purpose [of the Jews' activity] is to achieve its black goals: Destroying the Al-Aqsa Mosque, building the 'alleged Temple,' taking over the Muslim and Christian holy sites, and destroying its [Jerusalem's] institutions in order to empty it, uproot its residents, and continue its occupation and Judaization."[7]

Not to be outdone by their Palestinian enemies in the effectiveness in spreading antisemitic accusations against Jews regarding Al Aqsa, Hamas broadcast a television cartoon for children in which Jews excavate under the Al Aqsa in order to topple it.[8]

There are many people who have bad desires and intentions but little ability to act upon them. This antisemitic notion that Jews seek to destroy the Al Aqsa conveys clearly to all who believe it that the Jews are a profoundly dangerous evil. The Jews also have the capacity to destroy the Al Aqsa, so goes the automatic thinking, a most threatening material and symbolic assault on the sacred, a powerful component in the Jews' putative war to destroy Islam itself. Any people of such demonic intent and dangerous capacity would be seen by those they threaten and, for that matter, by other people of goodwill as having their independence to act, their sovereignty over the vehicle of their power — in this case their country — be *delegitimized*, namely that their right to have such a country, and therefore their country's right to exist, is not legitimate. This delegitimization, together with the obvious need and the concomitant right of the threatened people to defend themselves against such a demonic and dangerous foe, justifies, and not only justifies, but suggests, even propels forward the seemingly obvious conclusion, that such an entity, and its people, need to be eliminated, in other words *destroyed*.

The power of this one accusation is immense. It is not perfectly analogous to the most damaging calumny of all time, the Christian one that

Adel Abd Al-Rahman, columnist for the official PA daily
Islamic-Christian Council for Jerusalem and the Holy Places
Official PA TV news readers and reporters
WAFA, the official PLO and PA news agency
The PA's official daily *Al-Hayat Al-Jadida*

Dig! Dig!

*Children's video of Jews seeking to destroy the Al Aqsa Mosque under the protective watch of an Israeli soldier.*

the Jews murdered God's son and are therefore guilty and cursed for all time, but it parallels it in important ways. It renders the Jews willfully desirous of committing an unimaginably heinous and evil act—an assault upon a religion, all its adherents, truth, goodness, and God himself. It rouses that religion's members individually and collectively against the Jews. And it justifies, even suggests, that any and every act in defense of the path to salvation, its adherents, and their God as permissible, even necessary. That the Jews have not yet carried out their plan against Islam is a difference of some distinction (probably not all that much to believers).

This one antisemitic accusation about Al Aqsa thus inheres and brings into sharp relief almost all the essential elements and the basic structure (plus an elaborated charge) of the contemporary Arab and Islamic antisemitic discourse, and of global antisemitism.

Jews are demonic. This is an account of their nature. Ultimately, it does not matter to antisemites today the way it once did in the nineteenth and early part of the twentieth century, when the issue of ontology, that is, understanding the nature of being, was of burning cultural and political importance for two reasons: a sea change was taking place away from religion as the major source of identity to an ethnic and national notion of identity, which became grounded in notions of biology, conceived of at the time as race and rooted in pseudoscience. At the time, the issue of the source of a person's, a group's, a people's nature was hotly contested and a critical component of the paradigm for understanding much else in the social, cultural, and political world. The second reason was that Europeans' obsession with expressing and organizing society and life around ethnicity and nation meant that a deeply contested conception of nation had to be worked out. This became one of the central concerns (and often the central concern) of politics, which in so many areas of Europe focused on forging nations on disputed territories and ensuring that the right kind of people were included as members, and the wrong kind of people were occluded, so that the nation, conceived as an organism, would be healthy and strong, not weakened by alien elements, particularly malignant ones, such as, or often particularly, Jews.

Today, ontology in even a broader sense, that is, understanding the source of a person's or nation's nature (or merely the country's populace—times are much more multicultural, de facto), is not a generally salient issue, as it was when the modern world was being forged politically, but a latent theme. The world is fully organized into sovereign countries, so the source of belongingness (while contested in some countries and on the margins in others) is, by and large, settled. Second, a silent revolution has taken place in people's conception of human beings, from being grounded in a fundamental identity, which often then had to be contested (is it religion, ethnicity, or citizenship?), to being grounded in multiple identities (you can be a Muslim *and* an Egyptian, or a Christian of ethnic Polish background *and* a citizen of Germany). So it is understood that people have multiple sources of their nature and multiple allegiances. One of the primary characteristics of contemporary life is the minor concern with determining what is taken for granted as being multiple and often elusive, and ultimately not that important. This has changed the plausibility structure for antisemitism, turning what was once an obsession with race and origins into a more pluralistic prejudicial orientation that takes Jewness for granted from whichever of its multiple sources and in whichever of its multiple forms it comes.

This leads to several considerations about today's antisemites' and the antisemitic discourse's view of Jews. It is that much more striking that Jews, rare if not alone among people internationally, are not accorded these multiple identities, or at least far less frequently. Such is antisemitic prejudice's power that it so reduces Jews to this one, often ascribed, identity, their Jewness, even against such powerful contemporary currents. More germane to demonization, antisemites remain both divided and less interested in the source of Jews' nature, in the source of Jewness, so therefore concentrate not on the problem's *sources* but on diagnosing the problem's *character,* which is a problem of Jews and their existence — or put differently, a problem of Jewish civilization, namely those larger structures and forms and practices that Jews produce or that loosely define them.

Because we live in a more politicized world and because Jews have a country, most everything of significance is understood to be political or have a political dimension as never before, when many of the same issues were considered more personal, social, and cultural. This too leads people to focus less on the issue of the source of Jewness and more on the problem that it and its political expression, principally Israel, pose.

Although European norms — and in many countries, laws against hate speech — prevent people from explicitly saying this in the public sphere, it can be, and is, snuck in visually, as in the cartoon that appeared in 2003 in the United Kingdom in the *Independent,* named in 2004 newspaper of the year:[9] Not only is Israel's prime minister, Ariel Sharon, portrayed as a monstrous, fearsome cannibal eating a Palestinian child, not only does this activate the Christian blood libel, not only is the entire

*The* Independent's *prizewinning political cartoon of the year.*

scene one of apocalyptic destructiveness wrought by Israel, but Sharon's deed is presented as appealing to the Jews of Israel. It conveys that Jews' essence is such that such a scene would not horrify the Jews but rather that the image function like an attractive election poster — sexualized with the "VOTE LIKUD" ribbon as a fig leaf over his genitals — that is calculated to win votes by leading people to think that the candidate and his party is like them or expresses their deepest wishes. The cartoon was not some aberrant doodle, and appealing not only to the antisemitic leftist readers of the *Independent:* broadly thought to be a masterpiece in the United Kingdom, it, obviously appealing to those across the political spectrum, won the award as the political cartoon of the year.

We have already seen the character of Israel's demonization. It is a commonplace of European thought and public expression that Israel is the new Nazi Germany or that Israelis are like Nazis or that the Israelis are treating the Palestinians just as the Nazis treated the Jews. Forty to 50 percent of Europeans surveyed hold Israel to be a Nazi-like country. No other country or regime or people — not the most murderous of our time, not Rwanda or the Hutu in 1994; not concentration camp–like and mass-murderous North Korea; not Saddam's Iraq or the Sunni who supported him in Saddam's mass murdering of half a million; not colossally genocidal Sudan and its political Islamic majority — none has been equated to Nazi Germany on as regular, reflexive, and broad basis, certainly in no manner resembling Israel. And roughly half of the Europeans assert that Israel is explicitly engaged in the wholesale extermination of Palestinians. These and other antisemites focus their fire, naturally, on the harm Israel and Jewish Israelis allegedly or actually inflict on Palestinians, or potentially will. Such injuries range from small indignities to supposedly seeking to destroy these wholly innocent people, including everything and anything in-between. Some of the catalogue of such alleged injuries, of course, is real, given the intensive and ongoing and long-lasting conflict, requiring Israelis to defend themselves, sometimes with lethal force, against violent and armed attacks — and, of course, in the conflict's context, Israelis have committed excesses. In the antisemitic informational flow, these get unconscionably inflated and distorted, rendering Jewish Israelis' justifiable or even excessive acts into monstrous events that prove nothing less than Israel's and its Jews' demonic nature. And within the Arab and Islamic world, such offenses are taken as additional proof of Israel's threat to other countries and to Islam itself. Until the Arab Spring's ferment, nothing was seen more generally (except among Al Qaeda, which focused its ire overwhelmingly on the United States) to threaten Islam and Muslims, and Arab countries and Arabs, more than Israel, Israel's Jews, and Jews around the world, especially as they allied with and allegedly controlled the American superpower.

Israel's alleged plot to destroy the Al Aqsa Mosque also conveys a third central element of the antisemitic discourse, which follows from the first two. If Israel is *demonic* and if the *danger* it poses is so acute, then how can its existence be deemed legitimate? It cannot be, and therefore, according to such thinking, it is right and necessary to *delegitimize* Israel's existence. Israel, by its own nature and actions, proves that it has no legitimate right to exist.

The *logic* of the Al Aqsa calumny and surrounding discourse, which, as we have seen, also suggests a fourth core element of the antisemitic anti-Israel discourse, namely, that *destroying* Israel is right and necessary, not surprisingly is the logic of the broader antisemitic discourse that presents Israel as illegitimate and therefore needing to be eliminated.

This discourse that delegitimizes Israel and leads to calls for its destruction takes place on many levels, has many overlapping and mutually reinforcing strands, and is calculated to be persuasive if it gains a person's assent, often only to one of its aspects. The delegitimizing discourse targets the people of Israel, that is, its Jews, as having no right to be on Palestinian land, which is said to include all of Israel, West Bank, and Gaza, or occupying any aspect, let alone a central place of the Islamic caliphate, a place that belongs forever only to Muslims. (Islamic and Arab antisemites disagree over how many Jews should be allowed to remain in these lands as a [small] minority and without political control. Not a formal point of the discourse, it is usually left vague.) The Jews' conquest, as it is characterized, of this land shows only how illegitimate their presence is in what is considered Palestine generally, and the Islamic holy city of Jerusalem most specifically. The delegitimizing discourse targets specific policies and governments as being especially heinous, with the explicit or implicit argument that Benjamin Netanyahu's government, in its horrifying stances, reveals the real illegitimate nature of the people who would willfully elect Netanyahu, and of the country producing them and which they in turn shape. Because these elements are all interconnected, or could easily be deemed to be interconnected (even though many Jewish Israelis do not support any given government or any given policy), and because the framework of antisemitism's anti-Israel component makes keeping clear distinctions among the different elements difficult, articulating an antisemitic attack on one element easily and at least implicitly conjures up the others, reinforcing the general case that the country of Israel is illegitimate. There is even shorthand for communicating this, which is encapsulated in the name for the Jews' national movement: Zionism (at least when antisemites or the global antisemitic discourse use it). Zionism is the proper name for the national movement of the Jews—the equivalent of many national movements of the past or present, including those of the Italians and Germans in the nineteenth century, of the Irish, Indians, Ugandans, and Algerians in the twentieth, or the Kurds and Palestinians today. Yet antisemites long ago managed to rebrand the term—alone among national movements—into an international epithet that connotes, indeed epitomizes, racism, oppression, and fundamental illegitimacy.

When delegitimizing Israel, antisemites target Israel in a variety of ways. Israel had no right to be founded. Even if it did, it rescinded that right with its founding's original sin. Even if it had not, its essential nature and conduct has since nullified that right. When speaking the language that is seemingly more grounded in international law's language and norms, antisemites turn an actual tragic history—which is like so many others between peoples contesting common land in Europe, Africa, and Asia—into a one-sided, false narrative of the Jews' usurpation and predations in order to present Israel as not meeting, alone among the world's countries, the test for international legitimacy.

While people around the world are deeply prejudiced against other people, they as a rule do not delegitimize those people's country and its right to exist. Americans prejudiced against Mexicans do not say Mexico has no right to exist. Europeans prejudiced against Germans or Poles do not say Germany (even after it perpetrated genocide) or Poland (although after World War II it annexed considerable territory that had been part of Germany) has no right to exist. Koreans prejudiced against Japanese do not say that Japan has no right to exist. And it is not merely one prejudiced people or one country that holds such a position against

Jews and Israel, it is an international coalition of peoples and states that not only has no parallel today, and none in the past, except, not surprisingly, against Jews.

Antisemitism's anti-Israel stream *demonizes* Israel and *delegitimizes* it. It also casts Israel and its Jews as an ongoing grave *danger*. It elaborates the danger in a panoply of ways, deems it to be acute, even ratchets it up to existential levels against the Palestinians, against surrounding countries (especially given Israel's nuclear weapons), and against Islam. What follows from the demonization, namely that Israel and its Jews are evil, from the delegitimization, that Israel has no legitimate right to exist and that Jews have no right to a country, and from the acute danger it poses to other countries and peoples and faiths, seems obvious, and it is the obvious conclusion that the anti-Israel antisemitic discourse has at its core: it is right, and it is necessary, to *destroy* Israel and, in some of this discourse's central variants or streams, to *destroy* its Jews.

Global antisemitism, fueled by its anti-Israel core, has achieved an explicit eliminationist and exterminationist level that goes well beyond medieval Christianity, which for all its demonization of Jews and for all its theology that called for the Jews to disappear did not preach that it was right and normative to physically destroy them and their communities. In the now dated language of pre-Oslo times, when the Palestinian Liberation Organization did not in any rhetorical or actual sense recognize Israel's right to exist and would not even utter the country's name, the PLO was unmistakable in its conviction and intent that (in the stock phrase of the time) *the Zionist entity must be liquidated!* The anti-Israel antisemitic discourse is clear on this point. Israel must be destroyed. In May 2012, a person to be taken very seriously, the chief of staff of the Iranian Armed Forces, Major General Hassan Firouzabadi, could not have been more plainspoken and serious about Iran's armed forces' strategic goal, which they have been pursuing by supporting Hezbollah and Hamas. Addressing a defense gathering, he declared, citing Iran's Supreme Leader Ayatollah Khomeini's authority: "The Iranian nation is standing for its cause that is the full annihilation of Israel."[10] No furtive statement, but meant to be transmitted to the world, it was reported by Iran's semi-official Fars News Agency.

Multiple views and considerable uncertainty exist over the means of the upcoming expected annihilation and the likely timeline for achieving it. Iran is building a nuclear weapon, which Iran's leaders and one of its architects have alike said or intimated might or could be used to this end against Israel. After Mostafa Ahmadi Roshan Behdast, a senior scientist of Iran's nuclear weapons program, died in a bomb blast in Tehran in January 2012, his widow Fatemeh Bolouri Kashani with evident pride explained to the Fars News Agency, which imparted her message at home and internationally, that "Mostafa's ultimate goal was the annihilation of Israel."[11] But whatever the means, there is a firm and growing view that success is only a matter of time. Tiny, fragile, and surrounded, Israel will sooner or later either implode, owing to these constant features and pressures of its existence, or be overwhelmed demographically by the more fertile Palestinians, or be defeated by the ascendant Arab and Islamic forces. Thus, in antisemites' thinking and speaking, the inevitability of such a propitious ending to their attempts to destroy Israel is a foregone conclusion. Hassan Nasrallah, in the Arab and Islamic world a longtime celebrity anti-Israel leader of Hezbollah, has explained:

> To free your land, you don't need tanks, a strategic balance, rockets, and cannons; you need to follow the way of the past self-sacrifice martyrs who disrupted and horrified the coercive Zionist entity. You, the oppressed, unarmed, and restricted Palestinians, can force the Zionist invaders to return to the places they came from. Let the Falasha [Ethiopian Jews] go to Ethiopia, and let the Russian Jews return to Russia. The choice is yours, and the model lies right in front of your eyes. An honest and serious resistance can make the freedom dawn arise. Our brothers and beloved Palestinians, I tell you: Israel, which owns nuclear weapons and the strongest war aircraft in the region, is feebler than a spider's web — I swear to God.

Here Nasrallah invokes the well-known parable of the spider web from the Qur'an, lending his conclusions religious authority: "The parable of those who take [beings or forces] other than God for their protectors is that of the spider which makes for itself a house: for behold, the frailest of all houses is the spider's house. If only they understood this!"[12] Israel, he and so many others believe, is, appearances notwithstanding, like the spider's web, which at the right time Allah's faithful will sweep away.

Lest anyone mistake Nasrallah's antagonism and aspiration to be merely a reaction to Israel's policies or even its existence, Nasrallah and Hezbollah have repeatedly gone out of their way to correct this view. The term *the Zionist entity,* long in existence among Israel's enemies for Israel, the political collectivity of the Jews, has not in itself been linguistically adequate to express Nasrallah and Hezbollah's conception of the country and the source of their enmity for it, hence they have taken to a more explicit term, *the Jewish entity. Jewish* is considered by Hezbollah such a vile term that Hezbollah uses it as an epithet for *Zionist* — as if the latter term were not in itself strong enough. This, of course, makes that much more sense when we learn that Nasrallah, this leading spokesman for Israel's Arab and Islamic enemies, emphatically explained already in 1997 that it is not Israel and Israelis whom he most fundamentally hates, but Jews themselves: "If we searched the entire world for a person more cowardly, despicable, weak and feeble in psyche, mind, ideology and religion, we would not find anyone like the Jew. Notice, I do not say the Israeli."[13] It is Jewness itself that Nasrallah and others combat, and that must be destroyed among them, if not everywhere. Recall that Hezbollah's very first Facebook posting, in October 2011, was in English so the entire world would know that Nasrallah and Hezbollah were eliminationist antisemites, whose focus was not on Israel and its Jews, but globally on the world and on Jewness: "O Allah, Please Clean This World From Jewish Contamination."[14] For Hezbollah and for Nasrallah, and in this respect, they speak for tens upon tens of millions in the Arab and Islamic world, individually it is "the Jew," collectively it is Jewness ("the Jewish contamination"), and politically, it is "the Jewish entity" whom they hate and wish to destroy.

Mahmoud Ahmadinejad, addressing the entire world through the media to mark the opening of the United Nations General Assembly in September 2012, chose to proclaim Israel's destruction on the holiest day in the Jewish calendar, Yom Kippur. He engaged in classic history denial and Israel denial (these are further discussed below), delegitimizing Israel's right to exist: "Iran has been around for the last seven, ten thousand years. They [the Israelis] have been occupying those territories for the last sixty to seventy years, with the support and force of the Westerners. They have no roots there in history." Ahmadinejad explained that the passing phase of Israel's illegitimate existence will close with its extermination: "We do believe that they have found themselves at a dead end and they are seeking new adventures in order to escape this dead end. Iran will not be damaged with foreign bombs. We don't even count them as any part of any equation for Iran. During a historical phase, they [the Israelis] represent minimal disturbances that come into the picture and are then eliminated."[15] Speaking the explicit language of eliminationism, Ahmadinejad reaffirmed what Iranian leaders had already often proclaimed. In the quest to destroy Israel, Iran would be willing to suffer damages, because, as mentioned earlier, political Islamic leaders, ordinary political Islamists, and even children preaching to the masses often say to characterize the critical differences between their people and the Jews in Israel: *we love death and they love life.* The lovers of life can hold out for only so long against people willing to die and to kill for their ultimate goal: Israel and its Jewish people's destruction.

The opening declaration of the Hamas Charter is a call to arms: "Israel will rise and will remain erect until Islam eliminates it as it had eliminated its predecessors."[16] As with Hamas and so many in the Arab and Islamic world categorically opposed to making peace with Israel, it stands to reason that they (or at least a huge number of them) think they can defeat Israel sooner or later. And the survey data confirm that what their leaders say is what Palestinians, and presumably other Arabs and Muslims, believe. Eighty percent of the Palestinians affirm the Hamas Charter's assertion that the struggle against "the Jews" must continue "until the enemies are defeated and Allah's victory prevails," which 73 percent avow will include the mass murder of the Jews, which 62 percent agree means that "jihad" is necessary to undo "the usurpation of Palestine by Jews," which 45 percent say is the only way to solve "the Palestinian problem."[17]

The global anti-Israel antisemitic discourse explicitly elaborates all of prejudice's core elements and fills each element with strikingly pernicious content. It provides an extensive and powerful description or characterization of Israel and its Jews' nature, which is *demonic.* It explains the *danger* they pose—extreme and existential. It renders a moral judgment of *delegitimization,* which means that Israel and Jewish Israelis have no right to exist or, in the case of the Jews, no right to exist in such numbers or as sovereign over this territory. It prescribes a solution, elimination: Israel and the capacities of Jewish Israelis, if not the people themselves, must be *destroyed*. In this eliminationist, indeed exterminationist, systematic logic, the anti-Israel antisemitic discourse, and therefore the global antisemitic discourse, is far more complete and explicit than medieval Christianity, or even much modern antisemitism.

These clearly articulated elements, and the anti-Israel antisemitic discourse as a whole, have all the features of a political ideology, which, by any reasonable yardstick, it is. It specifies the problem: Israel and Jews. Indeed, it is a very serious problem. It lays the blame directly on the Jews themselves. It calls for a solution: destruction. Moreover, the problem and the solution (1) are considered above all political, (2) are at the center of the politics of movements, governments, and countries, (3) are used to mobilize and sway people politically, and (4) serve as the centerpiece of foreign policy-making, (5) including military preparations and repeated violent conflicts from rocket attacks and genocide bombing to full-scale war.

Antisemites in Arab and Islamic countries and around the world have produced, as a powerful and growing element of the global antisemitic discourse, a systematic and complete dismantling of the core elements of Jews' history and existence, which undergirds and cuts across the four elements — Israel is *demonic, dangerous, delegitimized,* and must be *destroyed* — that we have seen as constitutive of the antisemitic anti-Israel political ideology. This stream of the global antisemitic discourse goes beyond and, in that sense, is still more pernicious than the powerful delegitimizing assault that focuses on Israel: it *denies* the Jews' peoplehood, their history's essential facts, and that the Israel of antiquity and Jews in the land area of today's Israel ever existed.

This broad-based *denialism* constitutes a fifth central element of the anti-Israel antisemitic political ideology and discourse. This *denialism,* which has Holocaust denial (which probably inspired it) as a core element, essentially asserts about Jews and their history what Holocaust deniers say about the Holocaust: they are hoaxes. The antisemitic denial movement's breadth is breathtaking, sometimes manifestly focusing more on Jews as people, yet even when doing so ultimately pointing toward Israel. An inventory of major denial discourses, a brief account of each, and their rationales reads like a textbook of annihilative notions.

- Holocaust denial. This denies that the Holocaust occurred or casts doubt on any of its central aspects, such as that the Germans used gas chambers to exterminate Jews. This is meant to erase from the public discourse and people's knowledge the fact of the Holocaust — the knowledge of which having done more to delegitimize anti-semitism than anything else, done more to gain sympathy for Jews than anything else, and used often to explain why Jews, obviously and like other peoples, need the political protection of a sovereign country, namely Israel. No lesser personage than Abbas, the president of the Palestinian Authority, penned a Holocaust denial book in 1984, *The Other Side: The Secret Relationship Between Nazism and Zionism,* in which he declares the Nazis' slaughter of six million Jews a myth and their use of gas chambers a "fantastic lie."[18]

- Israel denial. This denies that the country as a morally or internationally legitimate country exists — it is a "Zionist entity" or a "Zionist state" — or that it is of the character of other countries, protecting its people's security and interests, as opposed to being fundamentally of a different genus, a "Nazi state."

- Biblical denial. This denies that the Jewish bible is the province of Jews. Some maintain that it is a forgery in its entirety. Others maintain that it no longer belongs to Jews, but to others.

- History denial. This denies that the Jews have had a historical home in the land of present-day Israel, including a country during antiquity.

- Temple denial. This denies that the temples of David and Solomon, the holiest of sites in the history of Judaism, existed at all, or if they existed, that they did so in Jerusalem on the Temple Mount, for which the Western Wall is one of the retaining walls. This is meant to wrest from Jews any broad claim to Jerusalem as their holy city, and the narrower claim to the holiness of the Temple Mount for Judaism and Jews. Muslims assert that the Temple Mount is solely an Islamic holy site, from which Muhammad ascended to heaven, and maintain today that it should be exclusively Palestinian territory.

- Jerusalem denial. Not only is Jerusalem not deemed a holy city for Jews, but this denies their very historical presence in Jerusalem, and any claim they make to present-day Jerusalem.

- Dead Sea Scrolls denial. This denies that these most famous religious and legal manuscripts, including hundreds of texts from the Jewish bible, dating from antiquity, had anything to do with Jews or Judaism.
- Jesus denial. This denies that Jesus was a Jew, maintaining instead that he was a Palestinian. Yasser Arafat, subsequent Palestinian leaders, and Palestinian and other Arab and Islamic media have steadily denied that Jesus was a Jew, regularly proclaiming that Jesus was a Palestinian, to inaugurate Christmas in Bethlehem. The Palestinian Authority's prime minister, Salam Fayyad, declared, as he lit Bethlehem's fifty-foot Christmas tree in December 2011, "Christmas is an opportunity to celebrate the Palestinian identity of Jesus Christ." Indeed, the Palestinian leaders have created a chain of Jews' victimization of Palestinians from Jesus all the way to the present day, including by explicitly linking him to contemporary leaders. In 2011, on Palestinian Authority Television, Fatah Central Committee member Jibril Rajoub declared: "The greatest Palestinian in history since Jesus is Yasser Arafat."[19] As amazing as all this may sound to Western ears—and specifically to Christian ears, the comparison of Arafat to Jesus—there is actually an age-old practice of denying or concealing that Jesus was a Jew. Christian churches (including the Catholic Church) for centuries either denied or did not inform its followers of Jesus' origins. In Germany, before and especially under the Nazis, this was a common practice. This, like many other antisemitic European and especially Nazi tropes and initiatives, has been adopted and is now persistently employed by Palestinians and Arabs and Muslims.
- Peoplehood denial. This denies that the Jews are a people like other people. The contemporary version of this in the Arab and Islamic world hearkens back to the Nazi notion that the Jews are not a people, or a Volk, but a pseudo-people. There is also an age-old Christian variant of this, which is supersessionism.
- Humanity denial. It finds expression in various forms of dehumanization, most notably in the widespread discourse, grounded in the Qur'an, that Jews are not human beings but the descendants of "apes and pigs." This is meant to wrest from Jews two things: any claim to the things, including a country, that peoples, composed of

human beings, have, and any claim to the moral consideration and protection that is accorded to peoples.

- Right-to-life denial. This is an explicit and implicit discourse that Jews do not have the right to be alive, that they are, in their essence, in their Jewness, evil and irredeemable, and, indeed, must be destroyed.

- Antisemitism denial. This is a widespread discourse, especially in Europe and North America, whereby antisemites deny that anti-semitism (except perhaps as a minor or fringe prejudice) exists at all. It has many streams within it. Some deny that antisemitic discourse is antisemitic—after all, it can't be the *prejudice* of antisemitism, because it is true. Others maintain that antisemitic assaults, namely assaults on people who are Jews merely because they are Jews, are not antisemitic, but random acts of violence, or justified acts of violence. Others maintain that the blatant antisemitism that is an overt part of the discursive and material assault on Israel, or that so manifestly undergirds the assault, has nothing to do with antisemitism at all and instead is but a cool and rational response to Israel's and its people's real or imputed conduct.

Holocaust denial is by far the best known as a denial campaign, but as insidious as it is, it is hardly the most sinister. It is probably misnamed in a strict denotative sense, as it takes many hues, from denying that the Germans slaughtered Jews, to treating the Holocaust in an antiseptic, falsifying way, in order to minimize or conceal its horror, to admitting that the Germans exterminated Jews but saying that, owing to the Jews' nature or the danger they posed, the Germans were justified in eliminating them, or to saying that the Holocaust was not such a major historical event and does not warrant the attention it receives, because eliminationist assaults against other peoples have also been perpetrated— and that whatever actually happened to the Jews, the most significant fact, as usual, is that Jews exploit the past to harm other peoples, especially Germans and Palestinians.

Similar to its core element of Holocaust denial, *denialism* in general has different facets that do not always perfectly harmonize. Its subsidiary denial campaigns are each similarly pluralistic. Denialism and its many architects and adherents seek not intellectual coherence, let alone veracity, but to broadly assault, deny, cast doubt on, create bogus controversies over, and ultimately to weaken Israel's and Jews' status as a country or people. By constructing many assaults of varying claims and types or argumentation, the antisemites win if a given person latches onto any one of them, no matter if it is not the one the antisemites would optimally choose. Also, because they speak differently to different audiences, as political movements and politicians are wont to do, they tailor or alter their message to appeal to the given audience, regardless of intellectual consistency. Furthermore, in constructing denial discourses about such a range of fundamental issues about Israel and Jews, antisemites create an overall aura that Israel and Jews are hoaxes and are perpetrating hoaxes in asserting that they are a country and a people. Finally, by implication or openly, this turns Jews into transgressors against all those who believe they perpetrate hoaxes and all those who allegedly suffer under their material consequences. This is apparent in the Holocaust denial movement. Like all these movements, it at once concentrates on denying basic historical or contemporary facts, and more fundamentally and encompassingly turns the victimized Jews into the big lie's perpetrators — from which they profit monetarily (reparations) and politically (support for Israel) and fulfill their evil intentions (dispossess, dominate, and even destroy Palestinians) — and thus by implication or openly transform Jews into transgressors.

Much of this can be seen in the Palestinian satellite television broadcast on Al-Quds in April 2013 of the denialist diatribe by the International Union of Muslim Scholars' Tareq Hawwas, which, grounded extensively in the foundational antisemitic paradigm, covered a range of antisemitic calumnies, including that "deception are engrained within them [the Jews]," and that the Prophet Muhammad "died from the poison given to him by the Jews." Regarding the Holocaust, Hawwas begins with a classic denialist statement: "Incidentally, most of what is said about the massacre is exaggeration and lies." But he wishes that it were true, and more, by throwing his lot in with Hitler, musing, "If only Hitler had finished them off, thus relieving humanity of them." Hawwas then declares the Jews venal compared to Hitler, explaining that "Hitler was more merciful than they are themselves." And then he adds the by now common trope that the Jews, lying about their victimization, victimize others: "They exploited this minor incident in order to extort the world."[20]

Holocaust denial, like other powerful denial discourses, augments and furthers the general public antisemitic discourse and its various proponents' antisemitic programs, whether by lifting the Holocaust's shadow from Germany and antisemites more broadly, creating more common ground and sympathy between Arab and Islamic antisemites and European antisemites, working for Israel's destruction, laying claims to Christian religious suzerainty, neutering Jews in American politics and society, or just fomenting for antisemites satisfying hatred of Israel and Jews.

For no other people, no other history, and no other present political life is there such a range of denials, let alone about so many fundamental issues that strike at that people's heart and standing in the world. And the denialisms are widely believed. How widely we do not know, but we do know that where it counts most, in the Arab and Islamic world, including among Palestinians, they are so broadly subscribed to as to approach articles of faith. Take Jerusalem denial, about which we have data. Seventy-two percent of Palestinians deny "that Jews have a long history in Jerusalem going back thousands of years." More than nine out of ten Palestinians say that in any future settlement Jerusalem should be the capital only of Palestine and in no way the capital, including the shared capital, of Israel.[21] Holocaust denial, Israel/state/country denial, Jesus denial, humanity denial—the evidence suggests that for all of them, to varying degrees, there are an enormous number of adherents, spanning regions, countries, and peoples. As with the antisemitic discourse in general, the denial discourse is also unprecedented and has no parallel for any other people and their country, in that so many people in different countries and cultures accept and participate in it, effectively forming an international denial and falsification coalition. Like antisemitism itself, many of its contributors self-consciously and knowingly lie (to serve a subjective higher truth), while many others, duped, take its assertions as true. Like today's antisemitism, the denial discourse is global.

Denialism, as the fifth d, contributes in overt and subtle ways to the other four d's—that Israel is *demonic, dangerous, delegitimized,* and must be *destroyed*—which together form the core of the anti-Israel discourse, in addition to being central to the antisemitic discourse more generally. The denial discourse, which turns Israel and Jews into or

*Al-Watan, Qatar, July 27, 2002. A Jewish devil—possibly Ariel Sharon—walks over the skulls of its victims.*

back into the sixth *d,* the original *d,* the devil, further conveys that Israel, this fictive country of a wholly or at least partly fictive people, like the devil of lore himself, ought to be destroyed.

# 13

# Global Unification

THINK OF A naive person who is curious about Jews. Or think of a person who has come across disturbing things that seem credible about Jews and who wants to learn more. Or think of a person with antisemitic tendencies, but who is not yet an impassioned antisemite, seeking to investigate the nature of Jews. Or think of a dyed-in-the-wool antisemite who wishes to keep current on the latest dangers Jews are said to pose. Each of them might type "Jew" into his or her browser. In Google and Bing often the second or third item that comes up is a website called "Jew Watch," which any of these people might or would be likely to click on. After all, except for the Wikipedia entry, it is perhaps the most prominent item on the Internet about Jews. Once clicking on it, each of these people enters a vast world of information and images—news, articles, videos, lists of deeds—about Jews, their nature, their many activities, with the information well organized by category, and alluring for each of these people to explore.

What kind of a world will these people descend into? At the top of the homepage, it states:

*This Scholarly Library of Facts about Domestic & Worldwide Zionist Criminality*

# Jew Wat✡h

*The Jew Watch Project Is The Internet's Largest Scholarly Collection of Articles on Zionist History*

*Free Educational Library for Private Study, Scholarship, Research & News About Zionism*

*We Reveal Zionist Banksters, News Falsifiers, PR Liars, Neocons, Subversives, Terrorists & Spies*

*The Jew Watch Project's 1.5 Billion Pages Served Demonstrate Our Focus on Professionalism*

*An Oasis of News for Americans Who Presently Endure the Hateful Censorship of Zionist Occupation*

The website's homepage contains a dizzying offering of tabs, each with links to articles, videos, and other websites, often with a pseudo-scholarly apparatus of source citations, etc., of the most inflammatory and damaging antisemitism. Some of the major homepage tabs are:

- Zionist Occupied Governments
- Jewish Genocides Today and Yesterday
- Jewish Leaders, Conspirators, Power Lords…
- Jewish Banking & Financial Manipulations
- Jewish Communist Rulers and Killers
- Jewish Mind Control Mechanisms
- Jewish Hate Hoaxes
- Jewish Criminals
- Jewish Oppression of Gentiles — The Hate Crime Boondoggle
- Jewish-Christian Murders
- Jewish Supremacist Lists & The Associations They Dominate
- Jewish Controlled Press
- Jewish Hate Groups (e.g., The World Jewish Congress, the ADL)
- Jewish World Conspiracies

To spend time on Jew Watch, with its self-proclaimed 1.5 billion pages, is to descend into a world of utter fantasy, obsessiveness, hatred, and demonization, which is hard to convey to anyone unwilling to devote time to exploring its mad world. The most shocking thing about such madness—whether or not you choose to immerse yourself in it as the craziness is paraded, elaborated upon, and celebrated on Jew Watch—is that you need not go to somewhere as manifestly off-balanced (though not hard to find) as Jew Watch to encounter what the site proffers. Indeed, Jew Watch is an aggregator site of material that originates all over the Internet. And its wares, its discourse, which centers on the foundational antisemitic paradigm, grounded in a demonic image of Jewness, and its many constitutive discourses—political Islamist, leftist, rightist, anti-globalization, etc.—are the stock-in-trade of antisemites the world over. Its wares, its discourses, its presentation of Jewness, constitute the ordinary, taken-for-granted public discourse of countries, governments, institutions, peoples, and cultural production around the world. Moreover, an endless stream of websites, blogs, and proliferating social networks on YouTube, Facebook, Twitter, Tumblr, and more are devoted to similar themes or purvey them as part of their ordinary and broader discourses. Who knows how many countless tens of millions come across these sites and pages, let alone spend considerable amounts of time on them and absorb truth as these sites and networks represent it.

Jew Watch's antisemitic fare is striking for another reason. It functions as a clearinghouse, a mall, or supermarket for antisemitism, containing all brands of antisemitic discourse, assaults, accusations. It does have its particular hyper-obsessions (Jews as communists) within the multi-obsessive world of antisemitism, yet it welcomes and directs users to any brand of antisemitism they might choose. This is one of global antisemitism's characteristics and crucially successful features, namely cross-fertilization and mutual deepening. It is as if the old orthodoxy, which focused on what a Jew is, and which was so tied to the understanding of the Jews' nature as derived from the understanding of the source of Jews' malfeasance, matters little or no more. It is as if the source of Jews' alleged perniciousness, and the need for a kind of antisemitic purity, has become too academic a thing to argue about, too arcane a demand of the anti-semite, even if antisemites certainly spend plenty of time decrying the Jews' alleged original sin, whatever they might conceive it to be. In the world of Jew Watch and in the world of global antisemitism, the crucial issue is not *why* a person thinks ill of Jews. It is not what his foundational reason, grounded in an understanding of Jews' ontology or Jewness, is for thinking bad things about Jews. The crucial issue, regardless of the reason or justification, is simply *whether* a person holds antisemitic beliefs or animus, whether a person signs on to the antisemitic orientation. That the antisemites may disagree about everything else, including the exact source and character of Jews' Jewness is of secondary, tertiary, indeed often of no importance. That's why political leftist groups (who passionately support women's and gay rights) and political Islamists (who are fervently against women's equality and would want to see gays executed), such as Britain's Respect Party (an electoral political party dominated by an alliance of the Socialist Workers' Party and the Muslim Alliance), can march in antisemitic lockstep at rallies applauding one another's speeches of antisemitic imprecations, hatred, and fantasy about Israel and Jews. The enemy of my enemy, the Jews, is my antisemitic friend.

Perhaps the emblematic statement conveying the unification of antisemitisms was delivered by José Saramago in an article he published on April 21, 2002, in Spain's and one of Europe's leading newspapers, *El País*.

> Intoxicated mentally by the messianic dream of a Greater Israel which will finally achieve the expansionist dreams of the most radical Zionism; contaminated by the monstrous and rooted "certitude" that in this catastrophic and absurd world there exists a people chosen by God and that, consequently, all the actions of an obsessive, psychological and pathologically exclusivist racism are justified; educated and trained in the idea that any suffering that has been inflicted, or is being inflicted, or will be inflicted on everyone else, especially the Palestinians, will always be inferior to that which they themselves suffered in the Holocaust, the Jews endlessly scratch their own wound to keep it bleeding, to make it incurable, and they show it to the world as if it were a banner. Israel seizes hold of the terrible words of God in Deuteronomy: "Vengeance is mine, and I will be repaid." Israel wants all of us to feel guilty, directly or indirectly, for the horrors of the Holocaust; Israel wants us to renounce the most elemental critical judgment and for us to transform ourselves into a docile echo of its will.
>
> Israel, in short, is a racist state by virtue of Judaism's monstrous doctrines — racist not just against the Palestinians, but against the entire world, which it seeks to manipulate and abuse. Israel's struggles with its neighbors, seen in that light, do take on a unique and even metaphysical quality of genuine evil — the quality that distinguishes Israel's struggles from those of all other nations with disputed borders, no matter what the statistics of death and suffering might suggest.[1]

Most, perhaps the vast majority of, Europeans would read this and nod, thinking and saying among themselves in private that Saramago expressed publicly what everyone knows and is afraid to say. Virtually all Arab and Islamic antisemites would agree to its every point. Christian antisemites would, in addition to much else they would undoubtedly like, certainly concur with the age-old Christian charges of Jews and their God being vengeful and the effrontery of the Jews' stiff-necked "certitude" of their chosenness and therefore casting doubt on Christians' claims that they are the rightful proprietors of the Judaic tradition. Leftists could find many finely expressed points, especially the condemnation of Zionism and the condemnation of the imputed drive to create a "Greater Israel." Rightists might in particular latch on to the Holocaust inversion, casting the Jews as abusers of the past to justify their own predations, and, in effect making the Jews coequal to or worse than any of those who may have afflicted them. Internationalist human rights or global antisemites, who relentlessly focus on the international dimension of antisemitism, might applaud the notion that Israel is trying to subjugate and control a good part of the world.

Saramago's antisemitic diatribe, grounded in the foundational antisemitic paradigm, is a distillation and concentration of the common notions that are to be found piecemeal and usually more genteelly expressed around the European media and in surveys. It easily slides among Jews, Judaism, Zionism, and Israel, presenting them as inextricably interrelated entities. Its range of antisemitic tropes draws on different antisemitic streams and traditions, binding the old and the new. Its amalgam of accusations and perspectives can appeal to all manner of antisemites, and, in its clever interweaving of them, persuade someone who agrees with one or another of them of the veracity of others. It renders a collage of Jewness that has historical, religious, psychological, intentional, political, and, of course, diabolical elements. Jewness is rooted in the Jewish religion, in the Jews' historical experience, in their essential psychology, in their malevolence ("genuine evil" ), in the boundlessness of the harm they willfully and with a feeling of justification inflict on others, in the quality of that harm, in their singularity, in their cosmic scope of evildoing (not just against their neighbors, the Palestinians, but against the whole world), and perhaps most of all in the illegitimacy, alone among the nations, of their country, which in sum and in a totalizing and essentializing manner is reduced to a "racist state," which Saramago is clear to explicitly emphasize is rooted in "Judaism's monstrous doctrines."

For Saramago, Jews are different. They have always been different, as it is grounded in their foundation. It is now rooted in their psychology. They want it to be that way. They are malevolent. They are powerful. They are "racist," "monstrous," and "evil" in their religion, their beings, their country, which are all linked in a mutually interlocking set of causes and effects. For Saramago, it boils down to the evil of Jewness and its current most catastrophic manifestation in the evil of its political expression, the Jews' country.

Saramago was a Nobel Prize winner for literature, and a major European intellectual and voice until his death in 2010. It is hard to imagine a prominent European intellectual penning such a racist diatribe against another ethnic group or people, describing them as inveterate evil going back thousands of years and being worse than ever in the present. It is hard to imagine one of Europe's leading newspapers publishing such a hate-filled, racist diatribe against any other ethnic group. It is hard to imagine that if such a luminary would harbor such profound prejudices against some other ethnic group, say against Germans, and if he would dare to want to parade his racism before the world, and if somehow a major European newspaper would give him a forum to express his rank bigotry, that there would not have been a withering pan-European outcry and condemnation, rendering the offending person unfit for further respectable public life. But not against Saramago, because his bigotry regarded Jews.

Grounded in an age-old and powerfully current notion of Jewness, with an elaboration built upon it that draws on and integrates in a manner that is at once guttersnipe and highly sophisticated, a causal and frightening argument about Jews' cosmic danger, and presenting the Jews as world-historical evil and Israel as the criminal par excellence among countries, Saramago—who also described the conditions existing in Palestinian Ramallah, owing to Israel, as "a crime comparable to Auschwitz"!—exemplifies the integration and unity of antisemitisms and of the fluid character of global antisemitism, which ultimately sees Jews and Israel as an international menace. Whatever an antisemite, or just someone sympathetic to some antisemitic notions, might understand to be the source of the Jews' character and differentness, this elaboration on the foundational antisemitic paradigm, this presentation of Jewness and its evil, can be accepted by and feed into that conception, whether it is racist, religious, cultural, or political at its core, and whether it originates in an Arab and Islamic, Christian, leftist, rightist, or more internationally oriented antisemitism. Pluralist accounts of the sources of Jews' unfitness for society and often for remaining alive are commonplace in today's global antisemitic discourse and amalgam—even among the most fervent Islamic antisemites, who would ordinarily rely so heavily or exclusively on the Islamic tradition. Recall that when Saudi Sheikh Abd Al-Rahman Al-Sudayis of Mecca elaborated on what the Qur'an and Hadith and Muslims' "belief" and "history" say about the source of the Jews' "evil," he explained that it is the Jews' "belief, identity, and existence"[2]—a set of, here mutually reinforcing, options among which virtually any antisemite can find at least one, and often all three, that speaks to his own beliefs about Jews. The Jews' beliefs are evil. Check. Their chosen identity, which when political is to be Israeli or to support the Jews' political existence in Israel, is evil. Check. And their very existence is evil and ought to be eliminated. Check. Racist, religious, cultural antisemites, those of the left, right, or center or from virtually any tradition can see here a foundation for their demonology and animus toward Jews.

In the world of global antisemitism, there are clearly defined antisemitic discourses or brands, which have or could be given labels. You can be an Islamic or political Islamic antisemite. Many are. You can be a Christian antisemite. Many are. You can be a particular kind of Christian antisemite, a Catholic antisemite. Many are. You can be an anti-Zionist or anti-Israel antisemite. Many are. You can be a neo-Nazi antisemite. Many are. You can be a white supremacist antisemite. Many are. You can be a leftist antisemite. Many are. You can be an antiglobalization antisemite. Many are. You can be an international human rights antisemite. Many are. You can be a strategic antisemite. Many are. You can be any or all of these and other kinds of antisemites, or you can be an amalgam of two or three or more of them. A Christian antisemite can believe not only that all Jews are guilty for Jesus' death, but also that they provoked the Germans into killing them or exaggerate the Holocaust today and are in the process of exterminating the Palestinians. An antiglobalist antisemite can be left or right wing, believing that the Jews are responsible for the predations of globalization but specifying them quite differently, the leftist condemning their alleged responsibility for capitalism's ills and the rightist seeing Jews undermining national purity, strength, or independence with their alleged responsibility for foreign elements infiltrating the country. In today's world, it is likely that people, even if it is not known to them, have imbibed antisemitic elements that have nothing to do with the core discourse from which their antisemitisms come.

This is one of global antisemitism's crucial points and features. The discourses, whatever their differences, have merged. They incorporate elements from one another. And they simultaneously coexist around the world, and not just on Google, Bing, or on search-engine-dominant websites devoted to antisemitism, such as Jew Watch, so that as in a vast market, people, whether new to antisemitism or dyed-in-the-wool antisemites, can go shopping there, picking out or picking up whatever aspect of the distinct and now also overlapping lines they find appealing, all the while rubbing shoulders with a veritable United Nations of fellow and diverse antisemites. They are available as any number of apps from Apple or Google, which have offered to their innocent or not-so-innocent users the *Protocols of the Elders of Zion,* the world's leading antisemitic conspiracy tract.

*A* Protocols *app.*

Some teenager, or some curious adult, young or old, may innocently download an Apple or Google app and plunge into the world of antisemitism, with its conspiracies and dangers and explanations for the ways the world, perhaps his world, is awry. Or he may stumble across the book on Amazon.com, which then leads him to other books, including *Conspiracy of the Six-Pointed Star: Eye-Opening Revelations and Forbidden Knowledge About Israel, the Jews, Zionism, and the Rothschilds* and *The Synagogue of Satan.* Or he or she may be drawn to Jew Watch innocently, wishing to learn about Jews, or may use it as a go-to website for fortifying his already existing antisemitism or just to get the latest information it offers about Jews and their predations. The pluralism of Jew Watch's offerings is its virtually comprehensive menu of antisemitisms, ways into their respective discourses, and array of antisemitic accusations, images, and tropes. Jew Watch's antisemitisms are connected to broader bodies of thought, discourses, or ideologies, but that is secondary to Jew Watch's overwhelming focus on the Jews themselves.

For another kind of antisemitic pluralism and another path into the netherworld of antisemitic hatred, many websites and social networking media that are principally devoted to political, religious, ideological, economic, or cultural matters extensively interweave, and therefore powerfully integrate, into their broader discourses and worldviews antisemitic constructs of Jews and Jewness. A person who goes to Stormfront, the oldest and most prominent political rightist, white supremacist website, descends into a fantasy world of devilish Jews, much of it in the explicitly racist-biological cast of the contemporary neo-Nazi or right-wing stream of antisemitism. In Stormfront, Jews are inimical to the well-being of the white "race" as they sponsor conspiratorially or openly a panoply of movements, policies, corrosive ideas, and initiatives that undermine the well-being of whites and Christians, as well as the national health and wealth of the Stormfront country or countries of a language group (it has nineteen language-affiliated websites) being visited, with the American one in English being the mainstay. In the Stormfront website's introduction for new users, Stormfront directly addresses the crux of the white race's and the world's problems:

> The attentive reader may wonder at how the situation has gotten as grave as it has. How could people have become so detached from reality to believe the delusion of racial equality? Why would anyone in their right mind allow immigration from places like Iraq, Somalia and Mexico into the United States and Europe?
>
> Which brings us to the horrible truth of the "Jewish problem."
> *It was the Jews.*
> The Jews have been working together behind the scenes to gain control of all the TV stations, schools, newspapers, radio stations, governments, movie studios, banks, etc.—an all encompassing "Matrix" of lies to destroy all potential rival groups and rule the

*A Stormfront image of Jews' power and predations.*

world. And they are very close to achieving it. They managed to get our people's heads so far up their butts that Whites think that allowing millions of third worlders into the US and Europe will somehow "improve" those lands with "diversity" and economic prosperity.

The origin of the problem with the Jews is, once again, in the blood. As a group, a *race,* they suffer from psychopathy—a mental disorder whose main symptom is the ability to lie like there is no tomorrow. They seem to be able to talk entire nations into believing just about anything they want. That is the little secret to their success.[3]

The Stormfront English language website is a cascade of antisemitism integrated into its broader discourse of racism, hatred, and violence. And it informs its users that they are part of an enormous community of like-minded people, by citing an astonishing degree of activity on it: almost three-quarters of a million discussion threads and ten million posts.

Like Jew Watch, Stormfront is a clearinghouse of antisemitism, but unlike Jew Watch, it is one where antisemitism serves as a master theme — the ideational glue — to the pluralism of its broader brand of hatred and fantasy, which is against all those who are imputed to stand against whites and Christians. Stormfront and Jew Watch are each portals not only into the world of bigotry and hatred against Jews but also to other websites and social media, to which its visitors easily link to continue their path of exploring and deepening their antisemitic views of Jews by finding like-minded individuals, notions, and virtual and real communities.

Global antisemitism means that whatever the prepackaged brands, which is another way of conceptualizing the individual antisemitic discourses, antisemites are free to and have the resources to assemble their individual brands, to create their personal combinations, and to do so precisely by listening to, clicking through to, and rubbing shoulders with varieties of antisemitisms and antisemites and varieties of antisemitic narratives and accusations. Just as today's general global market, and the proliferating choices it offers, includes material and intellectual wares from different continents, traditions, and sensibilities, which are all at a person's fingertips for him to pick and choose as he sees fit, so too is this true of antisemitism and antisemites. Pluralism is one of globalism's central features. It is also, as never before, one of antisemitism's central features, not only in that antisemitic discourses and antisemitisms now stream in so many varieties around the world, but also in the opportunities individual antisemites have to tailor their views according to what makes sense — or, put differently, what makes the most persuasive emotionally satisfying nonsense — to them.

Nevertheless, global antisemitism has core elements that structure it and give it its distinctive cast. Whatever the elaborations, the religious or other cultural bents or inflections, the specific charges, the means the Jews use, the Jews seen this way (all Jews or a major subset, such as Jews in Israel), and the implied or articulated courses of anti-Jewish action — they are grounded in, coalesce around, and find commonality in the foundational antisemitic paradigm: Jews are different. Their differences are essential. They are pernicious in intent or deed. They are mightily powerful and dangerous.

And then there is global antisemitism's crucial feature, which differentiates it from past antisemitisms: its overwhelmingly political orientation. Problems in the global world and problems with Jews are ever more cast not principally economically, socially, or culturally but politically, or at least with a strong political dimension, to be solved through political action, particularly on the global stage, in the international arena. Although antisemites do not agree on all aspects of the international dimension of the problems and dangers Jews allegedly pose, they keep coming back to several themes: Jews' international political nature and predations and, whatever their national citizenship, that they operate conspiratorially; Jews' international financial predations; Israel's predations and the general disorder it sows; and the Jews' predations through their manipulation of the American superpower. Thus, antisemites' focus on fighting fire with fire fills the international realm and floods the globe with antisemitism, especially in the overarching international forums, which are the nodes that connect all governments, all countries, all cultures, all peoples, all individuals. Hence, their concerted and successful efforts to capture international institutions, starting with but by no means restricted to the United Nations, to co-opt international law and its institutions, especially for the anti-Israel antisemitic component of the agenda, and to turn the Jews' central emblem, their peoplehood's central expression, their central political institution and locus of

*The eliminationist consensus.*

life—the country of Israel—into an international pariah and to keep its misdeeds and deeds (which are cast as misdeeds) in the world's eye and insinuated into its consciousness. Ultimately, they seek to use politics and policy to delegitimize, attack, weaken, diminish, or destroy Israel. On this, antisemites of all the major streams can agree and unite.

One significant development among Jews has enhanced global antisemitism's plausibility and has spurred antisemites to globalize antisemitism relentlessly. Jews finally find communal expression in its universal form: a country. The global order is one of countries. Thus, when Jews achieved communal and political expression's global form, and then became a significant actor in global politics—first as an important player during the politically and strategically hegemonic Cold War, which heightened and locked in place Israel's visibility, and then at the center of the most conflict-ridden and problematic and threatening significant region in the post–Cold War era—antisemitism was likely to globalize in some form, and antisemites' attempts to globally broaden and further antisemitism became a natural and winning strategy.

The global antisemitic story has a second half. Even though Jews finally have their own country, they also remain a dispersed people with a real or imagined presence in many countries, which many non-Jews have long enveloped in antisemitism, seeing Jews as composing a fantasized powerful nefarious network around the world, as having infiltrated into the heart of the world's sole superpower, and as being the focus of the global order and of attempts to alter it. No other people is seen this way, as continuing to exist as a deracinated *politically powerful* people, indeed as a vast network of such people—and to exist this way even when other members of their people have their own country. In global antisemitism's presentation, Jews remain a networked people spanning the globe, powerful string-pullers in country after country, especially the United States, but in the global era the conspiracy is hyper-concentrated politically, because its alleged goal is to secure and further the power and predations of the world's two putatively most destructive or dangerous political entities, Israel and the United States. This creates visible and ready political targets for antisemites' antipathies, in country after country, regarding real or imagined problem after problem, especially as the United States and Israel are effectively always in the news. That the global antisemitic discourse can tap into age-old antisemitic notions and tropes, in addition to global

*The global threat of the Jews*

antisemitism's central features of the Jews' putative international preda-tions and political nature and conduct, means that directing, activating, and inflaming existing antipathies for Jews, and spreading them to those who may not share them yet, can be done in the major realms of human existence. The political dimension of contemporary antisemitism is clear. The economic tropes about Jewish power and predations are age-old. The social, cultural, and spiritual notions about Jews undermining society, a country's or a people's culture, or defying, threatening, or defiling God or his people are very much alive.

Except in much of the United States, almost everywhere Jews are wary. That is because Jews everywhere, seen both as part of interna-tional Jewry and as the dispersed co-conspirators serving Israel's Jews, are potential targets. This is apparent from the high-profile attacks that take place in Europe, including the Toulouse school mass murder, the attacks in Berlin, Malmö, Venice, Vienna, and elsewhere. It is apparent in the fortress-like security that Jewish communal and religious institu-tions have in country after country. It is apparent in the string of Fatwas that Islamic leaders promulgate justifying or urging the murder of Jews around the world, which include such statements as "May Allah send, from the One Billion [Muslim] Nation, only one thousand to carry out suicide attacks, and destroy their [the Jews'] interests and centers everywhere so that they be humiliated and exterminated."[4] It is apparent in the virtually endless, implied or open, incitements to violence against Jews coursing through the Internet. It is apparent in the publication of names and addresses of prominent Jews on antisemitic websites, such as Stormfront posting its "Jew Traitors Master List" of prominent Jews in politics and policy making in the United States, and Italian Stormfront posting a list of "influential Italian Jews" in politics, business, media, and culture. The incitements to violence emanating from Arab and Islamic digital media and social media (in addition to conventional newspapers and public occasions and Friday sermons, many of which end up on the web) are so common and so much a part of the web's infrastructure of hatred that they hardly, if ever, receive coverage or a concerted push back. Sometimes calls to kill Jews that originate from non-Arab and Islamic sources do elicit outraged responses, which only bring to the awareness of Jews and broader interested publics the threat they at least implicitly pose. This has happened with the repeated appearance on Facebook sites calling for "Kill A Jew Day" and "Burn A Jew Day," which have explicitly exhorted people to kill and burn Jews and invited everyone to relevant events, which themselves have elicited a flood of antisemitic comments and violent and licentious fantasies, including "Can't wait to rape the dead baby Jews."[5]

That Jews are potential targets and must be wary is apparent in what more and more ordinary people are saying. Thirty-seven percent of British Muslims have said regarding the use of violence that British Jews are "legitimate targets as part of the struggle for justice in the Middle East."[6] As with so many other numbers, it is easy to read this and just move on. But the figure is astonishing: more than one out of every three Muslims in Britain says that people who have nothing to do with a conflict two thousand miles away are legitimate targets for violence, only because these Muslims define those people by, and reduce them to, a characteristic that they treat as an essence shared with the people party to that conflict. The people whom British Muslims want to target are British, may support a variety of political parties or foreign policies, may be wholeheartedly supportive or extremely critical of Israel's policies, may be friendly or not to Muslims, and may have dozens of other qualities that distinguish them as individuals and differentiate them from one another. But all this is irrelevant for the British Muslim antisemites who reduce them to only one aspect of their identity, which may be of little importance to the people anyway, namely that they are Jews, who by definition share the most fundamental attribute with the Jews of Israel, a common and essential Jewness. This astonishingly high figure—of people supporting such violence against a civilian population only because they see them as Jews—exists, significantly, in the rather pacified country of Britain and, significantly, in a Muslim community that is overwhelmingly, perhaps as high as 80 percent, not from or without ancestry in the Middle East, not from the countries whose people have been directly (or even tangentially) in the conflict with Israel and its Jews, but overwhelmingly from Pakistan, Bangladesh, and India. This finding confirms how profound and widespread the antisemitism is that is rife in the Arab and Islamic world even beyond the confines of their majoritarian countries.

And it shows how little antisemites differentiate between Israel the country and its people, and Jews in general. And why should they, as their opinion leaders and the institutions they look to not only fail to distinguish between Israel and Jews in general, but repeatedly explicitly do the opposite, which is to link the two or treat the two as being of an indistinguishable whole. Recall that the Hamas Charter grounds its annihilationism toward Israel in the fact that it is a country for Jews: "Israel, by virtue of its being Jewish and of having a Jewish population, defies Islam and the Muslims." And Hamas conceives of "the Jews" as "the merchants of war" whom Hamas depicts in its racist way as inveterate and eternal enemies of Muslims: "We have cast among them [the Jews] enmity and hatred till the day of Resurrection. As often as they light a fire for war, Allah extinguishes it. Their effort is for corruption in the land, and Allah loves not corrupters." That Jews are eternal enemies and merchants of war is, among the other reasons Hamas enumerates, why Arabs and Muslims ought to both destroy Israel and slaughter Jews in general.[7] With such racist thinking, common among antisemites, implicating, and frequently calling for the death of, Jews everywhere, it is no surprise that more and more ordinary antisemites in Britain and Europe as well as the Middle East share this view and that some are acting upon it. In essence, Jews in general are no longer seen as civilians. For ever more antisemites, Jews, whether they are in Tel Aviv, New York, London, Berlin, Malmö, Venice, or wherever, are by definition, namely according to antisemites' definition of them and their Jewness, seen as foot soldiers in the antisemitic war against Israel. As Rabbi Abraham Cooper of the Simon Wiesenthal Center in Los Angeles noted, Mohammed Merah, the murderer of Jewish *children* in Toulouse, articulated this when justifying his deed: "...If I would have killed civilians, the French population would have called me another mad Al Qaeda terrorist..." Merah further explained, "...killing military and Jews passed the message....But my message is different....I kill Jews in France as these are the same Jews who kill innocents in Palestine."[8] Jews are not civilians. And Jews in France are the same as Jewish soldiers in Israel. Ipso facto, they—and this pertains to Jews everywhere—must be killed.

These two features of Jews in the global age—having achieved their own country, making them finally part of the global order, *and* remaining a dispersed people—are crucial elements of global antisemitism's development, of its distinctiveness compared to past antisemitisms and compared to other prejudices, and of its power. Regarding the Jews' country of Israel, an entirely new body of demonological thought and accusations and intensive hatreds has developed. Regarding Jews as a dispersed people, Jews remain mostly figmentally imagined as networked in a conspiracy (even people who do not use this explicit language rely upon it, or use it, as their frame) to cause acute problems and threaten countries and peoples (which they allegedly do). Crucially, these two features of Jews in our global age are linked into an ever more distinctive and tighter antisemitic web, with the Jews living dispersed around the world serving the powerful, demonized country, and with Israel serving as a demonic control center mobilizing the Jews of different countries to undermine their countrymen and betray their countries' interests.

Antisemites today share their views through the media available regionally, internationally, indeed globally, through television and radio and distinctively and devastatingly on the Internet. Antisemites have an international television and general news network in Al Jazeera, which is accepted around the world as being reliable, indeed for many a leading news source, allowing its incendiary antisemitic reports to be taken as truthful news. They have co-opted a second international network, the BBC, which steadily demonizes, delegitimizes, and—but not overtly—in its anti-Israel drumbeat implicitly gives succor to those who support or might consider supporting Israel's destruction.* They have a state-run Iranian English language television network, Press TV, which broadcasts a stream of antisemitic invective around the world. Reuters, the international news and wire service that feeds stories to newspapers, magazines, television, and radio around the world in twenty languages, even though it is not particularly known for antisemitism, nevertheless is colossally biased, which is one indicator of antisemitism, in its reporting of events in the Middle East. A study of fifty news and news-oriented articles about Israel's conflict with Palestinians and other Arab countries over a three-month period uncovered "over 1,100 occurrences of reporting/ethical failures" as judged by Reuters' own reporting and ethical guidelines. And the effects of such antisemitic bias and reporting are devastating, as the study shows that people, starting off with relatively neutral views of the conflict between Israel and the Palestinians, who read such biased stories shift their views substantially toward being more hostile toward Israel.[9]

In country after country, antisemites have countless national and local networks and outlets. They have their views carried and spread in national wire services, major and minor newspapers, magazines, blogs, and around the Internet-connected world. They have their thousands, tens of thousands—who knows how many—websites, Facebook networks, blogs, Twitter accounts, newsfeeds, and more. The Simon Wiesenthal Center monitors more than fifteen thousand websites in its project to combat antisemitism and hate on the Internet, but even this huge number vastly understates the problem's extent, as social networking means that "a single posting can reach untold thousands [of sites] beyond." Cooper explains: "The explosive rise in Internet usage in the

---

* Owing to withering criticism of its bias, the BBC was compelled to commission an internal report of its practices, which it then (presumably owing to damning findings) refused to release, even going so far as fighting in court a Freedom of Information Act demand for it—a stunning, self-condemning position for a news organization that champions the use of the act and what it stands for. For this and a more general account of the BBC's documented hostility and bias toward Israel, see Melanie Phillips, "An Open Letter to the Culture Secretary in the UK," *Spectator,* April 12, 2011, as posted at http://www.ruthfullyyours .com/2011/04/13/melanie-phillips-an-open-letter-to-the-culture-secretary-in-the-uk/.

present century has brought with it a new way of transmitting a wide range of classic anti-Semitic images and messages. Terrorist, racist, bigoted and anti-Semitic sites have emerged in large numbers and are often linked to each other. Traditional hate groups such as neo-Nazis, the Ku Klux Klan and skinheads, proliferate on the Net. Very different activist groups have built coalitions in the name of anti-globalization, anti-Americanism and attacking Israel."[10]

Jew Watch and Stormfront are but prominent exemplars of a far more widespread and already deeply rooted problem of the antisemitic world, with its many and overlapping antisemitic communities that have colonized the Internet.

Antisemitism has gone viral. It has gone viral not only in the principal sense that "going viral" is meant on the web, which is to multiply and spread widely, but in the four dimensions of a virus' original sense. Like a highly contagious viral disease, antisemitism has multiplied and spread. It does not merely harmlessly entertain Gangnam style, but in exposing itself to people antisemitism infects them, turning them into carriers and sources of further infection. Like such a viral disease, antisemitism's form of infection is not benign, but injurious. And like such a viral disease, antisemitism casts a pall over others who know the virus spreads, injures, and threatens them and virtually anybody.

The viral power of the Internet for antisemitism has been barely discerned and dimly understood. Its contribution to global antisemitism's reach and character is critical and vast, and it is growing in expanse and intensity. Through television and radio, in the Islamic world through the weekly institution of Friday prayers so often devoted to spreading antisemitism, through daily newspapers and weekly magazines, millions upon millions of people — often at one time — receive regular, repeated, powerful, if sometimes fleeting doses of antisemitism, which are cumulatively devastating. So many of these antisemitic installments, unlike in the past, have an ongoing life, as they are posted on the Internet and then reposted and reposted on Facebook, YouTube, Twitter, blogs, and multiplying social media that are international in reach, country specific in language, and community centered in locale. Arabic antisemitic videos quickly get posted and reposted onto hundreds of sites. As if this were not enough to guarantee a world turning and teeming with ever proliferating antisemitism, there is the vast uncharted world of antisemitic production that is original to individuals and gets appended to articles and videos that are themselves not antisemitic—such as newspaper and magazine reports about the financial crises or problems—but which deal with any of the many themes that antisemites think are related to Jews or Israel and which get posted in social media, uploaded, reposted, spread to websites and Facebook and Twitter networks, and from them to still other ones. Who knows how many Twitter followers antisemitic tweeters have, how many antisemitic *friends* on Facebook share their malignant beliefs and impassioned hatreds of Jews, how many videos are posted on the video sites that multiply around the globe, how many antisemitic photos, cartoons, and images are shared on Tumblr? This avalanche of material is encountered by dyed-in-the-wool antisemites, more casual antisemites, and innocents who just come across it and may be vulnerable to its messages, with a cumulative viral, poisonous effect of unknown though certainly enormous size.

The Internet has made the swirling streams of antisemitism possible, and made them instantly and 24/7 available to everyone. These developments have been further enhanced by a virtually uncommented-upon feature of the global era that is relevant to antisemitism's proliferation: the spread of English. Today, 1.5 billion people use English. When the speakers of just three other major international languages, Spanish, Arabic, and French, totaling one billion, are added, the number of people who can be reached by posting a video, an antisemitic news story, or a conspiratorial rant in just four languages approaches 2.5 billion, including people, especially including opinion leaders, in the vast majority of countries of the world. Add translations into two geographically constricted languages that nevertheless have vast numbers of speakers, Chinese and Hindi, and your potential audience increases by another 1.5 billion people. The internationalization of language, especially English, makes spreading and deepening antisemitism, whatever the day's accusation may be, a thousand times, or rather an Internet-times easier than it was prior to the global age. Today, one person knowing four languages, or three people each knowing two of the four—English, Spanish, Arabic, and French—can post an antisemitic article or video, or cartoon or image, or accusation in those languages, potentially reach more than two billion people, and readily seed the entire world for translations or transcriptions into every language and for every community in the world. Think of how long it used to take, and how arduous a process, and the cost involved, and therefore how rarely it was done, for an incendiary antisemitic story to spread around the world. It was a virtual, which means nonvirtual, pony express. Today, in twenty-four hours or less, such a story can be everywhere, available to almost anybody. Today, new notions of the alleged conspiracies of Jews can take on a vast life almost overnight.

Plan Andinia is a wild Jewish conspiracy notion that has coursed through the Internet. It may sound crackpot to the many who are not aware of the raging antisemitism on the Internet, but fantastical news of Jews' potential predations are the common cyber-currency of untold millions. Plan Andinia is the plan that Jews are said to have hatched and to be preparing to implement to take over Argentinean and/or Chilean Patagonia. That's right, to go halfway around the world from where most of them are and to seize from two countries a rugged, mainly wilderness region of the world. And why would Jews do such a far-fetched thing? Because conquest and theft is what Jews today do.

A common antisemitic trope, known to anyone who pays the least bit of attention to the antisemitic barrage coming from Arab and Islamic countries and anti-Israel agitation in general, is that Jews seek to conquer ever more territory, colonize ever more of the world, wrest the land and homes from ever more peoples. This is, of course, one of the standard fantastical charges against Israel and its Jews, namely that they seek to conquer the entire Middle East. That Jews are minuscule in number according to the world's population and would have few people to settle these places is only one of reality's many irrelevances to those spreading and consuming these stories of Jews' predations. In the last few years, the notion has spread that Jews were intending to conquer, of all places, Patagonia, even though it made no logistical, material, geostrategic, or human sense. Once on the Internet, this perhaps latest and certainly among the most bizarre of Jewish conspiracy tales became an article of faith to vast numbers of people—if it is judged by the measure that we have, which is the number of postings. There are now fifty thousand items on the Internet, reaching who knows how many millions or tens of millions of people, about the Jews' plan to take over Patagonia. There are many accounts as to how they will do it. The Chilean website The Truth Now explains its version: "The plan is based on burning the region of Patagonia, so that the government of Chile […] would create a law to protect the area […]

in order to declare the area 'under UN's protection' and then will allow the establishment of a Jewish State, as they did in Palestine." As we have often had cause to wonder, about which people other than Jews would such lunacy even be broadly contemplated let alone articulated publicly let alone become an article of faith for many in the public sphere, let alone be supported by the most prominent public figures? No less than Chilean parliamentarians fan the flames of such antisemitic conspiracy thinking. Senator Eugenio Tuma, the Chilean Senate's president of the Commission on Foreign Relations, has pointed to a stealth Israeli reconnaissance of Patagonia, whereby Israel has sent ten thousand former soldiers as tourists to this vast region shared by Chile and Argentina. When an Israeli tourist was accused of having started a fire in Patagonia, another Chilean member of parliament issued on Twitter an antisemitic salvo: "I bet that the Israeli 'tourist' who caused the blaze is one of those sent by his government after killing Palestinian children."[11] Such is the hold of the foundational antisemitic paradigm halfway across the world from where the vast majority of Jews reside in our globalized age.

The capacity of antisemites to invent a powerful antisemitic conspiracy or just some antisemitic accusation, to have it take root among the faithful and then spread and spread until it becomes a prominent fixed part of the antisemitic landscape, so much so that it enters the mainstream public discourse as fact and enters even parliaments, is one aspect of how the Internet has become an unprecedented antisemitic multiplier and contributes to the new character of global antisemitism. Another is how it can give an otherwise marginal and therefore ineffectual antisemitic voice a worldwide platform and perniciousness. Carlos Latuff, a Brazilian cartoonist whose creative talent rivals his cartoons' malevolence, would have remained an obscure local cartoonist in Brazil but, owing to the Internet, he has become an international antisemitic cartooning superstar, with his cartoons (see next page) regularly streaming around the world, after they are launched by him or by the Iranian news agency that carries them, and then relaunched again and again by the enormous number of repostings that lard websites and social media with them. An Internet search turns up a cascade of his copyright-free cartoons available to everyone, and for everyone to use, which, as Internet sites show, they liberally do.

We see in the Internet both the unification and the plurification of antisemitism. The Internet is available everywhere. It brings together if

*Israel's prime minister Ehud Olmert falling asleep peacefully with a dead Palestinian baby, like a child's stuffed animal, comforting him, and dreaming of how this murder will win him popularity and votes with the approving Israeli public.*

*Israel's prime minister Ariel Sharon and Adolf Hitler.*

not merges different antisemitic streams, discourses, tropes, and accusations. It houses and contributes to English's ever-expanding reach and universalism and, owing to English together with the use of a few other languages, antisemitism's easily near blanketing of the globe, especially elite and media circles. It provides for vast and ever growing networks of major websites and social media offerings overtly and covertly spreading antisemitism, not to mention such sites' and networks' strategic use by antisemitic governments and nongovernmental organizations and movements (which we will explore in-depth in the next chapter). All of this is the medium and the message of the unification of antisemitisms. Yet within this unity remains an enormous diversification of all kinds of antisemitisms and all kinds of accusations, many particular to different streams of antisemitism, different countries, different communities, different locales. Jew Watch is an English-language clearinghouse for all antisemitisms. Stormfront is a home site for white racist antisemitism that integrates it into a broader worldview and ideological streams, with its home in English and subsidiary sites in a score of languages. You-Tube, Facebook, Twitter, and other social media have individual power-ful antisemitic postings and established and ad hoc networks that are too plentiful to track. Plan Andinia is a dangerous antisemitic conspiracy known most prominently in the Spanish-language world and particu-larly in the would-be afflicted countries of Argentina and Chile. And all of this is said without reference to the avalanche of antisemitism—unified and plurified, pure and connected to broader political and religious ideologies, general and particular in message—coming from the Arab and Islamic world. Antisemites and Eurocentric racists have even created an alternative to Wikipedia called Metapedia: The Alter-native Encyclopedia, a growing compendium and clearinghouse of misinformation—currently with more than seventeen thousand arti-cles in English!—which on its mission statement explains that it wishes to counteract hostile researchers from the Anti-Defamation League and the Simon Wiesenthal Center, which are two of only four such organi-zations listed. With Metapedia, antisemites and Euroracists seek to pro-vide a legitimate-looking and -sounding alternative universe "about culture, art, science, philosophy and politics" in which Jews and their predations compose a good part of the world's structure and a pervasive threat to countries and peoples, to culture, society, economy, and poli-tics. With sufficient computing power to track the growth of antisemitic content, we might realize that something more or less akin to Moore's Law for the doubling of the microprocessor's power every eighteen months might be the rule of antisemitic expansion on the web.

Not only the foundational antisemitic paradigm but also antisemi-tism, with its elaborated accounts of Jews, has become plural. This means it can attract all different kinds of people. It speaks the language of politics, which is universal (organized around rights, legitimacy, and transgressions) and which is available to everyone. Its elements have been recast fundamentally in international terms, adopting an interna-tional paradigm (including conspiracy) as its frame. It insinuates itself in the institutions of the world. It uses as its means the most effective global instruments of transmission yet devised: the international information substructure and global network, digital media, especially the Internet.

This global antisemitism complements and overtakes the various streams of antisemitism on which it is constructed, bringing them together like so many small steel cables twisted together to form a far stronger cable. Yet those individual streams remain independently powerful. Among them, Christian antisemitism is making a notable comeback. Its tempering as a consequence of its custodians' reckoning with the Holocaust and with the undeniable Christian roots of Nazi antisemitism, and the recognition of the myriad ways that Christian teaching had contributed to the Jews' violent elimination, including by motivating many Christians to kill and to help to kill Jews, has had profound and lasting effects for the good. Yet the return of the partly repressed animus has been under way for some time.

Having explored Christian antisemitism's features, as well as the others', we touch on the relevant ones here but briefly. It is both amazing and not amazing that so many tens of millions of Christians believe the nonsense about Jews' alleged guilt for Jesus' death, then and today. The Christian biblical claim's sheer implausibility that *all* Jews were present calling for Jesus' death, and the moral blindness of deeming individuals born two thousand years after an alleged event guilty for it, is mind bending to those who see such damaging prejudice for what it is, and differently mind bending for those whose minds it actually bends.

Nevertheless, energized and informed by some of the classic Christian tropes about Jews, notably the deprecation of Jews for the Jewish bible's designation of them as the Chosen People, a revival is under way. This is one of the many taken-for-granted antisemitic weapons, and because it is taken for granted and repeated so frequently as an unquestioned matter of fact, people far and wide believe the force of its accusation, including those who have otherwise no antisemitic inclinations. The bible states that Jews are God's chosen people. You might say: *So what?* The people of one religion after another consider themselves special, even chosen. Christians consider themselves chosen — in many forms of Christianity they called themselves *the elect,* and more, cast those who do not follow Jesus into an eternity in hell! But leave aside that such religioncentric claims are commonplace, you still might say: *So what?* It was authored in a book from antiquity, when many things were said that few if any people take seriously, just as few take seriously many of the Christian bible's statements. Any person familiar with ancient books should be skeptical about their contents' germaneness, unless the specific passages can be shown to tangibly influence people. So aside from this claim of specialness being a commonplace among peoples and groups, and aside from it being part of a book that, when written, recommended acts such as stoning people, as was the practice in the ancient world, the claim has no effective force today, except perhaps among ultra-orthodox Jews. Today, when self-imposed limits, owing to social and political post-Holocaust norms, constrain what antisemites might express in polite circles about Jews without delegitimizing themselves, it is not surprising that more and more we hear the accusation—and it is presented as an accusation and treated as a damning attribute—that Jews consider themselves the chosen people: chosen, better than others, and, explicitly or by implication, seeking to dominate others. Its use invokes and activates for the listeners or readers the foundational antisemitic paradigm and all it implies.

Yet when do Jews assert that they are the chosen people and that this alleged status confers on them privileged political or other rights? I cannot recall hearing any Jew in private or in a public gathering, let alone Jewish institutions, make this claim, except in the formulaic incantation of certain age-old liturgy. And if one or another did, *so what?* But Jews don't. It is not Jews who speak about it, but antisemites who do, regularly, in order to tar Jews with an alleged claim of superiority. The real historical source of keeping this claim alive as socially relevant, namely as anything but part of a biblical story of God's selection of Abraham and as a feel-good moment for Jews, has been Christians' competition with Jews for the Judaic tradition and its God's custodianship, and how it has stuck in Christians' throats that the Jewish bible says explicitly something that has undercut Christians' attempt to delegitimize Jews and Jews' claim to possess their own tradition, the Abrahamic God and religious covenant.

The blood libel, a derivative of the accusation that Jews committed deicide, has through the ages cast Jews in various ways as supposedly reenacting this original sin, supposedly for their Satanic purposes, by actually killing Christians, usually to use their blood. This was an article of faith among Christians for hundreds of years, that Jews used Christian blood, usually of Christian children, for baking Passover matzos. As hard as it may be to believe, such charges are increasingly being leveled at Jews, especially by Arab and Islamic leaders and in Islamic media around the world, including especially among Palestinians. In 2007, Ra'ad Salah, head of the Islamic Movement in Israel's Northern Branch, explained to an East Jerusalem rally and the assembled media the difference between Muslims and Jews: "We have never allowed ourselves to knead [the dough for] the bread that breaks the fast in the holy month of Ramadan with children's blood." And the Jews? "Whoever wants a more thorough explanation, let him ask what used to happen to some children in Europe, whose blood was mixed in with the dough of the [Jewish] holy bread."[12]

In 2012, Saudi cleric Salman Al-Odeh, who was casting the Jews in the most demonological terms, explained on Saudi television, on a network that is also beamed throughout the Arab world:

> It is well-known that the Jews celebrate several holidays, one of which is the Passover, or the Matzos Holiday. I read once about a doctor who was working in a laboratory. This doctor lived with a Jewish family. One day, they said to him: "We want blood. Get us some human blood." He was confused. He didn't know what this was all about. Of course, he couldn't betray his work ethics in such a way, but he began inquiring, and he found that they were making matzos with human blood....
>
> They eat it, believing that this brings them close to their false God, Yahweh. This caused a scandal. The same thing would happen in Damascus. As you may know, Naguib Al-Kilani wrote a book titled *Blood for the Matzos of Zion*. This is the best story he ever wrote. It discusses what would go on in the Jewish neighborhood of Damascus or elsewhere. They would lure a child in order to sacrifice him in the religious rite that they perform during that holiday.

*Hook-nosed Jew eating Palestinian child, published in several Arab newspapers.*

This was part of the foundation for his exploration of how Jews, who "believe they have the right to kill anyone who does not adhere to their religion" and who miscast and misuse the Holocaust in order to commit the most heinous crimes themselves: "Through this Holocaust, the Jews began to extort many governments worldwide—in Europe and in the US. The Jews even began to perpetrate the same thing themselves against the Palestinian people, carrying out a Holocaust in Gaza and the occupied land. They attack children, women, and the elderly under the pretext of the Holocaust that they are trying to substantiate."[13]

Blood-libel charges are by no means confined to the Middle East. In Russia, in Poland, and elsewhere they live on or are invoked for contemporary antisemitic assaults. In Canada in 2010, the Canadian Muslim newspaper *Al Ameen Post* reported that Jews kidnapped "some 25,000 Ukrainian children into the occupied entity [the newspaper's antisemitic term for Israel] over the past two years in order to harvest their organs." This news article, poisoning Canadian Muslims and others against Jews as few accusations can, drew on the information that Iran's Press TV Network had disseminated worldwide.[14] (Note the blood libel's updating in keeping with today's plausibility structure, grounding itself in the technological capacities of medicine to illicitly, indeed unconscionably, serve the kinds of needs that people are known to have.)

This followed a prominent blood-libel accusation in high-minded Sweden. The country's largest daily newspaper, *Aftonbladet,* blared the headline "They plunder the organs of our sons" as the irresistible sensational invitation to read about Israeli soldiers abducting Palestinians to cut out and steal their internal organs. The article, authored by Swedish journalist Donald Boström, presented such blood-libel accusations from Palestinians as fact: "'Our sons are used as involuntary organ donors,' relatives of Khaled from Nablus said to me, as did the mother of Raed from Jenin as well as the uncles of Machmod and Nafes from Gaza, who all had disappeared for a few days and returned by night, dead and autopsied." Boström and the Swedish newspaper had no evidence that any of this was true (as the newspaper and Boström himself were later compelled to admit), and no justification for their linking of this fabrication to a crime syndicate in New Jersey in which some American rabbis were implicated. Yet once in existence, blood libels, as with antisemitic accusations of all kinds, live on and propagate, especially in our digital age, getting repeated again and again as fact, which is what it then becomes in the minds of committed antisemites and innocents alike. In our globalized antisemitic world, blood libels travel rapidly across borders—in this case through the mouthpiece of George Galloway, a British Member of Parliament who cavorts with Hamas' leadership, into the pages of Scotland's leading circulation tabloid newspaper, *Daily Record:* "But the revelation in the Israeli parliament in recent days that the body parts of Palestinian prisoners were systematically harvested without the knowledge or consent of their families has had an impact in these parts which it is difficult to overstate. When the story first broke, on Swedish TV [sic], I frankly did not believe it." Galloway clinches his demonizing fabrication with another: "Israel has admitted this evil, wicked crime and declared it no longer practises it."[15]

Central Christian antisemitic tropes' and accusations' recent and intensifying revival—including calling, as the World Council of Churches did in 2011, Israel a "sin"—is, of course, hardly the most significant of Christian antisemitism's contributions to the global antisemitic discourse and complex. One of the most important and powerful of these is, no surprise, the Palestinians' adoption and exploitation of the figure of Jesus, and more so the trope of the murdered child of God, and even more so the trope of identifying Palestinians as the new Jesus. This can be seen all over Palestinian media and in the assertions of Palestinian leaders, including in the official newspaper of the Palestinian Authority: Palestinians assert that Jesus was a Palestinian and seek to turn Palestine and Palestinians today into Jesus-like victims of Jews' persecutions. Emblematic is an "Easter message" from the Palestinian Sabeel Ecumenical Liberation Theology Center in Jerusalem in 2001: "It seems to many of us that Jesus is on the cross again with thousands of crucified Palestinians around him…Palestinian men, women, and children being crucified. Palestine has become one huge golgotha. The Israeli government crucifixion system is operating daily. Palestine has become the place of the skull."[16] Even the leading Palestinian "moderate" Mustafa Barghouti, who ran for president of the Palestinian Authority against Abbas as a democratic reformer and is a member of parliament, has spread this Jesus Denial and blood-libel trope, asserting on Fatah's Palestinian TV in a Christmas Eve interview in 2009, "We always remember that Jesus was the first Palestinian who was tortured in this land." And a

*The word on the cross: "Palestine."*

recent installment, from May 2012, in the continuous stream of antisemitically Palestinizing Jesus and appropriating his death to blacken Israel, Palestinian Minister of Prisoners' Affairs Issa Karake on Palestinian TV: "We are standing at Jesus' Plaza, in front of the Church of the Nativity, [to convey] to those who uphold human rights: Take action before it is too late, take action to save [the Palestinian prisoners] the sons of Nativity, the sons of Jerusalem, and the sons of Jesus, the Palestinian, and the sons of Jesus, the Palestinian, the first prisoner and the first Martyr (*Shahid*) in history."[17] By invoking and updating Jesus and the blood libel against Jews, Palestinians, other Arabs, and Muslims merge useful aspects of the two traditions that can feed antisemitism, particularly its anti-Israel variant, to demonize and inflame hatred of Israel and Jews and thereby, both as a natural corollary to such thinking and with explicit exhortations, to win Christian converts and sympathy to their causes. They often do this in arresting visual form. The cartoon on the next page, published in April 2001 in *Al Ahram,* the largest Egyptian newspaper, during the so-called Second Intifada, depicts two joyous Israeli soldiers slaughtering children, one of whom is labeled "The Palestinian People," in a meat-grinder, and two Jews, one resembling Israeli Prime Minister Ariel Sharon, drinking the children's blood. They toast each other with "Cheers to peace."

All of this is yet another reminder that the Christian antisemitic discourse has supplied the global antisemitic paradigm's heart. The Islamic antisemitic discourse, particularly in its hypertrophied political Islamic forms, has infused global antisemitism with its impassioned and violent soul.

*Demonizing Jews.*

Certainly since Israel's establishment, and ever more in the last few decades, Arab and Islamic antisemitism has become overtly eliminationist. Whereas before the antisemitic Qur'anic verses and Hadithic stories and parables were known and invoked, now they have been elevated from minor chords to the major themes, indeed often the central melody, of Arab and Islamic public discourse. The same phrases and stories once occasionally told have, during the last few decades, and often on a daily basis, and certainly on a weekly basis at Friday prayers in mosques across the Islamic world, been drummed into the heads of Arabs and Muslims all around the Middle East and beyond. Earlier, Muslims kept Jews in their place with traditional autocratic control and taxed them heavily. Today the prescribed mode and, as much as possible, the practiced mode for doing so is violent and openly murderous. Muslims and the overwhelming weight of the Islamic public discourse have replaced calls for the Jewish infidels to be merely kept in check, in their rightful subordinate place, with calls for their elimination or extermination.

The power and the ubiquity of the antisemitism that is grounded in the Islamic tradition and given its most potent political form in political Islam is immense. Arab and Islamic antisemitism drives much of global antisemitism's discourse, both in its particular forms in Arab and Islamic countries and, more generally, the world over. Several aspects stand out: the antisemitic passions it unleashes among Arabs and Muslims (and among sympathetic non-Muslim Arabs continuously exposed to it)—with Friday prayer crowds chanting in mosques *death to Israel* or *death to Jews*—infuses the discourse and the people promoting it with a drive and intensity that rivals that of any antisemitic era or historical moment. (Can you imagine Christians in churches around the world, led by priests and ministers, chanting for the death of any ethnic group or people?) Second, Arab and Islamic antisemitism has relentlessly provided the general political orientation, and the specific orientation about the need to destroy the Jews *politically,* that fundamentally shapes global antisemitism's new nature. Third, Arab and Islamic antisemitism has helped merge Israel with all Jews as one and the same and imbued the antisemitic imagination, and to a great extent the global antisemitic discourse, with the understanding that they be treated as a unity. Fourth, it has steadily fueled the global information streams with continuous flows of antisemitic notions and tropes, an antisemitic world export unprecedented in volume and reach, but which in this rapidly changing global age is already no longer an export but an integral part of the global marketplace of views, ideas, and passions.

The Western political left's and the international human rights community's antisemitism has given global antisemitism's political nature—its political essence cannot be emphasized enough—additional powerful global glue. Leftist and internationalist human rights antisemitism comes in various guises: its long-standing, reflexive identification with the developing world's people, believed to be oppressed by the West, and the demonizing of those who allegedly oppress them, notably Israel; siding with and applauding any country or people opposing the American hegemon, with which they intimately identify Israel; the Marxian- and Christian-derived antipathy for the Jews, and for the Jews as symbols and especially as the incarnation of capitalism; the antiglobalization forces that see Israel and the Jews as one of the globalization complex's central parts; the privileging of the United Nations' orientation, international law, and abstract and partial notions of justice over geostrategic concerns, which casts Israel (because Israel's enemies have captured these institutions) as a law-breaking nation and its people, essentialized, as a law-breaking people; the concomitant suspicion, indeed condemnation, especially pronounced in Europe, of countries using force to defend the West, which rests on the beliefs that the downtrodden people's complaints are just and if they find redress, then conflicts would be defused; the need for some of these elements to find a unifying cause after the Soviet champion's disintegration, and socialism and communism's utter discrediting as viable forms of domestic organization, which turned the political left's attention to the international realm and redirected to it the anti-Soviet international human rights organizations, where one big cause, demonizing and combating Israel, could be elevated to a common crusade.

Leftist and international human rights antisemitisms' various elements include political parties, labor organizations, NGOs, intellectuals, and, critically, university campus groups and have a powerful presence in Western media and therefore shaping public perceptions and opinion more broadly. Although partly divergent, like global antisemitism in general, they come together in their fixation on Israel as the demonized state that contributes to the predations that prevent a range of groups and peoples from realizing their various cherished goals. The political left's antisemitism and the left-liberal international human rights community, which though on other matters diverge, have converged over critical international issues, principally Israel though also their opposition to neocolonialism. Virtually every antisemite around the world can agree on some aspect of their overlapping litany against Israel. In this sense, Marx's prophecy that the political left — he thought the working class and its class representatives — would one day become the bearer of the universal ideology and champion the universal cause, has, if partially, come true, though in a form radically different from his expectation (an outcome to which he unwittingly contributed with his polemical essay universalizing antisemitism, "On the Jewish Question"). In adopting anti-Israel antisemitism, the political left has, more than it ever did with any other intellectual and programmatic stance, finally found common cause with an enormous part of humanity, cutting across class, ethnic, national, religious, gender, and about every other relevant line. The developing world's people and the downtrodden have, for the left, de facto become the substitute of the working class as imputed bearers of universal values, and have in the globalized world become the favorites of those who oppose the powerful (capitalist and Western) hegemons. At least for many of them, the Palestinians have become an agreed upon and unifying symbol.

The political right's contribution to global antisemitism is mainly as an auxiliary though multi-dimensional catalyst. Content-wise its crucial component has been its profound and lasting influence on Arab and Islamic antisemitism, with its by now deep and broad legacy of Nazified notions about Jews. Related to this, the antisemitic political right feeds the Holocaust denial movement, which, though most potent now in the Arab and Islamic world, Western deniers nonetheless legitimized and gave cover to, and still lend it an international cast and therefore, for many, an air of legitimacy because even when Arab or Muslim countries or movements or individuals put forward its notions, they sound less parochial, owing to their Western fellow deniers. Also, the Holocaust denial movement's influence in spawning the broad panoply of antisemitic denial insurgencies and discourses composing this new and heretofore unrecognized phenomenon of denialism has been quietly monumental.

The antisemitism of the political right has been an integral part of several prominent European political movements, substantially fueling local antisemitisms in countries where nationalism and right-wing politics have produced potent brews of hatred, such as Russia and Hungary. The avowedly antisemitic Jobbik party in Hungary is the most spectacular such example, as it has powerfully entered the mainstream, gaining overnight the sizable electoral support of one in six Hungarians in the 2010 election, and a firm parliamentary presence. In other places, such antisemitism exists more on the fringe of politics, and powerfully in communities and families outside the public sphere's spotlight. This has been so in Germany, Austria, and in other northern European countries and, still less so, in the United States. Aside from the support such antisemitism generates and receives, by violating the taboo on bald, uncoded antisemitic expression, it creates political and media space for such prejudicial notions. It also makes other less overtly objectionable antisemitic notions seem less extreme and more reasonable, and, as always, legitimizes, encourages, and deepens the mostly concealed antisemitism of civil society.

In Hungary, Jobbik has done all of this and managed to catapult from being virtually nonexistent to a prominent opposition party, in some ways dominating the public discourse. Levels of intensive antisemitism in Hungary have jumped during Jobbik's ascendancy from, by one composite index (which greatly understates the extent of antisemitism), from 47 percent of the population in 2009 to 63 percent in 2012, an increase of one-third in three years, an alteration of the sort that hardly ever occurs in already slow-moving and deeply antisemitic Europe. Whereas in 2009 this index of intensive antisemitism grouped Hungary together with Poland and Spain as the most antisemitic of European countries, in 2012 Hungary far outstripped them all and was close to three times the already high levels of Germany and France and four times those of the Netherlands, Norway, and the United Kingdom.[18] The relationship among the political activation of antisemitism into the public sphere and the poisoning of the public discourse with antisemitism, in this instance by the political right, and the encouragement and fanning of antisemitism among ordinary people could not be clearer.

Today's global antisemitism is a vast market under a big tent for antisemites, the equivalent of a majoritarian catch-all political party (though, importantly, without the formal organization) that can satisfy and bring together diverse peoples with widely varying sensibilities on many issues, because they can agree on the core values of the institution, in this case global antisemitism, which such institutions often define negatively by standing against the opposition or enemy. This quality of antisemitism has always existed. It has become substantially more pronounced with antisemitic expression's great upsurge in the last two decades, and its dissemination, proliferation, and transformation on the Internet and digital media. In domestic politics, conventional catch-all, big-tent parties have organized and mobilized vast parts of the electorate around standard political cleavages over the size of the free market, or the degree to which the state should regulate personal liberty. *We are not socialists.* Or *We must wrest power away from the moneyed interests.* Such classic positions, which at once encapsulate the putative danger and what must therefore be done to protect society from such danger (defeat socialism, or take power for the people), can appeal to people who otherwise disagree on many, including fundamental, things.

Global antisemitism is similar. The danger is the Jews. Because it is global, it is heard and experienced from multiple angles and seems to be part of the global fabric; it has become as familiar and, for many, as taken for granted as the pluralist global world we live in. British sociologist and commentator Frank Furedi experiences this in London:

> I am standing in a queue waiting to buy a train ticket from London to Canterbury. A well-dressed lady standing behind me informs her friend that she "can't wait till Israel disappears off the face of the earth." What struck me was not her intense hostility to Israel but the mild-mannered, matter-of-fact tone with which she announced her wish for the annihilation of a nation. It seems that it is okay to condemn and demonize Israel. All of a sudden Israel has become an all-purpose target for a variety of disparate and confused causes. When I ask a group of Pakistani waiters sitting around a table in their restaurant why they "hate" Israel, they casually tell me that it is because Jews are their "religion's enemy." Those who are highly educated have their own pet prejudice. One of my young colleagues who teaches media studies in a London-based university was taken aback during a seminar discussion when some of her students insisted that since all the banks are owned by Jews, Israel was responsible for the current global financial crisis.

A well-dressed woman, working-class Muslims, university students. Dispassionate and matter-of-fact, impassioned hatred, insistent belief. Israel must be eliminated, the Jews are Islam's enemy, the Jews and Israel are responsible for the global financial crisis. Different peoples, different tenors and temperatures, different accusations. One is openly annihilationist, the others we do not know about but the character of their beliefs readily leaves open the possibility. The substantial differences among them and the different streams of antisemitism they represent notwithstanding, the danger is the Jews as international or global actors. As Furedi, echoed by a small legion of other observers living or spending time in Europe, explains, "Increasingly expressions of aversion toward Israel have assumed the status of a taken-for-granted sentiment in many sections of polite European society."[19]

Through its discourses and institutions, global antisemitism mobilizes disparate peoples—both engaging their thinking and their persons, and as political beings and actors—against the Jews in order to safeguard people, society, a religion and its civilization, or the global order. Global antisemitism coalesces not around domestic problems in country after country, which are almost always highly particular issues that do not unify these peoples' countries with one another—it is fueled variously by different religious or political traditions and contemporary orientations. But because its political orientation is international, in other words, global, it unifies people around its political message. By not fixating on the source of the Jews' supposed predations, and by keeping its focus on the political and the international realm, global antisemitism has established itself as the preeminent *international* prejudice and animus, a kind of universal political ideology to which people the world over can subscribe.

How else can we understand that so much of the world, hundreds of millions upon hundreds of millions of people, is so preoccupied with, and directs active antipathies and enormous passion against, a people comprising only thirteen million out of seven billion, less than two-tenths of 1 percent of the world's population, and against one country out of two hundred, which happens to be democratic, to the virtual exclusion of systematic and sustained criticism of the many others that are dictatorships, repressive of freedom, or mass murderous? As part of the world's substructure of prejudice, antisemitism ably fuels hatred to those seeking local comfort or broad explanations for privations or dangers. Global antisemitism is at once at the amorphous foundation of world prejudice and also its most highly visible, best articulated, and most concrete and tangible and dangerous prejudicial ideology. The foundational antisemitic paradigm with its particular elaborations in different places still predominates, and antisemitism is typically also integrated into the broader cognitive structures that form the foundations of today's worldviews and ideologies.

For many people, communities, and discourses, the utterance of the word *Jew* itself conjures up and reinforces the foundational antisemitic paradigm and the beliefs and animus built upon it. This is an all but ignored aspect of antisemitism. Yet it is fundamental. Think of what you think whenever you hear the word *Nazi* or the name *Hitler*. Probably some component of or variation upon *evil, mass murder, death, destruction.* Visual images probably come to mind—of SS uniforms, swastikas, men marching in goose step, of Hitler raising his fist shouting at a political rally, death, corpses, barbed wire and guard towers, destruction. Imagine if you heard that a Nazi moved into a house on your street.

*A classic image of Nazism.*

What would you think? When antisemites hear *Jew* or encounter a Jew on their street or neighborhood, in their communities, in a caricature or piece of graffiti drawn on a building, in newspapers or television, in politics, on the Internet, the same processes and much of the same content applies. For antisemites, and for countries in which there is a broad and accepted public antisemitic discourse, uttering, hearing, or reading the word *Jew* — almost no matter how it is meant — subtly or overtly activates, reinforces, deepens the antisemitism of those involved.

In many countries, cultures, and times antisemitism has so encrusted the word *Jew* with prejudicial thoughts, images, and emotions — not to mention an undertone or overtone of eliminationism and violence — that Jews themselves have recoiled from its usage. To hear the phrase "he's a Jew" was enough to make Jews across time and place look up for danger, recoil in anticipation of something unpleasant or worse, be on guard for what might follow either verbally or physically. As a consequence, in many countries, Jews have often, consciously or not, avoided using the noun *Jew* to describe themselves, preferring the adjective *Jewish,* or even to eschew all references to the word or its offshoots by calling themselves Israelites or people of the mosaic faith. Joseph Goebbels, the inveterate antisemite and Nazi propaganda wizard, was as attuned as anyone to language's uses, power, and nuances and its effective deployment in society and politics in general. Goebbels wrote an article in 1929, before the Nazis came to power, when the Jews, as he understood it, still ran riot in Germany. The article, entitled simply "The Jew," has as its starting point that the Jew with his stealth, cunning, and lies ceaselessly assaults Germans and those who would oppose him. Goebbels explains: "One cannot defend himself against the Jew. He attacks with lightning speed from his position of safety and uses his abilities to crush any attempt at defense." Goebbels laments that the usual self-defense methods against such an enemy are ineffective: "The Jew is immunized against all dangers: one may call him a scoundrel, parasite, swindler, profiteer, it all runs off him like water off a raincoat." What then could be done to expose the Jew? What could he be called so that he cannot escape the truth with his lies? Goebbels knows: "But call him a Jew and you will be astonished at how he recoils, how injured he is, how he suddenly shrinks back: 'I've been found out.'"

The foot-in-the-door phenomenon is real. Once a person latches onto one aspect of the antisemitic litany, it leaves him open to, and more vulnerable to adopting, new antisemitic elements. Whether or not he (consciously or not) will be on the lookout for them, he will certainly be more receptive to them, as he already believes things that make antisemitic notions more plausible, and often compelling. Adding to that process, the cognitive factors promoting the internalization of our global age's foundational antisemitic paradigm, already powerful, will likely increase effectiveness in our linked and informationally dense era, when the range and type of activities available so vastly outstrip those of the past, when time is that much more prized and in short supply, when a cacophony of messages compete for a person's cognitive and emotional attention, and when attention spans are shorter than ever.

At Jew Watch, a plethora of antisemitic offerings await the many who go there. Yet even if the wares are bewildering in their multiplicity, or even if the site's different users are attracted to very different aspects of the vast antisemitic demonology, they all know where they are: Jew Watch. They know why they are there: because of *the Jew*. They know what they must do: watch *the Jews*. And they know what they might need to do: something about *the Jews*.

# 14

# Strategic Politics, Eliminationist Ends

NOTWITHSTANDING ANTISEMITISM'S MULTIPLE locations and multiple themes, and its variations and elements, antisemitism is today, in its essence, a global phenomenon. It is global not only because the foundational antisemitic paradigm underlies and structures the various antisemitic streams and elaborations that compose in aggregate the antisemitic discourse and practice, thus lending it a global coherence. It is global also because it blankets the globe and it exists within the muscles and tissue of the world order.

Part of the complexity of understanding antisemitism is our need to treat both its global coherence and its many constituent and overlapping, or partly overlapping and diverging, aspects: Antisemitism is composed of beliefs, images, and emotions. It is composed of people as individuals and in shared communities of belief and hatred. It has stable, varying, and overlapping discourses. It is grounded in institutions. It is expressed through media, the Internet, and other organs. It finds particular expression and homes in politics, most significantly in governments. It is composed of plans and policies. It is composed of acts — systematic acts that are the execution of policies and, when systematic, can be called campaigns, or uncoordinated social and discriminatory acts that are not centrally directed. It is composed of violence and the violence's consequences, which is destruction, injury, eliminationism, and death. Each of these is related, often in complex ways, to one another. The part that is at once most obvious and, in fundamental ways, least recognized and least understood is antisemitism's powerful strategic political component, especially in its relentless internationalism or globalism.

Globalization has been regularly seen as an economically driven phenomenon—with global trade's increase, countries' economic integration, and financial instruments' rapid flow—that greatly compromises, if not ends, national economies' independence and integrity. What happens economically in Italy or Spain or France affects American industries, trade balance, banks, and more, and what happens in China, in manufacturing, resource use, fiscal policy, currency policy, and more, affects the United States and Europe. What happens economically in the United States or China affects the fortunes and politics of smaller and poorer countries even more. Globalization has also been seen as a communications-driven phenomenon, with television and the Internet blanketing the world, with instantaneous news about the world appearing in people's living rooms and on computer screens and phones, and with the ability to communicate with everyone anywhere inexpensively or for free. Globalization has also been seen as a cultural phenomenon, with cultures becoming more influenced by dominant culture makers, especially American popular culture of music and television and now video games, all of which, as globalization proceeds, themselves become internationalized.

Much less central to the treatments of globalization than the interpenetration of economies, peoples, and cultures, and less noticed, are two additional aspects: the assertion of a principled and necessary universal standard of human rights, and politics' globalization. The notion that all peoples have certain rights, such as not to be killed or tortured, to be able to speak and worship as they wish, and to live free of oppression took a place on the world stage and became institutionally significant with the United Nations' founding in 1948. The notion that redress might exist against the worst violators gained recognition and a powerful legal foundation a bit earlier with the Nuremberg Trials of the leading German perpetrators of aggressive war and eliminationism starting in 1945 and 1946 and with the Tokyo Trials of their Japanese counterparts beginning in 1946 (the earlier legal tribunal that tried the Turkish leaders who masterminded the eliminationist and genocidal assault on the Armenians had no similar legacy), which led then to various United Nations and international legal conventions to strengthen such international action. In both cases the genuine recognition and actual implementation of the institutions' promises to create a respected and defended standard of human rights remained, for decades, sketchy to nonexistent, but the institutions did lay down important norms and foundations that had two effects: to establish a basis to be built upon when the world's countries finally decided to take their promises at least semi-seriously, and to spread their norms among ordinary people, particularly but not only on the left, who naively enough, but with some real effects, actually did take them seriously.

Prior to globalism, few people paid attention to, let alone cared substantially about, the rights of people outside their countries, unless it pertained to the call for freedoms for the people suffering from colonialism or under the real or alleged predations of the other side, whether it be capitalism or communism. Indeed, human rights remained for decades little more than a verbal stick with which the United States and the West beat the Soviet Union and other communist countries, while ignoring (and sometimes promoting) the same rights' violation among their client states run often by the most brutal and mass-murderous tyrants. Human rights, including the often complicated to apply right to national self-determination, got a boost with American president Jimmy Carter adopting its language as the basis for American positions on international affairs, especially because he applied it to Latin America, where some of the worst dictators and violators were aligned with the United States. In the ensuing decades, and certainly by the time the Soviet Union fell and the age of globalism began, human rights as a battle cry—albeit an uninvestigated and uncontested mantra of many, including states, nongovernmental organizations, international organizations, and ordinary people—had become a fixed and central part of the world's political landscape.

Picking up steam later, though really not until the 2000s, the call for justice and legal redress in the form of criminal prosecutions followed suit. To be sure, in both instances the call for the application of these laudable principles was selective and highly politicized, making them at least as often a tool for governments and others rather than the genuine moral or humanitarian expression. The result was to make them dubious components of the international order, even though we should welcome them, recognizing that they do more than some good, and vigorously promote them further.

Before this development, people paid little heed to foreigners' rights, so antisemites did not dwell on accusing Jews with harming people beyond their specific country's borders. Medieval antisemites oriented themselves overwhelmingly *locally*. Modern antisemites, notions of international Jewish conspiracies notwithstanding, oriented themselves *locally* and *nationally*. Global antisemites, however, decidedly survey the *entire world* as the natural terrain for expressing their animus against Jews and Jewness.

With the spread and increased force of the cry for human rights and for international justice, global antisemites and the public antisemitic discourses, which already oriented themselves to the international scene, acquired a range of powerful additional tools for assaulting Israel and Jews. They could now adopt and speak the unimpeachable language of universal human rights and international justice, which both legitimized them and effectively camouflaged their underlying antisemitic animus. They obtained ready-made and winning appeals to others not already sharing their antisemitism to join their assault. And they augmented or even transformed the antisemitic litany in a critical way. In a world where human rights and international justice are central, they turned Jews into a threat not just to a country's people or to those people's rights, but also to international human rights and justice — in other words, to the very foundational principles of world order and goodness. This is the elaboration of the foundational antisemitic paradigm updated.

This kind of justification, legitimation, and cover for antisemites never existed before. Antisemites had previously cast the beliefs, appeals, and justifications for their animus and agitation against Jews in particularistic and overtly prejudicial terms: the Jews are bad because they are bad. Or in the most general though vague terms: they violate goodness and threaten humanity. To be sure, in medieval Europe, the Christian antisemitic idiom was as universal as Christianity's claims to universality, even if those claims were false, and it existed in a world where Christianity reigned mostly uncontested as the universal salvation. Marxists, as Marx himself did in his deeply antisemitic tract "On the Jewish Question" and as the communist regimes sought to treat Zionism as a stand-in for the international oppression of peoples, have mainly sought to clothe their animus toward Jews in universal terms just as they unsuccessfully sought to cast communism. But certainly most modern antisemites and antisemitic discourse, animated and oriented toward notions of race and nation, cast their imprecations against Jews in the particularistic terms of their race or nation being preeminent and the Jews undermining or threatening them.

Today, in our global world, a world where human rights and international justice are gaining an ever greater sway on public discourses, political and policy aspirations of many groups and institutions, and even (slowly) among governments, antisemites finally have a universal language and justification — that is in tune with the times — for their beliefs and hatreds, albeit somewhat transformed and concealed, to gain universal appeal. If you believe that human beings have human rights, they say or imply, then you must stand against Israel, and against the people who run Israel and those who support it — that is, the Jews. And no matter where or who you are, in whatever country of the world, whatever ethnicity, religion, profession, social class, or political ideology regarding your domestic politics, you can agree that the central violator of human rights on the international scene, which means in the world, is to be condemned and condemned and condemned, both as necessary and good for its own sake, and also as a hortatory example to other actual or would-be violators. That is the power, and for antisemites the beauty, of the advent of human rights as a universal principle, and the primary standard for evaluating states' and peoples' conduct. It can appeal to everyone, persuasively so.

To be sure, this condemnation of Israel and Jews, as malefactors extraordinaire against human rights, and international human rights law, is selective and in bad faith to a degree that is well beyond even the antisemites' usual biased norm regarding Jews (leaving aside the accusations' falseness). Yet in this instance, it is precisely the antisemites' claim to applying *universal* principles which highlights that they do anything but that. This is a transparently sham internationalism. As we have seen, antisemites, with most of their other accusations against Jews, pay little regard to universally applicable principles. They openly champion and justify their animus against Jews. They say that the Jews are noxious, predatory, and injurious, or evil for this or that reason, and must be resisted or eliminated because they do or threaten to do this or that. Whether they are completely, partially, or not at all inventing the bill of transgressions that they lay on Jews, the hypocrisy of antisemites' accusations over the centuries has been unmistakable. Their hypocrisy has been their evident lack of interest, let alone concern, and their silence when other peoples are, or are doing, the things they say Jews are or do, which is different from using universal terms to champion their condemnations of Jews, which by definition apply to all non-Jewish people and all countries—and not only to Israel.

Survey research and candid insiders both reveal the intimate relationship of anti-Israelism—which includes, indeed is distinguished by, its selective condemnation of Israel and its Jews—and antisemitism. Anti-Israelism or anti-Zionism is overwhelmingly grounded in antisemitism. Speaking in November 2012 of the burgeoning anti-Israel initiatives that Protestant churches are undertaking, all in the name of universal principles and humanitarianism, Reverend Andrew Love of the United Church of Canada, who knows the Protestant world as an insider, exposes their real motive: "What really emerged from this story was just how deep-seated the hatred [for Jews] is." This shows that "the humanitarian concern" is anything but that. According to Love, grounded in hatred of Jews, "the humanitarian concern is the veil that covers, or is the rationalization for ultimately what I believe to be anti-Semitic ideas and anti-Semitic policies."[1] He would know, because Protestant churches are at the center of the anti-Israel international human-rights movement, as well as at the center of the pan-European anti-Israel public discourse, which share the same "universal" and "humanitarian" principles. Christian groups, many funded by the European Union, are the motor force behind much of the divestment campaign against Israel, with Pax Christi, the most important international Catholic peace movement urging an economic boycott of Israel—with no irony intended—"in the name of love."[2] Andrew Love might as well have been speaking for the movement and for the European antisemitic public discourse as a whole, about which Manfred Gerstenfeld, intimately familiar with the continent's antisemitic scene, has said, "Europe is hiding behind a false mask of humanitarianism."[3]

Global antisemitism's rhetorical adoption of an international standard of human rights is related to various groups' discontent with power's constellation around the world, which still resides to an overwhelming extent in the United States. When Mahmoud Ahmadinejad and other political Islamists refer to the United States as the Great Satan and Israel as the Little Satan, they express a view widely shared among political Islamists regarding each one's place vis-à-vis Arab and Islamic countries. They also express a view that many governments and peoples in other parts of the world can embrace for reasons that have nothing to do with any particular interest they may have for the Middle East or its peoples—an interest that has certainly been absent for decades before the Arab Spring gained force in 2011 and since then so far has been in evidence mainly in lip service. Antisemitism thereby becomes a strategic and symbolic assault on the United States, against which there remains considerable hostility in the developing world, because the more that Israel and Jews can be demonized, and the more that the United States can be identified with Israel and said to be controlled by its own Jews working for Israel, the more animus that can be created toward the United States. This is strategically useful for those regimes and people who wish to roll back American power and influence, and those who hate what the United States stands for—democracy, liberalism, and pluralism, social, cultural, and religious freedom, women's and gays' rights and equality—and the values the United States espouses (whatever its failures to live up to them). But it is even effective for regimes and elites that are not hostile to the United States, and may also have a good and cooperative relationship with it, because antisemitism and anti-Americanism have been enormously useful for deflecting local discontent.

Especially in Arab and Islamic countries, antisemitism becomes the basis for diverting dissatisfaction from domestic malefactors and miseries, whether they are repressive governments, corrupt practices, the failure to provide basic necessities for people, economic development's absence, social inequality, or intellectual and scientific life's retrograde state. This is not to say that regimes and elites have all used antisemitism to explain why the conditions of so many of these societies have been so poor in these ways, but it is to note that regimes and elites have used and therefore further promoted antisemitism because they know it effectively diverts people's attention away from their real problems and, even more so, encourages people to let off steam by venting against the

Jews. Agitating against Jews becomes a legitimized way for people to protest, gain satisfaction for their anger, and, crucially, find common cause with the governments and regimes they might otherwise have little in common with. The enemy of my enemy is my friend, or if not my friend, then at least my ally in this matter. Such is the logic of governments and of political and other elites, which includes the genuine expression of their own prejudicial beliefs about and animus toward Israel and Jews. It is worth saying again and again, belief and cynical pragmatism often work hand in glove for antisemites who also fan the antisemitic flames within their own countries.

Global antisemitism has not only been useful and therefore deployed as a domestic politics and policy-making tool. It has also been used as an international political and foreign-policy-making tool. In this respect as well, global antisemitism's balance has shifted away from the domestic to the international. This has happened in four intertwined ways.

The first is an international analogue to its domestic policy use. Governments and ruling elites tell the world, as political Islamists both in and out of power have, that various regions' problems, and their sources, are Israel and its Jews and the Jews in the United States. Arab and Islamic leaders have employed this technique to appeal to the overt or latent antisemitism that courses around the world, and it has long been found also in the capitals and halls of power, especially in Europe, so as to preempt or reduce pressure from abroad for the political, social, economic, and cultural changes that various Arab and Islamic countries have sorely needed and continue to need. It has never been explained in any sustained and coherent way how Israel's policies toward the Palestinians, or Israel's existence more generally, are supposed to have blocked change or progress in countries near and far (unless we point to those countries' antisemitic pathologies themselves) that have so compromised their people's capacities to focus on their real problems, or how, absent such Israeli policies, or absent Israel itself, these countries would have quickly become democratic, more pluralistic, less intolerant, more economically developed, more culturally productive scientifically and in other ways. Yet this myth, dovetailing with other antisemitic myths, became a fixed idea among many people and was eagerly latched on to by active antisemites around the world and in the West, especially in Europe. The argument was something along the lines that democracy failed to flourish because the Middle East's repressive regimes could so effectively use Israel to deflect discontent from themselves that their oppressed people's other important everyday and existential concerns paled in significance. This was never credible, and never persuasively articulated. It was not credible not only because it defies what we know about how acutely attuned and overwhelmingly concerned people are with their own economic circumstances and freedoms, but also because it presented antisemitism as an elite diversionary tactic rather than what it has been: a widely and profoundly shared prejudice among a country's people. Furthermore, it was, as we now indisputably know, utter nonsense: the Arab Spring's rebellions wiped away almost overnight a host of such regimes, even though the conflict between Israel and the Palestinians appeared at the time as intractable as it had in decades.

The second way that global antisemitism has been used as an international political tool follows and is suggested by the first. Arab and Islamic countries have worked individually and in concert to exclude Israel from international associations and forums, to get international associations and forums to condemn Israel, and more generally to get many countries around the world, from the developing world and from Europe, to join their antisemitic assault on Israel, even if it is not couched in openly antisemitic terms. The Arab and Islamic countries, constituting a substantial voting and power block in international institutions, have made it clear that countries that do not line up behind them in their various initiatives against Israel will not garner their support regarding matters that are dear to those countries, including membership in international institutions such as the United Nations Security Council. Partly as a consequence, the politics of denying Israel's legitimacy and of condemning Israel in an unprincipled manner is intensive and regularly practiced by countries around the world.

This leads to the third way that foreign policy making and international relations take on an antisemitic cast. Many countries' governments, which would otherwise have little to no interest in pursuing antisemitic politics or contributing to the public antisemitic discourses, nevertheless promote antisemitism internationally and also at home in order to find favor with Arab and Islamic governments. The intensive and unprincipled condemnations of Israel and, even more so, the unparalleled frequency with which it is done are meant to please and find support from the world's committed antisemitic governments and to prevent unnecessary difficulties with them. This occurred first before globalization's advent, during the post–World War II era's gestation period, when the OPEC countries began to flex their petrodollar muscle during the October 1973 Arab-Israeli war, with an oil embargo against Israel's supporters to complement the enduring Arab boycott (started already in 1945 but suddenly having new teeth) of companies doing business with Israel or its companies. With many Arab countries' formal recognition of Israel after the Oslo Accords of 1993, this boycott has been mainly lifted—formally abandoned by Jordan and the Palestinian Authority—or weakened during the 1990s, especially the provisions to punish companies or countries doing business with Israel. Still, the temptations of adopting this by now well-established antisemitic measure, made famous by the Nazis and continued by Arab and Islamic countries, has proven irresistible to different groups and ideologues— including Christian churches, governments, labor unions, academic groups, and cultural groups—around the world, perhaps most notably the Teachers' Union of Ireland, which decided in 2013 to prohibit all collaboration with Israelis, and the British academic unions, who voted in 2006 to boycott Israeli academics (a vote seen as so self-condemning that it was soon thereafter overturned in Britain in an emergency meeting). Such individual institutional calls to boycott—as the passion expended to bring them about suggests—have resulted mainly from people's antisemitic orientations rather than the exigencies of power and politics. More generally, the Boycott, Divestment and Sanctions movement, known as BDS, which was established in 2005 after a call for such action in the official final declaration of the NGO Forum at the United Nations' World Conference Against Racism 2001 in Durban (discussed more below as the antisemitic conclave that it was), is driven mainly by Palestinian NGOs. Tapping into the world of NGO alliances that Arab and Palestinian politics have formed, and employing the antisemitic tropes and rhetoric discussed here, it has been gaining steam since its founding.

Finally, the heart of the international arena itself, the international institutions in which much of international relations take place and some of which help compose the international arena itself, has become global antisemitism's hotbed. This too started during globalization's gestation period, when Arab and Islamic countries began deploying their petro-dollars and international diplomatic muscle during and after the 1973 war, and achieved their first and perhaps paradigmatic success by getting the United Nations to pass the antisemitic Zionist Is Racism resolution in 1975. Picking up steam after the fall of the Soviet empire, which opened up the international arena to a reshuffled, non-East-West-dominated politics, Arab and Islamic countries, with their many allies of conviction and convenience in the developing and Western worlds, have systematically turned international institutions into antisemitic bastions, which have become the foci and vehicles for spreading antisemitism, reinforcing it in countries and among people around the world, and have become the basis for promulgating antisemitic policies. The Zionism Is Racism resolution, paradigmatic development that it was for the demonization of Israel and Jews, has been built upon systematically and intensively. Perhaps the signal moment in this international campaign came at the United Nations antiracism summit in Durban, South Africa, in 2001, which, its name notwithstanding, turned into, as its planners intended, an antisemitic hatefest at its core and in its proceedings. (No small irony there, as we will explore below.) Many national and international institutions, including legions among the vast world of nongovernmental organizations (NGOs), centered around but by no means restricted to the United Nations, are antisemitism's objects, bastions, and intensive promoters. NGOs, as a group systematically and overwhelmingly prejudicially hostile toward Israel, form a vast antisemitic international institutional infrastructure that disseminates antisemitism, especially anti-Israel antisemitism, which is cloaked in the impartial language of international human rights and stamped with the imprimatur of human rights' seemingly foremost defenders. Cumulatively, this has had a devastatingly pernicious power to shape media perceptions and reporting, demonizing Israel and its Jews in the eyes of the world in general as effectively as any other contributor to the contemporary antisemitic context. Both in their drumbeat of condemnations of Israel, in their outsized influence on media reporting, and in their own political initiatives — protests, boycott movements, support for local, national, and international forums, lobbying of governments, and formal and informal advisory and collaborative roles with international law-making and policy-making institutions — it is NGOs that have done so much to disproportionately and falsely focus the world's attention and outrage on Israel, branding it as the number one violator of human rights in the world, and projecting Israel as the greatest threat to world peace. They have been so effective in this regard that they have created a near negative identity between *human rights* and *Israel*. When international institutions and NGOs of all kinds are more important than ever, when the global arena ever more shapes and houses antisemitic expression and policy making, it would be hard not to conclude that, in this respect as well, the very sinews of the international system have become imbued with antisemitism and reconstituted as antisemitic.

For global antisemitism, the explicit *international* orientation — including foreign-policy making of various kinds, and appropriating and working through international institutions and organizations — began incipiently, as we have seen, already during the post–World War II period of antisemitism's lull in public expression, agitation, and spread in the West. Arab and Islamic states' international and foreign-policy-making initiatives, which were to become, in sum, one of the global age's pillars, took place not under the radar, as Arab and Islamic countries' domestic antisemitic developments and expression mainly did, but spectacularly and with devastating effect in the international arena itself. During the global era, international institutions, including the United Nations itself and NGOs, have become more intensively and prominently antisemitic, and, as they and many countries' powerful domestic antisemitisms complement and reinforce one another, have produced an international stranglehold against Israel and its Jews, and to a considerable, though not complete, extent against Jews themselves, who experience the international arena's antisemitism as what it is, deeply hostile and injurious.

This returns us to the theme of why people become antisemitic, which we need to consider anew when confronting global antisemitism. Three modes of faulty thinking have predominated. The first, itself antisemitic, is to blame the victims by attributing antisemitism to a reasonable (if sometimes exaggerated) reaction against the Jews' own conduct. The second, an unwritten and unspoken frame of understanding about prejudice, and particularly about antisemitism, is that it just happens: Some people, so goes the thinking, become antisemitic just because they do, perhaps owing to personality defects. Some people learn it from their families or just happen to pick it up. This folk theory of antisemitism is accurate for some people, but they are the exception, the small minority. Antisemitism, as we have seen, has identifiable, systemic sources— including widespread public discourses of various kinds—which in a patterned and methodical manner instill, support, reinforce, and spread it to vast numbers of people around the world. The third erroneous conception of why people become antisemitic does point to a systemic source, which is the allegedly universal psychological propensity for people to blame economic problems or other social stressors on others. In this view, this magically happens to be—nearly regardless of country, culture, past historical time period, or level of economic development— the Jews. We have already seen myriad problems with this view, which, although repeatedly and overwhelmingly falsified by experience, still exerts a hold on the popular and scholarly imagination. We have witnessed this view's problems particularly when assessing antisemitism historically, in part because this notion about what is called antisemitism's economic origins is invoked mostly reflexively *for the past.* In other words, though once supposedly *the* cause of antisemitism, it has miraculously stopped in recent years. For global antisemitism, this imputed economically or socially caused psychological reaction appears almost irrelevant.

If the rise of antisemitic expression was once said to be related to economic downturns, in our global age it supposedly derives from Middle Eastern political conflicts. Both views of antisemitism (note that they are views of the prejudice and not of its variability in expression) cannot be right, which means, given the underlying facts, that neither is right. If people's envy or their need to explain suffering owing to the economy and the Jews' real or alleged place in it has historically produced antisemitism, then there would be no way to explain why Israel's policies or existence would produce *the same animus,* and do so particularly during good economic times (and even in oil-rich Saudi Arabia, not to mention in the wealthy West)! If today, antisemitism's cause is Israel's policies and Jewish Israelis' conduct vis-à-vis the Palestinians, which is an ideological and political phenomenon, then no reason would suggest that historically economic factors would have produced the same or a highly similar animus.

These, the two predominant structural explanations—each locating antisemitism's cause in the Jews and not in the antisemitic people—have nothing to do with each other. (And the conditions underlying each one falsify the other.) Yet they are magically supposed to generate the same prejudice. We can finally put to bed the untenable economic view of antisemitism.* We should also put to bed the nonsensical, indeed antisemitically informed, view of contemporary antisemitism—particularly in light of the copious evidence we have seen here—that Israel is the reason people the world over have fantastical prejudice against Jews.

We do need to explain antisemitism's *expression,* as it differs in its trends from antisemitism's *existence,* which is rooted in the foundational antisemitic paradigm and well-established public discourses and institutional practices. Antisemitic expression can and does fluctuate substantially in a given country or region, and sometimes considerably even over a short period. This contrasts from antisemitism's *existence,* which is much more constant, extensive, and intense, even though it does evolve, whether it is in a phase of gradual increase or decrease. This discrepancy between antisemitism's existence and its expression is especially pronounced in Western societies, which still powerfully taboo or criminalize many forms of antisemitic expression in the public sphere. The variability in antisemitism's expression is explained, unlike its underlying beliefs and animus, by two things: Political leaders' strategic decisions to inject antisemitism into the public sphere and publicly fan its flames, or not to do so. And, more organically, fluctuations in societal and political stressors—notably of late events in the Middle East, such as Israel's Operation Cast Lead in Gaza in 2009—which can catalyze the foundational antisemitic paradigm and its higher-level elaboration, to produce temporary or variable changes in antisemites' desire to vent against or blame the Jews.

Antisemitism's sources have always included cultural and social ones (we have already explored Christianity's and Islam's textual sources and

---

* Note also that antisemitic expression returned to already economically well off Western Europe not during an economic downturn but during the especially economically and politically prosperous years of the 1990s. It is a region, moreover, where few genuinely believe that the tiny Jewish minority who survived the genocide of their people are economically so powerful, and most important, objectively Jews are not at all powerful. This means that the antisemitic belief that Jews constitute a collective economic hegemon, to the extent that it exists, is itself a manifestation of the problem—antisemitism—it is supposed to cause!

their interpreters' teachings) and at times have included political ones. Global antisemitism's sources include strategically created ones that political and religious leaders deeply committed to intensifying the bigotry and hatred against Jews have deployed, and championed. This strategic political dimension has become ever more prominent and effective.

Discussing global antisemitism's sources starts with the long-standing cognitive and emotional antipathies toward Jews. Had there not been such a preexisting, deeply rooted, and widespread prejudice against Jews, grounded in two thousand years of Christian teaching, thirteen hundred years of Islamic teaching (in other words, a core part of more than three billion people's central religious and cognitive traditions), which had also metamorphosed into a modern pseudoscientific doctrine that provided the basis for an international genocidal coalition that set out to slaughter an entire continent's and ultimately the world's Jews, then global antisemitism would not exist today. Put differently, it is inconceivable that without all this, in other words, had there been abso-lutely no prejudice against Jews in the world, say in 1989—at the Cold War's end and shortly before Israeli-Palestinian relations thawed with the Oslo Accords—we would have today the *worldwide* phenomenon global antisemitism. It would not have the vast number of adherents that it does. It would not consist of the content—the beliefs, accusa-tions, tropes, and images—that it does. It would not have the diversity of believers that it does. It would not have the fantastical quality that it does. It would not be producing the violence and threat of violence that it does. It would not be as eliminationist as it is or as exterminationist as many antisemites would have it be. It would simply not exist, in any size or form resembling what it does.

This is significant for three reasons. The first is analytical: these facts must center our understanding of global antisemitism, even though many other factors are at work, some of which might deserve equal or for certain topics more attention. The second is discursive and political: the crucial foundation, including the foundational antisemitic para-digm, that these long-standing sources provide for global antisemitism, and how these sources continue to powerfully fuel them, is elided from much discussion of antisemitism and of anti-Israel agitation. This long-existing antisemitic foundation's continuing power and relevance are actively denied by those who say either that such antisemitism does not exist or is not so prevalent, or that today's Jews and Israel's policies and actions produce the animus toward them. Therefore, it is discursively and politically crucial to keep the record honest and to speak the truth to the many deniers and ideologues, and for the general publics, whether their members are antisemitic or not. The third is remedial and restorative: to make progress in combating antisemitism, in lessening its reach, and reducing its danger, and in protecting the many people who are at risk—of lives being distorted (this includes non-Jews), of having to live in cultures of hate, of being subject to physical attacks, to being killed—we need to recognize the global nature of antisemitism, and above all its political nature, and to recognize that antisemites with different means in different places are conducting a multipronged offensive against Jews in what constitutes a partly declared and partly undeclared one-sided war.

The several-decades-long happenstancial, impermanent, and ultimately ineffective damper that the Holocaust's horror produced on antisemitism's further expression and public spread may have made little difference in antisemitism's evolution. It may be that antisemitism, in any case, would have been transformed into global antisemitism because this world-leading prejudice would have naturally adapted to the globalized world, with the added development of the Jews' acquisition of the political focal point Israel for the antisemites to fixate upon. Antisemitic discourse's move to the Internet, some of its new tropes, its unmooring from its original sources, its politicization, and its many cross-cultural flows leading to the cross-fertilization of antisemitic traditions and a degree of sharing and growing closeness would likely more or less have similarly come to be. After all, the hallmark of antisemitism's mutability is to incorporate its era's features, ethos, and mechanisms, and to adapt itself to the reigning plausibility structure in order to utilize that structure. Its capacity to so readily metamorphose itself derives precisely from its free-floating nature divorced from the reality of Jews' and their communities' constitutions and deeds.

The foundational antisemitic paradigm's power leaves no doubt that without further post–World War II and post–Cold War developments that directly or indirectly powerfully nurtured this prejudice, antisemitism would still be a powerful and global force of anti-Jewish thought, animus, and practice. Yet its evolution was, in fact, not wholly natural or unaided by design. Other sources came into play. Drawing and building upon the foundational antisemitic paradigm — grounded in Christianity and adopted by Islam, with each tradition's powerfully prejudicial and highly emotive elaborations, to produce deeply prejudicial beliefs and antipathies toward Jews — global antisemitism's other sources had a vast reservoir of notions and ready adherents to draw upon.

After World War II, the world was turned upside down. The Cold War created the East-West conflict and divided much of the world, including the countries of the Middle East, into one side's or the other's allies or clients. Decolonization proceeded rapidly, replacing Western global occupation and dominance's fixed point with peoples and elites the world over trying to establish their new bearings, which included ever many more in the developing world coming to see how economically and technologically and, subjectively, culturally lagging they were. Israel's founding posed an unceasing challenge by its very existence to Arabs' and Muslims' self-understanding and self-regard, as Israel's ability to withstand the combined power of a good part of a civilization seeking to destroy it bitterly reminded Arabs and Muslims of their collective weakness, which in their Islamic-governed or -inflected minds seemed to mock Islam's claims to being the world's sovereign. A few years after Israel came into being, King Saud of Saudi Arabia, speaking for the Arab world, expressed this sentiment: "Israel is a serious wound in the Arab world body, and we cannot endure the pain of this wound forever. We don't have the patience to see Israel remain occupying part of Palestine for long.... We Arabs total about 50,000,000. Why don't we sacrifice 10,000,000 of our number to live in pride and self-respect?"[4] So powerful has this humiliation been that again and again Arab and Islamic leaders have been willing to contemplate massive defeats and massive losses along the way, so long as it would eventually end that humiliation. It was one thing to be defeated and ruled by the British or French, with European and Christian civilization's might behind them, with which the Arabs and Muslims had been locked in the combat of civilizations for centuries. It was another thing to be defeated by the weakling Jews, despised and deprecated in the Qur'an and the Islamic tradition, the remnants of a people just slaughtered as helpless animals might be, who had previously no martial tradition, no country, no army, no power at all. The humiliation and the hatred Israel's existence and flourishing engendered among Arab and Islamic peoples, elites, and political leaders was titanic. Antisemitism became ever more strategically appealing and ever more strategically useful for Arab and Islamic leaders and people alike.

Arabs' and Muslims' broad distemper with the state of Arab and Islamic culture, with Islam's place in the world, and with their countries' economic and technological backwardness composed a fertile situation for melding contemporary dissatisfactions with an ancient and powerful prejudice, recently augmented by its even more intensive modern racial version, owing to the Nazis' effective, if often indirect, antisemitic ambassadorship and cultural missionizing. It was as if central casting sent the Jews for the perfect part to induce a widespread and enormous upsurge in disordered thinking, prejudice, animus, hatred, and the desire to strike out. Ascendant Israel and its Jews were the darlings of the West's major powers, eventually becoming the close ally and protégé of the world's true superpower, the United States. Israel and its Jews had defeated the Arab world's combined military might. They were economically prodigious. They became a technological and scientific powerhouse. They made, in what became a cliché of the time, the desert bloom. The sudden rise and victory, and further rise of this, in Arabs' and Muslims' eyes, infidel and servile people, tiny in number, were already combustible enough without a series of further related factors coming into play.

The Arab countries and peoples suffered under monarchical and nonmonarchical dictatorships that (as dictatorships do) ranged from the stifling to the brutal to the mass murderous. But as violence is an expensive, difficult, inefficient, and ultimately self-injurious way to rule, the dictators also used nonviolent techniques to bond with the populace and deflect attention from their rule's social and economic pathologies. The principal tool kit readily available included demonizing Israel, inflaming the existing antisemitism and inculcating more of it into the public sphere and people's minds and hearts, and representing the dictatorial regime as the nation's defender against the Jews and as their would-be vanquisher. The roster of political dictators who did this is a who's who of the most famous—infamous, really—Arab leaders of modern times, including the Grand Mufti of Jerusalem Mohammad Amin al-Husayni, Iraq's Saddam Hussein (who fancied himself the new Saladin), Egypt's Gamal Abdel Nasser, Syria's Hafez al-Assad, Lebanon's and Hezbollah's Hassan Nasrallah, Libya's Muammar Gaddafi, the PLO's Yasser Arafat, Hamas' Khaled Mashal, Iran's Ayatollah Ruhollah Khomeini, and Iran's Mahmoud Ahmadinejad. This roster of scoundrels, abrogators of freedom, peddlers of the big lie, totalitarians, or perpetrators of wanton violence, including mass murder — any number of whom were rivals or enemies of one another — rallied around one cause, a cause they shared with Hitler among others: spreading demonizing views and hatred of Jews, and seeking to turn such antisemitism into eliminationist action. That this roster of dictators and mass murderers did this, and with such fervor and persistence, should perhaps be enough to persuade anyone of the evils of any kind of antisemitism, any kind of deprecation of Jews, any kind of singular, not to mention obsessive, hostile focus on them or their country. Thus, the dictators and their regimes infused the public sphere, at first in newspapers, on radio, and on television, with antisemitism and an incessant focus on Israel's real and mainly alleged deeds and transgressions. It was a win-win emotionally even no matter that it was politically self-injurious for the Arab and Muslim peoples: if expressing your dissatisfaction toward the regime, not to mention antagonism toward it, may cause you difficulties, then blaming your problems on Israel and the Jews becomes a psychologically and emotionally, comparatively satisfying option.*

The Arab and Islamic dictatorships also became aware of how they could politicize discontent in ways that support rather than undermine their regimes, most effectively by infusing the public sphere with antisemitic content. They could thus draw upon the powerful Islamic antisemitic tradition and antisemitism's considerable popular reservoir, making

---

* It should be clear that blaming Israel for Arab and Islamic leaders using Israel's existence to divert their people's attention from the people's real material and political needs of developing their countries and toppling dictatorships is but a form of antisemitism. It is not the Jews' fault that Arabs and Muslims were broadly antisemitic in the first place, and that such antisemitism was easily mobilized by sincere or cynical political leaders. Egypt, after all, maintained a dictatorship for three decades after making peace with Israel, which shows that war footing vis-à-vis Israel or an Arab or Islamic regime's call for Israel's destruction was not the cause of dictatorship or of retarded development.

this the dominant strategy of regimes, even those somewhat less hostile to Israel, across the Arab and Islamic worlds.

Antisemitism's resurgence in Europe has been crucial for global antisemitism's character, spread, and efficacy. If the Europeans had continued to toe the post-Holocaust line that this prejudice must not see the light of day, not return to the public sphere, if the European taboo on its expression had not been eroded and eventually all but overthrown, then the Arab and Islamic discursive and institutional onslaught against Jews and Israel would have remained a parochial matter, important and threatening but parochial, maintaining itself as another developing world gripe against the developed world. But Europeans, aside from the adherence of so many tens of millions in country after country to the foundational antisemitic paradigm, and aside from the proliferation of elaborations upon it by varieties of Christian antisemites and of modern racist antisemites, had a new powerful impetus to think ill of and deprecate Jews. Ever since the Holocaust, Europeans, whether they had any connection to the eliminationist onslaught or not (this includes those born after the war), have had to hear about what they or their countrymen once did to Jews or—and this is a big, unappreciated caveat— knew, as in the Netherlands, that such a reckoning might come one day. After all, the Holocaust was the product of an international genocidal coalition, spearheaded to be sure by the German government and Germans and joined in by many countries' governments and peoples. This is essential to mention here because, owing to the faulty paradigm of understanding, in which virtually all peoples and all governments were deemed to be either terrorized by or the stooges of the mythically all-powerful Nazi leadership and its mythically omniscient and ever-present terror apparatus, Europe's peoples and what they willfully did to further or carry out the elimination and extermination of the Jews— in Poland, Ukraine, France, the Netherlands, Slovakia, and in other countries—had been overlooked and therefore they were let off the hook. But just because the Holocaust's historians for decades had written about the deed's commission without placing its perpetrators at the center, and also neglected the Holocaust's complicit wider circle of ordinary Germans, ordinary Poles, ordinary Dutch supporters, we might say ordinary Europeans at the center (of which there were countless tens of millions), it did not mean that those very same people—Germans,

Poles, Dutch, French, Lithuanians, Ukrainians, and others—and even many of their descendants did not know the truth.[5] Of course they did. They knew how much they and their countrymen hated Jews, how much they wanted to be rid of them (even if many condemned the mass murder itself), how little empathy there was for the Jews in their plight, and how many of their countrymen tangibly lent aid, in one way or another, to the eliminationist measures. It was a truth they wanted to cover up, or to minimize in potential impact. Blaming the Jews themselves helped enormously. This temptation was not just too hard to pass up, as many temptations are, but was also their broader antisemitic orientation toward Jews' natural corollary. So Europeans proceeded to blacken the Jews, subject them to charges of hypocrisy, divert attention from their own deeds by shining accusatory scrutiny's spotlight on the Jews. Over the past two decades, this theme has been well explored for Germans. But due to the failings of the scholarship on the Holocaust's perpetration also beyond Germany, it has still not been well explored for other countries. The failure to recognize the culpability of so many ordinary Poles, Dutch, French, Ukrainians, et cetera—which apologetic authors and opinion leaders in those countries vehemently denied and still often deny—obviated the need to investigate the ways, including the antisemitic ways, these same people and their societies might seek to deal after the war with the huge problem of that culpability.

The sense of culpability for what is often characterized as the greatest horror in human history is burdensome or unbearable for most people for whom a salient (often the principal) locus of group identity is the nation, the image and standing of which they typically, especially in the eyes of people outside their countries, want to bolster. If we consider how much people bristle at unflattering stereotypes about their national or ethnic or religious group, and how afflicted it makes them feel personally, we should magnify such reactions a figurative hundred or thousand times to understand how disturbing it is to be implicated in the Holocaust. Germans, the French, the Dutch, Norwegians, the Swiss, Poles, Ukrainians, Lithuanians, Latvians, Slovaks, Greeks, Hungarians, Christians in general, and Catholics in particular, even Danes face this problem albeit to different degrees. Yet there is no easy way around it other than burying it or, even more effective, shifting blame to the Jews themselves. The strategic impulse to deprecate contemporary Jews, or to incriminate them in something similar, so that the horror's burden is shifted from implicated people and countries alike to the Jews, becomes not only attractive but, for many, a near psychological imperative.

This phenomenon has been identified in Germany correctly, but dubbed erroneously, as *secondary antisemitism*. This antisemitism is a reaction of the peoples implicated, if only by association, with the Holocaust's perpetration. For Germany in particular it has been analyzed as weariness from hearing about the Holocaust — in Walser's (false though resonant) formulation, from being beaten with the Holocaust "cudgel." Such vexation exists — and there is something to the notion that some Germans feel put upon by the *extent* of media and other attention the Holocaust gets, angering them at Jews, whom they blame for this state of affairs. But such aggravation does not credibly explain the more extensive and profound animus. The frequently repeated phrase *Germans will never forgive the Jews for the Holocaust* points the way toward the real issue. The phrase rightly does not say that Germans will never forgive Jews for *talking* about the Holocaust. It is for the Holocaust itself, meaning that Germans must live with the burden of knowing, and of having others know, that their country and their countrymen and -women were (whatever the help of other peoples) principally responsible for or widely supportive of the eliminationist and exterminationist assault on Jews. This is the burden many seek to lift, not the lesser, or indeed phantom, burden of Jews wanting to remember what happened to themselves, their families, their people.

That Germans blame Jews for having to hear about the past's horrors is *in itself an expression of antisemitism*. In Germany, most media attention on the Holocaust is generated by non-Jewish Germans. The German authors of the general histories and monographs, who produce the vast majority of scholarship and general-interest books on Nazism and the Holocaust, are with the rare exception not Jews. *Spiegel, Süddeutsche Zeitung, Zeit, Frankfurter Allgemeine Zeitung*, the television networks ARD and ZDF cover the Holocaust and the Nazi era with great frequency. These media institutions are not seen, even in Germany, as Jewish outfits. So why attack the Jews, when it is Germans doing it? Not because of what Jews do — so it is not secondary antisemitism, but primary. To understand so-called secondary antisemitism as resentment against Jews, instead of as a strategy, if somewhat reclad, straight out of the old antisemitic playbook is naive.

This strategic assault on Jews is the only credible explanation for so many Germans (true of other Europeans) coming to the strange, totally not obvious, indeed fantastical notion of equating how Israel and Jewish Israelis treat Palestinians (who themselves have sought to destroy Israel) with what the Nazi leadership and Germans did to Jews (who in Germany wanted nothing more than to be good Germans), and for how Germans (and Europeans) can say that the Jews are conducting a war of extermination against the Palestinians. If the people victimized by the Nazis are themselves Nazis, then how can those who treated them harshly or hated them be blamed? After all, Nazis must be stopped, and stopped with all available means. This, to be sure, is not usually spelled out in this manner, but it is the logical conclusion for those who think of what one might or should do to today's Nazis conducting a war of extermination against men, women, and children. At the very least, when those same putative Nazis—the Jews—make claims to having been victimized, or when such claims are made by others on their behalf, it lessens the sting, if not inoculating others against it altogether.

This complex, namely the problem many—though decidedly not all—Germans have with accepting their countrymen's eliminationist and exterminationist deeds for what they were, and without, as psychic and emotional compensation, lashing out at Jews, pertains to other European countries and peoples as well. One observer living in the Netherlands for a decade comments on her extensive everyday experience. The Dutch

> don't like talking about it because the Holocaust forces ordinary Europeans to face their own antisemitic roots.... [M]ost Dutch people do not like to talk about antisemitism in their own ranks. Most quickly move from this topic preferring instead to talk about Israel's treatment of the Palestinians, something which they are uncharacteristically passionate about. I am not sure why it is that they avoid talking of this chapter in their history, maybe not only because Dutch people suffered greatly during the war and those who are alive who lived through it still carry deep scars which don't take

much pulling at to make them raw. But I also think, they don't like to face their own collective guilt for not doing more to protect Dutch Jewry from the gas chambers.[6]

And the issue is not just facing what they did not do, but also what they actively did to help Germans round up Jews, and how all of this is wrapped up in and incriminates their antisemitism. In Poland, Ukraine, Croatia, the Netherlands, France, Denmark, and Switzerland, and cutting across national borders, among Christians generally and Catholics in particular, having their countries or churches, their countrymen and women, and their religious traditions and its leaders (including Pope Pius XII) implicated or potentially implicated in the Holocaust has produced resistance and push back across Europe. This part of the global antisemitic complex's most hyperbolic and unmistakable manifestation of likening Israel and Jewish Israelis to Nazi Germany and to Nazis is in evidence in colossal proportions across Europe. The visual equation, typically in cartoons, of the Star of David with a swastika is a commonplace. How visually and immediately satisfying this must be to antisemites across Europe! That this equation of Israel and Jews with Nazism

*In the Spanish press: a hook-nosed Israeli prime minister Ariel Sharon, wearing a yarmulke and sporting a swastika inside a Star of David, proclaims: "At least Hitler taught me how to invade a country and destroy every living insect."*

and Nazis occurs in the European countries which themselves suffered such violence and destruction at the hands of the Germans, meaning that they know how incommensurately brutal and destructive the Germans actually were, only reveals how much more their assessments of Israel and its Jews are unmoored from reality testing. Because the victims were not only Jews: the Germans enslaved millions of non-Jewish Europeans across the continent. They slaughtered or created the conditions to starve to death millions of non-Jewish Europeans. They were turning central and Eastern Europe into a vast German colony and imperium and eradicating, literally eradicating, the existence of various nations as nations, including the Polish nation. They responded to attacks upon them with utter brutality, often murdering — lining up and gunning down — local civilians at a ratio of one hundred to one for every German killed. They created death factories, outfitted with gas chambers and crematoria. This was the reality of Nazism, of the Germans' occupation of the European landmass. In five and a half years, the Germans slaughtered close to twenty million people.

This specific post-Holocaust impetus across Europe to denigrate Jews by tapping into the region's existing deep and broad antisemitic reservoir, and then to augment it and substantially intensify it, is a transparent attempt to shed the subjective sense of guilt or to free one's country, religion, or people from accusations of guilt and from their association with the Holocaust. In Europe and among elites and the general public alike, this probably has more to do with generating the anti-Israel antisemitism, and its withering orientation and animus, than anything Israel has done. Europeans' wild, fantastical anti-Israel antisemitic accusations are otherwise incomprehensible. Their political and cultural elites' bad faith, in their long-enduring preference for dictators over democrats in the Middle East, further fuels this. Put bluntly: instead of Europeans saying that Jews' subversive influence allows them to control and distort United States' policy toward the Middle East, it is far more plausible, indeed easily demonstrable (as the 1973 OPEC oil embargo's success in Europe, discussed below, shows), that the substantial Arab economic influence has corrupted the European countries' discourses and stances toward Jews and Arabs alike. European countries' economic interests, especially access to oil but also to massive business contracts, swing them against what was for decades the region's lone democracy, which remains the region's only liberal democracy that respects political freedoms. Yet this goes generally unsaid, the more to persuade others and themselves that it is legitimate to blacken the image of Israel and Jews more broadly. Hence the synergistic elements—widespread antisemitism, lashing out to lift the burden of guilt, and economic pragmatism—of Europeans' hyperbolically critical treatment of Israel. And the final irony is that the warping of European political and ideological sensibilities into demonizing democratic and existentially threatened Israel is covered up with antisemitic accusations of a Jewish conspiracy to warp the United States and Americans into what?—into supporting a democracy and an existentially threatened people and country!

This overall psychological logic to defame Israel probably also has more to do with the very different orientation of Europeans and Americans toward Israel than the so-called power of Jews in the United States, and certainly more to do with the antisemitic fantasies than the alleged Jewish conspiracy running American foreign policy and controlling American public opinion and utterly duping the immensely confident American power elites and the American public into supporting the otherwise obviously unsupportable Israel. Such a charge demonizes Jews in a *secular political* way—in line with global antisemitism's shifting the locus of antisemitic charges to the political sphere, which for people in the West is, almost by definition, a secular sphere. It turns Israel and its Jews into a contemporary political and secular devil, which neatly draws upon and gains plausibility by the long-existing practice of identifying Jews with the devil or seeing them as devils, the first being the province of Christian antisemitism and the second of modern racial antisemitism. This is hardly a coincidence or a trivial development. It is but another of antisemitism's unsurprising metamorphoses, cloaking a consistent underlying view and animus in attire more fitting for the times, and creating the prejudice's profound, new aspect.

The critical importance of Europeans' displacement of guilt onto Israel and its Jews by Nazifying them is still greater. It creates a direct bond with Arab and Islamic antisemites of shared demonizing of Israel and Jews, and allows the two regional discourses to overlap, meaning in particular that it makes Europeans immediately more receptive to the virulently antisemitic Arab and Islamic discourse about Jews and particularly about Israel. For those who liken Israel and its Jews to Nazis, there is, in principle, no antisemitic trope or accusation (excluding those that dwell explicitly on Islam specific Qur'anic or Hadithic moments) that is not plausible. This matters greatly because the Arab and Islamic antisemitic public discourse is far less restrained, more accusatory, wilder, and more openly eliminationist than Europe's. When Europeans who see Jews as Nazis hear, whether it be a lengthy disquisition or a snippet, that Jews have allegedly committed this or that atrocity, or that their intention is to undertake some malevolent or eliminationist campaign against Arabs, Muslims, or Islam itself, they are predisposed to give them a ready hearing if not accept this at face value. Arab and Islamic antisemites, and inveterate anti-Israel antisemites elsewhere who are part of the Arab and Islamic anti-Israel discourse, are surely aware of this appeal. (Its stunning success is such that they could hardly not be.) And so they play to this antisemitic propensity of Europeans shamelessly.

In 2000 Palestinians perpetrated one of their many fraudulent claims of Israeli atrocities, which was eagerly latched on to by Western media and publics, broadcast around the world, and turned into a cause célèbre. It was an incident during the Second Intifada that seemed to show a Palestinian boy, Muhammad Al Dura, huddling behind his father and then being supposedly murdered by Jewish Israelis soldiers. Yet elements of this episode, if not its core elements, were surely staged. That the claims that Israeli forces simply murdered him were at best dubious was apparent from the full videotape of the incident, which shows Muhammad *alive* after he was supposedly murdered. This part of the video footage — which did not coincide with the claims journalists and others made about what happened — was pointedly not included in the French 2's television broadcast, which presented the deceptively edited images that were rebroadcast on European networks and around the world, and posted on the Internet, falsely blackening the image of Israel and Jews. Witness testimony, forensic evidence, and findings of investigations, all belie the repeated claims about Muhammad's fate (who likely was not killed or even hit by bullets), yet none of this mattered to the substantial, antisemitically inclined portions of the Western media and public. Particularly relevant here was one of the powerful ways that this version of the blood libel was constructed and calculated to be more devastating in its antisemitic effects. The caption of the incident's signature photo was uttered by the French journalist Catherine Nay: "The Death of Muhammad cancels out, erases that of the Jewish child, his hands in the air from the SS in the Warsaw Ghetto."[7] The antisemitic intention and effect, and the appeal, to Europeans could not be stated more plainly or truly: to equate the Jews with Nazis as willful murderers of children, to give the Palestinians primacy as the victims of today's Holocaust, and to deny that the Holocaust gives Jews legitimacy to have, like other peoples, their own country.

The global antisemitic complex's final contingent source is a genuine critique of Israel gone bad or, one might reasonably say, mad. We have already explored its hyperbolic and fantastical and obsessive nature. Still, we should note that without Israel's victory in the 1967 war—before which the leaders of Arab countries and the Arab and Islamic political discourses regularly threatened to imminently annihilate not just Israel but also its Jews—and Israel's subsequent strategic occupation of Palestinians in West Bank and Gaza owing to the Arab countries' unwillingness to trade land for peace, which Israel offered them shortly after the war, the antisemitic fixation on Israel and its effective widespread appeal would likely not have occurred to the same degree. Many people are not particularly knowledgeable about the region's geopolitics and are not aware of how thoroughgoing the Palestinians' and other Arab countries' rejection was first of Israel's very existence starting with their attempts to destroy it in 1948, and second of any Israeli peace offer for decades after 1967, including to relinquish conquered territories, to which the infamous and unanimous Arab League Khartoum Resolution directly responded with the three *no's:* "no peace with Israel, no recognition of Israel, no negotiations with it." Many other people have been duped by the vast, continuous stream of disinformation that falsifies the history and demonizes Israel. To such people Israel's control over Palestinian territories has come to look like pure aggrandizing colonization and the denial to a people of self-government, which many deem selectively *and* reflexively to be an inalienable human right—although, of course, they have not done the same for decades when Arab peoples have suffered under dictators and kings (who are actually dictators), or when Turks deny Kurds the same right, or in the many other comparable or worse instances of oppression. How the counterfactual of Israel not occupying

West Bank and Gaza would have affected global antisemitism's development cannot be known. The Arab and Islamic antisemitic discourse, and its broad appeal, would have likely been similar in its basic stance and orientation, because Arabs and Muslims' antipathy toward a Jewish country at their world's heart has always been the underlying animus driving their antisemitism—as they themselves openly declared and have sought to do for decades. Recall Palestinian Authority's Fatwa Council Sheik Ahmad Abu Halabiya's Friday prayer declaration broadcast by Palestinian Authority official television that Muslims should kill Jews wherever they find them, "because they established Israel here, in the beating heart of the Arab world, in Palestine."[8] Aside from the invocation in Arab and Islamic, including Iranian, antisemitic discourses of the Jews' enmity toward Allah, Muhammad, and Islam, Israel's existence in the heart of the Arab and Muslim world is perhaps the foundational evil most frequently ascribed to the Jews.

For the Christian antisemitic discourse, the absence of the occupation might have robbed it of seeing or projecting onto the Palestinians the role of Jesus being crucified by the Jews, but this has not been driving Christian antisemitism, which has its own powerful sources, embedded in its tradition and in the minds of countless millions, which are independent of Israel's rule over Palestinians. Similarly, rightist or neo-Nazi antisemitism, happy enough to exploit Israel's real or alleged transgressions against Palestinians, has its own independent concerns, including rehabilitating Nazi or radical-right politics, which has at its core the denial of the Holocaust or the minimizing of its horrors.

Global antisemitism's stream most fueled by the polemical and emotional potential of Israel's continuing occupation of West Bank and recently concluded occupation of Gaza specifically, as opposed to Israel's existence in general, has been leftist antisemitism and the soft version of it that has been central to the dishonest human-rights orientation of much of Europe and the international human-rights community. Had the occupation never occurred, it is possible, even likely, that the political left and the international human-rights community, after the Soviet empire's fall and the end to the effectiveness of the rallying cry of socialism of any kind, when casting about for a new signal cause, would not (given the many mass-murdering and brutal regimes in Africa and Asia) have latched on to Israel as the symbol and one of the central agents of the world's evil. This would also likely have been true of the humanitarian international human-rights community seeking a focal point for its fire. In this regard, Israel's occupation's contingent feature has been important for aspects of global antisemitism's development. This is so although that development itself was predicated upon the foundational antisemitic paradigm, its existence encouraging the left and left-liberal human-rights groups to easily and quickly adopt Israel as its new cause, shape how its members apprehended Israel and its deeds, and lead it to take its genuine critique of Israel's policies to the hyperbolic extreme of obsessively demonizing Israel and its Jews.

This fixation on demonizing Israel has, as would be predicted, led increasingly to those on the left and in the international human-rights community, and through their loud voices critically contributing to the public discourse over Israel, even to people not on the left, to question, then doubt, then deny that such an entity as Israel has the right to exist in the first place. If this country, so goes the thinking, is Nazi-like, is robbing other people of their inalienable rights, is pursuing policies and regular acts of wanton butchery and cruelty, is carrying out a war of extermination, how can people of good conscience support this country's continuing existence, especially when it was founded on the territory of another people? Indeed, how can people of good conscience say that its founding was anything but illegitimate? In this way, Israel's occupation of West Bank and Gaza produced a political discourse in the West that naturally, given the discourse's assumptions, gradually developed an ever more powerful eliminationist strand that otherwise would likely not have been present, or certainly not to the degree it has become.

Global antisemitism constituted by once-distinct streams of anti-Jewish prejudice and animus has come together into a new foundational synthesis. The discourse of global antisemitism, in performing many relational and psychic functions, and with a self-generating and self-perpetuating quality, is even much more robust than any single one of its multiple constituent discourses. Individual and global antisemitic discourses are grass-roots affairs with democratic participation and life that merely reflects people's thinking, however erroneous, and their inclinations to express those thoughts, imbibe them from others, exchange them in their attempt, heartfelt or cynically disingenuous, to understand the world and Jews' place in it. Yet global antisemitism is not merely such a bottom-up grass-roots phenomenon. It is also pushed from above. Purposive people, institutions, and states also powerfully fuel global antisemitism. An international political, social, economic, and cultural insurgency that is unprecedented and singular spreads *this* prejudice's hatred, demonizes the Jewish people, and ultimately seeks an eliminationist campaign against them, or at least the ones in Israel. That this is occurring is apparent to anyone willing to look, and not something we need to infer or speculate about. And this cannot be emphasized enough: to say that political leaders and institutions actively promote antisemitism is in no sense analogous to saying, as antisemites do, that Jews work behind the scenes to perpetrate evil. So many of antisemitism's state and institutional sponsors do so *openly* in word and deed, with policy and politicking.

Global antisemitic discourse's most striking aspect is the great extent to which governments around the world promote, drive, and shape it, not only, as we have seen, at home, but also *abroad,* especially in two respects: to have antisemitism enshrined in international institutions' and forums' ethos and practices, and to get other states and international institutions, including corporations, to practice antisemitism as a matter of conviction or of prudential politics and economic interest. An international antisemitic alliance, or rather a core alliance with somewhat shifting parts, has come firmly into existence. No other ethnic group is the target of systematic multiple-state and interstate programs and policies of fomenting prejudice. Only the Jews. And it is not a small and marginal phenomenon where there is no other. It is massive. Many countries carry it out, and it is a notable part of international politics.

Arab and Islamic governments originated the new international antisemitic alliance and have been its driving spirit. Ever since Israel's founding in 1948 many Arab and Islamic countries were openly antisemitic and dedicated to Israel's destruction, for which they naturally fostered support. With their principal patron, the Soviet Union, they sought to enlist other countries, mainly unsuccessfully during the next two decades. It was first with the OPEC oil embargo during the 1973 Yom Kippur war (started by Egypt and Syria in a surprise attack on Israel) that Arab and Islamic states were able to muster the economic and political muscle, and a coherent strategic plan, to create an antisemitic anti-Israel bloc and to push their agenda internationally with success. That success was stupendous. Overnight, they threatened Western economies, quadrupled oil prices, brought on a great recession and the new alarming phenomenon of stagflation (simultaneous high unemployment and inflation), and got all governments, elites, and publics to reckon with the Arab and Islamic countries' new international economic and political might, congealed in OPEC, the suddenly powerful oil cartel that controlled the world economy's oil lifeblood.

The price of receiving oil from Arab- and Islamic-dominated OPEC was to abandon support for Israel, and to do so when, owing to Israel being caught off-guard, in October 1973 Israel initially faced military defeat, and its enemies threatened its existence, and that of its people, with destruction. This attack occurred after Israel — to deaf Arab ears — had offered to return virtually *all* territory it had occupied after the 1967 war. Clearly, the fate of the Palestinians and the territories they inhabited, West Bank and Gaza, had *nothing* to do with Arab and Islamic enmity toward Israel, *nothing* to do with antisemitism's framing and growth, *nothing* to do with the incipient European de facto alliance with the anti-Israel coalition, and *nothing* to do with Arab states' lip-service to the Palestinians' well-being. Except the Netherlands, Europe's countries succumbed to OPEC's demands, and Israel found itself virtually without international support, save for the United States. And thus began the capture and distortion of European countries' foreign policy toward Israel and the Middle East by antisemitic economic pressure.

In the 1973 war, Israel managed to reverse the battlefield and win a considerable military victory, which, unlike its enemies' dire intentions for Israel, did not translate into either Israeli territorial gains or an Israeli eliminationist assault against Arabs. Quickly thereafter, the Arab and Islamic countries consolidated support for their antisemitic program. Still, their most visible, though not their only or perhaps even their most significant success, was their formal colonizing of the principal international institution, the United Nations, marked by the General Assembly's overwhelming adoption of the previously mentioned, enduringly infamous Zionism Is Racism resolution. Of the 139 countries voting, only 35 voted against it. Faced with what was an out-and-out antisemitic hate resolution against Jews, for Zionism is nothing more than the

name of the Jews' national movement, no different from any other people's national movement, 32 governments, either moved by this prejudice or not wanting to incur the wrath of the Arab and Islamic bloc,
abstained. Seventy-two countries affirmed their support for the United
Nations to sanction unabashed antisemitism.

The Arab and Islamic countries and peoples understood their newfound power and put it to antisemitic use. From then on, the United
Nations and international institutions have been a bastion of antisemitic
discourse and initiatives, with a vast record of concerted assault upon
Israel and its Jews, which so obviously violates any legitimate criteria of
reasonable criticism or censure, and so obviously can be classified only as
antisemitic by the neutral criteria for identifying prejudice (of any kind)
that we have seen here. And the United Nations' antisemitic assault
upon Israel and its Jews has lasted for more than thirty-five years since
the infamous antisemitic resolution.

In the last ten years the United Nations has passed more resolutions
against Israel than against all Arab and relevant Islamic countries combined, and by a wide margin of 288 against Israel versus 97 against all
the others. By this measure the United Nations deemed Israel three
times as bad as all these undemocratic, mainly highly repressive, and
often murderous regimes combined! Fully two out of every five human-
rights resolutions the United Nations passed during the most recent ten-
year period attacked Israel. That's right: the United Nations deemed
Israel alone to be worthy of total condemnation that comes close to
equaling that which it doled out to the rest of world, with all the world's
dictatorships, violence, war making, eliminationism, and mass murder.
The United Nations passed more than six times as many resolutions
against Israel than the forty-seven resolutions over ten years it passed
against Sudan (the second-most-censured country), which had been
perpetrating a massive eliminationist and exterminationist drive that
had the world's attention during this time. Iran, which has been in
ongoing conflict with much of the world and with the United Nations
itself over nuclear weapons and suffers under a brutal repressive dictatorship that openly sponsors international terrorism, was the target of
only twelve United Nations resolutions over the ten years, *4 percent* of
the number attacking Israel. Syria, governed by a ruthless regime
employing an archipelago of camps and torture chambers, and for the

last year of the period engaged in a violent and enormously destructive suppression of those wishing to free its populace of its yoke — which has received massive international media attention — has had only twelve resolutions passed against it, one for every twenty-five passed against Israel.

And on and on. In the Arab and Islamic world one repressive or murderous regime after another — known to be flagrant human-rights violators — has generated only scant United Nations condemnation compared to Israel, including Libya (eight resolutions), Egypt (zero), Saudi Arabia (zero), Turkey (one), Yemen (three), Lebanon (twelve), South Yemen (zero). While the Arab and Islamic countries are extremely powerful in the United Nations, that is not the reason they have received so little censure proportionate to Israel when they deserve by many orders of magnitude so much more. The condemnation directed at Israel also dwarfs that which is directed at the world's other worst regimes. Genocidal Democratic Republic of the Congo, with millions slaughtered, was the object of only forty-two resolutions. Brutally repressive Myanmar: twnty-one. North Korea, a regime employing a gulag and essentially starving hundreds of thousands if not considerably more of its people to death: fifteen. Kenya, which had an eliminationist assault in 2008 that riveted the world: one.

During a singular historical moment, on the heels of the Soviet empire's destruction and therefore the loss of much of the developing world's patron and a counterweight to the United States, and with Israel demanding a rescission of the infamous Zionism Is Racism resolution as a prerequisite for its participation in the Madrid negotiations to produce an agreement with the PLO for a move toward Palestinian statehood, the Arab and Islamic power bloc — perhaps for the only significant time in recent decades — was unable to hold in line the other countries of the world, and the General Assembly voted in 1991 to rescind the Zionism Is Racism resolution. This is the only time that the General Assembly has revoked one of its own resolutions. Had it not been revoked at that propitious moment, there is little doubt it would have almost certainly survived the past decade, as the antisemitic agitation in the United Nations has intensified.

This upsurge in antisemitic animus and expression, in the increasingly dense antisemitic public discourse, and in the antisemitic international political assault on Jews and Israel—in a word, in global antisemitism—was symbolized and given substance during the 2001 United Nations first international antiracism conference held in Durban, South Africa. What was billed as, and perhaps originally conceived as, a celebration of pluralism, diversity, and tolerance, together with the need to mobilize the world community to fight prejudice of many kinds, was quickly hijacked and turned into—and this is not hyperbole—a United Nations global antisemitic conclave. Not a word of criticism was officially uttered, and no meetings were held to investigate the racism of the world's worst offending states, including all the antisemitic and brutal and mass-murderous governments in the Arab and Islamic world. Durban was instead almost wholly dominated by meeting after meeting devoted to Israel's alleged racism, replete with antisemitism, antisemitic denunciations by delegates of country after country, and, owing to this atmosphere and permissive context, also physical assaults on the street against Jews and, of course, resolutions attacking Israel and calling for its elimination. Indeed, the entire Durban Declaration names only one country for criticism: Israel. United States congressman Tom Lantos, a member of the United States' delegation and founder of the Congressional Human Rights Caucus, offered a detailed account of what went on:

> Another ring in the Durban circus was the NGO forum, taking place just outside the conference center. Although the NGO proceedings were intended to provide a platform for the wide range of civil society groups interested in the conference's conciliatory mission, the forum quickly became stacked with Palestinian and fundamentalist Arab groups. Each day, these groups organized anti-Israeli and anti-Semitic rallies around the meetings, attracting thousands. One flyer which was widely distributed showed a photograph of Hitler and the question "What if I had won?" The answer: "There would be NO Israel…." At a press conference held by Jewish NGO's to discuss their concerns with the direction the conference was taking, an accredited NGO, the Arab Lawyers Union, distributed a booklet filled with anti-Semitic caricatures frighteningly like those seen in the Nazi hate literature printed in the 1930s. Jewish leaders and I who were in Durban were shocked at this blatant display of

anti-Semitism. For me, having experienced the horrors of the Holocaust first hand, this was the most sickening and unabashed display of hate for Jews I had seen since the Nazi period.

Lantos adds that "the official NGO document that was later adopted by a majority of 3,000 NGOs in the forum branded Israel a 'racist apartheid state' guilty of 'genocide.'"[9] Durban alone—and there is much more beyond Durban—is compelling proof of the international community's and the international human-rights community's thoroughgoing antisemitism: it is, with the United Nations at its epicenter and radiating out to thousands of NGOs and to their millions of members and supporters, and with their antisemitic accusations vis-à-vis Israel and its Jews disseminated by all manner of media as though these accusations were born of impartial concern to see universal humanitarian principles applied, a global community of antisemitism. To any fair-minded person, Durban had more the character of a Nazi conclave than anything resembling an august international gathering to combat racism. The naked antisemitism in Durban was beyond anything that had hitherto been seen at a world gathering. Israel walked out. The United States withdrew its delegation. That they were the only ones that were

*Handout at the NGO Forum.*

sufficiently revolted not to want to participate shows how acceptable antisemitism had become. It is hard to imagine that, had such a bigoted hatefest been directed at any other people — black, American, French, Japanese, Christian, Palestinian — it would not have led to legions of defections. Different countries stayed with different attitudes. Some Western countries' delegates were distressed by the overwhelming, raw, and unbridled antisemitic hatred and incitement they witnessed. Yet the vast majority remained to celebrate hatred at a forum devoted to combating it — as did, demonstrably, the legions of NGOs.

The United Nations being turned into an antisemitic institution is a singular development in prejudice's history. The UN is the world's most respected and visible international institution, created to foster peace and mutual understanding and accommodation, enshrining the international human-rights doctrine and machine and, as a general principle, decrying all bigotry and prejudice; but it has been so captured by antisemitic countries, and so purposely used to further their agenda, including its eliminationist component, that it does more than any other non-media international institution to spread prejudice and animus against one people, the Jews. In a global age, the age of global antisemitism, the world's antisemitic forces quite naturally sought to capture, successfully, the leading global institution from which much of international relations, international law, international coordination, and international development takes place. What is true of the United Nations is true of its subsidiary institutions — especially its high- profile Human Rights Council — prominent people who work for it and its institutions, and international institutions more broadly. The examples are effectively endless. The UN's special rapporteur on human rights in the Palestinian territories, the American professor Richard Falk, likens the Israelis to Nazis, and in an article in 2007 called "Slouching Towards a

*The streets of Durban during the 2001 UN Antiracism Conference.*

Palestinian Holocaust," wrote that Israel "threatens to produce a new holocaust" of Palestinians in Gaza. Falk received his UN appointment in March 2008 not despite such antisemitic canards, but undoubtedly because they bolstered his qualifications for the UN post. As indefensible as Falk's fantastical characterization of Israel is, he unmistakably revealed the character of his true animus when he endorsed Gilad Atzmon's blatantly antisemitic book and posted on his website an out-and-out incendiary antisemitic cartoon, showing a ferocious American dog wearing a kippa with a Jewish star (in other words, under the control of the Jews), eating bloody human bones and urinating on blindfolded justice.[10] Falk, this overt antisemitic incitement notwithstanding, kept his position as what is supposed to be the United Nations' impartial guide to evaluating how Israelis treat Palestinians in their territories.

In April 2012, the United Nations committee devoted to supporting the Palestinians' cause against Israel convened a two-day conference, where the keynote address was delivered by the Palestinian Authority's Minister for Prisoner's Affairs, who fabricated the notion that the Israeli government was contemplating, if not planning, a genocide, asserting that "there was a call at the highest level of the Israeli state for concentration camps to be set up for the rounding up and extermination of Palestinian people." His speech, which included a litany of antisemitic accusations, including that "the Chief Rabbi of Israel" has called "for the establishment of extermination camps for Palestinians," was posted on the United Nations website,[11] which not only was a way to endorse these views, but to make them available to everyone and to spread the

*An 'impartial' UN official's antisemitic posting.*

hatred of Jews. The UN watcher Anne Bayefsky, who covered the conference, summarized:

> When the combination of U.N. experts and officials, diplomats and non-governmental participants, had finished analogizing Israelis to Nazis and Palestinians to Holocaust victims, claiming Jews have no historical ties to the land of Israel, and declaring open season on Israeli men, women, and children in the name of self-determination, Riyad Mansour, the Palestinians' lead U.N. representative, was given a final word: "We thank the U.N. for organizing this very important conference in this very important location of the U.N.... the capital and center of human rights."[12]

The self-parodic closing flourish before this dyed-in-the-wool antisemitic body was a truer-than-true and fitting ending: antisemitism effectively equals human rights.

That the United Nations' agencies are so deeply enmeshed in the propagation and promotion of antisemitism should come as no surprise because they are governed and run by the same states and their personnel that make up the antisemitic United Nations majority, the central and controlling bloc of which are the fifty-seven Arab and Islamic countries, which formally organize as the United Nations' Organisation of the Islamic Conference. And, as mentioned, the United Nations is the template for other international institutions, the model for them, or is deeply enmeshed with them. The self-styled human-rights community, with epicenters in countries and national law, holding a powerful presence in international affairs and international law, and anchored in the United Nations and its organizations, is augmented mainly by several thousand NGOs, which on the whole seek to achieve laudable goals: alleviate poverty, promote democracy, protect the rights and security of people, teach skills of various kinds, empower people economically, and more. But just as the Catholic Church or other Christian churches during the Middle Ages and modern period pursued laudable goals of bringing people to their understanding of God and saving souls, so too are many of these otherwise well-intentioned organizations beholden to an ideology of demonization and often elimination of Jews and their country. Replete with antisemitic anti-Israelism, they form part of antisemitism's international institutional infrastructure, together with the United Nations, governments, and far-reaching religions and their transnational organizations. Broad-based international and marquee NGOs, such as Human Rights Watch, which in 2004 devoted *more than one-third* of its efforts in the entire world to alleged Israeli violations, provide the overarching human-rights legitimation to this concerted assault on Israel. Movement-based and Western national NGOs, such as Christian Aid, have specific expertises and audiences that trust them and whom they reliably reach. The large and powerful bloc of Arab and Islamic NGOs are spearheaded by the many Palestinian NGOs operating in a concerted way under the umbrella organization Palestinian Non-Governmental Organizations Network, which comprises 132 NGOs. Together, they often lead the way in steering the NGO community and discourse about Israel. In turn, in their alliance with the leading and broad-based NGOs and in the other Western NGOs, they receive cover for their antisemitism, which legitimizes what might otherwise be seen as naked bad-faith politics. Together these NGOs form a vast, interlocking network, with a certain division of labor, that, in part because they are seen to be humanitarian and impartial, have their reports, statements, and attacks on Israel taken at face value and simply repeated by a credulous international media.

All in all, this extensive NGO network has devastatingly steered the international community and discourse onto an antisemitic fixation on Israel. Over one period that has been systematically assessed, the two gold-standard and discourse-setting international human-rights NGOs, Human Rights Watch and Amnesty International, almost obsessively focused human-rights condemnatory discourse on Israel. During the five years from 1999 to 2004, Amnesty International issued 380 reports on Israel, averaging about seventy-six per year, or one every five days. Before Sudan's political Islamic regime began its eliminationist and genocidal assault on Darfur that would take the lives of four hundred thousand and expel on the order of 2.5 million beginning in early 2003, it was conducting an even more destructive mass elimination and genocide in Southern Sudan, slaughtering perhaps two million people and expelling millions more. Over almost eight years Amnesty International produced fewer than thirty reports per year on this murderous regime. According to the number of noncombatant deaths and of lives utterly ruined by expulsion, Amnesty International's treatment of Israel compared to Sudan constituted an incalculable disproportionate focus of many thousands of times to one. Similarly, Human Rights Watch from the early 1990s to 2004 issued twice as many documents on democratic Israel than on Sudan, the most murderous, genocidal regime of the last quarter century, which was in the midst of slaughtering the people of Southern Sudan the entire time, during which it was also enslaving many tens of thousands of people.[13]

Can it be any surprise that, on the website of one of Finland's largest newspapers, the head of Amnesty International in Finland, Frank Johansson, characterized Israel in 2010 as a "scum state"? When challenged, he defended the appellation (which in Finland is considered "highly derogatory" and frequently translated as "scum bag" or "douche bag") as being applicable to only one country in the world: Israel. (He added that it would apply to some Russian officials, but not to Russia.) Even though he denied being an antisemite, he confirmed his antisemitic bona fides by his crude labeling and in the selectivity of his vitriol focused exclusively on the country of the Jews. Johansson said his comprehensive condemnation was based on his "personal experiences inside and outside of Israel with meeting Israelis."[14] Can it be any surprise that an NGO such as Amnesty International, which has obsessively condemned Israel and done so in such bad faith, kept him in his leading position?

Indicative of the character of NGOs, large and small and from all over the world, was their conduct and tenor at Durban. Canada's former justice minister Irwin Cotler recounts: "The atmospherics at the WCAR [World Conference Against Racism] was that of a Festival of Hate — particularly at the NGO Conference. Every 'thematic' or 'regional' tent, every street march, every demonstration, every communication or information medium, was festooned with or disseminated booklets, placards, leaflets, bumper stickers that proclaimed Israel's 'Racism', 'criminality', and 'illegality', with the notion of Israel as an Apartheid state having particular resonance in South Africa."[15] The template laid down and solidified at the forum, which was a vast international conclave of the who's who of NGOs as well as legions of NGO lesser lights, put the demonization of Israel and its Jews at the absolute center of concerns, and turned going along with, if not adopting, such a stance into a sine qua non of NGO good standing. It also turned the antisemitic demonizing and political targeting of Israel into the one cause around which NGOs, whatever their other many differences, can rally. Of course, for people who enter or work in such organizations who might otherwise not begin with strong views about Jews and Israel, surrounded by likeminded people devoted to fighting poverty or bringing democracy to undemocratic countries, the antisemitic milieu becomes powerfully persuasive. Would so many good-hearted people devoting themselves to the well-being of others be wrong about Jews and Israel? And let's not underestimate in such circumstances the power of self-justification, the power of not wanting to think oneself unjust, so that when people find themselves in such a milieu, having to participate, and without perhaps having well-formed or powerful views about Israel that depart from the norm and without institutional support for them—but precisely the opposite—they find themselves more quickly or slowly coming to genuinely accept the paradigm of antisemitic prejudice and its many elaborate and wild notions. Such is the nature of the spread of prejudice and of antisemitism in particular.

Some might think that in 2001 the antisemitic character of Durban came about because of an unusual confluence of contingent features, because there was not adequate leadership or enough oversight. Yet the subsequent conduct of the NGOs and of the United Nations—including their antisemitic fixation on Israel—belies such notions. The effects of Durban, and the ongoing concerted campaigns to delegitimize and demonize Israel and its Jews, to present them as the new Nazis, have powerfully inflamed Western domestic antisemitic expression, as European Jewish leaders across the continent attest. Recent events further show that Durban was not an aberration but the new normal.

Durban II was a conference held in 2009 at the United Nations offices in Geneva to review the implementation of the resolutions and principles promulgated at Durban I. Although it was not meant to be a large antiracism festival similar to the original Durban conference, the nine most anti-antisemitic governments in the world, including Israel, the United States, and Germany, nevertheless boycotted it, and most European countries sent low-level delegations. The boycotters had good reason for their refusal to participate. Durban II was organized by United Nations leadership to follow the unabashed antisemitic blueprint of

Durban I, and it did. Iran's leader, Mahmoud Ahmadinejad, perhaps the most internationally influential and notorious antisemite in the world today, graced the conference's opening day with his usual mix of antisemitism, Holocaust denial, and demonization of Israel. He attacked Israel, then the region's only democracy, as a country of "genocidal racists" and preached that "global Zionism is the complete symbol of racism." In the expanded text of the speech Ahmadinejad handed out at the conference, he called for "eradicating this barbaric racism," by which he meant "world Zionism." In a passage of Nazi-like rank antisemitism, Ahmadinejad declared:

> The egoist and uncivilized Zionism have been able to deeply penetrate into their political and economic structure including their legislation, mass media, companies, financial systems, and their security and intelligence agencies. They have imposed their domination to the extent that nothing can be done against their will.... So long as Zionist domination continues, many countries, governments and nations will never be able to enjoy freedom, independence and security. As long as they are at the helm of power, justice will never prevail in the world and human dignity will continue to be offended and trampled upon. It is time the ideal of Zionism, which is the paragon of racism, to be broken.

Ahmadinejad further put his stamp on his speech by again invoking and embedding a world Jewish conspiracy in a compacted series of classic antisemitic tropes: "The world Zionism personifies racism that falsely resorts to religion and abuse[s] religious sentiments to hide their hatred and ugly faces."[16]

What was the institutional response to Ahmadinejad's blatant racism at the United Nations' antiracism conference? To attack the victims. When two Jewish NGOs and one anti-Ahmadinejad Iranian NGO protested Ahmadinejad's racism, the United Nations kicked them out of the conference, revoking their members' credentials. This followed the pattern set down at one of the original Durban preparatory conferences for the NGO Forum held in Tehran, under the antisemitic political Islamic Iranian regime, which barred Jewish and Israeli human-rights delegates, and which produced the infamous preliminary document that accused Israel of "committing holocausts" (note the plural) and of itself "being anti-Semitic."[17] At the end, Navi Pillay, the notorious anti-Israel antisemite UN High Commissioner for Human Rights, after the world's most murderous and criminal regimes had given speeches to denounce Israel and themselves received no criticism, declared Durban II an enormous success.

Durban III, held in New York in September 2011, was meant to be more of the same, an official commemoration of Durban I, and it was. Thirteen countries boycotted this latest United Nations antisemitic hatefest allegedly devoted to fighting racism, with the United States' representative explaining that "the United States will not participate in the Durban Commemoration. In December, we voted against the resolution establishing this event because the Durban process included ugly displays of intolerance and anti-Semitism, and we did not want to see that commemorated." But it was commemorated by most of the world, as it has been for decades including before Durban I, with the world's premier international institution the United Nations stamping it with its august authority's approval. Most people assume that the United Nations stands on the side of the oppressed and for justice, and so, sadly, the continuous grind of the antisemitism that it issues, and the spectacular moments of focused antisemitic conferences, festivals, reports, resolutions, and condemnations which often receive immense worldwide media attention, damages enormously and prejudicially Jews and Israel.

The media assault on Israel and its Jews has no more prominent example than Al Jazeera, the satellite and Internet television and information behemoth that is the tool of its owner the Qatar state. Al Jazeera beams all over the Middle East and, in an English-language version on cable and satellite, around the world, including in most European countries and ever more in the United States, as well as streaming live on the Internet in Arabic and in English. Its purposeful and systematic antisemitic agitation and demonization of Israel has helped cement in people's minds everywhere that the antisemitic charges against Israel and its Jews are to be believed. Al Jazeera's credibility on this matter, which has been fortuitous for buttressing the antisemitic discourse's power, has been enhanced by its pioneering and critical stance toward the dictatorial Arab and political Islamic regimes that once uniformly ruled the Middle East. If Al Jazeera tells the truth like no one else (certainly in the Arab and Islamic world) about these governments, so goes the thinking, then why should we not believe it regarding the Jews and Israel? In Arab and Islamic countries this added credibility for demonizing Israel and validating the foundational antisemitic paradigm and its particular elaborations has been icing on the cake because such notions were already solidly central in public discourse and private belief. But for the rest of the world, especially Europe, where such notions are less universal, less firm, more contested, such a "credible" television and Internet network substantially influences people's understanding, inflames their emotions, solidifies their animus, and shapes the public discourse, of which it is a significant part.

Government after government in Arab and Middle Eastern countries have had their own media networks, and with the transition from old-style dictatorships in many countries to new regimes of various kinds, new stations, such as the Muslim Brotherhood's in Egypt, have gained influence. Significantly, in the four areas of greatest confrontation with Israel, and which may be the most crucial for any possible resolution of the Middle East conflict — Palestinian Authority–governed West Bank, Hamas-ruled Gaza, Hezbollah-dominated Lebanon, and political Islamic Iran — each ruling regime's broadcast network is Nazi-like in its antisemitism, explicitly demonizing Israel, explicitly demonizing its Jews, and explicitly demonizing Jews in general. This is also true of other regime-run or -influenced media, including daily newspapers, and the non-regime-run media, which is subject to each regime's often heavy-handed influence. Beyond these areas, in country after country, state-run media — television, radio, newspapers, magazines, and Internet — are virulently antisemitic, purposively spreading the official state antisemitic doctrine, focusing on Israel and its Jews but also openly or tacitly discursively blackening the image of Jews in general.

State-sponsored antisemitism's effects at home are also consequential abroad. In our global world, with grass-roots global flows of all kinds, a state spreading and intensifying bigotry among its own people can have, and regarding antisemitism demonstrably has, a large cumulative effect in other countries and internationally. It creates more participants for the antisemitic discourse, on both the producer and the consumer side. The more people who are antisemitic, the more they spread their antisemitism to others, including today over the Internet—on websites, and through the ever-proliferating social media. The vast numbers of people, including immigrants, flowing from the most dedicated antisemitic countries to lesser and less-intensively antisemitic countries, bring their worldviews and their passions with them, which augments their new countries' antisemitic numbers, increases their strength, and deepens the antisemitic discourse. This has been evident the world over, as people from Arab and Islamic countries have migrated out around the world, though most tellingly to Europe, where throughout the continent they now form a powerful antisemitic bloc and have demonstrably increased the hostility to Israel and to local Jews and also imperiled the Jews' safety. Significantly enough, while most Europeans have adhered to global antisemitism's norms of not publicly attacking their own country's Jews, either rhetorically with old-style antisemitic charges or physically, the Arab and Islamic antisemites in Europe have shown no such restraint. As they make little to no distinction between Israel's Jews and Jews elsewhere, they combat the demonized Jews everywhere. Moreover, to them, at least those who still see their countries of origin as their real homes, Europe's Jews are Jews abroad and are responsible for Israel's and its Jews' predations.

Whatever common views Arab and Islamic antisemites in Europe share with European majorities regarding Jews, the restraints that many in Europe impose on themselves or feel imposed on them by public norms (owing to the identification of classic antisemitic charges with the Nazis and the Holocaust), are weak to nonexistent among Arab and Islamic antisemites across Europe. Nineteen million Muslims populate the European Union, composing almost 4 percent of the population, and only 1.1 million Jews, not even one-half a percent. Muslims' sway as voting and lobbying blocs, not to mention on the street, often organized through religious institutions or with foreign-state sponsorship, has also been growing. Even though prejudice in Europe against Muslims is considerable, many Europeans and Muslims share common ground and find common cause regarding Israel and often even Jews, including the foundational antisemitic paradigm. (Even for those who find the Islamic and Muslim antisemitism excessive, defending Jews is not an issue that merits having conflict with impassioned Muslim communities.)

Religious institutions also form part of global antisemitism's institutional structure and sinews. Many in the Islamic world are state sponsored or influenced, or exist with state understanding that they may or should spread antisemitism. Such is the case with the Wahhabi Sunni madrassas (religious educational institutions), which the Saudi government sponsors or supports inside and outside Saudi Arabia, including in Europe, where these antisemitically radical institutions have, owing to Saudi governmental funding, crowded out Islam's more moderate, tolerant branches. The Saudis have constructed fifteen hundred such madrassas around the world, financing them and their operations, including their teaching materials, with perhaps as much as one hundred billion dollars over the last two decades. The Saudis and others intently focus such efforts on non–Arab and Islamic countries. The Saudis also fund Islamic schools in the United Kingdom, which use antisemitic texts (violating British law) and inculcate the conventional Islamic antisemitism into their students, most of whom are British or will become so, shaping the British public discourse and exercising their voices in United Kingdom policy making. One partial investigation found that Saudi textbooks in use in at least forty British Islamic schools and clubs in 2010 promoted dehumanizing and demonizing antisemitism, including the notion that Jews descend from "monkeys" and "pigs," and tasking the schoolchildren to list the "reprehensible qualities of Jews,"[18] all the more effective because the children are asked to think hard about all the antisemitic things they have learned or heard about Jews. As discussed earlier, various Christian denominations, including the Catholic Church, often without malicious intention but knowingly nonetheless, still spread antisemitism in scripture, theology, doctrine, teachings, declarations, and preachings both verbal and written. Many Christian denominations' and individual religious leaders' renewed participation in and sustenance of the antisemitic discourse have partly reversed decades of progress in repudiating or deemphasizing Christianity's antisemitic component. Many such churches are transnational or international institutions, and the Christian bible, like the Qur'an and the Hadith, is a transnational, indeed a global, work, informing hundreds of millions if not billions, which churches present as the word of God thereby, without such intent, consecrating its antisemitism as sacred.

Secular educational institutions are another significant institutional pillar of global antisemitism. Even in the United States many university campuses have become enormously hostile to Israel and its Jews and, if only by seemingly natural extension, to Jews more generally. Middle Eastern Studies, the association of scholars in academia for studying the region, including Israel, is a bastion of antisemitic anti-Israelism. Ever more academic chairs and funding come from Saudi and other sources opposed to Israel's existence. Middle Eastern Studies is so hostile to Israel and Jews that young scholars who fail to toe a radical anti-Israel line would face enormous obstacles to acquiring academic posts in the field. This, of course, means that what is being taught at universities around the world, what is being inculcated into the students and citizens of country after country, is often radical anti-Israelism and, at best, coded antisemitism. It is no surprise that with such mentors, but also driven by youthful leftist idealism, antisemitism and antisemitic initiatives against Israel find no more hospitable place than universities, which have created such a hostile environment for Jews and for ordinary expressions of Jewish life and political activity that many Jewish students report being intimidated on campus. In 2011, 43 percent of Jewish students in American universities reported general antisemitism on their campuses as well as anti-Israelism in the classroom.[19] It is in universities that the antisemitic BDS movement to boycott Israel—its economy and products, its scholars and people, the country itself—is most powerful, and exists, among the professoriate and students alike. Of course, such academic developments of the last two decades should cause additional concern for anyone not supporting antisemitism, as the professors who spearhead such movements are becoming ever bolder in activating a public antisemitic discourse by writing in newspapers, appearing on radio and television, participating in social media, et cetera. The students imbued with these views, including those at elite universities, gradually move into positions of ever greater social and political standing and influence, creating an ever more receptive and tolerant milieu for antisemitism's expression and further spread in public discourses and public life.

Global antisemitism's institutional pillars interlock and intersect in various ways. Politics and its leaders, media and its opinion makers, religion and its authoritative clergy, academia and its wise men and mentors, which form global antisemitism's many institutions and people, all contribute to the spread and reinforcement of antisemitism domestically and globally. States, the principal and most powerful institutional actors, take a hand at all levels. Nowhere can this integration be better seen, and nowhere is it more pronounced today, than in many Arab and Islamic countries and areas, from Iran and Saudi Arabia to Lebanon, West Bank and Gaza, to Egypt. There antisemitism's vertical integration through state leadership and state policy of demonizing Israel and Jews and centrally pursuing hostile or eliminationist policies against them, which permeates the media, subjects the populace to a continuous stream of antisemitic content and invective. It runs through religious institutions as a prominent feature of how to understand good and evil, how to achieve salvation, and what good Muslims ought to work for, with Friday prayers providing a weekly forum for antisemitic agitation to the assembled (often in huge numbers) faithful. It is a core element at all levels of educational curricula and teaching.

These sorts of institutional integration and alliance, which take place both within given countries and internationally, are not the only kind. Alliances and mutual reinforcement also exist among institutions of the different streams of antisemitism. The alliances, as we have seen, sometimes make for strange bedfellows, but the power of shared enmity to paper over profound differences and antagonisms has been one of anti-semitism's hallmarks historically and in the contemporary world. So there is by now a firm and decades-long alliance, if perhaps only tacit, between Christian antisemites and Arab and Islamic antisemites, in which each incorporates elements of the other's litany of antisemitic accusations and tropes into their own messages. In July 2000, perhaps at the time of greatest Palestinian hope for a peace agreement with Israel, Palestinian TV broadcast artist's Yasser Abu Ciedo's portrayal of Christians' and Palestinians' age-old and eternal conflict with Jews: "Our struggle today against the other (Israel) is an eternal one. It started 2000 years ago and continues until today. I demonstrate this through the figure of Jesus, who came to the world with a message of justice and the other side did what they did to him. Here [he shows a painting] I demonstrate the following idea: the Israeli soldiers are wearing army uniforms while Jesus has nothing except for the truth. This is the Palestinian from the beginning of the struggle until its end—if it will ever end." A decade later, in December 2010, Fatah's Palestinian TV, picking up the theme of Jesus the Palestinian and today's Palestinians' symbiotic martyrdom, broadcast a religious interview program with author Samih Ghanadreh:

> **Ghanadreh:** The Shahid (Martyr) President Yasser Arafat used to say that Jesus was the first Palestinian Shahid (Martyr); I heard that phrase from him many times.
>
> **PA TV Host:** He [Jesus] was a Palestinian; no one denies that.
>
> **Ghanadreh:** He was the first Palestinian Shahid. In other words, he [Arafat] attributed this Shahada [Jesus' Martyrdom], too, to Palestine.[20]

Thus we see Arab and Islamic antisemites, who otherwise consider Christians also to be infidels and with whom they have ongoing conflict, eagerly adopt and regularly repeat the most powerful antisemitic charge of all time, that Jews murdered Jesus, and a host of subsidiary Christian-based accusations against Jews, as well as pointing to Christians' antisemitic and eliminationist acts over the centuries as proof positive of the predations of Jews and as models of how to deal with them. In turn, Christian antisemites adopt and tacitly accept the antisemitic Palestinian, Arab, and Islamic account of the Palestinians' plight as their own, which includes a fair quantity of Jesus-like tropes and imagery, put most pointedly as that of Palestinians as crucified or martyred at the hands of Jews. In what may be a signal moment of this, symbolizing its merging into a Christian antisemitic politics, a Scottish Baptist minister invited in 2010 to give a devotional address to Scottish members of Parliament, "spoke about the hope of Christmas being found in the birth of another Palestinian child, born a refugee, living under military occupation."[21] Even an American middle-school social-studies textbook, *The World,* has adopted this fictive stance, stating that "Christianity was started by a young Palestinian named Jesus."[22]

The antisemitic alliance that takes place thoroughly on the discursive level also extends to institutional cooperation and support. The Catholic Church's hostility to Israel and Jews' political existence in Israel, which is self-condemning in light of the Church's horrifying role in promoting antisemitism and persecuting Jews, including during the Holocaust, is long standing and, though considerably tempered, continues to this day. In this sense, the Catholic Church has, probably mainly unwittingly, given enormous succor to the eliminationism that is the commonplace among

Arab and Islamic antisemites. In doing so, the Church has clearly made a strategic, as well as perhaps a heartfelt, decision to sacrifice Jews' well-being on the altar of its foreign policy, which is focused on supporting Catholics in Arab countries and gaining converts from Islam wherever it can, and in not further intensifying the simmering conflict between the Church and Muslims. A signal moment of the Church tacitly or explicitly supporting antisemitism occurred in 2001. Pope John Paul II in important ways tried to improve the Church's stance toward Jews, including by becoming in 1986 the first pope ever to visit a synagogue when he went to the Great Synagogue of Rome and there publicly declaring Jews to be "our elder brothers."[23] Nevertheless, John Paul II stood by as the mass murderer and dictator of Syria Bashar al-Assad portrayed him as his ally against Israel and Jews in general. With the pope at his side, Assad unleashed an antisemitic diatribe that was televised to the entire Christian world. Jews, Assad conveyed in the most demonizing and dehumanizing of terms, are the ontological enemies of God. They oppose "heavenly tenets" and "try to kill all the principles of divine faiths." Assad even, or perhaps, in the world of global antisemitism, "naturally," invoked the Christian blood libel of Jews as Christ-killers, and hitching Islam to Christianity, claimed that just as Jews "betrayed" and "tortured" Jesus, the Jews "in the same way" also "tried to commit treachery against Prophet Mohammad." Regardless of having certainly found some of this offensive, and its expression in such a blatant form deeply at odds with the Church's own pubic stance, neither John Paul II nor other Church officials walked out on, tried to stop, or took issue with this most blatant and damaging antisemitic poisoning of the minds of millions, which the pope's presence seemed to consecrate in interfaith unanimity.[24]

Politics, pressure, institutional interests, money, natural affinities, cynical exploitation, genuine belief. All these work together to create an enormous and powerful web of incentives for institutional and group cooperation and alliances in promoting, furthering, spreading, and deepening antisemitism, for mobilizing support behind other kinds of antisemitic stances and actions, for creating a reservoir of antisemites who can form the political and social support for such action, and for creating a stable and extensive institutional foundation for ensuring that the global antisemitic discourse will be robust and perpetuated, will be political and strategic.

In fact, today a higher proportion of antisemitism serves broader political goals, and this politics' global strategic orientation, when added to global antisemitism's inherently incendiary quality, has made antisemitism today particularly dangerous for Jews just about anywhere. All Jews, because they are Jews, and because they are Israel's imputed supporters — for both reasons — are fair game around the world. All over Europe, Jews, communally and individually, as they fear walking the streets with visible marks of their Jewishness, live in a state of siege, with their institutions guarded like fortresses because otherwise they would be subjected to violence, including being bombed or set ablaze. This is also true of smaller South American Jewish communities, from which many of their members have emigrated owing to the violence. Only in the United States do Jews not feel wary or not threatened in their cities, homes, and streets. Canada, for example, a country much more like the United States than European countries are, with a more similar *relatively* benign history of its treatment of Jews, is considered to be among the most pluralistic and tolerant countries in the world. Yet Canada has a rate of attacks upon Jews proportionate to the country's overall population that is almost ten times higher than in the United States. If measured by the number of Jews in each country, the similar absolute number of antisemitic incidents means that the Jews of Canada are afflicted at roughly twenty times the rate of Jews in the United States. Jews of Canada, France, Germany, and elsewhere in Europe, Jews of Argentina, Chile, Venezuela, and elsewhere in South America, and Jews elsewhere around the world are not reacting to imaginary threats or dangers. Attacks on Jews in Europe — which necessitate around-the-clock police protection for their communal buildings — could give the impression that they are even more frequent today than in the years before the Holocaust, especially in proportion to the enormously diminished size of the contemporary Jewish communities! The situation in Arab and Islamic countries is so far gone that it is not even thinkable for Jews in any large number to live in them — they would in any case not be welcomed. In fact, the hostility and danger to Jews is so great that the number of countries no longer hospitable to Jews has reached an all-time high — and has no parallel or even near parallel for any other people.

Not only have Jews been the objects of attacks and threats of attack by local peoples, whether neo-Nazis and skinheads in Germany and northern

Europe or Muslims in France and all over Europe, but they also live under the specter of terrorist attack, as few if any other people do. Palestinians and political Islamists invented international terrorism, and its most fearsome form of genocide (aka suicide) bombing, specifically to assault and strike fear into Jews. Unceasing terrorism has targeted Israel and Jewish Israelis since the late 1960s, though its effectiveness has waxed and waned, and more concerted genocide bombing has targeted them than any other country or people, except perhaps in the last decade in Iraq.

The most emblematic moment, and the moment when the multiple strands of the danger that Jews face owing to global antisemitism could also be seen, was back in Durban in 2001: South Africa is far from the center of old antisemitism, whether Christian, Islamic, or modern racist. It is a full continent away from the Middle East conflict. It has a notable, if small, Jewish community, then numbering about seventy thousand in a country of forty-five million, which had been known to be, among the whites, liberal and far more anti-apartheid than the Afrikaner majority. For the United Nations antiracism conference, tight security greeted presidents and prime ministers, the international diplomatic community, and many other dignitaries who came to South Africa, affording it its first real chance to be a showpiece country for the world. What happened? In addition to being, as we have already seen, an international coalescing of global antisemitism's forces and discourse, a United Nations–organized assault on Israel and Jews, it became a symbolic and actual pogrom of sorts and produced a pervasive sense of justifiable physical insecurity for Jews in the street, as there were physical assaults upon them. Even a few attacks strike fear into an entire community in our media-driven, global antisemitic, age, when antisemitic assaults in one country can be experienced as an attack on Jews everywhere. This is particularly so when such antisemitic violence takes place under the auspices of the United Nations and the international community itself.

The greatest danger to Jews goes well beyond these local actual and potential assaults afflicting or endangering Jews like no other people, almost everywhere in the world. The form of the ongoing multiple eliminationist threats to Israel's existence and the desire of various governments — most notably of nuclear-arming political Islamic Iran — and peoples to eliminate Israel and its people imperils Jews collectively and on a grand scale. To global antisemites, because the problem is international and political and colossal, the solution must be international and political and colossal. The problem includes the existence of a country deemed demonic, dangerous, delegitimized, and fit for destruction, which makes Jews the perpetrators of one of the worst transgressions, if not the worst, in the world. Jews in Israel and Jews everywhere, or certainly those who support Israel, which antisemites presume Jews do, are essentially — according to the global antisemitic discourse's text and subtext — in a state of war with humanity and goodness. So, the means to be used against them, and the means actually used, have in principle no limits. And never before has antisemitism been so openly and diversely eliminationist in its rhetoric — not even during the Nazi period, when Germany and an international genocidal coalition of governments and people were carrying out a full-scale genocide, yet did not so clearly broadcast their intentions, let alone their deeds, to the world. Global antisemitism brings together the major streams of antisemitism's diverse eliminationist impulses into a loose and sometimes not so loose informal eliminationist coalition, where what needs to be eliminated and the accepted means may vary but the overall eliminationist impulse or goal does not.

For its part, Christianity's eliminationist underpinning and supersessionist and doctrinal core, it must be emphasized, remains today predominantly latent and — aside from the confines of regular liturgical, theological, and doctrinal presentations, which focus on the nullification of Judaism by Christianity — when articulated as part of the larger public discourse, speaks mainly about Israel, and generally in a quiet and measured voice. (Many Christian churches, owing to the Holocaust, have formally stopped proselytizing Jews.) Yet it retains the potential to be galvanized and to become much more publicly explicit, strident, and expansive in its demands. It could do so as part of the global antisemitic complex and it might find enormous resonance — given the hundreds of millions of Christians whose thinking is grounded in the foundational Christian antisemitic paradigm. This just points to global antisemitism's further incendiary potential, which is greatly underestimated — indeed, it is hardly recognized — in public discourse. Time and again, antisemitism, of which there is currently a vast reservoir, has been rapidly and unpredictably activated, bursting forth and being translated into program and action, taking just about everyone by surprise.

The radical political right's antisemitism regarding Jews is deeply rooted in the Christian foundational antisemitic paradigm and has repeatedly drawn explicitly on Christian notions and tropes about Jews, often grounding its attacks in Christian thought and teachings, which it has regularly taken to extremes. The radical antisemitic right has for a long time been openly and aggressively eliminationist. Nevertheless, it is even more appropriate to see the radical right's bearing toward Jews as the heir of modern racist antisemitism, specifically of Nazism. Most critically, as we saw earlier, it formed and forms the eliminationist bridge between Christian antisemitism and Islamic and Arab antisemitism, infusing the once generally nonmurderous Islamic antisemitic tradition with radical right and Nazified notions about Jews and the need to extirpate them, infusing the age-old Islamic antisemitic stream with a new, far more threatening image of Jews and a far more lethal set of desires, policy potential, and, on the part of many, program. While the political right's antisemitism retains, almost as a matter of course, an eliminationist orientation toward Jews, sometimes, as in Hungary, focusing on local Jews (it is the only major antisemitic stream that does this), its current eliminationist contribution to global antisemitism remains more parochial and of relatively less importance than that of the others. This, of course, includes the bulk of Western Holocaust deniers, who themselves often seek to justify explicitly or implicitly the past and current need to eliminate the Jews.

The antisemitism of the political left and the international human-rights community, fully engaged in the discourse of the five *d*'s, is differently eliminationist. It overwhelmingly targets Israel in global antisemitism's anti-Israel vein, calling in various ways for the country's *destruction,* whether by implication in *demonizing* it and wildly exaggerating the *danger* it poses to Palestinians and others, by indirection in calls for the chimeric one-state solution (a code word for Israel's destruction), or openly *delegitimizing* Israel by asserting that it has no right to exist and the Jews have no right to be there. Left antisemites by and large do not spell out the means of such elimination, but their support (this includes many Europeans) for the eliminationist, even openly exterminationist, Arab and Islamic governments, groups, and people, and their contributions to the antisemitic and eliminationist discourse more generally, reveal their comfort with the thrust of such messages, planning, programs, and deeds.

The final, most forceful, and most dangerous eliminationist stream within global antisemitism is the open, aggressive, relentless, and lethal Arab and Islamic one. It is global eliminationism's leading component, even without all other global antisemites subscribing to it chapter and verse. The mere existence of a robust discussion about possibly destroying Israel already substantially legitimizes such a horrifying discourse and makes such thoughts and such planning conceivable and plausible.

Global antisemitism is strongly, though not exclusively, eliminationist. Its various major streams contribute in contrasting and complementary ways to this most radical form of prejudice and hatred. Global antisemitism presents a continual bombardment of threats of elimination, extinction, and mass murder. Verbal annihilation is common. And it has inured people the world over to accept it, as it is hardly commented upon. Since prior to the 1967 Six Day War, when Egyptian dictator Gamal Abdel Nasser repeatedly threatened to drive the Jews into the sea, perhaps the only time that even those who are not eliminationist and not antisemitic have publicly and forcefully recoiled was when at the end of 2005 Mahmoud Ahmadinejad successively threatened to wipe Israel off the map and denied the Holocaust. Indeed, curiously and significantly in the public global discourse, Holocaust denial appears to be deemed a more serious transgression than threatening another Holocaust. As we have seen, Arab and Islamic antisemites, including political and religious leaders and other men of prominence, speak and write regularly of the need and intention to annihilate Israel and mass-murder Jews in Israel and beyond. This hardly gets a notice in the rest of the world and certainly does not elicit concerted outrage and condemnation.

The most stunning example of the stream of such exterminationist threats is one that has not merely been uttered in general terms but that an authoritative, high-level Iranian political leader has publicly put forward as detailed operational plans for the annihilation of Israel and its Jews. On February 3, 2012, Iranian supreme leader Ali Khamenei characterized Israel during his Friday speech to be a "cancerous tumor"—itself an eliminationist metaphor—"that must be removed." Coming from Iran's supreme ruler, as Iran drives to acquire nuclear weapons, this is already a major genocidal threat, which he had, among other times, clearly stated as a New Year's greeting in 2000 to usher in the new millennium: "There is only one solution to the Middle East problem, namely the annihilation and destruction of the Jewish state."[25] Yet no outcry ensued in the West.

The next day, in what appears to be a transparently coordinated move, former governor of Iran's Kish province Alireza Forghani, a steadfast supporter of his Imam Khamenei, published an article in Farsi and English versions that was quickly reproduced by multiple proregime media and websites, including the authoritative Fars News Agency. The article called for Iran to attack and annihilate Israel, which he grounded as a religious duty based in the Qur'an and the teachings of Ayatollah Ruhollah Khomeini that must be carried out. Forghani lays down the specifics—including weapons and targets for how Iran would completely obliterate Israel, its military capabilities, its entire civilian infrastructure, and all its people. He explains how this utter destruction could be accomplished, using Iran's missiles, "in less than nine minutes." One characteristic portion reads: "Residents of Tel Aviv, Jerusalem, and H[a]ifa can be targeted even by Shah[a]b 3 [missiles]. Population density in these three adjacent areas composes about 60% of [the total] Israeli population. Sejjil missiles can target power plants, sewage treatment facilities, energy resources, [and] transportation and [communication] infrastructures; and in the second stage, Shahab 3, Ghadr, and Ashura missiles can target urban settlements until [the] final annihilation of Israel['s] people." Yes, the Iranian's plan is to target not just military targets but "urban settlements" in an explicit program of mass murder. So that no one would mistake the exterminationist intention for anything else, Forghani, and all those Iranian sites that disseminated the operational plans to Iranians and the world, take pains to make the explicitly genocidal character of the plans clear. Forghani itemizes the number of people the Iranians would target for extermination in each of Israel's major regions:

- Northern District (Mehoz HaTzafon). Population: 1,231,900; District capital: Nazareth
- Haifa District (Mehoz Heifa). Population: 880,700; District capital: Haifa
- Central District (Mehoz HaMerkaz). Population: 1,770,000; District capital: Ramla
- Tel Aviv District (Mehoz Tel Aviv). Population: 1,227,900; District capital: Tel Aviv
- Jerusalem District (Mehoz Yerushalayim). Population: 907,300; District capital: Jerusalem

• Southern District (Mehoz HaDarom). Population: 1,201,200; District capital: Beersheba

This itemized list of people whom Forghani proposes to slaughter totals more than seven million. That it is intended as a second Holocaust is explicit as Forghani declares that the "Israeli people must be annihilated."[26] All this is eerily reminiscent, perhaps not by accident, of the Wannsee Protocol, the record of the meeting in January 1942 at which the Nazi leadership detailed the further operations in the already ongoing program to exterminate all of European Jewry, which included a country-by-country itemized list of the number of Jews the Germans intended to kill, which they calculated to be more than eleven million. The Wannsee

| Land | Zahl |
|---|---|
| A. Altreich | 131.800 |
| Ostmark | 43.700 |
| Ostgebiete | 420.000 |
| Generalgouvernement | 2.284.000 |
| Bialystok | 400.000 |
| Protektorat Böhmen und Mähren | 74.200 |
| Estland        - judenfrei - | |
| Lettland | 3.500 |
| Litauen | 34.000 |
| Belgien | 43.000 |
| Dänemark | 5.600 |
| Frankreich / Besetztes Gebiet | 165.000 |
| Unbesetztes Gebiet | 700.000 |
| Griechenland | 69.600 |
| Niederlande | 160.800 |
| Norwegen | 1.300 |
| B. Bulgarien | 48.000 |
| England | 330.000 |
| Finnland | 2.300 |
| Irland | 4.000 |
| Italien einschl. Sardinien | 58.000 |
| Albanien | 200 |
| Kroatien | 40.000 |
| Portugal | 3.000 |
| Rumänien einschl. Bessarabien | 342.000 |
| Schweden | 8.000 |
| Schweiz | 18.000 |
| Serbien | 10.000 |
| Slowakei | 88.000 |
| Spanien | 6.000 |
| Türkei (europ. Teil) | 55.500 |
| Ungarn | 742.800 |
| UdSSR | 5.000.000 |
| Ukraine        2.994.684 | |
| Weißrußland aus-schl. Bialystok        446.484 | |
| Zusammen:        über | 11.000.000 |

*The Nazis' plans: itemizing the Jews to be exterminated.*

Protocol is perhaps the most chilling authoritative document in human history. If so, Forghani's detailing the more than seven million Jews the Iranians would exterminate might be a close second. And unlike the Germans' plan, which the Germans sought to hide from public view, the Iranians, with multiple full-color targeting maps and photos of the missiles to be used, broadcast this annihilative blueprint in English to the world.

We might have thought that such a semiofficial plan so reminiscent of the Germans' plan for the Holocaust would stir a world outcry, especially coming the day after Khamenei publicly expressed his genocidal ideal, and coming but a few months after the Iranian armed forces chief of staff Major General Hassan Firouzabadi declared, "The Iranian nation is standing for its cause that is the full annihilation of Israel," suggesting that this detailed genocidal blueprint is meant seriously.[27] But there was hardly a peep. Partly because the West and the world have become inured to the regular calls for mass murder directed at Jews. Partly because antisemitism is so powerful around the world among governments and media alike. Had such a detailed plan from a political leader—fleshing out the previous day's announcement of a genocidal intention by the country's supreme leader—been so prominently and brazenly published targeting another group, say, Christians in the Middle East or the people of Poland by, say, Russia or the people of Taiwan by China, the ensuing storm would have been fierce.

Christians' antisemitism is eliminationist in generally subdued tones and focuses mainly on all Jews, with but secondary though more public concerns for Israel. Leftists' and the human-rights community's antisemitism is eliminationist in overt ways, invoking the high-minded language of justice and rights, and focuses on Israel, while decidedly trying to stay away from Jews in general, even if it explicitly supports aspects of the more conventional and murderously oriented Arab and Islamic antisemitism. The rightists' eliminationism is more locally oriented, as they tend to be nationalists (less concerned with international affairs) and interested in safeguarding and purifying the nation narrowly conceived, and they come out of a violent and murderous antisemitic tradition, which their discourse reflects. Arab and Islamic antisemitism is the most explicitly and violently eliminationist, indeed openly murderous, unabashedly so regarding Israel and only slightly less so regarding its Jews, and even Jews in general.

The global antisemitic discourse thus has a diversity of eliminationist chords from the major antisemitic movements—all explicitly eliminationist for the first time or as never before—varying (aside from the myriad justifications) on three dimensions: which Jews or expressions of Jewness are targeted, how strident and explicit they are, and what eliminationist means are implied or specified. These differences notwithstanding, they all contribute to global antisemitic discourse's powerful overall eliminationist orientation. We live in an age of social and political efficacy and transformation, so the more powerful a prejudice is, the more likely it will be not confined to mere verbal expression but be oriented to politics and transformative action, and when the implications are eliminationist, so too will the orientation and policy desires be. Antisemitism's partly explicit and partly tacit global international eliminationist alliance must be recognized for being just that. Those participating in it should not be allowed to wiggle out by saying, well, we do not support the annihilation of the Jews of Israel, but only of the country itself and only by creating one majoritarian Palestinian state. The unwillingness of governments and opinion leaders to condemn Arab and Islamic antisemites' brazen eliminationist and exterminationist discourse, practices, and planning bespeaks a silent assent, or a failure to find the underlying animus, or even the more threatening pronouncements against Israel and Jews sufficiently abhorrent. Antisemites around the globe know that they choose to run with the devil and play with fire.

From the full menu and amalgam of antisemitic prejudice coursing around the web at Jew Watch and the thousands upon thousands of other sites; to the countries, societies, cultures, and subcultures discoursing their particular streams of antisemitism, whether it is Arab or Islamic, Christian, left, internationalist human rights, or right in its version and emphasis; to the transnational intensive anti-Israel antisemitic barrage; to the incessant demonization and delegitimization of Israel and politicization of anti-Jewish passion and animus; to this being both the substructure of prejudice around the world and its most spectacular agglomeration of superstructures of prejudice; to the hundreds upon hundreds of millions of adherents who can agree on the foundational antisemitic paradigm, who abhor Jewness, and who share an eliminationist orientation toward Jews; to the ever more widespread singular notion embodied in *The Protocols of the Elders of Zion,* which, given its ubiquity, is that much more powerfully resistant to being falsified and abandoned, that Jews act conspiratorially, hidden, behind the scenes in ways that cannot be seen; to the siegelike condition of Jewish communities and people in country after country; to the growing physical attacks on Jews; to the habituation of the discursive sphere and the world more generally to calls for Israel's or Jews' elimination and destruction; to the desire and the work of many to wipe out the political home and the political life of Jews; global antisemitism has all the elements, all the features, all the power of a most fearsome, enduring, and powerful ideology and movement. It has not even been recognized and conceptualized as such because of the many features of antisemitism that lead to such perceptual and rhetorical denial; it needs a name and a focus, and it must be combated. Global antisemitism has to be fought directly and concertedly in part because it is being supported and furthered directly and concertedly, though not always openly, by people, institutions, and governments. It is time to countermobilize.

The global hostility and agitation that exists against Jews is vast.

It exists not because of economic conditions. It exists not because Israel—whatever strategic, tactical, and moral mistakes it has made under inordinately difficult conditions of being under existential threat from many sides throughout its history—has been embroiled in conflict. It exists not because it is a natural state of affairs that people will be so prejudiced against Jews, as there is not analogous prejudice against other people, ethnic groups, and religious adherents. And antisemitism has taken the global form it has, with the merging of its various powerful streams into a new global version, with its distinctive features, not merely because that has been what has naturally happened. Some of those developments do have a natural, evolutionary quality. They have been natural in the sense that, given the prior existence of this world-historical powerful, deeply rooted, and unparalleled prejudice, and given the existence of the discourses that are at once built upon it, are its bearer, and are its most potent expression, and given the practice of this prejudice and discourse (as divorced from reality as it has always been), antisemitism easily and readily adapted its character to and incorporated features of the social, political, economic, and cultural contexts of the new social, cultural, and political circumstances and opportunities of the new global age.

Global antisemitism may yet further evolve into a still more powerful form where the redemonized international figure of the Jews will continue to bleed into Westerners' and others' conceptions of the Jews of their own countries, who will be similarly redemonized—in part owing to their actual or imputed support for Israel—with ever more classical antisemitic charges about their supposed malevolence and perniciousness toward their neighbors and their countries gaining expression, public legitimacy, and credence. That a pernicious image of Jews in general— and not just of Israel—is being ever more strategically promoted by the antisemitic states and organizations of the world only reinforces and accelerates this process. That the demonization of Israel and its Jews is spreading and accelerating still more quickly among all regions and peoples of the world, and that it so steadily conveys that the essence of Jews, their Jewness, is evil, makes general antisemitic notions and accusations ever more plausible and appealing to ever more people, and increasingly wins converts to the demonic ecumenical church of antisemitism. As Joschka Fischer, then foreign minister of Germany and one who *knows*—he is steeped in German elite culture, the German left from which he comes, the international human-rights movement in which he has been a major player, and in German society and culture more broadly—plainly says, "anti-Zionism inevitably leads to antisemitism."[28]

This process of redemonization, already under way, can be seen in many areas, including where the taboos on open antisemitic public expression cannot be enforced. In the crowds of European soccer matches, it is routine for mobs of fans to hurl antisemitic and mass-murderous antisemitic taunts and chants particularly at the clubs that are identified as "Jewish" but also at opposing fans as a general way to curse them. Given the widespread understanding of the essence of Jewness, what could be worse than rhythmically jeering opposing soccer fans and teams with *Jew, Jew, Jew*? The nonlinguistic repertoire of clapping as approval and whistling as disapproval has been augmented by the aforementioned regular collective hissing to signify that the fans want to send their opponents, dubbed Jews, to the gas chambers—a historical deed that they seem obviously to approve of, or not be horrified by, or at least see sympathetically in the sense of sharing the understanding of Jews that prompted Europeans to aid in the Jews' annihilation. This glimpse into the id of the European publics, across the continent in country after country, reveals the frightening potential of antisemitism, especially on the intensifying trajectory it is on, in an untrammeled

European public sphere, where norms of constraint are slowly and not so slowly eroding. What the anonymity of the soccer stadiums reveals is further substantiated by reports from country after country about the rank antisemitism that is regularly expressed out of earshot of the public sphere, including or especially at dinner parties or events among the social, cultural, and political elites. It is also further substantiated on a vast individual-by-individual case in the anonymity of the talk-back sections of websites, where articles on Israel, Jewish history, the Holocaust, genocide, human rights, or Jews in general elicit ferociously antisemitic responses of the kind that people do not yet dare speak uninhibitedly and nonanonymously in public. This process of redemonization, which is far from complete and which can still be arrested, is nonetheless well under way in Europe and is apparent even in the United States, as can be seen on college campuses and ever more in the media, where antisemitic expression in the guise of anti-Israelism or of a critique of American support for Israel grows more frequent.

*September 2012, the Jewish devil as the director of an anti-Islamic film,* Innocence of Muslims, *which was actually produced by non-Jews.*

Whatever the evolutionary character of antisemitism that has produced its new global form, global antisemitism (and even the incipient redemonization of countries' own Jews) has also been forcefully, purposely, and politically fashioned by a set of powerful institutional actors, from states and political movements and their leaders, to religions and their leaders, to media institutions and their leaders, to educational institutions and their leaders. Better than anyone, they have understood that the global world is a political world with a political worldwide discourse, and to achieve their political goals, they need to devise and pursue political policies to capture that discourse and shape the world's politics in an antisemitic manner. They have strategically built upon the vast existing antisemitism and exploited antisemitism's individual powerful streams that predated this new politics, and without which there would be no global antisemitism today, because the foundational antisemitic paradigm, and all the antisemitic calumnies, narratives, and discourses grounded in it, was the sine qua non for vast numbers of people today to be susceptible to believing the antisemitic nonsense and fantasies that pass for accounts of Jews, and their political lives, whether in Israel or in other countries. Nevertheless, without this purposeful and strategic politics, antisemitism today would still be powerful but would not be nearly as intense or nearly as eliminationist, or nearly as threatening as it is. Without antisemitism past, there would be no global antisemitism. Without the strategic purveyors of antisemitism present, antisemitism today would be far less extensive and far tamer, and would not be the acute threat it is to Israel and Jews the world over.

Antisemitism, the real devil that Christianity spawned, has not died and shows no prospect of dying anytime soon. In living, it has adapted and evolved and stalks the world ever more confidently as a global menace. Its raison d'être is to eliminate Jews, and it has done so by murdering them, by mass-murdering them, again and again. Even if we cannot stop this devil entirely, we all need to ensure that he does not again succeed in his worst predations, his eliminationism, and especially his mass murdering.

People of good conscience unite: Combat the devil that never dies, he who is named antisemitism.

# Thanks

---

Thanks, Esther, for finding the right publisher and editor for this book. Thanks, Geoff, for being the best editor imaginable. Thanks, Tattie and Mom, for all you have selflessly done. Thanks, Sarah, for your love, support, and deft touch.

# Illustration Sources

Pages 27, 272, 277, 341: Dale Hurd, "Anti-Semitic European Cartoons," CBN News, March 6, 2008, cbn.com/CBNnews/333778.aspx; p. 28: "Spreading Anti-Semitism: Arab Media Blame Jews/Israel for Pushing U.S. to Brink of War," Scottish Friends of Israel, 2003, scottishfriendsofisrael.org/arab_antisem.htm; p. 165: B'nai Brith Canada, "Antisemitism in Canada Remains at All-Time High, New Report Finds," April 30, 2012, app.streamsend.com/s/1/6N4X/TL0tWel/35ccr; p. 171: "Gunman Attacks Jewish School in France, Four Killed," Reuters/Jean-Philippe Arles, reuters.com/article/2012/03/19/us-france-crime -idUSBRE82I07N20120319; p. 179 [top]: Nazi Wandering Jew propaganda by David Shankbone.jpg, en .wikipedia.org/wiki/File:Nazi_Wandering_Jew_propaganda_by_David_Shankbone.jpg; p. 179 [bottom]: "Nazi Propaganda Illustrations," *A Teacher's Guide to the Holocaust*, fcit.usf.edu/holocaust/arts /ARTPROP.HTM; pp. 180 [top], 331: "Israel's Gaza Operation in the Arab and Iranian Media: The Use of Anti-Semitic Imagery to Vilify Israel (November 2012)," ADL, November 2012, adl.org/anti-semitism /muslim-arab-world/c/Cartoons-on-Gaza-Nov-2012.pdf; p. 180 [bottom]: Tom Gross, "Cartoons from the Arab World," tomgrossmedia.com/ArabCartoons.htm; p. 209: "Protocols of the Elders of Zion," Google images, google.com/search?q=protocols+of+elders+of+zion&client=firefox-a&hs=neS&rls=org .mozilla:en-US:official&source=lnms&tbm=isch&sa=X&ei=grHKUd _rGuit0AGdnICIBQ&ved=0CAkQ_AUoAQ&biw=1366&bih=536. Although fewer than 1,000 of Japan's 128 million residents are Jewish, millions of books based on the Protocols have been sold there. In this edition (middle protocol with bird), antisemtic ideologue Ota Ryu claims that Jews dominate the Western nations and that Japan must guard vigilantly against a Jewish takeover. Published in Tokyo, 2004. Credit: USHMM Collection; p. 211: "Protocols of the Meetings of the Learned Elders of Zion," iamthewit-ness.com/Protocols-of-Zion.htm; p. 237: "Egyptian President Morsi Joins Preacher in Prayer for Dispersal of the Jews," Channel 1 (Egypt) posted on MEMRI TV, October 19, 2012, memritv.org/clip/en/3614.htm; and "Columnist in Egyptian Daily Al-Ahram Says MEMRI TV Clip Embarrassed President Mursi [sic]," MEMRI, October 23, 2012, memri.org/report/en/0/0/0/0/0/0/6772.htm; p. 288: Adam Levick, "Anti-Semitic Cartoons at the Guardian," JewishPress.com, November 28, 2012, jewishpress.com/blogs/cif watch/anti-semitic-cartoons-at-the-gaurdian/2012/11/28; p. 303: "PA Depicts a World without Israel," Palestinian Media Watch, palwatch.org/main.aspx?fi=449; p. 317: Jabotinski International Center, "Greece: Anti-Semitism and the Arab-Israeli Conflict," FightHatred, March 23, 2012, fighthatred.com /anti-semitic-cartoons/western-cartoons/556-greece-anti-semitism-and-the-arab-israeli-conflict; p. 332: "Bush and Sharon (cartoon by Latuff)," Indymedia.be, archive.indymedia.be/news/2002/07/26628.html; p. 339: "Hamas TV Cartoon for Kids: Jews Endanger Al-Aqsa Mosque by Digging under It," uploaded by Palestinian Media Watch, youtube.com/watch?v=4y4lBqIXaU0&feature=player_detailpage#t=25s; p.355: "Anti-Semitic Incitement: Political Cartoons in the Arab Media," ADL, June–August 2002, adl. org/anti_semitism/arab/cartoon_arab_press_080702.asp; p. 357: Jew Watch, jewwatch.com; p. 363: Adam Kredo, "The Protocols of Apple: iTunes, Android Marketplace Selling Anti-Semitic Book," Washington Free Beacon, freebeacon.com/the-protocols-of-apple; p. 365: Stormfront, stormfront.org; p. 367: Planck's Constant blog, plancksconstant.org/blog1/image-pump/aaa_cartoon_destroy_israel.gif; pp. 369, 432: "Jewish Validation of Anti-Semitism from Richard Falk and Amira Hass," JG, Caesarea, July 9, 2011, jgcaesarea.blogspot.com/2011_07_01_archive.html; p. 378: Adam Levick, "How Low Will They Go? Guardian Publishes Cartoon by Notorious Anti-Semite, Carlos Latuff," CiF Watch, January 26, 2011, cif-watch.com/2011/01/26/how-low-will-they-go-guardian-publishes-cartoon-by-notorious-anti-semite-car los-latuff; p. 382: "Jew-Eating-Palestinian-Cartoon," Bare Naked Islam, ivarfjeld.files.wordpress .com/2009/09/jew-eating-palestinian-cartoon.jpg?w=450&h=331; p. 385: "Intifada," supplement to Al Hayat Al Jadida, December 11, 2000, posted in "Jesus Misrepresented as 'Muslim Palestinian,'" Palestinian Media Watch, broadcast of December 3, 2010, palwatch.org/main.aspx?fi=505: p. 386: "Egypt: Jews Drink Palestinian Blood," Fight Hatred, July 11, 2010, fighthatred.com/anti-semitic-cartoons?start=27; p. 393: CupOfJoe, flickr.com/photos/cup0fjoe/5746408807; p. 418: Tom Gross, "Middle Beast: Ariel Sharon as a Target of Anti-Semitism," *Jerusalem Post*, January 11, 2005, posted at tomgrossmedia.com/Ari elSharon.html; p. 430: "Photos from the 2001 UN World Conference Against Racism, Durban, South Africa," Human Rights Voices, humanrightsvoices.org/EYEontheUN/antisemitism/ durban/?l=36&p=350; p. 431: Benjamin Weinthal, "Where Is Europe in the Fight against UN-Sponsored Anti-Semitism?," Thecommentator, August 7, 2011, thecommentator.com/article/353/where_is_europe _in_the_fight_against_un_sponsored_anti_semitism; p. 452: "WannseeList.jpg," Wikipedia, en.wikipe dia.org/wiki/File:WannseeList.jpg; p. 457: Adam Levick, "Jewish Reaction to Thousands of Antisemitic Arab Cartoons: No Riots, No Injuries, No Deaths," CiF Watch, September 23, 2012, cifwatch .com/2012/09/23/jewish-reaction-to-thousands-of-antisemitic-arab-cartoons-no-riots-no -injuries-no-deaths.

# Notes

## Chapter 2: The Jews

1. Quoted in Marvin Perry and Frederick M. Schweitzer, *Antisemitism: Myth and Hate from Antiquity to the Present* (New York: Palgrave MacMillan, 2002), p. 125.

## Chapter 3: The Singular Prejudice

1. For a biographical account and sources, see "Horst Mahler," Wikipedia, http://en.wikipedia.org/wiki/Horst_Mahler.

2. Norman Finkelstein, *New Left Review*, July/August 1997, p. 83. For compilations of Finkelstein's statements, see Alan Dershowitz, "Letter to Professor Calahan," September 18, 2006, http://www.alandershowitz.com/publications/docs/depaulletter.htm, which also reproduces my essay on Finkelstein, "The New Discourse of Avoidance."

3. "Norman Finkelstein: Israel Is Committing a Holocaust in Gaza," Interview with Selçuk Gültaşli, *Today's Zaman*, January 19, 2009, http://www.todayszaman.com/newsDetail_getNewsById.action?load=detay&link=164483.

4. "Transcript of Hasan Nasrallah's Speech in Nabi Sheet on 24 February 2012, Lebanon's (Official) National News Agency, translation from "Hassan Nasrallah," Wikipedia, https://en.wikipedia.org/wiki/Hassan_Nasrallah#cite_note-47.

5. "Today, Facebook Removes Hizbullah Pages—Following Memri Series on Hizbullah Facebook Activity," MEMRI, October 17, 2012, http://www.memri.org/report/en/0/0/0/0/0/0/6755.htm.

6. Gilad Atzmon, *The Wandering Who: A Study of Jewish Identity Politics* (Washington: Zero, 2011), Kindle edition, location 774; and Gilad Atzmon, "Truth, History and Integrity," March 13, 2010, http://www.gilad.co.uk/writings/truth-history-and-integrity-by-gilad-atzmon.html.

7. "Helen Thomas Quits," *JTA*, June 7, 2010, http://www.jta.org/news/article/2010/06/07/2739488/helen-thomas-quits.

8. Allison Hope Weiner, "Mel Gibson Apologizes for Tirade After Arrest," *New York Times*, July 30, 2006, http://www.nytimes.com/2006/07/30/us/30gibson.html?_r=1&scp=1&sq=%22jews%20are%20responsible%22%20gibson&st=cse&; "Gibson's Anti-Semitic Tirade—Alleged Cover Up," *TMZ*, July 28, 2006, http://www.tmz.com/2006/07/28/gibsons-anti-semitic-tirade-alleged-cover-up/#. T04HmXmGiuI; and "Joe Eszterhas' Letter to Mel Gibson," *Wrap*, April 11, 2012, http://www.thewrap.com/movies/article/joe-eszterhas-letter-mel-gibson-36949. For an account of the antisemitism of *The Passion of the Christ*, see Daniel Jonah Goldhagen, "Mel Gibson's Cross of Vengeance," *Forward*, March 5, 2004, http://forward.com/articles/6452/mel-gibson-s-cross-of-vengeance/.

9. Angelique Chrisafis, "John Galliano Found Guilty of Racist and Antisemitic Abuse," *Guardian*, September 8, 2011, http://www.guardian.co.uk/world/2011/sep/08/john-galliano-guilty-racism-antisemitism.

10. "Berufsverbot für Horst Mahler," *Welt*, April 20, 2004, http://www.welt.de/print-welt/article308012/Berufsverbot_fuer_Horst_Mahler.html.

11. Quoted in Helmut Berding, *Moderner Antisemitismus in Deutschland* (Berlin: Suhrkamp, 1988), p. 79.

12. Marcus Dysch, "Academic Boycott of Israel Approved by Irish Union," *Jewish Chronicle Online*, April 5, 2013, http://www.thejc.com/news/uk-news/104739/academic-boycott-israel-approved-irish-union.

13. Fred Gottheil, "What Kind of Academic Signs These Anti-Israel Petitions?" *American Thinker*, September 5, 2010, http://www.americanthinker.com/2010/09/what_kind_of_academic_signs_th.html.

14. Michael Shain, Don Kaplan, and Kate Sheehy, "CBS Reporter's Cairo Nightmare," *New York Post*, February 16, 2011, http://www.nypost.com/p/news/international/cbs_reporter_cairo_nightmare_pXiU VvhwIDdCrbD95ybD5N#ixzz1E98g8gcr.

15. Yves Pallade, Christoph Villinger, and Deidre Berger, "Antisemitism and Racism in European Soccer," AJC Berlin Office/Ramer Center for German-Jewish Relations, May 2007, http://www.ajcgermany.org/atf/cf/%7B46AEE739-55DC-4914-959A-D5BC4A990F8D%7D/DB%20Racism%20in%20 European%20Soccer%20-%20for%20ajc.pdf; Jim Finn, "Shouts of Jews to the Gas Chambers: Dutch Soccer Chant Shouts 'Hamas, Hamas, Jews to the Gas,'" Thoughts of an Old Man, http://jpfinn7. com/2011/09/01/shouts-of-jews-to-the-gas-chambers/; and Tom McGowan, "Football Grapples with Anti-Semitism Storm," CNN, November 27, 2012, http://edition.cnn.com/2012/11/27/sport/football/ tottenham-west-ham-jewish-football.

16. Adolf Hitler, *Mein Kampf* (New York: Houghton Mifflin, 1969), p. 60, excerpted at Jewish Virtual Library, http://www.jewishvirtuallibrary.org/jsource/Holocaust/kampf.html.

17. The Gospel According to Luke, 3:9; and The Gospel According to Matthew, 24:37–38, *The New American Bible* (Wichita, KS: Fireside Bible, 2001–2002).

18. John Chrysostom "Eight Homilies Against the Jews," Fordham University, http://www.fordham. edu/halsall/source/chrysostom-jews6-homily1.asp.

19. Malcolm Hay, *Thy Brother's Blood: The Roots of Christian Anti-Semitism* (New York: Hart, 1975), p. 57.

20. Geoffrey Chaucer, *The Poetical Works* (London: Edward Moxon, 1843), p. 103.

21. Quoted in Andrew G. Bostom, ed., *The Legacy of Islamic Antisemitism: From Sacred Texts to Solemn History* (Amherst, NY: Prometheus Books, 2008), pp. 35–36.

22. Robert S. Wistrich, *Antisemitism: The Longest Hatred* (New York: Schocken, 1991), pp. 39–41, and Martin Luther, *On the Jews and Their Lies, 1543* (Philadelphia: Fortress Press, 1971), http://www. humanitas-international.org/showcase/chronography/documents/luther-jews.htm.

23. Quoted in Jacob Katz, *From Prejudice to Destruction: Anti-Semitism, 1700–1933*, (Cambridge: Harvard University Press, 1980), pp. 44–45 and 47.

24. Quoted in Walter Arnold Kaufmann, *Goethe, Kant, and Hegel: Discovering the Mind*, vol. 1 (New Brunswick, NJ: Transaction, 2009), p. 74; and Paul Lawrence Rose, *German Question/Jewish Question: Revolutionary Antisemitism from Kant to Wagner* (Princeton: Princeton, 1990), pp. 94 and 96.

25. Quoted in Katz, *From Prejudice to Destruction*, p. 71.

26. Joel Carmichael, *The Satanizing of the Jews: Origin and Development of Mystical Anti-Semitism* (New York: Fromm, 1992), p. 116.

27. Ibid., p. 117.

28. Quoted in Rose, *German Question/Jewish Question*, pp. 364–65.

29. Karl Marx, "On the Jewish Question," in *The Marx-Engels Reader*, Robert C. Tucker, ed. (New York: Norton, 1972), p. 47.

30. T. S. Eliot, "Gerontian," http://www.bartleby.com/199/13.html, and "Burbank with a Baedeker: Bleistein with a Cigar," http://www.bartleby.com/199/14.html.

31. Quoted in *Antisemitism: A Historical Encyclopedia of Prejudice and Persecution* (Santa Barbara: ABC-Clio, 2005), p. 200.

32. Eberhard Jäckel, ed., *Hitler: Sämtliche Aufzeichnungen 1905–1924* (Stuttgart: Deutsche Verlags-Anstalt, 1980), pp. 119–20.

33. Quoted in Joel Fishman, "A Stormy Romance of France and Israel," *Jewish Political Studies Review* (Spring 2006), http://www.jcpa.org/phas/phas-fishman-s06.htm.

34. Sayyid Qutb, "Our Struggle with the Jews," in Bostom, ed., *The Legacy of Islamic Antisemitism*, p. 357.

35. Anna Arco, "Lefevbrists Face Crisis as Bishop Is Exposed as 'Dangerous' Anti-Semite," *Catholic Herald,* March 5, 2008, http://archive.catholicherald.co.uk/article/7th-march-2008/1/lefebvrists-face-crisis -as-bishop-is-exposed-as-da.

36. "Former Al-Azhar Fatwa Committee Head Sets Out the Jews' 20 Bad Traits As Described in the Qur'an," April 6, 2004, http://www.memri.org/report/en/0/0/0/0/0/0/1102.htm.

37. *Qur'an* 58:14–19, quoted in Bostom, ed., *The Legacy of Islamic Antisemitism,* pp. 40–41.

38. *The Protocols of the Learned Elders of Zion,* http://ddickerson.igc.org/The_Protocols_of_the_ Learned_Elders_of_Zion.pdf.

39. Hitler, *Mein Kampf,* pp. 293-96, excerpted at Jewish Virtual Library, http://www.jewishvirtualli-brary.org/jsource/Holocaust/kampf.html.

40. "The Reich Citizenship Law: First Regulation (November 14, 1935)," Jewish Virtual Library, http://www.jewishvirtuallibrary.org/jsource/Holocaust/nurmlaw4.html.

41. Quoted in Daniel Jonah Goldhagen, *A Moral Reckoning: The Role of the Catholic Church in the Holocaust and Its Unfulfilled Duty of Repair* (New York: Knopf, 2002), p. 65.

42. United Nations General Assembly Resolution 3379, "Elimination of All Forms of Racial Discrim-ination," United Nations, http://daccess-dds-ny.un.org/doc/RESOLUTION/GEN/NR0/000/92/IMG/ NR000092.pdf?OpenElement.

43. Elaine Sciolino, "A Resistance Hero Fires Up the French," *New York Times,* March 9, 2011, http:// www.nytimes.com/2011/03/10/books/stephane-hessel-93-calls-for-time-of-outrage-in-france .html?pagewanted=all&_r=0.

44. *The Charter of Allah: The Platform of the Islamic Resistance Movement (Hamas),* http://www.theje-rusalemfund.org/www.thejerusalemfund.org/carryover/documents/charter.html.

45 Quoted in Eric Michaud, *The Cult of Art in Nazi Germany* (Palo Alto: Stanford University Press, 2004), p. 81.

46 "Anti-Semitism of the 'Church Fathers,'" Yashanet, http://www.yashanet.com/library/fathers.htm.

### Chapter 4: Fear and Trembling

1. For a more extensive discussion of eliminationism, including its principal forms, see Daniel Jonah Goldhagen, *Worse Than War: Genocide, Eliminationism, and the Ongoing Assault on Humanity* (New York: Public Affairs, 2009), pp. 14–21, from which these passages are adapted.

2. David Firestone, "Billy Graham Responds to Lingering Anger Over 1972 Remarks on Jews," *New York Times,* March 17, 2002, http://www.nytimes.com/2002/03/17/us/billy-graham-responds-to-lingering-anger-over-1972-remarks-on-jews.html.

3. Eric Fingerhut, "Nixon: If only the Jews would behave…," *JTA,* June 24, 2009, http://blogs.jta.org/ politics/article/2009/06/24/1006112/nixon-if-only-the-jews-would-behave; and Eric Fingerhut, "ADL: Nixon remarks 'reinforce' what we already know," *JTA,* June 24, 2009, http://blogs.jta.org/politics/ article/2009/06/24/1006117/adl-nixon-remarks-reinforce-what-we-already-know.

### Chapter 6: The Post–World War II Illusion

1. Paul Spiegel, "Die Deutschen waren Riesen, die durchs Land stapften und Kinder verschleppten," interview, *Stern,* January 17, 2002, pp. 68ff.

2. See Daniel Jonah Goldhagen, *Hitler's Willing Executioners: Ordinary Germans and the Holocaust* (New York: Vintage, 1997), and *Worse Than War: Genocide, Eliminationism, and the Ongoing Assault on Humanity* (New York: PublicAffairs, 2009), esp. p. 367.

3. Quoted in "To Bigotry No Sanction, to Persecution No Assistance,' George Washington's Letter to the Jews of Newport, Rhode Island (1790)," Jewish Virtual Library, http://www.jewishvirtuallibrary. org/jsource/US-Israel/bigotry.html.

4. "Justice Jackson's Opening Statement for the Prosecution," Title: "Second Day, Wednesday, 11/21/1945, Part 04," in *Trial of the Major War Criminals before the International Military Tribunal,* Volume II (Nuremberg: IMT, 1947), pp. 98–102. http://law2.umkc.edu/faculty/projects/ftrials/nuremberg/jackson.html#Crimes%20against%20the%20Jews.

5. Alina Cała, *The Image of the Jew in Polish Folk Culture* (Jerusalem: Magnes, 1995), pp. 218 and 227.

6. "Leaving Tracks Uncovered," interview with Joanna Tokarska-Bakir and Anna Zawadzka, *Academia*, n.d., http://www.academia.pan.pl/dokonania.php?jezyk=en&id=487.

7. Frederick D. Weil, "Survey Findings on Antisemitism: A Four-Nation Comparison," Table 1, p. 32, http://www.lsu.edu/faculty/fweil/Weil90AntisemitismFourNation-BergmannErb.pdf [An English translation of "Umfragen zum Antisemitismus: Ein Vergleich zwischen vier Nationen" in Werner Bergmann and Rainer Erb, eds., *Antisemitismus in der politischen Kultur nach 1945* (Opladen: Westdeutscher Verlag, 1990), pp. 131–78]. The more general index of antisemitism is ADL, "A Survey of American Attitudes Toward Jews in America," 2011, http://archive.adl.org/PresRele/ASUS_12/6154_12.

8. *The Charter of Allah: The Platform of the Islamic Resistance Movement (Hamas)*, http://www.thejerusalemfund.org/www.thejerusalemfund.org/carryover/documents/charter.html.

9. Ayaan Hirsi Ali, "Why They Deny the Holocaust: On Top of Nearly Constant Anti-Semitic Propaganda, Much of the Muslim World Hasn't Even Heard of It," *Los Angeles Times*, December 16, 2006, http://www.latimes.com/news/la-oe-ali16dec16,0,449142.story.

10. Quoted in Uli Hesse, "Straff organisiertes Netzwerk: Rechtsradikale Kameradschaften in Deutschland," *Deutschlandfunk*, May 15, 2004, http://www.dradio.de/dlf/sendungen/hintergrundpolitik/264534/.

## Chapter 8: Learning to See

1. David Rosenberg, "In the Arab World, Turkey's on Top," *Jerusalem Post*, February 12, 2002, http://www.jpost.com/Features/InThespotlight/Article.aspx?id=256964.

## Chapter 9: The ABCs of Global Antisemitism

1. B'nai Brith Canada, "Antisemitism in Canada Remains at All-Time High, New Report Finds," April 30, 2012, http://app.streamsend.com/s/1/6N4X/TL0tWel/35ccr.

2. Kantor Center for the Study of Contemporary European Jewry, *Antisemitism Worldwide 2012*, Appendices, http://kantorcenter.tau.ac.il/sites/default/files/doch-all-final-2012_0.pdf.

3. B'nai Brith Canada, "Antisemitism in Canada Remains at All-Time High, New Report Finds"; comparative data from Cara Dowden and Shannon Brennan, "Police-Reported Hate Crime in Canada, 2010," Statistics Canada, http://www.statcan.gc.ca/pub/85-002-x/2012001/article/11635-eng.htm.

4. "Odense: Strained Relations between Palestinians and Jews," *Islam in Europe*, January 5, 2009, http://islamineurope.blogspot.com/2009/01/odense-strained-relations-between.html.

5. Paulina Neuding, "Sweden's 'Damn Jew' Problem," *Tablet*, April 5, 2012, http://www.tabletmag.com/jewish-news-and-politics/96146/swedens-damn-jew-problem#; and Barbara Sofer, "The Human Spirit: Funny on the Way to the Forum," *Jerusalem Post*, September 13, 2012, http://www.jpost.com/Opinion/Columnists/Article.aspx?id=284958.

6. Giulio Meotti, "Jews Unwelcome on Campus: Western Universities Becoming Frightening Bastions of Anti-Israel, Anti-Jewish Hostility," Ynetnews.com, June 5, 2012, http://www.ynetnews.com/articles/0,7340,L-4225175,00.html.

7. Guilio Meotti, "EXPOSÉ: No-Go Areas for Jews in Europe," *Arutz Sheva*, December 18, 2012, http://www.israelnationalnews.com/Articles/Article.aspx/12605#.UT3SzzfNggo; Yedidya Kennard, "Antisemitism: Back to the Old Days," *Times of Israel*, January 31, 2013, http://blogs.timesofisrael.com/antisemitism-back-to-the-old-days/.

8. Annette Sach, "Mitten unter Uns: Antisemitismus," *Das Parlament*, December 5, 2011, http://www.das-parlament.de/2011/49-50/Thema/36909820.html.

9. "Rabbiner in Berlin attackiert und verletzt," *Jüdische Allgemeine*, August 29, 2012, http://www.juedische-allgemeine.de/article/view/id/13893.

10. Tzvi Ben Gedalyahu, "Anti-Semite Viciously Beats Buenos Aires Jewish Day School Rabbi," *Arutz Sheva*, May 11, 2011, http://www.israelnationalnews.com/News/News.aspx/144063#.ULyQk2dOSSo.

11. Tzvi Ben Gedalyahu, "Arabs Brutally Attack US Yeshiva Student in Italy," *Arutz Sheva*, January 2, 2012, http://www.israelnationalnews.com/News/News.aspx/163803#.UOX7X6xOSSp.

12. Gil Yaron, "More and More French Jews Emigrating to Israel," Spiegel Online, March 22, 2012, http://www.spiegel.de/international/world/jews-emigrating-from-france-to-israel-a-822928.html;

and Itamar Eichner, "Anti-Semitism Hits New Record in Europe," Ynetnews, June 24, 2013, http://www.ynetnews.com/articles/0,7340,L-4396159,00.html.

13. Shirli Sitbon, "Behind High Walls, France's Jews on High Alert," Haaretz, December 13, 2002, http://www.haaretz.com/jewish-world/behind-high-walls-france-s-jews-on-high-alert.premium-1.484565.

14. Meotti, "Jews Unwelcome On Campus."

15. Joachim Gauck, "Einweihung der Neuen Synagoge Ulm," Der Bundespräsident, December 2, 2012, http://www.bundespraesident.de/SharedDocs/Reden/DE/Joachim-Gauck/Reden/2012/12/121202-Synagogeneroeffnung.html.

16. Charlotte Knobloch, "Wollt ihr uns Juden noch?," Süddeutsche.de, September 25, 2012, http://www.sueddeutsche.de/politik/2.220/beschneidungen-in-deutschland-wollt-ihr-uns-juden-noch-1.1459038.

17. "Lauder Reacts to Malmö Attack: 'Time for Sweden to Stand by Its Jewish Community and Give It the Protection It Needs,'" World Jewish Congress, September 28, 2012, http://www.worldjewishcongress.org/en/news/12429/lauder_reacts_to_malm_attack_time_for_sweden_to_stand_by_its_jewish_community_and_give_it_the_protection_it_needs; and Itamar Eichner, "Anti-Semitism Hits New Record in Europe."

18. ADL, Surveys of antisemitism in Europe, 2007, 2009, and 2012, http://archive.adl.org/main_Anti_Semitism_International/Default.htm; and ADL, "A Survey of American Attitudes Toward Jews in America," 2011, http://archive.adl.org/PresRele/ASUS_12/6154_12.htm.

19. Sarah Wildman, "Iraq Assault Triggers Anti-Semitic Backlash in France," Christian Science Monitor, April 4, 2003, http://www.csmonitor.com/2003/0404/p07s02-woeu.html.

20. "Rabbiner in Berlin attackiert und verletzt."

21. Lee C. Bollinger, "Statement about President Ahmadinejad's Scheduled Appearance," September 19, 2007, http://www.columbia.edu/cu/president/docs/communications/2007-2008/070919-Statement-visit-Iranian-President.html.

22. Kantor Center for the Study of Contemporary European Jewry, Antisemitism Worldwide 2010, 2011, and 2012, Appendices, http://kantorcenter.tau.ac.il/general-analyses-1.

23. Steven L. Jacobs and Mark Weitzman, Dismantling the Big Lie: The Protocols of the Elders of Zion (Jersey City: KTAV, 2003), table of contents.

24. Matthias Küntzel, "The 'Protocols of the Elders of Zion' at the Frankfurt Book Fair," http://www.matthiaskuentzel.de/contents/the-protocols-of-the-elders-of-zion-at-the-frankfurt-book-fair; "'The Secret of Armageddon': An Iranian TV 'Documentary' Claims That 'a Jewish Plan for the Genocide of Humanity,' Includes a Conspiracy for the Takeover of Iran by Local Jewish and Bahai Communities," MEMRI, May–June, 2008, http://www.memritv.org/clip_transcript/en/1802.htm#.

25. "The Charter of Allah: The Platform of the Islamic Resistance Movement (Hamas), http://www.thejerusalemfund.org/www.thejerusalemfund.org/carryover/documents/charter.html.

26. For these and other instances of the Palestinian Authority's use and spread of the Protocols, see Itamar Marcus and Barbara Crook, The Protocols of the Elders of Zion: An Authentic Document in Palestinian Authority Ideology, in Richard Landes and Steven T. Katz, eds., The Paranoid Apocalypse: A Hundred-Year Retrospective on The Protocols of the Elders of Zion (New York: New York University Press, 2012), pp. 152–60; and Palestinian Media Watch, Libels: The Protocols of the Elders of Zion, http://palwatch.org/main.aspx?fi=783.

27. Anna Arco, "Lefebvrists Face Crisis as Bishop Is Exposed as 'Dangerous' Anti-Semite: SSPX Refuses to Distance Itself from Prelate Who Accuses Jews of Doing Work of the Anti-Christ," Catholic Herald, March 5, 2008, http://web.archive.org/web/20090606071534/http://catholicherald.co.uk/articles/a0000226.shtml; Ofer Aderet, "Pioneer of Global Peace Studies Hints at Link between Norway Massacre and Mossad," Haaretz, April 30, 2012, http://www.haaretz.com/news/diplomacy-defense/pioneer-of-global-peace-studies-hints-at-link-between-norway-massacre-and-mossad-1.427385; Hung Huang, "China, Anti-Semitic Conspiracy Theories and Wall Street," New York Times, October 2, 2008, http://economix.blogs.nytimes.com/2008/10/02/china-anti-semitic-conspiracy-theories-and-wall-street/; David G. Goodman, "The Protocols in Japan," in Landes and Katz, eds., The Paranoid Apocalypse, p. 135.

28. "Malaysian Prime Minister Mahathir Mohamad: On the Jews," ADL, October 27, 2003, http://www.adl.org/Anti_semitism/malaysian_1.asp.

## Chapter 10: Today's Demonology

1. Qur'an 5:60; 7:166–67, quoted in M. A. S. Abdel Haleem, *The Qur'an* (Oxford World's Classics), (Oxford University Press. Kindle Edition, 2005).

2. "Contemporary Islamist Ideology Authorizing Genocidal Murder," MEMRI, January 27, 2004, http://www.memri.org/report/en/print1049.htm.

3. Qur'an 2:90–91, quoted in Haleem, *The Qur'an*.

4. Daniel Jonah Goldhagen, *Worse Than War: Genocide, Eliminationism, and the Ongoing Assault on Humanity* (New York: PublicAffairs, 2009).

5. See Georges Vajda, "Jews and Muslims According to the Hadith," in Andrew G. Bostom, ed., *The Legacy of Islamic Antisemitism: From Sacred Texts to Solemn History* (Amherst, NY: Prometheus Books, 2008), p. 246.

6. "On Al-Aqsa TV, Hamas Deputy Minister of Religious Endowments Calls for Jews to Be Annihilated, Saying They Are Bacteria, Not Human Beings; Following President Obama's Election, Said in Friday Sermon: We Must 'First Check If His Heart Is Black or White,'" MEMRI, March 15, 2010, http://www.memri.org/report/en/0/0/0/0/0/0/0/4035.htm.

7. "Contemporary Islamist Ideology Authorizing Genocidal Murder."

8. Quoted in "Eyewitness to Ramallah Lynching," Jewish Virtual Library, http://www.jewishvirtuallibrary.org/jsource/History/lynchwit.html.

9. "Hamas Leader Mahmoud Al-Zahhar Justifies Persecution of Jews in History and Declares That Jews 'Are Headed to Annihilation,'" MEMRI, November 5, 2010, http://www.memritv.org/clip_transcript/en/2676.htm.

10. "Former Lebanese Defense Minister Mohsen Dalloul: George Washington Said the Jews Were 'Blood-Suckers,' Benjamin Franklin Called to Prevent Their Entry into the U.S.," MEMRI, September 4, 2011, http://www.memritv.org/clip_transcript/en/3108.htm.

11. "Bishop of Syrian Orthodox Church in Lebanon George Saliba: Jews Incite Unrest in the Arab World in Accordance with 'The Protocols of the Elders of Zion,'" MEMRI, July 24, 2011, http://www.memritv.org/clip_transcript/en/3047.htm.

12. Y. Mansharof and A. Savyon, "In Response to Escalating Threats between West and Iran, Iranian Official Calls on Regime to Attack Israel," MEMRI, February 7, 2012, http://www.memri.org/report/en/print6058.htm.

13. "Faraeen TV Owner and Egyptian Presidential Candidate Tawfiq Okasha: The Jews Plan to Rule the World through Schemes, Intrigues, and Civil Strife—Like They Are Doing in Egypt," MEMRI, July 17, 2011, http://www.memritv.org/clip_transcript/en/3038.htm.

14. "Egyptian Cleric Miqdam Al-Khadhari on the Benefits of Al-Azhar Curricula: The Only Textbooks to Militarize the Students and Teach Jihad and Hatred of Jews Extensively," MEMRI, December 23, 2010, http://www.memritv.org/clip_transcript/en/2835.htm.

15. "Child Preacher Ibrahim Adham Longs for Martyrdom, Fighting alongside the Palestinians," MEMRI TV, http://www.memri.org/clip/en/0/0/0/0/0/0/3644.htm.

16. "Egyptian President Morsi Joins Preacher in Prayer for Dispersal of the Jews," Channel 1 (Egypt) posted on MEMRI TV, October 19, 2012, http://www.memritv.org/clip/en/3614.htm; and "Columnist in Egyptian Daily Al-Ahram Says MEMRI TV Clip Embarrassed President Mursi," MEMRI, October 23, 2012, http://www.memri.org/report/en/0/0/0/0/0/0/6772.htm.

17. "Egypt's Morsi in 2010: Obama Insincere; We Must Nurse Our Children and Grandchildren on Hatred of Jews, MEMRI TV, January 10, 2010, http://www.memritv.org/clip/en/3713.htm; and "Morsi in 2010: No to Negotiations with the Blood-Sucking, Warmongering 'Descendants of Apes and Pigs'; Calls to Boycott U.S. Products," MEMRI TV, March 20 and September 23, 2010, http://www.memritv.org/clip/en/0/0/0/0/0/0/3702.htm.

18. Sarah Dilorenzo, "French Gunman's Brother Blames Parents in New Book," AP, November 11, 2012, http://www.boston.com/news/world/europe/2012/11/11/french-gunman-brother-blames-parents-new-book/MJX1YcrAj5aGwmwOmT5MkL/story.html.

19. "Hamas Suicide Terrorist Farewell Video: Palestinians Drink the Blood of Jews," Hamas website, February 1, 2006, posted at Palestinian Media Watch, http://www.palwatch.org/main.aspx?fi=740&fld_id=740&doc_id=2677.

20. For a discussion of this, see Daniel Jonah Goldhagen, *A Moral Reckoning: The Role of the Church in the Holocaust and Its Unfulfilled Duty of Repair* (New York: Knopf, 2002), p. 206.

21. Bishops' Committee on the Liturgy, National Conference of Catholic Bishops, *God's Love Endures Forever: Guidelines on the Presentation of Jews and Judaism in Catholic Preaching* (1988), http://nccbuscc.org/liturgy/godsmercy.shtml; and Bishops' Committee for Ecumenical and Interreligious Affairs, National Conference of Catholic Bishops, *Criteria for the Evaluation of Dramatizations of the Passion* (1988), http://www.sacredheart.edu/pages/12452_criteria_for_the_evaluation_of_dramatizations_of_the_passion_1988_.cfm.

22. Tom Kington, "Bishop 'Blames Jews' for Criticism of Catholic Church Record on Abuse," *Guardian*, April 11, 2010, http://www.guardian.co.uk/world/2010/apr/11/catholic-bishop-blames-jews.

23. Goldhagen, *A Moral Reckoning* (Vintage paperback afterword, 2003), pp. 270–71, and 310–11.

24. ADL, "A Survey of American Attitudes Toward Jews in America," 2011, http://archive.adl.org/PresRele/ASUS_12/6154_12.

25. Raphael Ahren, "At Interfaith Meet in Jerusalem, a Grim Picture of Jewish-Protestant Relations," *Times of Israel*, November 9, 2012, http://www.timesofisrael.com/at-interfaith-meet-in-jerusalem-a-grim-picture-of-jewish-Protestant-relations/.

## Chapter 11: Millions Upon Millions of Antisemites

1. Karl Barth's letter to Friedrich-Wilhelm Marquardt (5 September 1967): "I am decidedly not a philosemite," Jewish-Non-Jewish Relations, http://www.jnjr.div.ed.ac.uk/Primary%20Sources/contemporary/fischer_barthmarquardt.html, taken from *Karl Barth, Letters 1961–1968*. Jürgen Fangmeier and Hinrich Stoevesandt, eds. Translated and edited by Geoffrey W. Bromiley (Edinburgh: T.&T. Clark, 1981), No. 260, p. 261.

2. The best, consistent survey data assessing Europeans' antisemitism has been conducted by the Anti-Defamation League (ADL), which has asked a stable series of questions in multiple European countries in 2002, 2004, 2005, 2007, 2009, and 2012. Unless otherwise specified, the European survey data cited here comes from these surveys, and unless otherwise specified, from the most recent survey (usually 2012) for each of the countries discussed. The ADL has conducted an analogous series of surveys of antisemitism in the United States, in 2002, 2005, 2007, 2009, and the most recent one in 2011, which is the basis for the American data discussed here. For the surveys, see Anti-Defamation League, http://archive.adl.org/main_Anti_Semitism_International/Default.htm; and http://archive.adl.org/main_Anti_Semitism_Domestic/default.

3. Special Eurobarometer, "Social Values, Science, and Technology," June 2005, http://ec.europa.eu/public_opinion/archives/ebs/ebs_225_report_en.pdf.

4. Antoinette Kelly, "Anti-Israeli Mood Rife in Ireland Says New Survey Findings," *Irish Central*, May 29, 2011, http://www.irishcentral.com/news/Anti-Israeli-mood-rife-in-Ireland-says-new-survey-findings—122794539.html.

5. Khaled Abu Toameh, "Palestinians in Syria Killed, Injured, Displaced: Arabs, Human Rights Organizations, Media Yawn," Gatestone Institute, May 10, 2013, http://www.gatestoneinstitute.org/3706/palestinians-syria-killed-injured-displaced; and "UNRWA Condemns Mass Displacement of Palestine Refugees in Syria," *United Nations Relief and Works Agency for Palestine Refugees*, April 30, 2013, http://www.unrwa.org/etemplate.php?id=1735. The press release by UNRWA, itself tepid, was all but ignored by the international community and the media.

6. Andreas Zick and Beate Küpper, "Antisemitische Mentalitäten: Bericht über Ergebnisse des Forschungsprojektes Gruppenbezogene Menschenfeindlichkeit in Deutschland und Europa," Universität Bielefeld, 2010, http://www.bmi.bund.de/SharedDocs/Downloads/DE/Themen/Politik_Gesellschaft/Expertenkreis_Antisemmitismus/kuepper.pdf?__blob=publicationFile.

7. See Goldhagen, *A Moral Reckoning: The Role of the Church in the Holocaust and Its Unfulfilled Duty of Repair* (New York: Vintage, 2003), paperback afterword, p. 310.

8. Ian Traynor, "Anger at EU Chief's Middle East Outburst," *Guardian*, September 3, 2010, http://www.guardian.co.uk/world/2010/sep/03/eu-official-antisemitism-middle-east-peace-talks.

9. Benjamin Weinthal, "Finnish Politician: Jews Control Money, Media in US," *Jerusalem Post*, December 1, 2012, http://www.jpost.com/JewishWorld/JewishFeatures/Article.aspx?id=294146.

10. "Daniel Bernard," *Telegraph,* May 3, 2004, http://www.telegraph.co.uk/news/obituaries/1460855/Daniel-Bernard.html; and "Daniel Bernard," Wikipedia, http://en.wikipedia.org/wiki/Daniel_Bernard_%28diplomat%29.

11. Paulina Neuding, "Sweden's 'Damn Jew' Problem," *Tablet,* April 5, 2012, http://www.tabletmag.com/jewish-news-and-politics/96146/swedens-damn-jew-problem#.

12. "German Parliamentarian Calls Jews 'Race of Perpetrators,'" Deutsche Welle Online, http://www.dw.de/german-parliamentarian-calls-jews-race-of-perpetrators/a-1018003.

13. Thilo Sarrazin, interview in *Welt am Sonntag,* August 29, 2010, http://www.welt.de/politik/deutschland/article9255898/Moegen-Sie-keine-Tuerken-Herr-Sarrazin.html.

14. Giulio Meotti, "Of Music, Jews and Evil," *Arutz Sheva 7,* February 24, 2012, http://www.israelnationalnews.com/Articles/Article.aspx/11306#.UZtFWkrEV_4.

15. "Protocols of the Elders of Zion Read Aloud in Greek Parliament," *Haaretz,* October 26, 2012, http://www.haaretz.com/jewish-world/jewish-world-news/protocols-of-the-elders-of-zion-read-aloud-in-greek-parliament-1.472552.

16. Tuvia Tenenbaum, *I Sleep in Hitler's Room: An American Jew Visits Germany* (New York: Jewish Theater of New York, 2011).

17. Pew Global Attitudes Project, "Unfavorable Views of Jews and Muslims on the Increase in Europe," September 17, 2008, http://www.pewglobal.org/files/2008/09/Pew-2008-Pew-Global-Attitudes-Report-3-September-17-2pm.pdf. The publication's title notwithstanding, the survey is of twenty-four countries, eighteen of them outside Europe.

18. Eric T. Justin, "Protocols of the Elders of Crazy: On Anti-Semitism in the Arab World," *Harvard Crimson,* October 3, 2011, http://www.thecrimson.com/article/2011/10/3/arab-world-antisemitism-jews/.

19. Michael Kamber, "The Chosen One: Journalist Daniel Pearl Was Killed for Being a Jew," *Village Voice,* February 26, 2002, http://www.villagevoice.com/2002-02-26/news/the-chosen-one/full/.

20. "PA Depicts a World without Israel," Palestinian Media Watch, http://www.palwatch.org/main.aspx?fi=449.

21. Ibid.; and Paul Bogdanor, "Understanding the Arab-Israeli Conflict," citing *El Mundo,* Venezuela, February 11, 1980, and *London Times,* August 5, 1980, and *Jerusalem Post,* February 23, 1996, http://www.paulbogdanor.com/israel/quotes.html; "The Palestinian National Charter: Resolutions of the Palestine National Council July 1–17, 1968," *The Avalon Project,* Yale Law School, http://avalon.law.yale.edu/20th_century/plocov.asp.

22. Palestinian Center for Policy and Survey Research, Palestinian Public Opinion Poll Nos. 9 (October 2003) and 27 (March 2008), http://www.pcpsr.org/survey/.

23. "Religious War: Jews Are Evil and Threatening," Palestinian Media Watch, http://palwatch.org/main.aspx?fi=571; "Arab Spring and Frozen Peace: Palestinian Opinion, Summer 2011: Key Findings from a National Survey of 1,101 Palestinian Adults in the West Bank and Gaza," *The Israel Project,* June 20–July 8, 2011, www.theisraelproject.org, p. 22.

24. "Egyptian Cleric Muhammad Hussein Ya'qoub: The Jews are the Enemies of Muslims Regardless of the Occupation of Palestine; 'Believe That We Will Fight, Defeat, and Annihilate Them, Until Not a Single Jew Remains on the Face of the Earth,'" MEMRI, March 12, 2009, http://www.memri.org/report/en/0/0/0/0/0/0/3186.htm.

25. Pew Global Attitudes Project, "Unfavorable Views of Jews and Muslims on the Increase in Europe."

26. Anti-Defamation League (ADL) and New York Delegation of Argentinean Jewish Associations (DAIA), "Attitudes Towards Jews in Argentina," September 2011, http://archive.adl.org/anti_semitism/2010_Survey_of_Anti-Semitism_in_Argentina_20110921.pdf.

27. Survey published in *Wprost* of January 18, 2004, cited in Jan T. Gross, *Fear: Anti-Semitism in Poland After Auschwitz* (New York: Random House, 2006), p. 30.

## Chapter 12: The Nazified Fantasy

1. Jabotinski International Center, "Greece: Anti-Semitism and the Arab-Israeli Conflict," *FightHatred,* March 23, 2010, http://fighthatred.com/anti-semitic-cartoons/western-cartoons/556-greece-anti-semitism-and-the-arab-israeli-conflict.

2. Sonja Vogel, "Sprache, die tötet," taz.de, February 9, 2013, http://www.taz.de/1/archiv/digitaz/arti kel/?ressort=ku&dig=2013%2F02%2F09%2Fa0273&cHash=4655c48ca095c1f61b83f4b68efcdb4e.

3. All such estimates are rough, as population sizes for all the countries were always evolving and grew considerably from 1948 to today. For compilations of casualty figures, see "Israeli casualties of war," Wikipedia, http://en.wikipedia.org/wiki/Israeli_casualties_of_war.

4. Paul Bogdanor, "Understanding the Arab-Israeli Conflict," citing *New York Times*, January 10, 1954, http://www.paulbogdanor.com/israel/quotes.html.

5. Anne Barnard and Hania Mourtada, "An Atrocity in Syria, with No Victim Too Small," *New York Times*, May 14, 2013, http://www.nytimes.com/2013/05/15/world/middleeast/grisly-killings-in-syrian-towns-dim-hopes-for-peace-talks.html?hp&_r=0.

6. This closely follows a passage from Daniel Jonah Goldhagen, *Worse Than War: Genocide, Eliminationism, and the Ongoing Assault on Humanity* (New York: PublicAffairs, 2009), pp. 503–504. The quotes are from "Hamas Leader Khaled Mash'al at a Damascus Mosque: The Nation of Islam Will Sit at the Throne of the World and the West Will Be Full of Remorse — When It's Too Late," MEMRI, February 7, 2006, www.memri.org/bin/articles.cgi?Area=sd&ID=SP 108706&Page=archives; and Itamar Marcus and Barbara Crook, "Hamas Video: We Will Drink the Blood of the Jews," Palestinian Media Watch, February 14, 2006, www.pmw.org.il/Latest%20bulletins%20new.htm#b140206.

7. Itamar Marcus, "Abbas and the PA Used Term 'Alleged Temple' at Least 97 Times in 2011 and 2012 in Its Ongoing Campaign to Deny Jerusalem's Jewish History," Palestinian Media Watch, August 23, 2012, http://palwatch.org/main.aspx?fi=157&doc_id=7284.

8. "Libel: Israel to Destroy Al-Aqsa Mosque," Palestinian Media Watch, http://www.palwatch.org /main.aspx?fi=771.

9. Cartoonist Dave Brown, in Dale Hurd, "Anti-Semitic European Cartoons," CBN News, March 6, 2008, http://www.cbn.com/CBNnews/333778.aspx.

10. "Top Commander Reiterates Iran's Commitment to Full Annihilation of Israel," Fars News Agency, May 20, 2012, http://english.farsnews.com/newstext.php?nn=9102112759.

11. "Wife of Assassinated Scientist: Annihilation of Israel 'Mostafa's Ultimate Goal,'" Fars News Agency, February 21, 2012, http://english.farsnews.com/newstext.php?nn=9010175602.

12. "Full Speech of Secretary General of Hizbullah, His Eminence Sayyed Hassan Nasrallah, during the Festival of Victory in Bint Jbeil City on May 26, 2000," *Breaking the Spider's Web*, http://breakingthe spidersweb.blogspot.com/2011/05/nasrallahs-spider-web-speech.html.

13. Quoted in Amal Saad-Ghorayeb, *Hizbu'llah: Politics and Religion* (London: Pluto, 2002), p. 170.

14. "Today, Facebook Removes Hizbullah Pages — Following MEMRI Series on Hizbullah Facebook Activity," MEMRI, October 17, 2012, http://www.memri.org/report/en/0/0/0/0/0/0/6755.htm.

15. Quoted in "Israel Must Be 'Eliminated,'" *Wall Street Journal*. September 25, 2012, http://online .wsj.com/article/SB10000872396390443819404577633511664110678.html.

16. "The Charter of Allah: The Platform of the Islamic Resistance Movement (Hamas), http://www .thejerusalemfund.org/www.thejerusalemfund.org/carryover/documents/charter.html.

17. "Arab Spring and Frozen Peace: Palestinian Opinion, Summer 2011: Key Findings from a National Survey of 1,101 Palestinian Adults in the West Bank and Gaza" *The Israel Project*, June 20–July 8, 2011, www.theisraelproject.org, p. 22.

18. Benny Morris, "Exposing Abbas," *National Interest*, May 19, 2011, http://nationalinterest.org /commentary/exposing-abbas-5335.

19. Ryan Jones, "Israel: Jesus Was Not Born in Palestine!," *Israel Today Magazine*, June 13, 2012, http:// www.israeltoday.co.il/NewsItem/tabid/178/nid/23255/language/en-US/Default.aspx; and "Rewriting History: Jesus Misrepresented as 'Muslim Palestinian,'" *Palestinian Media Watch*, http://palwatch.org /main.aspx?fi=505.

20. "IUMS Member Tareq Hawwas in Antisemitic Diatribe: 'If Only Hitler Had Finished Them Off,'" MEMRI, April 18, 2013, http://thememriblog.org/antisemitism/blog_personal/en/42207.htm

21. "Arab Spring and Frozen Peace: Palestinian Opinion, Summer 2011: Key Findings from a National Survey of 1,101 Palestinian Adults in the West Bank and Gaza," *The Israel Project*, June 20–July 8, 2011, www.theisraelproject.org.

## Chapter 13: Global Unification

1. Quoted in Paul Berman, "Something's Changed Bigotry in Print: Crowds Chant Murder," in Ron Rosenbaum, ed., *Those Who Forget the Past: The Question of Anti-Semitism* (New York: Random House, 2004), pp. 18–19.

2. "Contemporary Islamist Ideology Authorizing Genocidal Murder," MEMRI, January 27, 2004, http://www.memri.org/report/en/print1049.htm.

3. "Intro Material for People New to StormFront," Stormfront, http://www.stormfront.org/forum /t538924/.

4. http://aljahad.com/vb/showthread.php?s=f4ab222c34783339ac5d84cf4f9bb9ab&t=23906; translation courtesy of Simon Wiesenthal Center, Los Angeles.

5. Yaakov Lappin, "'Kill a Jew' Page on Facebook Sparks Furor," *Jerusalem Post,* July 5, 2010, http://www.jpost.com/JewishWorld/JewishNews/Article.aspx?id=180456.

6. Survey of December 2005 by Populous, Findings Posted on Daniel Pipes, "More Survey Research from a British Islamist Hell," *Daniel Pipes Middle East Forum,* February 7, 2006, http://www.danielpipes .org/blog/2005/07/more-survey-research-from-a-british-islamist.

7. *The Charter of Allah: The Platform of the Islamic Resistance Movement (Hamas),* http://www.thejeru salemfund.org/www.thejerusalemfund.org/carryover/documents/charter.html.

8. Rabbi Abraham Cooper, "How a Terrorist's Words from the Grave Threaten France and Its Jews," FoxNews.com, August 23, 2012, http://www.foxnews.com/opinion /2012/08/23/how-terrorists-words-from-grave-threaten-france-and-its-jews/.

9. Henry I. Silverman, "Reuters: Principles of Trust or Propaganda?," *The Journal of Applied Business Research* (November–December 2011), http://journals.cluteonline.com/index.php/JABR/article/view /6469/6547.

10. "Terror and Anti-Semitism on the Internet," Rabbi Abraham Cooper interview with Manfred Gerstenfeld, *ArutzSheva,* August 20, 2012, http://www.israelnationalnews.com/Articles/Article.aspx /12072#.UMrx6axOSSo.

11. Anna Mahjar-Barducci, "Anti-Semitism in Chile: Jews Accused of Plotting to Take Over Patagonia," Gatestone Institute, January 23, 2012, http://www.gatestoneinstitute.org/2775/anti-semitism-chile.

12. Yoav Stern," Islamic Movement Head Charged with Incitement to Racism, Violence," *Haaretz,* January 29, 2008, http://www.haaretz.com/news/islamic-movement-head-charged-with-incitement-to-racism-violence-1.238209.

13. "Saudi Cleric Salman Al-Odeh: Jews Use Human Blood for Passover Matzos," MEMRI, August 13, 2012, http://www.memritv.org/clip_transcript/en/3536.htm.

14. Tzvi Ben Gedalyahu, "Muslim Blood Libels against Jews Spread to Canada," *ArutzSheva 7,* January 12, 2010, http://www.israelnationalnews.com/News/News.aspx/135481#.T_QbaZEk67s.

15. "The Medieval 'Blood Libel,'" Wildolive, http://www.wildolive.co.uk/blood_libel.htm; and Morten Berthelsen and Barak Ravid, "Top Sweden Newspaper Says IDF Kills Palestinians for Their Organs: Report Ties Claims to New Jersey Crime Syndicate, Prompts Accusations of Anti-Semitism from Rival Newspaper,"*Haaretz,* August 18, 2009, http://www.haaretz.com/news/top-sweden-newspaper-says-idf-kills-palestinians-for-their-organs-1.282166.

16. "Sabeel Ecumenical Liberation Theology Center," ADL, April 18, 2008, http://www.adl.org /main_Interfaith/sabeel_backgrounder.htm.

17. "Jesus Misrepresented as 'Muslim Palestinian,'" *Palestinian Media Watch,* broadcast of December 24, 2009, http://www.palwatch.org/main.aspx?fi=505.

18. ADL, Surveys of antisemitism in Europe, 2009 and 2012, http://archive.adl.org/main_Anti_Sem itism_International/Default.htm..

19. Frank Furedi, "Europe's Estrangement from Israel," PJMedia, January 17, 2009, http://pjmedia .com/blog/europs-estrangement-from-israel/.

## Chapter 14: Strategic Politics, Eliminationist Ends

1. Raphael Ahren, "At Interfaith Meet in Jerusalem, a Grim Picture of Jewish-Protestant Relations," *Times of Israel,* November 9, 2012, http://www.timesofisrael.com/at-interfaith-meet-in-jerusalem-a-grim-picture-of-jewish-Protestant-relations/.

2. Giulio Meotti, "The Churches Against Israel: Christian Blood Libels Revived, with Israel Being Painted as Evil, Having No Right to Exist," Ynetnews, July 3, 2011, http://www.ynetnews.com /articles/0,7340,L-4090528,00.html.

3. Benjamin Weinthal, " 'Hate Crimes Are a Reality in the EU,' Agencies Say," *Jerusalem Post,* November 28, 2012, http://www.jpost.com/International/Article.aspx?id=293845.

4. Paul Bogdanor, "Understanding the Arab-Israeli Conflict," citing *New York Times,* January 10, 1954, http://www.paulbogdanor.com/israel/quotes.html.

5. The revolution in understanding that my publication of *Hitler's Willing Executioners: Ordinary Germans and the Holocaust* produced, with the paradigm shift it initiated by replacing abstractions, such as the terror apparatus, the SS, and the monstrous Nazi leadership, with the human beings who committed the deeds and the understandings of the world they had, especially their antisemitism, clarified how many crucial aspects of the Holocaust had been for decades suppressed or fundamentally misunderstood. Although the "Goldhagen Debate," as it has come to be known, has produced voluminous new research and improved understanding of the Holocaust and even of its aftereffects, an obvious point that had not been conceptualized properly until a few years ago was that an international genocidal alliance formed to carry out the Holocaust. See Daniel Jonah Goldhagen, *Hitler's Willing Executioners: Ordinary Germans and the Holocaust* (New York: Vintage, 1997) and *Worse Than War: Genocide, Eliminationism, and the Ongoing Assault Against Humanity* (New York: PublicAffairs, 2009), p. 367; and *"Spiegel* Interview with Daniel Jonah Goldhagen: 'Mass Slaughter Is a Systemic Problem of the Modern World,' " *Spiegel,* October 8, 2009, http://www.spiegel.de/international/germany/spiegel-interview-with-daniel-jonah-goldhagen-mass-slaughter-is-a-systemic-problem-of-the-modern-world-a-653938 .html.

6. Dana Meijler, "In Europe, Even the Jews Are Anti-Semitic," *Times of Israel,* September 24, 2012, http://blogs.timesofisrael.com/in-europe-even-the-jews-are-anti-semitic/.

7. See Richard Landes, "Al Durah Affair: The Dossier," at The Augean Stables, http://www .theaugeanstables.com/al-durah-affair-the-dossier/. For a further discussion of the dubious evidence substantiating the anti-Israel account of the incident, and the welter of claims and counterclaims, see "Muhammad al-Durrah Incident," Wikipedia, http://en.wikipedia.org/wiki/Muhammad_al-Durrah_ incident, and for reports of an Israeli official commission's conclusions—after assessing the video, forensic, and eyewitness evidence—that, as the *New York Times* reports, "there was no evidence for the original account of the event, which was that the boy was hit by Israeli bullets—and that it was even possible that neither the boy nor his father had been struck by any bullets at all," see Isabel Kershner, "Israeli Report Casts New Doubts on Shooting in Gaza," *New York Times,* May 19, 2013, http://www .nytimes.com/2013/05/20/world/middleeast/israel-casts-new-doubt-on-muhammad-al-dura-episode .html.

8. "Contemporary Islamist Ideology Authorizing Genocidal Murder," http://www.memri.org /report/en/0/0/0/0/0/0/1049.htm#_ednref10.

9. Tom Lantos, "The Durban Debacle: An Insider's View of the World Racism Conference at Durban," *Fletcher Forum of World Affairs* (Winter/Spring 2002), p. 16, http://www.eyeontheun.org/assets /attachments/articles/568_durban_debacle.pdf.

10. Richard Falk, "Slouching Towards a Palestinian Holocaust," *Transnational Institute,* July 16, 2007, http://www.tni.org/archives/falk_palestinianholocaust; and Jeremy Sharon, "UN's Richard Falk Under Fire for 'Anti-Semitic' Cartoon," *Jerusalem Post,* July 8, 2011, http://www.jpost.com/International/Arti cle.aspx?id=228448.

11. Anne Bayefsky, "U.N.-Sponsored Meeting Equates Israelis with Nazis: Palestinian Minister Accuses Israeli Leaders of Advocating Extermination Camps," April 5, 2012, National Review Online, http://www.nationalreview.com/corner/295353/palestinian-authority-minister-accuses-israelis-calling-extermination-camps-anne-bayef. For United Nations posting of this article, http://www.un.org/depts /dpa/qpal/docs/2012%20Geneva/keynote%20Issa%20QARAQE%20FINAL%20EN%20rev1.pdf.

12. Ibid.

13. Adla Shashati, "The Darfur Effect," Sudaneseonline.com, September 5, 2005, http://www.suda neseonline.com/earticle2005/sep5-90664.shtml.

14. Benjamin Weinthal, "Amnesty Int'l Finland: Israel Scum State," *Jerusalem Post,* August 24, 2010, http://www.jpost.com/International/Article.aspx?id=185846.

15. Irwin Cotler, "Beyond Durban: The Conference Against Racism That Became a Racist Conference Against Jews," December 2001, posted at MEfacts.com, http://www.mefacts.com/cached.asp?x_id=11248.

16. "Ahmadinejad Speech: Full Text," BBC News, April 21, 2009, http://news.bbc.co.uk/2/hi/middle_east/8010747.stm; and "Statement by H. E. Dr. Mahmoud Ahmadinejad, President of the Islamic Republic of Iran, High Level Segment, Durban Review Conference, Geneva, 20 April 2009," http://news.bbc.co.uk/2/shared/bsp/hi/pdfs/20_04_09_ahmadinejad_geneva.pdf.

17. Gerald M. Steinberg, "The Centrality of NGOs in the Durban Strategy," *Yale Israel Journal,* Summer 2006, posted at NGO-Monitor, http://www.ngo-monitor.org/article.php?operation=print&id=1958.

18. David Goldberg, "Saudi Arabia's Intolerable Antisemitic Textbooks," *Guardian,* November 24, 2010, http://www.guardian.co.uk/commentisfree/belief/2010/nov/24/saudi-arabia-antisemitic-textbooks; and "Saudi School Lessons in UK Concern Government," BBC News, November 21, 2010, http://www.bbc.co.uk/news/uk-11799713.

19. Aryeh Weinberg, "Alone on the Quad: Understanding Jewish Student Isolation on Campus," *Institute for Jewish & Community Research,* December 2011, http://jewishresearch.org/quad/12-11/alone-quad.html.

20. "Jesus Misrepresented as 'Muslim Palestinian,'" *Palestinian Media Watch,* December 3, 2010, http://www.palwatch.org/main.aspx?fi=505.

21. Raphael Ahren, "At Interfaith Meet in Jerusalem, a Grim Picture of Jewish-Protestant Relations," *Times of Israel,* November 9, 2012, http://www.timesofisrael.com/at-interfaith-meet-in-jerusalem-a-grim-picture-of-jewish-Protestant-relations/.

22. *The World* (Scott Foresman/Pearson, 2004).

23. E. J. Dionne Jr., "Pope Speaks in Rome Synagogue, in the First Such Visit on Record," *New York Times,* April 14, 1986, http://www.nytimes.com/1986/04/14/international/europe/14POPE.html.

24. Goldhagen, *A Moral Reckoning: The Role of the Church in the Holocaust and Its Unfulfilled Duty of Repair* (New York: Knopf, 2002), p. 243.

25. "Friday Prayers sermons in Tehran (2012/02/03)," The Office of the Supreme Leader Ayatollah Sayyid Ali Khameini, http://www.leader.ir/langs/en/index.php?p=contentShow&id=9094; "Genocidal Rhetoric," http://www.stopiransnukes.org/IranGenocidalRetaric.asp.

26. Y. Mansharof and A. Savyon, "In Response to Escalating Threats Between West and Iran, Iranian Official Calls On Regime to Attack Israel," MEMRI, February 7, 2012, http://www.memri.org/report/en/0/0/0/0/0/0/6058.htm#_edn4.

27. "Top Commander Reiterates Iran's Commitment to Full Annihilation of Israel," Fars News Agency, May 20, 2012, http://english.farsnews.com/newstext.php?nn=9102112759.

28. "German Foreign Minister to Wiesenthal Center: 'Anti-Zionism Inevitably Leads to Antisemitism,'" Simon Wiesenthal Center, July 17, 2001, http://www.wiesenthal.com/site/apps/s/content.asp?c=1sKWLbPJLnF&b=4442915&ct=5850509.

# Index

# About the Author

Daniel Jonah Goldhagen, a former professor at Harvard University, is the author of *Hitler's Willing Executioners, A Moral Reckoning,* and *Worse Than War.* His writing has appeared in the *New York Times, Los Angeles Times, Washington Post, New Republic,* and newspapers around the world.